Sociology

sixth
edition

Sociology

A Brief Introduction

Alex Thio

Ohio University

PEARSON

Boston ■ New York ■ San Francisco
Mexico City ■ Montreal ■ Toronto ■ London ■ Madrid ■ Munich ■ Paris
Hong Kong ■ Singapore ■ Tokyo ■ Cape Town ■ Sydney

Senior Editor: Jeff Lasser
Development Editor: Tom Jefferies
Editorial Assistant: Sara Owen
Composition and Prepress Buyer: Linda Cox
Manufacturing Buyer: Megan Cochran
Cover Administrator: Linda Knowles
Marketing Manager: Krista Groshong
Editorial-Production Service: Communicáto, Ltd.
Text Design: Glenna Collett
Electronic Composition: Publishers' Design and Production Services, Inc.
Photo Researcher: Laurie Frankenthaler, F&F Associates
Cover Designer: Studio Nine

For related titles and support materials, visit our online catalog at www.ablongman.com.

Between the time website information is gathered and then published, it is not unusual for some sites to have closed. Also, the transcription of URLs can result in typographical errors. The publisher would appreciate notification where these errors occur so that they may be corrected in subsequent editions.

Library of Congress Cataloging-in-Publication Data

Thio, Alex.
    Sociology : a brief introduction / Alex Thio. — 6th ed.
      p.   cm.
    Includes bibliographical references and indexes.
    ISBN 0-205-40785-4
    1. Sociology.   I. Title.
  HM585.T48 2005
  301—dc22   2004047738

Photo credits appear on page 500, which comprises a continuation of the copyright page.

Printed in the United States of America

10 9 8 7 6 5 4 3 2 1   RRD-OH   09 08 07 06 05 04

Brief Contents

Contents

1 The Essence of Sociology   1

2 Society and Culture   32

Theoretical Thumbnails

Maps

Preface

Today, we are living in a world of swift social changes. Just reflect on how our society has changed because of the explosive growth of Internet use, the widespread loss of jobs, the enormous cost of bringing democracy to Iraq, the decline of international respect for the United States, and the constant threat of 9/11-like terrorist attacks. The need to use sociology to understand these and numerous other changes around us is greater than ever. We will explore them in this new edition of *Sociology: A Brief Introduction*. It is a significant revision, packed with up-to-date and useful information and new ideas from the latest sociological research.

This book is designed to help students have fun learning sociology. Thus, the fast-paced and lively writing style, the frequent use of interesting examples, and the abundance of thought-provoking illustrations should stimulate student interest in sociology. By studying this book, students will learn to think analytically and critically about the society and the world in which they live. Equipped with new information and better tools for thinking, they will look at their world, their society, and their own lives with enhanced clarity and insight and will be able to live their lives more productively and joyously.

FEATURES

A unique blend of style and substance makes *Sociology: A Brief Introduction* stand out from the rest. In addition to the trusted, hallmark features of the book, I have added a number of new features to this edition in order to make it easier and more enjoyable for students to learn sociology.

Myths and Realities

This text is unique for opening each chapter with a list of Myths and Realities about social behavior, which are then addressed at relevant points in the chapter. Many students assume that sociology is only common sense—that what it has to teach, they have

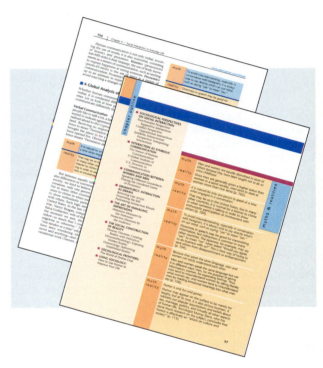

known all along. In this text, students will find some of their firmest assumptions challenged, and they will start to look at the familiar world around them with a fresh, critical eye. A Myth and Reality item in Chapter 10 (Families), for example, questions the popular belief that the high U.S. divorce rate has made Americans sour on marriage. This item appears again later in the chapter, near the point at which the topic is discussed, to reinforce student comprehension and retention.

Sociological Frontiers

Unique to this book, the Sociological Frontiers feature follows the text discussion in every chapter. It offers new, intriguing sociological studies and ideas, as well as sociological interpretations of the new events in our fast-changing world. Students are thus invited to explore and understand the frontiers of

both sociology and social life. In Chapter 11 (Education and Religion), for example, students are shown how religious fanaticism led to the terrorist attacks on the United States on September 11, 2001—an event that has transformed the United States into a new society, more unified than ever before, among other things.

■ Using Sociology

Presented as the last section in every chapter, Using Sociology deals with larger social policy issues, such as how to reduce gender inequality, how to stop terrorists, and how to revitalize large cities. By bringing home the relevance of sociology, this section also offers specific guidance that students can apply to their own lives, such as how to manage their drinking, how to become a millionaire, and how to achieve success and happiness in college.

■ Theoretical Thumbnail

The three major theoretical perspectives—functionalist, conflict, and symbolic interactionist—are introduced in the first chapter and then illustrated in a section on sports, a subject most students are familiar with. Having established this basic understanding, the text returns to these three perspectives consistently in every chapter, applying each to the topic at hand. At the end of this discussion, the three perspectives are summed up in a table called Theoretical Thumbnail. This approach, which is unique to this text, enables students to easily compare the perspectives so that they can clearly comprehend and remember how each one makes sense of the subject in question.

■ Photo Caption Titles

Distinct to this text is the use of short titles with all photo captions. New to this edition, these titles were carefully created to bring out the essence of the message showcased by each picture and commentary. Students will find the titles interesting to read and the messages easy to remember, which will enhance their enjoyment and learning of sociology.

■ Global Analysis

Again, unique to this book, every chapter contains a section that analyzes how people around the world live. These analyses not only enhance and deepen students' understanding of other cultures, but they also help students gain special insight into their own

society by looking at it more objectively—from an outsider's point of view. The global analysis section in Chapter 7 (U.S. and Global Stratification), for example, explores the link between women's participation in the labor force and the level of prosperity in a society, suggesting one reason for the relatively high level of economic success in the United States.

■ Social Diversity

The diversity of American society—which comprises various racial and ethnic groups, as well as women and men of different social classes and sexual orientations—is highlighted in sections on Social Diversity that appear in virtually all chapters. The text does not focus only on the *problems* of women and minorities; instead, their strengths and achievements are also revealed. Chapter 10 (Families), for example, discusses differences among Native American, African American, Hispanic American, and Asian American families, along with gay and lesbian marriages.

■ Feminist Views

Explanations of feminist views on various social issues are frequently provided throughout the text. Feminist theorists have made significant contributions to sociology by shedding light on many previously ignored subjects and offering new ways of looking at familiar social issues. In this book, students will learn from the feminist perspective about numerous important matters, such as how feminists contribute to the conflict perspective in sociology, why women run organizations differently than men, and how the oppression of women is related to environmental problems.

■ Continuing Update on the Web

Every day, events occur that challenge our perception of U.S. society and how it functions in the global arena. To address these events, this book will be updated continually after it has been published. These updates will appear in the form of original articles that bring a sociological perspective to today's issues and events, much like those discussed in the Sociological Frontiers sections of this text. Such articles will appear regularly at the text's Companion Website: www.ablongman.com/thio6e. Readers will find a reminder of the Continuing Update feature, including this web address, after the Sociological Frontiers section in every chapter.

▌LEARNING AIDS

The effective system of learning aids provided in this text will motivate students and facilitate their learning. Students are encouraged to think about the materials by themselves and then to prepare for class discussion of important concepts and issues. It is frequently through such active involvement with what they have read that students begin to sharpen their thinking skills. Then the understanding and absorption of ideas presented in this text and in the course will come easily.

■ Chapter-Opening Vignettes

Along with a chapter outline and a Myths and Realities box, each chapter opens with a thought-provoking vignette. This brief story will stimulate students' interest and fix their attention on the main themes of the chapter.

Questions for Thinking Critically

Critical-thinking questions are used to conclude the Using Sociology features and the commentaries that appear with all of the figures. These questions encourage students to think critically about their society and the world around them and to apply what they have learned from sociology to their own lives.

Stimulating Graphics

A wide range of colorful graphs, maps, photos, tables, and cartoons have been provided throughout the book. They have been designed not only to spark students' interest but, more important, to reinforce comprehension and retention of the content through the use of substantial captions for the photos and detailed commentaries for the figures.

Key Terms

Important terms and concepts are boldfaced and defined when introduced in the text. They are then listed and defined again at the end of each chapter, with a page cross-reference to the text location of each item to facilitate study. Finally, all key terms with their definitions are compiled in the Glossary at the end of the book, and the first appearance of each key term is identified in the Subject Index.

Questions for Discussion and Review

Near the end of each chapter are questions instructors can use as a springboard for lively discussion in class. Students can also use these questions, which are organized by major topic heading, to review the key ideas discussed in the chapter. Whether the questions are used in class, for individual review, or both, students will learn more as active thinkers than as recipients of ideas and facts.

Chapter Reviews

Each chapter ends with a substantive review of content in a question-and-answer format that is unique to this text. The standard form of summary that is typical of other texts tends to turn students into passive consumers of knowledge. In contrast, the question-and-answer format in this book encourages students to become actively involved by inviting them to join the author in thinking about important issues. Students who have actively thought about what they have read will more easily understand and remember the material later.

Suggested Readings and Additional Resources

To encourage further exploration of the chapter topic, suggestions for further reading are included at the end of each chapter. These suggestions include up-to-date books readily available in most college libraries. In addition, students are directed to Pearson's *ResearchNavigator* website to access relevant journal articles and to the text's Companion Website to view interesting and current articles from the *New York Times*.

UPDATED CONTENT

Sociology is a fast-growing field, and special care has been taken to present the significant changes that have recently taken place all over the world. Many of the studies and the data presented in this text are up to date. Current events, as reported in the nation's first-rate newspapers and newsmagazines, are also analyzed to demonstrate the relevance of sociology to today's world. In addition, no attempt has been made to gloss over or water down complex sociological issues, such as the death penalty, ethnic conflicts around the world, and welfare for the rich. Such issues are confronted head on but explained in a clear and interesting fashion.

The outpouring of sociological studies and news stories that have appeared over the last two years, since the previous edition of this text, has been reviewed and documented. As a result, this edition has been strengthened with a number of new materials, the most significant of which are listed here:

- *Chapter 1, The Essence of Sociology:* New data on the surge of patriotism in the United States, a new map showing the world as a global village, an updated U.S. map of suicide rates, recent research that debunks the "dumb jock" stereotype, a new discussion with a new map of women's participation in the Olympics, and an updated demonstration of how to conduct a survey
- *Chapter 2, Society and Culture:* A new discussion on how U.S. values have served Americans well in today's world, a new map on agricultural societies, a new figure on employment in postindustrial society, and new data on how Americans are working harder and longer than ever before
- *Chapter 3, Socialization:* New data on how teenagers talk with each other in New York City, an expanded discussion of the mass media to include the impact of the Internet on children, and a new map showing regional differences in parents' concern about their children having premarital sex and using drugs
- *Chapter 4, Social Interaction in Everyday Life:* An expanded discussion with new research on cooperation as a type of supportive interaction, a new map with new commentary about Internet communication around the world, a revision of the commentary about flying saucers, and an updating of a joke to include California's new governor, Arnold Schwarzenegger
- *Chapter 5, Groups and Organizations:* An expanded and revised discussion of the benefits of group diversity, a revised discussion with new data on the attributes of social networks, a revised discussion of the military, and a new section on the threat of organizations to privacy
- *Chapter 6, Deviance and Control:* A new chapter-opening vignette about two snipers terrorizing the residents of suburban Washington, D.C., in 2002, a new section about suicide bombing, a new global map showing where women have been raped during wars, a new world map of where suicide bombers operate, and a new map showing the global sex trade
- *Chapter 7, U.S. and Global Stratification:* An extensive revision of the section on class profiles, with new information about the upper-middle class, the middle class, and the working poor; an updated discussion with new data on poverty; new figures about the feminization of poverty and the changing percentages of the rich and the poor; and a new global maps of girls' primary school enrollment rates and women doing housework
- *Chapter 8, Race and Ethnicity:* A new chapter-opening vignette, new data on the cohesiveness of the Jewish community, a considerable update on the current status of affirmative action, and new information about the increasing prevalence of college-prep classes for minority students
- *Chapter 9, Gender and Age:* New data on gender difference in the duration of friendship, an updated discussion of female employment, an expanded discussion about elderly women faced with the difficulty of marriage, and new world maps portraying women in higher education and female genital circumcision

- *Chapter10, Families:* An expanded discussion with new data on two-career families, an updated discussion on gay and lesbian marriages, and new data on solving marital problems with acceptance therapy
- *Chapter 11, Education and Religion:* A revision with new data on Head Start, discussion of the U.S. Supreme Court's 2002 ruling on the voucher program in Cleveland, new data on Native American students and Christian fundamentalists, a new section on the current condition of global religion, and a revision of the section on religious fanaticism and terrorism
- *Chapter 12, The Economy and Politics:* A new section on the global economy, a new section on corporate corruption, and an updated discussion of how to stop terrorists
- *Chapter 13, Health and Population:* An updating of the section on social diversity in U.S. health, a new section on the U.S. health care system, new data on today's anti-immigration policy, and a new map on smoking-related deaths around the world
- *Chapter 14, Environment and Urbanization:* A revision of the section on diminishing resources, a new discussion on Tokyo's plan to create an underground city, and an expansion of the discussion on how to use the so-called smart growth policy to curb the expansion of edge cities and suburbs
- *Chapter 15, Collective Behavior, Social Movements, and Social Change:* An updated discussion on the relative rarity of panics during a disaster, a significant revision of the section on crowds, a revision of the section on public opinion, a new section about the consequences of social movements, and an expanded and updated discussion on the changes in U.S. society

SUPPLEMENTS

For Instructors

Instructor's Manual. For each chapter in the text, the Instructor's Manual provides this information: a chapter summary; learning objectives; a lecture outline; a list of what's new in the sixth edition; key terms with page cross-references; classroom discussion topics and activities; and video and Internet resources.

Test Bank. The Test Bank contains hundreds of questions in multiple-choice, fill-in-the-blank, and essay formats. Many of the multiple-choice questions test students' ability to apply what they've learned to new situations.

TestGen Computerized Testing. Allyn & Bacon's TestGen is an integrated suite of testing and assessment tools for Windows and Macintosh. Instructors can use TestGen to create professional-looking exams in just minutes by selecting from the existing database of questions, editing those questions, or writing their own questions.

Allyn & Bacon/ABC News Video Library. Instructors can use the up-to-the-minute video segments from ABC news programs such as *Nightline, World News Tonight,* and *20/20* to launch lectures, spark classroom discussions, and encourage critical thinking. The topics available include race and ethnicity, stratification, gender, deviance, and aging.

Allyn & Bacon Transparencies for Introductory Sociology. This revised package includes over 125 color acetates, featuring illustrations from the most current Allyn & Bacon sociology titles.

PowerPoint Presentation. The PowerPoint lecture outlines created for this text provide dozens of ready-to-use graphic and text images. The full presentation is available on a cross-platform CD-ROM. PowerPoint software is not required to use this program, as a PowerPoint viewer to access the images is included.

Digital Media Archive III for Sociology (DMA). This CD-ROM for Windows and Macintosh contains hundreds of graphs, charts, and maps, all organized by topic, for use in supplementing lectures and illustrating key sociological concepts. It also includes 40 topical lectures with 20 to 50 PowerPoint slides for each. For classrooms with full multimedia capability, the DMA contains video segments and links to sociology websites.

Online Course Management. *CourseCompass,* powered by Blackboard and hosted nationally, is Allyn & Bacon's own course management system. Instructors will find it useful in managing all aspects of teaching a course. It features preloaded content to support an Introduction to Sociology course. For colleges and universities with *WebCT* and *Blackboard* licenses, special course management packages are available in these formats as well.

The Blockbuster Approach: A Guide to Teaching Sociology with Video (by Casey Jordan, Western Connecticut State University). This manual describes hundreds of commercially available videos that represent sociological ideas and themes, and provides sample assignments.

Sociology Video Library. Qualified adopters may select from a wide variety of high-quality videos from such sources as Films for the Humanities and Sciences and Annenberg/CPB. Some restrictions apply. (Contact your Allyn & Bacon/Longman representative for details.)

■ For Students

Study Guide with Flashcards. This manual contains summaries of key information for every chapter and practice tests to help students prepare for quizzes and exams. Flashcards of the key terms for every chapter are also provided.

Companion Website. Students who visit the Companion Website for the sixth edition (www.ablongman. com/thio6e) will find an online study guide with practice tests, learning objectives, and links to useful sociology sites on the Internet. In addition, there is an *eThemes of the Times* collection: 30 articles from the *New York Times* on topics of sociological interest.

Intersections: Readings to Accompany Sociology: A Brief Introduction, **Sixth Edition (from Pearson Custom Publishing).** The author of this text, Alex Thio, assembled a brief, inexpensive anthology of readings (one reading per chapter) from the Pearson Custom Publishing *Intersections* database to complement his book. The reader can be purchased separately or packaged with this text at a special price.

Sociology Tutor Center (Access Code Required). After-hours tutoring from qualified sociology instructors by phone, e-mail, or fax is available free to students when a Tutor Center Access Code is packaged with this text upon request.

Research Navigator (Access Code Required). This online research database is available free to students when the text is packaged upon request with the *Research Navigator Guide for Sociology.* Searchable by keyword, it provides access to thousands of full-text articles from scholarly social science journals, popular newspapers and magazines, and a one-year archive of the *New York Times.*

■ Additional Supplements

Doing Sociology with Student CHIP: Data Happy! **Fourth Edition (by Gregg Lee Carter, Bryant College).** This workbook with CHIP software is de-signed for classes with an empirical orientation. The computer exercises allow students to explore sociological issues using real data.

Careers in Sociology, **Third Edition (by W. Richard Stephens, Eastern Nazarene College).** This supplement examines how people working as sociologists entered the field and describes how a degree in sociology can provide preparation for careers in areas such as law, gerontology, social work, and the computer industry. It is packaged free with the text upon request.

College and Society **(by Stephen Sweet, Ithaca College).** This supplemental text uses examples from familiar surroundings—the patterns of interaction, social structures, and expectations of conduct on a typical college campus—to help students see the ways in which the larger society operates.

Breaking the Ice, **Third Edition (by Daisy Kabagarama, Montgomery College).** This supplement aims to help students understand and appreciate cultural differences. It includes exercises to help readers identify their own biases. It, too, is packaged free with the text upon request.

Building Bridges: The Allyn & Bacon Guide to Service Learning **(by Doris Hamner).** This manual offers practical advice for students who must complete a service learning project as part of their required course work. It is packaged free with the text upon request.

■ ACKNOWLEDGMENTS

I am grateful to the numerous instructors all over the United States who have adopted past editions of this text. I am equally thankful for the invaluable help from many colleagues at various universities and colleges in reviewing the manuscript of the current edition. Unsolicited responses from adopters and insightful criticisms and suggestions from Allyn & Bacon's reviewers have helped me produce, I hope, the best brief text on introductory sociology available today. The reviewers for this current edition are as follows:

Naima Brown, Santa Fe Community College
Jared D. Cootz, Montgomery College
Nils Hovik, Lehigh Carbon Community College
Jay Hughes, Georgia Southern University
Jeanne Humble, Lexington Community College
Paul D. Roof, College of Charleston

Martha L. Shwayder, Metropolitan State College of Denver

I am also thankful to Professor Peter Morrill, Professor Lillian Dees, and Professor Naima Brown for their work on the Instructor's Manual, Test Bank, and Practice Tests. Finally, thanks go to the people at Allyn & Bacon, including Tom Jefferies, for his help in developing this new revision, and Donna Simons, for efficiently guiding the production of the book.

Alex Thio

About the Author

Alex Thio (pronounced TEE-oh) is Professor of Sociology at Ohio University. Born of Chinese parentage in Penang, Malaysia, he grew up in a multicultural environment. He acquired fluency in Mandarin (modern standard Chinese), two Chinese dialects (Fujianese and Hakka), Malay, and Indonesian. He also picked up a smattering of English and Dutch. He further took French and German in high school and college.

Professor Thio attended primary school in Malaysia and high school in Indonesia. He then came to the United States and worked his way through Central Methodist College in Missouri, where he majored in social sciences and took many literature and writing courses. Later, he studied sociology as a graduate student at the State University of New York at Buffalo, and he completed his doctorate while working as a research and teaching assistant.

Professor Thio regularly teaches courses in introductory sociology and deviance. In addition to teaching, he enjoys writing. Aside from this book, he is the author of the popular text *Deviant Behavior*, Seventh Edition (2004), and has written many articles. The author is grateful for the feedback he often receives from faculty and students, which he believes improves the quality of his books. If you have any comments, suggestions, or questions, please write to him at the Department of Sociology, Ohio University, Athens, OH, 45701, or via e-mail (thio@ohio.edu).

Professor Thio lives in Athens, Ohio. His hobbies include traveling, moviegoing, and reading.

The Essence of Sociology

myths & realities

myth	*Sociology is merely common sense, and nothing new can be found in it.*
reality	Sociology is more than common sense because it is based largely on scientific evidence. Often ideas or beliefs derived from common sense turn out to be false, contradicted by facts from sociological research. While common sense gives us familiar and untested ideas, sociology offers factually supported ideas as well as the excitement of discovering something new about ourselves (p. 2).
myth	*Normal people are more competent than people with disabilities. Sighted people, for example, can more easily walk from one spot to another than blind people can.*
reality	If the walking contest is a fair one, in which the sighted are blindfolded so they cannot see, they will lose to the blind (p. 4).
myth	*Life must be more stressful in densely populated states, such as New York and New Jersey, than in wide-open areas, such as Montana and Wyoming. Not surprisingly, people in densely populated states are more likely to commit suicide.*
reality	People in densely populated states have *lower* suicide rates (p. 8).
myth	*The sole purpose of going to college is to get an education.*
reality	Going to college also serves some latent functions, unintended and often unrecognized, such as enabling many students to find their future spouses (p. 13).
myth	*Problems, especially crises, are bad. They are just like failures and miseries.*
reality	Problems, even crises, are not necessarily bad. They can be good, providing opportunities for achieving success in our lives (p. 27).

On September 11, 2001, the day of the terrorist attacks in New York City and Washington, D.C., life changed for 52-year-old Kurt Stone. In his youth, he was an antiwar hippie, and for years, he didn't even stand when "The Star-Spangled Banner" was played at a sporting event. He did love the United States, but he showed it by protesting about the government. As he explained, "My form of patriotism was being grateful for the right to protest." But the day after he saw what the terrorists did to the World Trade Center and the Pentagon, he found himself flying Old Glory outside his home and wanting to see the enemy die. And the next time he's at a baseball game, Stone said, "I will be singing, and there will be tears in my eyes" (Simon, 2001).

Like Stone, Americans all over the country have felt a surge of patriotism following the events of September 11, but some have been more inclined than others to express extreme pride in their country (see Figure 1.1). Why this difference in reaction to the terror attacks? Also, why do many countries oppose the use of war to fight terrorism?

Such questions deal with the diversity of U.S. society as well as the diversity found in other parts of the world today. We can ask many other important and interesting questions about ourselves and others around the globe: Why do wars break out between nations? Why do some marriages succeed while others end in divorce? How will having a college education affect your income potential? How can you become a millionaire? Are men naturally more aggressive than women? As you will see in the following chapters, answers to these and numerous other questions can be found in **sociology:** the systematic, scientific study of human society.

THE STUDY OF SOCIAL LIFE

Virtually everybody has something to say about social behavior. Because we observe it around us every day, many people assume that they know all about it. But as Otto Larsen (1981) has noted, "Living in a family or working in an organization does not automatically make one a sociologist any more than swimming in the sea makes one an oceanographer or being an animal breeder makes one a geneticist." Sociologists have a special way of looking at human behavior and special tools for studying it.

More Than Common Sense

To many people, sociology appears to be a laborious study of the obvious, an expensive way to discover what everybody already knows. To these people, sociology is merely common sense. But sociology is more than common sense because it is based largely on scientific evidence. Often ideas or beliefs derived from common sense turn out to be false, contradicted by facts from sociological research. See, for example, the Myths and Realities section at the beginning of

this chapter, which demonstrates some differences between common sense and sociological facts.

myth	Sociology is merely common sense, and nothing new can be found in it.
reality	Sociology is more than common sense because it is based largely on scientific evidence. Often ideas or beliefs derived from common sense turn out to be false, contradicted by facts from sociological research. While common sense gives us familiar and untested ideas, sociology offers factually supported ideas as well as the excitement of discovering something new about ourselves.

Sociological findings such as those that contradict commonly held myths may surprise you. Of course, not every finding in sociology is surprising. In fact, some confirm what you have known all along. You should not be surprised, therefore, to learn from sociology that there is more joblessness among blacks than among whites or that there are more poor people than rich people in prison. But many other

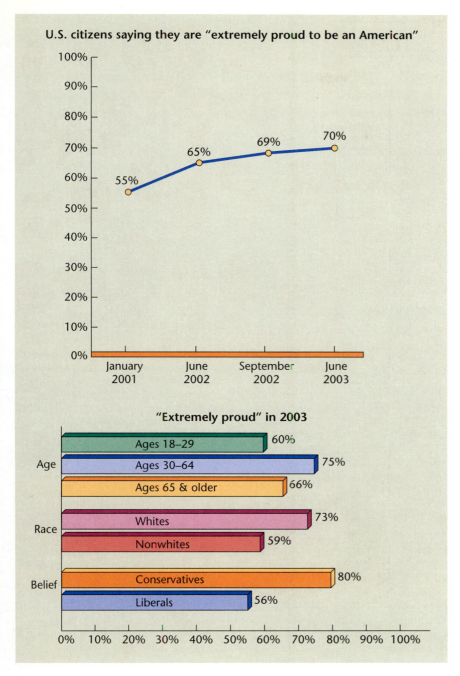

U.S. citizens saying they are "extremely proud to be an American"

"Extremely proud" in 2003

Age
- Ages 18–29 — 60%
- Ages 30–64 — 75%
- Ages 65 & older — 66%

Race
- Whites — 73%
- Nonwhites — 59%

Belief
- Conservatives — 80%
- Liberals — 56%

FIGURE 1.1

The Surge of U.S. Patriotism

Following the terrorist attacks on September 11, 2001, many more people in the United States have expressed their patriotism by saying they are "extremely proud" to be Americans. In late June 2003, 70 percent of Americans said they were extremely proud, compared to just 55 percent in January 2001—before the events of September 11. But some groups of Americans are more or less likely than others to proclaim extreme pride in their country.

Critical Thinking: *Are you extremely proud to be an American? Why or why not?*

Source: Gallup Poll, July 3, 2003.

commonsense ideas have turned out to be false, like the ones in the chapter-opening box. By systematically checking commonsense ideas against reliable facts, sociology can tell us which popular beliefs are myths and which are realities.

Sociology can also help reduce the confusion that sometimes arises from common sense. You may have read that "Birds of a feather flock together" but also that "Opposites attract." You may have heard the en-

couraging message that "Absence makes the heart grow fonder," but you may still remember the discouraging warning "Out of sight, out of mind." When facing such conflicting commonsense ideas, how can we tell which are correct and which are false? We can get the answer from sociological research. It has shown, for example, that the effect of one person's absence on another depends on the strength of the initial relationship. If two people have loved each other deeply, like Romeo and Juliet, absence will make their hearts grow fonder, but a high school romance tends to disintegrate because such relationships are usually not deep or serious enough to begin with (Epstein, 1997; Kohn, 1988).

In sum, it is *not* true that sociology is only common sense. If it were, we wouldn't bother to study sociology. Why would we spend our time learning something we already know? Common sense requires only a willingness to believe what it tells us. It cannot tell us whether those beliefs have any basis in fact. But sociology can. This is one of the reasons that sociology is exciting. It enables us to see that what has long been familiar—or just common sense—may turn out to be unfamiliar or uncommon. While common sense gives us familiar and untested ideas, sociology offers factually supported ideas as well as the excitement of discovering something new about ourselves.

■ The Appreciation of Social Diversity

For centuries, many people have followed the ancient Greek philosopher Plato's advice to "Know thyself" by looking into themselves rather than at others for understanding. Sociology suggests that we can know *ourselves* better by studying *others*. By doing so, we can see how others are similar to us in some ways and different in other ways. By a small leap of imagination, we may see that we are likely to behave similarly if we find ourselves under the same social conditions.

Our society offers great diversity in race, ethnicity, class, gender, age, sexual orientation, and other social characteristics. Studying these differences provides us with an excellent opportunity to know one another and gain insight into how society operates. We can learn much, for example, from people who experience **social marginality**—being excluded from mainstream society—such as racial and ethnic minorities, women, people who are poor and homeless, older persons, gays, people with disabilities, and so on.

myth	Normal people are more competent than people with disabilities. Sighted people, for example, can more easily walk from one spot to another than blind people can.
reality	If the walking contest is a fair one, in which the sighted are blindfolded so they cannot see, they will lose to the blind.

Consider people with disabilities. Often they are judged using criteria of competence that are *biased* in favor of nondisabled people. Compare, for example, an average blind person with an average sighted person. Who will be more competent in walking from one place to another? You might think that the

MODERN MOSAIC   In the United States, there is great diversity in race, ethnicity, class, gender, age, sexual orientation, and other social characteristics. Studying these differences offers us an excellent opportunity to know one another and gain insight into how society operates. We may know, for example, that in modern society we tend to learn something about others and come to appreciate and celebrate their lives. ■

sighted person will be more competent because the sighted person can see where he or she is going, but this is using an unfair criterion. If you think about competence based on the fairer criterion of who can best walk with the eyes closed, then the blind person will definitely be more competent. Such knowledge about people who are blind—and by extension, other socially marginal people—can make us appreciate them and celebrate their unique abilities as they really are, rather than discriminate against, pity, or patronize them for some incompetence that does not exist except as a figment of our traditional, prejudiced imaginations.

We can further grasp the reality of how various social conditions, such as prejudice and discrimination, powerfully affect socially marginal people. In doing so, we can understand how difficult it is for them to make it in a society that treats them like outsiders. On the other hand, we can also see how the social advantages enjoyed by members of mainstream society make it easier for them to succeed. In short, the study of social diversity can reveal the various ways in which society influences the lives of different groups and individuals—including our own—as we will see throughout this text.

■ The Importance of Global Analysis

We can gain further insight into ourselves and our society by going beyond our national boundaries to study other societies. Today the whole world has become a **global village**, a closely knit community of all the world's societies (see Figure 1.2, p. 6). Whatever happens in a faraway land can affect our lives here. Consider the various ways in which **economic globalization**—the interrelationship among the world's economies—can influence the U.S. economy and society at large.

First, the abundance of low-paid workers in relatively poor countries tends to decrease the wages of American workers because employers want to reduce production costs, including wages, in order to compete. The abundance of low-paid foreign workers also encourages U.S. corporations to turn to **outsourcing**, the practice of producing inexpensive products by building factories and hiring workers abroad. This may increase plant closings, unemployment, low-wage employment, poverty, and community breakdown in the United States. Outsourcing also tends to impoverish the government by reducing its tax base because U.S. companies and their employees abroad do not pay taxes to Uncle Sam. All this may cause the living standard in the United States to decline and its social problems to increase (Rubin, 1996).

On the other hand, economic globalization may have some positive consequences for the U.S. economy. Competing with foreign firms here and abroad forces U.S. corporations to become more efficient and productive. Shifting low-skilled jobs from the United States to poor nations is likely to raise those countries' incomes, making them bigger markets for U.S. goods. Globalization induces each country to specialize in what it does best—a poor country, for example, in making clothes and shoes and a wealthy country in producing biomedical devices and computer software. Competition in the global market may increase the availability of well-made but inexpensive products in all nations. The upshot is a better life not only for people in the United States but also for people in other societies as well (Krugman, 2001, 1996).

Given the importance of globalization in our lives, we can never emphasize strongly enough the significance of studying other societies. As Peter Berger (1992) says, "One can be an excellent physicist without ever having stepped outside one's own society; this is not so for a sociologist. . . . Thus sociologists must look at Japan in order to understand the West, at socialism in order to understand capitalism, at India so as to understand Brazil, and so on." In brief, by guiding us through the global village, sociology enables us to understand our lives better by opening our eyes to social forces that we may not see by looking at our society alone. We will return to this idea in all of the following chapters.

■ Sociology as a Science

The goal of science is to find order in apparent chaos. Scientists search for a pattern in what, on the surface,

BOON AND BANE Globalization induces each country to specialize in what it does best—for example, a poor country will make shoes and a wealthy country will produce computer software. This can increase the availability of well-made but inexpensive products to people all over the world. But globalization also causes corporations in rich countries, such as the United States, to build factories and hire low-paid workers abroad. As a result, many workers in affluent countries lose their jobs or find their paychecks shrinking. ■

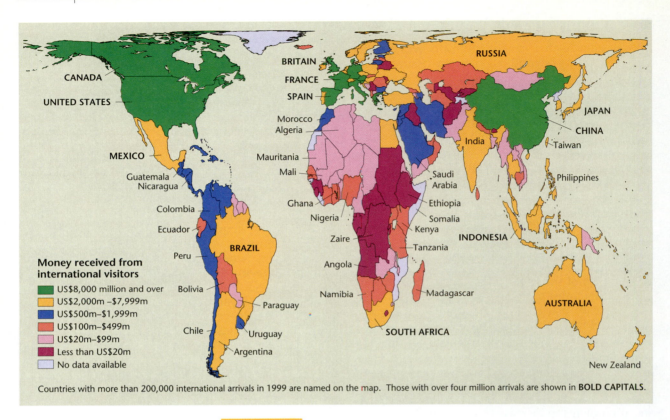

Money received from
international visitors

- US$8,000 million and over
- US$2,000m –$7,999m
- US$500m–$1,999m
- US$100m–$499m
- US$20m–$99m
- Less than US$20m
- No data available

Countries with more than 200,000 international arrivals in 1999 are named on the map. Those with over four million arrivals are shown in **BOLD CAPITALS**.

FIGURE 1.2

The Whole World Today as a Global Village

Today, virtually all societies interact with each other as if they live in a small village, thanks to low-cost travel and high-tech communication. In this global village, many societies are exposed to goods, services, ideas, fashions, movies, music, and other cultural items from distant lands. There are also frequent contacts with businesspeople, migrants, tourists, and others from foreign countries. But all societies are not equally integrated into the global village. Generally, more prosperous areas, such as the United States and Western Europe, are highly globalized, while poorer areas, such as many countries in Africa, are less globalized. As this map shows, more prosperous countries generally have more foreign tourists—an indication of being more globalized—than do poorer countries.

Critical Thinking: *Can foreign tourists create problems for the country that they visit? If yes, how? If no, why not?*

Source: David Burles, *The World Travel Atlas* (London: Columbus Publishing, 2002), p. 20. Reprinted with permission of Highbury Columbus Travel Publishing UK.

may look like random variations. They look for regularity, something that appears over and over, across time and space. Observation is usually a key element in this search. It is true that scientists, like everyone else, have preconceived ideas, beliefs, and values, and they use intuition to understand the world. But scientific methods require scientists to put aside existing views of what the world should be like and to rely, above all, on observation.

When scientists discover a pattern in the world, they describe it in the form of a **hypothesis**, a ten-

tative statement of how various events are related to one another. Then they test the hypothesis against systematic observations, producing evidence for or against it. Hypotheses must be related to one another to explain a broader range of phenomena. A set of logically related hypotheses that explains the relationship among various phenomena is called a **theory**. A good theory will apply to a wide range of existing observations and suggest testable predictions about what can be observed in the future.

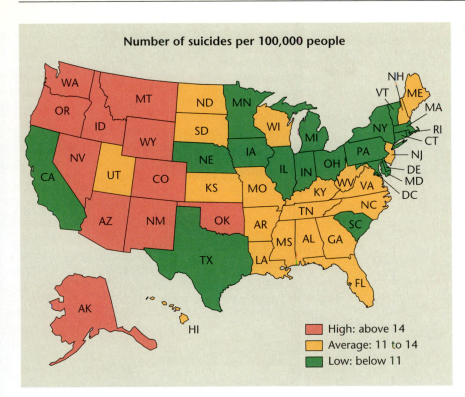

Number of suicides per 100,000 people

High: above 14
Average: 11 to 14
Low: below 11

FIGURE 1.3

Suicide More Common in Wide-Open Areas

A social cause of suicide is relative isolation from others. Isolated individuals must rely on themselves to solve personal problems and thus tend to be too subjective and emotional to find viable solutions. This may explain why suicide rates are generally higher in sparsely populated, wide-open areas, such as Alaska and the mountain states.

Critical Thinking: *If you knew someone who was extremely depressed and prone to suicide, what would you do to help?*

Source: Data from U.S. Census Bureau, *Statistical Abstract of the United States, 2002*, p. 83.

Suppose we are investigating the causes of revolutions. We find that most of the Asian and African nations gained their independence by revolting against their various European colonial rulers in the late 1940s and 1950s. Despite their differences, we come across one thing that all those revolutions had in common: *rising expectations.* For a period before each revolution started, the living conditions in the country had improved, causing the people to expect more than before. But the improvement was not adequate to meet these newly high expectations. With this observation, we could devise the hypothesis that revolutions are caused by rising expectations. If we were to test this hypothesis against systematic observations of other revolutions and find that the evidence consistently supports our hypothesis, then we would have a theory of revolution.

We would have proven our theory to be only tentatively, rather than absolutely, true, however. A scientific theory is always open to revision in the light of new evidence. Scientific findings are always subject to verification or refutation by other scientists. If the findings cannot be duplicated by other scientists, they are suspect. Scientists usually check whether their findings confirm or contradict those of their colleagues. This procedure increases the chances that mistakes, oversights, and biases will be detected. It ensures the objectivity of science.

■ The Sociological Imagination

To understand human behavior, sociologists stand back and look "from the outside" at individuals as members of society, rather than "inside them" to examine their thoughts, personalities, and motivations. Sociologists have long found that no matter how personal our experiences are, they are influenced by **social forces**—forces that arise from the society of which we are a part. Social forces exist outside the individual in the form of social relationships, such as those we share with friends, relatives, and people in educational, economic, religious, and other institutions. C. Wright Mills (1959b) referred to the ability to see the impact of social forces on individuals, especially on their private lives, as the **sociological imagination.** Through social forces, society exercises so much power on individuals that we can effectively see it through their behaviors.

Consider the case of suicide. It is reasonable to assume that those who kill themselves are frustrated and unhappy, since happy people rarely want to die. But suicide cannot be explained that simply. This explanation does not tell us why, for example, people who live in wide-open areas have much higher suicide rates than those who live in crowded areas (see Figure 1.3). There is no evidence that those who live in wide-open areas are more unhappy. How, then, do we account for the difference in suicide rates?

The sociological imagination leads us to look not at the individual personalities of those who commit suicide but at social forces. When French sociologist Émile Durkheim (1897/1951) examined suicide in the late nineteenth century, he described variations in the rates of suicide among different countries and groups. These rates constitute social, not individual, facts; to explain them, Durkheim turned to social forces. One force that he found to have a great impact on suicide was **social integration**, the degree to which people are tied to a social group. When there is either excessive or inadequate social integration, the suicide rate is likely to be high.

In the past, when elderly Inuit* committed suicide, the cause was usually *extreme* social integration. Obedient to the values and customs of their society, they did what they were expected by others to do: kill themselves when they could no longer contribute to the economy of their community. Similarly, Hindu widows used to follow the tradition of their society by ceremoniously throwing themselves onto the funeral pyres of their husbands. These ritual suicides were called *suttee* (literally, "good women"). The Hindu widows and elderly Inuit apparently felt pressured to commit suicide. If the Hindu widows did not kill themselves, they might be scorned as bad women. If the elderly Inuit refused to kill themselves, they might be stigmatized as selfish.

myth	Life must be more stressful in densely populated states, such as New York and New Jersey, than in wide-open areas, such as Montana and Wyoming. Not surprisingly, people in densely populated states are more likely to commit suicide.
reality	People in densely populated states have *lower* suicide rates.

On the other hand, a lack of social integration can also be found in high suicide rates. Divorced and widowed people, for example, are more likely than married people to be isolated from others and to receive little affection or moral support when they have problems. In other words, they are more likely to experience *inadequate* social integration. As a result, they are also more likely than married people to commit suicide. Similarly, people who live in sparsely populated states, such as Alaska, Montana, and Wyoming, are more isolated from others than those who live in densely populated states, such as New

York and New Jersey. Greater isolation tends to make people more individualistic, more dependent on themselves than on others. This individualism may underlie the higher rate of suicide in the wide-open areas. By relying on themselves to solve their personal problems, people tend to be too subjective and emotional to find viable solutions (Thio, 2004).

Suicide is an extreme, exceptional act, but all around us, we can see ordinary actions that are also molded by social forces. The distribution of income in the United States, for example, is a social fact. Your family's position in that distribution is one of your social characteristics. This characteristic influences your way of living and your chances in life—such as the likelihood that you will pursue a successful career. Our private worlds can never be totally sealed off from the larger world of society and global community. The technology, economy, customs, ideals, beliefs, government, and politics in the United States, like those in other countries, are all social characteristics and represent social forces that help shape our lives.

THE DEVELOPMENT OF SOCIOLOGY

Sociology as a formal field of study has a very short history. Of course, centuries before Christ was born, thinkers such as Plato and Socrates thought and argued about social behavior. But most of them did not make systematic observations to test their speculations against reality. They were social philosophers, not sociologists. The field of sociology emerged in the nineteenth century, when European social philosophers began to use scientific methods.

At least two factors combined to convert some philosophers into sociologists: the social upheavals of nineteenth-century Europe and the advancement of the natural sciences. The Western world was radically altered during the nineteenth century as the Industrial Revolution brought new industries and technologies and new ways of living. Almost overnight, societies that had long been rural and stable became industrialized, urbanized, and chaotic. They confronted problems such as the exploitation of factory workers, the migration of people from farms to cities, congestion and poverty in the cities, crowded and squalid housing, broken families, and rising crime. Meanwhile, the European political order had been shaken. In the aftermath of the French Revolution, many people began to question the legitimacy of their monarchies and the authority of their churches, demanding greater freedom for the individual. Many social philosophers felt challenged to find solutions to their societies' new problems and to

*Inuit are popularly called "Eskimo," a derogatory term meaning "eater of raw meat."

understand how and why such radical change could occur. At the same time, the natural sciences were highly respected because they were providing ways both to explain and control aspects of the physical world. Some social philosophers looked on the natural sciences to provide models for how they might go about understanding and controlling the social world.

As sociology developed, these two urges—to improve the world and to apply scientific methods to the study of society—continued to motivate sociologists.

■ The Pioneers of Sociology

The nineteenth-century French philosopher Auguste Comte (1798–1857) is sometimes called the "father of sociology." He coined the term *sociology* in 1838 to refer to the scientific study of society. Comte believed that every society goes through three stages of development: religious, metaphysical, and scientific. According to Comte, reliance on superstition and speculation characterizes the religious and metaphysical stages, and neither is adequate for understanding society. What is needed, he argued, is scientific knowledge about society based on social facts, just as scientific knowledge about the physical world is based on physical facts. He envisioned a science of society with two branches: *statics,* the study of the organization that allows societies to endure, and *dynamics,* the study of the processes by which

FOUNDING FATHER   Auguste Comte (1798–1857) was the first to argue for the need for scientific knowledge about society. He is regarded as the "father of sociology." ■

societies change. During the scientific stage, Comte believed, sociologists would develop a scientific knowledge of society and would guide society in a peaceful, orderly evolution.

In England, Harriet Martineau (1802–1876), the first woman sociologist, agreed with Comte. She thought it useful to translate Comte's ideas into English for wider accessibility. But Martineau, also an accomplished writer, found Comte's work—which ran to six volumes—"overloaded with words," and she finally pruned it to just two volumes. The result is considerably more lucid and forceful than the original, and Comte was so impressed that he wanted Martineau's version translated back into French. Also, as an independent thinker in sociology, Martineau studied British and U.S. societies and suggested that societal progress could be achieved by expanding scientific knowledge in general and by eliminating slavery and gender inequality in particular (Hill and Hoecker-Drysdale, 2002; Hoecker-Drysdale, 1992).

Herbert Spencer (1820–1903), an Englishman, had a different view of how society works. He believed that a society can be compared to a living organism. Each part of an animal—its heart, lungs, brain, and so on—has its own function to perform, yet all the parts are interdependent; a change in one part affects all the others. Moreover, each part contributes to the survival and health of the animal as a whole. If one organ becomes diseased, the others adapt by working harder to ensure the animal's survival. Similarly, in Spencer's view, each part of a society performs its own function and contributes to the survival and stability of the whole. The family, religion, government, and industry are all seen as parts of one organism: society.

Spencer concluded that society, if left alone, corrects its own problems; it tends naturally toward health and stability. Social problems work themselves out through the process of natural selection called *survival of the fittest.* The phrase suggests that rich, powerful, or otherwise successful people—the fittest—have been selected by nature to be what they are. On the other hand, poor, weak, or otherwise unsuccessful individuals—the unfit—have been doomed by nature to failure. If government interferes with this natural process by helping the unfit, society will suffer because the efforts of its successful people will be wasted. According to Spencer, the best thing government can do about social problems is to leave them alone. The fate of society, in his view, is governed by laws of nature. If nature is left to do its job without government interference, society will not only survive but evolve to become better.

Where Spencer saw harmony and stability, Karl Marx (1818–1883) observed underlying conflict, exploitation, and the seeds of revolution. According to

Marx, a German who spent much of his life writing in England, Spencer's stable, interdependent society was a myth. The primary features of society, Marx claimed, are not stability and interdependence but conflict and competition. He saw every society, past and present, as marked by social conflict.

In particular, Marx claimed that the primary feature of society is **class conflict**, the struggle between capitalists, who own the means of production, and the proletariat, who do not. These two classes, he said, are inevitably locked in conflict. The laborers, far from being naturally unfit, are destined to overthrow the capitalists and establish a classless society in which everyone will work according to ability and receive according to need.

Marx did not believe, as did Spencer, that the differences between laborers and capitalists are determined by natural selection. On the contrary, Marx believed that they are determined by the economic system. In fact, he argued, the economic system determines a society's religious beliefs, its values, and the nature of its educational system, government, and other institutions. He urged people not to let society evolve on its own but to change it.

Despite their differences, both Marx and Spencer, like Comte, recognized the value of science in the study of society, but they did not actually use scientific methods. They merely argued about how society worked and how its troubles might be eased. It was Émile Durkheim (1858–1917) who pioneered the systematic application of scientific methods to sociology. His ideas about suicide, discussed earlier, were not based on speculation. In his study of suicide, he made a research plan and collected a large mass of statistical data on suicide in various European countries. Then he analyzed the data in order to discover the causes of suicide. He not only used systematic observation, but he also argued that sociologists should consider only what they could observe and should look at "social facts as things." They should not look, he said, to the "notions" of people in order to explain society. People's subjective experiences should not be a concern of sociologists.

In contrast, German sociologist Max Weber (1864–1920) believed that sociologists must go beyond what people do, beyond what can be observed directly. He argued that individuals always interpret the meaning of their own behavior and act according to these interpretations. Sociologists must therefore find out how people feel or what they think about their own behavior. To do this, according to Weber, sociologists should adopt a method he called **Verstehen** (pronounced fair-SHTAY-in)—empathetic understanding of their subjects. By putting themselves mentally in the positions of their subjects, sociologists could obtain "interpretive understandings" of the meanings of particular behaviors. Then, he said, they should test these understandings through careful observation.

■ Sociology in the United States

By the turn of the twentieth century, sociology had made its way from Europe to the United States. Like their European predecessors, the first U.S. sociologists tried to understand and solve the problems of their time, such as crime and delinquency, broken homes, poor neighborhoods, and racial problems. But they dealt with social problems differently. The Europeans were more interested in developing large-scale social theories. So they examined the fundamental issues of social order and social change, trying to discover the causes of social problems as a whole. In contrast, the U.S. sociologists were more pragmatic. They were more inclined to focus on specific problems, such as prostitution, street gangs, or racial discrimination in employment, and to treat each problem separately (Ross, 1991).

A good example was Jane Addams (1860–1935), one of the founders of U.S. sociology and social work. In Chicago, she set up and directed a center for social reform and research, which she named Hull House. Most of the social activists working at Hull House

METHOD MAN Émile Durkheim (1858–1917) pioneered the systematic application of scientific principles to sociology. He was the first to use statistical methods to test hypotheses. ■

SERVING SOCIETY   Jane Addams (1860–1935) conducted scientific research on social problems with the aim of eliminating or alleviating them. She is the only sociologist ever to have received a Nobel prize. ◼

were women. Their goal was to solve social problems using sound sociological theory and research. In their projects, Addams and her colleagues would first identify a certain problem, gather data documenting the nature of the problem, and then formulate a social-action policy based on the data. Their final step was to organize citizens and lobby political and community leaders to eliminate or alleviate the problem. They dealt with a wide array of social ills, including poverty, worker exploitation, child labor, and juvenile delinquency. Addams was thus able to play a significant role in establishing many government programs—most notably, Social Security, the Children's Bureau, and workers' compensation—and various government regulations affecting health and safety standards. For all these contributions, Addams was awarded the Nobel Peace Prize in 1931 (Ross, 1991; Deegan, 1988).

Another sociologist with the same dedication to improving society was W. E. B. DuBois (1868–1963), an African American. He graduated from Fisk University in Tennessee and became the first African Amer-

ican to receive a doctorate from Harvard University. Then, at Atlanta University, he founded the nation's second department of sociology. (The first was at the University of Chicago.) He soon began a highly productive academic career that included, among many other things, founding two scholarly journals and writing numerous books and articles. He focused his research and writing on the racial problems in the United States. At the same time, however, he worked hard to apply his enormous knowledge to improving the society. He founded the Niagara Movement, an organization of African American intellectuals fighting for racial equality. He also helped create the National Association for the Advancement of Colored People (NAACP) and edited its influential magazine, *Crisis*. Later, he became a revolutionary Marxist, advocating the use of force to achieve racial equality. Finally, seeing little improvement in race relations, he moved in 1961 to the African nation of Ghana, where he died two years later.

For about 40 years after 1900, most U.S. sociologists, such as Addams and DuBois, concentrated on

ESPOUSING EQUALITY   W. E. B. DuBois (1868–1963) was the first African American to receive a doctorate from Harvard University. As a sociologist, he focused his research and writing on the racial problems in the United States. He further worked hard to apply his enormous knowledge to achieving racial equality. ◼

studying and solving social problems. However, the prosperity that followed World War II masked many social problems, causing the reformist fervor to begin to cool. Some sociologists turned their attention to general theories of society. The idea grew that sociology should be a *basic science,* seeking knowledge only, not an *applied science,* which puts knowledge to use. Moreover, many people believed that sociology must be objective and free of values. This left no room for a commitment to reform society according to certain values. From about 1945 to 1965, sociology was dominated by the attempt to develop scientific methods that could be applied to the study of societies and social behavior. During these two decades, sociologists developed increasingly sophisticated research techniques.

In the 1960s, however, the ideal of objective, value-free knowledge came under fire in just about all fields, including sociology. Renewed awareness of poverty and years of social unrest—marked by race riots, student revolts, and controversy about the Vietnam War—put pressure on sociologists to attack society's ills once again. Meanwhile, attitudes toward the major theoretical perspectives in sociology were also shifting. The conflict perspective, which emphasizes social conflict as a constant fact of social life, was becoming popular at the expense of the functionalist perspective, which stresses the persistence of social order.

American sociology has thus developed into a diverse discipline. Today, it is both a basic and an applied science, and sociologists use both objective and subjective methods. The soaring number of sociologists—from only about 3,000 in the 1960s to over 20,000 today—has further splintered sociology into numerous specialties, such as mathematical sociology, organizational research, and race and ethnic relations. Each of these specialties has been differentiated into many subspecialties. The specialty of race relations, for example, has broken down into studies of African Americans, Hispanics, Asians, and other specific minorities in the United States. Underlying the diversity of those studies are certain theoretical perspectives that sociologists employ to study and understand social behavior. We will examine three major perspectives in the next section.

MAJOR PERSPECTIVES IN SOCIOLOGY

Sociologists approach the study of human society in different ways. They can look at the "big picture" of society to see how it operates. This is a **macro view**, focusing on the large social phenomena of society,

such as social institutions and inequality. Sociologists can also take a **micro view**, zeroing in on the immediate social situations in which people interact with one another. From these two views, sociologists have developed various **theoretical perspectives**, each a set of general assumptions about the nature of society. There are three well-known theoretical perspectives in sociology: the functionalist and conflict perspectives, which both provide a macro view of society, and the symbolic interactionist perspective, which offers a micro view.

■ Functionalist Perspective: A Focus on Social Order

Both Spencer and Durkheim provided ideas that inspired the **functionalist perspective**, which focuses on social order. According to this perspective, each part of society—the family, the school, the economy, the state—performs certain functions for the society as a whole. Moreover, all the parts are interdependent. The family, for example, depends on the school to educate its children, and the school, in turn, depends on the family and the state to provide financial support. The state, in turn, depends on the family and the school to help children grow up to become law-abiding, tax-paying citizens.

Out of these interdependent parts of society comes a stable social order. If something happens to disrupt this social order, its parts will adjust in a way that produces a new stability. Suppose the economy were in bad shape, with high rates of inflation and unemployment. The family would adjust, perhaps by spending less and saving more. Schools would probably offer fewer programs and might emphasize vocational training to help students find work. The state might try to cut its budget. As a result, a new social order would emerge.

However, what holds the society together, enabling all of its parts to produce social order? The answer, according to functionalists, is **social consensus**, a condition in which most members of the society agree on what would be good for everybody and cooperate to achieve it. Durkheim assumed that social consensus can come about in the form of either mechanical or organic solidarity.

Mechanical solidarity is a type of social cohesion that develops when people do similar work and have similar beliefs and values. It exists in relatively small-scale, traditional societies. An example is a society in which almost everyone works at farming and believes in the same gods.

In contrast, **organic solidarity** is a type of social cohesion that arises when the people in a society perform a wide variety of specialized jobs and therefore have to depend on one another. Organic solidarity is characteristic of complex industrialized societies. The people in a U.S. city, for example, are likely to hold many very different types of jobs, to have grown up with different family customs, and to hold varying beliefs and values. There are bankers, teachers, engineers, plumbers, and people who work in many other businesses, professions, and occupations. Among these people, there are probably atheists and Christians, Jews and Muslims, reactionaries and radicals, and everything in between.

Thus, mechanical solidarity among the city's population is not likely to be strong. They cannot be bound together by conformity to the same ideas and ideals. But they can be more easily bound together by their need for each other. The banker needs the worker who deposits and borrows money, and both need the storekeeper, who needs the trucker who delivers food, who needs the mechanic and gas station attendant, and so on. The complex ties of dependence seem virtually endless. These people are bound together by organic solidarity.

During the 1940s and 1950s, the functionalist perspective became widely accepted by U.S. sociologists. In its European origins, functionalism was used to help explain the society as a whole—to clarify how order and stability were maintained. American sociologists, on the other hand, have been more interested in discovering the functions of specific types of human behavior.

myth	The sole purpose of going to college is to get an education.
reality	Going to college also serves some latent functions, unintended and often unrecognized, such as enabling many students to find their future spouses.

The most prominent among these U.S. sociologists is Robert Merton (1957). He classified functions into two types: manifest and latent. **Manifest functions** are those that are intended and seem obvious; **latent functions** are unintended and often unrecognized. The manifest function of going to college, for example, is to get an education, but going to college also has the latent function of enabling many students to find their future spouses. Another latent function is to force students to learn the valuable lesson of negotiating their way through bureaucratic mazes to get things done. After four years of learning to master preregistration, financial aid forms, major and general education requirements, course schedules, and add-and-drop policies, you will find it easier to work in even the most formidable business bureaucracy.

The functionalist perspective has been criticized, however, for focusing on the positive functions of social events and ignoring the negative ones. It has also been attacked for being inherently conservative; in effect, it justifies the status quo. By emphasizing what every current aspect of society does for its citizens, functionalism encourages people to dismiss social change as *dysfunctional* (harmful), even though change may, in fact, produce a better society.

■ Conflict Perspective: A Focus on Social Conflict

The conflict perspective produces a portrait of society strikingly different from that offered by functionalism. Whereas functionalism emphasizes society's stability, the **conflict perspective** portrays society as always changing and always marked by conflict.

General View of Conflict Functionalists tend to focus on social order, to view social change as harmful, and to assume that the social order is based largely on people's willing cooperation. In contrast, proponents of the conflict perspective are inclined to concentrate on social conflict, to see social change as beneficial, and to assume that the social order is forcibly imposed by the powerful on the weak. They criticize the status quo.

The conflict perspective originated largely from Karl Marx's writings on class conflict between capitalists and the proletariat, discussed earlier. For decades, U.S. sociologists tended to ignore Marx and the conflict perspective because the functionalist perspective dominated their view of society. Since the turbulent 1960s, however, the conflict perspective has gained popularity. Generally, conflict is now defined more broadly. Whereas Marx believed that conflict between *economic* classes was the key force in society, conflict theorists today define social conflict to mean conflict between any *unequal* groups or societies. Thus, they examine conflict between whites and blacks, men and women, one religious group and another, one society and another, and so on. They emphasize that groups or societies have conflicting interests and values and compete with each other for scarce resources. The more powerful groups gain more than the less powerful, but the former continue to seek more wealth and power, while the latter continue to struggle for more resources. Because of this perpetual competition, society or the world is always changing.

The conflict perspective leads sociologists to ask such questions as: Which groups are more powerful, and which are more weak? How do powerful groups benefit from the existing social order, and how are weaker groups hurt? Consider, for example, how the conflict perspective can shed light on prostitution. According to this perspective, prostitution reflects

CLASS CLASH Conflict theories focus on conflicts between unequal groups, such as whites and blacks, men and women, one religious group and another, and so on. The more powerful groups are seen as seeking more wealth and power, while the less powerful are viewed as struggling for more resources and better lives. Here, a former powerless Enron employee holds up protest signs at a rally against the corrupt, powerful corporation. ■

the unequal social positions of men and women. In prostitution, members of a dominant group, men, benefit from the exploitation of a weaker group, women. This exploitation is made possible by the existence of a social order in which women are subordinate to men. If the sexes were treated equally—with women having full access to and being equally paid for more respectable types of work as men—women would be unlikely to become prostitutes. Prostitution further reinforces the general dominance of men over women because it helps perpetuate the sexist idea that women are inferior beings who can be used as mere objects for pleasure. In short, prostitution reflects and reinforces the power of one group over another.

Feminist Theory Some sociologists in recent decades have used the conflict perspective to fashion a **feminist theory**, a form of conflict theory that explains human life in terms of the experiences of women. Details of the theory vary from one sociologist to another. But they suggest, in one way or another, how women's lives differ from men's, with the assumption that these gender differences shape the lives of all of us.

First, women's experiences are said to *differ* from those of men. There is a diversity of feminist views on what the gender differences are. However, most agree that being interested in bearing and caring for infants, tending to be gentle rather than tough, and tending to be peaceful rather than violent toward others are among the characteristics that generally distinguish women from men. To feminists, these feminine values are at least equal, if not superior, to

traditional masculine values. They deserve to be respected and recognized as valuable alternatives to, rather than as undesirable departures from, male values. But men have long regarded these traits as less valuable, which reinforces the devaluation of women's social position.

Second, feminist theory holds that women's position in most social situations is *unequal* to that of men. Compared with men, women have less power, freedom, respect, and money. This gender inequality goes hand in hand with the widely held sexist belief that women are inferior to men.

Third, feminist theory views women as *oppressed*—restrained, subordinated, controlled, molded, or abused—by a male-dominated society. This is the essence of **patriarchy**, a system of domination in which men exercise power over women. The oppression may involve overt physical violence against women, such as rape, wife abuse, and incest. It may assume more subtle forms such as unpaid household work, underpaid wage work, sexual harassment in the workplace, and the standards of fashion and beauty that reduce women to men's sexual playthings (Lengermann and Niebrugge-Brantley, 1992).

According to feminist theory, then, women are not only different from men but also unequal to men and oppressed by men. Given these negative experiences, the theory suggests, women are bound to challenge the status quo by seeking gender equality in education, career, marriage, and other areas of life. The theory is therefore useful for understanding the changes that have been taking place in the lives of both women and men throughout society. The theory has been criticized, however, for overemphasizing the oppressiveness of patriarchy. According to critics, not all men are oppressors and not all women are victims. In fact, in critics' views, most women are far from being victims of their fathers, husbands, and sons; instead, women receive love, assistance, and other benefits from them. In the same way, the conflict perspective itself has been criticized for overly stressing social conflict and other negative aspects of society while ignoring the order, stability, and other positive aspects.

Symbolic Interactionist Perspective: A Focus on Social Interactions

Both functionalist and conflict perspectives focus on larger social forces of order, conflict, and patriarchy, forces that simultaneously affect huge numbers of people across the country. In contrast, the **symbolic interactionist perspective** directs our attention to the details of a specific situation and the interaction between individuals in that situation. The combination of these countless interactions in various situations is seen to constitute society. We can trace the origins of symbolic interactionism to Max Weber's argument that people act according to their interpretation of the meaning of their social world. But it was George Herbert Mead (1863–1931), a U.S. philosopher, who introduced symbolic interactionism to sociology in the 1920s.

According to symbolic interactionism, people assign meanings to each other's words and actions. Our response to a person's action is therefore determined not by that person's action in itself but by our *subjective interpretation* of the action. When we speak to a friend, an observer can easily give an objective report of the words we have said. But our friend's response will depend not on the words we spoke but on his or her interpretation of the entire interaction; at the same time, our friend's response is influencing what we are saying. If our friend perceives by the way we speak that we are intelligent, this interpretation may make our friend respect and admire us and, perhaps, respond more positively to what we are saying. If we, in turn, catch this interpretation, we may feel proud and speak more confidently. In other words, the exchange is a *symbolic interaction*. It is an interaction between individuals that is governed by their interpretation of the meaning of symbols. In this case, the symbols are primarily spoken words. But a symbol can be anything—an object, a sound, a gesture—that points to something beyond itself. The marks on this paper are symbols because they point to things—they have meanings—beyond black squiggles.

The symbolic interactionist perspective suggests two things. First, people do not respond directly to physical things. Rather, they respond to their *own* interpretations of them. Second, because people constantly impose interpretations—on the world in general, on other people, themselves, and even their own interpretations—and then act accordingly, human behavior is fluid, always changing. How we act is constantly being altered by how we interpret other people's actions and their reactions to our own behavior. Human behavior is thus not real in itself but becomes real only after it has been subjected to *reality construction,* the process by which we interpret what a given action means and respond to it in accordance with the interpretation.

The symbolic interactionist perspective has been criticized, however, for ignoring the larger issues of national and international order and change. It has also been faulted for ignoring the influence of larger social forces, such as social institutions, groups, cultures, and societies, on individual interactions.

A Multiple View

After thinking about these three perspectives, you may ask: Which one is right? The answer can be found in the following story from sociologist Elliot Liebow (1993):

> Mr. Shapiro and Mr. Goldberg had an argument they were unable to resolve.
> It was agreed that Mr. Shapiro would present the case to a rabbi.
> The rabbi said to Mr. Shapiro, "You are right."
> When Mr. Goldberg learned of this, he ran to the rabbi with his version of the argument. The rabbi said to him, "You are right."
> Then the rabbi's wife said to the rabbi, "You told Mr. Shapiro he was right and you told Mr. Goldberg he was right. They can't both be right!"
> The rabbi said to his wife, "You are right too."

As the rabbi would say, each of the three perspectives in sociology is right in its own way. Each shows what our world looks like, but only when viewed from a certain angle. The Theoretical Thumbnail on page 16 provides an overview of the key features of each perspective.

Although different, the three perspectives are not really incompatible. To some extent, they are like different perspectives on a house. Looked at from the front, the house has a door, windows, and a chimney on top. From the back, it has a door and a chimney on top but probably fewer windows and maybe a porch. From the top, it has no doors or windows, but it has a chimney in the middle. It is the same house, but it looks very different, depending on perspective. Similarly, whether we see functions, conflict, or interaction depends on the position from which we are looking. Each perspective is useful because we cannot take everything about the complex social world

theoretical thumbnail

Major Perspectives in Sociology

Perspective	Focus	Insights
Functionalist	Social order or stability	Society consists of interdependent groups pursuing common goals. Social order is maintained through social consensus, whereby people agree to cooperate in order to contribute to social order.
Conflict (including feminist theory)	Social conflict or change	Society is made up of conflicting groups, such as women and men, each pursuing their own interests. Social order is maintained through coercion, whereby social order is imposed by the powerful over the weak, such as how patriarchy is imposed by men on women.
Symbolic interactionist	Interaction between individuals	Society is composed of individuals whose actions depend on interpreting each other's behavior. Social order is maintained through constant negotiations between individuals trying to understand each other's actions and reactions.

into account at once. We need some vantage point. Each perspective tells us what to look for, and each brings some aspect of society and human behavior into sharper focus. Brought together, these diverse perspectives can enrich our sociological knowledge of the world.

Suppose we want to study the interaction between whites and blacks or between upper- and lower-class people. Each perspective can be useful. Functionalist and conflict perspectives can clarify how the interaction is affected by larger social forces, such as the popular belief in democracy and equality, the long history of racial prejudice, and the differences in lifestyle or power between rich and poor. Symbolic interactionism can give us a richer, more detailed view of specific interactions and an understanding of why people who are exposed to the same social forces behave in different ways. Moreover, the three perspectives can be used to check each other to see if we have overemphasized any one perspective and missed the complex reality of the world in which we live. In the next section, we will see how the three perspectives can be used to shed light on sports.

SPORTS: ILLUSTRATING THE THREE PERSPECTIVES

The influence of sports reaches far and wide. Sports are particularly popular in the leisure-oriented American society. Most of us have had some experience with athletics as participants or spectators. Schools, from elementary to college, provide many sports opportunities. Many newspapers carry more news about sports than about politics, the economy, crime, or practically any other event. Radio and television newscasts rarely go on the air without a sports report. Football, basketball, baseball, and other games are often broadcast in their entirety, preempting regular programming. Sports exert so much influence on our lives that our everyday speech is full of sports imagery: "struck out," "touch base," "ballpark figure," "game plan," "teamwork," "cheap shot," "go all the way," and so on.

What, then, is the nature of this powerful aspect of our lives? From the three sociological perspectives, we can see that sports are beneficial to society in some ways, harmful in other ways, and, like any other social interaction, governed by individuals' definitions of each other's actions.

■ Sports as Beneficial to Society

According to the functionalist perspective, sports contribute to the welfare of society by performing at least three major functions.

First, sports are conducive to success in other areas of life. Being competitive, sports inspire athletes to do their utmost to win, thereby helping them to develop such qualities as skill and ability, diligence and self-discipline, mental alertness, and physical fitness. These qualities can ensure success in the larger society. In the words of General Douglas MacArthur: "Upon the fields of friendly strife are sown the seeds that, upon other fields, on other days, will bear the fruits of victory." In fact, while still in high school,

MORE THAN FUN AND GAMES To functionalists, sports help athletes develop such qualities as skill and ability, diligence and self-discipline, mental alertness, and physical fitness, which in turn help athletes be successful in the larger society. ■

athletes already benefit from playing interscholastic sports. As research by Beckett Broh (2002) shows, athletes turn the tables on the "dumb jock" stereotype by achieving higher grades in English and math than other students. Athletes also have higher self-esteem, friends who are more academically oriented, and stronger ties to their parents and school officials. These are qualities and experiences that will later help ensure success in a career and other aspects of life.

Second, sports enhance health and happiness. Participants can enjoy a healthy, long life. The health benefit is more than physical. It is also psychological. Runners and joggers, for example, often find that their activity releases tension and anger as well as relieves anxiety and depression. Moreover, many people derive much pleasure from looking on their participation as a form of beauty, an artistic expres-

sion, or a way of having a good time with friends. Similarly, sports improve the quality of life for the spectators. Fans can escape their humdrum daily routines or find pleasure in filling their leisure time, as many Americans do when watching baseball, long known as the national pastime (see Figure 1.4, p. 18). They can savor the aesthetic pleasure of watching the excellence, beauty, and creativity in an athlete's performance. The fans can therefore attain greater happiness, life satisfaction, or psychological well-being (Smith, 1996).

Third, sports contribute to social order and stability by serving as an integrating force for society as a whole. Sports are, in effect, a social mechanism for uniting potentially disunited members of society. Through their common interest in a famous athlete or team, people of diverse racial, social, and cultural backgrounds can feel a sense of homogeneity, community, or intimacy that they can acquire in no other way. Athletes, too, can identify with their fans, their community, and their country.

■ Sports as Harmful to Society

According to the conflict perspective, sports harm society by serving the interests of the relatively powerful over those of the powerless in at least two ways.

"Well, it sure seems to me that a $4 million a year pitcher should be able to strike out a $1.2 million a year hitter once in a while!"

Source: From the *Wall Street Journal*—Permission, Cartoon Features Syndicate.

FIGURE 1.4

Taking in the National Pastime

According to the functionalist perspective, sports contribute to the welfare of society by performing certain functions. One function involves improving the quality of life for the spectators of sports. Many Americans, for example, can escape their humdrum daily routines or find pleasure in filling their leisure time by watching baseball, long known as the national pastime. This map shows that these baseball enthusiasts live mostly outside the South.

Critical Thinking: *Why do you think baseball is less popular in the South than elsewhere?*

Source: Claritas, Inc., Simmons Market Research Bureau, as appeared in *Newsweek,* April 13, 1998, p. 8.

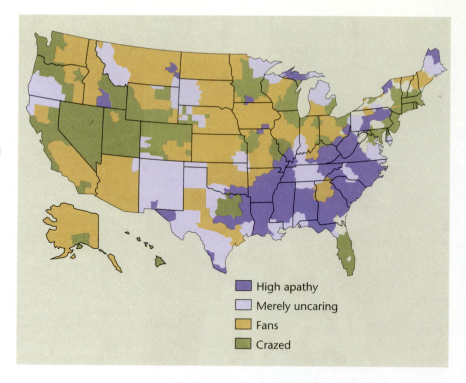

- High apathy
- Merely uncaring
- Fans
- Crazed

First, sports tend to act as an opiate, numbing the masses' sense of dissatisfaction with capitalist society. Involvement in sports as spectators tends to distract low-paid or unemployed workers from their tedious and dehumanizing jobs or frustrating joblessness. At the same time, sports tend to promote what Marx called "false consciousness," attitudes that support the established society rather than question it. The mostly working-class "soccer hooligans" in Great Britain are a good example. After their team loses in international soccer games, they often show "an exaggerated, embarrassing patriotism, a violent nationalism," by attacking foreigners (Buford, 1992). To divert their citizens' attention from their miserable lives, governments of many poor countries also seize any opportunity that arises to whip up the masses into a frenzy of patriotic support for their teams. Such a nationalistic frenzy can be carried to extremes, as it was in 1969 when Honduras and El Salvador went to war against each other after a World Cup soccer match. All this serves to maintain the capitalist system by which the rich and powerful exploit the masses.

Second, sports reinforce social, gender, and racial inequalities in society. With regard to social inequality, the overemphasis on competition and winning has caused the loss of something that all participants can enjoy equally—namely, the original elements of play and fun in sporting activities. This has turned many people into "couch potatoes," who spend more time watching than playing sports. Sports, then, have become big business, with powerful owners of professional teams exploiting the public and government. Aside from making enormous sums of money from the fans, team owners receive many tax breaks while enjoying the enviable position of being the only self-regulated (in effect, unregulated) monopoly in the nation. Team owners have further professionalized and bureaucratized sports. This, in turn, has led to an elitist system in which a very tiny group of owners and players become tycoons and superstars, while a huge number of potential players are transformed into mere spectators.

It is true that over the last two decades, sports participation among women has risen sharply, thanks to the women's liberation movement and the 1972 law that prohibits sex discrimination in school sports. Nevertheless, in many colleges and universities, more funds continue to be spent on men's sports, especially football and basketball, than on women's athletic programs. Because of gender bias, men are even more likely than women to get the top management and coaching jobs in *women's* programs (Chambers, 1997; Diesenhouse, 1990). The sports arena is still considered a "man's world" in which women's leadership skills are devalued. Even the skills of superb women athletes are discounted by the media, which often describe female athletes as "pretty," "slim," "attractive," "gracious," and "lovely," as opposed to male athletes, who are "brilliant," "cool," "courageous," "great," and "tough." In glorifying masculinity, sports further encourage male athletes to commit rape, sexual harassment, and physical abuse (Steiss, 2001; Nelson, 1994). Internationally, the United States ranks only average when it comes to women's participation in the Olympics, falling behind such countries as China, Peru, and the Central African Republic (see Figure 1.5, p. 20).

On the surface, the large number of remarkably successful African American athletes in basketball and football today may cast doubt on the existence of racial inequality in sports. But African Americans do suffer from racism in some ways, as indicated by the virtual absence of blacks in top positions as owners, managers, and coaches of professional teams.

Far more significantly, however, sports may help perpetuate the relatively high rate of poverty among African Americans. Traditionally, severe, widespread job discrimination has caused many poor African American youths to work extremely hard to develop athletic skills in order to make it in college and professional sports, which explains why most of the best athletes in the country are African American. Today, the enormous attention given by the white-dominated media to African American superstars further encourages many poor African American youths to give their all to athletics. But this intense concentration on sports has diverted attention from academic work. This is tragic because, given the same hard work, it is far easier to become a professional in business, government, education, or any other field. The

chances of becoming a professional athlete are extremely small. Only 1 or 2 percent of high school players with college athletic scholarships will end up in professional sports, while nearly 100 percent of their nonathlete peers with scholarships for academic achievement will become professionals in other, nonathletic fields. Understandably, the late black tennis star Arthur Ashe (1977) urged African American youths to spend two hours in the library for every hour spent on the athletic field.

■ Sports as Symbolic Interaction

While the functionalist and conflict perspectives focus on the larger societal issues of sports that affect most people, symbolic interactionism hones in on the smaller, immediate issue of how athletes—or other individuals involved in a sport, such as coaches and fans—behave. According to this third perspective, if we define a situation as real, it is real in its consequences. Thus, if athletes define a game as one that they will win, they will likely win it. This may explain why Tiger Woods is currently the world's greatest golfer. After watching many golfers being interviewed on TV, hockey legend Wayne Gretzky had this observation: "Most golfers can't believe they won. Tiger sounds like he expected to win or can't believe he didn't" (Gordon, 2001). Let's take a closer look at how definition influences performance.

Great coaches know that they can get their athletes to perform well by drumming certain ideas into their heads. Foremost is the idea that the players are winners, so that they will think only of winning and never about the possibility of losing. Chances are high that they indeed will win because the image of themselves as winners will force them to concentrate only on the moves that ensure winning. This is basically the technique Jack Nicklaus, perhaps the greatest golfer of the past several decades, used to enhance his performance. Before every shot, he formed a mental picture in which he saw three things: (1) the target area the ball would land in, (2) the flight path of the ball to the target area, and (3) himself using the appropriate swing for that particular shot (Vealey and Walter, 1998). In short, if athletes define themselves as winners, they are more likely to win. By the same token, if athletes define themselves as losers, they will very likely lose.

Whatever the content of self-definition, it does not necessarily come from within the person. It is more likely to originate from social interaction. Children under age 10, for example, often evaluate how good or bad they are at a sport based on what their significant others (parents, teachers, or coaches) say to them. Thus, children describe themselves in ways such as "I know I am a good runner because my mom

BIAS LINGERS Thanks to the women's movement and the law against sex discrimination in school sports, the number of women athletes on college campuses has risen sharply. Nevertheless, in most colleges and universities, more funds continue to be spent on men's sports than on women's athletic programs. ■

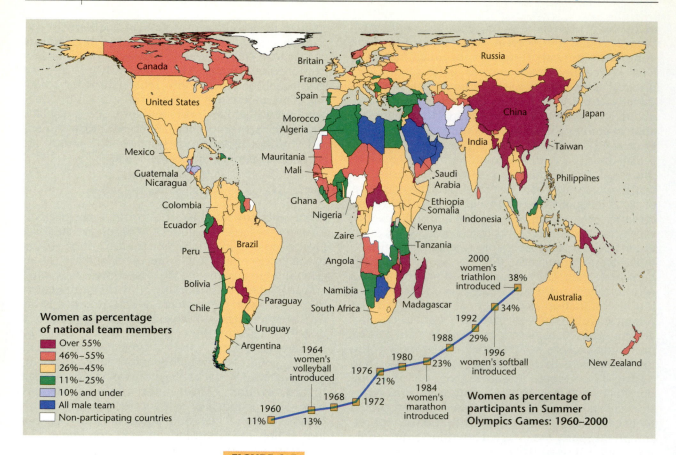

FIGURE 1.5

Women's Participation in the Olympics

More and more women from around the world have participated in the Olympics in recent years, but their participation rate still lags behind that of men, representing only 38 percent of the athletes at the latest Olympics in 2002. Gender inequality is greatest in Muslim societies, such as Saudi Arabia, Libya, Iran, and Turkey. But even the United States and most other Western countries are still a long way from achieving full equality. At least two factors discourage female participation in the Olympics: Athletic women and girls tend to be stigmatized as unfeminine, and less money and media attention are showered on female sports and athletes.

Critical Thinking: *What other reasons might explain the lower rate of women's participation in the Olympics?*

Source: From *The Penguin Atlas of Women in the World,* by Joni Seager, copyright © 1997, 2003 by Myriad Editions Ltd, maps & graphics. Used by permission of Penguin, a division of Penguin Group (USA) Inc.

says I am" and "I don't think that I'm a very good soccer player because my coach is always yelling at me" (Horn and Lox, 1998).

Indeed, how others see us when they interact with us can shape how we define ourselves. But just as we often derive our self-definition from our social environment, others also develop their image of us from *their* environment. In interacting with an African American athlete, for example, a coach tends to stereotype the athlete as naturally gifted in sports. This stereotype, part of the popular belief about African Americans in U.S. society, has a significant impact on the coach's interaction with the African American athlete. Most commonly, the coach will impose a higher standard of performance on an African American athlete than on a white athlete.

And the African American athlete will be forced to work harder to achieve that higher standard, which may partly explain why African American athletes usually outshine their white peers on the same team. Similarly, gender bias in the larger society has often led parents and teachers to discourage young women from playing basketball, soccer, and other so-called male sports, defining women who want to compete in these games as unfeminine. As a result, many women have responded by avoiding these sports and choosing the so-called female sports, such as aerobic dancing, swimming, gymnastics, and tennis. The popular definition of some sports as masculine and others as feminine can also influence the spectators. Masculine sports, such as football and soccer, for example, are more likely to cause fan violence than are feminine sports, such as gymnastics and swimming.

■ An Evaluation

We have observed how the three sociological perspectives can shed light on different aspects of sports. Combined, the perspectives can offer not only a *fuller* but also a *more balanced* view of the subject. The combination of functionalist and conflict perspectives, for example, provides the balanced view that sports are *both* beneficial and harmful—rather than either totally beneficial or totally harmful. Symbolic interactionism can also balance either of the other two perspectives.

Consider the conflict perspective's assumption that the British soccer hooligans' violence is an expression of patriotism. This cannot be taken to mean that the violence *completely* or *only* reflects the hooligans' patriotism because we know from symbolic interactionism that fans' violence may *also* reflect a unique interaction between players and spectators. In basketball, football, and other sports popular in the United States, players of both teams usually score some points, thrilling the fans. By contrast, points are rarely scored in soccer. In a typical game, fans of the losing team are repeatedly put through the wringer, waiting with heightened expectation for a goal that never comes. The cumulative effect of these repeated disappointments at the end of the game is likely to trigger violence among fans, such as the British soccer hooligans, who are already frustrated by their working-class lives. Also consider the functionalist assumption that sports enable athletes to develop qualities such as skill, diligence, and self-discipline that can ensure success in other areas of life. But this cannot be *always* true because symbolic interactionism suggests that most amateur athletes do not develop their skill to the level of a professional since they define their sports as fun rather than as hard work.

In conclusion, it is important to consider each of the three different perspectives. Together, they can offer not only a fuller but also a more balanced view of sports.

Major research methods

From the three major sociological perspectives, we can draw many ideas about how social forces shape our lives. Yet these ideas are merely idle guesswork unless they are backed up by scientific facts. The need for facts is one important reason sociologists conduct research. The purpose of social research, however, is not only to check the presumed validity of existing theories about people and society. It also is to produce information that describes our lives and to develop new theories that explain how our lives are influenced by various social forces. Thus, the production of sociological knowledge depends heavily on social research. It involves the use of four basic methods: survey, observation (including ethnography), experiment, and analysis of existing data.

■ Survey

Of the four research methods, the **survey**—which involves asking questions about opinions, beliefs, or behaviors—is most frequently used by sociologists. Suppose we want to know if there is a gender difference in the fequency of thinking about sex. We could take a survey and find that men think about sex much more than women do (see Figure 1.6, p. 22). Or suppose a theory suggests that students' social classes and geographical backgrounds (urban, rural, or suburban) are related to their sexual behavior. Survey data could be collected to determine whether this might be true.

Sampling To take a survey, we first select a **population**, the entire group of people to be studied. We can choose a population of any size, but all of its members must have something in common. Thus, a population may consist of all U.S. adults aged 30 to 40, all U.S. congresswomen, all of the students at a large university, or all the people in the world.

If a population is relatively small, all of its members can be approached and interviewed. If a population is very large, it would cost too much time and money to contact all of its members. In such a case, we need a **sample**, a relatively small number of people selected from a larger population. The sample, however, must accurately represent the entire population from which it is drawn. Otherwise, the information obtained from the sample cannot be generalized to the population. Failing to remember this may produce misleading conclusions.

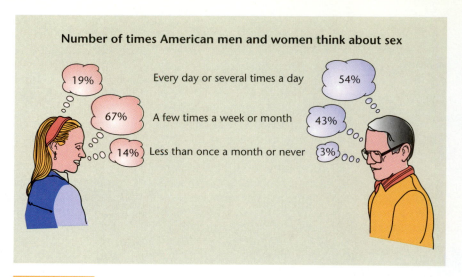

FIGURE 1.6

How to Conduct a Survey

To find out if gender influences how often people think about sex, a team of sociologists randomly chose a sample of 3,159 adults, aged 18 and older, from all over the United States. This randomly selected national sample can be said to represent the entire population of American adults because the process of random selection ensures that every adult has the same chance of getting selected. Then the researchers called up and asked the members of this random, representative sample the question "How often do you think about sex?" with the responses as given here. The results showed that men think about sex more often than women, leading the researchers to conclude that gender does influence the frequency of erotic thoughts.

Critical Thinking: *Do men really think more about sex or just feel freer to reveal to others their erotic thoughts? Defend or explain your answer.*

Source: Data from Judith Mackay, *The Penguin Atlas of Human Sexual Behavior* (London, England: Penguin Group, 2000), p. 21.

If a sample is to be representative, all members of the population must have the same chance of being selected for the sample. Selection, in effect, must be random, which is why a representative sample is often called a **random sample.** A crude way to select a random sample is to throw the names of all members of a population into a hat, mix them up, and then pull out as many names as needed for a sample. This method may be too cumbersome to use if the population is very large. There are more sophisticated and convenient techniques for drawing random samples from large populations. The methods most commonly used are systematic sampling and stratified sampling.

Systematic sampling is the process of drawing a random sample systematically rather than haphazardly. It involves using a system, such as selecting every tenth or hundredth person in the population. In contrast, *stratified sampling* is used when the population can be divided into various strata or categories, such as males and females or rural, urban, and suburban residents. To draw a stratified sample, we have to know what percentage of the population falls into each of the categories used and then select a random sample in which each category is represented in exactly the same proportion as it is in the population. Suppose we know that the population of a city is 52 percent female and 48 percent male; then our stratified sample should also be 52 percent female and 48 percent male. Thus, **stratified sampling** is the process of drawing a random sample in which various categories of people are represented in proportions equal to their presence in the population.

Questionnaires and Interviews   Given a representative sample, we can ask its members about their opinions, attitudes, or behaviors. This is usually done by using self-administered questionnaires, personal interviews, or telephone interviews.

In using *self-administered questionnaires,* the researcher simply gives or sends the people in the sample a list of questions and asks them to fill in the answers themselves. Usually the list consists of true-false or multiple-choice questions. The respondents

"We spent a lot of money educating him, so if you want Junior's opinion, you'll have to pay for it."

Source: Harley Schwadron.

are asked to answer "yes," "no," or "don't know" or to check one of the answers, such as "single," "married," "divorced," or "widowed."

Personal interviews may be either structured or unstructured. In a **structured interview**, the researcher asks standardized questions that require respondents to choose from among several standardized answers, comparable to those in self-administered questionnaires. But in an **unstructured interview**, open-ended questions are asked and respondents are allowed to answer freely, in their own words.

Telephone interviews have recently become popular in survey research and are routinely used in many public opinion polls. An even more convenient method, computer-assisted telephone interviewing, has become increasingly popular. The U.S. Census Bureau and commercial survey firms already use this method.

■ Observation and Ethnography

It is obvious from the preceding section that in surveys, we depend on others to tell us what has happened. By contrast, in observation, we rely on ourselves to go where the action is—and to watch what is happening. There are two ways to observe an ongoing activity. In **detached observation**, we observe as outsiders, from a distance, without getting involved. As detached observers, we may watch children playing in a schoolyard or bring them into a room and watch from behind a one-way mirror. Detached observation has the advantage of making it less likely that the subjects will be affected by the observer. But it has at least one disadvantage: The

detached observer has difficulty perceiving and understanding subtle communication among the subjects. The detached observer behind a one-way mirror might not see some important facial expressions or understand the emotions attached to some unconventional symbols.

The second type of observation avoids this problem. In **participant observation**, researchers take part in the activities of the group they are studying. Sometimes they conceal their identity as researchers when they join the group. This enhances the chances that the unknowing subjects will act naturally. If the subjects knew they were being observed, they might change their behavior. As members of the group, researchers have the opportunity to observe practically everything, including whatever secret activities are hidden from outsiders. As a result, researchers can discover some surprising facts about their subjects. Consider, for example, the following classic case of participant observation involving a concealed researcher identity.

Most people assume that if men engage in same-sex practices, they must be gay. If you make this assumption, the results of Laud Humphreys's (1970) classic research may surprise you. Humphreys concealed his identity as a researcher by offering to serve as a lookout for men engaging in same-sex activity in public restrooms, which was against the law. Without being suspected of being an outsider, Humphreys also succeeded in secretly jotting down his subjects' automobile license plate numbers, which he used to trace their addresses. A year later, he disguised himself, visited those men at their homes, and found that they were mostly conservative lower-class married men who were seeking the same-sex experience as a means of releasing tension. They considered themselves straight and masculine. Humphreys has been severely criticized for being unethical in deceiving his subjects. He has argued, though, that had he not concealed his identity, it would have been impossible to get scientifically accurate information because his subjects would have behaved differently or would have refused to be studied.

Many sociologists do identify themselves as researchers to the people they study. They do not worry that revealing their true identity will change their subjects' behavior. They are not overly concerned that subjects will hide secrets from them. Usually, they strive to minimize these problems by not getting too deeply involved with their subjects while simultaneously establishing a good rapport with them. This is not easy to accomplish. Nevertheless, such efforts have paid off, as indicated by some sociological insights that have emerged from their work. Herbert Gans (1982), for example, became a participant observer in a poor Italian neighborhood in Boston in the late 1950s. On the surface, the neighborhood looked like a badly organized place, an urban jungle of its period. Yet Gans discovered that it was a well-organized community—an urban village rather than a jungle—where the residents enjoyed close social relationships with one another.

But in participant observation, Gans and other traditional sociologists basically play the role of outsider to their subjects and therefore use the outsider's objective perspective to study their subjects' world. Many modern sociologists, however, get more involved with their subjects, living with them as friends and viewing their world from their own standpoint—namely, from the insider's subjective perspective (Neuman, 2000). These sociologists are engaged in **ethnography,** an analysis of people's lives from their own perspective. In ethnography, the researcher focuses more on *meanings* (what subjects think, believe, or ponder) than on *activities* (what subjects do or how they behave).

This research method has produced interesting insights. In their ethnographic study of people who are homeless in Austin, Texas, for example, David Snow and Leon Anderson (2003, 1993) made a startling discovery. Conventional people often associate some disabilities or pathologies—such as a drinking problem, drug abuse, or mental disorder—with homeless individuals. But Snow and Anderson found that the disabilities usually do not inhere in homeless persons but instead stem from the disabling situation called *homelessness.* As Snow and Anderson explain, "If the presumably troubled individual is removed from the disabling context or the context is repaired, the disabilities often disappear or at least lose salience."

Whether carried out with detachment, with participation as a disguised member, or with participation as a known researcher, observation has the advantage of providing firsthand experience with natural, real-life situations. This is particularly true of ethnography. The wealth of findings derived from these methods are useful for developing new theories. Gans's data, for example, can be used to suggest the theory that many poor neighborhoods in the city are actually well-organized communities. This very advantage, however, is also a disadvantage. Because rich findings from observation techniques are relevant to one particular case study but not necessarily generalizable to other cases, they may not be used for testing theories. To test theories, sociologists usually use surveys, which we have discussed, or experiments.

■ Experiment

Actually, a theory can be tested only indirectly, not directly. It must be translated into a hypothesis or a

LEAVE THEM ALONE Detached observation is one method of gathering data. From behind a two-way mirror, this researcher unobtrusively records the meeting of a focus group at an advertising agency. The validity of the results that will come from this study will be enhanced because the subjects are likely to behave as they would under normal circumstances and not change their behavior to please the observer. ■

series of related hypotheses that can be tested directly—more specific statements that can be demonstrated to be either true or false. To test a hypothesis, researchers first specify what they assume to be the *independent variable* (cause) and the *dependent variable* (effect). Then they create a situation in which they can determine whether the independent variable indeed causes the dependent variable. They are, in effect, conducting an **experiment,** a research operation in which the researcher manipulates variables so that their influence can be determined.

Consider an experiment conducted by Matthew McGlone (1998). He wanted to test the hypothesis that nice-sounding statements make even dubious notions more believable. He gave students a list of rhyming sentences, such as "Woes unite foes," and asked them how accurately the sentences described human behavior. Then he asked the same students to judge the accuracy of nonrhyming statements, such as "Misfortunes unite foes." The result was that the students considered the rhyming statements more accurate. Later, when asked whether they agreed that financial success makes people healthier, nearly all of the students said no. But they regarded "Wealth makes health" as somehow more plausible. All this led the researcher to speculate that at O. J. Simpson's 1995 murder trial, the defense lawyer's repeated intonation of "If the glove doesn't fit, you must acquit" may have had its desired impact on the jurors.

Quite often, sociologists design controls to ensure that a hidden intervening variable is not producing the apparent effect of the independent variable. To do this, they generally select two groups of people who are similar in all respects except for the way they are treated in the experiment. One group, called the **experimental group**, is exposed to the independent variable; the second, called the **control group**, is not. If the researchers find that the experimental group differs from the control group with respect to the dependent variable, they may reasonably conclude that the independent variable is the cause of this effect.

In a classic experiment, for example, Robert Rosenthal (1973) and his colleague Lenore Jacobson wanted to test the theory of the self-fulfilling prophecy. In applying this theory to the classroom, they hypothesized that teachers' expectations influence students' performance. That is, if a teacher considers certain students unintelligent and expects them to do poorly in class, the students will do poorly. If the teacher regards other students as intelligent and expects them to perform well, they will perform well. To test this hypothesis, Rosenthal and Jacobson gave all the children in an elementary school an IQ test. Then, *without looking at the test results,* they randomly chose a small number of children and told their teachers—falsely—that these children had scored very high on the test. The intention was to make the teachers expect these supposedly bright children to show remarkable success later in the year. Thus, the experimental group consisted of these "bright" children, who were exposed to high teacher expectations; the control group included the rest of the pupils. Eight months later, the researchers went back to the school and gave all the children another test. They found that the experimental group did perform better than the control group. They concluded that teachers' expectations (the independent variable) were indeed the cause of student performance (the dependent variable).

■ Analysis of Existing Data

So far, we have discussed methods for collecting data from scratch. Sometimes, it is unnecessary to gather new information because of the availability of data collected previously by someone else. Sometimes, it is simply impossible to conduct an interview, observation, or experiment because the people we want to study are long dead. Thus, sociologists often turn to analysis of existing data, which may be in the form of secondary analysis or content analysis.

In **secondary analysis,** the sociologist searches for new knowledge in the data collected earlier by another researcher. Usually, the original investigator had gathered the data for a specific purpose and the secondary analyst uses them for something else. Suppose we want to study religious behavior by means of secondary analysis. We might get our data from an existing study of voting behavior conducted by a political scientist. This kind of research typically provides information on each voter's religion, along with his or her education, income, gender, and other social characteristics. The political scientist may try to find out from this research whether, among other things, men are more likely than women to vote in a presidential election and whether the more religious are more politically active than the less religious. As secondary analysts, we can find out from the same data whether women attend church more often than men.

The data for secondary analysis are usually quantitative, presented in the form of numbers, percentages, and other statistics, such as the *percentage* of women compared to the *percentage* of men attending church once a week. But some of the existing information is qualitative, in the form of words or ideas. Such information can be found in virtually all kinds of human communication—books, magazines, newspapers, movies, TV programs, speeches, letters, songs, laws, and so on. To study human behavior from these materials, sociologists often do **content analysis**, searching for specific words or ideas and then turning them into numbers.

How can we carry out "this marvelous social alchemy" (Bailey, 1994) that transforms verbal documents into *quantitative* data? Suppose we want to know whether public attitudes toward sex have changed significantly in the last 20 years. We may find the answer by comparing popular novels of today with those of the past to see if one set is more erotic than the other. We would first decide what words will reflect the nature of eroticism. After we settle on a list of words, such as *love, kiss,* and *embrace,* to serve as indicators of eroticism, we will look for them in a novel. We will count the number of times those words appear on an average page, and we will use the number as the measure of how erotic the novel is. In repeating the same process with other novels, we will see which ones are more erotic.

Table 1.1 (p. 26) summarizes the key characteristics of the major research methods used in sociology, with their advantages and disadvantages.

■ Research Ethics

Sociological research can be very useful to society. It can, for example, help the government serve citizens better, politicians get more votes, businesses sell more products, and the general public live better lives. But research can also be harmful by producing data to help an organization overthrow the government or to

TABLE 1.1

Major Research Methods in Sociology

Method	Characteristics	Advantages	Disadvantages
Survey	Selecting a representative sample of people and asking them to fill out questionnaires, interviewing them in person or on the phone	Self-administered questionnaires inexpensive and useful; greater response from subjects in personal interviews; phone interviews convenient	Questionnaires not returned; personal interviews costly in time and money; phone interviews discourage subjects' cooperation
Observation and ethnography	Observing subjects' activities as a detached outsider or as a participating member identifying or concealing oneself as researcher to subjects	Provides firsthand experience with natural, real-life situations; reveals subjects' own perspectives; useful for developing new theories	Findings largely relevant to one particular case; not generalizable to other cases or useful for testing theories
Experiment	Manipulating variables to determine their influence on subjects in the field or laboratory	Relatively easy to test theories by determining the relationship between independent and dependent variables	Observer's presence in the field may influence subjects; subjects may not behave the same outside laboratory as inside
Analysis of existing data	Secondary analysis involves studying someone else's quantitative data; content analysis entails examining and converting qualitative into quantitative data	Both secondary and content analysis save much time and money; content analysis also unobtrusive to subjects and uniquely suitable for historical research	Both secondary and content analysis not sufficiently valid and reliable because interpretation of data tends to be subjective

help a tobacco company sell more cigarettes. Research can even further harm its subjects. It is unethical, or morally wrong, to conduct harmful research. Let's see how sociologists deal with these problems.

Ethical Guidelines   To conduct research ethically, sociologists generally follow three guidelines set by the American Sociological Association.

The first concerns responsibilities to the *profession*. Sociologists must report research findings fully, without leaving out significant data. They must also disclose details of their theories, research methods and designs, and data interpretations. Given these facts, it is possible to detect if the researcher is trying to deceive the professional community. In short, sociologists must be *honest* or their profession's integrity will be destroyed.

The second guideline involves being responsible for the *welfare of research participants*. Researchers should make sure that subjects do not suffer personally (such as being humiliated or embarrassed), psychologically (experiencing stress or losing self-esteem), or socially (hating or losing trust in others). Researchers should also avoid invading subjects' privacy. Confidential information provided by research participants, for example, must not be divulged to others.

The third guideline pertains to *responsibilities to the public*. Sociologists must refrain from doing research

that can be used to harm society, such as providing information for management to quiet labor unions or for the Central Intelligence Agency to instigate or suppress revolutions in foreign countries.

Problems and Risks   While sociologists generally accept these guidelines, ethical problems can still exist. Some researchers lie to their subjects, trying to justify the deceptions as necessary to their pursuit of knowledge. Otherwise, they argue, the subjects might refuse to be studied or their behavior might be altered in a way that would make the study useless.

But most sociologists find it morally offensive to deceive subjects to achieve scientific ends. They also fear that deception by researchers can undermine public trust. Suspecting researchers of being tricksters, subjects may lie or do what they think the investigator expects them to do. If deception escalates, we may reach a point where there are no longer credible subjects, only noncredible researchers cranking out bogus data.

To seek genuine data, then, most sociologists strive to be as ethical as possible. Ironically, though, being uncompromisingly ethical may run the risk of violating the law in cases where the research subject has committed a crime. To be ethical in their profession, researchers must protect the welfare of their subjects by keeping the information about them confidential. But this may land the researcher in jail, as it did sociologist Rik Scarce (1994). He was jailed in the state of Washington for five months because he refused to reveal to a grand jury the content of his interview with members of a radical animal rights group suspected of having committed a crime.

 ■ For more of the latest Sociological Frontiers, look up Continuing Update at www.ablongman.com/thio6e.

sociological **f r o n t i e r s**

Deconstructing Society

In recent years, a new sociological frontier has opened up in the form of postmodernist theory. The roots of this theory can be traced back to early twentieth century French philosophers who criticized the excessive objectivity in modern science for causing people to regard each other as objects and thus find it difficult to form genuine and close relationships. The French philosophers called for a greater emphasis on the *postmodernist* value of subjectivity, which would lead people to attaining richer, more meaningful lives.

The core of today's postmodernist theory is the concept of **deconstructionism,** the idea that to understand society, we should "deconstruct" it, or take it apart, and anything associated with it. Just as by taking apart a computer, we can see how it's built, the theory suggests that by deconstructing society, we can uncover its meanings, values, and ideologies.

Postmodernist theorists use feeling, intuition, and insight to reveal that society is made up of binary, paired opposites of all kinds. In each paired opposite, one feature is granted a privileged position by society while the other is relegated to the margin. In other words, individuals, ideas, and practices that are highly valued by society dominate those that are less valued (Leledakis, 2000; Smith, 1998; Derrida, 1997). Here are some examples of paired opposites in U.S. society:

Privileged Features	Marginal Features
Uniformity	Diversity
Conformity	Deviance
Marriage	Divorce
Toughness	Gentleness
Male	Female
Majority	Minority
Rich	Poor

Postmodernist theory looks like a hybrid of the conflict and the symbolic interactionist perspectives. It shares with the conflict perspective the notion that one group dominates the other, and it shares with symbolic interactionism the emphasis on the search for the meanings of society. To put it in terms of both these perspectives, we could say that postmodernist theory views society as being composed of conflicting groups, with each interpreting the other's position as privileged or marginalized and then acting accordingly.

u s i n g *sociology*

How to Change Our World

Sociology can be used in at least three ways. First, it can be used as *an intellectual exercise* that's pursued for its own sake, for the pleasure of tickling our curiosity, or for producing scientific knowledge. Second, sociology can be used to pursue *a specific career* in government (to help fight crime, improve education, reduce poverty, or solve some other social problem) or in the private sector (as a sociology teacher, researcher, social critic, political analyst or lobbyist, or some other position that requires sociological knowledge). Third, sociology can be used as *a general guide* for understanding our social world so that we can function more successfully in it.

No matter what career you end up in, sociology will be useful to you, as it has apparently been for these people in diverse fields of endeavor: Dr. Martin Luther King, Jr. (civil rights leader), Ronald Reagan (former U.S. president), Saul Bellow (Nobel Prize–winning novelist), Regis Philbin (host of TV shows), and Robin Williams (comedian and film actor), all of whom majored in sociology in college (Dreier, 2001). Sociology has proven useful primarily because of its special perspectives and insights, which can be applied to all aspects of our world and change it for the better.

myth	Problems, especially crises, are bad. They are just like failures and miseries.
reality	Problems, even crises, are not necessarily bad. They can be good, producing opportunities for achieving success in our lives.

One of the most useful insights we can gain from sociology is that problems can be seen as opportunities. Common sense causes people to see problems as failures or obstacles, but we can avoid this negative view of problems by letting the global perspective in sociology transport us to another culture. In the Chinese culture, the word for *crisis* consists of two characters: *wei ji,* meaning "danger" and "opportunity." Through this cross-cultural perspective, we may be able to stop seeing problems as setbacks and instead start looking for the opportunities they present. On the surface, these opportunities may not appear real but merely as perceptions. However, through the symbolic interactionist perspective, sociologists have long recognized the self-fulfilling prophecy that if people define something as real, it is real in its consequences. (We will see more of this idea in Chapter 4: Social Inter-

SILVER LINING   In Chinese culture, the word for *crisis* consists of two characters that mean "danger" and "opportunity." Symbolic interactionists, who believe that people act in accord with their interpretations of things, would argue that if we *see* problems as problems, they *will be* problems, but if we view them as opportunities, we can use them as chances for solving problems and achieving success in our lives. ■

action in Everyday Life.) Similarly, if we believe that problems are full of opportunities, we will probably find—and use—these opportunities to solve the problems and achieve success in our lives.

The same sociological perspective also offers the useful insight that *our own interpretation* of the world around us affects our lives more than the world itself. Suppose someone insults us. We may interpret the insult in a commonsensical way, as a justification to be angry at the individual, or we may define the insult in a sociological way, as a product of the individual's social circumstances, such as poverty, unemployment, or family problems. Both interpretations affect our lives but in different ways. The commonsense interpretation will make us feel vengeful or even violent toward the individual, but the sociological one will make us feel fortunate (for not being in the individual's circumstances ourselves) and perhaps tolerant or compassionate. In a larger sense, the commonsense interpretation will tend to worsen social life, whereas the sociological interpretation will likely improve it. Witness how Dr. Martin Luther King, Jr., improved race relations in a nonviolent way without advocating retaliatory action against racist individuals. This is an example of sociological imagination at work. It enables us to see the individual's problem from the social-structural standpoint (as represented by the functionalist and conflict perspectives), attributing the problem to social forces rather than blaming the victim.

Sociological perspectives and insights can be used in many other, more specific ways to improve various aspects of our lives, as we will see in each of the following chapters.

CHAPTER REVIEW

1. *How does sociology differ from common sense?* While common sense produces familiar and untested ideas, sociology provides factually supported ideas and the excitement of discovering something new about ourselves. *Why is it important to study groups and societies different from ours?* By studying others, we can understand our lives better because others may open our eyes to social forces that we have not seen before. *What is the nature of sociology as a science?* As a science, sociology seeks to discover relationships between one event and another, describe these relationships in the form of hypotheses and theories, and dig out evidence that supports or refutes these hypotheses and theories. *How does the sociological imagination help us understand our lives better?* By showing the influences of social forces on our private lives, the sociological imagination gives new insight into why we think and behave as we do.

2. *Plato and Socrates discussed social issues. Were they sociologists?* No, they were social philosophers, who thought and argued about the nature of the world but did not test their ideas against systematic observation. *What led to the transformation of social philosophy into sociology?* Seized with the desire to solve social problems and impressed with the contributions from the natural sciences, some nineteenth-century social philosophers tried to apply the scientific method to the study of society in the hope of curing social ills. This attempt to replace philosophical speculation with the scientific method of systematic observation transformed social philosophy into sociology.

3. *What did Spencer mean when he said that society is like a living organism?* In Spencer's view, each part of society, like each organ of an animal, performs its own function. If one part of society has problems, the other parts will adapt to the situation, ensuring the survival of the entire society. *What did Marx mean by class conflict?* Marx was referring to the struggle between the class of capitalists, who own the means of production, and the proletariat, who perform the labor. *What is the difference between* Verstehen *and Durkheim's objective approach?* Verstehen requires sociologists to adopt an attitude of understanding or empathy toward their subjects in order to understand how people interpret their own behavior. Durkheim, who pioneered the application of scientific methods to sociology, argued that sociologists should deal solely with observable aspects of human behavior.

4. *How did the early U.S. sociologists differ from their European predecessors?* The European sociologists were primarily interested in explaining the nature of society as a whole—the causes of social stability and change. In the United States, interest shifted to the study of specific social problems. Later, U.S. sociologists emphasized the search for sociological knowledge rather than its application to social problems, but their interest in social reform grew again during the 1960s. *What is the nature of modern sociology?* Modern sociology is a diverse discipline, one that is both a basic and an applied science and that uses both objective and subjective methods of investigation.

5. *What are the basic ideas of the functionalist perspective?* It focuses on social order and assumes that the various parts of a society are interdependent, forming a social structure in which each part serves a function that helps ensure the survival of the whole. *How does the conflict perspective differ from functionalism?* Whereas functionalism focuses on social order and stability, the conflict perspective emphasizes social conflict and change, showing how one group dominates another. *What are the basic ideas of feminist theory?* Women are different from, unequal to, and oppressed by men, which compels women to challenge the status quo of gender prejudice and discrimination. *What is a symbolic interaction?* It is an interaction between individuals that is governed by their interpretations of each other's actions. *What is the nature of sports as seen from the three perspectives?* Sports appear to be beneficial to society in some ways, harmful in other ways, and similar to any other social interaction.

6. *What research methods do sociologists use?* They use four major methods: survey, which gathers information on a population through interviews or questionnaires; observation and ethnography, which provides firsthand experience of the subject being studied; experiment, which allows the researcher to manipulate variables; and secondary and content analyses, which use existing data. *What are the ethical guidelines for conducting social research?* Researchers must protect the integrity of their profession, the welfare of their subjects, and the well-being of the public. Most sociologists adhere to these guidelines, but some ethical and legal problems can still occur.

7. *What does postmodernist theory reveal from deconstructing society?* Society is made up of countless binary opposites, each of which comprises a privileged item or position and a marginalized item or position. *How can we use sociology to change our world?* By using insights from such perspectives as the global, symbolic interactionist, and social-structural approaches, we can better understand our lives and how to go about changing them.

KEY TERMS

Class conflict Marx's term for the struggle between the capitalists, who own the means of production, and the proletariat, who do not (p. 10).

Conflict perspective A theoretical perspective that portrays society as always changing and always marked by conflict (p. 13).

Content analysis Searching for specific words or ideas and then turning them into numbers (p. 25).

Control group The subjects in an experiment who are not exposed to the independent variable (p. 25).

Deconstructionism The idea that to understand society, we should deconstruct it, or take it apart, along with anything associated with it (p. 27).

Detached observation A method of observation in which the researcher observes as an outsider, from a distance, without getting involved (p. 23).

Economic globalization The interrelationship among the world's economies (p. 5).

Ethnography An analysis of people's lives from their own perspectives (p. 24).

Experiment A research operation in which the researcher manipulates variables so that their influence can be determined (p. 24).

Experimental group The group that is exposed to the independent variable (p. 25).

Feminist theory A form of conflict theory that explains human life in terms of the experiences of women (p. 14).

Functionalist perspective A theoretical perspective that focuses on social order (p. 12).

Global village A closely knit community of all the world's societies (p. 5).

Hypothesis A tentative statement about how various events are related to one another (p. 6).

Latent function A function that is unintended and often unrecognized (p. 13).

Macro view A view that focuses on the large social phenomena of society, such as social institutions and inequality (p. 12).

Manifest function A function that is intended and seems obvious (p. 13).

Mechanical solidarity A form of social cohesion that develops when people do similar work and have similar beliefs and values (p. 12).

Micro view A view that focuses on the immediate social situations in which people interact with one another (p. 12).

Organic solidarity A type of social cohesion that arises when people in a society perform a wide variety of specialized jobs and therefore have to depend on one another (p. 12).

Outsourcing The practice of producing inexpensive products by building factories and hiring workers abroad (p. 5).

Participant observation A method of observation in which the researcher takes part in the activities of the group being studied (p. 23).

Patriarchy A system of domination in which men exercise power over women (p. 14).

Population The entire group of people to be studied (p. 21).

Random sample A sample drawn in such a way that all members of the population have an equal chance of being selected (p. 22).

Sample A relatively small number of people selected from a larger population (p. 21).

Secondary analysis Searching for new knowledge in the data collected earlier by another researcher or a public agency (p. 25).

Social consensus A condition in which most members of society agree on what is good for everybody to have and cooperate to achieve it (p. 12).

Social forces Forces that arise from the society of which we are a part (p. 7).

Social integration The degree to which people are tied to a social group (p. 8).

Social marginality Being excluded from mainstream society (p. 4).

Sociological imagination Mills's term for the ability to see the impact of social forces on individuals, especially on their private lives (p. 7).

Sociology The systematic, scientific study of human society (p. 2).

Stratified sampling The process of drawing a random sample in which various categories of people are represented in proportions equal to their presence in the population (p. 22).

Structured interview An interview in which the researcher asks standardized questions that require

respondents to choose from among several standardized answers (p. 23).

Survey A research method that involves asking questions about opinions, beliefs, or behaviors (p. 21).

Symbolic interactionist perspective A theoretical perspective that directs our attention to the details of a specific situation and of the interaction between individuals in that situation (p. 15).

Systematic sampling The process of drawing a random sample systematically rather than haphazardly (p. 22).

Theoretical perspective A set of general assumptions about the nature of society (p. 12).

Theory A set of logically related hypotheses that explains the relationship among various phenomena (p. 6).

Unstructured interview An interview in which open-ended questions are asked and the respondent is allowed to answer freely in his or her own words (p. 23).

Verstehen Weber's term for empathetic understanding of the subjects studied by sociologists (p. 10).

■ QUESTIONS FOR DISCUSSION AND REVIEW

THE STUDY OF SOCIAL LIFE

1. How does sociology differ from common sense?
2. Why is it important to study social diversity in the United States and the world?
3. What is the nature of sociology as a science?
4. What is the sociological imagination? How does it help us better understand our lives?

THE DEVELOPMENT OF SOCIOLOGY

1. How did Karl Marx's understanding of nineteenth-century European society differ from that of Herbert Spencer?
2. How did the development of U.S. sociology differ from the earlier work of European sociologists?

MAJOR PERSPECTIVES IN SOCIOLOGY

1. What is a theoretical perspective?
2. What are the main features of the three perspectives sociologists use today?
3. How do the basic assumptions of the conflict perspective differ from those of functionalism?
4. Why isn't any one of the three perspectives better than the others?

SPORTS: ILLUSTRATING THE THREE PERSPECTIVES

1. What are the differences between the functionalist and conflict perspectives on sports?
2. What is the nature of sports as seen through the symbolic interactionist perspective?

MAJOR RESEARCH METHODS

1. How do sociologists use surveys to study human behavior?
2. How do detached observation, participant observation, and ethnography differ?
3. How do you conduct an experiment to determine whether one variable causes another?
4. How does secondary analysis differ from content analysis?
5. What ethical guidelines do most sociologists follow when conducting social research?

SOCIOLOGICAL FRONTIERS/USING SOCIOLOGY

1. What is deconstructionism?
2. For what purposes can sociology be used?
3. In responding to an interpersonal conflict, how does the sociological approach differ from the commonsensical one?

■ SUGGESTED READINGS

Deutscher, Irwin. 1999. *Making a Difference: The Practice of Sociology.* New Brunswick, NJ: Transaction. Shows how sociological knowledge can be used to address a large variety of social problems.

Hacking, Ian. 1999. *The Social Construction of What?* Cambridge, MA: Harvard University Press. A clarification of the essence of a relatively new sociological perspective that has much in common with postmodernist theory.

Hardt, Michael, and Antonio Negri. 2000. *Empire.* Cambridge, MA: Harvard University Press. A thought-provoking and wide-ranging analysis of how the easy movement of goods, money, technology, and people across national boundaries has quickly produced a new global society that has a significant impact on every nation in the world.

Wallerstein, Immanuel. 1999. *The End of the World as We Know It: Social Science for the Twenty-First Century.* Minneapolis: University of Minnesota Press. Argues for a new social science to deal with an emerging world order that is faced with increasing deruralization (or urbanization), worsening environmental problems, growing democratization, and declining state power.

Wrong, Dennis. 1994. *The Problem of Order: What Unites and Divides Society.* New York: Free Press. Analyzes the basic sociological issues of order and conflict in society.

■ Additional Resources

The New York Times
expect the world®

nytimes.com

Expand your knowledge of the concepts discussed in this chapter by reading the following current and historical articles from the *New York Times.* Go to the "eThemes of the Times" section of the Companion Website (www.ablongman.com/thio6e):

"First Test for Freshmen: Picking Roommates"
"Want to Try Out for College Sports? Forget It"

Research Navigator.com

Research Navigator, a research database, provides immediate access to hundreds of full-text articles from EBSCO's ContentSelect Academic Journal Database. If the Research Navigator access code was included with your textbook, go to the website www.researchnavigator.com and read the following articles related to this chapter by typing in the article number:

Maynard, Mary. "Studying Age, 'Race' and Gender: Translating a Research Proposal into a Project." *International Journal of Social Research Methodology,* Jan–Mar2002, Vol. 5 Issue 1, p31, 10p. Accession Number: 5893583. Discusses the initial stages of a research project focusing on women, "race," and later life.

Richardson, Barbara. "Ellen Swallow Richards: 'Humanistic Oekologist,' 'Applied Sociologist,' and the Founding of Sociology." *American Sociologist,* Fall2002, Vol. 33 Issue 3, p21, 37p. Accession Number: 9373964. Examines the career of Ellen Swallow Richards, a progressive-era reformer.

chapter 2

Society and Culture

myths & realities

myth *Beauty is only skin deep. People do not consider a person competent just because he or she is good looking.*

reality Unfortunately, attractive persons are expected to be more capable than unattractive ones at most tasks. This may explain the research finding that people considered good looking earn more than those viewed as homely, even though both groups have similar education and employment experiences (p. 36).

myth *Although it is by no means perfect, the United States has the most egalitarian society in the world.*

reality Hunting-gathering societies are generally the most egalitarian because they do not attempt to accumulate food surpluses (p. 40).

myth *Language, aside from being useful for communication, is only a tool that allows people to express their thoughts.*

reality Language is more than a tool. It can determine, or at least influence, how we think. It can also be a source of our thoughts (p. 49).

myth *The values that the West considers highly important, such as human rights, individualism, equality, and liberty, must be popular with the rest of the world.*

reality An analysis of 100 studies on cultural values in different societies concludes that "the values that are most important in the West are least important worldwide" (p. 58).

myth *In India, the Hindus refrain from killing cows for food simply because they consider the animals sacred.*

reality The reason has to do with more than the Hindu belief in the sacredness of cows. India's peasant economy depends heavily on the cows performing various services, without which massive numbers of people would starve to death (p. 59).

33

Not long ago, on a nice spring afternoon, a senior at Ohio University was strolling with his girl-friend on the main street near the campus. As they passed by the town's courthouse, they saw two local unemployed youths loitering on its steps. Suddenly, one of these young men made a very offensive, lewd remark about the student's girlfriend. Enraged, the student stopped, walked up to the offender, and shouted, "What did you say?" The offender rose and repeated exactly what he had said. The student tried to slug him, but the latter swiftly took out a knife and thrust it into the student's chest. The student staggered back and fell. He died several hours later in the hospital.

When I first heard about this incident from a student of mine, I could not help recalling a similar event, but without the tragic consequence, that took place when I was in high school in Indonesia. During recess one afternoon, I saw four or five punks jeering, taunting, and even spitting on a Chinese friend of mine. Unknown to them, he had practiced kung fu since child-hood and could easily have made mincemeat of them. But he simply walked away, letting them laugh and call him "chicken." Later, when I asked him why he did not teach them a lesson, he said, "If a dog barks at you, you don't want to get down on all fours and bark back at it, do you?"

Why did these two individuals—the American student and the Chinese student—react so differently to harassment? The answer is that they lived in different kinds of society and cul-ture. In the United States, young men are expected to be tough and aggressive. It would be embarrassing or viewed as cowardly for a young American man simply to walk away from someone who has insulted his girlfriend. By contrast, the Chinese culture emphasizes the im-portance of being polite and civilized. If someone behaves like the hoods who harassed the Chinese student, that person is regarded as impolite and uncivilized, like an ani-mal. That's why the Chinese student refused to behave in the same way as his harassers. In this chapter, we will examine in more detail how society and culture shape human life.

▍**B**UILDING BLOCKS OF SOCIETY

Society is a collection of interacting individuals shar-ing the same way of life and living in the same terri-tory. Societies, especially large ones such as that of the United States, are highly complex. They have so many diverse characteristics—their customs, reli-gions, politics, economies, families, schools, and so on—that we may despair of making sense of what they are like. Nevertheless, sociologists have long been aware of certain patterns in the way societies operate. Most important, all societies can carry on in the face of differences and conflicts among their members because they have developed certain build-ing blocks—the foundation of society—called *sta-tuses, roles, groups,* and *institutions.*

▍Statuses

To the general public, status often means prestige, but to sociologists, **status** is a position in society. Peo-ple usually behave in accordance with their statuses. When interacting with a friend, you are likely to be relaxed, informal, uninhibited, but when talking with a professor, you are more likely to be a bit stiff and to act in a formal, inhibited way. The status of being a student differs from the status of being a friend.

In our complex society, we have so many statuses that it is impossible to name them all. Some we are born with, such as male or female or some racial or ethnic identity. These statuses of gender and race, as well as age, are called **ascribed statuses.** They are

WEARING DIFFERENT HATS
Ascribed statuses are given to us independently of what we do. Achieved statuses result from our own actions. Condoleezza Rice's position as National Security Advisor in the Bush administration is an achieved status, and her status as an African American and a woman are ascribed. ■

given to us independently of what we do. All other statuses result from what we do. We earn them in some way. You must *do* something to gain the status of a student or college graduate or married person or countless other things. These are called **achieved statuses** and are attained through our own actions. In modern societies such as the United States, achieved statuses have grown in influence at the expense of ascribed statuses. In place of a king or queen who inherits the position, for example, we have a president who must win the office.

Statuses are sometimes ranked, with one being considered higher than the other. In U.S. society, for example, the position of doctor is ranked higher than that of plumber. In a family, the father's status is higher than the son's. But other statuses are merely different, not higher or lower. A sociology major's status is different from but essentially equal to that of a history major.

Despite our many statuses, we are usually influenced by only one status when we interact with another person. If a woman interacts with her husband at home, she will behave primarily as a wife, not as a banker, employer, PTA leader, or athlete. Because the status of wife dominates her relationship with her husband, it is called the **master status** in this interaction. All of her other statuses—as a banker, an employer, and so on—are less relevant to the interaction; hence they are called **subordinate statuses**. On the other hand, when this same woman is at the office, her status as a banker is the master status, and her position as a wife becomes a subordinate status.

The nature of a society may determine which status becomes the master status. In an extremely sexist society, gender is the master status and all others are subordinate to it. A sexist person interacting with a woman surgeon would therefore be likely to use gender as the master status and profession as the subordinate status. As a result, the sexist person would not likely treat the woman physician with the respect usually given doctors. In such a case, the female doctor would encounter **status inconsistency**, the condition in which the same individual is given two conflicting status rankings, one high because of the victim's profession and the other low because of gender.

In U.S. society, the master statuses of gender and race also influence the way others treat us. Research has shown that women in mixed company and blacks in interracial groups, compared with their male and white colleagues, are often given fewer opportunities to interact, are less likely to have their contributions accepted, and usually have less influence over group decisions. This *interaction disability*, as imposed by the master statuses of gender and race, is difficult to overcome unless the minorities appear highly cooperative and agreeable to the majority. The influence of gender and race also appears in many other areas of social life, as we will see in Chapter 8 (Race and Ethnicity) and Chapter 9 (Gender and Age).

Even physical appearance can function as a master status. More specifically, physical attractiveness has a profound impact on how individuals are perceived and treated by others. Research has shown, for example, that attractive individuals are expected by college students to be more capable at most tasks than unattractive ones. Similar studies have found that teachers tend to expect attractive schoolchildren to be smarter than unattractive ones and that many people perceive attractive adults to be more likable, friendly, sensitive, and confident. Not surprisingly, research has consistently shown that people considered good looking earn, on average, about 10 percent more than those viewed as homely, even though both groups have similar education levels, employment experience, and other characteristics. This phenomenon is not limited to occupations where looks play a big part, such as modeling or acting. It also exists in jobs where appearance cannot conceivably enhance employer profits, such as bricklaying, factory work, and telemarketing (Gerencher, 2001; Jackson et al., 1995; Harper, 1993).

myth	Beauty is only skin deep. People do not consider a person competent just because he or she is good looking.
reality	Unfortunately, attractive persons are expected to be more capable than unattractive ones at most tasks. This may explain the research finding that people considered good looking earn more than those viewed as homely, even though both groups have similar education and employment experiences.

■ Roles

Every status has rights and obligations. Children enjoy the right to receive food, shelter, and love from their parents, but they are expected to show respect, obedience, gratitude, and affection in return. In other words, every status carries with it a **role**, the expectation of what individuals should do in accordance with their particular status. Because of your status as a student, you act in a certain way that is part of the student role. Thus, status and role seem like two sides of the same coin. But they are distinguishable. A status is basically static, like a label on a bottle. A role is dynamic, shaped by specific situations and persons.

Consider the role of nurse. In an emergency, nurses must be cool and professional, but they are also expected to convey warmth and concern to their patients. With doctors, nurses are expected to be obedient; with patients' relatives, they may be authoritative. The behaviors demanded by the role change with the situation.

In addition, various people play the same role differently, just as various actors perform the same role on stage in diverse ways, even though they are working from the same script. The script—the set of expectations about how a person with a particular status should behave—is the **prescribed role.** How a person actually carries out the role is the **role performance.** The prescribed role of college student calls for attending classes, reading, thinking, and learning, but students differ in how and to what extent they fulfill these expectations. They may understand the prescribed role differently and be more or less successful in fulfilling those expectations. They may simply differ in their manner of carrying out the role. Thus, some students may expect to get straight A's, while others will settle for B's and C's. The ambitious ones study harder. No matter how each individual defines and performs the student role, however, commitment to it is far from total. In fact, most students do not strongly identify with their role as student. The reason is that many other roles—such as friend, date, worker, and athlete—compete for the student's time.

Indeed, all of us play many roles every day. Some of these are bound to impose conflicting demands. The role of judge (person with the status of a judge) prescribes an emotionless, objective attitude; the role of father (person with the status of a father) requires emotional involvement. Usually, the conflicting demands of these roles present no particular problem because a person plays one role at a time. But if a judge found his or her daughter in court as the defendant, there would be a conflict. Similarly, if you are both a student and an athlete, you will find yourself in conflict when your professor gives an exam on the day your coach wants you to play a game away from your school. When we are expected to play two conflicting roles of our two different statuses at the same time, we experience **role conflict.**

We have so far implied that only one role is attached to a status. But there can also be a **role set**, an array of roles attached to one particular status. The status of a college professor, for example, may carry with it the roles of being a lecturer, an adviser, a researcher, a colleague, a committee member, and a writer. Sometimes two or more of these roles involve conflicting expectations and thus produce **role strain**, stress caused by incompatible demands from the roles of a single status. Thus, professors are torn between the expectation to teach classes and the expectation to do research. Supervisors, too, are expected to be friendly with their workers, to be one of the group. But they are also expected to be part of management and to enforce its rules. Role strain, as well as role conflict, is usually stressful, causing anxiety and other psychological aches and pains.

Figure 2.1 illustrates the differences among role conflict, role set, and role strain.

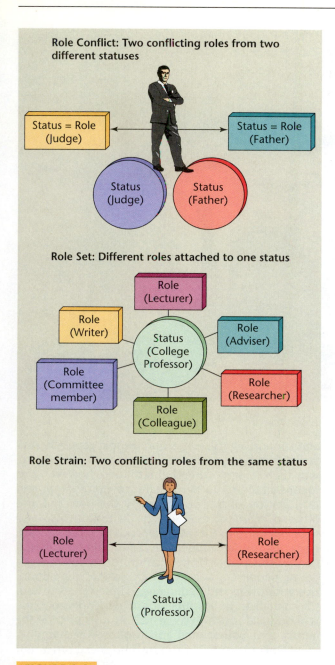

Role Conflict: Two conflicting roles from two different statuses

Status = Role (Judge) ⟷ Status = Role (Father)

Status (Judge)   Status (Father)

Role Set: Different roles attached to one status

Role (Lecturer)
Role (Writer)
Role (Adviser)
Status (College Professor)
Role (Committee member)
Role (Researcher)
Role (Colleague)

Role Strain: Two conflicting roles from the same status

Role (Lecturer) ⟷ Role (Researcher)

Status (Professor)

FIGURE 2.1

Role Conflict, Role Set, and Role Strain

We each have many different statuses and roles. Given our different statuses, we can play different roles. But we will experience *role conflict* if we simultaneously play two conflicting roles from two different statuses. We also have many *role sets*, each consisting of multiple roles attached to one particular status. But we will feel *role strain* if we have to play two conflicting roles from the same status.

Critical Thinking: *Given your status as a student, you play a number of different roles. Name two of these roles that can bring you role strain. Also, what other status do you have that can cause you to experience role conflict?*

Groups

When people interact in accordance with their statuses and roles, they form a **social group,** a collection of people who interact with one another and have a certain feeling of unity. A group can be a family, a class, or two businesspersons trying to strike a deal. A group differs, though, from a **social aggregate,** a number of people who happen to be in one place but do not interact with one another, such as the audience in a theater or the pedestrians on a street. Groups are so important to our daily lives that no society can survive without them.

There are two major types of groups: primary and secondary. A **primary group** is a group whose members interact informally, relate to each other as whole persons, and enjoy their relationship for its own sake. Families, friends, neighbors, and the like are primary groups. They are durable, often lasting for years.

By contrast, a **secondary group** is a group whose members interact formally, relate to each other as players of particular roles, and expect to profit from each other. A secondary group may consist of a salesclerk and a customer. In such a group, there are hardly any emotional ties, the communication is bound by formalities, and each person is interested only in getting what he or she wants, such as something to sell or buy. Once this self-centered goal is accomplished, the group dissolves.

Primary groups are more common in traditional preindustrial societies, and secondary groups are more prevalent in modern industrial societies. (We will discuss these two types of groups in greater detail in Chapter 5: Groups and Organizations.)

Institutions

Society cannot survive without social institutions. A **social institution** is a set of widely shared beliefs, norms, and procedures necessary for meeting the basic needs of society. The most important institutions are family, education, religion, economy, and politics. They have stood the test of time, serving society well. The family institution leads countless people to produce and raise children to ensure that they can eventually take over from the older generation the task of keeping society going. The educational institution teaches the young to become effective contributors to the welfare—such as the order, stability, or prosperity—of society. The religious institution fulfills spiritual needs, making earthly lives seem more meaningful and therefore more bearable or satisfying. The economic institution provides food, clothing, shelter, employment, banking, and other goods and services that we need

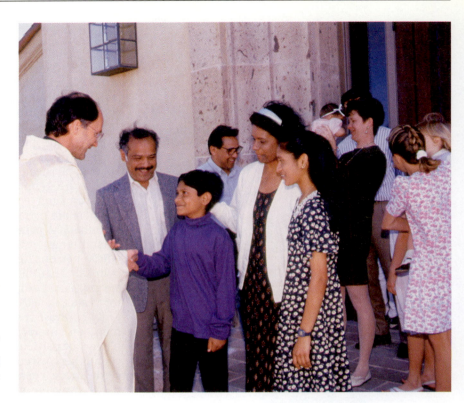

HEAVEN ON EARTH Social instutions are sets of widely shared beliefs, norms, and procedures that are needed to meet the basic needs of society. The institution of religion, illustrated by this Catholic church, fulfills people's spiritual needs, making their earthly lives seem more meaningful, bearable, and satisfying. With religion, then, we can easily find guidance on how to get blessed by God rather than endlessly searching for God on our own. ∎

to live. The political institution makes and enforces laws to prevent criminals and other similar forces from destabilizing society.

In ensuring the survival of society, institutions make life much easier for individuals. They are like the map of a country. With the map, we can easily find our way in driving from one place to another. Without the map, we may have to spend much time exploring, through trial and error, different ways of reaching our destination. Similarly, with institutions we know what to do in our lives. The institutions in our society help us do many things. If we want to have a family, we probably will have a few children rather than 10 or 20. If we want to pursue a career in science, law, medicine, or some other field, we can go to school instead of studying by ourselves. If we seek spiritual fulfillment, we can find guidance from various religions rather than endlessly searching for God on our own. If we need employment, we are free to find the best job possible instead of being forced by the government to accept a low-paying, unpleasant one. If we want to have a good government, we are allowed to vote or run for office rather than risk our lives by starting a revolution. These are only a few of the countless benefits we can enjoy by simply following the guidance of institutions.

Because institutions are so useful, it is not surprising that they tend to be *conservative*, resisting change

and supporting the status quo. People generally support institutions with the attitude "If it ain't broke, why fix it?" Supporting the status quo, however, also involves helping to perpetuate the domination and exploitation of the powerless by the powerful and other social injustices in society. Institutions also tend to be *integrated* in that they depend on one another as parts of a unified whole. The family and educational institutions in the United States, for example, teach young people the values of hard work, competition, free enterprise, and democracy. These values sustain the capitalistic and democratic activities of economic and political institutions, which in turn provide the family and educational institutions with employment, income, public funding, and social order. But the degree of institutional conservatism and integration varies from one society to another.

Generally, institutions are more conservative and integrated in traditional preindustrial societies than in modern industrial societies. Being more conservative and integrated, the institutions in traditional societies are less likely to generate social problems such as high rates of family violence, drug abuse, or crime. At the same time, however, the institutions in traditional societies are more likely to suppress individual freedom and creativity, forcing people to conform to age-old traditions, with threats of harsh punishment for nonconformity.

MEN HUNT, WOMEN GATHER
Hunter-gatherers move about in search of food. Limited food sources keep the size of the population in such a society small. Division of labor is largely based on gender, with men doing the hunting and women the gathering. Here, a !Kung man in the African country of Namibia shows two boys how to cut open a dead python that he has caught in the bush. ■

SOCIETIES IN SOCIOCULTURAL EVOLUTION

Since they first appeared on earth, most human societies have gone through different stages of **sociocultural evolution**, the process of changing from a technologically simple society to a more complex one, with significant consequences for social and cultural life. In the most technologically simple societies, the methods of producing food are so primitive and inefficient that practically the whole population is forced to do the same kind of work—food production—to survive. Social and cultural opportunities—such as meeting people with various ways of life and enjoying a wide range of entertainments—are therefore extremely limited.

In the most technologically advanced societies, where highly efficient methods are used in food production, only a tiny number of farmers are needed to produce enough food to support the whole population. This frees the overwhelming majority of people to pursue numerous other kinds of work, creating a huge and complex array of social and cultural opportunities. Food-producing technology, then, is the driving force behind sociocultural evolution. Societies can be classified into different types according to the technologies they use to produce food and the stage of sociocultural evolution they have achieved (Nolan and Lenski, 1999).

■ Hunting-Gathering Societies

Hunting-gathering societies hunt animals and gather plants as their primary means of survival.

Throughout 99 percent of humankind's presence on earth, or until about 10,000 years ago, all societies survived by using simple tools such as spears to hunt wild animals and to fish and by using human hands to gather wild roots, fruits, birds' eggs, wild bees' honey, and the like. Today, fewer than 0.1 percent of the world's people live this way. Among the few remaining hunting-gathering societies are the !Kung* of South Africa, the Batek Negritos of Malaysia, and the Alyawara of Central Australia.

Hunter-gatherers move about a great deal in search of food, but they cover only a small area. Because their food sources are so limited, hunting-gathering societies are very small, each including only 20 to 50 people. Their division of labor is based on gender: Men usually do the hunting; women, the gathering. Contrary to popular belief, though, hunter-gatherers do not live in total isolation and eat only wild foods. For thousands of years they have also practiced some herding and farming or have traded with herders and farmers (Headland and Reid, 1989). But hunting and gathering remain their *primary* subsistence technology.

The lives of hunter-gatherers are not necessarily hard. In fact, because their needs are simple, they may work only two or three hours a day. It has been estimated that a family can easily collect enough wild cereal grain in three weeks to feed itself for a year. Sometimes the food must be processed. Some nuts, for example, require roasting and cracking. Hence, hunter-gatherers may spend more time preparing food than finding it (Hawkes and O'Connell, 1981).

*The ! represents a click, a speech sound not used in English.

"I just don't trust gatherers!"

Source: From the *Wall Street Journal*—Permission, Cartoon Features Syndicate.

Nevertheless, they still have so much leisure time that anthropologist Marshall Sahlins (1972) has called them the "original affluent societies."

myth	Although it is by no means perfect, the United States has the most egalitarian society in the world.
reality	Hunting-gathering societies are generally the most egalitarian because they do not attempt to accumulate food surpluses.

Sharing food with one another is a central norm and value in these societies. The more successful hunters are denied the opportunity to create prestige and wealth with their skills. They are expected to be self-deprecating about their hunting success, and boasting is met with scorn. Because no one hoards, no one acquires great wealth. And because there are few possessions to fight about, hunter-gatherers are unlikely to engage in warfare. If a strong and skilled hunter tries to dominate others, he can be secretly killed because there is no effective means of protection (like the police in other societies) and because everyone has easy access to poisoned arrows, spears, and other hunting weapons. As a result, the !Kung and other hunting-gathering societies are generally the most egalitarian in the world.

These societies, however, are patriarchal. Men exclude women from hunting activities. They even impose strict and extensive taboos on menstruating women, prohibiting them from touching any man and from handling such "male" things as bows, arrows, and fishing gear. They believe that menstruating women are dangerous to men, possibly causing sickness, injury, or loss of magical power in the men they touch (Kitahara, 1982; Woodburn, 1982).

◼ Pastoral Societies

Pastoral societies domesticate and herd animals as their primary source of food. In deserts, mountains, and grasslands, plants are difficult to cultivate, but animals can easily be domesticated for use as a food source. About 10,000 years ago, some hunter-gatherers began to specialize in the domestication of animals. Today, there are a number of pastoral societies, mostly in the deserts and highlands of North and East Africa, the Middle East, and Mongolia. The Africans specialize in keeping cattle; the Arabs, camels and horses; and the Mongols, various combinations of horses, cattle, camels, goats, and sheep. These peoples are different racially and far apart geographically, yet they show a considerable degree of cultural uniformity.

Unlike hunter-gatherers, pastoralists accumulate a surplus of food, allowing their societies to include more members than hunting-gathering bands. There is also marked social inequality based on the size of an individual's herd and the number of a man's wives. Some anthropologists argue that animal holdings represent an unstable form of wealth because, as one herder puts it, "Owning animals is like the wind. Sometimes it comes and sometimes it doesn't." When a disaster such as an epidemic or a severe drought strikes, the wealthy herders are assumed to suffer such great losses that social inequality cannot be maintained. But in his study of the Komachi pastoralists in south-central Iran, sociologist Daniel Bradburd (1982) found that disasters cannot wipe out inequalities in animal wealth. "While disasters befall rich and poor alike, they do not befall each with quite the same effect," Bradburd explains. "A poor man who loses half his herd frequently finds it reduced to a size from which recovery is impossible; on the other hand, a wealthy man who loses half his herd will frequently be left with enough animals to rebuild the herd without great difficulty."

Usually, pastoral peoples are constantly on the move, looking for fresh grazing grounds for their herds. Consequently, they become fiercely independent and inclined to scorn land boundaries. They also become rather warlike, and some use horses to enhance their war-making capabilities. They are just as likely to raid settled villages as they are to attack each other. The aim of such aggression is to increase

FOOTLOOSE In pastoral societies, animals are domesticated for use as a major source of food. Since pastoralists can accumulate a surplus of food, social inequality develops in their societies. Because they are on the move in search of fresh grazing grounds for their herds, pastoralists are also fiercely independent and tend to disregard land boundaries. ■

their livestock numbers, as well as to warn others against encroachment. Sometimes they take captives and use them as slaves.

The religious beliefs of these societies reflect the pastoral way of life. The Hebrews, who founded Judaism and Christianity, and the Arabs, who founded Islam, were pastoral people, and in each religion we can find the image of a god who looks after his people in the same way that a shepherd looks after his flock. The Mongols have a religious taboo against farming, believing that plowing and planting offend the earth spirit. The African cattle herders, very proud of their pastoralism, regard horticulture as degrading toil. The non-Islamic tribes of the Hindu Kush mountains, on the borders of Afghanistan and Pakistan, treat their goats as sacred animals capable of appeasing the gods and mountain spirits (Parkes, 1987).

■ Horticultural Societies

Horticultural societies produce food primarily by growing plants in small gardens. About 10,000 years ago, while some hunter-gatherers became pastoralists, others became horticulturalists. Horticulturalists do their gardening by hand, with hoes and digging sticks. Because their soil cannot support continuous intensive farming, many horticulturalists rely on slash-and-burn cultivation. They clear an area in the forest by slashing undergrowth and cutting trees, allowing them to dry, and then burning them off, leaving ashes that help fertilize the soil. This procedure

also ensures that the plot will be free of weeds. After two or three years of growing crops, the soil becomes exhausted, so new fields are slashed and burned.

Unlike pastoralists, horticulturalists live in permanent settlements. Like pastoralists, their society is marked by a sexual division of labor: Men clear the forest, and women do the cultivation. Because horticulturalists can produce a food surplus, their societies are usually larger than those of hunter-gatherers. The existence of a surplus also gives rise to inequality in many horticultural societies, where the men can enjoy great prestige by possessing many gardens, houses, and wives.

Warfare, too, becomes common. Many tribes in a forest often raid each other, occasionally torturing, killing, or even eating their captives. Victorious warriors receive great honors. They preserve and display their defeated enemies' skulls and shrunken heads, much as athletes in other societies show off their trophies. In advanced horticultural societies, warriors hold power as well as prestige. These societies are usually divided into a small, powerful warrior nobility and a large mass of powerless common people.

This social inequality is reflected in the religious beliefs of horticultural societies. They generally believe in capricious gods who must be worshiped. And they perform religious rituals to appease not only the gods but also the spirits of their dead ancestors, perhaps because in permanent settlements the living remain physically close to their dead. Today, there are still some horticulturalists in the tropical forests of Africa, Asia, Australia, and South America.

■ Agricultural Societies

Agricultural societies produce food primarily by using plows and draft animals on the farm. The invention of the plow about 5,000 years ago touched off an agricultural revolution that radically transformed life in the Middle East and eventually throughout the world. When a field is plowed, weeds are killed and buried efficiently, fertilizing the soil. At the same time, nutrients that have sunk too deep for the plants' roots to reach are brought closer to the surface. Thus, the coming of the plow allowed peasants to obtain crop yields many times larger than the horticulturalists could obtain with their hoes. If farmers use animals to pull their plows, their productivity is increased further. As a result, unlike horticulturalists, farmers can cultivate a piece of land continuously and intensively.

The giant leap forward in food production enables large populations to emerge in agricultural societies. Because each farmer can produce more than enough food for one person, some people are able to give up farming and become tailors, shoemakers, tanners, and weavers. These people help cities emerge.

The towns, cities, and farms in an agricultural society come under the control of a central government, usually headed by a dictator with the power to enslave or even exterminate large numbers of people. This centralization of political control, coupled with the possession of valuable property, provides a strong stimulus for warfare. The common people who fight for their leader tend to believe that the leader has divine power. They also believe in a family of gods, in which one is the high god and the others are lesser gods. This hierarchy seems to mirror the peasants' experience with various levels of government officials, from the tax collector at the bottom to the leader at the top. In fact, agricultural societies, both past and present, have the greatest inequality of all types of society. Agricultural societies still predominate today in relatively poor countries in Africa and Asia (see Figure 2.2).

■ Industrial Societies

Industrial societies produce food for their subsistence primarily by using machinery. Since the Industrial Revolution started in England about 250 years ago, many agricultural societies have become industrialized and use machinery to till their lands. Today's industrial societies are relatively rich and can be found in Western Europe, North America, and parts of Asia (Japan, South Korea, Taiwan, and Singapore). Industrialism has been fueled by the use of increasingly powerful energy sources—flowing water, steam, internal combustion, electricity, and atomic fission—to power more and more efficient machines to do the work that had been done mostly by humans or animals in the past.

Consequently, only a tiny number of farmers are needed to produce enough food for the rest of the population. This phenomenon triggers an exodus from the countryside into towns and cities, creating large urban centers across the nation. There, huge masses of people work in numerous industries, producing an abundance of remarkable new things and

LONELY CROWD   In industrial societies, human relations have become weaker and more impersonal. Instead of working with family members on the farm, as in agricultural societies, most people in industrial societies are employed away from home and thrown into daily contact with others they hardly know. This impersonalization has led to a rise in individual concerns and a decline in social solidarity. ■

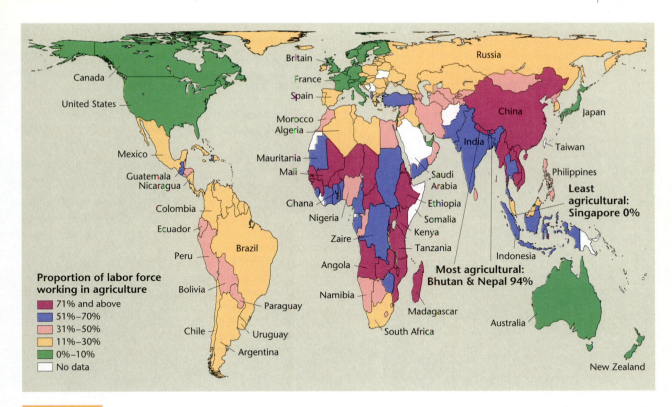

FIGURE 2.2

Agricultural Societies

Agricultural societies can be defined as having most of their population working on farms. These societies generally come under the control of a central government headed by a dictator. They are the most inegalitarian of all types of societies and are predominant in relatively poor countries in Africa and Asia.

Critical Thinking: *What can be done to improve the social conditions of these societies and the lives of their citizens?*

Source: From *The Penguin State of the World Atlas,* 6th edition, by Dan Smith, copyright © 1999 by Dan Smith. Illustrations © 1999 by Myriad Editions Ltd. Used by permission of Penguin, a division of Penguin Group (USA) Inc.

experiences. In the twentieth century alone, we have seen the invention and proliferation of automobiles, telephones, radios, movies, television, jet airliners, nuclear reactors, computers, fax machines, and other high-tech devices. All these and other modern technologies have affected our lives significantly.

For one thing, the functions of institutions have changed. The family alone no longer provides gainful employment for adults, education for children, and religious worship for both. These functions have been taken over by businesses, schools, and churches, synagogues, mosques, or temples. The economy is vast and powerful because virtually everybody depends on this institution for survival. The edu-

cational institution is equally powerful in another way: It serves all school-age youngsters, not just a few from wealthy families, which makes for a prosperous and democratic society. Religion, however, has lost its earlier influence as the dominant, unquestioned source of moral authority; this institution now faces challenges from varying beliefs of a more diverse population.

Second, human life has greatly improved. People are much healthier and live considerably longer. The standard of living has risen sharply for most people. Social inequality has declined significantly, although the income gap between rich and poor was great in the early stages of industrialism. Gender inequality has similarly declined. And political, religious, and other freedoms have become more easily attainable.

Third, war has become less likely to break out between industrial societies than between preindustrial societies. This change has much to do with the fear that modern weapons, such as nuclear bombs, can wreak massive, unthinkable destruction on warring nations. Perhaps not surprisingly, the former Soviet Union and the United States avoided a nuclear war, choosing instead the cold war. But in the poorer, less industrialized world, where weapons are unlikely to destroy an entire nation, war continues to be common, as in predominantly agricultural societies. Fighting is particularly likely to erupt between tribes or ethnic groups within a nation-state, such as the recent wars between the Tutsi and Hutu tribes in Rwanda and among the Serbs, Muslims, and Croats in Bosnia.

Fourth, human relations have become weaker and more impersonal. Instead of working with family members on the farm, as in agricultural societies, most people in industrial societies are employed away from home and thrown into contact with others they hardly know. Their social life also revolves increasingly around secondary groups rather than primary groups. Interaction with strangers becomes more and more common. All this has led to a rise in individual concerns and a decline in social solidarity. But life also has become more interesting and challenging: Greater social diversity offers experiences of meeting new people with different ways of life and enjoying their distinctive entertainment and food and other aspects of their subcultures.

■ Postindustrial Societies

Since the early 1970s, the most advanced and richest industrial countries—the United States, Canada, Japan, and the Western European nations—seem to have begun emerging as **postindustrial societies**, the type that produces food so efficiently that high technology and service industry dominate the society. It is impossible to predict with accuracy when those societies will become mostly postindustrial. But we can be certain that it will not take thousands or even hundreds of years, as it did for each of the earlier societal types to appear, because the speed of sociocultural evolution is remarkably greater today. It will be only a matter of decades, sometime in the twenty-first century, until the United States transforms into a primarily postindustrial society. The United States, along with the other richest nations, has already shown some unmistakable signs that it is in transition from industrialism to postindustrialism.

In recent years, biotechnology has made food production far more efficient than ever. When a mass-produced hormone called *bovine somatotropin (BST)* is injected into cows, milk production increases by 30 or even 40 percent. Within a decade, the use of BST will so sharply reduce the number of cows needed to meet U.S. milk requirements that the number of commercial dairy farms could be cut in half. Moreover, genetically identical bull calves have been produced from human-made embryos in Texas. This means that large numbers of cattle, pigs, and sheep can be cloned from a single embryo to produce uniformly healthier animals and higher-quality, lower-fat, tastier meat. Fish have also been genetically altered to mature faster. Applying genetic engineering to plants has produced supertomatoes that have built-in resistance to parasites, viruses, and herbicides. Various vegetables and fruits can be genetically made pest resistant, disease resistant, and frost resistant. Some biotechnologists are even trying to engineer the lowly potato so that it will offer higher-quality protein than beef. When these high-tech strategies become commonplace, far fewer people will be needed to farm, and the United States will truly become the leading postindustrial society.

By relieving people of physical labor, high technology has also begun to transform the economy from one that grows food and produces things to one that provides services or information. Thus, increasing numbers of *agricultural* and *manufacturing* jobs have been eliminated and growing numbers of *service* jobs have been created (see Figure 2.3). Americans have increasingly allowed less industrialized societies to produce their goods, largely because these societies can do so more cheaply, while Americans focus instead on designing and marketing the products.

At about the same time, the proportion of Americans with at least some college education has shot up to nearly 50 percent, the highest in the world. Consequently, the demand for service jobs has increased sharply; it has been met through an explosion of knowledge, particularly with the proliferation of computers. The numerous managerial, administrative, and technical jobs created by computer usage, along with product design and marketing, are high-wage service jobs. However, less educated workers, who used to earn high wages in the steel, auto, and other manufacturing industries, have largely been left out in the cold. When they move out of manufacturing, they are forced to settle for low-paying service jobs. Obviously, higher education is the key to success in the increasingly postindustrial knowledge society.

The transition to postindustrialism has begun to influence American's lives in at least three ways. First, more and more people have been moving from large cities to small towns and rural areas. In industrial societies, workers must live close to their work, swarming into places that become larger cities. In the

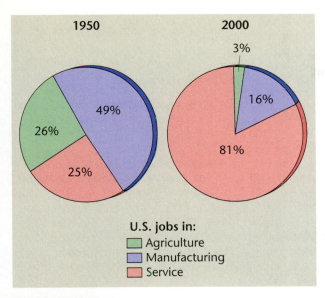

FIGURE 2.3

New Employment Structure in Postindustrial Society

In the United States, high technology has begun to transform the economy from one that grows foods and produces things to one that provides services and information. Thus, agricultural and manufacturing jobs have increasingly been eliminated and replaced by service jobs. Today, most Americans work in the service sector.

Critical Thinking: *Do you foresee the total or near-total disappearance of farm and manufacturing jobs in the United States when it becomes fully postindustrial? Why or why not?*

Source: Data from Mark Balnaves, James Donald, and Stephanie Hemelryk Donald, *The Penguin Atlas of Media and Information* (New York: Penguin Putnam, 2001), p. 13.

emerging postindustrial society, however, the cities are declining because urbanites are attracted to the quality of life in less populated places: low crime rates, inexpensive housing, recreational opportunities, and a return to community values. The migration is facilitated by computers, fax machines, e-mail, and overnight delivery service, all of which enable people to work anywhere. In the United States, there are now many more full-time home-based businesses and people working at home in computer-related jobs (Edwards et al., 2000).

Second, individuals enjoy more power and freedom than ever before. They receive so much information on government activity through television and other telecommunications that they can prevent misconduct among their leaders. Computers enable individuals to keep tabs on their government more efficiently than the government can keep tabs on all of them. With global television, fax machines, and computer networks, it seems difficult for a repressive

and dictatorial government to emerge in a postindustrial society. The government can seize radio and television stations and silence the press, but individual citizens can still get information from one another and from abroad through faxes, the Internet, and other telecommunications that the government cannot control (Watson, 1995).

Third, there now tends to be more gender equality. Postindustrialism depends on brain power more than does industrialism. Since women are just as likely as men to attend college today, they can be expected to be as likely to command high positions in the service and information economies. Well-educated women can advance fastest in the forefront of the emerging postindustrial information industry. At Apple Computer, for example, the proportion of women managers had already risen to 30 percent by 1989 and reached nearly 50 percent—parity with men—by the end of the 1990s (Linzmayer, 1999; Naisbitt and Aburdene, 1990).

The main characteristics of the various societal types just discussed are presented in Table 2.1 (p. 46).

COMPONENTS OF CULTURE

Culture is a design for living or, more precisely, a complex whole consisting of objects, values, and other characteristics that people acquire as members of a society. When sociologists talk about cultures, they usually are not talking about sophistication or knowledge of the opera, literature, or other fine arts—so-called high culture. While only a small proportion of a population may be sophisticated or interested in high culture, *all* members of a society possess a culture. Nor is *culture* the same as *society,* although the two terms are often used interchangeably. Society consists of people interacting with one another as residents of the same area. Culture, on the other hand, consists of (1) tangible, human-made objects that reflect the nature of society and (2) abstract entities—such as ideas—that influence people.

The tangible objects make up the **material culture,** which includes every conceivable kind of physical object produced by humans, from spears and plows to cooking pots and compact discs. Objects reflect the nature of the society in which they were made. If archaeologists find that an ancient society made many elaborate, finely worked weapons, then they have reason to believe that warfare was important to that society.

In their study of contemporary societies, however, sociologists are more interested in **nonmaterial culture,** the intangible aspect of culture. It includes *knowledge and beliefs* (its cognitive component),

TABLE 2.1

Societies in Various Stages of Sociocultural Evolution

Societal Type	When First Appeared, Where Today	Food-Producing Technology	Sociocultural Life
Hunting-gathering	Appeared when human life began on earth; extremely few remain today in South Africa, Malaysia, and Australia	Spears and other simple tools for hunting and fishing; hands for gathering wild plants	Gender-based division of labor, with men hunting and women gathering; generally, most egalitarian in the world
Pastoral	Appeared about 10,000 years ago; few remain today in deserts and highlands of North and East Africa, the Middle East, and Mongolia	Domesticating and herding animals	Fiercely independent; warlike; religions reflecting value of pastoralists' animals; great social inequality
Horticultural	Appeared about 10,000 years ago; few remain today in tropical forests of Africa, Asia, Australia, and South America	Simple hand tools (hoes, digging sticks)	Warlike and highly inegalitarian, warrior nobility dominating common people; inequality reflected in worship of capricious gods
Agricultural	Appeared about 5,000 years ago; still numerous in relatively poor countries in Africa, Asia, and Central and South America	Plows and draft animals	Create diverse occupations; cause cities to emerge; rulers believed to have divine power over common folk; many gods; most inegalitarian in the world
Industrial	Appeared about 250 years ago; many exist today in rich countries in Western Europe, North America, and parts of Asia (Japan, South Korea, Taiwan, Singapore)	Machinery	Create huge urban cities; educational and economic institutions more influential than in earlier societal types; religion no longer dominant; human life greatly improved; war less likely; human relations weaker and more impersonal
Postindustrial	Began to emerge about 1970; still in process of becoming fully postindustrial; led by the United States, Canada, Japan, and other richest nations	High-tech: biotechnology, genetic engineering; service industries	Increased replacement of manufacturing by service, knowledge, and information jobs; large cities in decline; more power and freedom for individuals increased gender equality

norms and values (normative component), and *symbols and language* (symbolic component).

■ Knowledge and Beliefs

Culture helps us develop certain knowledge and beliefs about what goes on around us. **Knowledge** is a collection of relatively objective ideas and facts about our physical and social worlds. Knowledge can be turned into technology, and as such it can be used to control the natural environment and to deal with social problems. The high standard of living in modern societies may be attributed to their advanced knowledge and sophisticated technology. Knowledge is best exemplified by science. By contrast, **beliefs** are ideas that are relatively subjective, unreliable, or unverifiable. They may include, for example, the idea

that God controls our lives. The best example of beliefs is religion, which we discuss in Chapter 11 (Education and Religion).

■ Norms and Values

Each culture has its own ideas, not only about what is important in the world but also about how people should act. This is the normative component of a culture, made up of its norms and values. **Values** are socially shared ideas about what is good, desirable, or important. These shared ideas are usually the basis of a society's **norms,** social rules that specify how people should behave. Whereas norms are specific rules dictating how people should act in a particular situation, values are the general ideas that support the norms. Thus, the specific U.S. norm against impris-

CULTURE COMPOSITION   Culture consists of both tangible objects (material culture) and intangible things (nonmaterial culture), both of which can differ markedly from one culture to the next. Here, a Geisha girl in Japan shows both material culture in the form of clothing and hair accessories and nonmaterial culture in terms of the norm of beauty expressed in her white body makeup and traditional costume. ■

oning people without a trial is based on the general U.S. value of freedom. Parents are required by a norm to send their children to school because society places a high value on mass education. We are allowed to criticize our government because we value freedom of speech. Even a norm as mundane as that against pushing to the head of a line is derived from a general value, one that emphasizes fairness and equal treatment for all.

Values and norms also vary from culture to culture. Because they are subjective, a value and its norms considered good in one society may appear bad in another. If someone says to us, "You have done an excellent job!" a U.S. norm requires that we respond with "Thank you." This may be traced to the value our society places on fair exchange: You scratch my back and I'll scratch yours; if you praise me, I'll thank you for it. In China, however, the same praise would elicit a self-effacing response like "Oh, no, not at all" or "No, I've done poorly." The reason for this is that humility ranks high in the Chinese value system. Thus, Americans might consider the Chinese odd for being unappreciative, and the Chinese might regard Americans as immodest.

Values and norms also change together over time. Forty years ago, most people in the United States supported the norm of school segregation because they did not value racial equality. Today, the norm has given way to school integration because the value has shifted toward racial equality. In China before the late 1970s, ideological purity was the country's reigning value: "We would rather have a poor country under socialism than a rich one under capitalism." One of its resulting norms was to send professors, students, scientists, and other intellectuals to farms to learn equality from the peasants. After the late 1970s, the new value of pragmatism ("It doesn't matter if the cat is white or black as long as it catches mice") took over, and one of its accompanying norms has been to send many intellectuals abroad to learn modernization from the West.

Norms   Day in and day out, we conform to norms. They affect all aspects of our lives. As a result, we usually are not aware of them. If someone asked why we say "Hi" when greeting a friend, we might be inclined to answer, "How else?" or "What a silly question!" We hardly recognize that we are following a U.S. norm, a fact that will dawn on us when we discover that people in other societies follow quite different customs. Tibetans and Bhutanese, for example, greet friends by sticking out their tongues. They are simply following their own norms.

These norms are **folkways,** weak norms that specify expectations about proper behavior. It's no big deal if we violate folkways; nobody will punish us severely. The worst might be that people would consider us uncouth, peculiar, or eccentric—not immoral, wicked, or criminal. Often society turns a blind eye to violations of folkways. When we go to a wedding, we are expected to bring a gift, dress formally, remain silent and attentive during the ceremony, and so on. If we violate any of these folkways, people may raise their eyebrows, but they will not ship us off to jail.

Much stronger norms than folkways are mores (pronounced *MORE-ayz*). **Mores** are strong norms that specify normal behavior and constitute demands, not just expectations. Violations of mores are severely punished. Fighting with the bridegroom, beating some of the guests, and kidnapping the bride would be violations of mores, and the offender

THE MORE THINGS CHANGE, THE MORE THEY REMAIN THE SAME Sometimes, norms persist even after the values from which they are derived have changed. For instance, the norm of showering a bride and groom with rice after their wedding can be traced back to the high value our ancestors placed on fertility. We hardly expect newlyweds today to have numerous children, yet the custom of throwing rice—or in this case, rose petals—continues. ■

would be dealt with harshly. Less shocking but still serious misbehaviors such as car theft, shoplifting, vandalism, and prostitution also represent violations of mores.

In modern societies, most mores are formalized into **laws,** norms that are specified formally in writing and backed by the power of the state. Violations of these mores are also considered illegal or criminal acts punishable under the law. Some folkways—such as driving safely, mowing the lawn, prohibiting liquor sales on Sundays—may also be turned into laws. Laws can effectively control our behavior if they are strongly supported by popular beliefs. If there is not enough *normative support*—support for the norms—the laws are hard to enforce, as in the case of legal prohibitions against prostitution, gambling, and teenage drinking.

In fact, all kinds of norms play an important role in controlling behavior, and society has various methods of enforcing them. These enforcement measures are called **sanctions,** rewards for conforming to norms or punishments for violation of norms. Positive sanctions, or *rewards,* range from a word of approval for helping a child cross a street to public adulation for rescuing someone trapped in a burning building. Negative sanctions, or *punishments,* can be as mild as a dirty look for heckling a speaker or as severe as execution for murder. Some sanctions are applied by formal agents of social control, such as the police and judges, but most often sanctions are applied informally by parents, neighbors, strangers, and so on.

Values By regularly rewarding good actions and punishing bad ones, the agents of social control seek to condition us to obey society's norms. If they are successful, obedience becomes habitual and automatic. We obey the norms even when no one is around to reward or punish us, even when we are not thinking of possible rewards and punishments. But human beings are very complicated and not easily conditioned, as animals are, by rewards and punishments alone. Thus, sanctions are not sufficient to produce the widespread, day-to-day conformity to norms that occurs in societies all over the world. To obtain this level of conformity, something more is needed: the values of the culture.

Because norms are derived from values, we are likely to abide by a society's norms if we believe in its underlying values. If we believe in the value our society places on freedom of religion, we are likely to follow the norm against religious intolerance. If employers cling to the traditional belief that a woman's place is in the home, they will violate the norm against job discrimination by not hiring married women. In developing countries, parents often carry on the norm of producing many babies because they continue to hold to the traditional value of big, extended families.

People are not always conscious of the values instilled in them, nor do they always know why they obey norms. Sometimes, norms persist even after the values from which they are derived have changed. Why, for example, do we shower a bride and groom with rice or birdseed after a wedding? It seems the proper thing to do, or a pleasant thing to do, or a vague sign of wishing the newlyweds well. In fact, the norm is derived from the high value our ancestors placed on fertility, which was symbolized by rice. Over time, a norm can become separated from the value that inspired it and come to be valued in itself. We may follow the norm simply because it seems the thing to do.

Values are not directly observable, but we can infer them from the way people carry out norms. When we see that the Japanese treat their elderly people with respect, we can safely infer that they put great value on old age. When we find that African Americans spend more time than other ethnic groups on church activities, we may conclude that they place a higher value on religion. When we discover that Hispanic Americans spend more time than others on child care, we can deduce that they put a higher value on family relations (see Figure 2.4, p. 50). When we see that many American women are dieting, some to the point of becoming anorexic, we know that U.S. culture places an enormous value on slenderness as the model for feminine beauty.

■ Symbols and Language

The components of culture that we have discussed so far—norms and values as well as knowledge and beliefs—cannot exist without symbols. A **symbol** is a word, gesture, music, or anything that stands for some other thing. A key example is language.

The Importance of Symbols   Symbols enable us to create, communicate and share, and transmit to the next generation the other components of culture. It is through symbols that we are immersed in culture and, in the process, become fully human. We can better appreciate the importance of symbols, particularly language, from Helen Keller's (1954) account of her first step into the humanizing world of culture. Blind and deaf, she had been cut off from that world until, at the age of 7, she entered it through a word:

> Someone was drawing water and my teacher placed my hand under the spout. As the cool stream gushed over one hand she spelled into the other the word water, first slowly, then rapidly. I stood still, my whole attention fixed upon the motion of her fingers. Suddenly I felt a misty consciousness as of something forgotten— a thrill of returning thought; and somehow the mystery of language was revealed to me. I knew that "w-a-t-e-r" meant the wonderful cool something that was flowing over my hand. The living word awakened my soul, gave it light, hope, joy, set it free! There were barriers still, it is true, but barriers that could in time be swept away.

Once Keller understood that her teacher's hand sign meant water, once she understood what a word was, she could share her world with others and enter into their world because she could communicate through symbols. All words are symbols; they have meaning only when people agree on what they mean. Communication succeeds or fails, depending on whether people agree or disagree on what their words mean. Keller's experience is a vivid example of the general truth that almost all human communication occurs through the use of language.

myth	Language, aside from being useful for communication, is only a tool that allows people to express their thoughts.
reality	Language is more than a tool. It can determine, or at least influence, how we think. It can also be a source of our thoughts.

The Influence of Language   According to many social scientists, language does more than enable us to communicate. It also influences the way we perceive the world around us. Edward Sapir (1929) was the first to hold this view. Human beings, he said, live "at the mercy of the particular language which has become the medium of expression for their society." Sapir also wrote that language has "a tyrannical hold upon our orientation to the world." When societies speak different languages, "the worlds in which societies live are distinct worlds, not merely the same world with different labels attached to it."

This view was developed by Sapir's student Benjamin Whorf (1956) and became known as the *Sapir-Whorf hypothesis*. It holds that language predisposes us to see the world in a certain way. Sometimes the hypothesis is put even more strongly: Language molds our minds, determining how we think about the world. Whorf found, for example, that the language

WINDOW ON THE WORLD   According to the Sapir-Whorf hypothesis, our language makes us see the world in a certain way. This may explain why the languages of societies that are surrounded by ice much of the year have numerous terms for the word *ice*. These terms enable people to see many different kinds of ice, which vary from one another in texture, strength, and depth—information that's useful for ensuring safety and comfort in an environment full of ice. ■

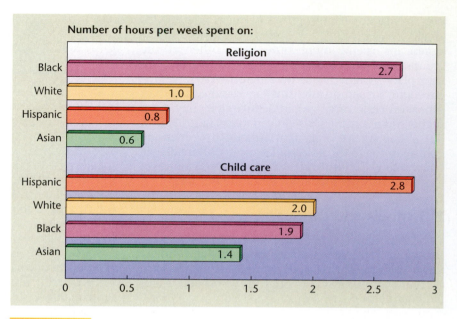

Number of hours per week spent on:

Religion

Black	2.7
White	1.0
Hispanic	0.8
Asian	0.6

Child care

Hispanic	2.8
White	2.0
Black	1.9
Asian	1.4

0   0.5   1   1.5   2   2.5   3

FIGURE 2.4

Ethnic Differences in Time Use

The "Americans' Use of Time Survey," conducted by researchers at the University of Maryland, reveals that various ethnic groups have different ways of spending time. Among the findings are that African Americans spend more time than other groups on religious activities and that Hispanic Americans spend more time on child care. Hispanics, whites, and Asians have one thing in common, however: They spend more time on child care than on religion.

Critical Thinking: *How we spend time reflects our cultural values. Can we change our values? Why or why not?*

Source: Data from *American Demographics,* June 1998, p. 20.

of the Hopi Indians of the southwestern United States has neither verb tenses to distinguish the past and the present nor nouns for times, days, seasons, or years. Consequently, according to Whorf, Hopi- and English-speaking people perceive time differently. Although English speakers see the difference between a person working *now* and the same person working *yesterday,* Hopi speakers do not, because their language makes no distinction between past and present. In his novel *1984,* George Orwell (1949) provided a dramatic presentation of the possibilities of the Sapir-Whorf hypothesis. In the dictatorship portrayed in the novel, a language called *Newspeak* has been created. Among other things, Newspeak has no word for *freedom,* so that people cannot even think about freedom, much less want it.

The Sapir-Whorf hypothesis has stirred controversy. A common criticism is that the hypothesis overemphasizes the power of language. According to the critics, language only influences—rather than

determines—how we think. If language determined thought, people who spoke different languages would always think differently, and it would be impossible for us to comprehend English translations of foreign languages. But the critics do admit that language has some influence on cognition. That is why people who speak different languages sometimes think differently, so that they cannot see eye to eye on some issues. Virtually all social scientists, then, agree that language influences perception and thinking, even though they disagree on the amount of influence (Bickerton, 1995).

The Sapir-Whorf hypothesis has further stimulated studies of language with the aim of understanding culture. An important finding is that the Garo of northeast India, living in an environment full of ants, have more than a dozen words for different kinds of ants but no general term for *ant.* The Garo apparently find it useful to distinguish one kind of ant from another. Ants play so small a role in our lives that our language makes no distinction between them. We lump them all together in one word, and to most of us, one ant looks just like another. On the other hand, in U.S. society, which is full of cars, there are many different words for *automobile,* such as *sedan, convertible, coupe, fastback, wagon, bus, van, SUV,* and *truck.* To people in another society with few automobiles, a car is a car, period (Whiteford and Friedl, 1992).

U.S. CULTURE

We can understand culture better by analyzing three aspects of the U.S. culture: basic values, multiculturalism, and pop culture.

Basic Values

According to sociologist Robin Williams (1970), 15 basic values are dominant in U.S. culture: success, hard work, efficiency, material comfort, morality, humanitarianism, progress, science, external conformity, individualism, in-group superiority, equality, freedom, patriotism, and democracy. Most of these values, such as success, hard work, and efficiency, are clearly related to one another, showing **cultural integration**, the joining of various values into a coherent whole. At the same time, however, the integration is never perfect in any society. If you take another look at Williams's list of U.S. values, you will see that the value given to *efficiency* and *success* often clashes with considerations of *morality* in the business world: Should companies pursue efficiency and success by selling unsafe products, engaging in deceptive advertising, or violating price-fixing laws? Or should they resist these immoral activities and risk losing out to competitors? The conflict between efficiency/success and morality shows a lack of cultural integration. So does the so-called culture war between traditionalists and multiculturalists, as we will discuss later. But all this should not be surprising because the cultures of large, modern industrial societies are generally less integrated than those of small, traditional ones.

Moreover, some of the values Williams identified have been changing. For one thing, people in the United States work harder than ever before. In the past 25 years, the typical adult's leisure time has shrunk to less hours a week and the work week has swelled to more hours, largely a result of the greater demands of employers and the rise of addictive consumerism. With less time for leisure, Americans are nonetheless trying harder to enjoy themselves, as indicated by the significant increase in personal expenditures on recreation over the last decade. Americans now spend more than a trillion dollars a

year in pursuit of leisure, far more than on health care, cars and trucks, or housing (U.S. Census Bureau, 2001; Kammen, 1999). Still, American workers get less vacation time than their counterparts in other prosperous countries (see Figure 2.5, p. 52).

Related to working harder is a greater interest in individual success. Concern with this personal value, however, has apparently caused a decline in community life and social responsibility. In relentlessly pursuing their personal ambitions, many people have little or no time left for their families, friends, and communities, finding themselves "suspended in glorious, but terrifying, isolation" (Putnam, 2000; Bellah et al., 1986).

Moreover, increased concern with one's own welfare has fostered a strong sense of individual rights but a weak sense of obligation to the community. Most U.S. citizens, for example, demand their right to be tried by a jury of their peers, but if asked to serve on such juries, many strive to evade the call. Consequently, a group of social thinkers called *communitarians* has emerged to encourage social responsibility. They urge that we move beyond the isolated self by spending more time with our families, seeking meaningful rather than casual relationships, and working to improve community life (Etzioni, 2001, 1993; Howard, 2001).

As a whole, however, U.S. values have served American society quite well. Other societies with different values have not been so lucky. Great Britain was the world's major power in the nineteenth century, but it is not so today. Japan and Germany, which just a decade ago seemed ready to become the world's economic giants, have been cut down to size. Twenty years ago Russia, as the former Soviet Union, was a superpower, but it isn't now. By contrast, the United States continues to be the world's most prosperous society and has become the world's only superpower (Samuelson, 2003).

Multiculturalism

The U.S. culture consists of many subcultures, such as the Anglo, Hispanic, and African subcultures. Figure 2.6 (p. 53) shows various linguistic subcultures in the United States, with non-English and bilingual speakers more concentrated in the West and Southwest, as well as in Hawaii and Alaska. The coexistence of such diverse subcultures can develop into **multiculturalism**, a state in which all subcultures in the same society are equal to one another. Multiculturalism varies in degree from one society to another. Switzerland seems to be among the most multicultural societies in view of the equality among its three subcultures—French, German, and Italian. Countries such as today's Bosnia, where minorities are not only

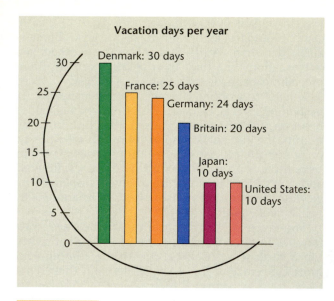

Vacation days per year

Denmark: 30 days
France: 25 days
Germany: 24 days
Britain: 20 days
Japan: 10 days
United States: 10 days

FIGURE 2.5

Less Vacation for Americans
People in the United States work harder than ever before. Over the last 25 years, work hours have swelled and leisure time has shrunk. There is a greater attempt to unwind by spending more on recreation, but when it comes to having a vacation, U.S. workers lag behind their counterparts in other developed countries.

Critical Thinking: *If you had to choose between more vacation time and higher pay, which would you go for? Why?*

Source: Data from Hewitt Associates, published in *Wall Street Journal,* March 27, 2003, p. D1.

despised but often killed, are the least multicultural. The United States is somewhere in between, closer to Switzerland than to Bosnia.

Mindful of the U.S. democratic ideal of equality for all, African Americans, women, gays, and other minorities have struggled since the early 1990s to move multiculturalism closer to reality. They remind others that, in their experience, the United States is far from a melting pot, where various subcultural groups join together to form one single people, as suggested by the U.S. national motto, *e pluribus unum,* or "Out of many, one." Instead, the advocates of multiculturalism argue, minorities are forced to adopt the white European male subculture, as if it is superior to all others.

Consider U.S. history. Written mostly by white European males, it has for the last two centuries largely ignored minority contributions to the development of this nation and concentrated instead on the exploits of white European males. Thus, many white European males, such as Christopher Columbus, are presented as heroes even though they

brought death, disease, and suffering to Native Americans, African Americans, and other minorities.

To counter **Eurocentrism**, the view of the world from the standpoint of European culture, a few multiculturalists have proposed the adoption of **Afrocentrism**, the view of the world from the standpoint of African culture. But most simply want better recognition of minority achievements and a more realistic assessment of white European male actions than has so far been presented. This presumably would help create an egalitarian society where all subcultures would be treated as respectfully as the white European male subculture.

DYNAMIC DIVERSITY Appreciation of multiculturalism has increased significantly in U.S. society. American history books have been broadened and enlivened by the inclusion of stories of blacks, Native Americans, women, and ordinary people. One such story is that of Frederick Douglass (1817–1895). Born a slave, he went North as a young man, where he worked, wrote his autobiography, and eventually bought his freedom with the proceeds of abolitionist lectures he gave. He then published a newspaper, recruited black regiments to fight for the North during the Civil War, and was consulted by President Lincoln several times on the problems of slavery. In 1872, Douglass was the first black vice-presidential candidate, running on the ticket of the Equal Rights Party. ■

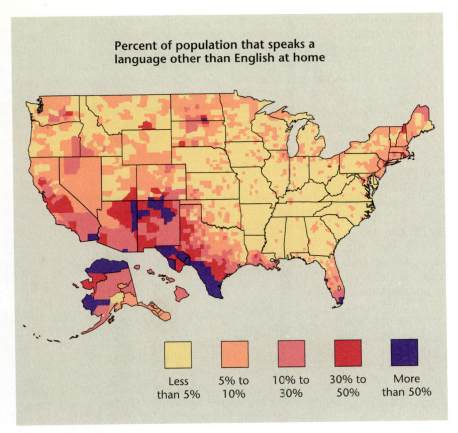

Percent of population that speaks a language other than English at home

| Less than 5% | 5% to 10% | 10% to 30% | 30% to 50% | More than 50% |

FIGURE 2.6

Linguistic Subcultures in the United States

There are many linguistic subcultures in the United States, with non-English and bilingual speakers more concentrated in the West and Southwest, as well as in Hawaii and Alaska. The coexistence of such diverse subcultures can develop into *multiculturalism,* in which all subcultures are treated equally and given the same respect.

Critical Thinking: *Does multiculturalism strengthen democracy or encourage divisiveness in U.S. society? How so?*

Source: Claritas, Inc., Simmons Market Research Bureau, as appeared in *Time,* January 30, 1995.

Some traditionalists have criticized multiculturalism for encouraging divisiveness in an already increasingly divisive society. Their reasoning is that members of each subculture would identify only with their own group rather than with the whole nation. Intergroup conflict or even violence would be expected to get worse. Other traditionalists have also criticized Afrocentrism for being as limiting as Eurocentrism because it is said to deprive African American children of a wide range of views necessary for success in a highly diverse U.S. society (Trotman, 2002; Schmidt, 1997; Lind, 1995).

Are such criticisms warranted? First, the divisiveness has stemmed largely from minority frustration born out of the feeling of being treated as second-class citizens. Thus, genuine recognition of minorities as equal to white European males may help reduce frustration and hence divisiveness. Second, critics are right for finding fault with Afrocentrism if it is offered as the *only* view for African American schoolchildren to learn. But Afrocentrism—or any other minority-centered view—can be useful if offered as merely one of the many views available for learning. It not only can foster self-esteem but also can challenge Eurocentrists to stop ignoring minor-ity contributions and exaggerating white European males' exploits.

In fact, appreciation of multiculturalism has increased significantly in U.S. society. Since 1994, for example, history textbooks for grades 5 to 12 have included the views and stories of African Americans, Native Americans, women, and ordinary people (Hancock, 1994). Multiculturalism has also kept alive the culture war between liberals and conservatives. For example, liberals are more likely to oppose military campaigns against terrorist targets, arguing that such actions only increase the cycle of violence while failing to eradicate the root causes of terrorism, such as U.S. foreign policy and global inequalities. But conservatives are more likely to support military action, arguing that without it, terrorists will get away with the horrendous crimes they commit and will therefore continue to kill innocent people (Bernstein, 2001; Lacayo, 2001; Leo, 2001).

■ Pop Culture

Popular culture consists of relatively unsophisticated artistic creations that appeal to a mass audience. Examples include movies, TV shows, musical performances, and other forms of entertainment that attract large audiences. American pop culture reflects the influences of certain aspects of our society while also influencing foreign cultures.

Democratic and Capitalistic Influences   Popular culture is by definition supposed to appeal to the masses. Yet today, the general public in the United States often complains that there is too much sex and violence on TV and in movies and rock music. Why, then, do leaders of the entertainment industry produce the offending product in the first place?

An apparent reason is that, as Figure 2.7 suggests, entertainment leaders are much less concerned than the public about the portrayal of sex in the media. This is because they are far less likely to believe that sex in movies or on TV contributes to casual sex, teen pregnancy, or extramarital sex in real life (Impoco, 1996). But the real reason for their relative lack of concern may be the influence of U.S. democracy, which protects, through the First Amendment of the Constitution, the right to free speech. Given this constitutional protection, many entertainment manufacturers strive to produce what they consider to be the best products, paying little attention to the possibility that the public may find their products offensive. The HBO series *The Sopranos* is a good example of this type of programming.

There is, however, a limit to how far the entertainment producers would exercise their free-speech right. The bottom line is that under the influence of capitalism, they have a strong interest in the pursuit of profit. There is thus an incentive to please the consumers, offering them the kind of entertainment they want. Not surprisingly, more Hollywood producers are responding to the growing public concern about TV portrayals of casual sex and excessive violence. According to one survey, 58 percent of producers said that they would include more discussions of abstinence in their shows, and 75 percent said that they would present more talk about contraceptive use and safe sex. TV violence, too, has declined. Most police shows portray violence less explicitly. In many episodes of *Law and Order: Special Victims Unit,* for example, there are gruesome murders. The acts of killing are not portrayed; only the corpses are shown. The only act of violence involves the police making an arrest (Dreazen, 2001; Impoco, 1996; Rowe, 1995).

Patriarchal Influence   The feminist perspective provides insight into how popular culture reflects the patriarchal influence of U.S. society. This was the case when Hollywood ostentatiously paid a special tribute to women in movies at the Academy Awards ceremony several years ago, proclaiming "Oscar Celebrates Women and the Movies" as the theme of the widely watched program. As a female film critic said, "That Oscar theme is a joke, because men are now playing *all* the best roles. They get the macho roles *and* the sweet-sensitive roles, and they play the sexual pinups too." Men also write, produce, and direct most feature films and television shows (Corliss, 2003; Bielby and Bielby, 2002; Walters, 1995).

The reason is that the mass audience, under the influence of patriarchy, prefers movies that seem to put women in their place. That's why Hollywood tends to produce blockbuster movies in which women play major roles as predators or sex kittens. Explaining the predator role, a woman director observed, "The general feeling is that if a woman is bright, aggressive and successful, she's got to be a bitch." Explaining the sex kitten role, a female screenwriter said, "Hollywood is trying to resexualize its women back into submission. . . . The women who do best in this society are the ones who are the most complacent in the role of women as sexual commodity, be it Madonna, Julia Roberts or Sharon Stone" (Schoemer, 1996; Walters, 1995; Corliss, 1993).

But patriarchy does not totally control Hollywood. There are always a few highly successful movies that feature aggressive women in top roles—without being predators or sex kittens. Examples are *Tomb Raider* and *Charlie's Angels* (Corliss, 2001).

Global Influence   American pop culture exerts a powerful influence on the world. The movies, TV programs, music, novels, and fashion produced in the United States have never been more dominant globally than today. U.S. movies in particular are the most popular around the world. Every year, the majority of the world's most popular films are produced in the United States. These cultural products, through which Hollywood gets half of its profit from abroad, are the second-biggest U.S. export, after aircraft.

This U.S. dominance has stirred some fear that American pop culture may destroy the traditional values of foreign countries. Some critics even argue that the bone-crunching, eyeball-popping violence on the screen may provoke violence on the streets. But the very popularity of U.S. movies tends to reflect the nature of foreign cultures. Apparently, foreign audiences find the American movie violence highly exciting, but they regard it as pure entertainment, not as a model for actual violence. Many foreign governments also do not seem as concerned as Americans are about movie violence. Fundamentalist Islamic governments, for example, often deface posters of semiclothed women but not lurid pictures of mayhem. The U.S. films would not have become hits around the world if they

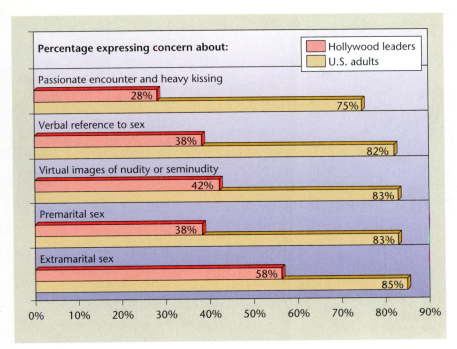

FIGURE 2.7

Divergent Views on TV Portrayals of Sex

Television and other entertainment producers are much less concerned than the general public about the portrayal of sex in the media because these producers are less likely to believe that the portrayal of sex contributes to casual sex, teen pregnancy, and extramarital sex in real life. But the real reason for the producers' view may be their belief that they have the Constitutional right to free speech.

Critical Thinking: *Does the media portrayal of sex have any impact on you and your friends? Why or why not?*

Source: Poll by Celinda Lake of Lake Research and Ed Goeas of the Tarrance Group, as appeared in *U.S. News & World Report,* April 15, 1996, p. 62.

did not meet a global need for highly exciting and entertaining violence (Tow, 2002; Patterson, 1994).

Another indication of how U.S. movies respond to the cultures of foreign audiences is the globalization of Hollywood. The U.S. movie industry is no longer as parochial as it used to be. The French and the Japanese now own some U.S. studios and invest heavily in U.S. films. Moreover, Hollywood constantly recruits successful foreign stars, such as Emma Thompson, Penelope Cruz, Mel Gibson, and Russell Crowe. Today, the U.S. movie industry can "boast an Austrian named Schwarzenegger as its biggest star . . . in action films," and he has tremendous appeal to foreign audiences, as well.

The global popularity of U.S. movies has enormous cultural and economic implications for the world. For generations, impressionable movie-going youths around the world have acquired the American habits of wearing blue jeans, drinking Coca-Cola, and eating McDonald's hamburgers. Under the influence of U.S. movies, then, people all over the world tend to adopt the U.S. way of life and to buy U.S. products (Rothstein, 2002). The reason is that, as one German film director explains, "People believe in what they see and they buy what they believe in. People use, drive, wear, eat, and buy what they see in the movies" (Robinson, 1995), and what they see in U.S. movies, according to a New Zealand writer, is a "materially better, freer, and more exciting world" (Lealand, 1994).

A GLOBAL ANALYSIS OF CULTURE

The world is full of cultures. But are cultures universally the same in some ways? Do cultural differences cause international conflict and violence? These are some of the questions of global significance that we will address here.

◼ Cultural Universals

Human beings everywhere are the product of the same evolutionary process, and all of us have the same needs that must be met if we are to survive. Some, such as the need for food and shelter, are rooted in biology. Others, such as the need for clothing, complex communication, peaceful coexistence, and aesthetic and spiritual experiences, are basic necessities of social life. Cultures are the means by which people everywhere meet these needs. Because these needs are universal, there are **cultural universals**—practices found in all cultures as the means for meeting the same human needs.

These universals appear in both material and nonmaterial cultures. To meet their need for food, all peoples have some kind of food-getting technology, such as food gathering, hunting, or farming. To meet their need for shelter, people in all societies build some

HOOFING AROUND THE WORLD   Cultural universals are those practices found in all cultures as the means for meeting the same human needs. Dance, for example, has been created all over the world to meet the human need for aesthetic experiences. Although the form it takes differs from culture to culture, dance is one of the more than 60 cultural universals. ■

kind of housing, such as a grass hut, igloo, wooden house, or brick building. To meet their need for complex communication, all societies develop symbols and language. To meet their need for aesthetic and religious experiences, peoples all over the world create art forms—such as music, painting, and literature—and believe in some kind of religion. There are more than 60 other cultural universals, including incest taboos, myths, folklore, medicine, cooking, bodily adornment, feasting, dancing, and so on.

Since the early 1980s, a new Darwinian theory called **sociobiology** has emerged to argue that human behavior is genetically determined. One of the sociobiologist's tasks is to explain how humans have acquired the cultural universals. With regard to the incest taboo, for example, the leading sociobiologist Edward Wilson (1980) argues that "human beings are guided by an instinct based on genes" to avoid having sex with their mothers, fathers, and other close relatives. In order to perpetuate and multiply themselves, our genes in effect tell us to avoid incest. If we do not, our offspring will become less fit than ourselves and less able to produce children. Through the logic of natural selection, then, individuals who avoid incest pass on their genes to more descendants than do those who practice incest. In other words, the prohibition on incest exists almost everywhere in the world because it serves to maximize the fitness and reproductive success of humans.

Most sociologists, however, find the sociobiological argument difficult to accept. In their view, if humans were already compelled by their genes to avoid incest, why would virtually every society in the world bother to prohibit it? Sociologists have instead suggested two reasons for the incest taboo. First, the taboo brings about marital alliances among many groups that are useful for security

against famine and foreign attack. Second, the taboo ensures family stability; without the taboo, sexual rivalry could tear the family apart. Sociological reasons such as these can also explain many other cultural universals.

■ Culture Clash

While cultural universals reflect the *general* means by which all societies meet their common needs, the *specific* content of these means varies from culture to culture. For example, religion is a cultural universal, but its specific content varies from one culture to another, as can be seen in the differences among Christianity, Islam, Judaism, Confucianism, and so on. These religions, along with other values, norms, and languages, constitute the specific cultures of various societies. These cultures can be classified into larger groupings called *cultural domains*, popularly known as *civilizations*. There are, according to Samuel Huntington (1996), about eight cultural domains in the world today (see Figure 2.8).

The differences among these cultural domains can be expected to generate most of the conflict around the globe. As Huntington (1996) observes, in the new world emerging from the ashes of the cold war, the dominating source of international conflict will no longer be political or economic but instead cultural. Huntington offers a number of reasons, including the following.

First, differences among cultures are real and basic. A common example is the differences in language around the globe. These linguistic differences have for centuries produced the most violent conflicts, as in the form of wars between tribes or nation-states in Africa and Asia.

Second, the world is shrinking, increasing interactions between peoples with different cultures. This reinforces awareness of the differences between cultures (such as American and Japanese cultures) and the commonalities within a culture (such as the Western culture shared by the United States, Canada, and Western Europe). This partly explains why the United States reacts far more negatively to Japanese investment here than to larger investments from Canada and Western Europe.

Third, economic modernization and social changes are destroying local traditions, the longstanding source of identity for much of the world. Religion has moved in to fill the gap, often in the form of fundamentalist religious movements. This may partly explain why terrorist Osama bin Laden and his followers became fanatic Muslims, blaming Western modernity for wrecking their traditional way of life by causing, among other things, their women to be "unveiled and in public places, taking buses, eating in cafes, and working alongside men" (Zakaria, 2001).

myth	The values that the West considers highly important, such as human rights, individualism, equality, and liberty, must be popular with the rest of the world.
reality	An analysis of 100 studies on cultural values in different societies concludes that "the values that are most important in the West are least important worldwide."

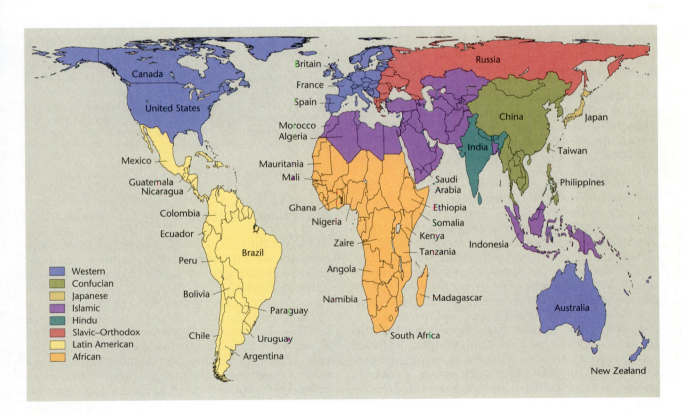

FIGURE 2.8

Cultural Domains of the World

Certain religions, languages, and other cultural norms and values constitute the specific cultures of various societies. These cultures can further be classified into larger groupings called *cultural domains,* more popularly known as *civilizations.* As shown in this map, there are eight cultural domains in the world: Western, Confucian, Japanese, Islamic, Hindu, Slavic-Orthodox, Latin American, and African. According to Huntington, the differences among these cultural domains can generate most of the global conflict.

Critical Thinking: *What do these different cultural domains have in common?*

Source: Reprinted with permission of Simon & Schuster Adult Publishing Group from *The Clash of Civilizations and the Remaking of World Order* by Samuel P. Huntington. Copyright © 1996 by Samuel P. Huntington. Base map © Hammond World Atlas Corp.

Fourth, Western notions of individualism, human rights, democracy, and the separation of church and state often run counter to Islamic, Confucian, Buddhist, Latin American, and other cultures. As Harry Triandis (1989) found in a review of 100 comparative studies of cultural values in different societies, "The values that are most important in the West are least important worldwide." This culture clash may explain why Western efforts to promote those values often provoke charges of "human rights imperialism" from the rest of the world (Huntington, 1996).

Because of these forces, culture clash may create more conflict and violence in the world. This may not happen if people learn to understand each other's cultures, especially the ways people in a different culture see their own interests. But there is strong resistance to such an understanding, and this resistance exists in the form of ethnocentrism. Let us analyze ethnocentrism and how we can deal with it.

■ Ethnocentrism

Almost from the time we are born, we are taught that our way of life is good, moral, civilized, and natural. At the same time, we learn to feel that other peoples' ways of life are not. The result is **ethnocentrism**, the attitude that one's own culture is superior to those of other peoples.

Ethnocentrism exists to some degree in every society. People in North America consider it psychologically unhealthy that children in some non-Western traditional countries sleep with their parents until they reach puberty. On the other hand, people in traditional countries tend to find it cruel that North Americans let their elderly parents live by themselves. Ethnocentrism can become so deeply ingrained in our bodies that we can become physically ill if we eat something our culture defines as sickening. Try eating toasted grasshoppers, which the Japanese relish, or ants, which some tribes in Brazil eat with gusto. Just the thought of eating either of these things might turn your stomach. Similarly, people in other cultures find many of our favorite foods nauseating. The Hindus in India abhor beef, and the Jews and Muslims in many countries spurn pork. Many Europeans consider corn on the cob fit only for animals. Numerous Asians and Africans recoil from cheese because they find it too smelly (Harris, 1985).

Ethnocentrism can serve as a glue to hold a society together. By declaring among themselves that "We're the greatest," people tend to feel a strong sense of unity as a nation. Usually, nations keep their ethnocentrism to themselves. But ethnocentrism can become excessive, leading to global violence, as suggested in the preceding section.

JUDGE OR JUDGE NOT   Cultural relativism is the belief that a culture must be understood on its own terms. Thus, to understand why people in another culture behave in a certain way, we should look at it from their own perspective. To some cultural relativists, bullfighting is acceptable behavior because it is seen as such from the perspective of the Spanish culture. But other cultural relativists may condemn it as cruelty to animals because they insist that understanding a culture on its own terms does not mean that they must also abandon their personal moralities. ■

■ Cultural Relativism

Although ethnocentrism is universal, it can be suppressed with **cultural relativism**, the belief that a culture must be understood on its own terms. By looking at the cultures of others from their own perspective, we can understand why they do things their way.

Such an understanding can bring a bonanza of profits to U.S. business operations around the globe. In our legalistic, rule-oriented culture, a written contract is usually required for conducting business. Once a contract is signed, negotiations should more or less cease. But to succeed in Greece, U.S. businesspeople have to look at the contract from the Greek point of view: The contract is only a charter for serious negotiations, which will stop only after the work is completed. In the Arab world, success in business requires acceptance of the Muslim view that a person's word, when given in a special kind of way, is just as binding as, if not more so than, most written contracts (Tiley, 2000; Morgan, 1989).

Cultural relativism can also contribute to international peace. Soon after Bill Clinton took office as president in 1993, he repeatedly pressured the Chinese government to correct its human rights abuses (which involved mistreating political dissidents). The pressure seriously strained U.S.–China relations. Clinton obviously refused to see the problem from China's perspective. The Chinese felt that Clinton was wrong to interfere in other countries' internal affairs and should focus instead on the United States' own human rights problems such as poverty, racism, and police brutality against African Americans. Finally, with an eye to China as a potentially huge market for U.S. products, Clinton seemed to adopt cultural relativism and came to understand the Chinese view. He stopped pressuring China on its human rights problem and started focusing on the task of increasing U.S. exports to China. As a result, U.S.–China relations began to improve.

But Clinton was criticized for kowtowing to China by ignoring its human rights abuses. This raises the question of how far cultural relativism should be carried. Should ethical judgment be suspended when others engage in such horrors as infanticide, genital mutilation, torture, or genocide? Only extremists would answer yes, arguing that no matter how repugnant they themselves find these horrors, their duty is only to understand them from others' perspectives, without passing judgment on them. They would pursue the "Live and let live" policy. But most cultural relativists would condemn the horrors because, to them, cultural relativism requires only understanding a culture on its own terms, *not* also abandoning one's own moral conscience (Tiley, 2000; Berreby, 1995).

SOCIOLOGICAL PERSPECTIVES ON CULTURE

So far, we have taken a close look at various aspects of culture. We may now step back, view culture as a whole, and ask: What is the essence of culture? Each of the three sociological perspectives provides an answer to this question.

■ Functionalist Perspective: Culture Meets Human Needs

According to the functionalist perspective, culture serves the important function of meeting human needs, ranging from the basic needs for food and shelter to the higher needs for psychological security, social harmony, and spiritual fulfillment. The most central function of culture is to ensure social order and stability. As functionalists see it, without culture, human society cannot survive. All this may seem obvious because the evidence is all around us. But the functionalist approach can help explain seemingly puzzling cultural practices. Consider how a key component of India's Hindu culture—the belief

in cows as sacred—serves the function of saving human lives and therefore ensuring social order.

In India, which has the largest number of cattle in the world, there are many poor and starving people, yet the slaughter of cows is forbidden. Moreover, their 180 million cows are treated as divine. They are given right of way in the street. They are even affectionately retired to "old-age homes" when they begin to become infirm. Why doesn't India feed its starving human population by killing these animals for food? The popular explanation is simply that the Hindus consider their cows sacred. But why?

myth	In India, the Hindus refrain from killing cows for food simply because they consider the animals sacred.
reality	The reason has to do with more than the Hindu belief in the sacredness of cows. India's peasant economy depends heavily on the cows performing various services, without which massive numbers of people would starve to death.

The reason suggested by the functionalist perspective is that the sacred cows serve several important, practical functions. First, they produce oxen, which Indian farmers desperately need to plow their fields and pull their carts. Second, when the cows die naturally, their beef is eaten by the poor lower castes and their hides are used by non-Hindu Indians to maintain one of the world's largest leather industries. Third, the cows produce an enormous amount of manure, which is used as fertilizer and cooking fuel. Fourth, the cows are tireless scavengers, eating garbage, stubble, and grass between railroad tracks, in ditches, and on roadsides. Thus, it costs nothing to raise the cows, and they provide many things of value. India's peasant economy depends heavily on the cows. If the Indians ate their cows, many more people would starve to death. In short, by enabling the cows to do all those things, the Hindu belief in their sacredness ultimately serves the function of saving the lives of people, thereby helping to ensure social order and stability in India.

■ Conflict Perspective: Culture Supports Social Inequality

While functionalism shows the positive side of culture, the conflict perspective reveals the negative side. At least two related ideas can be found in the conflict perspective.

First, culture reflects the interests of the rich and powerful in society. As Marx said, "The ruling ideas of society are the ideas of the ruling class." The value of competitiveness in our society, for example, benefits the powerful in two ways. One, it stimulates worker productivity, which enables employers to reap larger profits. Two, it discourages the poor and powerless from resenting the rich and powerful. If they believe in competition, the powerless will feel that the powerful deserve their riches and privileges because of their great intelligence and hard work. Therefore, the poor are likely to envy rather than resent the rich while blaming themselves for being poor. The powerless, in effect, join the powerful in supporting the status quo of social inequality.

Second, culture protects the status quo from the alienating effects of social and economic oppression. Suffering discrimination, exploitation, and poverty, some powerless persons may reject the competitive value as a hoax. But other values may still come to the rescue of the powerful. The most pertinent values are beliefs in morality and conformity, which may partly explain why most of the poor do not threaten the social order by committing crimes. Other, more tangible aspects of the culture further deflect the alienating impact of oppression from the powers that be. As Marvin Harris (1995) notes, such cultural artifacts as the movies, television, radio, and organized sports can effectively distract and amuse the exploited citizenry. This is similar to the way in which the ruling elite in the ancient Roman Empire controlled the masses by letting them watch gladiator contests and other circus spectaculars.

■ Symbolic Interactionist Perspective: Culture Reflects Shared Understandings

Both functionalist and conflict perspectives provide a structural view of culture as largely capable of *constraining* us. For functionalists, culture effectively forces us to depend on it because of the important functions it performs for us. Without these functions, we could hardly survive. To conflict theorists, culture oppresses the poor and the powerless by manipulating them into supporting the status quo of social inequality. Both functionalist and conflict theorists seem to offer a theme familiar to viewers of two movies, *Frankenstein* and *Jurassic Park:* Humans, through evolution, have created culture to free themselves from biological constraints, only to lose that freedom to the constraints of their own creation—namely, culture.

By contrast, symbolic interactionists are more likely to portray humans as being *free* to create and change culture. To them, culture is a set of shared understandings that people use to coordinate their activities. As a set of shared understandings, culture is both a *guide* to social interaction and a *product* of interaction. As a guide to humans, culture is fixed, mostly inherited from the past. But as a product of

humans, it is ever changing, continually created by people today. As Howard Becker (1982) explains, "On the one hand, culture persists and antedates the participation of particular people in it; indeed, culture can be said to shape the outlooks of people who participate in it." On the other hand, culture has "to be reviewed and remade continually, and in the remaking it changes."

As a guide, culture enables us to think and behave without first having to question the meaning of every thought and behavior. We do not, as Becker (1982) suggests, have to rack our brains trying to figure out how to shop (for example, whether to haggle over prices) every time we go to the grocery store. But culture has not always been a perfect or useful guide because the social environment changes continuously. A generation ago, most people bought their food at corner grocery stores, butcher shops, and poultry and fish stores. In those days, the shopping culture required store owners and employees to serve the customers. But that culture is no longer a useful guide today. Due to the rise of giant corporations capable of opening hundreds of stores across the country, most of us now buy our food in supermarkets, which requires a different way of shopping—we have to serve ourselves. In fact, many cultural practices in U.S. society change every 20 or 30 years. So, when new social conditions arise, people get together to create culture.

In short, while the functionalist and conflict perspectives are more likely to emphasize the importance of culture as a *constraint* on human behavior, the symbolic interactionist view tends to stress the importance of culture as a human *creation*. Together, both concepts of culture contribute much more than either one alone to our understanding of culture. The Theoretical Thumbnail on the next page provides a summary of these perspectives.

sociological **frontiers**

The New U.S. Society and Culture

Today, at the beginning of the new millennium, U.S. society is very different than it was a century ago. In that time, the life span of the average American has gone from 47 years to 77; the population has increased four-fold and become much more multicultural; and the average income of middle-class families, adjusted for inflation, has more than doubled (Wattenberg, 2001; Curry, 2000; Moore and Simon, 2000).

By objective measures, Americans are now living better than before, but subjectively, they are less happy, feeling that their culture has taken a turn for the worse. According to surveys cited by Robert Putnam (2000),

theoretical thumbnail

What Culture Does for People

Perspective	Focus	Insights
Functionalist	Culture serves important functions for meeting human needs so as to ensure social order.	In India, the Hindu belief that cows are sacred prevents mass killings of the animals, which are needed for farm work and other crucial economic benefits—ultimately saving the lives of people and ensuring social order and stability in the society.
Conflict	Culture supports social inequality by benefiting the rich and powerful as well as protecting the status quo from the oppressed masses.	The culture of competitiveness stimulates worker productivity, creating larger profits for employers. The belief in competition further makes the poor feel that the rich deserve their riches and privileges because of their great intelligence and hard work.
Symbolic interactionist	Culture reflects a set of shared understandings that works as a guide to social interaction and continually evolves as a product of interaction.	Culture shows people how to shop at a grocery store and do countless other things. Culture also changes as people create ways to deal with new conditions, such as by serving oneself in today's supermarkets.

most Americans believe that social and moral values have declined, that the average person is less trustworthy, and that the breakdown of community is a serious problem.

Certain signs of cultural renewal, however, have emerged in the last decade. The national rates of crime, divorce, and abortion have gone down significantly, as have the rates of teenage drug use and pregnancy. The level of charitable giving has risen, and a greater number of people attend large, new churches, many of them nondenominational. As one social observer concludes, "Across the land, Americans are hungering for something more than money and a new car. They are looking for answers that satisfy the soul and restore a sense of belonging to one another" (Gergen, 1999).

If this renewal continues, it will likely be some time before we see its complete impact on the culture. But in the meantime, a new culture is taking hold of U.S. society—the culture of *moral freedom,* in which individuals are expected to decide for themselves what is right and wrong, rather than let religious, moral, or other authorities make these decisions for them. Born in the 1960s, this culture has worked its way into every aspect of U.S. society today. As Alan Wolfe (2001) observes, "Even the most traditional Americans have been touched by the spread of moral freedom." Consider born-again Christians, who do not believe that individuals should be free to choose what they consider sinful—say, homosexuality. But they often reject the religion of their upbringing, start new churches, and homeschool their children. Interestingly, gays and lesbians have made similar lifestyle decisions, creating their own kinds of marriage and fam-

ily and founding houses of worship to serve their own spiritual needs. And so in this regard, these conflicting groups find common ground (Wolfe, 2001).

■ For more of the latest Sociological Frontiers, look up Continuing Update at www.ablongman.com/thio6e.

using *sociology*

How to Enhance Your Cultural Competence

As we saw earlier in this chapter, Americans are living in an increasingly multicultural society. With the presence of such diverse cultures come differences in how people interpret each other's behavior. When greeting someone, for example, people from France, Spain, Italy, Portugal, and the Mediterranean countries usually expect to be kissed on both cheeks. So do most Middle Easterners, especially Muslims, although they avoid body contact with the opposite sex. By contrast, Native Americans and Southeast Asians view a physical expression of greeting as an invasion of personal space. They also consider it discourteous to make direct eye contact or to stand too close to someone while in conversation. In many non-Western cultures, even calling older people by their first names is considered rude.

Given these and other cultural differences, it is important to develop *cultural competence,* the ability to accept, respect, and communicate smoothly with different cultures. Help in doing so is available from two keen observers of cross-cultural exchange. One is Divina Grossman (1994), a nursing professor who has studied interethnic interactions in socially diverse hospitals, and the other is Norine Dresser (1999), a professor whose firsthand experience as an EFL (English as a foreign language) teacher and extensive research on various cultures have led to the publication of *Multicultural Celebrations,* a guide to having effective and comfortable interactions with people of different cultures than your own. Grossman and Dresser offer these useful tips:

1. *Keep an open mind.* Try to look at the world through the eyes of culturally diverse peoples. Reading books and seeing films from different cultures may help provide such insight.
2. *Respect the differences among peoples.* Recognize that every group has its strengths and weaknesses. Appreciate the inherent worth of each culture, valuing it equally and not considering it inferior to your own.
3. *Be willing to learn.* Cultivate an interest in other peoples' values, beliefs, and practices. Get to know culturally diverse peoples through traveling, reading, and attending events held by local ethnic or cultural organizations.
4. *Learn to communicate effectively.* Develop proficiency in verbal and nonverbal communication. Be sensitive to the nuances of language and expression, emotion, posture, gestures, body movements, and use of personal space.

These four pointers reflect an attempt to combat *ethnocentrism* and acquire *cultural relativism,* two key concepts that have been discussed in this chapter. Thinking critically about these concepts, which of the four guidelines would you find easiest or most difficult to put into practice? Why?

◼ CHAPTER REVIEW
- -

1. *What are the basic components of society?* There are four basic components: statuses, roles, groups, and institutions. Statuses are the social positions occupied by individuals in a society. Roles are the expectations of what people should do in accordance with their statuses. Groups are collections of people who interact and have a feeling of unity. And institutions are sets of widely shared beliefs, norms, and procedures for meeting the basic needs of society.

2. *How do we get our statuses?* Statuses are either ascribed or achieved. *Are status and role equivalent?* No, although they are related. Whereas a status is a static label, a role is dynamic, varying with situations and persons. Different people may understand a

prescribed role in various ways and perform the same role differently. *How can roles be a source of conflict?* Role conflict occurs when we are expected to play two conflicting roles at the same time. Role strain arises when a single role imposes conflicting demands on us. *How do groups affect our behavior?* In a primary group, we interact with others informally, but in a secondary group, we interact formally. *Why are institutions so important to society?* Without institutions, society cannot survive because they are necessary for meeting its basic needs.

3. *What kinds of society can be found in various stages of sociocultural evolution?* They include hunting-gathering, pastoral, horticultural, agricultural, industrial, and postindustrial societies. Hunter-gatherers hunt animals and gather plants as their primary means for survival. Pastoralists domesticate and herd animals as their primary source of food. Horticulturalists produce food primarily by growing plants in small plots of land. Agricultural societies produce food primarily by using plows and draft animals on the farm. Industrial societies produce food for their subsistence primarily by using machinery. And postindustrial societies produce food for subsistence primarily by using high technology.

4. *What is culture?* It is a design for living. It consists of material culture, which includes all the things produced by members of a society, and nonmaterial culture, which comprises knowledge, beliefs, norms, values, and symbols. *What are norms and values?* Norms are social rules dictating how to behave. There are two types: folkways, which simply expect us to behave properly, and mores, which practically force us to behave morally. Both are derived from values, socially shared ideas about what is good, desirable, or important. *How does language affect our lives?* Language influences our perception and thinking, as well as reflecting our social life.

5. *What are the basic U.S. values?* Basic U.S. values include success, hard work, efficiency, material comfort, morality, humanitarianism, progress, science, external conformity, individualism, in-group superiority, equality, freedom, patriotism, and democracy. *What do advocates of multiculturalism want?* They want an egalitarian society in which all subcultures are treated equally. *What is U.S. pop culture like?* It reflects the democratic, capitalistic, and patriarchal nature of U.S. society while exerting an enormous influence all over the world.

6. *What are cultural universals?* They are practices found in all cultures as a means for meeting the same human needs. *Why can culture clash be expected*

to generate more global conflict and violence? Conflict and violence can be expected for a number of reasons: (1) Cultural differences are real and basic. (2) The world is shrinking. (3) Modernization is destroying local traditions. (4) The West's efforts to promote its own culture have provoked resistance from non-Western societies. *What should we do to understand other cultures?* We should get rid of ethnocentrism, the attitude that our own culture is superior to that of others, and adopt cultural relativism, which means judging other cultures on their own terms. Cultural relativism, however, should be tempered with moral conscience.

7. *What can we learn from the functionalist perspective on culture?* Culture serves important functions for meeting human needs so as to ensure social order and stability. *What does the conflict perspective suggest about culture?* Culture reflects the interests of the rich and powerful, helping to perpetuate social inequality. Culture also protects the status quo from the alienating effects of social and economic oppression. *What is the symbolic interactionist view on culture?* Culture comprises a set of shared understandings that is both a guide to social interaction and a product of interaction.

8. *What are the new U.S. society and culture like?* The society is healthier, more populous, more multicultural, and more wealthy. Americans are less happy due to a decline in social connections over the last several decades. That decline has recently stopped, however, while the culture of moral freedom has permeated society. *How can we become more culturally competent?* Keep an open mind, respect the differences among people, be willing to learn, and learn to communicate effectively.

KEY TERMS

Achieved status   A status that is attained through an individual's own actions (p. 35).

Afrocentrism   The view of the world from the standpoint of African culture (p. 52).

Agricultural society   A society that produces food primarily by using plows and draft animals on the farm (p. 42).

Ascribed status   A status that one has no control over, such as status based on race, gender, or age (p. 34).

Belief   An idea that is relatively subjective, unreliable, or unverifiable (p. 46).

Cultural integration   The joining of various values into a coherent whole (p. 51).

Cultural relativism   The belief that a culture must be understood on its own terms (p. 58).

Cultural universals   Practices found in all cultures as the means for meeting the same human needs (p. 55).

Culture   A design for living or a complex whole consisting of objects, values, and other characteristics that people acquire as members of society (p. 45).

Ethnocentrism   The attitude that one's own culture is superior to those of other peoples (p. 58).

Eurocentrism   A view of the world from the standpoint of European culture (p. 52).

Folkways   Weak norms that specify expectations about proper behavior (p. 47).

Horticultural society   A society that produces food primarily by growing plants in small gardens (p. 41).

Hunting-gathering society   A society that hunts animals and gathers plants as its primary means for survival (p. 39).

Industrial society   A society that produces food for its subsistence primarily by using machinery (p. 42).

Knowledge   A collection of relatively objective ideas and facts about the physical and social worlds (p. 46).

Laws   Norms that are specified formally in writing and backed by the power of the state (p. 48).

Master status   A status that dominates a relationship (p. 35).

Material culture   Every conceivable kind of physical object produced by humans (p. 45).

Mores   Strong norms that specify normal behavior and constitute demands, not just expectations (p. 47).

Multiculturalism   A state in which all subcultures in the same society are equal to one another (p. 51).

Nonmaterial culture   The intangible aspect of culture (p. 45).

Norm   A social rule that specifies how people should behave (p. 46).

Pastoral society   A society that domesticates and herds animals as its primary source of food (p. 40).

Popular culture   A collection of relatively unsophisticated artistic creations that appeal to a mass audience (p. 53).

Postindustrial society   A society that produces food so efficiently that high technology and service industry dominate it (p. 44).

Prescribed role   The expectation held by society regarding how an individual with a particular status should behave (p. 36).

Primary group   A group whose members interact informally, relate to each other as whole persons, and enjoy their relationship for its own sake (p. 37).

Role   A set of expectations of what individuals should do in accordance with a particular status that they hold (p. 36).

Role conflict   Conflict between the roles of two different statuses being played simultaneously (p. 36).

Role performance   Actual performance of a role (p. 36).

Role set   An array of roles attached to one particular status (p. 36).

Role strain   Stress caused by incompatible demands from the roles of a single status (p. 36).

Sanction   A reward for conformity to norms or punishment for violation of norms (p. 48).

Secondary group   A group whose members interact formally, relate to each other as players of particular roles, and expect to profit from each other (p. 37).

Social aggregate   A number of people who happen to be in one place but do not interact with one another (p. 37).

Social group   A collection of people who interact with one another and have a certain feeling of unity (p. 37).

Social institution   A set of widely shared beliefs, norms, and procedures necessary for meeting the basic needs of a society (p. 37).

Society   A collection of interacting individuals sharing the same way of life and living in the same territory (p. 34).

Sociobiology   A new Darwinian theory that human behavior is genetically determined (p. 56).

Sociocultural evolution   The process of changing from a technologically simple society to a more complex one, with significant consequences for social and cultural life (p. 39).

Status   A position in a group or society (p. 34).

Status inconsistency   A condition in which the same individual is given two conflicting status rankings (p. 35).

Subordinate status   A status that does not dominate a relationship; the opposite of master status (p. 35).

Symbol   A word, gesture, music, or anything that stands for some other thing (p. 49).

Value   A socially shared idea about what is good, desirable, or important (p. 46).

QUESTIONS FOR DISCUSSION AND REVIEW

BUILDING BLOCKS OF SOCIETY

1. What are statuses, and how do they influence our behavior?
2. How do prescribed roles differ from role performance?
3. How do primary groups differ from social aggregates and secondary groups?
4. What important functions do institutions have in society?

SOCIETIES IN SOCIOCULTURAL EVOLUTION

1. What are the differences among hunting-gathering, pastoral, and horticultural societies?
2. How do industrial societies differ from agricultural societies?
3. What consequences does our emerging postindustrial society have for our lives?

COMPONENTS OF CULTURE

1. How is sociologists' definition of *culture* different from that of the general public?
2. What are cultural values and norms, and how do they combine with sanctions to control people's behavior?
3. How does the language you use influence the way you see the world?

U.S. CULTURE

1. To what extent do your personal values agree with the 15 basic American values identified by Williams?
2. According to advocates of multiculturalism, what is wrong with the melting pot concept of U.S. culture?
3. What influences American pop culture? How does the world react to it?

A GLOBAL ANALYSIS OF CULTURE

1. What are cultural universals?
2. Why is culture clash likely to increase global conflict in the new world order?
3. What are the functions and dysfunctions of ethnocentrism and cultural relativism?

SOCIOLOGICAL PERSPECTIVES ON CULTURE

1. How can the functionalist perspective be used to explain the cultural value of cows in India?
2. How does the conflict perspective relate culture to social inequality?
3. How does the symbolic interactionist view of culture differ from those of the other two perspectives?

SOCIOLOGICAL FRONTIERS/USING SOCIOLOGY

1. What is new about U.S. society and culture today?
2. How can you become culturally competent?

SUGGESTED READINGS

Harrison, Lawrence E., and Samuel P. Huntington (eds.). 2000. *Culture Matters: How Values Shape Human Progress.* New York: Basic Books. A collection of articles on how cultural beliefs and values help some nations and ethnic groups to be more successful, economically and politically, than others.

Kammen, Michael. 1999. *American Culture, American Tastes: Social Change and the Twentieth Century.* New York: Knopf. Provides a historical perspective on how the U.S. mass and popular culture has evolved from about 70 years ago to today.

Putnam, Robert D. 2000. *Bowling Alone: The Collapse and Revival of American Community.* New York: Simon & Schuster. A study of how and why U.S. community has declined and what can be done to reverse this trend.

Warde, Alan, and Lydia Martens. 2000. *Eating Out: Social Differentiation, Consumption, and Pleasure.* New York: Cambridge University Press. Delves into the culture of dining out, in which diners are expected to enjoy the social experience at a restaurant more than the food itself.

Wolfe, Alan. 2001. *Moral Freedom: The Impossible Idea That Defines the Way We Live Now.* New York: Norton. Shows how U.S. culture has changed from demanding economic freedom in the nineteenth century to political freedom in the twentieth century and to moral freedom—the freedom to decide for oneself what is and isn't moral—in the twenty-first century.

■ Additional Resources

The New York Times
expect the world®
nytimes.com

Expand your knowledge of the concepts discussed in this chapter by reading the following current and historical articles from the *New York Times*. Go to the "eThemes of the Times" section of the Companion Website (www.ablongman.com/thio6e):

"Love on Campus: Trying to Set Rules for the Emotions"

"Western Farmers Fear Third-World Challenge to Subsidies"

Research Navigator.com

Research Navigator, a research database, provides immediate access to hundreds of full-text articles from EBSCO's ContentSelect Academic Journal Database. If the Research Navigator access code was included with your textbook, go to the website www.research navigator.com and read the following articles related to this chapter by typing in the article number:

Agre, Philip E. "Cyberspace as American Culture." *Science as Culture*, Jun2002, Vol. 11 Issue 2, p171, 19p. Accession Number: 6790432. Examines the cultural aspects of the Internet.

Potter, Garry. "*Sui Generis* Micro Social Structures: The Heuristic Example of Poker." *Canadian Journal of Sociology*, Spring 2003, Vol. 28 Issue 2, p171, 32p. Accession Number: 10109355. Looks at the social structures of a poker game.

Socialization

myths & realities

myth *Intelligence is either inherited or learned.*

reality Intelligence is both inherited and learned. Nature sets limits on what we *can* achieve, and socialization plays a very large role in determining what we *do* achieve (p. 69).

myth *Infants will not die as long as they are well fed.*

reality Despite being well fed, infants can become physically and psychologically impaired and even die if deprived of human contact (p. 69).

myth *To be a genius, you must be born one.*

reality Geniuses such as Einstein and Picasso are not only born but also made. From childhood, these men worked intensely to develop their potential abilities under the guidance of parents who valued learning and achievement (p. 70).

myth *Born with the ability to have feelings, children do not have to learn how to be happy, fearful, or anxious.*

reality Emotions are not innate; they must be learned. Through parents and other caretakers, children learn to feel happy when receiving a compliment, fearful when being threatened, or anxious when facing uncertainty (p. 72).

myth *Men and women know what morality is because they both have learned how to be moral in the same way.*

reality There is a gender difference in moral development: While men have learned to be more concerned with *justice*, women have learned to be more concerned with *relationships and the welfare of others* (p. 75).

myth *Schools only help students develop their potential as creative, independent individuals by teaching them knowledge and skills.*

reality Schools also mold students into social conformity. This includes the so-called hidden curriculum of training students to be patriotic, to believe in their country's cultural values, and to obey its laws (p. 85).

Soon after 3-year-old Rebecca and her family moved to another town, her mother wanted to find a good pediatrician. She talked to many new neighbors and friends, and they all recommended the same doctor. After five minutes of watching Rebecca undergo a checkup, the mother was extremely pleased at how well her little girl was responding to the doctor. He was very friendly, talking gently to her and explaining everything he was doing. When it was time to test her reflexes, he said, "Rebecca, I'm going to hit your knee very lightly with a hammer." Immediately, Rebecca let out a bloodcurdling scream. Shaken and puzzled, the doctor turned to her mother and asked, "What did I do wrong?"

"Her father," said the mother, "is a carpenter" (Espinosa, 1992).

Actually, Rebecca is just like all of us. To a significant degree, she is a product of **socialization**, the process by which a society transmits its cultural values to its members. Socialization is carried out through society's agents, such as parents and teachers. Without socialization, Rebecca could not have become a truly human being, a person who could take part in society and its culture, like most children her age.

Simultaneously, though, Rebecca has developed through socialization a **personality**—a fairly stable configuration of feelings, attitudes, ideas, and behaviors that characterizes an individual—that is different from those of most of her peers. As we have seen, unlike other children, Rebecca reacts fearfully to the word *hammer*. She obviously associates the physician's harmless little hammer with the carpenter's powerful hammer, a result of being socialized by a carpenter father.

In this chapter, we will explore how personality develops and how socialization transmits society's values to its young members.

THE SIGNIFICANCE OF HEREDITY

Are children like clay, waiting to be shaped in one way or another? The roles of *nature* (heredity or what we inherit) and *nurture* (environment or what we learn) in making us what we are have long been argued. To the seventeenth-century philosopher John Locke, the mind of a child was a *tabula rasa* (blank slate). People became what they were taught to be. By the second half of the nineteenth century, however, a quite different view was popular. Instead of looking to nurture—what people are taught—to explain human behavior, many social scientists looked to nature—what people inherit. The pendulum of opinion has swung back and forth ever since.

Obviously, we do inherit some of what makes us who we are. But what? Physical traits such as skin color and sex are inherited, but how they affect human behavior and personality depends to a great extent on what society makes of them.

People also appear to inherit *temperament*—an inclination to react in a certain way. Some people are inclined to be active, nervous, or irritable. Others, even when brought up in a similar environment, tend to be passive, calm, or placid. Psychologists have found that even infants show consistent temperaments. For instance, some are active most of the time, whereas others move rather little. Some cry and fuss a lot, and others rarely do. These differences may influence personality development. Very active infants, for example, are more likely than passive ones to become aggressive and competitive adults (Pinker, 2002; W. Gallagher, 1996).

The role of heredity in determining intelligence and aptitude is more controversial. **Intelligence** is the capacity for mental or intellectual achievement, such as the ability to think logically and solve problems. **Aptitude** is the capacity for developing physical or social skills, such as athletic prowess. The *extent* to which intelligence, in particular, is inherited has been the subject of some of the most bitter, emotional debates in all of social science. Richard Herrnstein and Charles Murray (1994) assume that more than half of our intelligence comes from genes. But most social scientists consider intelligence to be largely learned from the social environment. The debate is far from settled, as can be seen in Judith Harris's (1998) and Steven Pinker's (2002) controversial books attacking the nurture assumption.

myth	Intelligence is either inherited or learned.
reality	Intelligence is both inherited and learned. Nature sets limits on what we *can* achieve, and socialization plays a very large role in determining what we *do* achieve.

For our purposes, what is significant is that although nature sets limits on what we *can* achieve, socialization plays a very large role in determining what we *do* achieve. Whatever potential is inherited may be *enhanced or stunted* through socialization. Suppose certain infants are born with overly aggressive tendencies. They will likely grow up violent if raised by abusive parents but less aggressive if raised by affectionate parents. Similarly, an intellectual parenting style, which includes frequent reading to children, can boost children's inherited intelligence while nonintellectual parenting can keep their IQs low. Thus, heredity offers only a probability that a given trait will emerge, not a guarantee, and what is inherited can be changed—either encouraged or suppressed—by socialization (Ridley, 2003; Reiss, 2000).

THE SIGNIFICANCE OF SOCIALIZATION

What makes socialization both necessary and possible for human beings is their lack of *instincts,* biologically inherited capacities for performing relatively complex tasks. Whatever temperament and potential abilities human infants may be born with, they are also born helpless, depending on adults for survival. What may be more surprising is the extent to which traits that seem very basic and essential to human nature also appear to depend on socialization. Evidence of the far-reaching significance of socialization comes both from case studies of children deprived of socialization and from instances in which children are socialized into geniuses.

Impairing Development

Since the fourteenth century, there have been more than 50 recorded cases of *feral children*—children supposedly raised by animals. One of the most famous is the "wild boy of Aveyron," who was captured in the woods by hunters in southern France in 1797. He was about 11 years old and completely naked. The "wild boy" ran on all fours, had no speech, preferred uncooked food, and could not do most of the simple things done by younger children (Lane, 1976; Malson, 1972). The French boy had obviously been deprived of socialization.

In the United States, there have been three similar well-known cases. The first, Anna, was born in Pennsylvania in 1932 to a young unwed mother, a fact that outraged the mother's father. After trying unsuccessfully to give Anna away, the mother hid Anna in her attic and fed her just enough to keep her alive. Anna was neither touched nor talked to, neither washed nor bathed. She simply lay still in her own filth. When she was found in 1938 at the age of 6, Anna could not talk or walk. She could do nothing but lie quietly on the floor, her eyes vacant and her face expressionless (Davis, 1947).

Like Anna, Isabella was born to an unwed mother in Ohio. Her grandfather kept her and her deaf-mute mother secluded in a dark room. When Isabella was discovered in 1938, she, too, was 6 years old. She showed great fear and hostility toward people. Unable to talk, she could only make a strange croaking sound (Davis, 1947).

Genie, who was found in California in 1970, had been deprived of normal socialization for nearly 13 years—twice as long as Anna and Isabella. Since birth, Genie had been isolated in a small, quiet room. During the day, she was tied to her potty seat, able only to flutter her hands and feet. At night, her father straitjacketed and caged her in a crib with an overhead cover. He beat her if she made any noise. He never spoke to her except occasionally to bark or growl like a dog at her. Her terrified mother, forbidden to speak to Genie, fed her in silence and haste. Discovered at age 13, Genie could not stand straight, was unable to speak except to whimper, and had the intelligence and social maturity of a 1-year-old (Rymer, 1993; Pines, 1981).

myth	Infants will not die as long as they are well fed.
reality	Despite being well fed, infants can become physically and psychologically impaired and even die if deprived of human contact.

These four cases are, to say the least, unusual. But even less severe forms of deprivation can be harmful. In 1945, researcher René Spitz reported that children who received little attention in institutions suffered very noticeable effects. In one orphanage, Spitz found infants who were about 18 months old that were left lying on their backs in small cubicles most of the day without any human contact. Within a year, all had become physically, mentally, emotionally, and so-

NATURE NEEDS NURTURE
We inherit most of our physical makeup, including eye, hair, and skin color. But much debate revolves around whether we inherit nonphysical characteristics, such as intelligence, aptitude, and personality. Sociologists maintain that although nature sets limits on what we *can* achieve, socialization plays a large role in determining what we *do* achieve. ■

cially impaired. Two years later, more than a third of the children had died. Those who survived could not speak, walk, dress themselves, or use a spoon.

■ Creating Geniuses

While the lack of normal socialization can destroy minds, specialized socialization can create geniuses. A young woman named Edith finished grammar school in four years, skipped high school, and went straight to college. She graduated from college at age 15 and obtained her doctorate before she was 18. Was she born a genius? Not at all. Ever since she had stopped playing with dolls, her father had seen to it that her days were filled with reading, mathematics, classical music, intellectual discussions and debates, and whatever learning he could derive from the world's literature. When she felt like playing, her father told her to play chess with someone like himself, who would be a challenge to her (Hoult, 1979).

myth	To be a genius, you must be born one.
reality	Geniuses such as Einstein and Picasso are not only born but also made. From childhood, these men worked intensely to develop their potential abilities under the guidance of parents who valued learning and achievement.

Like Edith, many geniuses have been deliberately subjected to a very stimulating environment. A well-known example is Norbert Wiener, a prime mover in the development of computers and cybernetics. He entered college at age 11 and received his Ph.D. from Harvard at 18. According to his father, Norbert was "essentially an average boy who had had the advantage of superlative training." Another example is Adragon Eastwood DeMello, who graduated with a degree in mathematics from the University of California at age 11. When he was a few months old, his father gave up his career as a science writer to educate Adragon (Radford, 1990). In his study of Einstein, Picasso, Gandhi, and other world-renowned geniuses in various fields, Howard Gardner (1993) found that they were all born into families that valued learning and achievement and that had at least one loving and supportive adult.

These people may have been born with a *potential* for becoming geniuses, but that potential was transformed into reality only through extraordinary socialization. Without socialization, no infant can naturally grow into a genius. Consider ace test pilot Chuck Yeager. He may have been born fearless. But if his parents had been overprotective and kept him from jumping off barns, he might never have grown up to be the first flier to break the sound barrier.

▮ PROCESSES OF SOCIALIZATION

Children go through various processes of socialization that help them become who they are. The most important processes involve learning how to think, how to feel, how to be normal, how to be moral, and how to be a man or woman. We can learn much about these socialization processes from traditional and modern theories and research data.

■ Learning How to Think

From close observation, Swiss psychologist Jean Piaget (1896–1980) concluded that children learn how to think by passing through certain stages of *cognitive* (mental or intellectual) development:

1. *Sensorimotor stage (birth to age 2):* Infants lack language and cannot think in order to make sense of their environment. In their view, something exists only if they can see or touch it. Thus, to the infant, a parent no longer exists after leaving the child's field of vision. Unlike older children, who interact with the world by using their brains, infants use their senses and bodily movements to interact with the environment. Infants, for example, use their hands to touch, move, or pick up objects, and they put things in their mouths or suck on some objects.

SHOW AND NOT TELL   Jean Piaget described four stages of cognitive development that each child goes through. At the third, concrete operational stage (ages 7–12), children can perform simple intellectual tasks, but their mental abilities are restricted to dealing with concrete objects, such as lining up blocks in order of size. However, children cannot solve a similar problem stated verbally in abstract terms. ■

2. *Preoperational stage (ages 2 to 7):* Children are not yet capable of performing simple intellectual operations. Precausal, they cannot understand cause and effect. When Piaget asked 4-year-olds what makes a bicycle move, they replied that the street makes it go. When he asked 6-year-olds why the sun and moon move, the youngsters said that the heavenly bodies follow us in order to see us. These children are also *animistic:* They attribute human-like thoughts and wishes to the sun and moon. Moreover, they are *egocentric,* seeing things only from their own perspective. If we ask a young boy how many brothers he has, he may correctly say "One." But if we ask him "How many brothers does your brother have?" he would say "None." He has difficulty seeing himself from his brother's perspective.

3. *Concrete operational stage (ages 7 to 12):* By now, children can perform simple intellectual tasks, but their mental abilities are restricted to dealing with concrete objects. If children between ages 8 and 10 are asked to line up a series of dolls from the tallest to the shortest, they can easily do so. But they cannot solve a similar problem stated verbally—in abstract terms—such as "John is taller than Bill; Bill is taller than Harry; who is the tallest of the three?" The children can correctly answer this question only if they actually see John, Bill, and Harry in person.

4. *Formal operational stage (ages 12 to 15):* Adolescents can think and reason formally (abstractly). They can follow the form of an argument while ignoring its concrete content. They know, for example, that if A is greater than B and B is greater than C, then A is greater than C—without having to know in advance whether the concrete contents of A, B, and C are vegetables, fruits, animals, or other items that can be seen or touched.

Today's sociologists find Piaget's stages of cognitive development, summarized in Figure 3.1 (p. 72), useful for understanding how children learn new cognitive skills—such as perception, reasoning, and calculation—as they grow up. Piaget has been criticized, however, for treating cognitive development as if it occurred in a social vacuum. Obviously, children cannot learn any cognitive skill by themselves, without some help from parents, teachers, and other important people in their lives. Piaget did not necessarily ignore the influence of these people on a child's cognitive development. He simply chose to focus on what new intellectual skills children develop at each stage of their lives. Moreover, research has proved Piaget right in suggesting that virtually all children go through the sequence of mental development he laid out. All children, for example, think concretely before thinking abstractly, rather than the reverse.

■ Learning How to Feel

While developing their cognitive abilities, children also learn to understand their own emotions. This knowledge contributes significantly to how well they will function as adult members of society. Emotional socialization involves two tasks: how to identify feelings and how to manage them.

myth	Born with the ability to have feelings, children do not have to learn how to be happy, fearful, or anxious.
reality	Emotions are not innate; they must be learned. Through parents and other care-takers, children learn to feel happy when receiving a compliment, fearful when being threatened, or anxious when facing uncertainty.

Human emotions abound, ranging from such basic feelings as fear, anger, and happiness to more refined emotions such as frustration, love, and jealousy. Children are taught how to *identify* these feelings because by themselves, they cannot know what they are. Suppose a little boy at a day-care center engages in such expressive behaviors as fidgeting, sulking, biting, and kicking while waiting for his mother to pick him up. He may learn from an adult that what he feels is anger. Here is how such a scenario may occur (Pollak and Thoits, 1989):

> Boy [restless]: My mom is late.
> Staff member: Does that make you *mad?*
> Boy: Yes.
> Staff member: Sometimes kids get *mad* when their moms are late to pick them up.

The adult, in effect, teaches the child to identify an emotion by making a causal connection between a stimulus event (mother being late) and an emotional outcome (boy being angry). Through socialization—not only by parents and other caretakers but also by television, movies, and other mass media—children learn that a compliment is expected to give pleasure, a threat is expected to arouse fear, and uncertainty is expected to give rise to anxiety. While they learn that it is logical to feel resentful toward someone who has mistreated them, they also learn that it is not logical to feel affectionate toward that person. It is crucial for children to acquire this emotional logic. Failure to do so is popularly considered a symptom of mental disorder. If a 10-year-old boy tells you with a big smile that his mother has

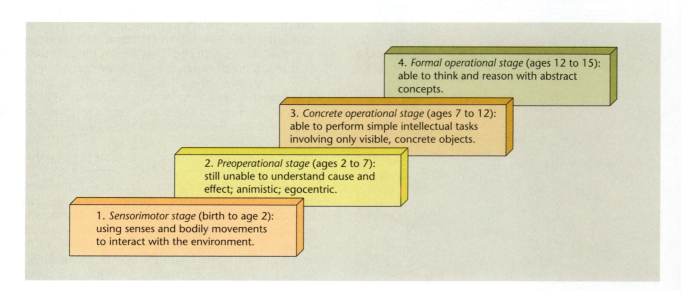

FIGURE 3.1

Piaget's Stages of Cognitive Development
Piaget suggested that virtually all children go through the same sequence of mental development. For instance, they think concretely (stage 3) before thinking abstractly (stage 4), rather than the other way around.

Critical Thinking: *As a child, how did you learn to think concretely and then abstractly? Give examples of the things that you learned.*

just died, you may suspect him of having abnormal psychological development (Smith-Lovin, 1995; Rosenberg, 1990).

Children also learn how to *manage* their emotions in at least three ways. First, they learn how they *should* feel. For example, they should love their parents and they should feel guilty for displeasing their parents.

Second, children learn how to *display* or *conceal* emotions. They should look happy at a wedding, seem sad at a funeral, and appear reverent at a religious service. Sometimes children learn to display an emotion that they do not have in them or to conceal a feeling that they do have. If a grandparent gives them a present they do not like, they are taught to show how much they like it. If they dislike their teachers, they learn to conceal the negative feeling.

Finally, while they learn to display or conceal certain emotions, children also learn how to *change* some feelings in themselves. When children are feeling sad, they may learn to manipulate that feeling by, for example, telephoning or visiting a friend (Smith-Lovin, 1995; Rosenberg, 1990).

Not all children learn to feel in the same way. Social forces, particularly gender roles and social classes, exert a strong influence on emotional socialization. Compared with boys, girls are taught to be more empathetic, more loving, less able to feel and express anger, but more able to feel and express fear and sadness (Thoits, 1989; Hochschild, 1983). Because middle-class and upper-class people tend to work more with people than with things, they are more attuned to emotional management, such as smiling at customers even when they do not feel

like smiling. Therefore, in teaching emotional management to their children, they are more likely than people of the lower classes to show respect for the youngsters' feelings by using reasoning and persuasion. Suppose a child says "I don't want to kiss Grandpa—why must I kiss him all the time?" Parents of the higher social classes would respond, "I know you don't like kissing Grandpa, but he's unwell and he's very fond of you." By contrast, lower-class and working-class parents, who tend to be less sensitive to their offspring's feelings, would answer, "Children should kiss their Grandpa" or "He's not well—I don't want any of your nonsense." In effect, they order the child to kiss his or her grandfather (Hochschild, 1983).

■ Learning How to Be Normal

One of the most influential theories of how children develop their personalities is that of Sigmund Freud (1856–1939). In his view, personality consists of three parts: the id, ego, and superego. The **id** is the part of personality that is irrational, concerned only with seeking pleasure. The id is our inborn desire to live, enjoy ourselves, make love, or celebrate life in one way or another. But such desires cannot be successfully fulfilled unless we have learned *how* to fulfill them. Thus we have learned innumerable ways to live as best we can.

The knowledge that results from this learning becomes the **ego**, the part of personality that is rational, dealing with the world logically and realistically. In trying to help us enjoy ourselves, our ego tells us that there is a limit to the satisfaction of our id. If we

WHEN NOT TO BE A COLD FISH   Children learn how to manage their emotions in at least three ways. First, they learn how they *should feel,* such as feeling guilty for displeasing their parents. Second, they learn how to *display emotions,* such as looking happy at a wedding or sad at a funeral. Third, they learn how to *change their feelings,* such as seeking consolation from a friend when sad. ▪

want to satisfy our sexual desire, we cannot simply make love anywhere, such as on a street corner. This limit to our self-enjoyment is imposed by society in the form of rules and injunctions—"You should not do this. You should not do that."

Our acceptance of society's rules and injunctions becomes the cornerstone of the **superego**, the part of personality that is moral; it is popularly known as *conscience*. The ego, in effect, advises the id to obey the superego so that we will enjoy life in a normal, socially acceptable way.

Freud proposed that these three parts of personality develop through a series of five stages in childhood. Influenced primarily by interaction with parents, these early experiences will have a significant impact on adult personalities. Table 3.1 shows how children may grow up to be normal or abnormal, depending on whether their experiences are mostly positive or negative (Kahn, 2002).

Sociologists have often criticized Freud for explaining human behavior in terms of inborn or unconscious motivations, particularly the id. Feminists have further criticized Freud for devaluing women with his concept of *penis envy*—the unconscious desire to be men. Nevertheless, Freud's work is sociologically significant in at least three ways: (1) the emphasis on the role played by parents in children's development; (2) the view that childhood experiences have a great impact on adult personality; and (3) the assumption that the superego, which has a great influence on human personality, reflects society's norms and values.

■ Learning How to Be Moral

According to U.S. psychologist Lawrence Kohlberg (1981), children go through three levels of moral development. This idea came from his research on how youngsters of different ages deal with moral dilemmas. The children were presented with a hypothetical situation: A man did not have the money to buy a drug that might save his dying wife. He became desperate and broke into a store to steal the drug. Should he have done that?

TABLE 3.1

Freud's Stages of Personality Development

Stage	Characteristics	Normal and Abnormal Personalities
Oral stage (birth to age 1)	The infant is at the mercy of the id (because the ego and superego have not emerged) and seeks pleasure through oral activities such as sucking.	If the drive for oral pleasure is adequately met, the child may grow up to engage in oral activities, such as eating and talking, in moderation, but if the drive is overindulged or frustrated, the pursuit of oral pleasure may become extreme, such as overeating or talkativeness.
Anal stage (ages 1 to 3)	The infant seeks pleasure from holding in and pushing out feces. The ego emerges, aided by toilet training, through which the child learns self-control and self-dependence.	If toilet training and other self-control lessons are satisfactory, the child may grow up to be self-composed and autonomous, but if the lessons are too lax or strict, the child may turn out to be extremely messy and wasteful or too concerned with order, cleanliness, and possessions.
Phallic stage (ages 3 to 6)	The child feels sexual love for the opposite-sex parent and learns that this desire must be suppressed. Through learning restrictions, the child internalizes society's norms and values, and thus the superego develops.	If the superego develops adequately, the child may grow up to be moralistic or law abiding, but if the superego fails to develop adequately, as an adult, the person may be inclined to engage in unconventional or antisocial activities.
Latency stage (ages 6 to 11)	The id quiets down, and the child focuses on developing intellectual and social skills. The ego and superego become stronger.	If there are adequate opportunities for learning and socializing, the child may grow up to be self-assured and sociable; if not, the child may turn out to be withdrawn or extremely individualistic.
Genital stage (adolescence)	The id resurges, and interest in sex develops, with which the habits of modesty and sympathy give way to pleasure in exhibitionism and aggressiveness; but gradually the adolescent learns to cope with these problems.	If frustrations are few or often successfully dealt with, the youth will get along well sexually with others as an adult and, if married, may have few or no serious problems. If frustrations repeatedly occur without resolution, the adult may have many sexual and marital problems.

Some children answered yes; others said no. But Kohlberg was more interested in the responses to a crucial question: *Why* did they answer as they had? He found three distinct patterns of response, each reflecting a certain level of moral development.

At the first level, generally under the age of 10, children have a **preconventional morality,** the practice of defining right and wrong according to the *consequence* of the action being judged. The consequence involves reward or punishment. Thus, some of these children said that it was all right to steal the drug because it could save the wife (reward), while others regarded the stealing as wrong because the offender could be arrested (punishment).

At the second level, between ages 10 and 16, children have a **conventional morality,** the practice of defining right and wrong according to the *motive* of the action being judged. Thus, most of these children said that they could not blame the man for stealing the drug because of his love for his wife.

At the third level, over age 16, most young adults have a **postconventional morality,** the practice of judging actions by taking into account the importance of *conflicting norms.* Some of these young adults supported the stealing but still believed in the general principle that stealing is wrong. They felt that the man was justified in stealing the drug for his wife, but they also believed that the stealing was not right. Other young adults opposed the drug theft but were nevertheless sympathetic to the thief. To such young adults, the ends do not justify the means, but the caring husband cannot be completely blamed for stealing the drug. In sum, adults are more likely than youngsters to appreciate the conflict between norms in a moral dilemma.

myth	Men and women know what morality is because they both have learned how to be moral in the same way.
reality	There is a gender difference in moral development: While men have learned to be more concerned with *justice,* women have learned to be more concerned with *relationships and the welfare of others.*

This view of moral development, outlined in Figure 3.2, has been criticized for being applicable to males more than females because it was based on research on males alone. According to Carol Gilligan (1989; 1982), Kohlberg focuses on men's interest in *justice,* which is impersonal in nature, and neglects women's lifelong concern with *relationships,* which are personal. In Gilligan's view, the moral development of most women differs from that of men. It involves progressing from an interest in one's own

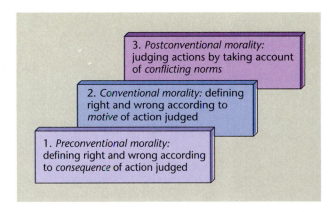

FIGURE 3.2

Kohlberg's Levels of Moral Development

According to Gilligan, in growing up, men may have gone through these levels of moral development, but most women may not have. Instead of being concerned with the impersonal issue of justice, women tend to develop morally by progressing from an interest in their own survival to a concern for others' welfare.

Critical Thinking: *Which type of moral maturity would you consider more beneficial to society: that of women or that of men? Why?*

survival to a concern for others. Thus, women are said to have achieved a great deal of moral maturity if they have developed a compassionate concern for others.

■ Learning How to Be Masculine or Feminine

From feminist theory, we can see how boys and girls learn to be masculine and feminine by developing **gender identities,** images of who they are expected to be on the basis of their sex. Under the influence of a patriarchal society, gender development involves socializing males to be dominant over females.

A major source of gender development is the family. In a patriarchal society, child care is assigned primarily to the mother, and children consequently spend much time with her. During the first 2 years or so after birth, children of both sexes lack self-awareness and see themselves as a part of their mothers. But beginning at about age 3, when children begin to see themselves as separate individuals, girls and boys start to develop different gender identities.

As gender identity develops, girls continue to identify with their mothers because they are of the same sex. Girls consequently develop the traditionally feminine appreciation for relationships and nurturance. By contrast, boys begin to differentiate themselves from their mothers because of the sexual difference. Further influenced by their fathers' primarily dominant role in the family, boys try to suppress the feminine traits they have acquired from their mothers, learn to devalue anything they consider feminine, and identify with their fathers by being independent and aggressive (Small, 2001).

Another important source of gender development is the school. Also influenced by patriarchal society, teachers tend to socialize girls to see themselves as less important than boys and boys to see themselves as more important than girls. Thus, teachers praise boys' contributions more lavishly and call on boys more frequently. Teachers also tend to socialize girls to be quiet and polite and boys to be assertive and aggressive. This involves, among other things, accepting answers that boys shout out but reprimanding girls for speaking out of turn (Corsaro and Eder, 1995; Wood, 1994).

The mass media also help socialize girls to be submissive and boys to be dominant. Analyzing some 80 television series and more than 500 characters, the National Commission on Working Women found a preponderance of women working as secretaries and homemakers and a world of young, beautiful, scantily dressed women. Even in advertisements that portray women as being in charge of their own lives, the women are shown "literally being carried by men, leaning on men, being helped down from a height of two feet, or figuratively being carried away by emotion" (Sidel, 1990). There is, though, a growing trend toward presenting successful and assertive women in the media (Baehr and Gray, 1996; Sengupta, 1995).

SOCIOLOGICAL PERSPECTIVES ON SOCIALIZATION

The preceding section has focused on the process by which children are socialized to become what they are. Here, we turn our attention to the nature of socialization, as explained by the three main sociological perspectives.

■ Functionalist Perspective: Social, Psychological, and Economic Functions

To functionalists, socialization serves a number of functions for society. By far the most important one is the social function: ensuring social order. With socialization, the norms and values of society can be instilled within the child. Society, in effect, can become a part of the individual's innermost being. It is therefore natural for socialized individuals to support their society, such as by working to contribute to its prosperity and obeying the law to help ensure its stabil-

ity. In addition, socialized individuals keep society going after the older generation dies. Without socialization, anarchy would likely reign, threatening the survival of society.

Socialization also provides important psychological benefits. Most parents enjoy holding and cuddling their infants, as well as watching them and helping them play and learn. As children grow older, their love and respect for parents are also highly valued. Socialization of children further teaches parents to be patient, understanding, and self-sacrificing, qualities useful for enhancing human relations in society. Socialization also provides children with love, affection, and other emotional support that is indispensable to having a happy life.

Socialization further serves an economic function for the family. Although this function has sharply declined in significance in modern Western societies, it is still very important for many traditional communities around the globe. First, children are socialized to grow up to support their parents in old age. Second, in many peasant villages, children are crucial contributors to the family's economic well-being. In Javanese villages in Indonesia, for example, girls aged 9 through 11 contribute about 38 hours of valuable work per week, while boys aged 12 to 14 put in 33 hours a week. Much of the work involves making handicrafts, processing foods for sale, and working in petty trade. Further, the children, especially girls, do most of the rearing of their younger siblings so that their mothers can go out to work (Harris, 1995). From the conflict perspective, however, this child labor can alternatively be seen as a case of exploitation of the powerless by the powerful.

■ Conflict Perspective: Exploitation and Abuse of Children

Viewed from the conflict perspective, some aspects of socialization are harmful to children. Because children have to depend heavily on adults to survive, an enormous power accrues to parents, who can thus be tempted to exploit and abuse children. Examples of child exploitation include child labor and child slavery, which are more prevalent in poor countries, and the use of children for pornographic profit, more common in wealthy countries. Child abuse ranges from beating to raping to murder. Every year, about 3 million children in the United States are abused, including more than 1,200 who are killed by their parents (Thio, 2004).

Occupying the top of the age hierarchy, parents usually regard children as their personal possessions, denying them many rights that adults enjoy as members of society. Consider the right to *physical integrity*. In virtually all societies, children do not have that right, as physical punishment is widely considered appropriate for disciplining children. This contrasts with the world of adults, where, for example, U.S. Army sergeants may *not* discipline recruits by hitting them (Leach, 1994).

It is understandable, from the conflict perspective, that powerful people usually justify their maltreatment of subordinate individuals under their control. Thus, adults often defend the physical punishment of their children by saying that "It is for their own good." As shown in Figure 3.3, most parents in the United States, for example, approve of spanking children (Costello, 2000). More tragically, parents in an extremely poor region in northeast Brazil tend to commit infanticide by withholding medical assistance from infants who at birth are considered not healthy or strong enough. Some of the reasons given by the parents for this infant killing are "It is best for them to die" and "It is a blessing that the child will soon be an angel" (Harris, 1995). In Western societies, when extremely stressed or depressed parents commit suicide, they often kill their young children first, rationalizing that the family will be happily reunited in the hereafter (McCormick, 1994).

In sum, the conflict perspective reveals the dark side of socialization as exploitive and abusive, reinforcing age inequality at the expense of children. It

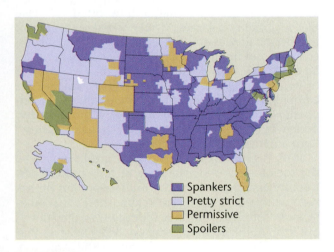

■ Spankers
□ Pretty strict
■ Permissive
■ Spoilers

FIGURE 3.3

Who Spanks Children?

According to a recent survey, some 70 percent of Americans say that it is OK to spank children. Spanking is most popular among folks in small towns, especially in the South. But most city dwellers, particularly those with more education, frown on corporal punishment.

Critical Thinking: *Is spanking really a good approach to disciplining a child who misbehaves? Why or why not?*

Source: Claritas, Inc., Simmons Market Research Bureau, as appeared in *Newsweek,* April 20, 1998, p. 6.

complements the functionalist view of socialization as a positive force in society.

■ Symbolic Interactionist Perspective: Developing Self-Image from Interactions

Unconcerned with the larger issue of whether socialization is a positive or a negative force in society, symbolic interactionists focus on how children develop a *self*—a sense of who they are—from interactions with their parents and other people in their lives. In these interactions, children see how others treat them and learn how to take the roles of others.

Cooley: The Looking-Glass Process   U.S. sociologist Charles Horton Cooley (1864–1929), a founder of symbolic interactionism, viewed society as a group of individuals helping each other to develop their personalities. According to Cooley, the core of personality is the concept of oneself, the *self-image.* And self-image, Cooley said, is developed through the *looking-glass process:* "Each to each a looking glass, Reflects the other that doth pass."

We, in effect, acquire a **looking-glass self,** the self-image that we develop from the way others treat us. Their treatment is like a mirror reflecting our personal qualities. According to Cooley, if we have a positive image, seeing ourselves as intelligent or respectable, it is because others have treated us as such. Just as we cannot see our own face unless we have a mirror in front of us, we cannot have a certain self-image unless others react to our behavior.

The self-image that emerges from the looking-glass process can affect our personality and behavior. If children have a favorable self-image, they tend to be self-confident, outgoing, and happy; behave relatively well; get good grades; and even show great creativity. If youngsters have a poor self-image, they are inclined to be timid, withdrawn, and unhappy. The consequences are likely to be, among other things, delinquent behavior and lower academic achievement (Miserandino, 1996; Moeller, 1994).

Mead: The Role-Taking Process   Like Cooley, George Herbert Mead (1863–1931), the other founder of symbolic interactionism, assumed that the development of a self-concept is made possible by interaction. But while Cooley stressed the importance of using others as mirrors by observing their reactions to our behavior, Mead emphasized the significance of getting "under the skin" of others by taking their roles (DeWaal, 2001).

According to Mead, children develop their self-concept in three stages. First, during their initial 2

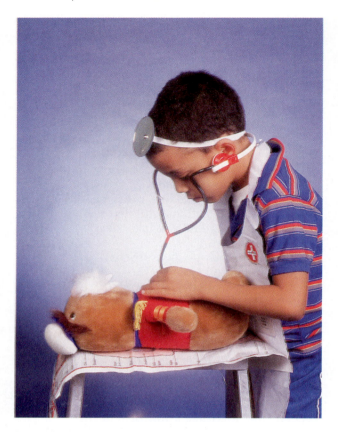

PLAYING DOCTOR   George Herbert Mead emphasized role-taking, by which children internalize the values and attitudes of significant others. Children imitate their parents, for instance, without actually knowing the meanings of their actions; then, in play, they pretend to be their parents, thus internalizing parental values. The boy in this photo is taking the role of a doctor, a generalized other, thereby beginning to be part of the larger society outside his own family. ■

years, they go through the *preparatory stage* by simply imitating other people in their immediate environment. When they see their mother reading a newspaper, they will pretend to read it, too. When they see their father talk on the phone, they may later pick up the phone and talk on it. In this imitation stage, however, they are not yet playing the role of father or mother because they have no idea of what they are doing. They simply learn to act like others without knowing the meanings of those actions.

Then, at about age 3, children begin to go through the *play stage* by taking the roles of **significant others**—people who have close ties to a child and exert a strong influence on the child. Children pretend to be their mother and father, examples of their significant others, while they play. In this world of make-believe, they learn to see themselves from their

parents' perspective. In the process, they internalize their parents' values and attitudes, incorporating them into their own personalities. When they tell their baby dolls not to be naughty, they, in effect, tell themselves not to be naughty.

As they grow older, children also come into contact with doctors, nurses, bus drivers, salesclerks, and so on. These people outside the family circle are not as significant as their parents, but they are representative of society as a whole. Mead called them **generalized others,** people who do not have close ties to a child but who do influence the child's internalization of the values of society. By this time, children are passing through the *game stage* by playing the roles of the generalized others. In this third stage, they learn to internalize the values of society as a whole. Participation in organized games, such as baseball and basketball, also promotes this internalization. These games involve a complex interaction among the players that is governed by a set of rules. When they play such games, children are, in effect, playing the game of life. They are learning that life has rules, too.

Internalized social values become only one part of our personality, which Mead called the *me.* Whenever we feel like obeying the law, following the crowd, and the like, we are sensing the presence of the me. It represents society within our personality. On the other hand, a portion of our personality cannot be easily invaded by society, no matter how often we have played childhood games. Mead referred to this part of our personality as the *I.* It is basically spontaneous, creative, and impulsive. Unlike the *me,* which makes all of us look alike in our behavior, the *I* makes each of us unique. These two aspects of personality are complementary: Without the *I,* there would be no individual creativity or social progress; without the *me,* there would be no social order or individual security. Both are inevitable and necessary.

With his concept of the *me,* Mead greatly advanced the sociological understanding of how human personality emerges from social interaction. But he has been criticized for failing to explain where the *I* comes from. According to Norbert Wiley (1979), the *I* develops from both the *me* and the *we.* Wiley believes that infants first develop the *me* in about the same way Mead indicated, except at a younger age. Through the *me,* infants identify with their parents so totally that they believe themselves to be an inseparable part of their parents. Then, through a tactile, giggly love experience between parents and infants, which Wiley calls a *we experience,* the adults, in effect, say to the youngsters, "You exist; you are a different person; and I love the person you are." The infants then learn to see themselves as independent of their parents, at which point they develop the *I.* Figure 3.4 summa-

theoretical thumbnail

Characteristics of Socialization

Perspective	Focus	Insights
Functionalist	The bright side of socialization: social, psychological, and economic benefits for society, parents, and children.	Socialization ensures social order by instilling society's norms and values in individuals, provides parents and children with emotional satisfaction and support, and teaches children to contribute to the family's finances.
Conflict	The dark side of socialization: exploitation and abuse of children by parents.	Given their enormous age inequality, parents usually regard children as their personal possessions, denying them many rights enjoyed by adults, such as freedom from corporal punishment.
Symbolic interactionist	Socialization can be bright or dark, depending on what self-image children develop from interactions with parents and other adults.	If children are treated like smart adults and then take and play that role, they will see themselves as smart people. But their self-image will turn negative if the adults in their lives are negative role models.

rizes the stages of self-development according to the symbolic interactionist theories of Mead and Wiley.

The Theoretical Thumbnail provides an overview of the three sociological perspectives on socialization.

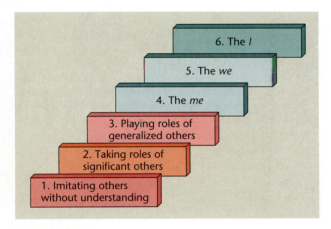

FIGURE 3.4

Stages of Self-Development

According to symbolic interactionists, we become who we are by interacting with our parents and other adults. As children, we first depend on these others to develop a self-image largely tied to them in the form of the *me* and then the *we*. Ultimately, we become an independent and creative person as the *I*.

Critical Thinking: *What, specifically, would your life be like if your I were much more fully developed than your me and we or vice versa?*

SOCIAL DIVERSITY IN SOCIALIZATION

In a multicultural society like that of the United States, there are different ways of socializing children. Consider the issue of how to deal with a misbehaving child. In many cities, most native-born U.S. parents would give a young child time out or ground an older child. But most immigrant parents would spank the child. While this is a widely accepted form of discipline in their homelands, they quickly learn that in the United States, they could be charged with child abuse. Many are shocked when their children threaten, "If you hit me, I'll call 911." They sigh, believing that native-born parents spoil their children by sparing the rod (Dresser, 1996; Dugger, 1996a).

Just as immigrants have different ways of socializing children, so do various minority groups. How these children are socialized will have an increasingly greater impact on American society because their percentage makeup of the population has grown significantly (see Figure 3.5, p. 80).

Socialization of Native American Children

Children of Native American parents are traditionally socialized through an extensive network of relatives. Along with grandparents, uncles and aunts participate with parents in child care, supervision of children, and assurance of love, and cousins are thus

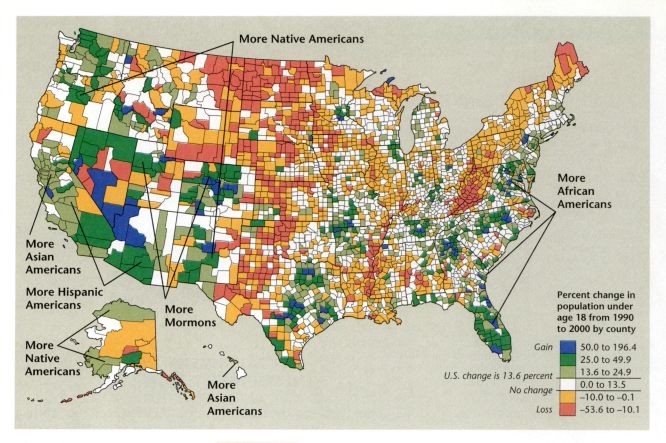

More Native Americans

More African Americans

More Asian Americans

More Hispanic Americans

More Mormons

More Native Americans

More Asian Americans

Percent change in population under age 18 from 1990 to 2000 by county

Gain

	50.0 to 196.4
	25.0 to 49.9
	13.6 to 24.9

U.S. change is 13.6 percent

| | 0.0 to 13.5 |

No change

| | −10.0 to −0.1 |

Loss

| | −53.6 to −10.1 |

FIGURE 3.5

Where American Children Are

In the U.S. population, the proportion of minority children, including Mormon children, has been growing significantly over the last decade. Today, many more children are found in places with a high concentration of minority children. Such places include parts of the South, where there are many African Americans; Hawaii and California, where there are many Asians and Pacific Islanders; and portions of the Southwest, Northwest, and Alaska, where there are many Native Americans. Areas where the Mormon influence is strong or gaining rapidly—namely, Utah, western Colorado, and northern Arizona—also boast a high concentration of children.

Critical Thinking: *In the future, what opportunities and challenges will this social diversity present to U.S. society?*

Source: Data from U.S. Census Bureau, 2001.

considered as close as siblings. Members of this extended family also teach children their tribal values and beliefs along with traditions and rituals. Reflecting a group-oriented culture, the values of cooperation and sharing are emphasized, while competitive behavior is discouraged (Berns, 1993). Children and adolescents are further encouraged to participate in tribal ceremonies and develop an appreciation for their cultural heritage.

The socialization is carried out with a considerable amount of tender, loving care, as well as pleasure.

Adults do not merely enjoy caring for and playing with children; they cherish the time spent with them. Thus, milestones in early childhood, such as the first steps, first smile, and first word, are celebrated. Even as they grow older, children are rarely hit because physical punishment is generally prohibited. Even shouting to correct a misbehaving child is disapproved of. Yet with so much love and respect for children, adults rarely praise them for performing some routine task well. This is because Native Americans believe that praise should be reserved for special accomplishments,

TRIBAL TOGETHERNESS
Children of Native American parents are socialized to absorb their tribal values and beliefs. Reflecting a group-oriented culture, the values of cooperation and sharing are emphasized, while competitive behavior is discouraged. Young people are further encouraged to develop an appreciation for their cultural heritage, such as tribal ceremonies. ■

not for doing something that is already required of the individual (Hamner and Turner, 1996).

■ Socialization of African American Children

Like Native Americans, African Americans generally have strong kinship bonds, but grandmothers and older siblings tend to share child-care responsibilities more than in other ethnic groups. There is also a unique tendency to informally adopt children, whether related or not, when their parents cannot care for them. Compared with white mothers, African American mothers are more permissive in the feeding and weaning of their children (Pinkney, 1993; Slonim, 1991).

But concerned about spoiling their youngsters, parents usually use strict discipline to discourage inappropriate behavior. The discipline ranges from casting an "evil eye" to spanking (Pinkney, 1993; Slonim, 1991). African American parents are more likely than white parents to teach obedience with physical punishment. Thus, African American children are more often physically punished for being disrespectful to elders, for disobeying adults or older siblings, and for being irresponsible with money. Generally, however, African American children are socialized to be strong and independent earlier than their white peers. African American children are less likely to continue being treated like babies at age 3 and more likely to assume responsibility during preadolescence for the care of younger siblings and the household (Hamner and Turner, 1996).

■ Socialization of Hispanic American Children

Seen as a gift from God, children occupy a central position in Hispanic American families and accompany their parents almost everywhere they go. Children are taught to be obedient and respectful toward their elders by avoiding eye contact and listening with bowed heads. Strong *familism*—family loyalty or identification with the family—is given top priority in the socialization of children. They are taught, for example, that if their grandmother is ill, they must drop everything, even school, to visit or care for her. Even first-graders will stay home to take care of younger siblings if their mother has to go to work (Dresser, 1996; Berns, 1993).

Hispanic American children are also socialized to develop great sensitivity to the needs and feelings of others in general. They are taught to be quick in offering assistance so that people in need of help do not have to feel embarrassed by asking for it. But Hispanic American children tend to be reluctant to ask for help, such as with their schoolwork, when they need it (Berns, 1993).

As in other ethnic groups, male and female Hispanic children are brought up differently, especially during adolescence. It has been observed that in Hispanic culture, *el amor de madre,* or motherly love, is stronger than wifely love (Ramirez, 1997). But Hispanic mothers are much closer to their daughters, tending to confine them to the home so that their femininity and innocence or premarital chastity can be preserved. Fathers, on the other hand, assume the primary responsibility for disciplining sons and en-

TABLE 3.2

Social Diversity in Socialization

U.S. Ethnic Group	Characteristics of Socialization
Native Americans	Teaching by an extensive kinship group, with emphasis on tribal tradition, cooperation, and sharing.
African Americans	Often with the help of grandmothers and older siblings, teaching focuses on strict discipline and the importance of being strong and independent at a young age.
Hispanic Americans	Teaching emphasizes family loyalty, sensitivity to others' needs, and helpfulness to others.
Asian Americans	Emphasis on identification with family, respect for elders, studying hard, and avoiding confrontation with others.

courage them to gain worldly knowledge outside the home. Young Hispanics, however, are increasingly challenging this gender inequality (Hamner and Turner, 1996).

■ Socialization of Asian American Children

Parents in Asian American families try to cultivate a strong sense of acceptance and security in their young children by indulging them, letting them have practically anything they want and letting them behave—or misbehave—in any way they want. But the pampering stops at the age of understanding, which is usually when the child is about 5 years old. From then on, parents set limits and impose discipline, often using psychological punishment by inducing guilt or shame to discourage improper behavior (Dresser, 1996; Min, 1995; Berns, 1993; Slonim, 1991).

Children are taught a number of things during the age of understanding. First, children are taught to identify themselves strongly with their family so that they will do whatever they can to bring happiness to their parents and other family members—and thereby to themselves. Second, children are taught to practice *hsiao,* or filial duty, by respecting elders, so that they will grow up to support or help their parents in some way when the latter reach old age. Third, children are taught to pursue academic excellence in order to ensure a financially secure future, as well as to bring glory to the family and, in the process, to themselves. Fourth, children are taught to avoid confrontation with others, that is, to appreciate the values of politeness, cooperation, and conformity as opposed to boldness, aggressiveness, and independence. In short, children are taught to cultivate largely group-oriented rather than individual-centered attitudes and behavior (Hamner and Turner, 1996; Min, 1995).

Table 3.2 summarizes the different ways in which the four ethnic groups socialize children.

A GLOBAL ANALYSIS OF SOCIALIZATION

All over the world, socialization appears largely the same in some ways and different in other ways. Researchers rarely study socialization using a global approach, but the existing findings reveal some interesting similarities and differences.

In a study of three significantly different cultures—American, French, and Japanese—researchers found similarities in how mothers respond to their 5-month-olds. When infants cry, mothers respond with nurturance. If the babies simply vocalize, showing no distress, mothers respond with imitation. Mothers generally respond more to infants' vocalizing than to infants' looking (Bornstein et al., 1991). Such uniformities across different societies suggest the influence of biological factors on socialization.

But most of the studies that have been conducted suggest the powerful influence of culture on socialization. This is most vivid in the differences between the West and the rest of the world. First, young children in the West are supposed to play, whereas their peers in many non-Western countries are expected to work. As previously stated, Javanese girls in Indoneesian villages, although only 9 years old, work to contribute substantially to the family income. Even younger children, 4 or 5 years old, work, mostly by taking care of younger siblings while their mothers work on the farm. In many African agricultural societies, the importance of child caregivers is so great that women with infants often recruit relatives' children from distant villages to help out (Small, 2001; Morelli and Tronick, 1991).

Second, in the West, responsibility for the daily care and long-term upbringing of children is often

CHILDREN BRINGING UP CHILDREN Whereas the primary role of young children in the West is to play, young children in many non-Western countries, such as this child in Mozambique, are also expected to work, mostly by taking care of younger siblings. In many African agricultural societies, the importance of child caregivers is so great that women with infants often recruit relatives' children from distant villages to help out. ■

left entirely to parents. Increasingly, strangers such as child-care workers take care of children more for money than out of affection. This kind of socialization tends to foster individualism in their charges. By contrast, in much of the rest of the world, extended family groups, clans, and even communities pitch in to care for each other's children. This kind of socialization is more likely to develop trust in others and thereby attachment to groups (Clawson and Gerstel, 2002; Leach, 1994).

Third, Western parents start socializing their children to be self-reliant at an extremely young age— virtually right after birth. Babies are placed in a crib, often in their own room. But at least initially, the trauma of being left alone causes the infant to cry at bedtime or on waking up. By contrast, infants in many non-Western societies are spared that trauma. They are allowed to sleep with their parents, often until age 5 or 6 (Small, 2001; Harrison, 1992). With this sleeping arrangement, the children may have a slow start in learning to be on their own. But they are effectively socialized to develop a strong sense of security. This may partly explain why the insurance industry, which is supposed to meet customers' need for security about their future, is not as prosperous in non-Western countries as it is in Western countries.

Fourth, Western parents begin earnestly socializing children to curb their impulses and behave well at a very young age—before age 4. This may have much to do with Westerners' assumption that people are born bad, as suggested by Judeo-Christian beliefs about being born sinners or by Freud's widely accepted idea about being born with animal instinct.

By contrast, in Japan, China, and other East Asian societies, children are assumed to be innately good and therefore given much freedom to do what they want. But this parental indulgence and permissiveness toward children usually gives way to strict disciplining after age 4 or 5. From then on, Asian parents become more authoritarian while their Western peers more permissive. The content of Asian and Western socialization also differs. Asian parents tend to emphasize emotional control, filial piety, politeness to others, and other traits that promote social relationships and conformity. By contrast, Western parents stress spontaneity, autonomy, assertiveness, and other characteristics that promote individual freedom and creativity (Small, 2001; Harrison, 1992; Papousek and Papousek, 1991).

AGENTS OF SOCIALIZATION

Every society tries to socialize its members. It slips the task into the hands of several groups and institutions, which sociologists call the *socializing agents* of society. Some of them, including the family and the school, are in a sense appointed by society to transmit its cultural heritage to the young. Other agents, including the peer group and mass media, are not appointed by society. Their socialization of children is mostly unintentional.

■ The Family

The family is the most important socializing agent, especially during the first few years of life. A review of various studies has concluded that warm, supportive, moderately restrictive family environments usually produce happy and well-behaving children; cold, rigid, and overly restrictive families tend to cause youngsters to become rebellious, resentful, and insecure. "The power and the importance of parents," says the lead author of a massive survey on adolescents, "continue to persist, even into late adolescence" (Brazelton, 1998; Resnick et al., 1997).

Various social forces, however, influence the way parents socialize their children. The most significant of these forces is social class. Research has long shown that lower-class families tend to be more authoritarian and strict than middle-class families. In authoritarian families, parents tend to train children to respect and obey parental authority. Middle-class parents are more permissive and lenient, emphasizing the value of independence. Compared with lower-class mothers, middle-class mothers are also more child centered and sensitive to the child's feelings. For example, they spend considerably more time conversing and playing with their 3-year-olds. And if a child, while playing, pretends to make a toy puppy bite off a larger toy dog's head, they refrain from jumping in with an accusatory remark, such as "Oh, that's terrible!" Instead, they respect the child's feeling by saying something like "Wow! It looks as if the baby doggy is really angry at the daddy doggy" (Crossen, 1991; Farran and Haskins, 1980).

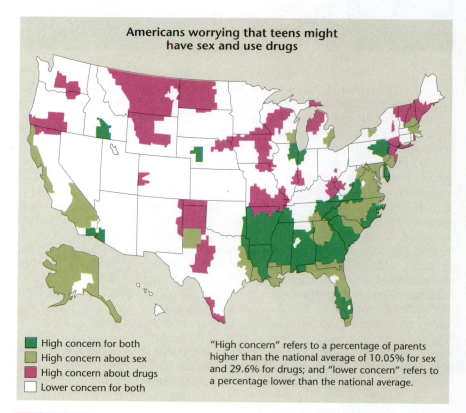

Americans worrying that teens might have sex and use drugs

- High concern for both
- High concern about sex
- High concern about drugs
- Lower concern for both

"High concern" refers to a percentage of parents higher than the national average of 10.05% for sex and 29.6% for drugs; and "lower concern" refers to a percentage lower than the national average.

FIGURE 3.6

American Parents Worrying about Teenagers

Teenagers today are no longer considered immature but rather capable of taking care of themselves when it comes to sex, drugs, crime, and other risky behaviors. Thus, most parents in the United States seem to have little concern that their adolescent children will recklessly engage in these activities. Reflecting the social diversity of U.S. society, however, parents in the more traditional or conservative South are more concerned than others that their children will turn to both premarital sex and drugs.

Critical Thinking: *When you were in high school, did your parents show concern that you might get involved in sex and drugs? Why or why not?*

Source: Michael J. Weiss, *The Clustered World* (Boston: Little, Brown, 2000), p. 58.

BIRDS OF A FEATHER
The influence of the peer group varies at different ages. Early adolescents are most willing to accept conformity and thus are most deeply involved with their peer group. An important function of the peer group is to teach its young members the value of friendship and companionship among equals. These values are relatively absent in the socialization by authority figures, such as parents and teachers. ■

As an agent of socialization, the family has changed a great deal over the last 30 years. In the past, young children were regarded as innocent and teenagers as immature, so they were protected from what were considered the evils and temptations of the world outside the family. Today, young children are considered competent rather than innocent. Thus, even 4- and 5-year-olds are taught about acquired immune deficiency syndrome (AIDS) and child abuse and provided with toys that simulate pregnancy. All this has prompted researchers to remark that kids grow up too quickly these days (Hymowitz, 2001; Elkind, 1992).

Similarly, teenagers are no longer considered immature but rather sophisticated in the ways of the world, knowledgeable about sex, drugs, crime, and much more. Thus, most parents do not seem to worry that their children may recklessly engage in these activities (see Figure 3.6). Teenagers are consequently left to fend for themselves, with little guidance or supervision from adults. This is particularly true for children whose parents seem more committed to a career than to parenting. But these children are more likely than traditional children to learn understanding and mature behavior instead of unthinking obedience (Hochchild, 1997; Greenberger and Goldberg, 1989).

■ The School

At home, children are treated as unique, special persons. At school, they are treated more impersonally, the same as all their schoolmates. One of their first tasks at school is to learn to fit in by getting along with others. In fact, the school often provides children with their first training in how to behave in secondary groups.

Whereas socialization by families often contributes to the diversity of society, schools are more likely to contribute to uniformity. Society, in effect, officially designates schools as its socializing agents. They are expected both to help children develop their potential as creative, independent individuals and to mold them into social conformity—two goals that seem contradictory. To meet the first goal, the school teaches its formal curriculum of academic knowledge and skills. The pursuit of this goal becomes increasingly important as students rise to progressively higher educational levels. By cultivating their intellectual abilities, students are expected to become intelligent citizens capable of making a living and contributing to the prosperity of their society.

myth	Schools only help students develop their potential as creative, independent individuals by teaching them knowledge and skills.
reality	Schools also mold students into social conformity. This includes the so-called hidden curriculum of training students to be patriotic, to believe in their country's cultural values, and to obey its laws.

The pursuit of the second goal—social conformity—is more earnest at the lower grade levels. It involves teaching history and civics. But also important is the *hidden curriculum,* which trains students to be patriotic, to believe in their country's cultural val-

TABLE 3.3

Peer-Group Jargon: "Teen Speak" in New York City

Word/Phrase	Definition	Used in a Sentence
"Be easy"	Relax; calm down	"Yo, son, be easy. Sit down."
"Grimy"	Something very mean	"That was really grimy of Vanessa to tell your mom."
"Jump off"	Hot; really happening	"That party is the jump off."
"Mad" or "madd"	A lot; very	"This shirt is mad cool."
"Deep"	The number of people at a location	"The party was at least 50 deep."
"Cheesin'"	Smiling broadly	"Yo, that chick is cheesin.'"

Source: Based on "From the Mouths of Teens," *American Demographics*, May 2003, p. 16.

ues, and to obey its laws. It is also implicit in classroom rituals (such as saying the Pledge of Allegiance), in demands that classroom rules be obeyed, in the choices of books assigned in English classes, and in a host of other activities (such as glorification of the competition and discipline of sports).

■ The Peer Group

As children grow older, they become increasingly involved with their **peer group**, a group whose members are about the same age and have similar interests. As a socializing agent, the peer group differs from both the family and the school. Whereas parents and teachers have more power than children and students, the peer group is made up of equals.

The peer group teaches its members several important things. First, it teaches them to be independent of adult authorities. Second, it teaches social skills and group loyalties. Third, the peer group teaches its members the values of friendship and companionship among equals—values that are relatively absent in the socialization received from authority figures like parents and teachers. On the other hand, a peer group can socialize its members to thumb their noses at authorities and adults. If there is a rule against bringing toys from home to nursery school, some children will ignore it, and some may even end up getting into trouble with the law one day. But many others may only innocently poke fun at adults behind their backs (Harris, 1999; Corsaro and Eder, 1990; Elkin and Handel, 1988).

Freeing themselves from the grip of parental and school authorities, peer groups often develop distinctive subcultures with their own values, jargon, music, dress, and heroes (see Table 3.3). Whereas parents and teachers tend to place great importance on scholastic achievement, adolescent peer groups are likely to put a higher premium on popularity, social leadership, and athletic attainment (Harris, 1999; Corsaro and Eder, 1990; Corsaro and Rizzo, 1988).

The divergence between parental and peer values does not necessarily lead to a hostile confrontation between parents and teenagers. In fact, most youngsters are just as friendly with parents as with peers. They simply engage in different types of activities— work and task activities with parents, play and recreation with peers. Concerning financial, educational, career, and other serious matters, such as what to spend money on and what occupation to choose, youths are inclined to seek advice from parents. When it comes to social activities, such as whom to date and what clubs to join, they are more likely to discuss them with peers. This reflects the great importance placed by the peer group on *other-directed behavior,* looking to others for approval and support as opposed to reliance on personal beliefs and traditional values. Peer groups, in effect, demand conformity at the expense of independence and individuality (Harris, 1999; Corsaro and Eder, 1995).

Early adolescents are most willing to accept conformity; hence, they are most deeply involved with peer groups. As young people grow into middle and late adolescence, their involvement with peers gradually declines because of their growing independence. When they reach the final year of high school, they tend to adopt adult values, such as wanting to get good grades and good jobs (Goodstein and Connelly, 1998; Larson, 1994; Steinberg, 1994).

■ The Mass Media

The mass media include popular books, magazines, newspapers, radio, movies, television, and the Internet. Today, television and increasingly the Internet have become children's major sources of information about the world. They have been found to affect children in certain ways.

First, children may come to expect their lives, their parents, and their teachers to be as exciting as those portrayed on television. Even the widely praised *Sesame Street* makes children expect their schools to be fast paced and entertaining. Thus, children are likely to be disappointed, finding their parents inadequate and their teachers boring. Second, television tends to impoverish its young viewers' creative imaginations. If they watch TV frequently, they may find it difficult to create pictures in their own minds or to understand stories without visual illustration. Third, through its frequent portrayal of violence, television tends to stimulate violence-prone children to actual violence, to make normal children less sensitive to violence in real life, and to instill the philosophy that "Might makes right." Finally, television destroys the age-old notion of childhood as a period of innocence. It reveals the secrets of adulthood that have been hidden from children for centuries. The spectacle of adults acting stupidly and breaking down and crying teaches children that adults know no more than children (Mifflin, 1999; Kolbert, 1994; Clark, 1993; Cullingford, 1993).

On the other hand, television has the redeeming quality of enlarging young children's vocabulary and knowledge of the world. Moreover, whatever negative effects TV may have on young children, they are likely to dissipate as the children age. Thus, beginning at age 12, youngsters increasingly find commercials unreal and misleading. With more sophistication, older teenagers also take TV violence for what it is— fake and intended for entertainment only (Rice et al., 1990; Freedman, 1986).

The Internet brings different kinds of experiences to children today, who are known as the *wired* or *digital generation*. Some of these experiences are negative, including being exposed to pornography and being contacted by adult strangers. Other experiences are positive, such as doing homework, playing games, listening to music, and chatting with friends. In addition, computer use has been found to improve test scores and social relationships (Livingstone, 2003; Palser, 2003).

ADULT SOCIALIZATION

The socialization process does not end with childhood. It continues with the emergence of adulthood and molds individuals throughout their entire lives.

■ Learning New Roles

Being socialized includes learning new roles. Like children, adults learn many new roles as they go through various stages of life. At the same time, adults' specific socialization experiences differ from those of children. We can see this in the three types of socialization that all of us undergo.

One is **anticipatory socialization**, the process by which an individual learns to assume a role in the future. Many young children learn to be parents in the future by playing house. Young adults prepare themselves for their future professions by attending college. Generally, as people get older, they tend to be less idealistic or more practical. Many first-year medical students, for example, expect to acquire every bit of medical knowledge and then to serve humanity selflessly. Toward the end of their medical schooling, they usually become more realistic: They strive to learn just enough to pass exams and look forward to a lucrative practice as a reward for their years of hard work. In brief, as people get closer to the end of their anticipatory socialization, their earlier idealism tends to gradually die out, to be replaced by realism.

Like children, adults go through **developmental socialization**, the process by which people learn to be more competent in playing their currently assumed role. This is much like receiving on-the-job training. Children learn their currently acquired roles as sons or daughters, students, and members of their peer groups. Adults learn their newly assumed roles as full-time workers, husbands, wives, parents, and so on. The learning of these roles can mold the adult personality. For example, the more complex the worker's job, the more likely the worker will experience self-direction in the workplace and end up valuing autonomy in other aspects of life. On the other hand, the more simple and routine the work, the more likely the individual will be supervised by some higher-up and eventually will value conformity (Kohn, 1980).

A third form of socialization is less common: **resocialization**, the process by which people are forced to abandon their old selves and develop new ones. This happens to adults more often than to children. Resocialization can take place in prisons, psychiatric hospitals, prisoner-of-war camps, military training centers, and religious cults. Such settings are **total institutions**, places where people are not only cut off from the larger society but also rigidly controlled by the administrators. Resocialization in total institutions is usually dehumanizing.

In a state-run psychiatric hospital, for example, the staff tends to treat patients as objects rather than humans. The staff may verbally or physically abuse patients or may prevent them from talking to the staff unless spoken to first. The staff may also enter patients' rooms and examine their possessions at any time. The staff may even monitor patients' personal hygiene and waste evacuation in the bathroom. Such dehumanization is intended to strip the patients of whatever self-concept they have brought into the institution from their prior social life. Then rewards and punishments are used to mold them into docile conformists. Such patients usually develop *institutionalism*—a deep sense of hopelessness, pervasive loss of initiative, deterioration of social skills, and inability to function in the larger society (Thio, 2004).

■ Continuing Development

As we saw earlier, Freud suggested that once the adult personality has been shaped by childhood experiences, it stops growing or changing. But his student Erik Erikson (1902–1994) theorized that personality continues to develop throughout life. According to Erikson, personality development goes through eight stages, as shown in Figure 3.7. In each stage, people are faced with a crisis that must be resolved, with either a positive or a negative result.

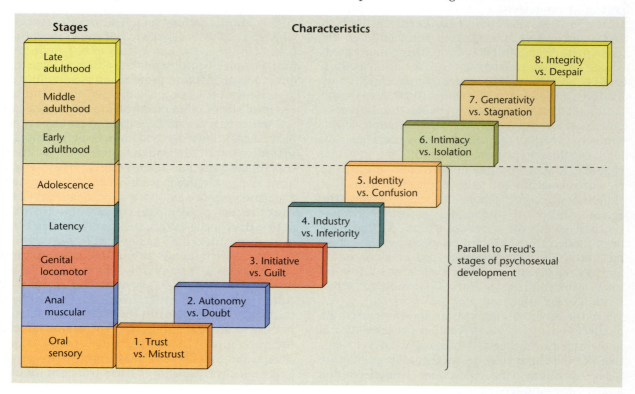

FIGURE 3.7

Erikson's Stages of Psychosocial Development

In each of the eight stages of developing personality, we are faced with a crisis that must be resolved with either a positive or a negative result. The crisis involves some conflict between two elements of ourselves. Adolescents, for example, are caught between identity and confusion—between knowing and not knowing who they are and what their goals in life are. As a result, they will either have a clear sense of self-identity, which will ensure success in life, or suffer from a lack of self-identity, which will bring a lot of problems.

Critical Thinking: *Compared to their peers in traditional societies, teenagers in modern societies have a harder time solving their identity crisis. How have you dealt with your own identity crisis?*

The first five preadult stages parallel those identified by Freud. According to Erikson, the child normally develops a sense of *trust* during what Freud called the oral stage, *autonomy* during the anal stage, *initiative* during the genital stage, *industry* during the latency stage, and *identity* during adolescence. Negative childhood experiences, however, lead to mistrust, doubt, guilt, a feeling of inferiority, and confusion. Consider, for example, how trust and mistrust develop. During the oral stage, from birth to age 1, the totally helpless infant must depend on an adult to survive. If the infant's need for life-sustaining care is well met, the infant will develop a sense of trust in others; otherwise, mistrust will develop.

After people enter adulthood, they will, in Erikson's view, go through three more stages of development. In early adulthood, which lasts from ages 20 to 40, people face the crisis of having to resolve the conflicting demands for love and work. They usually meet the demand for love by falling in love, getting married, and raising a family. If they are too attached to their families, they may not be able to achieve great success in their careers. But if they are too eager to work extremely hard, they risk losing intimacy with and becoming isolated from their families. In this stage, the young adult is confronted with the conflict between enjoying *intimacy* and suffering *isolation*.

In middle adulthood, which lasts from ages 40 to 60, people become acutely aware that their death will come, that their time is running out, and that they must give up their youthful dreams and start being more concerned with others rather than themselves. Usually, they choose to be what Erikson calls *generative*—nurturing or guiding the younger generation. This gives them an elevating sense of productivity and creativity, of having made a significant contribution to others. On the other hand, they are also inclined to continue hanging on to their youthful dreams, to try to be active and feel young again. Because this is difficult at this stage, individuals risk getting weighed down with a depressing sense of disappointment, stagnation, and boredom. In short, the middle-aged adult is faced with the conflict between *generativity* and *stagnation*.

In late adulthood, from age 60 until death, people find themselves in conflict between achieving *integrity* (holding oneself together) and sinking into *despair* (emotionally falling apart). Those who are able to maintain integrity are likely to have accepted whatever they have attained so far. But those who sink into despair regret that their lives have been full of missed opportunities and that the time is just too short for them to start another life. Death loses its sting for those who have learned to hold themselves together and to accept death as the ultimate outcome of life. But those who fall apart emotionally cannot accept death and are gripped with fear of it (Hoare, 2001; Welchman, 2000).

Feminists have criticized Erikson's theory for applying to men more than to women. The crisis of having to choose between intimacy and isolation, for example, is less likely to confront women in early adulthood because they have long been socialized to appreciate personal relationships. But research has established that most people do experience the two conflicting forces in most of the stages (Ochse and Plug, 1986; Varghese, 1981). Especially significant to sociology is Erikson's emphasis on how society influences personality development. He observes, for example, that teenagers in modern societies have a hard time solving their identity crisis because they are bombarded with a staggering array of lifestyle and career choices unimaginable in traditional societies.

■ Aging and Dying

Unlike traditional societies, modern societies do not adequately socialize individuals for old age. In traditional societies, older people are more valued and respected. It is quite an accomplishment to survive to old age in a traditional society, where most people die relatively young. Further, the experiences that the elders have accumulated over the years are invaluable to younger generations because their societies change so little and so slowly that old knowledge and values do not seem to lose their relevance. Since the aged in these societies live with their children and grandchildren, are given an honored role, and are often observed to dispense wisdom and advice, young people are easily socialized to accept old age when it occurs.

In modern societies, older people typically live alone. By not living with their elderly parents and grandparents, younger people have little chance of learning how to grow old gracefully. Although they may visit their older relatives often, they do not relish the prospect of growing old themselves because they believe that older people live unrewarding, lonely, or even degrading lives.

Modern societies also have come up short in socialization for death. In traditional societies, people see their loved ones die at home, handle their corpses, and personally bury them. But in modern societies, we seldom witness a dying scene at home because most deaths occur in hospitals. As Sherwin Nuland (1994) says, "We have created the method of modern dying. Modern dying takes place in the modern hospital, where it can be hidden, cleansed of its organic blight, and finally packaged for modern burial." The method of modern dying has in effect robbed us of the important realization that death is

DREADING LIFE'S FINAL CHAPTER Modern societies come up short in socializing their young members about aging and death. By not living with grandparents and by only occasionally visiting and playing with them, young people do not learn to grow old gracefully. Consequently, they are afraid of growing old themselves. They also seldom witness an old relative dying at home because most deaths take place in hospitals. As a result, young people find it hard to accept death as natural and unavoidable and become afraid to die. ■

the natural culmination of life. Not surprisingly, many of us find death frightening.

Because the older population in the United States is increasing, we will see many more deaths in our lives. Common sense would suggest that this should make us less afraid of the "horsemen of death." But it is not the number of deaths but *how society treats death* that affects our feelings about the end of life. We will likely continue to fear death as long as our society continues to depersonalize it, rendering it more distant and more forbidding than in traditional societies (Nuland, 1994).

ARE WE PUPPETS OF SOCIETY?

Through socialization, we internalize the norms and values of society. We become conformists, doing what our parents, teachers, and other socializing agents have taught us to do. Does this imply that we become puppets of society, individuals who basically enjoy giving up freedom and following the rules society sets down? The answer is yes—and no.

In many respects, we do behave like society's puppets. We are glad to follow society's expectation that we be nice to our friends and love our parents. We are happy to do many other similarly good things every day, as expected of us by society. It just happens that we enjoy doing all these things because others have made us happy by responding positively when we do them.

Living in a highly individualistic society, though, many of us may not see ourselves as society's puppets when we act in those ways. This is especially true

today because the new technology has made us even more independent than ever before. The Internet puts a wealth of information at our fingertips, broadening our perspective and sharpening our awareness. But even our society, which promotes individual freedom, imposes a limit on what we as individuals can do. Not surprisingly, then, day in and day out, the overwhelming majority of us conform to the norms of our society by not making waves or committing crimes.

But our conformity is not total. We may exert our independence by doing things differently than as dictated by society. We may get drunk, fool around a bit too much, protest what we perceive to be a social injustice, or do other similar things that raise others' eyebrows. By engaging in such activities, we express the unsocialized aspect of our selves, no longer behaving like puppets. Dennis Wrong (1961) has suggested that we can never be puppets all the time because it is impossible to be entirely socialized. There are at least four reasons socialization can never turn us into total puppets.

First, we have certain *imperious biological drives* that always buck against society's attempt to mold us in its image. Our sex drive, for example, sometimes gets the better of us, causing us to engage in sexual acts that our society condemns as deviant.

Second, socializing influences are not always consistent and harmonious with one another. Our ethnic group, social class, and professional and occupational associations may not socialize us in the same way. They may teach conflicting roles, norms, and values.

Third, even if society could socialize us consistently and completely, we would still violate its laws and rules. In the very process of learning to obey the rules, we might also learn how to break them without getting caught, which is a great temptation for most, if not all, people. Even some of the most respectable citizens have committed crimes.

Finally, if we were completely socialized, we would become extremely unhappy and probably neurotic or psychotic. This is why, as Sigmund Freud said, civilization tends to breed discontent in the individual. No normal persons want their drives for self-expression, freedom, creativity, or personal eccentricity to be totally suppressed.

sociological frontiers

Overpermissive Parenting

As we saw earlier in this chapter, a global analysis of socialization suggests some differences in parenting between relatively traditional non-Western societies and modern Western societies. In traditional societies, children are treated like helpless little humans who need to be told what to do. They are taught to obey their parents and other authorities so that they will grow up to become obedient conformists, curbing their own impulses and desires so as to enjoy good relationships with others (or at least to avoid conflict with others).

In Western societies, such as that of the United States, however, children are treated more like adults. Instead of ordering their children around like subordinates ("Do this" and "Do that"), as non-Western parents tend to do, Western parents are more likely to talk respectfully to and treat their children as equals ("Please do this" and "Don't you think it's a good idea to do that?"). In treating their children as peers, Western parents are effectively more permissive, allowing children to think for themselves and do things their own way. In essence, then, the authoritarian parenting style in non-Western societies emphasizes the development of social conformity—including self-control, civility, and obedience to authority—but the permissive, peer parenting in the West stresses the values of individual freedom, self-reliance, and creativity.

Increasingly, though, permissiveness may be turning into overpermissiveness. Recently, in an affluent Atlanta suburb, for example, many youths as young as 13 years old were found to have engaged in group sex with abandon. They got together after school to watch the Playboy cable TV channel and then imitated everything they saw. Sometimes, they had drunken parties at which one boy or girl was "passed around"; a number of the youths had upward of 50 partners.

While these teens may be very unusual, their parents are not: They are ordinary soccer moms and dads, coaching their children's teams, cooking dinner with

"Thank you, Adrian. Parenting is a learning process, and your criticisms help."

Source: © The New Yorker Collection 1998 Robert Weber from Cartoonbank.com. All rights reserved.

them, and going on vacations together. When asked for her view of those after-school activities, the mother of one of the teens said, "They have to make decisions, whether to take drugs, to have sex. I can give them my opinion, tell them how I feel. But they have to decide for themselves." When parents have such an overly permissive attitude, their children definitely know it. As one girl said of her parents, "We're pretty much like best friends or something. I mean, I can pretty much tell 'em how I feel, what I wanna do and they'll let me do it" (Hymowitz, 2001).

Overpermissive parenting has been attributed to an intense ambivalence about authority among many of today's parents. In one study, when asked how they feel about disciplining their children, parents gave such answers as "I feel mean," "I feel guilty," and "I quake all over—it's almost like having dry heaves inside." This discomfort with exercising authority may have stemmed from the parents' own experiences growing up during the Vietnam War in the 1960s and 1970s, an era that was characterized by protests against the authority of parents, teachers, the police, the military, and the government (Hymowitz, 2001). Parents' reluctance to tell their children what to do may be part of the emergent culture of moral freedom that sociologist Alan Wolfe has observed (see Chapter 2: Society and Culture). More research is needed, however, to determine the prevalence of overpermissive parenting in the United States.

 ■ For more of the latest Sociological Frontiers, look up Continuing Update at www.ablongman.com/thio6e.

u s i n g *sociology*

How to Make Latchkey Kids Safe and Smart

Children who are left alone at home after school are likely to get into trouble. The reason is that these so-called *latchkey kids* are deprived of proper socialization by caring adults and exposed to improper socialization by troublesome peers in empty homes or on the street. Not surprisingly, then, the juvenile crime rate *triples* after 3 P.M., when the schoolday ends. More than 75 percent of first-time sexual encounters take place in the afternoon at the house of someone whose parents are still at work. And compared with those who have some adult supervision, youngsters who are home alone are more likely to smoke, drink, and use marijuana, as well as to get poor grades and otherwise behave badly. Unfortunately, only 30 percent of U.S. schools provide after-hours care and supervision, and the majority of such schools charge fees that most low-income parents cannot afford (Alter, 1998; Powell, 1988).

Today, a number of individuals and organizations are seeking solutions to this problem. Among the strongest backers of after-school programs are mayors, police chiefs, and the federal government. The U.S. Department of Education, for example, has provided grants to turn public schools into *community education centers,* places where children can be kept safe in the after-school hours. Nonprofit groups and corporations have also worked together to create safe places for children, including schools, YMCAs, boys' and girls' clubs, houses of worship, and playgrounds. Both community centers and safe places provide children with access to home-work helpers, tutors, and mentors along with programs for cultural enrichment, recreation, and nutrition (U.S. Department of Education, 2000).

In general, youths who are regular participants in after-school activities have better peer relations and emotional adjustment, as well as lower incidences of juvenile crime, drug and alcohol use, violence, and pregnancy. These youths also have improved their grades and achieved higher reading and math scores. The factors behind the success of these after-school programs include low staff-student ratios, strong family involvement, and coordination of learning with the regular schoolday (U.S. Department of Education, 2000). Thinking critically, were these factors important in how your school socialized you? Why or why not? What other factors were important?

❙ CHAPTER REVIEW

1. *What is socialization?* It is the process by which a society transmits its cultural values to its members.

Can either nature or nurture alone explain human behavior? No. Both heredity and environment make us what we are. The importance of heredity can be demonstrated by how our temperament, intelligence, and aptitude influence the development of our personality. The significance of socialization can be seen in the case studies of children who are feral, isolated, institutionalized, or gifted.

2. *How do children learn to think?* They develop increasingly advanced forms of mental ability as they grow from birth through adolescence. *How do they learn to feel?* Largely through their parents, they learn to identify and manage their emotions. *How do they learn to be normal?* With their parents' help, they learn to be normal by resolving the conflicts among their id, ego, and superego. *How do they learn to be moral?* They develop morally from a low, preconventional level of judging right and wrong to higher levels. *How do they learn to be masculine or feminine?* They develop their sex-based identities through the influence of patriarchal society via its parents, schools, and media.

3. *What do the three major sociological perspectives tell us about socialization?* According to functionalists, socialization helps ensure social order, as well as provide psychological and economic benefits. To conflict theorists, due to parents' enormous power over their children, socialization can lead to child exploitation and abuse. The symbolic interactionist perspective suggests that children develop their self-image from the way others see them and from taking and playing the roles of others with whom they interact.

4. *How do various minority groups in the United States socialize their children?* In Native American socialization, emphasis is placed on the importance of extensive kinship, tribal traditions, and cooperation and sharing. Children are brought up with love and pleasure. Among African Americans, grandmothers and older siblings offer help with child care, strict discipline is used to discourage inappropriate behavior, and children are taught to be strong and independent at a young age. Among Hispanic Americans, children are taught family loyalty, sensitivity to the needs of others, and helpfulness to others. In Asian American families, children are pampered until about age 5, after which they are taught to identify with the family, respect elders, study hard, and avoid confrontation with others. *What can a global analysis of socialization reveal?* Socialization is both similar and different from society to society, suggesting the influence of both biological and cultural factors.

5. *What is distinctive about each of the major socializing agents?* The family is the most important socializing agent for the child. The school is charged both with helping children develop their potential as independent individuals and with securing their conformity to social norms. The peer group socializes its members as equals, offering a set of values largely different from those presented by adult authorities. The mass media, particularly television, influence the child's values and behavior, but this influence tends to wear off as the child grows up.

6. *Does socialization end with childhood?* No. Adults continue to experience socialization, just as children do. They go through anticipatory socialization, developmental socialization, and resocialization. According to Erikson, adults continue to go through three more stages of psychosocial development after emerging from five preadult stages. Each stage involves struggling to resolve a crisis. *How does modern society deal with aging and dying?* Not very well. Generally, older people are not as highly respected in modern societies as in traditional ones. Death also is not treated as a normal, inevitable part of life to be accepted.

7. *Are we puppets of society?* Yes, we are puppets to the extent that we enjoy doing many things in accordance with social norms, but no, we are not to the extent that we occasionally engage in activities frowned on by others.

8. *What is permissive parenting, and how can it be carried too far?* Permissive parenting involves treating children as peers and encouraging them to think for themselves. It can be carried too far when parents avoid exercising authority and let children do whatever they want. *What has been done to keep latchkey kids safe and smart?* Efforts have been made to provide these children with schools and other safe places where they can engage in cultural, recreational, and nutritional programs.

KEY TERMS

Anticipatory socialization The process by which an individual learns to assume a role in the future (p. 87).

Aptitude The capacity for developing physical or social skills (p. 68).

Conventional morality Kohlberg's term for the practice of defining right and wrong according to the *motive* of the action being judged (p. 75).

Developmental socialization The process by which people learn to be more competent in playing their currently assumed roles (p. 87).

Ego Freud's term for the part of personality that is rational, dealing with the world logically and realistically (p. 73).

Gender identity People's images of what they are socially expected to be and do on the basis of their sex (p. 75).

Generalized others Mead's term for people who do not have close ties to a child but who do influence the child's internalization of society's values (p. 78).

Id Freud's term for the part of personality that is irrational, concerned only with seeking pleasure (p. 73).

Intelligence The capacity for mental or intellectual achievement (p. 68).

Looking-glass self Cooley's term for the self-image that we develop from the way others treat us (p. 77).

Peer group A group whose members are about the same age and have similar interests (p. 86).

Personality A fairly stable configuration of feelings, attitudes, ideas, and behaviors that characterizes an individual (p. 68).

Postconventional morality Kohlberg's term for the practice of judging actions by taking into account the importance of *conflicting norms* (p. 75).

Preconventional morality Kohlberg's term for the practice of defining right and wrong according to the *consequence* of the action being judged (p. 75).

Resocialization The process by which people are forced to abandon their old selves and to develop new ones (p. 87).

Significant others Mead's term for people who have close ties to a child and exert a strong influence on the child (p. 78).

Socialization The process by which a society transmits its cultural values to its members (p. 68).

Superego Freud's term for the part of personality that is moral; popularly known as *conscience* (p. 74).

Total institutions Places where people are not only cut off from the larger society but also rigidly controlled by the administrators (p. 88).

QUESTIONS FOR DISCUSSION AND REVIEW

THE SIGNIFICANCE OF HEREDITY

1. How does heredity influence personality?

THE SIGNIFICANCE OF SOCIALIZATION

1. What happens to children deprived of socialization?
2. How can children become geniuses?

PROCESSES OF SOCIALIZATION

1. According to Piaget, what mental abilities develop from birth through adolescence?
2. How do children learn to identify and manage their emotions?
3. In Freud's view, what does personality consist of, and how does it develop?
4. How does moral development differ between males and females?
5. How does feminist theory explain the development of gender identity?

SOCIOLOGICAL PERSPECTIVES ON SOCIALIZATION

1. In what ways can socialization be functional?
2. In what ways can socialization be exploitive or abusive?
3. How do children develop the *I* and the *me?*

SOCIAL DIVERSITY IN SOCIALIZATION

1. Compare and contrast how the various ethnic groups in the United States socialize children.

A GLOBAL ANALYSIS OF SOCIALIZATION

1. In what ways is childhood socialization about the same throughout the world?
2. In what ways does childhood socialization vary from Western to non-Western societies?

AGENTS OF SOCIALIZATION

1. Why is the family the most important agent of socialization?
2. What is the hidden curriculum of the school, and how does it help ensure social order?
3. How does the peer group influence adolescents differently than does the family?
4. How does television influence children?

ADULT SOCIALIZATION

1. How do anticipatory and developmental socialization differ from resocialization?
2. What are Erikson's three development stages of adult life, and what personal crisis does each stage contain?
3. Why is the fear of death relatively common in modern societies?

ARE WE PUPPETS OF SOCIETY?

1. In what ways do we behave like society's puppets?

SOCIOLOGICAL FRONTIERS/USING SOCIOLOGY

1. What is permissive, peer parenting, and how can it be carried too far?
2. What problems are latchkey kids likely to have, and what can be done to help them?

■ SUGGESTED READINGS

Gallagher, Winifred. 1997. *Just the Way You Are: How Heredity and Experience Create the Individual.* New York: Random House. An introduction to groundbreaking research on how our biology and environment interact in shaping our personality.

Gardner, Howard. 1993. *Creating Minds: An Anatomy of Creativity Seen through the Lives of Freud, Einstein, Picasso, Stravinsky, Eliot, Graham, and Gandhi.* New York: Basic Books. Shows how their families and other social forces affected the development of these seven geniuses.

Hymowitz, Kay S. 1999. *Ready or Not: Why Treating Children as Small Adults Endangers Their Future—and Ours.* New York: Free Press. Shows the consequences of the current tendency to treat children as rational, independent, self-motivated miniature adults.

Reiss, David. 2000. *The Relationship Code: Deciphering Genetic and Social Influences on Adolescent Development.* Cambridge, MA: Harvard University Press. An important finding of how certain parenting styles reinforce and retard genetic influences on children's behavior and temperament.

Small, Meredith F. 2001. *Kids: How Biology and Culture Shape the Way We Raise Our Children.* New York: Doubleday. A highly readable book about various aspects of how children grow up to become adults.

■ Additional Resources

expect the world®

The New York Times

nytimes.com

Expand your knowledge of the concepts discussed in this chapter by reading the following current and historical articles from the *New York Times.* Go to the "eThemes of the Times" section of the Companion Website (www.ablongman.com/thio6e):

"3-Year Mideast Conflict Shapes Life on Both Sides"

"First Study on Patients Who Fast to End Lives"

Research Navigator.com

Research Navigator, a research database, provides immediate access to hundreds of full-text articles from EBSCO's ContentSelect Academic Journal Database. If the Research Navigator access code was included with your textbook, go to the website www.research navigator.com and read the following articles related to this chapter by typing in the article number:

Warren, Ron. "Do As I Say, Not As I Do: Video Stores and Parental Mediation of Children's Video Con-sumption." *Mass Communication and Society*, Feb 2001, Vol. 4 Issue 1, p77, 25p. Accession Number: 4274308. Charts the influence of video rental stores on parents' decisions about what their children watch.

Yeung, King-To, and Martin, John Levi. "The Looking Glass Self: An Empirical Test and Elaboration." *Social Forces*, Mar 2003, Vol. 81 Issue 3, p843, 37p. Accession Number: 9426360. Tests whether a person's self-perceptions are based on his or her perceptions of the views of others.

chapter 4

Social Interaction in Everyday Life

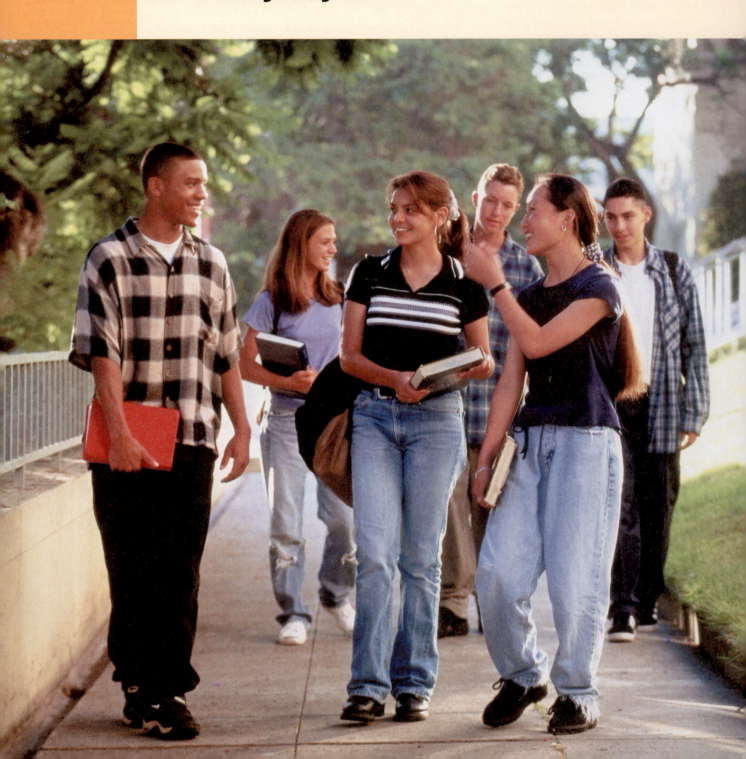

myths & realities

myth *Men and women are equally disinclined to stare at others because they have been taught not to do so since childhood.*

reality Since men are generally given a higher status than women in a sexist society, men tend to stare at women more than vice versa (p. 102).

myth *It is natural for only one person to speak at a time when engaged in a conversation.*

reality That may be so in the United States, but in many other countries, it is normal for a listener to chime in when someone is talking in order to show enthusiastic participation or involvement with others (p. 104).

myth *To avoid misunderstanding, especially in conversation with foreigners, it is always wise to say directly what's on our mind, such as saying "yes" to mean "yes."*

reality Directness in speech may be good for transmitting information, but *indirectness* is common in many other countries. The Japanese, for example, may say "yes" to mean "no" when asked "Would you agree to do business with us?" This is their way of trying to save others from disappointment or embarrassment (p. 104).

myth *Because they speak the same language, men and women can easily understand each other.*

reality Men and women speak the same language but use it in different ways: men, for the purpose of giving information; women, for expressing feelings. Thus, men tend to misunderstand women by taking literally what women say, and women tend to misunderstand men by reading emotional meanings into what men say (p. 106).

myth *Humor is only fun and games.*

reality Humor may appear on the surface to be merely for laughs, but at its core, it is also serious business. It subverts our popular assumptions and beliefs about sex, marriage, politics, and virtually all other aspects of human life. Sociologist Murray Davis, who has done much research on the subject, concludes that humor is effectively an "attack on culture and society" (p. 113).

John and Mary, a married couple, teach college in different cities. They spend three days a week far away from each other. People frequently express sympathy with remarks such as "That must be rough" or "How do you stand it?" Mary readily accepts their sympathy, saying things like "We fly a lot" and "The worst part is packing and unpacking all the time." But John reacts differently, often with irritation. He emphasizes the advantages of his marriage: As professors, he and his wife have long vacations throughout the year and even benefit from those days when they are separated because they can work without interruption. All this is true, but Mary is surprised that her husband reacts differently than she does. He explains that he senses condescension in others' expressions of concern, as if they are implying "Yours is not a real marriage. I pity you, and look down on you, because my spouse and I do not have your kind of misfortune." In a nutshell, John tends to see others as adversaries, but Mary does not (Tannen, 2001c).

SOCIOLOGICAL PERSPECTIVES ON SOCIAL INTERACTION

What John and Mary experience is **social interaction**, the process by which individuals act toward and react to others. Interactions can be classified into three types, roughly reflecting the three major perspectives in sociology. John tends to engage in **oppositional interactions**, treating others as competitors or enemies. Mary tends to have **supportive interactions**, treating others as supporters or friends. This gender difference reflects the different social worlds in which John and Mary live. Reflecting the conflict perspective, John's world is more hierarchical, more like a contest, where "people try to achieve and maintain the upper hand if they can" (Tannen, 2001c). Reflecting the functionalist perspective, Mary's world is more egalitarian, with a greater tendency to nurture relationships by seeking and giving confirmation and support (Tannen, 2001c).

To symbolic interactionists, all interactions, whether oppositional or supportive, are also **symbolic interactions**, in which people actively interpret each other's actions and reactions and behave in accordance with the interpretation. Thus, John and Mary react differently to the same comments from others because they *interpret* the comments differently.

In short, the three perspectives spotlight different patterns of social interaction. Functionalism focuses on the supportive nature of interaction; the conflict perspective, on the oppositional nature; and symbolic interactionism, on the symbolic or interpretive nature. In this chapter, we will study everyday social interactions from these three perspectives. But sociologists rely mostly on the symbolic interactionist perspective to study social interaction, as we do in this chapter.

■ Functionalist Perspective: Supportive Interactions

From the functionalist perspective, we can see two types of supportive interactions: exchange and cooperation. An **exchange** is an interaction in which two individuals offer each other something in order to obtain a reward in return. **Cooperation** is an interaction in which two or more individuals work together to achieve a common goal.

Exchange   If you help a friend study for an exam and your friend, in turn, types a paper for you, you have engaged in an exchange. The reward we expect to get for what we do for others may be material, such as a salary or a gift, or it may be nonmaterial, such as a word of praise or gratitude. We find exchanges in all types of situations. Representatives of nations trade votes at the United Nations, employees exchange their labor for a salary, friends exchange advice and gratitude, children trade toys, and so on.

Social exchanges are usually governed by the norm of *reciprocity*, which requires that people help those who have helped them. If a favor has been extended to us, we will be motivated to return the favor. Conversely, if others have not been helpful to us, we are not likely to be helpful to them. Therefore, if social exchanges are fair, the social structure involved tends to be solid. The exchange reinforces the rela-

IT TAKES A VILLAGE It used to be a custom in parts of the American frontier for neighbors to come together to build a barn. This traditional cooperation is still alive and well among people such as the Amish and members of Habitat for Humanity. Cooperation adds stability to the social structure by boosting community spirit and solidarity. ■

tionships and provides each party in the exchange with some needed good. But if exchanges are seen as unfair, the social structure is likely to be shaky. A friendship in which one person constantly helps another, expecting but not getting gratitude in return, is likely to be short lived (Molm, Takahashi, and Peterson, 2003).

But friends cannot be too fussy about the fairness of exchange, unless they want the relationship to be something less than friendship. If you give someone $5 and expect to get exactly the same amount back from that person later, chances are that he or she is not your friend. Thus, in exchanges between classmates, coworkers, or business associates who are not friends, the participants give benefits with the expectation of receiving precisely comparable benefits in return. In friendships, however, members actively avoid the exactly equitable exchange because it seems too impersonal, businesslike, or unsentimental. Instead, they work out complicated exchanges of noncomparable benefits. Such an exchange would occur if you were to offer help and consolation to a friend who is ill and later received $100 from that friend when you were broke.

Cooperation In an *exchange,* a task can be adequately performed by only one of the parties. In *cooperation,* an individual needs another person's help to do a job or to do it more effectively. Within this broad category of interactions, there are some differences (Nisbet, 1970).

When neighbors come together to help a family whose house has just burned down or been destroyed by a tornado, that is *spontaneous cooperation.* This type of cooperation is the oldest, but it is unpredictable.

Over time, some forms of cooperation occur frequently enough for them to become customary in society. It was a custom in parts of the U.S. frontier, for example, for neighbors to work together to build a barn. This type of cooperation, *traditional cooperation,* brings added stability to the social structure.

Because modern societies, such as the United States, include people with diverse traditions, they are more likely to depend on a third type of cooperation, *directed cooperation,* which is based on the directions of someone in authority. We are directed by government, for example, to abide by the law and pay taxes. In return, the government provides us with such services as education, police protection, and national defense.

A fourth type of cooperation is equally useful in complex modern societies: *contractual cooperation.* It does not originate from tradition or authority but from voluntary action. Nor does it happen spontaneously; instead, it involves some planning. In contractual cooperation, individuals freely decide, for example, whether to embark on a business project together, and they spell out the terms of the cooperation.

Whatever the type, cooperation prevails throughout society. Functionalists argue that without cooperation, society cannot survive, let alone prosper. According to a cultural transmission theory, most people cooperate because they have personally benefited from cooperation with others or observed how others benefitted (Mark, 2002).

FAIR AND SQUARE In competition, each participant tries to achieve the same goal before the others do. But competition involves some degree of cooperation because the competitors must cooperate with each other by "playing the game" according to the rules. In a track-and-field event, for example, the athletes must cooperate by starting to run at the same time and by not taking performance-enhancing drugs. ▪

▪ Conflict Perspective: Oppositional Interactions

Oppositional interaction can consist of competition or conflict. **Competition** is an interaction in which two individuals follow mutually accepted rules, each trying to achieve the same goal before the other does. **Conflict** is an interaction in which two individuals disregard any rules, each trying to achieve his or her own goal by defeating the other.

Competition In competition, some degree of cooperation exists because the competitors must cooperate with each other by "playing the game" according to the rules. In a boxing match, for example, the fighters must cooperate by not hitting each other on certain parts of the body—by not turning the fight into a free-for-all. In politics, candidates competing for the same office must cooperate by following certain rules, the major one being that all contenders, especially the losers, must accept the outcome.

It is widely believed that competition brings out the best in us. The economic prosperity of Western capitalist nations, as opposed to the lower standard of living in formerly communist countries, is often attributed to the high value placed on competition. Compelled to compete fiercely with Japan and other countries in the global market, U.S. industries seem to have become more efficient and productive. It is apparently true that competition can stimulate economic growth. Certain types of professionals, such as athletes, politicians, and lawyers, are also known to thrive on competition. In our everyday lives, how-

ever, we usually perform less well—or more poorly—when we are trying to beat others than when we are working with them.

Several scholars have reviewed more than 100 studies conducted over the last 70 years that dealt with competition and cooperation in classrooms (Kohn, 1997, 1988; Kohn and Nelson, 1992; Azmitia, 1988). The scholars found that in 65 of the studies, cooperation promoted higher achievement than competition. In only 8 studies did competition induce higher achievement; 36 studies showed no statistically significant difference. Research on college students, scientists, and workers has produced further data challenging the popular belief in the benefits of competition.

Competition seems to hamper achievement primarily because it is stressful. The anxiety that arises from the possibility of losing interferes with performance. Even if this anxiety can be suppressed, it is difficult to do two things at the same time: trying to do well and trying to beat others. Competition can easily distract attention from the task at hand. Consider a teacher asking her pupils a question. A little boy waves his arm wildly to attract her attention, crying, "Please! Please! Pick me!" Finally recognized, he has forgotten the answer. So he scratches his head, asking, "What was the question again?" The problem is that he has focused on beating his classmates, not on the subject matter (Kohn, 1997, 1986).

Conflict In competition, the contestants try to achieve the same goal in accordance with commonly accepted rules. The most important rule is usually that the competing parties should concentrate on winning the game, not on hurting each other. When competing parties no longer play by these rules, competition has become conflict. In conflict, defeating the opponent, by hook or by crook, has become the goal. To use an extreme contrast, we can see competition in sports and conflict in wars.

Conflict exists in all kinds of social situations. It occurs between management and labor, criminals and police, and among different races but also between friends, lovers, family members, and fellow workers.

Conflict can both harm and help a social structure. Wars between nations and violent confrontations between hostile groups clearly are harmful. Yet being engaged in a war may also unify the members of a society. This is most likely to occur if various segments of society, such as leaders and the ordinary people, agree that the enemy is a real menace to the entire country, that it warrants going to war and defending the nation, and that internal conflict, if any, can be resolved (Markides and Cohn, 1982). Thus, the Vietnam War divided the American people because many did not agree with their government that South Vietnam was worth defending. In contrast, World War II unified Americans because virtually the entire population looked on the threat posed by Nazi Germany and Japan in the same way. Similarly, the September 11 terrorist attacks brought Americans together to support the wars in Afghanistan and Iraq.

■ Symbolic Interactionist Perspective: Interpreting Interactions

Both the functionalist and conflict perspectives enable us to see the different forms of interaction by watching from a distance how people interact. What we get from these perspectives is the *outside* view of interaction. We do not know what is going on *inside* people when they interact. According to symbolic interactionists, we can learn much about interaction by analyzing people's interpretations of each other's actions.

Supportive Interactions Erving Goffman (1971) referred to supportive interactions as "supportive interchanges," "mutual dealings," or "acts of identificatory sympathy." Examples range from "the congratulations at marriage, the careful commiserations at divorce, and the doleful condolences at deaths" to "the neighborly act of lending various possessions and providing minor services" to inquiries about "another's health, his experience on a recent trip, [or] his feelings about a recent movie." To symbolic interactionists, all these words or actions should *not* be taken at face value because they are not what they

READING BETWEEN THE LINES To symbolic interactionists, people usually don't take supportive interactions at face value but pay more attention to the hidden meanings behind expressed words and actions. When friends ask "How are you?" we know they are not really interested in the condition of our health in the same way that our doctor would be. Instead, they mean that they are happy to see us. ■

appear to be. This is because the people involved in these supportive interactions pay more attention to the hidden, intended meanings behind the expressed words or actions.

When people ask us, for example, "How are you?" they are not really interested in finding out the condition of our health in the same way our doctor is concerned. Instead, if they are strangers, they may actually mean to say "You can trust me," "I want to know you," or "I want to be your friend." If they are already our friends, they may mean to express their joy at seeing us, their desire to reaffirm our friendship. There are many other possible meanings, depending on the people and circumstances we encounter. All such meanings are not literally or explicitly expressed, but the listener nonetheless grasps them.

Oppositional Interactions While supportive interactions usually involve individuals of about the same social status, oppositional interactions are more likely to involve people of different statuses. In such situations, higher-status people tend to perceive lower-status people as less worthy of respect than

theoretical thumbnail

The Nature of Social Interaction

Perspective	Focus	Insights
Functionalist	Supportive interactions: Exchange and cooperation	In exchange, we pay others to build a house; in cooperation, we work with them to build the house.
Conflict	Oppositional interactions: Competition and conflict	In competition, we try to win a boxing match by following the rules of the game; in conflict, we try to knock out the opponent by any means available.
Symbolic interactionist	Interpreting interactions	In supportive interactions, we heed others' well-intended meanings behind their expressed words and actions; in oppositional interactions, we see others as less worthy of respect and act toward them accordingly.

they themselves are. Higher-status people are consequently likely to behave disrespectfully toward lower-status people. One common way of showing this disrespect involves symbolically invading the personhood of others.

myth	Men and women are equally disinclined to stare at others because they have been taught not to do so since childhood.
reality	Since men are generally given a higher status than women in a sexist society, men tend to stare at women more than vice versa.

Consider, for example, the interactions between men and women in a sexist society. Since they are generally given a higher status than women, men tend to stare at women more than vice versa. Men are also more likely to touch women's bodies, such as letting their hands rest on women's shoulders, while women rarely reciprocate. When members of both sexes participate in a group discussion, men are far more likely to interrupt women than the other way around. In one study, only 4 percent of the interruptions in male–female conversations came from women; 96 percent came from men (Karp and Yoels, 1998).

The Theoretical Thumbnail above summarizes the three perspectives on social interaction.

INTERACTION AS SYMBOLIC COMMUNICATION

We have just seen how power, respect, and other aspects of social relationships are communicated with symbols, such as words and gestures. Without sym-

bolic communication, humans would have to interact like other animals. Symbolic communication, then, is the essence of human interaction.

■ The Nature of Human Communication

Animals communicate, too. If you try to catch a seagull, it will call out "hahaha! hahaha!" to signal its friends to watch out for an intruder. A squirrel may cry out to warn other squirrels to flee from danger. But these signal systems are not symbols, and animal communication differs in fundamental ways from human communication.

First, symbols are *arbitrary*. The meaning of a word is not determined by any inherent quality of the thing itself. Instead, a word may mean whatever a group of humans have agreed it is supposed to mean. If you do not speak Chinese, you would not know that *gou* is the Chinese word for *dog*. There is no inherent connection between the word and the animal itself. The Spaniards, after all, call the same animal *perro,* and the French call it *chien*. Even "dingdong" is an arbitrary symbol: A bell may sound like "dingdong" to us but not to the Germans, to whom a bell sounds like "bimbam."

The meaning of a word is *socially constructed* because it is determined by people through their social experiences as members of a specific society. It is no wonder that many different symbols are used in human communication to represent the same thing. Animals, by contrast, do not freely and arbitrarily produce different symbols to indicate the same thing because their communication is largely determined by instinct. This is why, for example, all seagulls throughout the world make the same sound to indicate the presence of danger. Unlike humans, they cannot express a particular thought in more than one way (Goodman, 1996).

Second, animal communication is a *closed system,* but human communication is an *open system.* Each animal species can communicate only a limited set of messages, and the meaning of these signals is fixed. Animals can use only one signal at a time; they cannot combine two or more to produce a new and more complex message. A bird can signal "worms" to other birds but not "worms" and "cats" together. Animal communication is also closed in the sense of being stimulus bound; it is tied to what is immediately present in the environment. The bird can signal "worms" only because it sees them. It is impossible for an animal to use a symbol to represent some invisible, abstract, or imaginary thing. As the philosopher Bertrand Russell said, "No matter how eloquently a dog can bark, he cannot tell you that his parents are poor but honest."

In contrast, we can blend and combine symbols to express whatever ideas come to mind. We can create new messages, and the potential number of messages that we can send is infinite. Thus, we can talk about abstractions such as good and evil, truth and beauty. It is this creative character of language that leads many people to believe that language is unique to humans. Language also makes possible the exchange of ideas through the information superhighway around the world (see Figure 4.1).

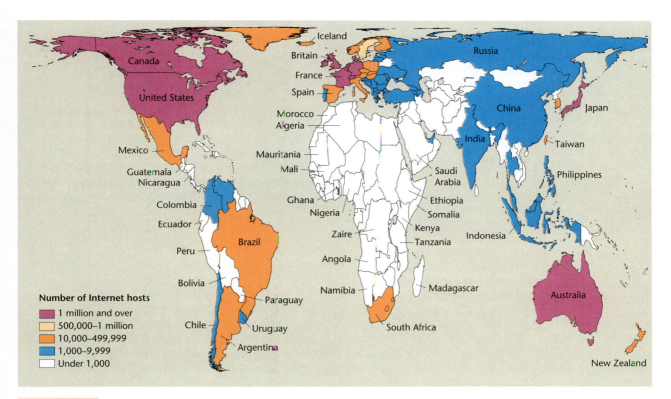

FIGURE 4.1

Communication via the Internet

At the core of symbolic communication, human language enables us to create a potentially infinite number of messages. With language, we can also exchange ideas with people all over the world through the information superhighway known as the Internet. Most Internet hosts, or websites, are still concentrated in relatively rich, developed countries. The small developed nation of Iceland, for example, has 20 times as many websites as all the world's 100 poorest countries combined. But the Internet is becoming increasingly accessible in poor, developing countries.

Critical Thinking: *What impact does the globalization of the Internet have on our lives?*

Source: From *The Penguin Atlas of Media and Information* by Mark Balnaves, James Donald, and Stephanie Hemelryk Donald, copyright © 2001 by Myriad Editions Ltd. Used with permission of Penguin, a division of Penguin Group (USA) Inc.

Human communication is not only verbal, involving the use of words; it is also nonverbal, consisting of kinesics and proxemics. **Kinesics** (pronounced *kuh-NEE-sicks*) is *body language,* the use of body movements as a means of communication, such as smiling to express happiness at seeing someone. **Proxemics** (*procks-EE-micks*) is the use of space as a means of communication. Proxemics occurs when we snuggle up to an intimate to express affection or when we avoid touching a stranger to show respect.

■ A Global Analysis of Communication

Whether human communication is verbal or nonverbal, it is conducted differently in different societies. Let us look at how people in other countries communicate differently than we do.

Verbal Communication In some cultures in which people like to talk a lot, a listener's silence is often assumed to indicate agreement. Once an Egyptian pilot radioed ahead to the Cyprus airport for permission to land. Receiving no response, the pilot took the silence to mean "Permission granted." But as the pilot brought the plane in for a landing, the Cypriot air force opened fire. Obviously, to the Cypriots, the silence meant "Permission denied" (Tannen, 1986).

myth	It is natural for only one person to speak at a time when engaged in a conversation.
reality	That may be so in the United States, but in many other countries, it is normal for a listener to chime in when someone is talking in order to show enthusiastic participation or involvement with others.

But between equally talkative cultures, there are also differences in conversational style. In American society, we tend to believe that even in casual conversation, only one person should speak at a time. Yet in many other countries, it is normal for a listener to chime in when someone is talking in order to show enthusiastic participation or involvement with others. Such logic seems to elude many in the United States. In the late 1980s, the U.S. president's wife, Nancy Reagan, complained to the press about Raisa Gorbachev, wife of the Soviet president: "From the moment we met, she talked and talked and *talked*—so much that I could barely get a word in, edgewise or otherwise." Probably unaware of the "one speaker at a time" ethic, Mrs. Gorbachev might have been wondering why her U.S. counterpart never said anything—and made her do all the conversational work (Tannen, 2001b, 2001c).

myth	To avoid misunderstanding, especially in conversation with foreigners, it is always wise to say directly what's on our mind, such as saying "yes" to mean "yes."
reality	Directness in speech may be good for transmitting information, but *indirectness* is common in many other countries. The Japanese, for example, may say "yes" to mean "no" when asked "Would you agree to do business with us?" This is their way of trying to save others from disappointment or embarrassment.

When Americans talk, they tend to express directly what is on their minds. People in many other cultures are more likely to speak indirectly. In China, if you visit an acquaintance on a hot day and feel thirsty, you would not ask your host point-blank, "May I have a glass of water?" Instead, you would convey the same request by saying "Isn't it hot today?" In Japan, if at the end of a lengthy business meeting you ask, "Do you then agree to do business with us?" the Japanese will always say "yes" even if they mean "no." They are reluctant to say "no" directly in order to save others' face and spare them embarrassment. Used to directness in speech, many Americans cannot understand how "yes" can possibly mean "no." But the Japanese can say "yes" in a certain way to mean "yes" and then say "yes" in another way to mean "no."

Nonverbal Communication Like verbal communication, body language varies from one culture to another. People in the United States nod their heads to mean "yes" and shake them to mean "no." But in Bulgaria, head nodding means "no" and head shaking means "yes." The Semang of Malaya thrust their heads forward to signal "yes" and cast their eyes down to signal "no." When North Americans use a thumb and forefinger to form a circle, they mean "A-OK," but to South Americans, the same gesture is equivalent to "Screw you!"

In proxemics, the amount of space we take up around us also varies from one society to another. In North America, when we talk to a person whom we do not know well, we ordinarily stand about 3 feet away. If one person moves in more closely, the other will find it too close for comfort. This may reflect the North American values of individual independence and privacy. But South Americans and Arabs are inclined to stand much closer. In entering others' space, they do not mean to be rude. On the contrary, they are expressing their desire for human connection (Dresser, 1999; Axtell, 1991).

TOO CLOSE FOR COMFORT?
Nonverbal communication may involve *proxemics,* the use of space as a means of communication. The amount of space we take up around us varies from one society to another. In North America, when conversing with people we do not know, we usually stand about 3 feet apart, but in Arab countries, people tend to maintain a closer conversational distance. ■

■ U.S. Diversity in Communication

Both verbal and nonverbal communication also vary from one group to another within U.S. society.

Verbal Communication   Various groups of Americans speak English with different accents. The Midwestern accent is different from the New York accent, which is distinct from the Southern accent, which is distinguishable from the New England accent, and so on. Accents also vary within each of these regional categories. Different races, ethnic groups, and social classes have their own accents. Most interestingly, there are variations in English usage and conversational style.

The middle class seldom uses the double negative ("I can't get no satisfaction"), whereas the working class often does. The middle class rarely drops the letter "g" in present participles ("doin'" for "doing," "singin'" for "singing"), perhaps because they are conscious of being correct. The working class often drops the "g," probably to avoid appearing snooty. They also tend to say "lay" instead of "lie," as in "Let's lay on the beach," without suggesting a desire for sex. On the other hand, the middle class has a weakness for euphemism. To them, drunks are "people with alcohol problems" and a prison is a "correctional facility." They also tend to choose words that they consider sophisticated—"vocalist" instead of "singer" or "as of this time" rather than "now." The upper class distinguishes itself by its tendency to use such words as "tiresome" or "tedious" instead of "boring" (Fussell, 1992).

Inner-city African Americans speak a dialect that their white counterparts may find hard to understand. Here is an example of how Black English (or Ebonics) was used to explain why God cannot be African American:

> Why? I'll tell you why. 'Cause the average whitey out here got everything, you dig? And the [black] ain't got shit, y'know? Y'understan'? So—um—for—in order for *that* to happen, you know it ain't no black God that's doin' that bullshit. (Nanda, 1994)

The quote can be roughly translated as follows: "No way God can be an African American. If he was, he wouldn't have screwed up our lives." To some whites, Black English is deficient, but for its speakers, it is a lively, useful tool for communication in the inner city.

Similarly, whites often say things in everyday conversation that would sound peculiar to Apache Indian listeners. Whites would say to mere acquaintances or even strangers, "Hello, my friend! How're you feeling?" Apaches would not call somebody "my friend" unless that person is truly a friend. They would not ask mere acquaintances how they feel because it is considered an invasion of personal privacy, reflecting an unnatural curiosity about others' inner feelings. Also, to Apaches, whites' frequent use of one another's names ("Glad to see you, *Mary,*" "How you doing, *Joe?*") smacks of disrespect because a personal name is the individual's sacred property (Nanda, 1994).

Nonverbal Communication   In his classic study of a Chicago slum, Gerald Suttles (1970) found some ethnic diversity in the use of body language and personal space:

> The other ethnic groups think it odd that a group of Mexican men should strike a pose of obliviousness to others, even their nearby wives and children. Puerto Ricans, on the other hand, are disparaged because they stand painfully close during a conversation. . . . Whites say that [African Americans] will not look them in the eye. The [African Americans] counter by saying that whites are impolite and try to "cow" people by staring at them.

But among whites themselves, when talking with members of the same sex, men are less likely than women to look at others. Researchers have observed a series of casual conversations between two subjects of the same sex. In these studies, men often "looked outward, away from each other, and around the room, rather than directly at each other," while women more frequently looked straight at each other. The men did occasionally look at each other, but their eye contact did not last as long as that among women (Tannen, 2001b, 2001c).

What does this gender difference mean? It is possible that to men, looking at others as long as women do seems like staring, hence a hostile action, a display of threat, which they try to avoid. But it is more likely that by looking away from each other, men may be avoiding friendly connection or intimacy, which women tend more to seek and express by looking at others (Tannen, 2001b, 2001c). This has much to do with the nature of the world in which men live, which differs from that of women. In the next section, we will explore these two worlds and see how they affect communication between the sexes.

COMMUNICATION BETWEEN WOMEN AND MEN

In the world of women, connection and intimacy are the primary goals of life, and individuals cultivate friendship, minimize differences, seek consensus, and avoid the appearance of superiority. Status and independence are the primary goals of life in men's world, however, so individuals seek status by telling others what to do, attain freedom from others' control, avoid taking orders, and resist asking for help. Thus, when the two sexes communicate with each other, women tend to use the language of connection and intimacy and men the language of status and independence. Both may use the same English

language, but in effect they speak and hear different dialects called **genderlects**, linguistic styles that reflect the different worlds of women and men (Canary and Dindia, 1998; Tannen, 2001b, 2001c).

■ Speaking Different Genderlects

Failure to understand each other's genderlect can spell trouble for intergender communication. Consider a married couple, Linda and Josh. One day, Josh's old high school buddy from another city called to announce that he would be in town the following month. Josh invited him to stay for the weekend. When he told Linda that they were going to have a houseguest, she was upset. Often away on business, she had planned to spend that weekend with Josh alone. But what upset her the most was that Josh had extended the invitation without first discussing it with her. Linda would never make plans without first checking with Josh. "Why can't you do the same with me?" Linda asked. But Josh responded, "I can't say to my friend, 'I have to ask my wife for permission!'" To Josh, who lives in the men's world of status, checking with his wife means seeking permission, giving up his independence, and having to act like a kid asking his mom if it's OK to play with a friend. In Linda's female world of connection, checking with her husband has nothing to do with permission. In fact, Linda likes to tell others "I have to check with Josh," because it makes her feel good to reaffirm that she is involved with someone, that her life is bound up with someone else's (Tannen, 2001c). In short, Linda and Josh speak and hear different genderlects: one having to do with connection and intimacy, the other with status and independence.

myth	Because they speak the same language, men and women can easily understand each other.
reality	Men and women speak the same language but use it in different ways: men, for the purpose of giving information; women, for expressing feelings. Thus, men tend to misunderstand women by taking literally what women say, and women tend to misunderstand men by reading emotional meanings into what men say.

There are other ways the different genderlects can throw a monkey wrench into the communication between women and men. Accustomed to speaking for the purpose of giving *information* only, men tend to misunderstand women by taking literally what women say. On the other hand, women, more habituated to talking for the purpose of expressing *feelings,* tend to misunderstand men by reading emotional meanings into what men say (Tannen, 2001b, 2001c; Canary and Dindia, 1998).

Thus, women and men tend to communicate at cross-purposes. If a woman says to her husband, "We never go out," he may upset her by responding, "That's not true. We went out last week." The husband fails to grasp the feeling the wife is trying to convey. In saying "We never go out," she is in effect saying something like "I feel like going out and doing something together. We always have such a fun time, and I enjoy being with you. It's been a few days since we went out." If on another occasion, the woman asks her husband, "What's the matter?" and gets the answer "I'm OK," she may respond by saying, "I know something's wrong. What is it? Why aren't you willing to share your problem with me? Let me help you." The wife fails to understand that by saying "I'm OK," her husband means "I am OK; I can deal with my problem. I don't need any help, thank you" (Gray, 1992). In his male world, dealing with one's own problem is a hallmark of independence, which he tries to assert, and getting help from others is a sign of weakness, which he tries to avoid.

Genderlects are not confined to communication between intimates. They also influence communication in public. A sociolinguist once sat alone in a dining room where bank officers had lunch and listened to what they were talking about at adjacent tables. When no women were present, the men talked mostly about business and rarely about people. The next most popular topics were food, sports, and recreation. When women talked alone, their most frequent topic was people, especially friends, children, and partners in personal relationships. Business was next and then health, including weight control. Together, women and men tended to avoid the topic that each group liked best and settle on topics of interest to both, *but they followed the style of the men-only conversations.* They talked about food the way men did, focusing on the food and restaurant rather than on diet and health. They talked about recreation the way men did, concentrating on sports figures and athletic events rather than on exercising. And they talked about housing the way men did, dealing mostly with location, property values, and commuting time rather than whether the house is suitable for the family, how safe the neighborhood is for the children, and what kinds of people live next door. In other words, in public communication between the sexes, the male genderlect tends to dominate, mostly centering on things and activities, thus ignoring the female genderlect, which primarily concerns people and relationships (Tannen, 2001a, 2001b; Canary and Dindia, 1998).

■ Playing the Gendered Game of Proxemics

In mixed-gender groups, men's proxemics differs from women's. Men usually sprawl, with legs spread apart and hands stretched away from the body, taking up considerable space around them. Women are more likely to draw themselves in, using little space and modest postures, such as closing or crossing the legs and placing the hands near the body

A more direct way for men to dominate women in proxemics involves invading their personal space. As has been suggested, men often let their hands rest on women's shoulders, but women rarely do the same to men. A similar proxemic domination prevails in interactions of mutual affection. When an intimate couple walk down the street, the man may place his arm around the woman's shoulders, but the woman is far less likely to put her arm around the man's shoulders. Doesn't this merely reflect the fact that the man is usually taller, so that it would be uncomfortable for the sexes to reverse positions? No. The same ritual of man playing the powerful protector and woman the helpless protected is often observed when both are of about the same height or even when the man is slightly shorter. If the man is too short to stretch his arm around the woman's shoulders, they still will not reverse positions but will in-

GIVE AND TAKE Reflecting men's dominance of women, proxemics differs between the genders. When sitting in gender-mixed groups, women are likely to give up space around them by drawing themselves in—for instance, closing their legs and placing their hands near their body. But men are more likely to take up a lot of space. They sprawl, with their legs spread out and hands stretched away from their body. ■

stead settle for holding hands. If a tall woman does put her arm around a shorter man's shoulders, chances are that she is a mother and he is her child (Tannen, 2001b, 2001c). In the world of gender inequality, a man is likely to cringe if his girlfriend or wife treats him like a child by putting her arm around his shoulders.

Even in the most intimate moments between a man and a woman, male domination reigns. When both lie down in bed, he typically lies on his back, flat and straight, but she lies on her side, her body nestled against his. She further places her head on his shoulder, and he places his arm around her. It is a picture of an unequal relationship, with the man appearing strong and protective and the woman weak and protected (Tannen, 2001b, 2001c).

DRAMATURGY: INTERACTION AS DRAMA

Underlying the diversity of communication that we have just analyzed is the same tendency for people everywhere to interact with others as if they were performing on the stage of a theater. Shakespeare captured the essence of social interaction as a staged drama with his famous line "All the world's a stage, and all the men and women merely players." American sociologist Erving Goffman (1922–1982) developed the theatrical analogy into **dramaturgy**, a method of analyzing social interaction as if the participants were performing on a stage.

■ Behaving Like Actors

When we interact, we behave like actors by following scripts that we have learned from our parents, teachers, friends, and others (see Chapter 3: Socialization). These scripts essentially tell us how to behave in accordance with our statuses and roles (Chapter 2: Society and Culture). But the stage analogy does have limitations. On stage, the actors have a clearly written and detailed script that allows them to rehearse exactly what they will say and do. In real life, our scripts are far more general and ambiguous. They cannot tell us precisely how we are going to act or how the other person is going to react. It is therefore much more difficult, if not impossible, to be well rehearsed. In fact, as we gain new experiences every day, we constantly revise our scripts. This means that we have to improvise a great deal, saying and doing many things that have not crossed our minds before that very moment.

One example is how a woman may react to a pelvic examination in the office of a gynecologist. Women tend to dread this event, when they have to subject their most private body areas to public

scrutiny, very often by a male physician. The occasion is potentially embarrassing to both doctor and patient. How can a woman best minimize this risk? One way was revealed in a classic study by James Henslin and Mae Biggs (1971), who analyzed the data on several thousand pelvic examinations that Biggs had observed as a trained nurse. A typical examination unfolded like the scenes in a play.

In the prologue, the woman enters the waiting room and thus assumes the role of patient. In the first act, she is called into the consulting room, where she describes her complaints. The doctor assumes his role by responding appropriately, listening closely, asking the necessary questions, and discussing the patient's problems. If a pelvic examination is indicated, he so informs the patient and then departs, leaving the patient in the nurse's hands.

The second act begins as the nurse ushers the patient into an examining room and asks her to disrobe. At the same time, the nurse tries to help the patient make the transition from a dignified, fully clothed person to little more than a scientific specimen. The patient appears nervous. The nurse is sympathetic and reassuring. The nurse shows the patient where to leave her clothes and how to put on her hospital gown. The interaction with the nurse creates a strictly clinical situation.

The third act is the examination itself. Lying on the table with her body covered, the patient is transformed into a nonperson, the object of the doctor's scrutiny. She cannot see the doctor, who sits on a low stool. She also avoids eye contact with the nurse. She simply stares at the ceiling and says little or nothing. Similarly, the doctor tries to refrain from talking. All this serves to desexualize the situation, reassuring everybody that it is only a medical examination.

The fourth and final act begins as the examination ends. The doctor leaves, allowing the patient to dress in solitude. Then, fully clothed, she is ushered back into the consulting room, where both doctor and patient resume the roles they played in the first act. Now the doctor again treats his patient as a person, and the patient behaves as though nothing unusual has happened. Finally, she departs, going back to her everyday roles.

This analysis suggests that despite the lack of a script showing how doctor and patient should interact, they nevertheless manage, with the help of the nurse, to play their roles. We also learn that each participant tries to save the other's face with what Goffman calls "tactful blindness" to an embarrassing situation, acting as if it did not exist. This mutual cooperation makes it possible for the performance to go on. According to Goffman, the performance is the heart of social interaction and as such involves *presenting the self* to the other.

Presenting the Self

In presenting our selves to others, we are the actors and they the audience. They also do the same, with themselves as actors and us as the audience. The playing of these two opposite roles by each participant in social interaction ensures that when each performs poorly in presenting the self, the audience will empathize, ignore the flaw, and form the impression desired by the actor. One will help the other pull off the performance because of the expectation that the favor will be returned. This explains the avoidance of embarrassment through tactful blindness in many situations comparable to the pelvic examination. If our houseguest stumbles on arrival or belches after dinner, we usually pretend not to see or hear the contretemps.

Although others want to help us succeed with our self-presentation, we still strive to do so on our own. Generally, we try to display the positive aspects of ourselves and conceal the negative ones. When we date someone for the first time, we shower and dress properly and use a deodorant to mask any unpleasant smell. When we listen to a story, we try to be all ears, but even if we become bored to the point of yawning, we cover our mouths with our hands. In conversation, we try to say the right thing and avoid saying the wrong thing. In fact, to ensure a smooth interaction, we often have to say or do things we truly don't want to. That is why store clerks appear friendly even to pesky customers and polite people laugh at bad jokes. Doesn't all this destroy our true self, self-identity, or dignity? No, because we maintain what Goffman calls **role distance**, the separation of our role-playing as outward performance from our inner self. Thus, we may outwardly appear servile to some people but inwardly scorn them.

The outward performance is similar to what the actor does *onstage,* and the inward feeling is comparable to what the actor does *backstage.* Goffman takes this stage analogy seriously in his analysis of self-presentation, which he divides into *front-region* (or *frontstage*) performance and *back-region* (*backstage*) behavior. In the front region, people present their selves in ways expected by others, the audience. In the back region, they reveal their true selves, with no concern for the audience. Often, the backstage behavior contradicts the frontstage performance. Consider, for example, the goings-on in a funeral home. The body-preparation room is the backstage, where the funeral director and staff often show no respect to the dead, such as by joking about the corpse or complaining about its size or smell. But in the frontstage interaction with the bereaved family and friends, the mortuary personnel exhibit great respect to the deceased. Even though in the back region they have drained

THE WORLD'S A STAGE According to Goffman, self-presentation can be divided into *frontstage* and *backstage* performances. On the frontstage, people present their selves in ways expected by others, the audience. This server in a restaurant, for example, smiles and appears friendly and helpful to her customers, showing her frontstage performance before her audience. On the backstage, in the kitchen, she may alter her behavior and reveal her true self, with no concern for the audience. ■

and stuffed the corpse, in the front region the personnel never touch it, always respectfully keeping a distance from the casketed body (Howarth, 1996; Turner and Edgley, 1990).

Onstage performances are not necessarily dishonest or intended only to manipulate or fool the audience. Often, we do present who we really are. Generally, the onstage performance is more honest with families and friends than with strangers. But even with strangers, a dishonest performance cannot be pulled off without the apparent collusion of the audience. In fact, the appearance of mutual cooperation between performer and audience is an important characteristic of interaction rituals.

Performing Interaction Rituals

In religious rituals, the worshipers perform certain acts to show reverence to the deity. Similarly, in

interaction rituals, the participants perform certain acts to show reverence to each other. Some people may not genuinely feel reverent but only show reverence, with the intention of manipulating others. But in dramaturgy, they can be said to be engaged in an interaction ritual because the essence of interaction rituals is the *appearance* or *display* of reverence rather than actual reverence. Just as anybody can participate in religious rituals, whether or not they truly believe in God, anybody can participate in interaction rituals. The only requirement is that the participant act as if the other's self is sacred, producing an action that exudes respect for the other.

Interaction rituals are performed every day. In a restaurant, on a sidewalk, or in some other public place, any two strangers can be observed quickly glancing at each other and then just as quickly looking away. The split-second eye contact suggests that the two strangers consider each other worthy, important, or respectful enough to have their presence recognized. Their instant withdrawal of attention from each other expresses even greater mutual respect. In effect, they treat each other like gods. As Goffman (1967) observed, "This secular world is not so irreligious as we might think. The individual is a deity of considerable importance. He walks with some dignity and is the recipient of many little offerings," such as the fleeting eye contact from strangers.

Without these rituals, interaction in everyday life would be difficult, if not impossible. Imagine how you would feel if strangers kept staring at you. But violations of interaction rituals do occur. A common violation involves *loss of poise,* such as spilling a drink at a friend's apartment. Another interaction-ritual violation involves *incorrect identification,* as when we get someone's name wrong or say "How's your wife?" to a man whose wife has died. A third form of violation involves *situational impropriety,* such as dressing improperly at a social event or giving sad news to a happy couple at their wedding.

When these and other ritual violations occur, most people pitch in by doing what Goffman calls "remedial work of various kinds." The culprit is likely to say "Excuse me" or "I'm sorry" or to provide an excuse ("The drink made me a little drunk") or disclaimer ("I *don't mean* to be insensitive, but I have to tell you something"). The offended others graciously accept the apology, excuse, or disclaimer. In doing so, they help the ritual violator save face, rescuing the individual from embarrassment so that the derailed interaction can be put back on track. As we will see in the next section, however, there are strategies for preventing the problems in the first place, helping the self get the desired impression from others.

THE ART OF MANAGING IMPRESSIONS

In Goffman's dramaturgy, all performances in social interaction are aimed at creating a desired, favorable impression. The performer can achieve the objective by *using defensive measures* with the help of the audience. The audience assists by *offering protective measures.*

■ Defensive Measures by the Performer

Goffman divides these measures into three types. The first has to do with *dramaturgical loyalty,* in which members of a team of performers support each other before an audience or keep their team secrets from outsiders. This involves treating each other so well that everyone enjoys being part of the team.

The second defensive measure has to do with *dramaturgical discipline.* This requires self-control, such as refraining from laughing about matters that are supposed to be serious and from taking seriously matters that are supposed to be humorous. Dramaturgical discipline also involves managing one's

DINNER AS THEATER   Goffman found that social performances involve defensive measures on the part of the performers, with cooperative assistance from the audience. At a dinner party, for example, the guests—the audience—often will stay discreetly away from the backstage area—the kitchen—to help the hosts maintain the frontstage performance of ease, elegance, and control. ■

face and voice to display appropriate feelings and conceal inappropriate ones. In dealing with pesky customers, for example, disciplined performers suppress their annoyance with a cheerful smile and a friendly voice.

The third defensive measure is *dramaturgical circumspection*. This involves carefully looking for the right things to do to ensure success in performance. One tactic is to adapt a performance to the audience, relaxing the performance when we are with those we have known for a long time while choreographing the performance when among those new to us. One should also adjust one's presentation to the nature of the thing presented to the audience. For example, clothing merchants take extreme care not to make exaggerated claims about their merchandise because customers can test them by sight and touch, but furniture salespersons need not be so careful because few customers can judge what lies behind the varnish and veneer of the product shown.

■ Protective Measures by the Audience

By themselves, those defensive techniques of impression management cannot guarantee success. The performer also needs the audience's cooperation. According to Goffman, the audience has the "tactful tendency" to act in a protective way to help the performers carry off their show.

First, audience members tend to stay discreetly away from the backstage unless invited. If audience members want to enter the back region, they will give the performers some warning, in the form of a knock or a cough, so that the performers will stop activities that are inconsistent with their frontstage performance.

Second, if the performer commits a social blunder, the audience usually will tactfully not see it. Audience tact is so common that we may even find it among mental hospital patients, who are well known for their unconventional behavior. To illustrate, Goffman (1967) cites this research report:

> [Once] the staff, without consulting the patients, decided to give them a Valentine party. Many of the patients did not wish to go, but did so anyway as they felt that they should not hurt the feelings of the student nurses who had organized the party. The games introduced by the nurses were on a very childish level; many of the patients felt silly playing them and were glad when the party was over.

According to Goffman, audiences are motivated to act tactfully for one of several reasons: (1) immediate identification with performers, (2) desire to avoid a scene, or (3) ingratiating themselves with performers for the purpose of exploitation. Goffman re-

gards the third as the best explanation for audience tactfulness, citing for illustration the case of successful prostitutes "who are willing to enact a lively approval of their clients' sexual performance."

THE SOCIAL CONSTRUCTION OF REALITY

In discussing interaction as symbolic communication or staged performance, we have focused on how people interact with *others*. But while interacting with others, people are also simultaneously interacting with *themselves,* somewhat like talking to themselves. In this internal interaction, they create within themselves images of the other people and then interact with *these images* rather than with the other people. Thus, when people are interacting outwardly with others, they are, in reality, interacting inwardly with their own images of those people.

This process refutes the popular belief that the world "out there"—such as the other person—is, by itself, real. If the world out there is real without being defined as real by us, we will all interact in the same way with the other person, who, after all, is exactly the same person. But we do not all interact in the same way because we are not really interacting with the same person but instead with our own different images of that person. In brief, reality does not exist out there, in the form of the other person, but within ourselves, in the form of our image of that person.

Nevertheless, reality cannot be created in a social vacuum; it is *socially* constructed through social interaction. Our past as well as current encounters with others help us develop all the ideas, feelings, and attitudes that shape our image of the other person at a given moment. Let us take a closer look at this **social construction of reality**, the process by which people create through social interactions certain ideas, feelings, and beliefs about their environment.

■ Thomas Theorem: Creating Reality with Definition

After constructing reality, we do not just let the reality lie idle within ourselves. We act it out by doing something in accordance with the constructed reality. This is what sociologist W. I. Thomas (1863–1947) had in mind when he made the famous pronouncement known today as the **Thomas theorem:** "If people define situations as real, they are real in their consequences." In other words, people can turn their socially constructed inner realities (perceptions, ideas, beliefs, attitudes, or feelings) into socially observable outer realities (behaviors, actions, or activities).

"Stock prices fell sharply today on the fear that stock prices would fall sharply."

Source: From the *Wall Street Journal*—Permission, Cartoon Features Syndicate.

For instance, if people believe that God exists, God is just as real to them as are humans, things, ideas, and other features of their social and physical worlds. They will *act as if God is real* by worshiping God. Similarly, if people believe that extraterrestrials exist, they will *act as if they are real* by telling others about alien beings and flying saucers (see Figure 4.2). Moreover, if people believe that they will become successful in the future, they will *do something to make it real,* such as working hard, which will likely lead to success.

This third illustration suggests two ways in which situations defined as real are real in their consequences: working hard *now* and achieving success *later.* This is why the Thomas theorem is sometimes called the *self-fulfilling prophecy.* But many instances resemble only the first two examples: Definition of the situation produces merely one kind of consequence, such as currently worshiping God or telling others about aliens and flying saucers. In sum, if we define something out there as real, we will act as if it is real or do something to make it real.

■ Ethnomethodology: Exposing Hidden Reality

We have just seen how the Thomas theorem focuses on the outer behavioral consequences of defining situations. But we are not shown the inner subjective reality. To delve into that reality, we need **ethnomethodology**, the analysis of how people define the world in which they live. Taken from Greek, *ethno* means "folk" and *methodology* means "a systematic or standard method." So *ethnomethodology*

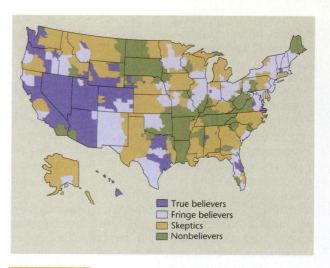

FIGURE 4.2

Look, It's a Flying Saucer!

Thirty percent of Americans believe, to one degree or another, that extraterrestrials exist. Believers are more likely to live in the West and Southwest. They are relatively well educated, upper middle class, and married.

Critical Thinking: *Why are Westerners and Southwesterners more likely than other Americans to believe in flying saucers?*

Source: Newsweek, May 25, 1998, p. 8.

literally means "folk method," implying that the method is popular, traditional, conventional, and widely shared.

But what exactly is the folk method people use to define their world in everyday interaction? To find out, Harold Garfinkel (2002, 1967), the founder of ethnomethodology, asked his students to interact with relatives, friends, and others in an antifolk, antitraditional, anticonventional manner. From such experiments, the students and Garfinkel discovered that the folk method generally involves *defining the world in a vague, ambiguous manner,* leaving out a lot of specific details. Consider the following two interactions: one involving a student and her husband; the other, a student and the student's friend:

Interaction 1
On Friday my husband remarked that he was tired.
I asked, "How are you tired? Physically, mentally, or just bored?"
"I don't know, I guess physically, mainly," he responded.
"You mean that your muscles ache or your bones?" I asked.
A little irritated, he said, "I guess so. Don't be so technical."

Interaction 2

Friend: How are you?

Student: How am I in regard to what? You mean my health, my finances, my school work, my sex life, my peace of mind, my . . .

Friend: Look, I was just trying to be polite. Frankly, I don't give a damn how you are.

Why do people interacting with one another define things vaguely and leave out the details? The reason is the popular assumption that *people understand one another without the specific details.* But this assumption of shared understanding, or the folk method based on it, is so often employed, widely shared, and taken for granted that most people are not aware that it exists. Only when it is questioned, as in the examples given above, do people suddenly recognize not only that they have long held it but also that it can be incorrect. As a consequence, they may become irritated, angry, dumbfounded, or embarrassed. Such negative reactions show the discomfort of having their cherished and taken-for-granted assumption taken away.

Not surprisingly, Garfinkel found the same negative reactions in many other experiments in which he instructed his students to bargain for small items in supermarkets, violate the rules in playing tic-tac-toe, or move increasingly close to someone in conversation until they were nearly nose-to-nose with them. Once again, these experiments demonstrated, through the subjects' negative reactions, that their cherished assumption of shared understanding can be questionable.

But we may not need Garfinkel's experiments to discover the shakiness of the shared-understanding assumption. As was previously discussed, women and men do not always have the same understanding, even when they use the same words to communicate. When we interact with people of different racial, ethnic, religious, or other backgrounds, we are also likely to find that they, like Garfinkel's students, do not share our definition of the situation. Generally, the more diverse the society, the more untenable the assumption of shared understanding.

This is particularly true in today's global village, where people of different cultures often interact. Without cross-cultural understanding, we may erroneously assume that people in other countries share our definitions of situations. We may believe, for example, that it is polite to inquire about a man's wife, but to do so in Saudi Arabia would provoke an angry reaction because the Saudis consider such an inquiry rude. Similarly, we may think that giving a gift such as a letter opener or a clock to a college friend is a nice gesture of friendship. But in Latin America, the presentation of a letter opener may be construed as our desire to sever the relationship, and in China, the clock may be taken as our wish for the person to die soon.

In instances such as these, people in other cultures effectively expose as untenable our socially shared assumption that we understand one another. Simultaneously, we also question the same assumption held by the foreigners, in about the same way as Garfinkel's students did with their subjects. When this happens, both interactants—we and the foreigners—may be dumbfounded, angry, irritated, or embarrassed.

■ Humorology: Subverting Established Reality

While ethnomethodology exposes our hidden, widely shared assumptions about our world, **humorology**—the study or practice of humor—takes this practice a step further by subverting them. On the face of it, humor is only for fun and games, as common sense suggests. At its core, however, humor is also serious business, serving the latent function of attacking, undermining, or subverting our taken-for-granted beliefs and practices—and, by extension, our established, conventional, and widely accepted culture and society as a whole (Provine, 2000; M. Davis, 1993). Thus, a joke appears funny not only in the positive sense of amusing us but also in the negative sense of ridiculing our established way of life. This fun-making, in effect, turns our established, conventional world upside down. Consider the following joke from a Woody Allen movie:

A boy goes to a psychiatrist, saying, "Doctor, you must help us; my brother thinks he's a chicken."

The psychiatrist exclaims, "You must have him committed at once."

But the boy retorts, "We can't, we need the eggs."

myth	Humor is only fun and games.
reality	Humor may appear on the surface to be merely for laughs, but at its core, it is also serious business. It subverts our popular assumptions and beliefs about sex, marriage, politics, and virtually all other aspects of human life. Sociologist Murray Davis, who has done much research on the subject, concludes that humor is effectively an "attack on culture and society."

With this joke, the humorologist *subverts* our conventional assumption that shared understanding exists between us and others, just as it does between the psychiatrist and the boy. In addition, humorology can subvert not only the assumption about shared understanding but also myriad other estab-

SERIOUSLY FUNNY   On the face of it, humor is only for fun and games. At its core, however, it is also serious business, serving the latent function of attacking, undermining, or subverting our taken-for-granted beliefs and practices. Thus, a joke appears funny not only in the positive sense of amusing us but also in the negative sense of ridiculing our established way of life. This fun-making effectively turns our established, conventional world upside down. ■

lished realities involving friendship, sex, marriage, politics, and virtually all other aspects of human life. In doing so, humor makes us laugh.

But what is it about humor that makes us laugh? The clue can be found in the fact that almost all jokes contain an *incongruity* between two realities, usually an established, conventional one and a subversive, unconventional one (M. Davis, 1993; Helitzer, 1987). These two realities represent conflicting definitions of the same situation. To make people laugh, we first make them clearly aware of their taken-for-granted conventional definition of a situation and then surprise them by contradicting that definition with an unconventional one.

Take another look at the Woody Allen joke just presented. The first sentence sets up a situation to be defined. In the second, the psychiatrist defines the situation to mean that the boy is normal, thereby reinforcing the audience's conventional belief that people who consider their relatives abnormal are normal themselves. But the last sentence, also aptly called the *punch line,* crushes the psychiatrist's definition with the unexpected reality that the boy himself is abnormal. More generally, the punch line shatters the popular belief with the unconventional reality that people who appear normal can indeed be abnormal.

A similar incongruity exists in the following joke from a study by Murray Davis (1993):

My wife comes home and says, "Pack your bags. I just won $20 million in the California lottery."

"Where are we going, Hawaii, Europe?" I ask jubilantly.

She says, "I don't know where you're going, Doug, as long as it's out of here."

The first two sentences set up in our minds the widely accepted assumption that the married couple will share the joy of winning the lottery. The punch line strikes down that assumption with the unexpected, subversive reality that a presumably loving wife wants to be free of her husband.

The reality in the punch line does not always have to be unconventional. It can be any kind of reality as long as it is incongruous with the one just presented. The punch line in the following joke, for example, is hardly unconventional, but it does unexpectedly subvert or contradict a reality previously defined—though with purposeful ambiguity:

Question: Schwarzenegger has a long one, Bush has a short one, the pope has one but doesn't use it, and Madonna doesn't have one. What is it?

Answer: A last name.

The question leads the audience to expect a raunchy answer, only to be contradicted by an innocent one.

sociological frontiers

The World of Online Chat

As suggested earlier, the information superhighway now runs through virtually every country in the world. One link to this superhighway is via an online chat room. Until recently, computer chat had a somewhat shady reputation. It was seen as a way to waste time, the equivalent of talking endlessly on the phone with a dozen friends at once. Even worse, chat brought cybersex into homes around the globe, and many once legitimate chat rooms turned into virtual back alleys where pedophiles and other sexual deviants would lurk.

The character of online chat has improved as its use has quickly spread to other sectors of society, including education, business, and consumer service. It has been estimated that of the over 110 million people using the Internet worldwide, at least 37 to 47 percent use chat in some fashion. America Online, the largest Internet service provider in the United States, has found that its users spend more time in chat rooms than surfing the net. According to a senior producer at Yahoo, chat has become so popular because it is a ubiquitous "every person's tool that can be used in any way anyone would want to use it" (Marriott, 1998b).

Sociologically, online chat is different from face-to-face interaction. This comes through clearly when chat is used as a tool for initiating and carrying on personal relationships, such as friendships and romances. In a chat room, people can mask their true identities, lying about their looks, skills, personalities, and the like. Even if they don't mean to be deceptive, they may not be able to represent themselves as faithfully and accurately as they intend to. If they are shy, for example, they may feel and appear more bold online simply because they are physically and safely alone, rather than in the intimidating presence of the other individuals to whom they're talking. Online chat is also devoid of certain unconscious cues, such as facial movement, body language, tone of voice, and clothing style, all of which can be picked up in face-to-face interactions. In essence, what people present to others in cyberspace are mostly their "virtual selves," which are different from their "real selves" (J. Cohen, 2001).

Consider for example, the case of a man in Holland and a woman in the United States, who met online and finally decided to get married. After their wedding, they had to "start all over," this time trying to know each other's real self. As the woman explained, "I was braver online. . . . You expose yourself more." And her new husband added, "No matter what happens online, it's different. You haven't met for real" (Herbert, 1999a).

 ■ For more of the latest Sociological Frontiers, look up Continuing Update at www.ablongman.com/thio6e.

using *sociology*

How to Use Humor to Improve Your Life

In this chapter, you have seen what humor is made of and what makes things funny. But can you use humor to make yourself happy and healthy? The answer is yes, according to various research findings. One study in Canada showed that stressed people who laugh at funny stories become less depressed than those who do not. Researchers in Pennsylvania found that college students are likely to be in a better mood if they use humor to cope with unpleasant experiences. In a New York study of elderly people who were depressed and suicidal, those who demonstrated an ability to laugh were much more likely to recover. Finally, there is medical evidence that laughter strengthens our immune system, making us less likely to become ill (Lefcourt, 2001a, 2001b; Doskoch, 1996).

You can use laughter in two ways to improve your spirit and health. First, figure out your *humor profile*. Monitor yourself for a few days to see what makes you laugh out loud. Be honest with yourself, though. Don't pretend to like sophisticated humor, such as French farces or Woody Allen's jokes, if your heartiest laughter comes from watching slapstick movies featuring Jim Carrey or the Three Stooges. Next, use your humor pro-

file to set up your own humor library: books, magazines, CDs, videos, and the like. House this collection in a portion of your bedroom or den as a "humor corner." Whenever life gets you down, go in there for a few minutes of laughter (Doskoch, 1996).

Besides using humor to benefit yourself, the functionalist perspective would also suggest that humor could serve some *social* functions. Thinking critically, do you find humor useful in your interactions and relationships with others? If so, in what ways is it useful? If not, why not?

■ CHAPTER REVIEW

1. *How do the three perspectives differ in dealing with social interaction?* The functionalist perspective focuses on the supportive types of interaction: exchange and cooperation. The conflict perspective deals with the oppositional types: competition and conflict. Both perspectives are structural, offering the outside, objective view of interaction. But the third, the symbolic interactionist perspective, delves into the subjective world of social interactants. While the structural perspectives concentrate on the objective, external characteristics of supportive and oppositional interactions, symbolic interactionism penetrates into the subjective internal meanings of these interactions.

2. *How does human communication differ from animal communication?* Animal communication is largely governed by instincts. It is also a closed system, tied to the immediate present, enabling animals to communicate only a limited set of messages. In contrast, human communication is socially constructed, arbitrarily determined by people through their social experiences. It is also an open system in which people are able to create an infinite number of messages.

3. *How does communication differ globally?* Verbal communication varies from one society to another. There is, for example, a greater adherence to the "One speaker at a time" rule in the United States than in other countries. Nonverbal communication also differs; making a circle with a thumb and forefinger has a positive meaning in the United States but a negative one in South America. *What is the nature of diversity in communication in the United States?* Various groups use the same language with different accents, words, and sentences, as well as conversational styles. Group differences also exist in the use of body language and personal space. *How do women and men differ in communication?* They tend to use different genderlects, one emphasizing connection and

intimacy and the other, status and independence. The sexes also differ in proxemics, with men more likely to dominate women by invading their personal space.

4. *What is the dramaturgical view of interaction?* Interaction involves people acting toward each other as if they were performers and audiences in a theater. *How do people present themselves to others?* They display the positive sides of themselves and conceal the negative ones. This frontstage behavior, designed to create a desired impression on others, may differ from backstage activities, in which the performers reveal their true selves. *What is the essence of interaction rituals?* They comprise a show of reverence or respect among people engaged in social interaction. *What is the art of impression management?* To create a desired impression on others, we must use defensive measures, with others offering protective measures.

5. *What is the Thomas theorem?* If people define, see, or believe that something is real, they will act as if it is real or do something to make it real. *What can we learn from ethnomethodology?* When people interact with one another, they define their world in an ambiguous manner, leaving out many specific details, assuming that everybody understands them. *What is the nature of humor that makes people laugh?* Humor consists of the surprising subversion of an established, conventional, or widely accepted reality by a contradicting, unconventional, or unexpected one.

6. *What is the world of online chat like?* Online chat has been spreading rapidly throughout the United States, but the selves people present to others in chat rooms are mostly virtual rather than real. *What can humor do for us?* It can lift our spirit and improve our health.

KEY TERMS

Competition   An interaction in which two individuals follow mutually accepted rules, each trying to achieve the same goal before the other does (p. 100).

Conflict   An interaction in which two individuals disregard any rules, each trying to achieve his or her own goal by defeating the other (p. 100).

Cooperation   An interaction in which two or more individuals work together to achieve a common goal (p. 98).

Dramaturgy   A method of analyzing social interaction as if the participants were performing on a stage (p. 108).

Ethnomethodology   The analysis of how people define the world in which they live (p. 112).

Exchange   An interaction in which two individuals offer each other something in order to obtain a reward in return (p. 98).

Genderlects   Linguistic styles that reflect the different worlds of women and men (p. 106).

Humorology   The study or practice of humor (p. 113).

Interaction ritual   A form of interaction in which the participants perform certain acts to show reverence to each other (p. 110).

Kinesics   The use of body movements as a means of communication; also called *body language* (p. 104).

Oppositional interaction   An interaction in which the participants treat each other as competitors or enemies (p. 98).

Proxemics   The use of space as a means of communication (p. 104).

Role distance   Separating role-playing as outward performance from the inner self (p. 109).

Social construction of reality   The process by which people create through social interaction a certain idea, feeling, or belief about their environment (p. 111).

Social interaction   The process by which individuals act toward and react to others (p. 98).

Supportive interaction   An interaction in which the participants treat each other as supporters or friends (p. 98).

Symbolic interaction   An interaction in which people actively interpret each other's actions and reactions and behave in accordance with the interpretation (p. 98).

Thomas theorem   Sociologist W. I. Thomas's famous pronouncement that "If people define situations as real, they are real in their consequences" (p. 111).

QUESTIONS FOR DISCUSSION AND REVIEW

SOCIOLOGICAL PERSPECTIVES ON SOCIAL INTERACTION

1. What is the difference between *exchange* and *cooperation?*
2. How does *competition* differ from *conflict?*

3. What is the symbolic interactionist view of supportive and oppositional interaction?

INTERACTION AS SYMBOLIC COMMUNICATION

1. In what ways does human communication differ from animal communication?
2. How does communication differ from one society to another?
3. How do various groups in the United States differ in communication?

COMMUNICATION BETWEEN WOMEN AND MEN

1. What are *genderlects,* and how do they affect communication between women and men?
2. How do men and women play the gendered game of proxemics?

DRAMATURGY: INTERACTION AS DRAMA

1. What does Goffman mean by "tactful blindness"? How does it help ensure the success of, for instance, a pelvic examination?
2. How do people present themselves to others?
3. What are interaction rituals? How can these rituals be violated?

THE ART OF MANAGING IMPRESSIONS

1. How can a performer obtain the desired impression from the audience?
2. How does the audience help the performer pull off the show?

THE SOCIAL CONSTRUCTION OF REALITY

1. Why can people be said to be actually interacting with themselves when they are apparently interacting with others?
2. How can we create realities with definitions?
3. How do ethnomethodologists expose the socially constructed reality that guides interaction?
4. How does humor make people laugh?

SOCIOLOGICAL FRONTIERS/USING SOCIOLOGY

1. Is it easier to present your virtual self than your real self in an online chat room? Why or why not?
2. What benefits can we get from humor?

Ⓢuggested readings

Glassner, Barry. 1999. *The Culture of Fear: Why Americans Are Afraid of the Wrong Things.* New York: Basic Books. An easy-to-read analysis of how the media construct scary social realities about such problems as crime, drug abuse, and road rage by exaggerating them.

Goffman, Erving. 1959. *The Presentation of Self in Everyday Life.* New York: Doubleday. The sociological classic on the dramaturgical analysis of social interaction.

Katz, Jack. 1999. *How Emotions Work.* Chicago: University of Chicago Press. A study of how people experience and express such emotions as anger, laughter, shame, and crying in face-to-face interactions with others.

O'Brien, Jodi, and Peter Kollock (eds). 2001. *The Production of Reality: Essays and Readings on Social Interaction,* 3rd ed. Thousand Oaks, CA: Pine Forge Press. A collection of articles about various aspects of social interaction.

Tannen, Deborah. 1994. *Gender and Discourse.* New York: Oxford University Press. An insightful sociolinguistic study of the gender differences in communication.

■ Additional Resources

The New York Times expect the world®
nytimes.com

Expand your knowledge of the concepts discussed in this chapter by reading the following current and historical articles from the *New York Times*. Go to the "eThemes of the Times" section of the Companion Website (www.ablongman.com/thio6e):

"When Schools Feared Only Nuclear Blasts"

Research Navigator.c⊛m

Research Navigator, a research database, provides immediate access to hundreds of full-text articles from EBSCO's ContentSelect Academic Journal Database. If the Research Navigator access code was included with your textbook, go to the website www.research navigator.com and read the following articles related to this chapter by typing in the article number:

Robinson, Dawn T., and Smith-Lovin, Lynn. "Getting a Laugh: Gender, Status, and Humor in Task Discussions." *Social Forces*, Sep2001, Vol. 80 Issue 1, p123, 36p. Accession Number: 5248852. Explores functions of humor within task-oriented group discussions.

Wiggins, Sally. "Talking with Your Mouth Full: Gustatory Mmms and the Embodiment of Pleasure." *Research on Language and Social Interaction*, Jul2002. Accession Number: 7362313. Examines expressions of eating pleasure.

chapter 5

Groups and Organizations

myths & realities

myth *When we look for a job, we can get more help from friends than acquaintances.*

reality Acquaintances are more effective in helping us find a job. We may already be aware of the job openings known to our friends, but we may not know of the many other job opportunities our acquaintances can tell us about (p. 122).

myth *In a group situation, you will never accept someone else's view when you are certain that it is wrong.*

reality The pressure to conform can make you accept that view if it is held by the majority (p. 124).

myth *Universally known for their politeness, the Japanese find it easy to be polite to fellow passengers on a crowded train.*

reality Even Japanese people become rude on a crowded train because a great increase in group size makes it difficult to maintain proper interpersonal relationships and individual recognition (p. 125).

myth *A nice, compassionate person will help a victim whether or not others are around.*

reality People are less likely to help a victim when others are present than when they are alone with the victim (p. 125).

myth *Having a network of friends and relatives can only bring joy and chase away loneliness, worries, and trouble, especially for widows.*

reality Intimates can also make widows feel miserable. According to a study of 120 widows, more than two-thirds of the people who made their lives more difficult were friends and relatives (p. 128).

myth *It's always nice to be your own boss. In small businesses owned and operated by the workers themselves, the workers generally have an easy, pleasant life.*

reality Although workers in such organizations are highly satisfied with their jobs, they tend to work too hard and often suffer stress and burnout as a result (p. 134).

119

A *female university president* was expecting a visit from a male member of the board of trustees. When her secretary told her that the visitor had arrived, she left her office to greet him in the reception area. Before ushering him into her office, the woman handed a letter to her secretary and said: "I've just finished drafting it. *Do you think you could* type it right away? I'd like to get it out before lunch. And *would you please do me a favor* and hold all calls while I'm meeting with Mr. Smith here?" After they were inside her office, with the door closed, Mr. Smith told her that he thought she had spoken inappropriately to her secretary. "Remember," he said, "*you're* the president!" To Mr. Smith, the president seemed self-deprecating and lacking in self-confidence, not giving orders like a man (Tannen, 2001a).

Mr. Smith didn't get it: that many women can run an organization effectively without playing a macho game of domination with their subordinates. In fact, the egalitarian style of management, as shown by the university president's expression of respect to her secretary, has made many female managers more successful in running organizations than their male counterparts, who tend to throw their weight around. To gain a deeper insight into this female approach to management, let us first analyze the basic characteristics of groups and organizations.

SOCIAL GROUPS

In a classic experiment, Muzafer Sherif (1956) took a group of white, middle-class, 12-year-old boys to a summer camp at Robbers' Cave State Park in Oklahoma. Sherif pretended to be a caretaker named Mr. Musee. For the first three days, the boys lived on one site at the camp and became acquainted. Then they were separated. Half of the boys were given one cabin and one set of activities, and the other half were given another. Soon each group had chosen a name, one group calling itself the Eagles and the other the Rattlers. Each group had its own insignia on caps and T-shirts, its own jargon, and its own jokes and secrets.

Each band of boys, in short, had formed a **social group**—a collection of people who interact with one another and have a certain feeling of unity. A social group is more than either a social aggregate or a social category. A **social aggregate** is just a number of people who happen to be in one place but do not interact with one another, such as the boys when they first arrived at the camp or the shoppers at a store lining up to buy something. A **social category** is a number of people who have something in common but who neither interact with one another nor gather in one place. Men as a whole constitute a social category. So do women as a whole, college students as a whole, and so on. A social category becomes a social

group when the people in the category interact with one another and identify themselves as members of the group. Thus, the boys at Robbers' Cave were members of a social category—12-year-old boys—but they became a social group when they began to interact with one another and consider themselves members of the Eagles or the Rattlers. A closer look at Sherif's experiment can give us a clearer idea of the significance of groups.

In-Groups and Out-Groups

A few days after Sherif had put the boys in separate cabins, he arranged for the groups to compete against each other in baseball, tug of war, and other games. The winners of the games were awarded points toward a prize—camp knives. At first, the Eagles and Rattlers were very friendly with each other, but soon the games turned into fierce competitions. The two groups began to call each other stinkers, sneaks, and cheaters. They raided each other's cabins, and scuffles became common.

The boys' behavior showed that in forming each group, the youngsters set up a boundary between themselves as an in-group and the others as an out-group. An **in-group** is the group to which an individual is strongly tied as a member, and an **out-group** is the group of which an individual is not a member. Every social group defines a boundary between itself and everyone else to some extent, but a cohesive in-group has three characteristics. First, members of the in-group normally use symbols such as names, slogans, dress, and badges to identify themselves so that they will be distinguishable from the out-group. As we have seen, one group of boys in Sherif's experiment called itself the Eagles, and the other called itself the Rattlers. Second, members of a cohesive in-group view themselves in terms of positive stereotypes and the out-group in terms of negative stereotypes. Sherif's boys, for example, liked to say things like "We are smart, and they are dumb!" We can also witness similar social behavior among college students: rating their own fraternity, sorority, or organization higher in prestige than someone else's and disparaging others as objectionable. Third, the in-group is inclined to compete or clash with the out-group.

Sherif's experiment showed how easily loyalty to an in-group can generate hostility toward an out-group and even aggression when there is competition for some resource (in this case, prizes). Competition with another group can also strengthen the unity within each group. But there was another phase in Sherif's experiment. He set up situations in which the groups had to work together to solve a common problem. When the camp's sole water tank broke down, he told the groups to work together to repair it. As they cooperated, friendships began to emerge between Eagles and Rattlers. In short, cooperation between the groups eroded the hostility and divisions that competition had spurred.

■ Reference Groups

An in-group can become a **reference group**, a group that is used as the frame of reference for evaluating one's own behavior. Members of a street gang, for example, may evaluate themselves by the standards of the gang and feel proud about a successful mugging. This positive self-evaluation reflects the *normative effect* of a reference group whose members share the same view of themselves. If other members of your reference group (say, your parents) have high self-esteem, you, too, are likely to share that norm and have high self-esteem. The normative effect basically involves imitating the reference group. However, reference groups can also have *comparison effects* and *associative effects* on self-appraisals. If most of your classmates shine in academic achievement, you are likely to compare yourself with them. As a result, you may have a negative self-evaluation, feeling that your academic performance is not up to par. Being associated with the brilliant group, though, makes you feel proud of yourself, "basking in reflected glory" (Felson and Reed, 1986).

"Of course you're going to be depressed if you keep comparing yourself with successful people."

Source: © The New Yorker Collection 1991 William Hamilton from Cartoonbank.com. All Rights Reserved.

These reference groups are at the same time in-groups. But we do not have to be members of a group to use it as our reference group. As a student, you might have professional athletes as your reference group. If that is the case, you will probably judge your athletic skills to be inadequate—even if they are excellent compared with those of most amateurs—and perhaps you will work harder in an effort to meet professional standards.

Whether we are members of reference groups or not, they frequently exert a powerful influence on our behavior and attitudes, as has been suggested. In fact, their impact became well known long ago, after Theodore Newcomb (1958) published his study of the students at Bennington College, a very liberal college in Vermont. Newcomb found that most of the students came from conservative families and that most of the freshmen were conservative. A small minority remained conservative throughout their time at the college, but most became more liberal the longer they stayed. These students, Newcomb concluded, used the liberal faculty or older students as their reference group, whereas the minority continued to look to their conservative families as their reference group.

Primary and Secondary Groups

It is not at all surprising that some students used their families as a reference group. After all, families are the best examples of the groups Charles Cooley (1909) called *primary* chiefly because they "are fundamental in forming the social nature and ideals of the individual." As mentioned in the preceding chapter, in *primary groups,* the individuals interact informally, relate to each other as whole persons, and enjoy their relationship for its own sake. Families, peer groups, fraternities, sororities, neighbors, friends, and small communities are all examples of primary groups. They are marked by *primary relationships.* This is one of the two main types of social groups. In the other type, *secondary groups,* the individuals engage in *secondary relationships.* The people in such relationships do not know each other personally. They may have little face-to-face interaction. If they interact, they do so formally. They relate to each other only in terms of particular roles and for certain practical purposes.

Consider salesclerks and their customers. In these secondary groups, there are likely to be few if any emotional ties, and the people know little about each other. Their communications are bound by formalities. Salesclerks are not likely to kiss their customers or to cry with them over the death of a relative. The clerk will treat the customer as a customer only—not as a person who is also a mother of three, a jazz lover,

a victim of an airplane hijacking, or a person who laughs easily but worries a lot. In contrast, we expect our families to treat us as whole persons, to be interested in our experiences, preferences, and feelings. The clerk is also likely to treat one customer much like another. We expect this attitude in a clerk, but the same attitude in our family or friends would hurt our feelings. Finally, the clerk and the customer have a relationship only because each has a specific task or purpose in mind: to buy or sell something. They use their relationship for this purpose.

The relationship among family members, in contrast, is not oriented to a particular task but is engaged in for its own sake. In fact, if we believe that a person in a primary group is interested in us only as a means to some end, we are likely to feel used. Parents are hurt if they feel their children are interested only in the food, shelter, and money the parents provide.

myth	When we look for a job, we can get more help from friends than acquaintances.
reality	Acquaintances are more effective in helping us find a job. We may already be aware of the job openings known to our friends, but we may not know of the many other job opportunities our acquaintances can tell us about.

TIES THAT BIND   As members of a primary group, these sorority sisters have strong emotional ties. They interact informally and relate to one another as unique, whole persons. They also enjoy their relationship for its own sake. Primary relationships are thus precious and helpful to us, especially when we are going through hard times. ■

Primary relationships—with our relatives, friends, and neighbors—are precious to us. As research has shown, they are particularly helpful when we are going through stressful life events. They help ease recovery from heart attacks, prevent childbirth complications, make childrearing easier, lighten the burden of household finances, and cushion the impact of job loss by providing financial assistance and employment information. However, primary relationships are not always more beneficial than secondary relationships. Our close friends cannot help us get as good a job as our acquaintances can. Our friends move in the same social circle we do, but our acquaintances, to whom we have only weak ties, move in different circles. Hence, we may already be aware of the job openings known to our friends, but we may not know of the many other job opportunities our acquaintances can tell us about (Bridges and Villemez, 1986; Granovetter, 1983).

GROUP CHARACTERISTICS

All social groups possess certain characteristics. The ones that sociologists have often studied or analyzed include group leadership, idiosyncrasy credit, group conformity, group size, and social diversity.

■ Group Leadership

In most groups, there are three types of leaders. **Instrumental leaders** are those who achieve their group's goal by getting others to focus on task performance. They may say something like "Let's get to work!" or "I think we're getting off the track." Such tactics show the leaders as overseers, whose exchange with followers involves a unidirectional downward influence and a weak sense of common fate. This is why such leaders are also known as *autocratic leaders*. Although this kind of leadership can get the group to move toward a goal, it can also rub people the wrong way. Not surprisingly, most people tend not to like their instrumental leaders.

On the other hand, most people tend to like their **expressive leaders**, who achieve group harmony by making others feel good. They are also known as *democratic leaders*. This second type of leader is more concerned with members' feelings, making sure that everybody is happy, so that cohesiveness can reign in the group. The exchange between such leaders and their followers reflects a partnership, characterized by reciprocal influence, a strong sense of common fate, and mutual trust, respect, and liking.

The third type of leader, the **laissez-faire** (from French, pronounced le-say-FAIR, meaning "let do")

CALLING THE SHOTS Instrumental leaders are primarily task oriented, concerned about achieving goals. Expressive leaders are person oriented, more concerned with their followers' feelings, making sure that harmony and cohesiveness can prevail in the group. Laissez-faire leaders are independence oriented, letting followers perform largely on their own. The coach of this football team exhibits one or more of these three leadership styles. ■

leader, lets others work more or less on their own. It is widely assumed that people, especially those with much education or special skill, will perform well if left relatively alone—with a minimum of direction, instruction, or supervision from above. This independence, however, often exacts a price: little or no social support. Understandably, most people like the laissez-faire leader less than the expressive, democratic leader but more than the instrumental, autocratic leader.

Of the three types, instrumental leadership is most effective in achieving group productivity. Expressive leadership is less effective, and laissez-faire leadership is least effective (Johnson and Johnson, 1997). A combination of these three leadership styles is typically found in the same person, except that one style usually predominates over the others.

■ Idiosyncrasy Credit

Because they are seen as competently performing certain tasks for the group, leaders are usually given an **idiosyncrasy credit**, the privilege that allows leaders to deviate from their groups' norms or, by extension, their society's norms. Understanding this point may go a long way toward understanding a social phenomenon that defies common sense. For nearly a year in 1998, former President Bill Clinton was first widely suspected to have had a sexual affair with a young White House intern and was later widely known to have lied about it to the grand jury and the nation. In the midst of all this scandal, however, Clinton continued to be popular with the U.S. public. His approval rating even shot up one day after the incriminating videotape of his grand-jury testimony was telecast all over the country. Clinton's job rating was also even higher than that of the Republican-dominated Congress, which impeached but failed to remove him from office.

Clinton is not the only president in U.S. history who flourished in the midst of a sex scandal. A number of other presidents, including Jefferson, Jackson, Cleveland, and Wilson, were equally popular with the general public despite an enormous amount of publicity about their sexual indiscretions. Cleveland, for example, was widely known in the 1880s to have fathered an illegitimate child but was elected president, and in the next two elections, he received the most votes despite widespread stories about wife beating and alcoholism (Collins, 1998).

The idiosyncrasy credit stems from people's favorable perceptions of their leaders, especially the perception that their leaders are highly competent. Thus, every time an American president proves his worth to the masses, he accumulates some idiosyncrasy credit in the bank of public opinion, which he can spend later by engaging in deviant acts with relative impunity (Estrada et al., 1995; Hollander, 1986).

■ Group Conformity

While leaders are often given an idiosyncrasy credit, the rank and file are expected to conform to the group's norms. In a group, the pressure to conform is so powerful that individual members tend to knuckle under, going along with the majority even though they privately disagree with it (Hogan, 2001).

myth	In a group situation, you will never accept someone else's view when you are certain that it is wrong.
reality	The pressure to conform can make you accept that view if it is held by the majority.

This point has been driven home by Solomon Asch's (1955) classic experiments. Asch brought together groups of eight or nine students each. He asked them to tell him which of the three lines on a card was as long as the line on another card, as shown in Figure 5.1. In each group only one person was a real subject; the others were the experimenter's

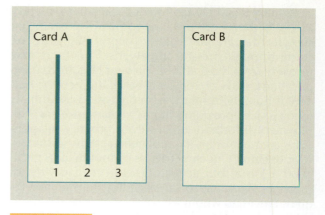

FIGURE 5.1

Would You Conform?

Asch's experiments suggest that if you are asked privately which line on card A is as long as the line on card B, there is a 99 percent chance that you will correctly pick line 2. But if you find yourself in a group in which all the other members choose line 3—an obviously wrong answer—there is about a 33 percent chance that you will yield to the group pressure to conform by choosing line 3.

Critical Thinking: *What repercussions might you face if you speak out against a majority decision?*

secret accomplices, who had been instructed to give the same obviously wrong answer. Asch found that nearly a third of the subjects changed their minds and accepted the majority's answer even though they were sure that their own answer was correct and that the answer of the others was wrong.

Perhaps it was no big deal for Asch's subjects to conform by matching lines. But would they have conformed if the task was much more serious? This is exactly what Asch's former student, Stanley Milgram (1974), tried to find out. He told each of his subjects to play the role of teacher and work with two other supposed teachers, who actually were Milgram's accomplices. They were asked to decide how much electric shock to give to a person who took the role of student every time the student gave the wrong answer to a question. Actually, this student was also Milgram's accomplice. Whenever the subjects pressed the shock machine, they could see the student's painful expression. Unknown to the subjects, the machine was a fake and the student was faking, but the subjects were led to believe that they were really administering electric shocks. When the other two teachers suggested increasing the level of shock with each wrong answer the student made, most of the subjects went along and did it, even though they saw and believed that the student was screaming with excruciating pain.

The groups to which Asch's and Milgram's subjects felt compelled to conform were strangers. The pressure to conform is even greater among people we know. It usually gives rise to what Irving Janis (1982) calls **groupthink**, the tendency for members of a cohesive group to maintain a consensus to the extent of ignoring the truth. Groupthink may lead to disastrous decisions, with tragic consequences. It caused President John F. Kennedy and his top advisors to approve the CIA's unsound plan to invade Cuba, and it caused President Lyndon B. Johnson and his advisors to escalate the Vietnam War. Groupthink is also what caused President George W. Bush and his advisors to exaggerate the nuclear threat posed by Iraq's dictator. In each case, a few members had serious doubts about the majority decision but did not speak out.

It is even more difficult to voice dissent if the leader rules with an iron hand. About 40 years ago, when Nikita Khrushchev, ruler of what was then the Soviet Union, came to the United States, he met with reporters at the Washington Press Club. The first anonymously written question he received was: "Today you talked about the hideous rule of your predecessor, Stalin, who killed thousands of his political opponents. You were one of his closest aides and colleagues during those years. What were you doing all that time?" Khrushchev's face turned red. "Who asked that?" he shouted. No one answered. "Who asked that?" he shouted again. Still no answer. Then Khrushchev said, "That's what I was doing: keeping my mouth shut" (Bennis, 1989). Because of this fear of questioning authority, most people will follow orders from an authority in the same way as the German Nazis did when told by their leaders to commit atrocities against the Jews. This is the conclusion Stanley Milgram (1974) reached after he saw that most of the subjects in his best-known experiment inflicted severe pain on the student when told to do so by him as an authority figure.

■ Group Size

In addition to pressuring people to conform, social groups also cause them to behave in other ways. This has a lot to do with the specific size of groups.

The smallest group is a *dyad,* which contains two people. As German sociologist Georg Simmel (1858–1918) suggested long ago, a dyad can easily become the most cohesive of all the groups because its members are inclined to be most personal and to interact most intensely with each other. This is why we are more willing to share our secrets in a dyad than in a larger group, secrets such as our parents getting divorced or a relative having been committed to a mental hospital. A dyad, however, is also the least

durable or the most likely to break up. If just one person leaves, the group will vanish.

Such a threat does not exist for a *triad,* a three-person group. If one member drops out, the group can still survive. A triad also makes it possible for two people to gang up on the third or for one member to patch up a quarrel between the other two. But triads lose the quality of intimacy that is the hallmark of dyads. As the saying goes, "Two's company; three's a crowd."

If more people join the group, it will become even less personal, with each individual finding it extremely difficult to talk and relate to each of the other members. The increase in group size, then, weakens interpersonal relationships. But it also enhances group durability by greatly increasing the number of relationships among its members. As Figure 5.2 (p. 126) shows, the addition of only one person to a group increases significantly the number of relationships. The larger the number of relationships, the more subgroups there are, and the more power they have in coming together to prevent anyone from breaking up the larger group.

myth	Universally known for their politeness, the Japanese find it easy to be polite to fellow passengers on a crowded train.
reality	Even Japanese people become rude on a crowded train because a great increase in group size makes it difficult to maintain proper interpersonal relationships and individual recognition.

Generally, however, as a group grows larger, it changes for the worse. Its members become less satisfied, participate less often in group activities, are less likely to cooperate with one another, and are more likely to misbehave. Even the Japanese, universally known for their politeness, may become rude on a crowded train. This is because an increase in group size makes it difficult to maintain interpersonal relationships and individual recognition (Levine and Moreland, 1990; Mullen et al., 1989).

myth	A nice, compassionate person will help a victim whether or not others are around.
reality	People are less likely to help a victim when others are present than when they are alone with the victim.

There are other, more fascinating effects of group size. In a dyad or triad, the host usually has the edge over the visitor; the host is more likely to get his or

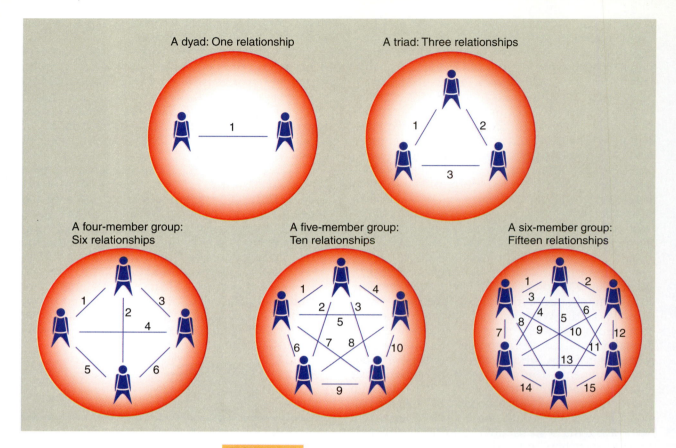

FIGURE 5.2

How the Number of Relationships Increases

The addition of only one person to a group greatly increases the number of relationships. This makes the group more durable, but its members become less satisfied, participate less in group activities, cooperate less with each other, and misbehave more often.

Critical Thinking: *Other than being more durable, what benefits can a larger group offer its members?*

her own way. Thus, a businessperson can strike a better deal by inviting the other person to his or her office. But such territorial dominance—the so-called home court advantage—may disappear if the group is larger than a triad. In public places, a large group may also inhibit an individual from helping someone in distress. More than 50 studies have shown consistently that people are less likely to help a victim if others are around than if they are alone with the victim. A major reason is that the knowledge that others are present and available to respond allows the individual to shift some of the responsibility to others. The same factor operates in "social loafing": As the size of a group performing a certain task increases, each member tends to work less hard (Latané and Nida, 1981).

■ Social Diversity

Some groups are more diverse than others, such that a larger number of members differ in ethnicity, gender, personality, skill, or other qualities. Generally, the more diverse a group, the more effective it is in achieving its goal. Research has found, for example, that athletic teams with a wide range of different skills among their members often outperform teams with less diverse skills, and in banking, the more heterogeneous the personnel, the more likely the bank

WHAT ARE FRIENDS FOR?
A social network acts as a support system for its members. Although friends can often place demands on our time and resources, at the same time, they boost our self-esteem, provide companionship and activity, and often give instrumental support to help us through tough times. ■

is to adopt innovative practices, make high-quality decisions, and become successful (Johnson and Johnson, 1997).

Why is diversity so useful? Diverse groups have more ways of solving a problem than less diverse ones. Suppose each member of any group has only one way of solving a problem. Now, a group of, say, five people who think differently and see the world differently will devise five different ways of solving a problem, while a group of five people who think alike and see the world the same way may have only one way of solving the problem. A diverse group, then, can draw on an ample supply of ideas and data, but a homogeneous group is more likely to suffer from a shortage of ideas and data. In addition, a diverse group is unlikely to have the problems that often plague a homogeneous group, such as the tendency to engage in groupthink and difficulty in adapting to changing conditions (Johnson and Johnson, 1997).

If you join a diverse group, it can benefit you. For one thing, it can help you get a good job because its variety of members will know about many more different jobs than you are likely to know about on your own. But members of your homogeneous group are likely to know about the same jobs already known to you. The diversity of a group can further make you healthier by providing a lot of new information about health, diet, and exercise. Belonging to a diverse group can even make you happier because, as the saying goes, "Variety is the very spice of life" (especially compared to the boring sameness in social

background among members of a homogeneous group) (Erickson, 2003).

SOCIAL NETWORKS

Regardless of size, groups can develop **social networks**, webs of social relationships that link individuals or groups to one another. We are all involved in numerous networks. Since birth, we have been constantly developing or expanding our networks by forming social ties with various people who come into our lives. As soon as we were born, our parents drew us into their networks, which became our own. When we began to attend school, we started to develop social ties with children in our neighborhoods, with our schoolmates and teachers, and with children in our churches, synagogues, or other places of worship. As adults, we often get involved in all kinds of networks, such as those at the college we attend, the place where we work, and the social organizations we belong to. These networks, however, are quite different from the ones that we joined before we turned 17 or 18. Our current adult networks are more diffuse, more loosely organized, and characterized by weaker social ties.

Individuals are not the only ones who join and develop social networks. Groups, organizations, and even nation-states also forge ties with each other. That is why there are numerous intergroup networks (for example, among lawyers, judges, doctors, business executives, and other professional groups), intercommunity networks (such as the U.S. Conference of Mayors), and international networks (such as the United Nations). Thanks to the emergence of cyberspace, people everywhere are being increasingly drawn into the worldwide computer network, as well.

■ Attributes

To make it easier to see what networks look like, sociologists use such devices as points (technically called *nodes*) and lines (or *links*) to represent them. A point can be a person, group, or nation-state. A line can be any kind of social relationship connecting two points. The relationship can be a friendship; an exchange of visits; a business transaction; a romantic entanglement; the flow of information, resources, influence, or power; or an expression of feelings such as affection, sympathy, or hostility.

Consider what your college network may look like. Let's make A in Figure 5.3 represent you and B, C, D, and E your friends. The lines show that all five of you are *directly* connected to one another. Your college network also comprises 12 other people, namely, F through Q. This is because four of you—A, B, C, and D—are *indirectly* tied, through E, to those individuals. Because of your (A's) friendship with E and E's friendship with F, you belong to the same network as F and all the other individuals, whom you may not know. Thus, a social network can consist of both directly and indirectly connected individuals. Because each of the numerous individuals to whom you are indirectly linked knows, directly and indirectly, numerous other people, you may ultimately belong to a network involving millions of people all over the world. This is especially true today because easily accessible air travel or telecommunication has made it possible for people from many different countries to establish links with one another.

Given the massive network to which we belong, we should not be surprised to meet a total stranger in some faraway city, state, or foreign country and discover that the stranger happens to know somebody that we know. On such an occasion, that stranger and we are likely to exclaim, "What a small world!" Indeed, one study showed that most Americans know someone who knows someone who died in the September 11 terrorist attacks, although they may not be aware of this connection (Mattson, 2002).

■ Effects

A social network usually acts as a support system for its members. It helps members maintain good physical and mental health or prevent physical and mental breakdown. It also reduces the risk of dying prematurely or of committing suicide. There are several reasons for this. Our friends, relatives, and coworkers, as part of our social network, can make us feel good by boosting our self-esteem despite our faults, weaknesses, and difficulties. Being more objective than we are about our own problems, they can open our eyes to solutions that we are too distressed emotionally to see. The companionship and camaraderie of our network, fortified by frequent participation in joint recreational activities, can bring us joy while chasing away loneliness, worries, and trouble. Finally, our friends and relatives often give us *instrumental support*—money and service—to help us cope with our problems. All these social-psychological factors have a physiological impact on our health: They keep our blood pressure and heart rate at low levels, presumably by lowering our brain's secretion of stress hormones (Pescosolido and Georgianna, 1989; House et al., 1988; Lin, 1982).

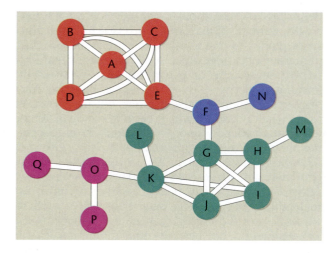

FIGURE 5.3

A Social Network

In this network, individuals A, B, C, D, and E are directly linked to one another. But through E's friendship with F, the other four members (A, B, C, and D) are indirectly connected to F, and all five of them (A, B, C, D, and E) are also indirectly linked to G, H, I, and so on. Thus, a social network can consist of both directly and indirectly connected individuals.

Critical Thinking: *How does your membership in any one social network affect your life?*

myth	Having a network of friends and relatives can only bring joy and chase away loneliness, worries, and trouble, especially for widows.
reality	Intimates can also make widows feel miserable. According to a study of 120 widows, more than two-thirds of the people who made their lives more difficult were friends and relatives.

On the other hand, our intimates make many demands on our time and personal resources. They can irritate us by criticizing us or invading our privacy. In fact, in a study of the social networks of 120 widows, the women reported that more than two-thirds of the people who made their lives more difficult were their friends and relatives.

These negative experiences seem to drag down people's sense of well-being more than the positive experiences of receiving social support raise it. Negative encounters usually have a stronger impact than positive ones because an argument sticks out like a sore thumb against a background of generally pleasant experiences. Thus, a pleasant exchange at a wedding that is already filled with strife between in-laws can restore only a little peacefulness, but a single heated exchange at an otherwise tranquil wedding can ruin the whole experience. In sum, social networks can have both positive and negative consequences for people's lives (Scott, 2002; Fischman, 1986).

▌FORMAL ORGANIZATIONS

Of the various kinds of social groups that we have discussed, secondary groups are the most likely to develop into **formal organizations**, groups whose activities are rationally designed to achieve specific goals. Not all secondary groups become formal organizations, though. Some secondary groups are small and transitory, without explicitly stated goals and rules. A salesclerk and a customer interact on a temporary basis to achieve a generally known but unstated objective without following any explicitly described rules for carrying out the business transaction. This is not a formal organization. Other secondary groups are large and more permanent, with explicit goals and working procedures. Government agencies, for instance, often last well beyond their members' lifetimes and are large and complex. Their goals and rules must be stated explicitly so that the work of their many members can be coordinated. These agencies—along with hospitals, colleges, business firms, political parties, branches of the U.S. military, groups such as the Sierra Club, and so on—are examples of formal organizations.

▪ Types of Formal Organizations

According to Amitai Etzioni (1975), virtually every organization includes *higher participants* (such as the administrators) and *lower participants* (the rank and file). The function of the higher participants is to exercise power over the lower participants so that the latter will help the organization achieve its goals. Three kinds of power are available to higher partici-

pants: (1) *coercive power,* the use of physical force; (2) *remunerative power,* the use of material rewards such as money and similar incentives to ensure cooperation; and (3) *normative power,* the use of moral persuasion, the prestige of a leader, or the promise of social acceptance.

There are also three kinds of involvement by lower participants: (1) *alienative,* in which they do not support the organization's goals; (2) *calculative,* in which they are moderately supportive; and (3) *moral,* in which they strongly support the organization.

From these kinds of power and involvement, Etzioni constructed the following typology of organizations:

	Kinds of Involvement		
Kinds of Power	Alienative	Calculative	Moral
Coercive	1	2	3
Remunerative	4	5	6
Normative	7	8	9

Of the nine types, only three—1, 5, and 9—represent the huge majority of organizations. These, then, are the most common types; the remaining six are rare. Etzioni called the three most common types *coercive organizations* (type 1), *utilitarian organizations* (type 5), and *normative organizations* (type 9).

Coercive Organizations Prisons, concentration camps, and custodial psychiatric hospitals are examples of coercive organizations. In each, force or the threat of force is used to achieve the organization's main goal: keeping the inmates in. The inmates obviously do not enjoy being imprisoned; they will run away if they have the chance. They are alienated from the organization and do not support its goals at all. Understandably, the higher participants—such as prison administrators—have to act tough toward the inmates, seeking compliance by threatening solitary confinement if they try to escape. In brief, in this kind of organization, coercion is the main form of power used, and the involvement by lower participants is alienative.

Utilitarian Organizations Factories, banks, and other businesses are all utilitarian organizations in Etzioni's classification. The higher participants (employers) use incentives such as money to ensure that the lower participants (employees) work to achieve the organization's goals. The employees tend to be moderately supportive of those goals. They are likely to calculate whether it is worth their while to work hard, asking, "What's in it for me?"

In general, the more attractive their remuneration—in money, fringe benefits, and working

MONEY TALKS In a utilitarian organization, the higher participants—such as Bill Gates, the chairman of Microsoft—use incentives such as money to ensure that the lower participants—the employees—work hard to achieve the organization's goals. In general, the more attractive the remuneration offered, in the form of money, fringe benefits, and working conditions, the harder the rank and file will work for the organization. ■

conditions—the more committed lower participants are to the organization. Thus, the major form of power used in utilitarian organizations is remunerative, and the typical form of involvement by lower-level participants is calculative.

Normative Organizations If Mormons do not pay their tithes, they may be denied access to religious services, but they are not subject to arrest and imprisonment. If a political party wants you to vote for its candidates, it may send you letters, phone you, or knock on your door, and it will certainly advertise, but it does not offer you money. Churches and political parties are examples of a type of organization very different from coercive and utilitarian organizations. Their power over lower participants is based on persuasion, exhortation, social pressure, public recognition, or even a leader's appeal. This normative power is sufficient because most of the participants generally want to do what the organization is asking; they are strongly committed to its goals. For this reason, normative organizations are sometimes called *voluntary associations*. In addition to religious and political organizations, examples include colleges, social clubs, and charitable organizations. In Etzioni's terms, their primary form of power is normative, and involvement by the rank and file is moral.

Mixed Organizations In fact, no organization relies entirely on just one type of power. All three types can be found in most organizations. Still, the majority do use one type of power far more than the other two. Prisons, for example, may use normative power through rehabilitation programs, but they still rely mostly on coercion. A business may use speeches to inspire its workers, but it depends mostly on wages to ensure their involvement.

Although rare, some organizations do depend on two or three types of power each to about the same degree. A good example is the military. In many countries in which military service is *compulsory* (see Figure 5.4), it is not necessary to rely on remunerative power by offering large sums of money to induce citizens to become soldiers and risk life and limb. But once they have been drafted, both coercive and normative powers are used to control them. Thus, the military applies coercion by confining uncooperative soldiers to the base and by imprisoning or executing mutineers and deserters. The military further applies normative power through basic training, military schools, and patriotic pep talks. However, in some countries, such as the United States, where serving in the armed forces is *voluntary*, renumeration is added as the third type of power. When there is a draft, as during the Vietnam War, volunteer soldiers are paid much better than their drafted counterparts.

An Evaluation Etzioni's typology is useful for knowing the characteristics of practically all organizations. It also explains why some organizations flounder while others sail smoothly. As Etzioni suggests, organizational effectiveness depends on running an outfit for what it is. A prison managed like a coercive organization, a business firm operated like a utilitarian organization, and a political party run like a normative organization can all be expected to do well. On the other hand, a prison run like a political party and a business firm operated like a prison would both probably be in trouble.

However, because Etzioni concentrates on what goes on inside organizations, his typology ignores environmental, contextual, and external influences.

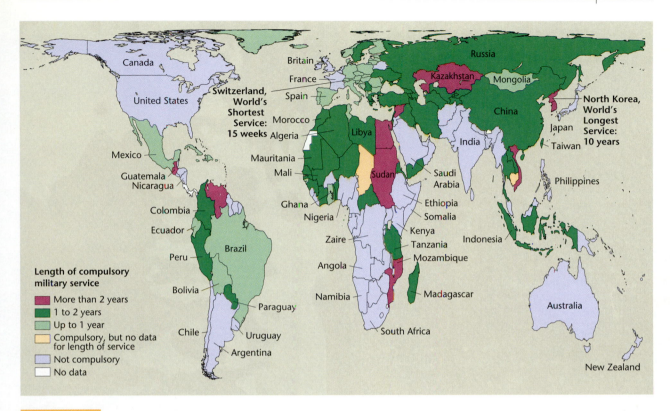

FIGURE 5.4

The Military as a Mixed Organization

In many countries in which serving in the armed forces is *compulsory*, the military is both a coercive and normative organization. It uses physical force, such as imprisonment and execution, to punish disobedience and desertion and employs persuasion, such as pep talks, to instill pride in its membership. The length of compulsory service varies greatly from one country to another. In some countries, however, military service is *voluntary*. In them, military organizations are still coercive and normative, but in addition, they are utilitarian, using monetary reward to turn volunteers into professional soldiers.

Critical Thinking: *Should the U.S. military service be compulsory or voluntary? Why?*

Source: From *The Penguin Atlas of War and Peace,* by Dan Smith, copyright © 2003 by Dan Smith. Used by permission of Penguin, a division of Penguin Group (USA) Inc.

Outside factors do affect organizations significantly. For example, societal and cultural differences make Swedish prisons less coercive than U.S. prisons. Also, because of social and cultural differences, Japanese firms are run more like normative organizations, whereas U.S. companies are managed more like utilitarian organizations.

■ Classifying Organizational Theories

All around us, we find organizations using the types of control Etzioni described. Much as we might try to stay in the warmer world of friends and family, we cannot escape these organizations and their power. How the organizations use power affects how they operate, as well as our ability to achieve goals we share with them.

Many attempts have been made to analyze just how organizations operate and what types of operations are most efficient. Under what circumstances, for example, can an organization do without moral persuasion? What is the most effective way to offer remunerative rewards? How should managers and workers interact if the organization is to be effective? Answers can be found in organizational theories.

A large number of theories have been proposed since the early twentieth century. Some describe what organizations are like; most suggest what they *should* be like to achieve their goals. These organizational theories can be classified into three types according to how they may have been influenced by the three major sociological perspectives:

1. Theories that may be considered *functionalist* portray organizations as conflict-free, harmonious systems in which members cooperate to achieve a common goal. Two such theories suggest that the goal can be attained by encouraging employees, through *scientific management* and *human relations,* to work harder.

2. Organizational theories influenced by the *conflict* model are critical of social inequality, regarding it as harmful to organizations. Two such theories (*collectivist* and *feminist*), therefore, emphasize social equality as the key to organizational success.

3. Theories that may be regarded as *symbolic interactionist* focus on definitions of the situation in organizations. One such theory says that an organization can succeed if its members share a positive view of the organization. Another such theory suggests that the Western view of rationality ensures bureaucratic efficiency.

In the following sections, we will take a closer look at how these three types of theories suggest different ways of running an organization successfully.

FUNCTIONALIST PERSPECTIVE: COOPERATING TO ACHIEVE A COMMON GOAL

For functionalists, organizations are essentially free of human conflict. Members come together to cooperate in achieving a common goal. Given such a harmonious environment, it is relatively easy to induce members to increase their productivity for the betterment of everybody in the organization. Two well-known theories have been proposed to show how this can be done.

■ Scientific Management

Early in the twentieth century, U.S. engineer Frederick Taylor (1911) published the first systematic presentation of what was soon called *scientific management.* Taylor assumed that the primary goal of an organization is to maximize efficiency. For a manufacturing company this means getting maximum productivity, the highest possible output per worker per hour. The achievement of this goal, Taylor argued, depends on three elements: maximum division of labor, close supervision of workers, and an incentive system of piecework wages.

To obtain maximum division of labor, production must be broken down into numerous simple, easy-

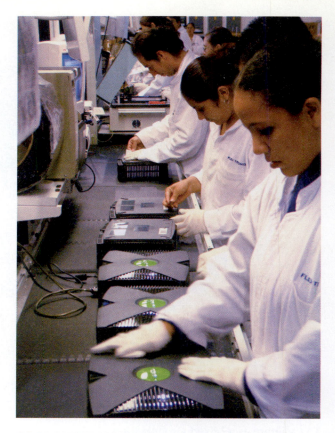

COGS IN THE MACHINE   The scientific management model of industrial organization suggests that a company can achieve maximum productivity if its workers do a simple repetitive task under close supervision. Scientific management works best in manufacturing companies, where the work is mostly routine, but it has been criticized for treating workers as machines. ■

to-perform tasks. Each of these tasks is then defined down to the tiniest detail so that it can be completed in the shortest time possible. One of Taylor's specific recommendations was that zigzag motions of the hands must be avoided; workers should begin and complete their motions with both hands simultaneously. To ensure that the task is properly carried out, the worker must be closely and continuously supervised. Taylor suggested that there be four types of supervisors—setting-up boss, speed boss, quality inspector, and repair boss—and that the supervisors, in turn, should be controlled by a planning department. Finally, to be sure that they work as hard as possible, workers should be paid by the piece: The more units each worker produces, the higher the pay.

Today, many companies still apply Taylor's basic principles. Productivity appears to decline if the basic features of this model are not applied to some degree.

Scientific management works particularly well in the world of production, where the work is mostly routine. But the theory ignores many aspects of organizations and human behavior. It looks only at the *official* organization, the formal relationships between workers and supervisors. Most sociologists have criticized the theory for treating human beings as machines, arguing that such treatment contributes to worker dissatisfaction and ultimately to lower productivity.

■ Human Relations

In the early 1930s, industrial psychologist Elton Mayo (1933) challenged practically all the assumptions of the scientific management theory. His argument consisted of several points:

1. Workers' productivity is not determined by their physical capacity but by their *social capacity,* their sensitivity to the work environment. No matter how fast they *can* do their jobs, they will not produce a lot if their fellow workers frown on the idea of working too fast.
2. Noneconomic rewards, such as friendship with coworkers and respect from management, play a central role in determining the motivation and happiness of workers. Thus, wages are less important than Taylor claimed.
3. The greatest specialization is not the most efficient division of labor. Extreme specialization creates problems for those coordinating the work. Supervisors are hard put to know all the details of very specialized tasks.
4. Workers react to management and its incentives not as isolated individuals but as members of a group. They will reject management's offer of high pay for maximum productivity if their fellow workers are against working too hard.

These points make up the *human relations theory.* In contrast to scientific management, it emphasizes that productivity depends on social forces, especially the informal relations among workers. The key to increased productivity is not the official organization, as Taylor assumed, but the **informal organization**, a group formed by the informal relationships among members of an organization—based on personal interactions, not on any plan by the organization.

Empirical support for this theory came from the classic study at the Hawthorne plant in Chicago in the 1930s (Roethlisberger and Dickson, 1939). The study showed that workers increased their productivity regardless of changes in the physical environment. Productivity went up, for example, when the experimenter brightened the workplace, but it also when he dimmed the lights. The researchers concluded that the employees worked harder because the presence of the researcher made them feel important; management seemed to be treating them as people, not as mere machines.

Another study at the same plant examined whether output was determined by financial incentives. Surprisingly, it was shaped by an informal norm. The norm forbade working too quickly, as well as working too slowly. Anyone working too quickly was ridiculed as a "rate buster," and anyone working too slowly was scorned as a "chiseler." As a result, each worker tried to produce as much as the other workers rather than meet management's goals. These studies clearly showed that informal relations can increase worker productivity.

The human relations theory covers parts of the organization ignored by scientific management, but it too has limitations. First, it exaggerates the importance of informal group life at the workplace. Most workers do not wake up every morning feeling that they cannot wait to go to work in order to be with their coworkers. They are more interested in their families and friends outside the workplace. Second, informal social relations may create more pleasant conditions in the plant, but they cannot significantly reduce the tediousness of the manual job itself. While a person may enjoy working with certain individuals, that cannot transform an inherently boring job into an exciting one. Relations with coworkers, though, may be more significant to white-collar and professional workers, whose jobs often involve a great deal of interaction with coworkers, than to blue-collar workers.

CONFLICT PERSPECTIVE: EQUALITY AS KEY TO ORGANIZATIONAL SUCCESS

According to the conflict perspective, the major problem with the scientific management and human relations theories is that they fail to take into account the reality of conflict in organizations. Given the inequality in income, status, and other rewards between management and workers, the lower participants cannot be expected to give their all to fulfill the higher participants' wish for maximum productivity. The inequality severely limits how far management can successfully use scientific management or human relations to manipulate workers into becoming superproducers. By contrast, the practice of equality can help ensure organizational success. This is the main point of the collectivist and feminist models of organization, which have been influenced by the conflict perspective.

■ Collectivist Model

According to Karl Marx, capitalist organizations—or business corporations—are the capitalists' tool for exploiting the working class. Eventually, Marx claimed, the corporations will be abolished in a classless, communist society. They will be replaced by *collectivist* organizations in which managers and workers work together as equals and for equal pay. The workers will be much more productive than the exploited ones of today. In the meantime, an approximation of this organizational model exists to some extent in the United States.

The typical U.S. corporation is bureaucratic, paternalistic, and undemocratic: Those on the top dictate to those below, and those at the bottom may not choose who is above them or who influences their decisions. Power, then, flows from the top down. By contrast, in a collectivist organization, power flows from the bottom up.

myth	It's always nice to be your own boss. In small businesses owned and operated by the workers themselves, the workers generally have an easy, pleasant life.
reality	Although workers in such organizations are highly satisfied with their jobs, they tend to work too hard and often suffer stress and burnout as a result.

In the United States, this element of the collectivist model can be seen in some 5,000 so-called alternative institutions established since the 1970s. These free schools, free medical clinics, legal collectives, food cooperatives, communes, and cooperative businesses are a legacy of movements during the 1960s against authority and the Establishment. These enterprises are collectively owned and managed, with no hierarchy of authority. They tend to exist in craft production and other special niches of the economy that exempt them from competing directly with conventional companies. Most of them are quite small, averaging six employees, but this size helps preserve full worker participation. The workers are highly satisfied with their jobs and strongly identify with their firms. Because they are also owners, the workers tend to work too hard and often suffer stress and burnout as a result (Rothschild and Russell, 1986).

The collectivist idea of giving workers control over their jobs has also been tried on a limited basis in nearly all of the 500 largest U.S. corporations as a way to combat worker alienation and low productivity. In these companies, small groups of employees work together as equals, similar to what are known in Japan as *quality circles*. They do not await orders from the top but take the initiative. They are encouraged with rewards and recognition—merit raises, cash bonuses, and bulletin-board praise—to contribute ideas on how to increase productivity and sales. They operate with the open-door policy, whereby employees report directly to top management. This policy, now popularly known as *participatory democracy*, further encourages employees to work harder because it makes them feel important and respected (Florida and Kenney, 1991; Rothschild and Russell, 1986).

Practically all the companies that first implemented quality circles were in the manufacturing sector of the economy. Good examples are Lockheed, IBM, and General Motors. The quality-circle style of worker participation has also begun to invade the service sector in such fields as banking and insurance. Collectivist practices such as these can boost not only worker morale but also productivity, as demonstrated in the successful operation of a Honda auto plant and other Japanese businesses in the United States (Florida and Kenney, 1991; Rothschild and Russell, 1986; Scott, 1986).

■ Feminist Model

We have seen how the collectivist model of organization achieves success through social equality. The model proposed by feminist theorists does more than simply get everybody to work together as equals. It also calls for emotional support from one's coworkers, as typically exists in a group of close friends. Instead of urging people to leave their personal problems behind when coming to work, as do most conventional organizations, the feminist model tolerates—even encourages—the opposite. The equality espoused in the feminist model is personal, subjective, and spontaneous. This is in contrast to the impersonal, objective, and rule-oriented type of equality found in organizations that have hired women and minorities only because federal law has forced them to do so.

The feminist model originates from studies of predominantly female organizations, as well as from studies of female executives of conventional, gender-mixed organizations. An example is Judy Rosener's (1990) landmark study. Her comparison of 456 successful female executives with their male counterparts in similar positions at similar companies fou[nd] significant gender differences in leadership sty[le]. Men tend to prefer a command and control wa[y of] dealing with subordinates—relying on orders, app[eals] to self-interest, rational decision making, an[d re]wards for manipulative purposes. By contrast, [women] are more likely to prefer an intuitive, antihier[archical]

WOMEN'S WAYS   The feminist model emphasizes personal relationships and emotional support in organizations. Although not all women have the same leadership style, studies of predominantly female organizations, as well as female executives of gender-mixed organizations, have found that women tend to prefer an intuitive, antihierarchical style typified by the sharing of experiences, ideas, and power. ■

style. They are more willing to share power, ask for guidance from subordinates, and humanize their workplace, as demonstrated to some degree by the female university president in the vignette at the beginning of this chapter.

In another study, Sandra Morgen (1994) found that the women who work at feminist health clinics generally cater to each other's *personal* needs, not just the instrumental, bottom-line needs of the organization. Considerable personal sharing goes on in the organization: Members tend not only to greet each other with hugs and kisses but also to share personal problems rather than leave them at home. Not surprisingly, members identify closely with their organizations, committed with heart and soul to them.

We should be careful, however, not to stereotype all women as having the same organizational style. Personal, subjective, and spontaneous egalitarianism does not exist exclusively among women or equally among all women. Some men have it, and some women do not. It is only as a group that women are more likely than men to have that kind of organizational style. This gender difference is far from innate; rather, it is largely a product of socialization. Generally, women are more likely than men to have learned from parents, peer groups, schools, and various social cl..periences the values of supporting and nurturing th..hers, protecting long-term relationships, seeking so-stucions in which everyone wins, and sharing emotivit..s. For example, boys tend to play in groups such ment..rarchical sports teams, where they learn how to experin..te, take criticism, and win, but girls are more went up..

likely to play in leaderless groups, where they learn to get along, be fair, and reach a consensus (Rothschild and Davies, 1994; Heim and Golant, 1993).

SYMBOLIC INTERACTIONIST PERSPECTIVE: DEFINING THE SITUATION IN ORGANIZATIONS

The basic ideas of many organizational theories can be related to the symbolic interactionist perspective. Here we analyze two such theories. One that is relatively new emphasizes the significance of organizational culture, suggesting that the way people define the situation they are in shapes their organization. The other theory is older and is known as *Weber's theory of bureaucracy;* it essentially portrays bureaucracy as the embodiment of the Western—or the male—definition of rationality as the proper and effective way to run an organization.

■ Organizational Culture: Shared Definitions

In the 1990s, many new organizational theories emerged, variously labeled cultural, interpretive, and hermeneutic. All are related to the symbolic interactionist perspective. *Cultural theories* emphasize how organizational members' values or beliefs, which reflect how they interpret the world around them, influence their behavior in the organization. *Interpretive theories* focus on the individual's "perspective on life in organizations." *Hermeneutic theories* show how interpretations of the meanings of organizational documents influence members' interactions (Pheysey, 1993; Turner, 1992; Aldrich, 1992; Morgan, 1989). Roughly translated into the language of symbolic interactionism, all of these theories essentially say that organizational culture, popularly called *corporate culture,* consists of members' shared definitions of what the organization is like and therefore significantly affects what goes on in the organization.

Studies of corporate culture often reveal why some organizations succeed while others fail to achieve their goals. Tandem, a successful computer manufacturer, was found to owe its success largely to the widely shared belief among its employees that it is a wonderful company to work for. Slogans extolling the company as an outstanding employer appear on T-shirts and bulletin boards and are spread by word of mouth. A related belief is that everybody is treated equally, as suggested by the absence of name tags and reserved parking spaces. When questioned by researchers, Tandem employees also revealed the relative lack of hierarchy, with comments such as "Everyone here, managers, vice-presidents, and even janitors, communicate on the same level. No one feels better than anyone else."

Like Tandem, many more companies today emphasize team work at the expense of competition. In short, organizations can be successful if they have a positive culture (Russo, 2001; Morgan, 1989). On the other hand, a positive organizational culture cannot exist without real support, such as in the form of recognitions and rewards. If Tandem's employees were not given enough praise and salary raises for their hard work, its gung-ho culture would disappear.

■ Bureaucracy: Embodiment of a Rational Worldview

According to Max Weber, modern Western society makes a specific form of organization necessary: **bureaucracy**, a modern Western organization defined as being rational in achieving its goal efficiently. "In the place of the old-type ruler who is moved by sympathy, favor, grace, and gratitude," Weber (1946) said, "modern culture requires . . . the emotionally detached, and hence rigorously 'professional' expert." In every area of modern life there is a tendency toward **rationalization**, Weber's term for the process of replacing subjective, spontaneous, informal, and diverse ways of doing things with a planned, objective, formally unified method based on abstract rules. Applied to organizations, rationalization means the development of bureaucracies.

What specifically is bureaucracy? It is an organization that differs sharply from a collectivist organization, as shown in Table 5.1. It is as rational as a machine, as Weber (1946) wrote:

> The fully developed bureaucratic mechanism compares with other organizations exactly as does the machine with the non-mechanical modes of production. . . . The strictly bureaucratic administration succeeds in eliminating from official business, love, hatred, and purely personal, irrational, and emotional elements which escape calculation.

By squeezing out the human element of emotion, bureaucracy is, in Weber's view, the most efficient form of organization. This can be so if, as symbolic interactionism suggests, organization members define the machinelike rationality as reasonable, legitimate, acceptable, or agreeable.

TABLE 5.1

Bureaucratic versus Collectivist Organizations

Bureaucratic Organizations	Collectivist Organizations
1. Maximum division of labor	1. Minimum division of labor
2. Maximum specialization of jobs—monopolization of expertise	2. Generalization of jobs—diffusion of expertise
3. Emphasis on hierarchy of position—justifying reward differentials	3. Striving for egalitarianism—restricting reward differentials
4. Authority in individual officeholders; hierarchical control; bureaucratic elitism	4. Authority in collectivity as a whole; democratic control; subordinate participation
5. Formalization of fixed and universal rules	5. Primacy of ad hoc decisions
6. Worker motivation through direct supervision	6. Worker motivation through personal appeals
7. Impersonality as ideal of social relations in organization	7. Comradeship as ideal of social relations in organization

How to Make an Organization Work

Perspective	Focus	Insights
Functional	Cooperating to achieve a common goal	*Scientific management theory:* Maximize the division of labor, supervision of workers, and wage incentives. *Human relations theory:* Strengthen informal relations in the workplace.
Conflict	Using equality as the key to organizational success	*Collectivist model:* Let workers participate as equals in managing the organization. *Feminist model:* Encourage both equality and emotional closeness among all members.
Symbolic interactionist	Defining the situations in organizations positively	*Cultural theory:* Use recognition and reward to help members define the organization as a good, friendly place to work. *Bureaucratic theory:* Eliminate human emotion by defining for members the organization's rules and regulations as rational.

However, this definition is increasingly rejected in today's socially diverse organizations. As our previous discussion of feminist theory suggests, women are likely to define the emotionless, impersonal, dehumanizing form of rationality as *irrational*. They tend more to define the subjective, personal, empathetic form of rationality as *rational*. With increasing female participation in organizations, we can expect bureaucracies to become increasingly humanized, like the feminist organizations that we have analyzed.

The Japanese also define the Western impersonal form of rationality as *unreasonable* for running organizations. And they define their own traditional values of mutual obligations and loyalties as *reasonable* because they help, among other things, strengthen a company's lifetime commitment to its employees and employee commitment to the company. This may explain why those traditional and emotional values that Weber regarded as obstacles to achieving organizational efficiency have made Japanese companies rank among the most efficient in the world.

Although bureaucracy is not the most efficient form of organization in the world, it is still the most efficient in predominantly individualist cultures such as that of the United States. Still, bureaucracy is also deficient in some ways. We will discuss both the efficient and deficient aspects of bureaucracy later.

All of the organizational theories we have discussed are basically **normative theories**, theories that suggest what we should do to achieve our goals. The Theoretical Thumbnail above summarizes what each of the theories prescribes as the key to achieving or-

ganizational efficiency. But the drive for efficiency can threaten personal privacy.

THE THREAT OF ORGANIZATIONS TO PERSONAL PRIVACY

To operate efficiently as an organization, the government, an employer, and a company must, among other things, protect national security, maintain a productive workforce, and seek and serve customers. But achieving these objectives tends to involve invading the personal privacy of citizens, employees, and consumers.

For example, in its effort to search for terrorists, the U.S. government may track people's e-mail and Internet use, obtaining their sensitive personal records and covertly searching their homes and offices (Margulis, 2003). But in the wake of the September 11 attacks, many Americans today are willing to give up some privacy for the sake of increased national security. As shown in Table 5.2 (p. 138), a large majority favor granting greater investigative powers to law enforcement agencies in searching for terrorists, which inevitably entails invading the privacy of ordinary citizens. The table also shows, however, that blacks are less likely than whites and Hispanics to support increased government intrusion. Blacks apparently feel more strongly about that intrusion as an infringement on civil rights, perhaps because they have experienced such infringement more than the other

TABLE 5.2

Americans' Support of Greater Investigative Powers
The figures below indicate the percentages of Americans who favor giving law enforcement agencies greater power in dealing with people suspected of terrorist activities.

	Male	Female	White	Black	Hispanic
Stronger document and physical security checks for travelers	80%	89%	87%	75%	93%
Stronger document and physical security checks for access to government and private office buildings	77%	88%	85%	65%	87%
Expanded undercover activities to penetrate groups under suspicion	78%	84%	85%	57%	87%

Source: Data from Simona Covel, "Getting Pragmatic about Privacy," *American Demographics,* June 2003, p. 14.

groups. Still, a majority of African Americans support greater investigative powers for law enforcement.

In their attempt to maintain a productive workforce, employers must collect and store personal information about employees, such as their age, past employment, and letters of reference. Some employers also use closed-circuit cameras, video-display terminals, and other devices to monitor worker performance and to catch deviant behavior, such as drug use and theft. Some go as far as taping employees' telephone conversations and reviewing their e-mails. All these activities effectively violate employee privacy, yet most employees express little concern. Why? The fear factor seems to play a role: Just as most citizens are afraid of being attacked by terrorists, most employees are afraid of losing their jobs, so they comply with clearly intrusive practices (Marx, 2003; Westin, 2003).

There is, however, much more expressed concern among consumers over losing their privacy to businesses that aggressively try to find customers and sell them products. Most Americans, for example, complain about receiving *spam,* or junk e-mails, which sell everything from insurance to penis enlargers. Consumer complaints about dinnertime telemarketing calls have become so widespread that the government has established a national "do not call" list and threatened telemarketers with fines for violating the list. Government actions such as this will pressure many marketers to respect consumer privacy. More generally, in seeking and using consumer personal data to sell products, many businesses are increasingly abandoning the business-oriented policy of "We must know you to serve you" and adopting the consumer-friendly policy of "Let me decide what you know about me" (Westin, 2003).

THE REALITIES OF BUREAUCRACY

Despite widespread dislike of bureaucracy, this form of organization is still pervasive. Most people in the United States continue to work in bureaucracies, and even more must deal with bureaucratic organizations when they enroll in school, have a phone installed, pay a hospital bill, or handle any number of countless other arrangements that are part of living in a modern Western society. The prevalence of bureaucratic organizations affects both the small details of everyday life and the overall functions of the government and the economy. The benefits and problems of bureaucracy are thus worth a closer look.

■ Bureaucratic Benefits

If so many people don't like bureaucracies, why does this kind of organization continue to exist? In part, it's because bureaucracies are not all bad. Even red tape has its advantages: One person's red tape can be another person's safeguard against problems. The process of getting a government permit to open a hazardous waste dump may seem to be an endless, expensive obstacle course of paperwork to the company that wants to operate the dump. But to the people living near the proposed site, the rules and regulations that make up that red tape may seem the best guarantee of proper precautions to safeguard their health.

Similarly, the impersonality of bureaucracies, especially in government, is sometimes welcome. If you need a government-subsidized student loan, you are probably glad that impersonal rules—not political pull or personal friendships—determine whether

RULES RULE The efficiency of bureaucracy can be attributed primarily to reliance on impersonal rules. Rules ensure that employees treat equally all the people they serve. Unfortunately, the consequences of bureaucratic efficiency may include rigidity on the part of personnel, such as being unable to help customers with unusual needs or special requests. ■

you can obtain the loan. Bureaucracy encourages equality and discourages discrimination.

Even for employees, bureaucracies may bring some benefits. The widely held assumption that bureaucracies tend to stifle individual creativity and imagination seems groundless. Data collected by sociologist Melvin Kohn (1983) suggest that bureaucracies make their workers intellectually flexible, creative, and open minded. Kohn defined *bureaucrats* as people who work in large organizations with complicated hierarchies of authority and nonbureaucrats as people who work in small organizations with only one level of supervision.

Kohn found that, compared with nonbureaucrats, bureaucrats demonstrated a higher level of intellectual performance on tests administered by an interviewer. Bureaucrats also placed greater intellectual demands on themselves during their leisure time. They were more likely than nonbureaucrats to read books and magazines, attend plays and concerts, and go to museums. They also put greater value on self-direction, rather than conformity, and were more likely to take personal responsibility for whatever they did. Finally, they were more open minded and more receptive to change.

Skeptics may argue that the bureaucrats' wonderful traits did not *result* from working in a bureaucracy. Perhaps the bureaucrats were better educated,

more intellectually flexible, and more receptive to change in the first place. This argument assumes that bureaucracies hold some special attraction for people with these qualities. But because most people believe that bureaucracies suppress creativity, this assumption is far from convincing.

Kohn contended that bureaucracies themselves encourage the development of the positive traits he found in their employees. He argued that the more complex a job is, the more intellectually flexible the worker becomes, and employees of bureaucracies tend to have more complex jobs than people with comparable levels of education who work for an organization with just one or two levels of supervision.

■ Bureaucratic Problems

In Weber's view, bureaucracy is inescapable but not very likable. "It is horrible," he once said, "to think that the world would one day be filled with nothing but those little cogs, little men clinging to little jobs and striving toward bigger ones" (Bendix, 1962). Finding a person to say a good word about bureaucracy is about as hard as finding a landlord who likes rent control. Why? The reason is that certain problems are often associated with bureaucracy.

The first problem has to do with rules and regulations. Since they are based on what is already known, rules cannot tell us what to do about the unanticipated. Blind adherence to rules can therefore wreak havoc in people's lives. If we have lost an important document like an ID card, bureaucrats cannot do for us anything that requires the presentation of that document. A more common problem is the tendency of bureaucracies to produce a seemingly endless array of rules and regulations. Public bureaucracies, in particular, are notorious for mountains of rules, all of which slow action by officials and fall like an avalanche on private citizens and businesses that must comply with them. The nation's small businesses alone spend an immense amount of money every year just to complete government forms.

Another problem is that bureaucracy tends to grow unnecessarily bigger. This problem has been called **Parkinson's law:** "Work expands to fill the time available for its completion." The author of this law, C. Northcote Parkinson, believed that the natural tendency of bureaucracy is to grow and keep on growing by at least 6 percent a year. Wanting to appear busy or important or both, officials increase their workload by writing many memos, creating rules, filling out forms, and keeping files. Then, feeling overworked, they hire assistants. At the same time, powerful incentives—such as bigger salaries, more perks, higher status, and greater power—encourage officials to increase their agency workforces, budgets, and missions. As a result, many bureaucrats are doing the same work at great cost to taxpayers. "As a rule," a White House official once said, "virtually any task being done by government is being done by 20 or more agencies" (Church, 1993).

There is yet another bureaucratic problem: Deadwood tends to pile up. This problem is known as the **Peter principle:** "In every hierarchy, every employee tends to rise to his or her level of incompetence." Competent officials are promoted, and if they prove to be competent in their new jobs, they are promoted again. The process continues until they are promoted to a position in which they are incompetent. And there they remain as deadwood until they retire. The bureaucracy functions only because there are always employees still proving their competence before they are promoted beyond their abilities. Like Parkinson's Law, however, the Peter Principle is based on impressionistic observation rather than rigorous scientific research. Both problems are widely thought to be common, but precisely how common is not known.

The Future of Bureaucracy

Bureaucracy will probably continue to thrive. Many organizations in the United States seem to be getting larger, as suggested by the growth of big government agencies, multinational corporations, multicampus universities, and agribusinesses. Large organizational size usually leads to greater bureaucratic control, requiring numerous workers to follow standard rules and operating procedures so that chaos can be avoided.

At the same time, less bureaucratic control is imposed on higher-ranked technical experts and specialists within giant organizations. There is also less administrative control throughout the corporations on the frontier of technology. In many successful U.S. corporations today, highly trained specialists already enjoy a large degree of autonomy. They resent taking orders from managers who have less technical knowledge.

Because of the increasing shift from manual to knowledge work in the composition of the U.S. workforce, the pressure will mount to replace hierarchical bureaucracies with much flatter, more egalitarian organizations made up of numerous smaller units with 6 to 10 employees each. In fact, there is some evidence that since the early 1990s, the information revolution has begun to force many centralized bureaucracies, from education to business, to give way to this collectivist, egalitarian model. Some public schools, for example, are managed by teams of teachers and parents rather than bureaucrats. The increase

in female participation in organizations also contributes to the replacement of bureaucratic control with egalitarian cooperation (Pinchot and Pinchot, 1993).

In sum, bureaucracy appears to be moving in two seemingly opposite directions. On the one hand, bureaucracy will probably increase in *form,* with more and more organizations across the United States and around the globe becoming giant bureaucracies. On the other hand, the *content* of bureaucracy will become increasingly antibureaucratic, with more and more participants working as equals.

A GLOBAL ANALYSIS OF ORGANIZATIONS

It is important to look at organizations from a global perspective. Without that perspective, we would have believed Weber's *erroneous* assumption that the traditional non-Western organization cannot be as efficient as a Western bureaucracy.

Writing about organizations around 1910, Weber, like most Westerners of that time, did not have the global sensitivity that many of us have today. Thus, he tended to see in non-Western traditionalism only its *negative* aspects, such as hiring the boss's incompetent relative rather than the best-qualified person.

GUNG HO Influenced by their countries' traditional cultures, which are group oriented rather than individual oriented, Japanese and other East Asian companies are often run like families and involved in every aspect of a worker's life. Employees may begin each day singing their company song or reciting slogans of devotion to the company. Here, workers at a Chinese auto plant do group calisthenics at the start of the workday. ■

But today, a more sensitive global analysis can reveal the *positive* aspects of non-Western traditionalism, such as the cooperation and commitment demonstrated by Japanese organizations.

Basically, the Japanese traditional culture is group oriented rather than individual centered, as in the West. As group members rather than independent individuals, Japanese tend to have stronger relations with one another. Therefore, at the heart of the Japanese organization is concern with group achievement. Employees begin each workday by singing their company song or reciting slogans of devotion to their company. They work in sections of 8 to 10 people headed by the *kacho* (section chief). Each section, now well known as a *quality circle,* does not await orders from the top but takes the initiative on its own, and all of its members work together as equals. Personnel from different sections often get together to discuss how best to achieve company objectives. Executives then rubber-stamp most of the decisions made by employees at the section level. Workers, moreover, look upon the company as their family because they enjoy the security of permanent employment. Executives also feel secure and regard the company as their family. Not surprisingly, both workers and executives are strongly committed to the company and work hard to make it highly efficient and productive.

Traditionalism has also contributed to organizational efficiency in other East Asian societies such as South Korea, China, and Taiwan. But why can't it do the same in many developing countries? The answer is hard to find because most research has focused on the negative aspects of their traditionalism. If the focus of research is shifted to the positive, then we may find out what—possibly other than foreign exploitation—prevents clan centeredness and personal ties from building efficient organizations in traditional African, Latin American, and other developing countries. Interestingly, in the meantime, these countries have begun to learn from the Japanese model of organization (French, 1996). In fact, many organizations in the West have already followed the Japanese lead by becoming more humanized and less impersonal.

sociological frontiers

Is Cyberspace Lonely?

According to a 2000 Stanford University study, cyberspace is a lonely frontier. A nationwide sample of 4,113 people were asked what impact the Internet has on their daily activities, from watching television to attending social gatherings. The researchers found, among other things, that the more time people spend online, the *less time* they spend with family and friends, shopping in stores, and attending social events and the *more time* they spend working at home after hours. In short, the more often people go online, the more isolated they become from real social groups. Thus, the researchers concluded, the Internet may be creating a new wave of social isolation across the United States by luring people away from traditional family, community, and other group-oriented activities (Markoff, 2000; Perry, 2000).

Similar findings resulted from a 1998 study of 93 families in Pittsburgh: Internet users "talked less to family members and reported being lonelier and more depressed" (Perry, 2000).

So, is cyberspace really a lonely place? It may be, but only to 13 percent of the people who spend 5 or more

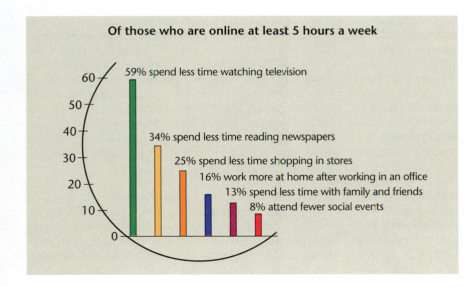

Of those who are online at least 5 hours a week

59% spend less time watching television

34% spend less time reading newspapers

25% spend less time shopping in stores

16% work more at home after working in an office

13% spend less time with family and friends

8% attend fewer social events

FIGURE 5.5

The Social Consequences of the Internet

To some extent, the more time people spend alone in the virtual world, the less time they spend with others in the real world. Even so, a large majority of regular Internet users do not become socially isolated.

Critical Thinking: *How much time is too much time to spend online?*

Source: Data from Stanford Institute for the Quantitative Study of Society, 2000.

hours a week on the web (see Figure 5.5). The large majority (more than 85 percent) of regular Internet users do not experience any change in the time spent with family and friends. In fact, many get closer to their primary groups through the net, as suggested by the fact that e-mail is the most popular online activity. In another recent study by the Pew Internet and American Life Project in Washington, DC, more than 60 percent of regular net users have a greater connection to family and friends. Finally, in a follow-up to the 1998 Pittsburgh study, researchers found a significant decline in depression and loneliness among respondents, thanks largely to the great increase in the number of family members and friends going online (Guernsey, 2001).

Taken together, then, the data suggest that the Internet has a negative impact on a few people but a more positive effect on many. Why the difference? The clue can be found in the latest Pittsburgh study: By using the Internet regularly, people who are already gregarious tend to become even more sociable, while those who are introverts tend to get more isolated (Kraut et al., 2002; Guernsey, 2001). This suggests that how the virtual world affects people may depend on what they are like in the real world.

 ■ For more of the latest Sociological Frontiers, look up Continuing Update at www.ablongman.com/thio6e.

using *sociology*

How to Reduce Wait Time in Lines

As you may recall from the beginning of this chapter, a *social group* consists of people who interact with each other, but a *social aggregate* is a number of individuals who just happen to gather in one place without interacting. An example of a social aggregate is a collection of customers standing in line to make a purchase or to be served at a popular business establishment. Because these people are strangers to each other, they do not interact by, for example, engaging in chitchat to make the time pass more quickly. Waiting in lines is thus an unpleasant experience. How, then, can the wait time in lines be reduced? This question has generated a lot of research, and the findings mean a great deal to businesses that serve throngs of customers. Ignoring the data could seriously hurt sales and reduce customer satisfaction.

Various researchers have observed lines in all kinds of business establishments and asked customers how they felt about standing in particular lines. As a result, the majority of the researchers have recommended, and most businesses have adopted, the single-line system as opposed to the multiple-line system. Thus, in all U.S.

post offices, airports, and banks, and in most fast-food restaurants, for example, customers stand in a single line, and as they reach the head of the line, they step up to the next available salesclerk. Only in a few businesses, particularly supermarkets, do customers still wait in multiple lines.

Why is the single-line system far more popular? Not only does the single-line system reduce the wait time for the average customer, but more importantly, this system also ensures customer satisfaction by eliminating the stress that the multiple-line system tends to create. Imagine yourself walking into a McDonald's that still uses the multiple-line system. First, you size up how quickly the various lines are moving and try to avoid a line with somebody placing a huge order. Then, after picking a line, you keep looking from one line to another to see if any are moving more quickly than yours. If they are (which happens all the time), you feel like a loser for having chosen a slower line. And so you develop an urge to hop from line to line to improve your position. All this can provoke anxiety (Gibson, 1998).

Of course, like everything else, the anxiety-free single-line system is not perfect. Owners of fancy hotels find it dehumanizing because its long ropes corral customers like cattle. Still, this system remains the favorite of most businesses (Gibson, 1998).

Regardless of the system used—single or multiple—what would you recommend a business do to help its customers feel better about waiting in line?

CHAPTER REVIEW

1. *What is a social group?* It is a collection of people who share some characteristics, interact with one another, and have some feeling of unity. *What are in-groups and out-groups?* An in-group is a group to which a person is strongly tied as a member. An out-group is a group of which an individual is not a member. *What is a reference group?* It is a group that people use as a guide for their behavior. *What are primary and secondary groups?* A primary group is one whose members interact informally, relate to each other as whole persons, and enjoy their relationship for its own sake. In a secondary group, the individuals interact formally, relate to each other as players of particular roles, and expect to achieve some practical purpose through the relationship.

2. *What is the nature of group leadership?* Leadership can be instrumental, trying to achieve goals by focusing on task performance. It can be expressive, being concerned with others' psychological well-being and working to enhance it. Or it can be laissez-

faire, letting others work largely on their own. *Why are leaders less likely than followers to conform to the group?* Leaders usually enjoy an idiosyncrasy credit extended to them by followers. *Is it unusual for people to go along with the majority even though they disagree with it?* No. It has been established by experiments that people tend to conform to groups. *Does the size of a group matter?* Yes. The larger a group, the more durable it is but the more impersonal it becomes and the less likely a member is to help someone in distress. *How can social diversity benefit a group and its members?* It can enhance group performance by providing many ideas for solving problems as well as help members get good jobs and make them healthier and happier.

3. *What draws us into a social network?* Friendship, business transactions, sexual contacts, expressions of admiration, and other kinds of social relationship draw us into social networks. *Can networks affect our lives?* Yes. Smaller, denser networks of friends and relatives can help us maintain good health by giving us social support. But they can also make our lives miserable by putting many demands on our time and personal resources, criticizing us, and invading our privacy.

4. *What is a formal organization?* It is a group whose activities are rationally designed to achieve specific goals. *What are the most common types of organizations?* According to Etzioni, they are coercive, utilitarian, and normative organizations.

5. *According to scientific management theory, what must an organization do to achieve its goal?* It must have maximum division of labor, close supervision of workers, and a piecework system of wages. *How does the human relations theory differ?* Whereas scientific management focuses on the official organization and the effect of wages on efficiency, the human relations theory emphasizes the influence of social forces—in particular, the informal relations among workers—on job satisfaction and productivity.

6. *What does a collectivist organization look like?* Its members participate as equals in the management of the organization. *What does a feminist organization look like?* In addition to practicing equality, a feminist organization fosters close personal relations among its members.

7. *What is organizational culture?* It consists of people's shared definitions of what their organization is like. *To Weber, what is bureaucracy like?* Bureaucracy is the embodiment of the Western definition of ratio-nality as the proper and effective way to run an organization.

8. *How can organizations threaten personal privacy?* In order to operate efficiently, organizations must engage in certain activities and in the process tend to invade individuals' privacy. The individual shows less concern if the invasion is considered justifiable or moderate than if unjustifiable or excessive.

9. *What are some of the benefits of bureaucracy?* When tasks are stable and routine, bureaucracies are very efficient; their reliance on rules and their impersonality can protect people from the exercise of arbitrary power and favoritism. In addition, bureaucracies may foster among their workers intellectual flexibility, creativity, and openness to change. *What are the problems of bureaucracy?* Bureaucracies tend to produce an ever-increasing number of rules, to grow unnecessarily large, and to retain incompetent officials. *What changes are occurring in bureaucracy?* Bureaucracies seem to be increasing in size but becoming more egalitarian.

10. *How does a global perspective enhance our understanding of organizations?* It enables us to see how non-Western traditionalism can contribute to organizational efficiency. *What are the social consequences of regular Internet use?* A few people become more isolated from others, but most people become more sociable. The nature of the consequence may depend on what kind of person the individual is in real life. *What can businesses learn from social research about standing in lines?* Single lines are better than multiple lines for reducing customer waiting time and enhancing customer satisfaction.

▌KEY TERMS

Bureaucracy   A modern Western organization defined by Max Weber as being rational in achieving its goal efficiently (p. 136).

Expressive leaders   Leaders who achieve group harmony by making others feel good (p. 123).

Formal organization   A group whose activities are rationally designed to achieve specific goals (p. 129).

Groupthink   The tendency for members of a cohesive group to maintain a consensus to the extent of ignoring the truth (p. 125).

Idiosyncrasy credit   The privilege that allows leaders to deviate from their group's norms (p. 123).

Informal organization A group formed by the informal relationships among members of an organization—based on personal interactions, not on any plan by the organization (p. 133).

In-group The group to which an individual is strongly tied as a member (p. 120).

Instrumental leaders Leaders who achieve their group's goal by getting others to focus on task performance (p. 123).

Laissez-faire leaders Leaders who let others do their work more or less on their own (p. 123).

Normative theories Theories that suggest what we *should* do to achieve our goals (p. 137).

Out-group A group of which an individual is not a member (p. 120).

Parkinson's law The observation that "Work expands to fill the time available for its completion" (p. 139).

Peter principle The observation that "In every hierarchy, every employee tends to rise to his or her level of incompetence" (p. 140).

Rationalization Max Weber's term for the process of replacing subjective, spontaneous, informal, and diverse ways of doing things with a planned, objective, formally unified method based on abstract rules (p. 136).

Reference group A group that is used as the frame of reference for evaluating one's own behavior (p. 121).

Social aggregate A number of people who happen to be in one place but do not interact with one another (p. 120)

Social category A number of people who have something in common but who neither interact with one another nor gather in one place (p. 120)

Social group A collection of people who interact with one another and have a certain feeling of unity (p. 120).

Social network A web of social relationships that link individuals or groups to one another (p. 127).

QUESTIONS FOR DISCUSSION AND REVIEW

SOCIAL GROUPS

1. What are some social functions of in-groups and reference groups?
2. Why are primary groups fundamental for human existence?

GROUP CHARACTERISTICS

1. What are the different types of leadership, and how can leaders earn idiosyncrasy credit?
2. How does the concept of groupthink help explain experiences you have had in social groups?
3. How does group size affect our behavior?
4. What advantages does a diverse group have over a homogeneous one?

SOCIAL NETWORKS

1. What does a social network consist of?
2. How can social networks affect our lives?

FORMAL ORGANIZATIONS

1. What are the principal features of a formal organization?
2. How do coercive, normative, and utilitarian organizations differ from each other?
3. In general, what do organizational theories tell us?

FUNCTIONALIST PERSPECTIVE: COOPERATING TO ACHIEVE A COMMON GOAL

1. What are the basic features of the scientific management theory?
2. What is the essence of the human relations theory?

CONFLICT PERSPECTIVE: EQUALITY AS KEY TO ORGANIZATIONAL SUCCESS

1. What is the most important characteristic of a collectivist organization?
2. What does a feminist organization look like?

SYMBOLIC INTERACTIONIST PERSPECTIVE: DEFINING THE SITUATION IN ORGANIZATIONS

1. How does organizational culture contribute to corporate success?
2. What are the major characteristics of Weber's bureaucratic model of organization?

THE THREAT OF ORGANIZATIONS TO PERSONAL PRIVACY

1. How do organizations threaten personal privacy?
2. How do Americans today react to this threat?

THE REALITIES OF BUREAUCRACY

1. What are the benefits of bureaucracies?
2. What bureaucratic problems do Parkinson's law and the Peter principle illustrate?
3. What changes seem to be happening in today's bureaucracies?

A GLOBAL ANALYSIS OF ORGANIZATIONS

1. How can traditionalism contribute to organizational efficiency in East Asia?

SOCIOLOGICAL FRONTIERS/USING SOCIOLOGY

1. What impact does the Internet have on its regular users?

2. How can the research on standing in lines benefit businesses?

SUGGESTED READINGS

Iannello, Kathleen P. 1992. *Decisions without Hierarchy: Feminist Interventions in Organization Theory and Practice*. New York: Routledge. Discusses the emphasis on equality in the feminist theory and practice of organization.

Snook, Scott A. 2000. *Friendly Fire: The Accidental Shootdown of U.S. Black Hawks over Northern Iraq*. Princeton, NJ: Princeton University Press. A fascinating organizational study that shows how the lack of coordination between two military organizations caused U.S. Air Force fighter jets to accidentally shoot down two U.S. Army helicopters.

Tsutsui, William M. 1998. *Manufacturing Ideology: Scientific Management in Twentieth-Century Japan*. Princeton, NJ: Princeton University Press. A historical analysis of how the U.S. model of scientific management influenced Japanese industrial organizations while it was reshaped by Japan's predominantly collectivist culture.

Wajcman, Judy. 1998. *Managing Like a Man: Women and Men in Corporate Management*. University Park, PA: Penn State University Press. A study of how difficult it is for female managers to thrive in corporations if they are expected to manage like men.

Whitman, Marina N. 1999. *New World, New Rules: The Changing Role of the American Corporation*. Boston: Harvard Business School Press. An analysis of how global competitiveness, the spread of information technology, the high cost of regulation, and shareholders' demands for greater investment returns have forced management to cut costs, limit wages, use temporary workers, and reduce community services.

■ Additional Resources

The New York Times
expect the world®
nytimes.com

Expand your knowledge of the concepts discussed in this chapter by reading the following current and historical articles from the *New York Times*. Go to the "eThemes of the Times" section of the Companion Website (www.ablongman.com/thio6e):

"Uncoupling Campus and Company"

"Thousands Gather in Washington to Remember 1963 March"

Research Navigator.com

Research Navigator, a research database, provides immediate access to hundreds of full-text articles from EBSCO's ContentSelect Academic Journal Database. If the Research Navigator access code was included with your textbook, go to the website www.research navigator.com and read the following articles related to this chapter by typing in the article number:

Roberts, Alden E., Koch, Jerome R., and Paul Johnson, D. "Religious Reference Groups and the Persistence of Normative Behavior: An Empirical Test." *Sociological Spectrum*, Jan2001, Vol. 21 Issue 1, p81, 18p, 6 charts. Accession Number: 3892863. Tests the importance of religious reference groups in shaping normative as well as deviant behavior patterns.

Jamil, Ishtiaq. "Administrative Culture in Bangladesh: Tensions between Tradition and Modernity." *International Review of Sociology,* Mar2002, Vol. 12 Issue 1, p93, 33p. Accession Number: 6790672. Describes bureaucracy in Bangladesh.

chapter 6

Deviance and Control

myths & realities

myth *Strangers don't care about us as much as our relatives, friends, and acquaintances do. So it's no wonder that most murder victims were killed by strangers.*

reality Most murder victims were related to or knew their killers (p. 149).

myth *"Guns don't kill; people do." Therefore, it is futile to outlaw the possession of guns.*

reality Of course, guns by themselves cannot kill, nor can their absence reduce people's motivation to kill. But were guns less available, potential murderers would use less lethal weapons, which would result in fewer deaths (p. 150).

myth *Since sexually active men can easily get sex, they are unlikely to rape their dates.*

reality Sexually active men are more likely to rape their dates than men with little or no sexual experience (p. 151).

myth *Deviance is always harmful to society.*

reality Deviance can bring benefits to society if it occurs within limits (p. 157).

myth *Because of the feminist movement for gender equality, women today are about as likely as men to commit crimes.*

reality Men still greatly outnumber women in committing crimes because the recent increase in female crime has not been great enough to be significant (p. 161).

myth *The U.S. criminal justice system is, by any measure, soft on criminals.*

reality The United States appears to be soft on criminals because extremely few criminals are apprehended and punished. But compared with other democracies, the United States is tougher in imprisoning proportionately more criminals and imposing longer prison terms (p. 168).

147

n October 2002, two men terrorized the residents of suburban Washington, DC, for nearly three weeks. They drove around in their car and shot at people whom they picked out at random. Ten of the victims died instantly, and three were critically wounded. During this siege, area residents were afraid to leave their homes, causing local restaurants, stores, and other businesses to suffer a sharp decline in patronage. When schoolchildren got off the bus, they had to run for the cover of the building, and once inside, they had to stay inside. They were not even allowed to romp in the playground. High school football homecoming games had to be played at undisclosed places away from the Washington area. Owners of gas stations had to put up large sheets of tarp to shield customers from the snipers. In fact, due to the daily reports about the shootings on national TV, Americans all over the country couldn't help feeling less safe than before (Thomas, 2002).

With such horrible crimes popping up in the media, we may regard deviants as creatures so abhorrent as to be foreign to us. But deviance is widespread. Most of it is far less horrendous than what these two killers did. Yet even in a society of saints, as Durkheim long ago suggested, rules will be broken. Virtually everybody has committed some deviant acts, such as those listed in Table 6.1. But what exactly is deviance?

WHAT IS DEVIANCE?

Deviance is generally defined as any act that violates a social norm. But the phenomenon is more complex than that. How do we know whether an act violates a social norm? Is homosexuality deviant—a violation of a social norm? Some people think so, but others do not. At least three factors are involved in determining what deviance is: time, place, and public consensus or power.

First, what constitutes deviance varies from one historical period to another. Nearly 2,000 years ago, the Roman Empress Messalina won a bet with a friend by publicly having a prolonged session of sexual intercourse with 25 men. At the time, Romans were not particularly scandalized, although they were quite impressed by her stamina (King, 1985). Today, if a person of similar social standing engaged in such behavior, we would consider it extremely scandalous.

Second, the definition of deviance varies from one place to another. A polygamist (a person with more than one spouse) is a criminal in the United States but not in Saudi Arabia and other Muslim countries. Prostitution is illegal in the United States (except in some counties in Nevada) but legal in Denmark, Germany, France, and many other countries. As a married man, former President Clinton got into hot water for having an affair, but married leaders in China are fully expected to have girlfriends (Janofsky, 2001; Rosenthal, 1998a).

Third, whether a given act is deviant depends on public consensus. Murder is unquestionably deviant because nearly all societies agree that it is. In contrast, drinking alcoholic beverages is generally not considered deviant. Public consensus, however, usually reflects the vested interests of the rich and powerful. As Marx would have said, the ideas of the ruling class tend to become the ruling ideas of society. Like the powerful, the general public tends, for example, to consider bank robbery a serious crime but not fraudulent advertising, which serves the interests of the powerful.

In view of these three determinants of deviant behavior, we may define **deviance** more precisely as an act considered by public consensus, or by the powerful, at a given time and place, to be a violation of some social rule.

EXAMPLES OF DEVIANCE

Most of the deviant acts studied by sociologists—such as homicide, robbery, and rape—involve violat-

TABLE 6.1

Common Offenses Punishable by Fines or Jail Terms

- Gambling illegally, such as betting on a sport event or political election
- Evading taxes, such as failing to report or exaggerating deductible expenses
- Committing computer crime, such as copying software illegally
- Serving alcohol to minors
- Drinking in public, where prohibited
- Possessing marijuana in small quantities for personal use
- Committing adultery in states where it is illegal
- Patronizing a prostitute
- Appearing nude in public, such as nude sunbathing, where prohibited
- Stealing TV signals, such as with a satellite dish
- Speeding or other moving-traffic violations
- Parking illegally
- Smoking in public, where an ordinance prohibits it
- Failing to recycle where required

Source: Adapted from Stephen J. Adler and Wade Lamber, "Common Criminals: Just About Everyone Violates Some Laws, Even Model Citizens," *Wall Street Journal,* March 12, 1993, p. A6.

ing a criminal law; hence, they are *criminal deviance.* Some sociologists have, however, urged that more attention be focused on *noncriminal deviance,* such as homophobia, using pornography, and mental disorder (Bader et al., 1996). Here, we discuss both kinds of deviance.

■ Homicide

Homicide is mostly a personal crime, far more likely to be committed against acquaintances, friends, or relatives than against strangers, as shown in Figure 6.1. Swayed by common sense, we may find this incredible. But as sociologists Donald Mulvihill and Melvin Tumin (1969) explained, "Everyone is within easy striking distance from intimates for a large part of the time. Although friends, lovers, spouses, and the like are a main source of pleasure in one's life, they are equally a main source of frustration and hurt. Few others can anger one so much." As a crime

of passion, homicide is usually carried out under the overwhelming pressure of a volcanic emotion, namely, uncontrollable rage.

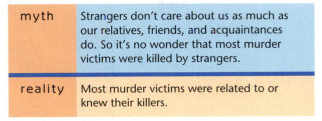

myth	Strangers don't care about us as much as our relatives, friends, and acquaintances do. So it's no wonder that most murder victims were killed by strangers.
reality	Most murder victims were related to or knew their killers.

Homicide occurs most frequently during weekend evenings, particularly Saturday night. This holds true largely for lower-class murderers but not for middle- and upper-class offenders, who tend more to kill on any day of the week. One apparent reason is that higher-class murders are more likely than lower-class homicides to be premeditated and hence are less likely to result from alcohol-induced quarrels during weekend sprees. Research has also often shown that most U.S. murderers are poor, including semiskilled workers, unskilled laborers, and welfare recipients (Levin and Fox, 2001; Parker, 1989).

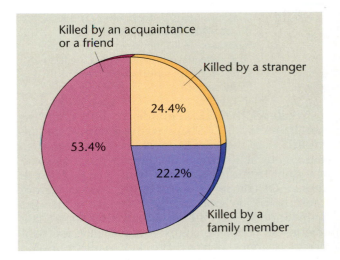

Killed by an acquaintance or a friend

Killed by a stranger

24.4%

53.4%

22.2%

Killed by a family member

FIGURE 6.1

Most Victims Know Their Killers

Most homicides involve killing acquaintances, friends, and family members, and only a few involve killing strangers. To explain this, sociologists have observed that while the people we know can give us great pleasure in life, they can also be a major source of unhappiness.

Critical Thinking: *Why can people we care about hurt us much more than total strangers?*

Source: Data from FBI, *Uniform Crime Reports,* 2003.

DIFFERENT STROKES The definition of *deviance* varies with time, place, and public consensus. Thus, women with tattoos were generally considered deviant in the past but are less so today. They are less likely to be treated as deviant in the United States than in more traditional societies. And in the eyes of the U.S. public, they appear less acceptable than their conventionally made up peers, but most Americans seem to hold a "live and let live" attitude toward them. ■

myth	"Guns don't kill; people do." Therefore, it is futile to outlaw the possession of guns.
reality	Of course, guns by themselves cannot kill, nor can their absence reduce people's motivation to kill. But were guns less available, potential murderers would use less lethal weapons, which would result in fewer deaths.

Whatever their class, murderers most often use handguns to kill. Perhaps seeing a gun while embroiled in a heated argument incites a person to murderous action. As Shakespeare wrote, "How oft the sight of means to do ill deeds, makes ill deeds done." Of course, firearms by themselves cannot cause homicide, nor can their absence reduce the motivation to kill. It is true that "Guns don't kill; people do." Still, were guns less available, less dangerous weapons such as fists or knives might be used instead. Thus, many heated arguments might result in aggravated assaults rather than murders, thereby reducing the number of fatalities. But given the enormous number of guns in private hands, it is not surprising that far more deaths result from gun attacks in the United States than in Canada, Britain, and other industrialized countries, where there are considerably fewer guns per person (Kim, 1999; Kristof, 1996a).

The easy availability of guns has contributed to a stunning upsurge in killings by teenagers and young adults before the early 1990s. Bus since then, the homicide rate among young people has declined, largely as the result of increased economic prosperity, tougher law enforcement, and greater protection of domestic violence victims (Rosenfeld, 2002).

■ Rape

Rape involves the use of force to get a woman to do something sexual against her will. It is a common problem in the United States but exactly how common? And why is it common?

Incidence and Characteristics   Every year, about 110,000 cases of rape in the United States are reported to the police, but the actual number of rapes is considerably higher, running into the millions. According to the most conservative estimate, at least 10 percent of women have been raped (Russell and Bolen, 2000; Berthelsen, 1999). Most of these rapes are not even legally defined as such, let alone reported to the police. A key reason is that the overwhelming majority of cases involve intimates such as lovers and close friends, whereas the popular perception of rape is associated with strangers or mere acquaintances.

In one survey, while 22 percent of the women said they had been forced to have sex, only about 3 percent of the men admitted to having committed forced sex. Why do the overwhelming majority of men fail to acknowledge what some women see as forced sex? The apparent reason, again, has much to do with the fact that most cases of forced sex involve intimates. Consider the following two scenarios given by Michael and his colleagues (1994).

One involves a married man coming home late after drinking a lot of beer with the guys. He wants sex, but his wife cringes when he approaches. She obviously does not want sex. He does and has his way. He does not think it was forced, but she does. Another illustration involves two young people on a date. She touches his hand, his arm, and then even his thigh while they are talking at dinner. She thinks she is only trying to get to know him, but he thinks she wants sex. Later, when he makes his move, she says no. But he thinks she means yes. He believes the sex was consensual. To her, it was forced.

But why do the males in such scenarios fail to see that they have committed forced sex? The reason seems to lie in the traditional patriarchal belief that a man should be aggressive to win a woman's heart. Resulting from such aggression gone out of control, forced sex is an extension of the traditional pattern of male sexual behavior. The belief about the importance of male aggressiveness is embedded in the culture that encourages rape.

The Culture of Rape   The culture of rape reveals itself through at least three prevailing attitudes toward women.

First, women traditionally have been treated like men's property. If a woman is married, she is, in effect, her husband's property. Thus, in most countries and some states in the United States, a man cannot be prosecuted for raping his wife. The reasoning seems to be: How can any man steal what already belongs to him? The property logic may also explain the difficulty of getting a man convicted for raping a "cheap, loose woman" or a known prostitute. Such a female is considered every man's property because she has had sex with many men. If a "good" woman is raped, we often say that she has been "ravaged," "ravished," "despoiled," or "ruined," as if she were a piece of property that has been damaged.

Globally, when conquering armies commandeer the conquered population's property, they also tend to rape the women as if they were part of that property. During World War II, German soldiers raped massive numbers of Jewish and Russian women after occupying many villages and cities in Europe, and the Japanese army systematically raped women and girls as it invaded Korea, China, and various Southeast Asian countries. In today's armed conflicts, foreign soldiers continue to rape local women (see Figure 6.2, p. 152).

Second, women are treated as if they are objects of masculinity contests among men. To prove his manhood, a man is culturally pressured to have sex with the largest number of women possible. The pressure

to play this masculinity game often comes from friends, who ask questions such as "Did you score?" "Had any lately?" If the answer is no, the friends may ask, "What's the matter? Are you gay or something?" Such social pressure tends to make young men want to show off their masculine qualities, such as aggressiveness, forcefulness, and violence.

Even without peer pressure, the popular belief in sexual conquest as a badge of masculinity encourages men to be aggressive toward women. If women say no, men are expected to ignore this response or even translate it into really meaning yes. Such lessons in sexual conquest often come from the stereotype of the movie or television hero who forcefully, persistently embraces and kisses the heroine despite her strong resistance, and who is rewarded when she finally melts in his arms.

myth	Since sexually active men can easily get sex, they are unlikely to rape their dates.
reality	Sexually active men are more likely to rape their dates than men with little or no sexual experience.

In real life, such sexual aggression can easily lead to rape. This is why many sociologists regard rape as an extension of the socially approved conventional pattern of male sexual behavior. It is also not surprising that members of the Spur Posse, a group of high school boys in California who compete with one another by scoring points for sexual conquests, were once jailed only for a few days on charges of molesting and raping girls as young as 10. It is also no wonder that other winners of the masculinity game, such as college men with considerable sexual experience, are more likely to rape their dates than are the so-called losers, who have little or no sexual experience (Nash, 1996; Schur, 1984; Kanin, 1983).

Third, there is a popular myth that, deep down, women want to be raped. This myth is often expressed in various ways: "She asked for it"; "She actually wanted it"; and "She lied about it (or consented to sex but later decided to 'cry rape')." In essence, the victim is held responsible for the rape. The victim is assumed to have done something that provoked the man to rape her. That something involves being in the wrong place (walking alone at night); wearing the wrong clothes (short shorts, miniskirts, or some other sexy dress); turning the man on (letting him kiss or pet her); or having an attitude (behaving assertively or independently) (Brinson, 1992).

Because of this blame-the-victim assumption, defense attorneys for alleged rapists tend to portray the victim as a willing partner. In one case, the victim was accused of having a "kinky and aggressive" sex

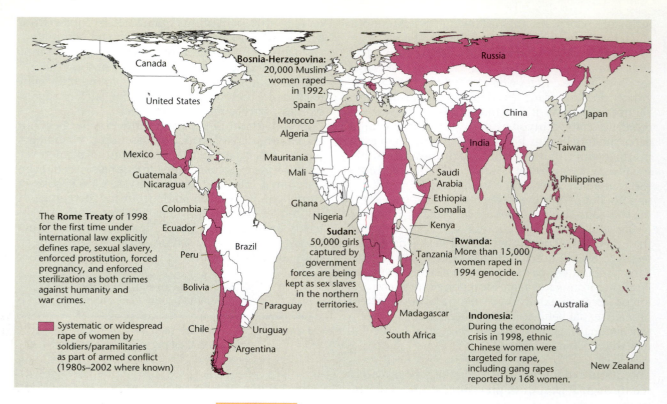

The **Rome Treaty** of 1998 for the first time under international law explicitly defines rape, sexual slavery, enforced prostitution, forced pregnancy, and enforced sterilization as both crimes against humanity and war crimes.

■ Systematic or widespread rape of women by soldiers/paramilitaries as part of armed conflict (1980s–2002 where known)

Bosnia-Herzegovina: 20,000 Muslim women raped in 1992.

Sudan: 50,000 girls captured by government forces are being kept as sex slaves in the northern territories.

Rwanda: More than 15,000 women raped in 1994 genocide.

Indonesia: During the economic crisis in 1998, ethnic Chinese women were targeted for rape, including gang rapes reported by 168 women.

FIGURE 6.2

Rape in War Zones

When a conquering army takes over the conquered population's property, they also tend to rape the women, as if they are part of that property. History is replete with instances in which women were raped by enemy soldiers, and this abhorrent practice continues to occur in today's armed conflicts worldwide.

Critical Thinking: *Could rape in war be stopped? If so, how? If not, why not?*

Source: From *The Penguin Atlas of Women in the World,* by Joni Seager, copyright © 1997, 2003 by Myriad Editions Ltd, maps & graphics. Used by permission of Penguin, a division of Penguin Group (USA) Inc.

life. In another case, the victim was said to be "sexually voracious" and to have "preyed on men" (Lacayo, 1987). The willing-victim myth is a major motivating force behind many rapes. In a study of convicted rapists, 59 percent denied their guilt and blamed their victims instead. They insisted that their victims seduced them, meant yes while saying no to the sexual assault, and eventually relaxed and enjoyed the rape. Not surprisingly, men who believe this dangerous myth about women are more likely to rape them (Smith, 2002; Scully and Marolla, 1984).

■ Binge Drinking

In recent years there have been many cases of college students dying from binge drinking, which involves having at least five drinks in a row for men or four

drinks in a row for women. According to Dr. David Anderson, of George Mason University in Fairfax, Virginia, at least 50 college students throughout the United States drink themselves to death every year. While endangering their own lives, binge drinkers also tend to disturb or hurt their fellow students, such as causing them to lose sleep, interrupting their studies, and assaulting them physically or sexually (Thompson, 1998; Winerip, 1998).

Although binge drinking is a serious problem, it has long been a tradition on many U.S. college campuses. And despite the raising of the legal drinking age to 21 in all states since the late 1980s, binge drinking continues to be about as prevalent today as it was 20 years ago. According to a nationwide survey, some 44 percent of college students (50 percent of the men and 39 percent of the women) have binged at least

GETTING INTO THEIR CUPS
Binge drinking has long been a serious problem on many college campuses. Some 44 percent of students have binged at least once during the past two weeks. One contributing factor is the stress from having to work hard for good grades. A more important factor is the social pressure to get drunk in order to fit in and not be seen as uptight or antisocial. ■

once during the past two weeks. There is also a relentless quality to the pursuit of intoxication among many students who drink: About 40 percent of students intend to binge or get drunk every time they drink (Wechsler, 1998; Wechsler et al., 1995).

Compared with their moderate or nondrinking peers, binge-drinking students are more likely to miss class, fall behind in schoolwork, have poor grades, engage in unprotected sex, get injured, damage property, fight, or get into trouble with the police. Binge drinkers are also more likely to be male, white, involved in athletics, or living in fraternity or sorority houses (Nelson and Wechsler, 2003; Thompson, 1998; Wechsler, 1998).

Why, then, do they binge drink? The stress from having to work hard for good grades is one contributing factor. A more important factor is the social pressure to get drunk so as to fit in and not to be seen by others as uptight or antisocial. This may explain why a large majority (81 percent) of fraternity brothers and sorority sisters are binge drinkers. The social pressure to fit in can also explain the unusually high incidence of binge drinking among those who regard parties as a very important part of their college life (Wechsler, 1998; Wechsler et al., 1995).

■ Corporate Crime

Corporate crimes are committed by company officials without the overt use of force, and their effect on the victims is not readily traceable to the offender. If a miner dies from a lung disease, it is difficult to prove beyond reasonable doubt that he died *because* the employer violated mine safety regula-

tions. Corporate crimes may be perpetrated not only against employees but also against customers and the general public. Examples include disregard for safety in the workplace, consumer fraud, price fixing, production of unsafe products, and violation of environmental regulations. Compared with traditional street crime, corporate crime is more rationally executed, more profitable, and less detectable by law enforcers. In addition, crime in the executive suite is distinguished from crime in the street by three characteristics that help explain the prevalence of corporate crime.

The Criminal's Noncriminal Self-Image Corporate criminals often see themselves as respectable people rather than common criminals. They maintain their noncriminal self-image through *rationalization*. Violators of price-fixing laws, for example, may insist that they are helping the nation's economy by "stabilizing prices" and serving their companies by "recovering costs." In their book, there is no such crime as price fixing.

The noncriminal self-image is also maintained through *seeing oneself as a victim rather than an offender*. Corporate criminals argue that they were just unlucky enough to get caught for doing something that practically everyone else does. As a convicted tax offender said, "Everybody cheats on their income tax, 95 percent of the people. Even if it's for $10 it's the same principle" (Benson, 1985).

The noncriminal self-image is further maintained through *denial of criminal intent*. Corporate criminals may admit that they committed the acts that landed them in prison, but they regard their acts only as mistakes, not as something motivated by a guilty criminal mind. As a convicted tax offender said, "I'm not a criminal. That is, I'm not a criminal from the standpoint of taking a gun and doing this and that. I'm a criminal from the standpoint of making a mistake, a serious mistake" (Benson, 1985).

The Victim's Unwitting Cooperation Primarily due to lack of caution or knowledge, many victims unwittingly cooperate with the corporate criminal. In a home improvement scheme, victims do not bother to check the work history of the fraudulent company that solicits them, or they sign a contract without examining its content for such matters as the true price and the credit terms. Some victims purchase goods through the mail without checking the reputation of the firm. Doctors prescribe untested drugs, relying only on the pharmaceutical company's salespeople and advertising. It may be difficult for victims to know they have been victimized, even if they want to find out the true nature of their victimization. Average grocery shoppers, for example, are hard put to detect such unlawful substances as residues of hormones, antibiotics, pesticides, and nitrites in the meat they buy.

Society's Relative Indifference Generally, little effort is made to catch corporate criminals. On the rare occasions when they are caught, they seldom go to jail or they receive a light sentence, if they are incarcerated. Their pleas for mercy are heard after they promise to repay their victims or to cooperate in prosecutions against others. They insist that a long

"It's time for your sentence. Which wrist would you like to be slapped on?"

Source: From the *Wall Street Journal*—Permission, Cartoon Features Syndicate.

prison term will do no good because their lives are already in ruins. Even when convicted of crimes that caused the death of many workers or customers, corporate offenders have never been sentenced to death, let alone executed, though numerous lower-class criminals have been executed for killing only one person.

■ Mental Problems

Mental problems are far more common than popularly believed. Every year, about 22 percent of U.S. adults suffer from a mental problem serious enough

CORPORATE CROOK Scott Sullivan (center), a former chief financial officer at WorldCom, a global communication corporation, was arrested on charges of masterminding a $7.2 billion securities fraud. Compared to traditional street crime, corporate crime is more rationally executed, more profitable, and less detectable by law enforcers. Perpetrators are also less likely to receive harsh punishment. ■

to require psychiatric help or hospitalization, and the figure for adolescents is 10 percent (NIMH, 2003). The most common problems are anxiety and phobia followed by depression and alcoholism (Regier et al., 1993). In fact, all of us have been or will be mentally ill in one way or another. Of course, most of our mental problems are not serious. We occasionally suffer from brief bouts of anxiety or depression, "the common cold of mental ailments."

This can be illustrated by what happened for a few days following the terrorist attacks on the World Trade Center and the Pentagon on September 11, 2001. After repeatedly seeing the horrifying images of death and destruction on television, Americans throughout the country suffered from anxiety, depression, and other stress-related symptoms such as fatigue and insomnia. These psychological complaints, in turn, led some to develop physical ailments including ulcers, hypertension, and irritable bowel syndrome (Spake and Szegedy-Maszak, 2001). For most people, though, these problems soon disappeared, thanks, in part, to the surge of social support from relatives, friends, and even strangers.

However, the types of mental problems that sociologists and psychiatrists usually study are more serious and durable. They include **psychosis**, typified by loss of touch with reality, and **neurosis**, characterized by a persistent fear, anxiety, or worry about trivial matters. A psychotic can be likened to a person who thinks incorrectly that 2 plus 2 equals 10 but strongly believes it to be correct. A neurotic can be compared to a person who thinks correctly that 2 plus 2 equals 4 but constantly worries that it may not be so (Thio, 2004).

Sociologists have long suspected that certain social forces are involved in the development of mental problems. The one most consistently demonstrated by research to be a key factor in mental problems is social class: the lower the social class, the higher the rate of mental problems. The poor are more prone to mental disorder because their lives are more stressful: more family problems and unemployment, more psychic frailty and neurological impairments, and less social and emotional support.

Other social factors, such as gender, ethnicity, and culture, give rise to certain types of mental problems. Thus, women are more likely to experience depression and anxiety attacks while men tend more to have antisocial personality, paranoia, and drug and alcohol abuse disorders. Jewish and Asian Americans have a higher incidence of depressive disorders, usually in the form of anger turned against oneself. Puerto Ricans and African Americans tend more to show paranoid and sociopathic propensities in the form of distrust and resentment against others. Finally, certain mental disorders take place in some cultures but never or rarely in others. In Latin America, for example, people experience *susto,* the pathological fear that their souls have left their bodies. In the United States, women get anorexia nervosa, an extreme fear of weight gain that is rarely found in other societies (Thio, 2004; Osborne, 2001).

■ Suicide Bombings

Since the September 11 terrorist attacks, many in the West have assumed that so-called suicide bombers must be psychotic, or at least irrational, and that they must be poor and uneducated. But evidence seems to suggest just the opposite. According to a study on the 149 Palestinian suicide bombers who tried to attack Israel between 1993 and 2002, the majority had about the same social background as the September 11 terrorists. They were young, male, and single. They came from relatively well-off, middle-class families, and they were better educated than most people in their countries. Thus, they were rational enough to know, for example, that they could resort to a suicide bombing as their ultimate weapon in perpetrating an asymmetrical war with Israel. They knew that, like the September 11 terrorists, they couldn't fight a conventional war with their enemy because they had no tanks, no artillery, and no air force, while their enemy had one of the world's most powerful and modern militaries (Dickey, 2002; Krueger and Maleckova, 2002; Ripley, 2002).

Why, then, do these individuals choose to get themselves killed while most other terrorists do not? One apparent reason is the suicide bombers' Muslim religious belief that by becoming martyrs, they will be rewarded in heaven, which includes being greeted by virgins. But this may not hold true for most of the Muslim Chechen suicide bombers in Russia, who are women, nor for the bombers in Sri Lanka and other countries, who are not Muslims (see Figure 6.3, p. 156). Again, what motivates not only the Palestinian terrorists and the September 11 attackers but also the female Chechen bombers and the non-Islamic terrorists to engage in suicide bombing?

The answer can be found with the aid of the sociological concept of *altruistic suicide* (Pedahzur, Perliger, and Weinberg, 2003). Individuals who commit altruistic suicide are so strongly tied to their group that they effectively lose their selves and stand ready to do their group's bidding. Examples from the past include the elderly Inuit and Hindu widows, who faithfully followed the tradition of their societies that encouraged people in their circumstances to commit suicide (see Chapter 1: The Essence of Sociology). Such suicide was relatively common in ancient societies, in which the group reigned supreme at the expense of the individual.

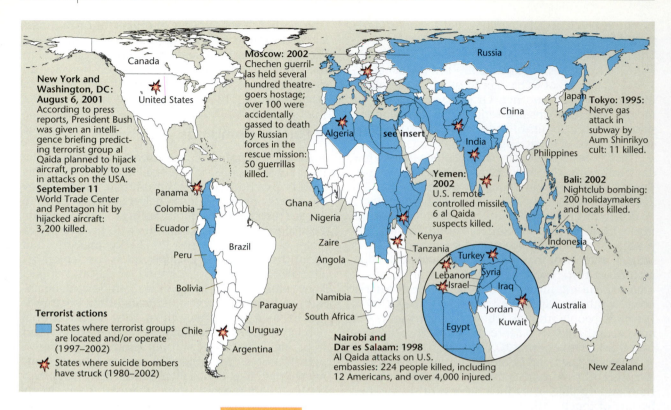

FIGURE 6.3

Suicide Bombers and Other Terrorists

Suicide bombers and other terrorists operate and strike in many countries other than Islamic ones. While the bombers in Islamic countries have the religious belief that they will be greatly rewarded in heaven for being martyrs, this is not true of non-Islamic bombers. What suicide bombers everywhere likely share is a strong bond to a terrorist organization, such that they will sacrifice their lives at its direction.

Critical Thinking: *Is it appropriate to call suicide bombing a form of altruistic suicide? Why or why not?*

Source: From *The Penguin Atlas of War and Peace,* by Dan Smith, copyright © 2003 by Dan Smith. Used by permission of Penguin, a division of Penguin Group (USA) Inc.

Not surprisingly, the suicide bombers of today typically live in traditional societies that give priority to conformity over individuality. And like the altruistic suicides of the past, the suicide bombers are too deeply integrated into their groups—terrorist organizations—and identify completely with them. A number of social factors support their all-consuming ties to these organizations. The candidates for suicide bombings are recruited and then subjected to intense spiritual and ideological indoctrination and terrorist training. In the Middle East, the bomber's surviving family is further provided with such rewards as cash bonuses, pensions, and health benefits. And the bomber is celebrated as a hero in the community. After a young man carries out a suicide attack, his parents may proudly announce his martyrdom in the newspaper (Ripley, 2002).

FUNCTIONALIST PERSPECTIVE: FUNCTIONS AND DYSFUNCTIONS

Most scholars other than sociologists generally attribute deviance to a certain biological or psychological abnormality in the individual. But sociologists have long assumed that there is nothing physically or mentally wrong with most deviants. This assumption is a legacy of the French sociologist Émile Durkheim (1858–1917), one of the founders of functionalism in the discipline. For him, deviance is not only normal but also beneficial to society because, ironically, it contributes to social order. Whereas Durkheim emphasized the functions or benefits of deviance, today's functionalists focus on society's dysfunctions or problems as the causes of deviance.

■ Durkheim: Functionalist Theory

According to Durkheim, deviance can serve a number of functions for society. First, it helps *enhance conformity* in society as a whole. Norms are basically abstract and ambiguous, subject to conflicting interpretations. Even criminal laws, which are far more clear-cut than other norms, can be confusing. The criminal act that a deviant commits and is punished for provides other citizens with a concrete example of what constitutes a crime. From deviants we can learn the difference between conformity and deviance, seeing the boundary between right and wrong more clearly. Once aware of this boundary, we are more likely to stay on the side of rightness.

myth	Deviance is always harmful to society.
reality	Deviance can bring benefits to society if it occurs within limits.

Second, deviance *strengthens solidarity* among law-abiding members of society. Differing values and interests may divide them, but collective outrage against deviants as a common enemy can unite them, as it did Americans in the aftermath of the terrorist attacks on September 11, 2001. Because deviance promotes social cohesion that decreases crime, Durkheim (1915) described it as "a factor in public health, an integral part of all healthy societies."

Third, deviance *provides a safety valve* for discontented people. Through relatively minor forms of deviance, they can strike out against the social order without doing serious harm to themselves or others. Prostitution, for example, may serve as a safety valve for marriage in a male-dominated society because the customer is unlikely to form an emotional attachment to the prostitute. In contrast, a sexual relationship with a friend is more likely to develop into a love affair that could destroy the marriage.

Fourth, deviance can *induce social change*. Martin Luther King, Jr., and other civil rights leaders were jeered and imprisoned for their opposition to segregation, but they moved the United States toward greater racial equality.

There is a limit, however, to the validity of Durkheim's functionalist theory. If deviance is widespread, it can threaten social order in at least two ways. First, it can wreck interpersonal relations. Alcoholism tears apart many families. If a friend flies into a rage and tries to kill us, it will be difficult to maintain a harmonious relationship. Second, deviance can undermine trust. If there were many killers, robbers, and rapists living in our neighborhoods, we would find it impossible to welcome neighbors into our home as guests or babysitters.

Nevertheless, Durkheim's theory is useful for demolishing the commonsense belief that deviance is always harmful. Deviance can bring benefits if it occurs within limits.

■ Merton: Strain Theory

In the 1930s, U.S. sociologist Robert Merton agreed with Durkheim that deviance is "an integral part of all healthy societies." More significantly, Merton drew on Durkheim's concept of *anomie* to develop a theory of deviance that later became well known among sociologists for a long time as *anomie theory* but has also been known since the 1980s as *strain theory*. Literally meaning "normlessness," **anomie** is a social condition in which norms are absent, weak, or in conflict. Anomie may arise, said Merton, when there is an inconsistency in society between the cultural goals and the institutionalized (socially approved, legitimate) means of achieving the goals. In the United States, such an inconsistency surrounds the issue of success.

According to Merton, U.S. culture places too much emphasis on success as a valued goal. From kindergarten to college, teachers prod students to achieve the American dream. Parents and coaches pressure even Little League players not just to play well but to win. The media often glorify winning not only in sports but also in business, politics, and other arenas of life. This emphasis on success motivates hard work, thereby contributing to society's prosperity. But at the same time, people are not equally provided with the legitimate means (such as good jobs and other opportunities) for achieving success. There is, then, an inconsistency between too much emphasis on the success *goal* and too little emphasis on the availability of legitimate *means* for achieving that goal. Such inconsistency produces a *strain* among people in the lower classes, pressuring them to achieve success through what Merton calls *innovation*—using illegitimate means of achieving success, such as committing a robbery or selling drugs.

But most people do not resort to innovation as a response to the goal–means inconsistency. In addition to innovation, four other responses are possible, depending on whether the cultural goal of success and the institutionalized means are accepted or rejected (see Table 6.2):

1. *Conformity,* the most popular form of response, involves accepting both the cultural goal of success and the use of legitimate means for achieving that goal.
2. *Innovation,* the response described earlier, involves accepting the goal of success but rejecting the use of socially accepted means to achieve it, turning instead to unconventional, illegitimate methods.
3. *Ritualism* occurs when people no longer set high success goals but continue to toil as conscientious, diligent workers.
4. *Retreatism* is withdrawal from society, caring neither about success nor about working. Retreatists include vagabonds, outcasts, and drug addicts.
5. *Rebellion* occurs when people reject and attempt to change both the goals and the means approved by society. The rebel tries to overthrow the existing system and establish a new system with different goals and means. An example would be attempting to replace the current U.S. competitive pursuit of fame and riches with a new system that enhances social relations through cooperation.

In short, Merton's theory blames deviance on society's failure to provide all people with legitimate means to achieve success. The theory is useful for explaining the higher rates of robbery, theft, and other property crimes among lower-class people, who are pressured to commit such crimes by their lack of good jobs and other legitimate means for success. But the theory fails to explain embezzlement, tax fraud, and other white-collar crimes because the people who commit such offenses are typically not deprived of the legitimate means for success, as the lower classes are. As a functionalist, Merton assumes that the same value—belief in *material* success—is shared throughout society. But this assumption runs counter to the pluralistic and conflicting nature of U.S. society, where many groups differentiated by class, gender, ethnicity, or religion do not share the same values. Some groups, for example, are more interested in pursuing strong relationships than in "big bucks."

■ Hirschi: Control Theory

A functionalist like Merton, U.S. sociologist Travis Hirschi (1969) assumed that the family, school, and other social institutions can greatly contribute to social order by controlling deviant tendencies in all of us. If such control is lacking or weak, in Hirschi's view, people will commit deviant acts.

According to Hirschi, the best control mechanism against deviance is our bond to others or, by extension, society. He proposed four types of social bond:

1. *Attachment to conventional people and institutions.* Teenagers, for example, may show this attachment by loving and respecting their parents, making friends with conventional peers, liking school, or working hard to develop intellectual skills.
2. *Commitment to conformity.* This commitment can be seen in the time and energy devoted to conventional activities—getting an education, holding a job, developing an occupational skill, improving professional status, building a business, or acquiring a reputation for virtue.
3. *Involvement in conventional activities.* Following the maxim that "Idleness is the devil's workshop," people keep themselves so busy doing conventional things that they do not have time to take part in deviant activities or even to think about deviance.
4. *Belief in the moral validity of social rules.* This is the conviction that the rules of conventional society should be obeyed. People show this moral belief by respecting the law.

If society fails to strengthen these four types of social bond, deviance is likely to flourish. Indeed, many studies have found that the lack of social bond *causes* deviance. But most of these studies, like the theory, have ignored the fact that the lack of bond can also be the *effect* of delinquency. Just as the loss of bond can cause youths to commit delinquency, delinquency can cause youths to lose their bond to society.

■ Braithwaite: Shaming Theory

While Hirschi sees how society controls us through bonding, Australian sociologist John Braithwaite

---

TABLE 6.2

Merton's Typology of Responses to Goal–Means Inconsistency

In U.S. society, according to Merton, there is too much emphasis on success but too little emphasis on the legitimate means for achieving success. Such inconsistency may cause deviant behavior, yet various people respond to it differently.

Response	Success goal	Legitimate means
1. Conformity	+	+
2. Innovation	+	−
3. Ritualism	−	+
4. Retreatism	−	−
5. Rebellion	− +	− +

Note: + signifies accepting; − rejecting; and − + rejecting the old and introducing the new.

OUT IN THE COLD Shackling prisoners to a chain gang is an example of disintegrative shaming, in which the wrongdoer is punished in such a way as to be stigmatized, rejected, or ostracized. Shaming theory suggests that disintegrative shaming is less effective in controlling deviance than reintegrative shaming, in which wrongdoers are made to feel guilty at the same time as they are shown understanding and forgiveness and welcomed back into conventional society. ■

(1989) looks at how society controls us through shaming. Shaming involves an expression of disapproval designed to evoke remorse in the wrongdoer.

There are two types of shaming: disintegrative and reintegrative. In **disintegrative shaming**, the wrongdoer is punished in such a way as to be stigmatized, rejected, or ostracized—in effect, banished from conventional society. It is the same as stigmatization. **Reintegrative shaming** is more positive and involves making wrongdoers feel guilty while showing them understanding, forgiveness, or even respect. It is the kind of shaming that affectionate parents administer to a misbehaving child. It involves "hating the sin but loving the sinner." Thus, reintegrative shaming serves to reintegrate—welcome back—the wrongdoer into conventional society.

Reintegrative shaming is more common in communitarian societies such as Japan, which are marked by strong social relationships or interdependence. Disintegrative shaming is more prevalent in less communitarian societies (characterized by weaker social relationships), such as the United States. Whereas reintegrative shaming usually discourages further deviance, disintegrative shaming tends to encourage more deviance. This is one reason why crime rates are higher in the United States than in Japan. Braithwaite concludes by arguing that the United States can significantly reduce its crime rates if it emphasizes reintegrative shaming in dealing with criminals, as Japanese society does, rather than stigmatization.

Braithwaite may be correct that the practice of reintegrative shaming can reduce crime, especially if it is applied to first-time offenders who have committed relatively minor crimes. But it can hardly have the same positive impact on hardened criminals with little sense of shame for their crimes. And this lack of shame is apparently the result of having been subjected to disintegrative shaming.

CONFLICT PERSPECTIVE: SOCIAL CONFLICT OR INEQUALITY

We have seen how functionalists describe the functions of deviance and attribute deviance to such dysfunctions of society as anomie, weak social bonds, and disintegrative shaming. Now, we will look at how conflict theorists regard social conflict—in the form of inequalities or power differentials—as the cause of deviance.

■ Conflict Theory

Many people assume that the law is based on the consent of citizens, that it treats citizens equally, and that it serves the best interest of society. If we simply read the U.S. Constitution and statutes, this assumption may indeed be justified. But focusing on the *law on the books,* as William Chambliss (1969) pointed out, may be misleading. The law on the books does indeed say that the authorities ought to be fair and just. But are they? To understand crime, Chambliss argued, we need to look at the *law in action,* at how legal authorities actually discharge their duties. After studying the law in action, Chambliss concluded that legal authorities are actually unfair and unjust, favoring the rich and powerful over the poor and weak and consequently creating more criminals among the latter.

Richard Quinney (1974) blamed unjust law directly on the capitalist system. "Criminal law," said Quinney, "is used by the state and the ruling class to secure the survival of the capitalist system." This involves the dominant class's doing four things. First, the dominant class defines as criminal those behaviors (robbery, murder, and the like) that threaten its interests. Second, it hires law enforcers to apply those definitions and protect its interests. Third, it exploits the subordinate class by paying low wages so that the resulting oppressive life conditions virtually force the powerless to commit what those in power have defined as crimes. Fourth, it uses these criminal actions to spread and reinforce the popular view that the subordinate class is dangerous in order to justify its concerns with making and enforcing the law. These factors and the relationships among them are shown in Figure 6.4. The upshot of these four related factors is the production and maintenance of a high level of crime in society (Quinney, 1974).

To Marxists, the capitalists' ceaseless drive to increase profits by cutting labor costs has created a large class of unemployed workers. These people become what Marxists call a **marginal surplus population**—superfluous or useless to the economy—and they are compelled to commit property crimes to survive. Marxists argue that the exploitive nature of capitalism also causes violent crimes (such as murder and assault) and noncriminal deviance (such as alcoholism and mental illness). As Sheila Balkan and her colleagues (1980) explained, economic "marginality leads to a lack of self-esteem and a sense of powerlessness and alienation, which create intense pressures on individuals. Many people turn to violence in order to vent their frustrations and strike out against symbols of authority, and others turn this frustration inward and experience severe emotional difficulties."

Marxists further contend that the monopolistic and oligopolistic nature of capitalism encourages corporate crime because "when only a few firms dominate a sector of the economy they can more easily collude to fix prices, divide up the market, and eliminate competitors" (Greenberg, 1981). Smaller firms, unable to compete with giant corporations and earn enough profits, also are motivated to shore up their sagging profits by illegal means.

Conflict theory is useful for explaining why most laws favor the wealthy and powerful and why the poor and powerless commit most of the unprofitable crimes in society (such as murder, assault, and robbery). The theory is also useful for explaining why crime rates began to soar after the communist countries of the former Soviet Union and Eastern Europe turned to capitalism. But the theory has been criticized for implying that all laws are unjust and that capitalism is the source of all crimes.

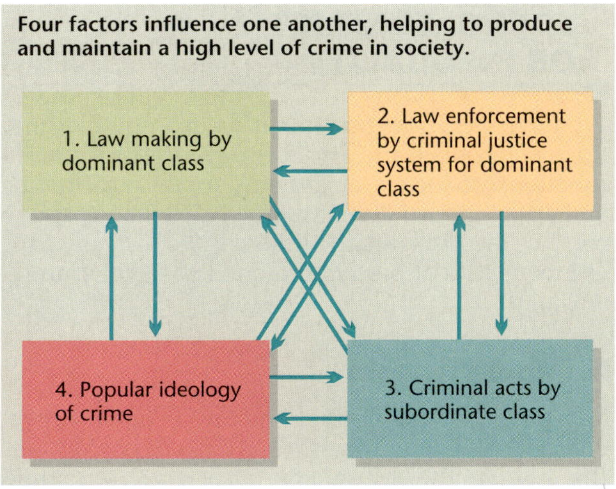

Four factors influence one another, helping to produce and maintain a high level of crime in society.

1. Law making by dominant class
2. Law enforcement by criminal justice system for dominant class
3. Criminal acts by subordinate class
4. Popular ideology of crime

FIGURE 6.4

Quinney's Conflict Theory

These four factors influence one another, helping to produce and maintain a high level of crime in society.

Critical Thinking: *This theory does not mention the crimes committed by the dominant class. Can it explain why people who are rich and powerful sometimes commit crime? If so, how?*

Source: Data from Richard Quinney, *The Social Reality of Crime* (Boston: Little, Brown, 1970).

■ Power Theory

It seems obvious that power inequality affects the quality of people's lives. The rich and powerful live better than the poor and powerless. Similarly, power inequality affects the *type* of deviant activities likely to be engaged in. Thus, the powerful are more likely to perpetrate profitable crimes, such as corporate crime, while the powerless are more likely to commit unprofitable crimes, such as homicide and assault. In other words, power—or the lack of it—largely determines the type of crime people are likely to commit.

Power can also be an important *cause* of deviance. More precisely, the likelihood of powerful people perpetrating profitable crimes is greater than the likelihood of powerless persons committing unprofitable crimes. It is, for example, more likely for bank executives to cheat customers quietly than for jobless persons to rob banks violently. Analysis of the deviance literature suggests three reasons why deviance is more common among the powerful (Thio, 2004).

First, the powerful have a *stronger deviant motivation*. Much of this motivation stems from **relative deprivation**—feeling unable to achieve relatively high aspirations. Compared with the powerless, whose aspirations are typically low, the powerful are more likely to raise their aspirations so high that they cannot be realized. The more people experience relative deprivation, the more likely they are to commit deviant acts.

Second, the powerful enjoy *greater opportunities for deviance*. Obviously, a successful banker enjoys more legitimate opportunities than a poor worker to make money. But suppose they both want to acquire a large sum of money *illegitimately*. The banker will have access to more and better opportunities that make it easy to defraud customers. The banker also has a good chance of getting away with it because the kinds of skills needed to pull off the crime are similar to the skills required for holding the bank position in the first place. In contrast, the poor worker would find his or her illegitimate opportunity limited to crudely robbing the banker, an opportunity further limited by the high risk of arrest.

Third, the powerful are subjected to *weaker social control*. Generally, the powerful have more influence in the making and enforcement of laws. The laws against higher-status criminals are therefore relatively lenient and seldom enforced, but the laws against lower-status criminals are harsher and more often enforced. Not a single corporate criminal, for example, has ever been sentenced to death for marketing an untested drug that "cleanly" kills many people. Given the lesser control imposed on them, the powerful are likely to feel freer to use some deviant means to amass their fortunes and power.

There is some evidence to support this theory, presented in greater detail elsewhere (Thio, 2004). It has been estimated, for example, that in the United States, about six industrial deaths are caused by corporate violation of safety regulations for every one homicide committed by a poor person. It is difficult, however, to get direct data on powerful deviants. Compared with their powerless counterparts, powerful deviants are more able to carry out their deviant activities in a sophisticated and consequently undetectable fashion.

■ Feminist Theory

Many theories about deviance are meant to apply to both sexes. But feminists argue that those theories are actually about men only. Consequently, the theories may be valid for male behavior but not necessarily for that of females.

Consider Merton's strain theory. First, this theory assumes that people are inclined to strive for material

success. This may be true for men but not necessarily for women. In a patriarchal society, women and men are socialized differently. Consequently, women are traditionally less interested in achieving material success, which often requires one-upmanship, and are more likely to seek emotional fulfillment through close personal relations with others.

Second, the strain theory assumes that women who have a strong desire for economic success but little access to opportunities are as likely as men in similar circumstances to commit a crime. Nowadays, given the greater availability of high positions for women in the economic world, the number of ambitious women in the so-called men's world is on the rise. But faced with the lack of opportunities for greater economic success, these women have *not* been as likely as men to engage in deviant activities.

Finally, the strain theory explicitly states that Americans are likely to commit a crime because their society overemphasizes the importance of holding high goals while failing to provide the necessary opportunities for all of its citizens to achieve those goals. But this may be more relevant to men than to women. Despite their greater lack of opportunities for success, women still have lower crime rates than men (Beirne and Messerschmidt, 2000).

The lack of relevance to women in strain and other conventional theories of deviance stems from a male-biased failure to take women into account. In redressing this problem, feminist theory focuses on women. First, the theory deals with women as *victims*, mostly of rape and sexual harassment. The crimes against women are said to reflect the patriarchal society's attempt to put women in their place so as to perpetuate men's dominance.

myth	Because of the feminist movement for gender equality, women today are about as likely as men to commit crimes.
reality	Men still greatly outnumber women in committing crimes because the recent increase in female crime has not been great enough to be significant.

Feminist theory also looks at women as *offenders*. It argues that the recent increase in female crime has not been great enough to be significant. This is said to reflect the fact that gender equality is still far from being a social reality. Like employment opportunities, criminal opportunities are still much less available to women than to men; hence, women are still much less likely to engage in criminal activities. When women do commit a crime, it tends to be the type that reflects their subordinate position in society: minor property crimes such as shoplifting, passing bad checks, welfare fraud, and petty credit card fraud (Miller, 1995; Steffensmeier and Allan, 1995).

In fact, recent increases in female crime primarily involve these minor crimes, largely reflecting the increasing feminization of poverty—more women falling below the poverty line. Not surprisingly, most women criminals are unemployed, high school dropouts, and single mothers with small children. They hardly fit the popular image of the newly empowered, liberated woman, who benefits from any increase in gender equality. There has been no significant increase in female involvement in more profitable crimes, such as burglary, robbery, embezzlement, and business fraud (Miller, 1995; Steffensmeier and Allan, 1995; Weisheit, 1992).

Feminist theory is useful for understanding female deviance. But its focus on female deviance cannot be easily generalized to male deviance.

SYMBOLIC INTERACTIONIST PERSPECTIVE: ASSOCIATION, REACTION, AND INTERPRETATION

Both the functionalist and conflict perspectives portray deviance as a *product* of society. In contrast, symbolic interactionists see deviance as a *process* of interaction between the supposed deviant and the rest of society. This process of interaction involves association, societal reaction, and subjective interpretations that shape the world of deviance.

■ Differential Association Theory

According to Edwin Sutherland (1939), deviance is learned through interactions with other people. Individuals learn not only how to perform deviant acts but also how to define these actions. Various social groups have different norms; acts considered deviant by the dominant culture may be viewed positively by some groups. Each person is likely to be exposed to both positive and negative definitions of these actions. An individual is likely to become deviant if the individual engages in **differential association**, the process of acquiring, through association with others, "an *excess* of definitions favorable to violation of law over definitions unfavorable to violation of law" (Sutherland, 1939).

Suppose a father tells his children that "It's all right to steal when you are poor." He is giving them a prodeviant definition. On the other hand, if the father tells his children that "It's wrong to steal," he is

providing an antideviant definition. If the youngsters pick up a greater number of prodeviant definitions, they are likely to become deviant.

While definitions play a crucial role in the process of becoming deviant, Sutherland emphasized more strongly the importance of social interaction because this is the source of definitions. Thus, Sutherland also stressed that deviance will arise if interactions with those who define deviant behavior positively outweigh interactions with those who define it negatively. Which definitions are most influential depends not just on the frequency and duration of the interactions but also on the strength of the relationship between the interactants.

Sutherland developed his theory to explain various forms of deviance, including white-collar crimes such as tax evasion, embezzlement, and price fixing. All these misdeeds were shown to result from some association with groups that viewed the wrongdoings as acceptable. Still, it is difficult to determine precisely what differential association is. Most people cannot identify the persons from whom they have learned a prodeviant or antideviant definition, much less whether they have been exposed to one definition more frequently, longer, or more intensely than the other.

■ Labeling Theory

Most theories focus on the *causes* of deviance. In contrast, labeling theory, which emerged in the 1960s, concentrates on the *societal reaction* to rule violation and the impact of this reaction on the rule violator.

According to *labeling theorists,* society tends to react to a rule-breaking act by labeling it as deviant. Deviance, then, is not something that a person does but merely a label imposed on that behavior. As Howard Becker (1963) explained, "Deviance is *not* a quality of the act the person commits, but rather a consequence of the application by others of rules and sanctions to an 'offender.' The deviant is one to whom that label has successfully been applied; deviant behavior is behavior that people so label." The label itself has serious and negative consequences for the individual even beyond any immediate punishment.

Once a person has been labeled a thief or a delinquent or a drunk, the individual may be stuck with that label for life and may be rejected and isolated as a result. Finding a job and making friends may be extremely difficult. More important, the person may come to accept the label and commit more deviant acts. Labeling people as deviants, in short, can push them toward further and greater deviance.

Much earlier, Frank Tannenbaum (1938) noted this process of becoming deviant. According to him,

NOT JUST "STICKS AND STONES" According to labeling theory, being called a "deviant" can make a person a deviant. Youngsters may annoy people, bully others, play hooky, and do other things that they innocently consider just a way of having fun. But if these pranks cause the police to label some of those youngsters as "delinquents" and haul them into juvenile court, they are likely to develop a delinquent self-image and try to live up to that self-image by getting increasingly involved in delinquent activities, like the members of this youth gang. ◼

children may break windows, annoy people, steal apples, and play hooky—and innocently consider these activities just a way of having fun. Edwin Lemert (1951) coined the term **primary deviance** to refer to these violations of norms that a person commits for the first time and without considering them deviant. Now, suppose parents, teachers, and police consider a child's pranks to be a sign of delinquency. They may dramatize the evil by admonishing or scolding the child. They may even go further, haul-

ing the child into juvenile court and labeling the child bad, a delinquent—a deviant. The child may develop a bad self-image and try to live up to this self-image by becoming increasingly involved in deviant behavior. Lemert used the term **secondary deviance** to refer to such repeated norm violations, which the violators themselves recognize as deviant. Secondary deviants are, in effect, confirmed or career deviants.

Labeling theory helps us understand how secondary deviance might develop, and it sensitizes us to the power of labels. But the theory has been criticized for at least two reasons. First, it cannot explain why primary deviance occurs in the first place. Second, it cannot deal with deviance that occurs in secret; unknown to others, it cannot be labeled as deviance. Without the label, logically the theory cannot define it as deviance.

◼ Phenomenological Theory

Phenomenologists delve into people's subjectivity (called *phenomenon*), including their consciousness, perceptions, feelings, and opinions about deviance. To really understand deviance, phenomenologists say, we must study people's subjective interpretations of their own deviant experiences.

Generally, phenomenological studies have revealed that deviants tend to see themselves and their deviance in some *positive* way and then behave accordingly. This is what Harold Garfinkel (1967) found in his classic study of Agnes, a hermaphrodite (a person with both male and female sex organs). Agnes was raised as a boy until high school. At 17, she developed an attractive female figure. She then dropped out of school, left home, moved to another city, and tried to begin a new life as a woman. A year later, she went to the UCLA medical center to request a sex-change operation. Garfinkel interviewed her extensively before she underwent surgery.

Garfinkel found that Agnes saw herself as a normal woman and did her best to convince others that that was what she was. She told Garfinkel that she was merely a normal woman who happened to have a physical defect comparable to any other deformity such as a harelip or clubfoot. Like any other normal person with a deformity, she felt it was only natural for her to want to have hers—the male organ—removed. Her self-concept as a normal woman further led her to claim that, as a sexual organ, her penis was "dead," that she had no sexual pleasure from it and felt no sexual attraction to women. She wanted it to be replaced by a surgically constructed vagina. Her self-concept as a normal woman also caused her to make sure that others would not suspect her of having the male organ, so she always wore a bathing

theoretical thumbnail

The Nature and Causes of Deviance

Perspective	Focus	Insights
Functionalist	Functions of deviance and dysfunctions of society	*Durkheim's functionalist theory:* Deviance benefits society by enhancing conformity, strengthening social solidarity, safely releasing discontent, and inducing social change. *Merton's strain theory:* Deviance is caused by society's stressing the importance of success without offering equal opportunities for achieving it. *Hirschi's control theory:* Deviance results from society's failure to develop strong social bonds among its members. *Braithwaite's shaming theory:* Deviance stems from society's frequent use of disintegrative shaming to punish wrongdoers.
Conflict	Deviance as a product of social conflict or inequality	*Conflict theory:* For Chambliss, law enforcement favors the rich and powerful over the poor and weak, thus creating more deviants among the latter. For Quinney, the dominant class produces deviance by making and enforcing laws, oppressing the subordinate class, and spreading the crime ideology. For Marxists, deviance comes from the exploitative nature of capitalism. *Power theory:* Because of their stronger deviant motivation, greater deviant opportunity, and weaker social control, the powerful are more likely to engage in profitable deviance than the powerless in unprofitable deviance. *Feminist theory:* Conventional theories are largely inapplicable to women, while the status of women as certain victims and offenders reflects the continuing subordination of women in patriarchal society.
Symbolic interactionist	Deviance as a process of social interaction	*Differential association theory:* Deviance arises from *association* with various others that yields an excess of prodeviant over antideviant definitions. *Labeling theory:* Being labeled deviant by society (i.e., negative *societal reaction* to certain behavior) leads people to see themselves as deviant and to live up to this self-image by committing more deviant acts. *Phenomenological theory:* Looking into people's *subjective interpretations* of their own experiences is key to understanding their deviant behaviors.

suit with a skirt and never undressed in her female roommate's presence.

In his more recent analysis of murderers, robbers, and other criminals, Jack Katz (1988) also found a similarly positive self-perception that conflicts with society's negative view of the deviant. Murderers, for example, tend to see themselves as morally superior to their victims. In most cases of homicide, because the victims humiliated them, the killers felt outraged and considered the killing a justifiable way of defending their identity, dignity, or respectability.

Phenomenological theory is useful for understanding the subjective world of deviants. But it is doubtful that all, or even most, deviants have a positive view of themselves and their deviance. Some are bound to develop a negative self-image from having been condemned or ridiculed by society, as suggested by labeling theory.

The key points of the theories presented under the functionalist, conflict, and symbolic interactionist perspectives are summarized in the Theoretical Thumbnail at the top of this page.

RUNNING AFOUL OF THE LAW
Contrary to popular belief, African Americans are not always more likely than whites to commit all kinds of crime. African Americans are more likely to commit and be arrested for relatively serious crimes such as murder and robbery. But self-report studies, in which teenagers are asked whether they have committed any offenses, reveal no significant racial differences in such minor deviant acts as petty theft, vandalism, and drunkenness. ■

SOCIAL DIVERSITY IN DEVIANCE

Race, class, and gender play a significant role in deviance, particularly crime and delinquency. As research has often shown, large differences in deviance rates exist among whites, African Americans, and other ethnic groups; between higher and lower income groups; and between men and women (Harris and Meidlinger, 1995; Hawkins, 1995; Steffensmeier and Allan, 1995).

■ Race and Deviance

Self-report studies, in which teenagers are asked whether they have committed any offenses, reveal no significant racial differences in the commission of such minor deviant acts as petty theft, vandalism, and drunkenness. But as the FBI's *Uniform Crime Reports* suggest, African Americans are more likely than whites to commit and be arrested for relatively serious crimes such as murder and robbery, and Asian Americans have lower crime and arrest rates than whites. Similarly, according to victimization surveys, crime victims are more likely to identify African Americans than whites as their offenders and are less likely to finger Asian Americans (Harris and Meidlinger, 1995).

These data, however, do not mean that the biological factor of skin color causes deviance. After all, whites in the United States have a much high-er crime rate than blacks in African countries. Why, then, do U.S. blacks have a higher crime rate than U.S. whites? Major reasons include a higher incidence of poverty and broken homes, largely the results of racism (Mann, 1995; Regulus, 1995). But why are Asian Americans, who also experience racism—though to a lesser degree—less likely to commit crimes than whites? A key reason is the close-knit Asian family, with which its members identify so strongly that they are disinclined to commit crime for fear of bringing shame to the entire family (Kitano and Daniels, 1995; Min, 1995).

■ Class and Deviance

Whether class is related to deviance depends on the *type* of deviance involved. Lower-income teenagers are just as likely as their higher-income peers to engage in nonpredatory victimless deviant acts, such as drug use, drunkenness, and truancy. But lower-income youths tend to commit more serious predatory crimes, such as aggravated assault, robbery, and auto theft, popularly referred to as "street crimes."

Lower-income adults are also more likely than those with higher incomes to commit predatory or street crimes. But higher-income adults tend to commit more profitable white-collar or corporate crimes, such as price fixing, tax evasion, and fraudulent advertising (Harris and Meidlinger, 1995). Reasons include greater motivation to be deviant, greater opportunity, and weaker social control among higher-

Greater Increase in Arrest Rates for Young Women

Since 1990, arrest rates for deviant activities have risen much more for young women than for young men. Still, young men of the same age continue to account for the majority (about 73 percent) of juvenile arrests.

Critical Thinking: *What might cause female teenagers to get more involved in deviant activities today than before? Why do you think females are still less inclined to engage in deviant behavior than their male peers?*

Sources: Data from American Bar Association; National Bar Association, 2001.

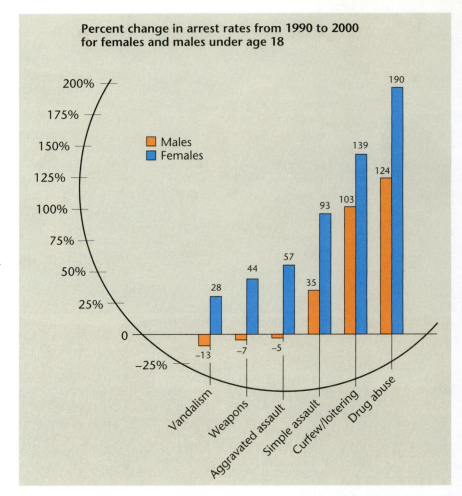

Percent change in arrest rates from 1990 to 2000 for females and males under age 18

Males
Females

Vandalism: Males –13, Females 28
Weapons: Males –7, Females 44
Aggravated assault: Males –5, Females 57
Simple assault: Males 35, Females 93
Curfew/loitering: Males 103, Females 139
Drug abuse: Males 124, Females 190

income people, as suggested earlier in reference to power theory.

Gender and Deviance

Deviance is mostly men's activity. With the exception of prostitution, men are more likely than women to engage in virtually all kinds of crime. The types of offenses more likely to be committed by men range from minor economic crimes (forgery, fraud, and petty theft) to serious economic and violent crimes (robbery, homicide, and aggravated assault). But over the last decade, there has been a great increase in female involvement in mostly minor deviances (see, for example, Figure 6.5). Men still outnumber women, though, in committing most deviant acts, especially the serious ones (Steffensmeier and Allan, 1995).

Several factors may explain the lower rates of deviance among women. One is socialization: Females

are taught to be less aggressive and violent than males. Another is social control: Females are subjected to greater parental supervision and social control than males. A third factor is lack of deviant opportunity: Women are less likely to enjoy deviant opportunities "as a spin-off of legitimate roles or activities." As Darrell Steffensmeier and Emilie Allan (1995) explain, "Women are less likely to hold jobs, such as truck driver, dockworker, or carpenter, that would provide opportunities for theft, drug dealing, fencing, and other illegitimate activities."

A GLOBAL ANALYSIS OF DEVIANCE

Analysis of deviance around the world reveals societal differences in a number of deviant activities (Thio, 2004). First, homicide is generally more likely to occur in poor than in wealthy countries, suggesting that poverty is a major contributing factor. Among wealthy countries, the United States has the highest homicide rate, largely because the poverty rate is considerably higher than in Western Europe, Canada, and Japan. But the ratio of property crimes to violent crimes is generally higher in rich than in poor countries. While poverty serves as a strong *motivation* for committing a crime, property crimes cannot occur without the necessary *opportunities,* namely, the availability of properties as targets for robbery or theft. Since such opportunities abound in more prosperous countries, more property crimes can be expected.

Second, prostitution has recently become a fast-growing global industry. Many unemployed women in formerly communist Russia and Eastern Europe have flocked to more prosperous Western Europe to sell sex. Some of these women, however, have been tricked into prostitution with promises of singing, dancing, modeling, or waitressing jobs from pimps posing as businessmen in their home countries. More women from poor Asian countries have been lured with promises of legitimate jobs to Japan, Western Europe, and North America, only to be sold to brothels (see Figure 6.6). Large numbers of Thai, Indian, and Filipino prostitutes who remain in their home countries cater to local men, as well as to hordes of Japanese and Western men on organized sex tours. Most of these prostitutes come from poor villages. Thus, poverty, along with exploitation by richer countries, contributes to the sex trade.

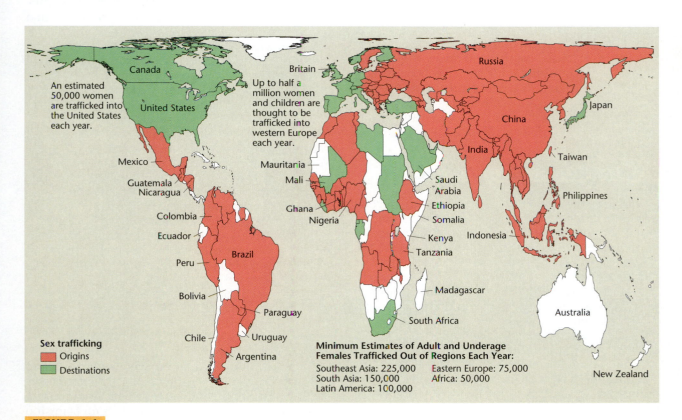

FIGURE 6.6

The Global Sex Trade

Prostitution has turned into a multibillion-dollar global industry, and it thrives on the inequality between rich and poor countries. Generally, women in poor countries in Asia, Latin America, and Eastern Europe are lured with promises of good jobs to rich countries such as Japan and those in Western Europe and North America, where they are forced into prostitution.

Critical Thinking: *What fuels the demand for foreign prostitutes? And how could the global sex trade be stopped?*

Source: From *The Penguin Atlas of Women in the World,* by Joni Seager, copyright © 1997, 2003 by Myriad Editions Ltd, maps & graphics. Used by permission of Penguin, a division of Penguin Group (USA) Inc.

Third, suicide is generally more common in modern than in traditional societies. But among modern societies, countries such as Finland, Denmark, and Austria have higher rates of suicide than do the United States, Spain, and Italy. The higher suicide rate seems related to greater social equality. In societies with greater equality, people are less subjected to social regulation—and weak regulation is a key contributor to suicide. As Durkheim (1915) suggested, less regulated individuals are more encouraged to expect too much from life and thus become more liable to greater frustration when expectations fail to materialize.

Fourth, organized crime differs across societies. Members' loyalty to crime organizations appears stronger in Japan and Hong Kong than in the United States. The syndicates in Hong Kong, Japan, Italy, and Russia have penetrated legitimate business and politics more deeply than those in the United States. Not surprisingly, antisyndicate measures fail more frequently in those countries than in the United States. There is one important similarity between U.S. organized crime and its counterparts in other countries: They all serve as a "crooked ladder of upward mobility" for the ambitious poor, who can become rich by joining a syndicate (Thio, 2004).

CONTROLLING DEVIANCE

As discussed in Chapter 3 (Socialization), society transmits its values to individuals through socialization. If families, schools, and other socializing agents do their jobs well, then individuals internalize the values of their society, accepting society's norms as their own. Even in poor inner-city neighborhoods, many people successfully internalize the norms of the society at large, becoming conformists and law-abiding citizens.

Internalization through socialization is the most efficient way of controlling deviance. It produces unconscious, spontaneous self-control. As a result, most people find it natural to conform to most social norms most of the time. Violating the norms makes them feel guilty, ashamed, or at least uncomfortable. They act as their own police officers.

Nevertheless, for reasons suggested by the various theories that we have discussed, a few people commit serious crimes, and everyone deviates occasionally, at least from some trivial norms. Thus, control by others is also needed to limit deviance and maintain social order. This control can be either informal or formal. Relatives, neighbors, peer groups, and even strangers enforce *informal* controls through discipline, criticism, ridicule, or some other treatments. *Formal* controls are usually imposed by police, judges, prison guards, and other law enforcement agents.

Compared with small traditional societies, large industrialized societies have a more extensive system of formal control. Perhaps formal control has become more important in modern nations because they have become more heterogeneous and more impersonal than traditional societies. This societal change may have increased social conflicts and enhanced the need for formal control, particularly the criminal justice system.

■ Criminal Justice

The criminal justice system is a network of police, courts, and prisons. These law enforcers are supposed to protect society, but they are also a potential threat to an individual's freedom. If they wanted to ensure that not a single criminal could slip away, the police would have to deprive innocent citizens of their rights and liberties. They would restrict our freedom of movement and invade our privacy—by tapping phones, reading mail, searching homes, stopping pedestrians for questioning, and blockading roads. No matter how law abiding we might be, we would always be treated like crime suspects—and some of us would almost certainly fall into the dragnet.

To prevent such abuses, the criminal justice system in the United States is restrained by the U.S. Constitution and laws. We have the right to be presumed innocent until proven guilty, the right not to incriminate ourselves, and many other legal protections. The ability of the police to search homes and question suspects is limited. Thus, our freedom, especially from being wrongly convicted and imprisoned, is protected.

In short, the criminal justice system faces a dilemma: If it does not catch enough criminals, the streets will not be safe; if it tries to apprehend too many, people's freedom will be in danger. Striking a balance between effective protection from criminals and respect for individual freedom is far from easy. This may be why the criminal justice system is criticized from both the right and the left, by one group for coddling criminals and by the other for being too harsh.

myth	The U.S. criminal justice system is, by any measure, soft on criminals.
reality	The United States appears to be soft on criminals because extremely few criminals are apprehended and punished. But compared with other democracies, the United States is tougher in imprisoning proportionately more criminals and imposing longer prison terms.

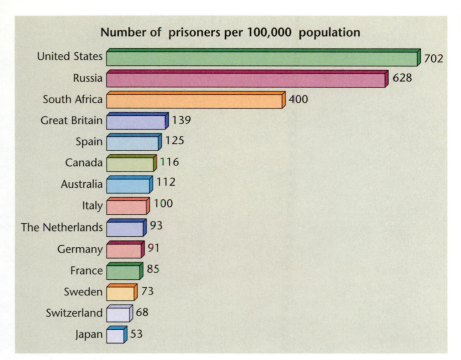

Number of prisoners per 100,000 population

United States	702
Russia	628
South Africa	400
Great Britain	139
Spain	125
Canada	116
Australia	112
Italy	100
The Netherlands	93
Germany	91
France	85
Sweden	73
Switzerland	68
Japan	53

FIGURE 6.7

Imprisonment around the World

The United States has the dubious distinction of being the number-one jailer in the world. At least half of the enormous prison population has ended up in jail because of the "get tough" policy toward criminals in the last 15 years.

Critical Thinking: *Can imprisoning more criminals reduce crime? Why or why not?*

Source: Data from The Sentencing Project, 2003.

Both criticisms have some merit. Most criminals in the United States are never punished. Of the 35 million crimes committed every year, less than half—about 15 million serious crimes—are reported to the police. Of these serious crimes, only 20 percent (3 million) result in arrest and prosecution. Of the 3 million prosecuted, 2 million are convicted, of whom 25 percent (500,000) are sent to prison. Ultimately, then, *less than 2 percent* of the original 35 million offenders are put behind bars. Moreover, most of these prisoners do not serve their full terms because they are released on parole. The average prisoners serve only about one-third of their sentences (U.S. Census Bureau, 2003; Anderson, 1998, 1994).

Does this mean that the U.S. criminal justice system is soft on criminals? Not necessarily. The United States punishes crime more severely than any other democratic nation. It has been for many years the number-one jailer in the world (see Figure 6.7). Since 1985, the U.S. prison population has more than doubled to about 1.6 million inmates—more than 2 million if local jail inmates are included. Imprisonment is also generally longer than in other democratic countries. The length of imprisonment is generally measured in weeks and months in Sweden but in years in the United States. The United States is also the only industrialized nation in the West that still executes convicted murderers (Anderson, 2003; Mauer, 1999; Currie, 1998; Gilliard and Beck, 1996).

Does the comparatively harsh treatment in the United States help reduce crime rates? The increasing rates of incarceration and the lengthening of prison sentences since the early 1980s have indeed reduced crime by removing from the streets many more hardcore criminals, who commit most of the crimes in society. But the decline in crime cannot be attributed to stepped-up imprisonment alone. Other factors are also involved, such as the economic boom in the 1990s, increases in citizen-led policing, and a dwindling population of teenagers—the age group with a very high crime rate. However, "we are sitting on a demographic crime bomb" because in the new millennium, the proportion of teenagers in the U.S. population will be much greater than it was in the 1990s (Rosenfeld, 2002; DiIulio, 1995).

■ The Death Penalty

In 1998, Karla Faye Tucker, age 38, was executed in Texas for murdering two people with a pickax 15 years earlier. She was the first woman put to death by the state since the Civil War and the second woman in the United States officially killed since 1976, the year when the U.S. Supreme Court reinstated the death penalty. Most Americans believe that the death penalty is an effective deterrent to murder. Many sociologists, however, have for a long time found otherwise, given the following forms of evidence.

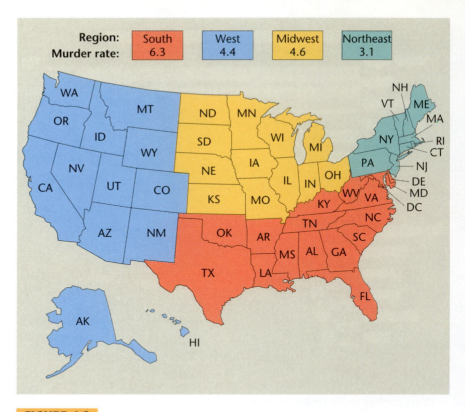

Region:	South	West	Midwest	Northeast
Murder rate:	6.3	4.4	4.6	3.1

FIGURE 6.8

Murder Rates Highest in the South

Generally, states that execute convicted murderers, such as those in the South, have higher murder rates than states that do not have the death penalty.

Critical Thinking: *Do you think the murder rate indicates how safe a region is to live in? Why or why not?*

Source: Data from FBI, *Uniform Crime Reports,* 2001.

First, the homicide rates in *states that have retained the death penalty law* are generally much higher than in *states that have abolished* it. As Figure 6.8 shows, Southern states, which still practice the death penalty, generally have higher murder rates than the states in other regions, which have mostly abolished capital punishment. This suggests that the death penalty does not appear to deter murder.

Second, within the same states, murder rates generally did not go up *after* the death penalty was abolished. Moreover, the *restoration* of capital punishment in states that had abolished it earlier did *not* lead to a significant decrease in homicides.

A third piece of evidence came from comparing the number of homicides *shortly before and shortly after executions* of convicted murderers that had been widely publicized. If the death penalty has a deterrent effect, the execution should so scare poten-

tial killers that they would refrain from killing, and the number of homicides in the area should decline. This may sound logical, but reality contradicts it. In Philadelphia during the 1930s, for example, the number of homicides remained about the same in the period from 60 days *before* to 60 days *after* a widely publicized execution of five murderers. This finding, among others, suggests that the death penalty apparently does not prevent potential killers from killing even when the state shows people that it means business.

Finally, similar findings have appeared in studies of various societies. As a classic study of 14 nations concludes:

If capital punishment is a more effective deterrent than the alternative punishment of long imprisonment, its abolition ought to be followed by homicide rate increases. The evidence examined

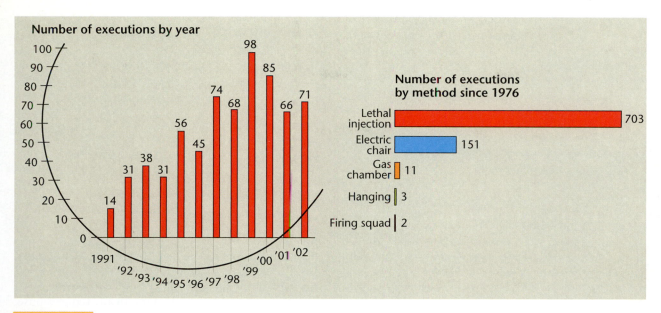

Number of executions by year

Number of executions by method since 1976

Lethal injection 703
Electric chair 151
Gas chamber 11
Hanging 3
Firing squad 2

The Death Penalty in the United States

Capital punishment is much more prevalent in the United States today than a decade ago. But since 1976, the methods of execution supposedly have become more humane, with lethal injection being by far the most often used.

Critical Thinking: *Do you think the death penalty deters people from committing murder? Why or why not?*

Source: Data from Death Penalty Information Center, 2003.

here fails to support and, indeed, repeatedly contradicts this proposition. In this cross-national sample, abolition was followed more often than not by absolute *decreases* in homicide rates, not by the increases predicted by deterrence theory. (Archer and Gartner, 1984)

Why doesn't the death penalty seem to deter murder? One reason is that murder is a crime of passion, most often carried out under the overwhelming pressure of a volcanic emotion, namely, uncontrollable rage. People in such a condition cannot stop and think about the death penalty. Another reason is that the causal forces of murder, such as severe poverty and child abuse, are simply too powerful to be neutralized by the threat of capital punishment.

Although it does not seem to deter murder, most Americans support the death penalty, and increasing numbers of people have been put to death in recent years (see Figure 6.9). There is, however, an apparent attempt to appear civilized in doing away with convicted killers. As Figure 6.9 further indicates, barbaric methods of execution, such as hangings and firing

squads, are for all intents no longer used; they have been replaced by the supposedly more humane methods of lethal injection and electrocution. Concern has also increased that innocent people are sometimes executed. In 2003, for example, the Illinois governor commuted the sentences of all the death-row prisoners in his state because he believed that "the capital system is haunted by the demon of error." The error of executing innocents usually comes from racial bias, coerced confessions, and unreliable witnesses (Cloud, 2003).

■ The Medicalization of Deviance

Deviance can be willful or unwillful. Increasingly in modern industrial societies, especially the United States, if deviance is considered willful, it tends to be defined as a crime, and the criminal justice system is called on to control it. But if deviance is considered unwillful, it tends to be defined as an illness, and medicine, as a social institution, is used to control it. This involves the **medicalization of deviance**, diagnosing and treating deviant behavior as a disease. A good example is the common practice of diagnosing hyperactivity in schoolchildren as a medical problem and then treating it with drugs such as Ritalin, Concerta, and Adderall (Zernike and Petersen, 2001).

Even more commonly, medical psychiatrists, who use drugs to treat mental illness like a physical disease, define many ordinary problems in our lives as mental disorders. Consider, for example, what the psychiatric profession calls the *disorder of written expression*. This so-called mental disorder consists of the poor use of grammar or punctuation, sloppy paragraph organization, awful spelling, and terrible handwriting. It is possible that some students who exhibit these traits may be mentally ill, but it is doubtful that most students with similar problems are mentally ill; they are simply weak or unskilled writers. Also, consider the *oppositional defiant disorder,* from which children are said to suffer if they often do any four of the following things: lose tempers, argue with adults, disobey adults, annoy people, blame others for their own behavior, or act touchy, angry, or spiteful. It is possible that in the heat of the moment, some parents may say that their disobedient kids are mentally ill. But it is doubtful that most parents believe that these irritating behaviors are signs of mental disorder (Kirk and Kutchins, 1994, 1992).

Once diagnosed as mentally ill, the individual is likely to be treated or controlled. Various social and government agencies, for example, often recruit psychiatrists to treat youngsters whose behaviors offend or disturb others, behaviors such as being defiant, using drugs, fighting, hating school, or being disrespectful. Actually, most of these youngsters have experienced poverty, child abuse, or family misery. But instead of dealing with the abnormal environment that causes troublesome behaviors, the psychiatrists label those normal children as mentally ill and then isolate or incarcerate them and give them drugs. In short, kids who stand out as different may be labeled mentally ill and controlled accordingly (Armstrong, 1993).

■ The War on Drugs

The war on drugs consists of two basic strategies. One is punitive: using law enforcement to stop the supply of drugs and punish drug sellers and users. The other is supportive: using drug prevention (or education) and treatment to reduce the demand for drugs and help drug addicts. The U.S. war on drugs is mostly punitive, as the government devotes most of its antidrug budget to law enforcement. (This has caused the U.S. prison population to double over the last 15 years, reaching 2.1 million in 2003.) But the war is targeted mostly at relatively powerless groups, particularly poor African Americans and Hispanics, who are much more likely than affluent whites to be arrested and convicted for drug offenses (Anderson, 2003; Musto, 2002; Currie, 1993).

The law enforcement approach has failed to reduce the general level of drug use, and this has led to calls for the legalization of drugs. Advocates of legalization contend that, like Prohibition (of alcohol) in the 1920s, current drug laws do more harm than good. They are said to generate many crimes, including homicides, and to encourage police corruption. By legalizing drugs, proponents argue, the government can take away obscene profits from drug traffickers, end police corruption, and reduce crime drastically. Finally, legalizers believe that with legalization, the huge amount of money currently spent on law enforcement can be used for drug treatment and education, which will dramatically reduce abuse.

Those who oppose legalization respond that if drugs are legalized, drug use and addiction will skyrocket (Forbes, 1996). As William Bennett (1989), a former national drug control policy director, points out, "After the repeal of Prohibition, consumption of alcohol soared by 350%."

Sociologist Elliott Currie (1999; 1993) has argued that neither drug warriors nor legalizers can solve the problem of widespread drug abuse and crime because they ignore the root causes of the problem—namely, poverty, racism, and inequality. Currie proposes that the government eradicate the causes of the problem by providing employment to all, increasing the minimum wage, expanding the Job Corps, boosting health care for the poor, offering paid family leave, providing affordable housing, and reducing social inequality.

Since 1996, California and eight other states have legalized the use of marijuana by patients with cancer, AIDS, and other serious diseases to ease their pain. More states are expected to follow suit. But the federal government has been challenging those laws and won a victory in 2001 when the U.S. Supreme Court effectively ordered a California group to stop distributing marijuana for medical use. The Court stopped short of invalidating those states' medical-marijuana laws, however, which meant individual patients still could obtain and use the drug. Even if the Court later finds those states' laws unconstitutional, juries are unlikely to convict sick people for pot possession, as polls have shown that the majority of Americans (nearly 75 percent) favor medical-marijuana use (Roosevelt, 2001).

Even so, it is doubtful that marijuana and other illicit drugs will soon be legalized for use by the general population throughout the United States. Most Americans seem viscerally opposed to the legalization of drugs. They particularly do not want to have heroin, cocaine, and other hard drugs as easily available as tobacco, alcoholic beverages, and other legal drugs (Bennett, 2001; Rosenthal, 1995).

sociological frontiers

Shyness as a New Disease

As we saw at the beginning of this chapter, what constitutes deviance varies from one historical period to another. Thus, what was not considered deviant in the past could become deviant today if it is labeled as such. This may explain why a fast-growing number of people are doing something they would not have thought of doing before: going to their doctors for a prescription drug to cure their shyness.

In the past, many people knew that they were shy, but it never crossed their minds that shyness was a pathology, a disease that requires medical treatment. Recently, though, a number of social forces have converged to turn shyness into a mental disorder. First, in 1980, the psychiatric profession labeled extreme shyness as a *social phobia* or *social anxiety disorder.* At that time, the condition was regarded as a *rare* disorder, as it involved experiencing not only a distracting nervousness at parties or before giving a speech but also a powerful desire to avoid these social situations altogether. Next, some movie stars, big-name athletes, and other celebrities appeared on talk shows, in magazines, and on other media to disclose their struggles with shyness. Finally, the pharmaceutical company Smith Kline Beecham entered the picture by advertising and selling its antidepressant Paxil as a medicine for shyness. And thus, Americans were left with the impression that shyness is far more serious and widespread than they had ever realized.

As a result, many people today regard shyness as a disease, a medical problem serious enough to require treatment with a drug. But shyness is a serious problem only for a very few—those who are extremely bashful or truly incapacitated by fears of others' disapproval and need relief through the use of psychoactive drugs. For the majority, however, shyness is only a mild problem. According to a recent survey, nearly half of all Americans consider themselves shy and still manage to carry on a normal social life. Also consider the fact that many of these Americans may actually not be shy at all. In American culture today, it is difficult *not* to feel shy given the ubiquitous media full of immodest and even brazen talkers, just as it is difficult not to feel fat with the media presentation of extremely thin beauties (Talbot, 2001).

In short, what was once considered a personality trait is now labeled as a disease and treated with drugs.

 ■ For more of the latest Sociological Frontiers, look up Continuing Update at www.ablongman.com/thio6e.

using *sociology*

How to Manage Your Drinking

As noted earlier, heavy drinking is a serious problem on many college campuses. The traditional approach to this problem has been simply to stop teenagers from drinking. Thus, since 1988, every state has raised the legal drinking age to 21. Doing so seems to have produced some positive results, such as a drop in drinking and in alcohol-related auto deaths among underage youths.

But a growing number of college administrators have argued recently that the higher drinking age has, in some ways, made drinking more dangerous. Before the enactment of the drinking age law, drinking took place in the open, where it could be supervised by police, security guards, and even health-care workers. When the drinking age went up, drinking did not stop, however. It simply moved underground to homes, cars, and frat-house basements, hidden from adults and authorities. In response to this development, campus administrators have tried to find another more effective way to solve the problem of excessive drinking.

A solution was found at Hobart and William Smith Colleges in New York. In 1996, one of the colleges' sociology professors, Wesley Perkins, did a survey at his school and found that students *believed* their peers were drinking five times a week when in *reality* they were drinking only twice a week. In another study conducted on 100 other campuses, students also overestimated their peers' drinking. These findings prompted Perkins to ask: If young people believe that most of their fellow students drink a lot, might they be more inclined to join them? But if they believe excessive drinking is relatively rare on their campus, might they drink more moderately? In short, Perkins hypothesized that students would drink in accordance with the social norm of drinking or, as has been suggested earlier in this chapter, the dictates of peer pressure at their school.

In 1997, Perkins's school spent about $2,000 to test the hypothesis. Using posters and newspaper ads, college officials publicized the fact that most students drank only twice a week and that just one-third of the students drank three-quarters of the alcohol on campus. Over the following two years, Perkins observed a significant (21 percent) drop in excessive drinking. When the same program was later carried out at other colleges, the reduction in frequent drinking was also significant— from a 20 percent drop at Western Washington University to a 44 percent plunge at Northern Illinois University (Kluger, 2001b).

What this study suggests is clear: If you drink, you should know that most of your fellow students actually drink less than you think, so you should not feel any pressure to drink heavily. Thinking critically, what would you do to overcome the pressure to drink heavily? Which deviance theory or theories provide the best ideas to deal with this problem and why?

CHAPTER REVIEW

1. *What is deviance?* It is an act considered, by public consensus or by the powerful at a given time and place, to be a violation of some social rule.

2. *In what ways does homicide occur?* Homicide involves nonstrangers more than strangers. It takes place most frequently during weekend evenings, especially for lower-class offenders. Guns are often used to commit homicide, and their easy availability has contributed to a startling upsurge in teen homicide. *What is the culture of rape?* It encourages men to rape women by treating women as if they are men's property, as if they are the trophies of men's masculinity contests, and as if they want to be raped. *Why do many college students binge drink?* One reason is stress from having to work hard for good grades; another reason is the social pressure to get drunk so as to fit in. *How does corporate crime differ from street crime?* Corporate crime is more rationally executed, more profitable, and less detectable. Corporate offenders do not see themselves as criminals, their victims unwittingly cooperate with them, and society does little to punish them. *What group is more likely than others to have mental problems?* People who are poor are most prone to mental problems primarily because their lives are more stressful than others'. Gender, ethnicity, and culture are also involved in the development of specific types of mental disorder. *Why do suicide bombers choose to die?* They choose to die because of their extremely stong ties to terrorist organizations, which indoctrinate and train them and also provide their surviving relatives with various benefits.

3. *What does Durkheim's functionalist theory tell us about deviance?* Deviance helps enhance conformity, strengthen social solidarity, provide a safe release for discontent, and induce social change. *According to Merton's strain theory, what is the cause of deviance?* U.S. society emphasizes the importance of success without providing equal opportunities for achieving it. One possible response to this inconsistency is deviance. *How are Hirschi's and Braithwaite's theories similar, and how are they different?* Both assume that social control leads to conformity and, therefore, the absence of control causes deviance. According to Hirschi, the absence of control arises from a lack of social bonds. To Braithwaite, the absence of control comes from disintegrative shaming.

4. *What does conflict theory say about deviance?* According to Chambliss, law enforcement favors the rich and powerful over the poor and weak. In Quinney's view, the dominant class produces crime by making criminal laws, hiring enforcers to carry out the laws, oppressing the subordinate class into deviance, and spreading the ideology that the lower class is crime-prone and dangerous. Marxists argue that the exploitative nature of capitalism produces violent crimes and noncriminal deviances. *How does the power theory explain deviance?* The powerful are more likely to engage in profitable deviance than the powerless are in unprofitable deviance because the powerful have a stronger deviant motivation, greater deviant opportunity, and weaker social control. *What is the feminist theory of deviance?* Conventional theories may be relevant to men but not to women. Women are likely to be victims of rape and sexual harassment, which reflect men's attempt to put women in their place. Although female crime has recently increased, it is not significant because most of the increase involves minor property crimes with very little profit, reflecting the continuing subordinate position of women in a patriarchy.

5. *How does differential association lead to deviance?* Deviance occurs if interactions with those who define deviance positively outweigh interactions with those who define it negatively. *How is being labeled deviant likely to affect people?* The label may cause them to look on themselves as deviant and to live up to this self-image by engaging in more deviant behavior. *What insight about deviance does phenomenological theory offer?* We can understand deviance better by looking at people's subjective interpretations of their own deviant experiences.

6. *How is deviance related to the social diversity of U.S. society?* African Americans are more likely than whites to be arrested for relatively serious crimes, whereas Asian Americans have the lowest arrest rates. Groups with lower incomes are more likely to commit predatory or street crimes than are their higher-income peers. Men are more likely than women to engage in practically all kinds of crime.

7. *How does deviance differ across societies?* Homicide is more likely to occur in poor countries or in rich countries with high rates of poverty. Property crimes

are more prevalent in wealthy countries because targets for such crimes are more abundant. Prostitution flourishes in poor countries as a result of both poverty and exploitation by richer countries. Suicide is more common in modern and egalitarian societies. Organized crime is stronger and more a part of legitimate business and politics in countries other than the United States, but it serves as an avenue to success for the ambitious poor in all countries.

8. *Is the U.S. criminal justice system soft on criminals?* It appears so because extremely few criminals are apprehended and punished, but compared with other democracies, the United States imprisons proportionately more people and imposes longer prison terms. *Why doesn't the death penalty deter murder?* Because murder is a crime of passion resulting from uncontrollable rage and because the larger social causes of murder are simply too powerful to be neutralized by the threat of capital punishment. *What is involved in the medicalization of deviance?* Medicine as a social institution is used to control what is considered unwillful deviance by diagnosing and treating it as a disease. *How does the government wage the war on drugs?* It focuses its efforts much more on law enforcement than on treatment and education. Failure of the drug war has led some to advocate legalizing drugs, arguing that it would take away obscene profits from drug traffickers, end police corruption, and reduce crime drastically. Opponents respond that legalization would cause rampant drug use and addiction without reducing crime.

9. *Why do some people today want to take medication for their shyness?* The primary reason is that shyness is now widely labeled a medical problem. *How can college students avoid excessive drinking?* By knowing that the social norm on their campus does not encourage excessive drinking, students can resist the peer pressure to drink.

▌KEY TERMS

Anomie   A social condition in which norms are absent, weak, or in conflict (p. 157).

Deviance   An act that is considered by public consensus, or by the powerful at a given place and time, to be a violation of some social rule (p. 148).

Differential association   The process of acquiring, through interaction with others, "an *excess* of definitions favorable to violation of law over definitions unfavorable to violation of law" (p. 162).

Disintegrative shaming   The process by which the wrongdoer is punished in such a way as to be stigmatized, rejected, or ostracized (p. 159).

Marginal surplus population   Marxist term for unemployed workers who are superfluous or useless to the economy (p. 160).

Medicalization of deviance   Diagnosing and treating deviant behavior as a disease (p. 171).

Neurosis   The mental problem characterized by a persistent fear, anxiety, or worry about trivial matters (p. 155).

Primary deviance   Norm violations that a person commits for the first time and without considering them deviant (p. 163).

Psychosis   The mental problem typified by loss of touch with reality (p. 155).

Rape   Coercive sex that involves the use of force to get a woman to do something sexual against her will (p. 150).

Reintegrative shaming   Making wrongdoers feel guilty while showing them understanding, forgiveness, or even respect (p. 159).

Relative deprivation   Feeling unable to achieve relatively high aspirations (p. 161).

Secondary deviance   Repeated norm violations that the violators themselves recognize as deviant (p. 163).

▌QUESTIONS FOR DISCUSSION AND REVIEW

WHAT IS DEVIANCE?

1. What determines whether a person has violated a social norm?

EXAMPLES OF DEVIANCE

1. What does it mean to call homicide a personal crime?
2. What is the culture of rape, and how does it encourage the crime?
3. How common is college binge drinking, and what causes it?
4. What distinguishes corporate crime from street crime?
5. How common are mental problems in the United States, and what does social class have to do with such problems?
6. What causes suicide bombings?

FUNCTIONALIST PERSPECTIVE: FUNCTIONS AND DYSFUNCTIONS

1. According to Durkheim, in what ways can deviance benefit society?
2. How did Merton explain the high crime rate in the United States?
3. How does Hirschi's control theory explain deviance?
4. In Braithwaite's view, how is shaming related to society and deviance?

CONFLICT PERSPECTIVE: SOCIAL CONFLICT OR INEQUALITY

1. How does conflict theory explain the nature of laws and the cause of deviance?
2. How does the power theory explain why deviance is more prevalent among the powerful?
3. How does feminist theory differ from other theories of deviance?

SYMBOLIC INTERACTIONIST PERSPECTIVE: ASSOCIATION, REACTION, AND INTERPRETATION

1. How does differential association lead to deviance?
2. What occurs when some people move from primary to secondary deviance?
3. What does phenomenological theory tell us about deviants?

SOCIAL DIVERSITY IN DEVIANCE

1. How are race, class, and gender related to deviance?

A GLOBAL ANALYSIS OF DEVIANCE

1. How do some forms of deviance vary from society to society?

CONTROLLING DEVIANCE

1. In what ways can the U.S. criminal justice system balance the need to catch criminals with the need to respect individual freedom?
2. Why doesn't the death penalty seem to deter murderers?
3. How does the medicalization of deviance affect people's lives?
4. How has the drug war been fought in the United States?
5. What are the pros and cons in the debate over drug legalization?

SOCIOLOGICAL FRONTIERS/USING SOCIOLOGY

1. How has shyness been turned into a disease?
2. How did some colleges and universities reduce the incidence of excessive drinking among their students?

SUGGESTED READINGS

Chambliss, William J. 2000. *Power, Politics, and Crime*. Boulder, CO: Westview Press. An analysis of how the prison population has grown greatly as a result of political, governmental, and media efforts to spread the fear of crime among the general public.

Goode, Erich, and Machman Ben-Yehuda. 1994. *Moral Panics: The Social Construction of Deviance*. Cambridge, MA: Blackwell. Explains why people react with unreasonable fear to a nonexistent or relatively harmless threat.

Mauer, Marc. 1999. *Race to Incarcerate*. New York: Free Press. Shows how incarceration does not necessarily reduce crime.

Russell, Diana H. 1998. *Dangerous Relationships: Pornography, Misogyny, and Rape*. Thousand Oaks, CA: Sage. Presents the thesis that pornography causes rape.

Thio, Alex. 2004. *Deviant Behavior*, 7th ed. Boston: Allyn & Bacon. A text that covers all the major theories in the sociology of deviance and a wide range of deviant behaviors.

■ Additional Resources

The New York Times
expect the world®
nytimes.com

Expand your knowledge of the concepts discussed in this chapter by reading the following current and historical articles from the *New York Times*. Go to the "eThemes of the Times" section of the Companion Website (www.ablongman.com/thio6e):

"A West Side Story: From Crime King to Mentor"
"Father Steals Best: Crime in an American Family"

Research Navigator.com

Research Navigator, a research database, provides immediate access to hundreds of full-text articles from EBSCO's ContentSelect Academic Journal Database. If the Research Navigator access code was included with your textbook, go to the website www.researchnavigator.com and read the following articles related to this chapter by typing in the article number:

Blankenship, Kevin L., and Bernard E. Whitley, Jr. "Relation of General Deviance to Academic Dishonesty." *Ethics and Behavior*, Jan2000, Vol. 10 Issue 1, p1, 12p, 3 charts. Accession Number:

3176620. Investigates the relationship between cheating and other forms of minor deviance.

Rock, Paul. "Rules, Boundaries and the Courts: Some Problems in the Neo-Durkheimian Sociology of Deviance." *British Journal of Sociology*, Dec98, Vol. 49 Issue 4, p586, 16p. Accession Number: 1422400. Investigates problems in the sociology of deviance and crime in Great Britain.

chapter 7

U.S. and Global Stratification

myth   As the world's leading democratic society, the United States has the most equal distribution of income.

reality   Although the U.S. income distribution is more equal than that of developing countries, it is less so than that of most other industrial nations, such as Japan, Sweden, and Germany (p. 180).

myth   Given the great diversity in the U.S. population, various groups are bound to disagree on whether a particular occupation is desirable.

reality   Virtually all groups, rich and poor, rate occupations in the same way. Even people in other countries evaluate occupations in the same way (p. 182).

myth   Homelessness is a new phenomenon in the United States.

reality   There have always been homeless people in the United States (p. 195).

myth   Most of the poor people in the United States are on welfare.

reality   Only one-third of the poor are on welfare (p. 195).

myth   As many rags-to-riches stories in the media show, it is not *uncommon* for a poor man's child to become a millionaire in this land of opportunity.

reality   It *is* uncommon for a poor person in the United States to become a millionaire. The success experienced by many in the past involved moving only a little way up the economic ladder. Since 1980, the rich have gotten richer and the poor poorer (p. 196).

myth   Because most immigrants are poor and need financial assistance, countries with unusually large numbers of them cannot become prosperous.

reality   The world's most prosperous societies, such as the United States, Canada, Israel, and Australia, have unusually large numbers of immigrants (p. 198).

Juliette Zinwue remembers how three years ago, when she was 7, a man paid her parents and took her along with other children from their village in the West African country of Benin to a city. There, she was put to work in the home of a relatively wealthy woman. Since then, Juliette has been rising at 6 A.M. every day to sweep the house and courtyard, wash the dishes, and clean out the garbage cans. For the rest of the day, she sells trinkets and hair accessories at the local market for her boss. Juliette's story is far from unusual in West and Central Africa, where, according to the United Nations Children's Fund, some 200,000 children are sold every year to work as slaves (Robinson and Palus, 2001).

The misery of the slaves reflects the most brutal form of **social stratification**, the system in which some people get more or fewer rewards than others. Most other types of stratification in today's world are far less brutal but nonetheless powerful enough to have a significant impact on human lives. In this chapter, we will discuss these and other aspects of social stratification.

THE BASES OF STRATIFICATION

Of the many rewards people can receive in life, sociologists have long identified three as the most important bases of stratification in the United States: wealth, power, and prestige. These three are, respectively, economic, political, and social rewards. They usually go together. People who are rich are also likely to have political power and social prestige. But possession of one reward does not guarantee enjoyment of others. Compared with teachers, some garbage collectors may make more money but have less prestige and power.

■ Wealth

In the nineteenth century, Karl Marx divided industrial society into two major classes and one minor class: the *bourgeoisie* (capitalists), the *proletariat* (workers), and the *petite bourgeoisie* (small capitalists). Marx differentiated them on the basis of two criteria: whether they own the means of production—tools, factories, offices, and stores—and whether they hire others to work for them. Capitalists are those who own the means of production and hire others. Workers neither own the means of production nor employ others; hence they are forced to work for capitalists. Small capitalists own the means of production but do most of the work themselves. Examples are shopkeepers, doctors, lawyers, and other self-employed persons. Marx considered these people a minor transitional class because he believed that they would eventually be forced down into the working class when their means of production were taken over by giant corporations.

In Marx's view, exploitation characterizes the relationship between the two major classes: capitalists and workers. Capitalists, bent on maximizing profits, compel workers to work long hours for little pay. Such exploitation was, indeed, extreme in Marx's time. Consider his description of child laborers:

> Children of nine or ten years are dragged from their squalid beds at two, three, or four o'clock in the morning and compelled to work for a bare subsistence until ten, eleven, or twelve at night, their limbs wearing away, their frames dwindling, their faces whitening, and their humanity absolutely sinking into a stone-like torpor, utterly horrible to contemplate. (Marx, 1866)

Marx believed that eventually workers would rise in revolt and establish a classless society of economic equals. But his prophecy of revolution has not materialized in any highly developed capitalist economy. Writing in the 1860s, Marx failed to foresee that the exploitation of workers would ease and that a large, prosperous class of white-collar workers would emerge, as it has in the United States.

myth	As the world's leading democratic society, the United States has the most equal distribution of income.
reality	Although the U.S. income distribution is more equal than that of developing countries, it is less so than that of most other industrial nations, such as Japan, Sweden, and Germany.

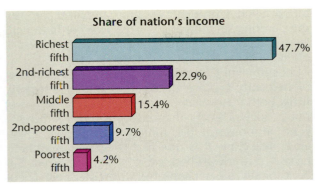

FIGURE 7.1

Unequal Income Distribution in the United States

The incomes of richer Americans far exceed those of poorer Americans. The richest fifth of the U.S. population, for example, receives nearly 48 percent of the nation's income, whereas only 4 percent goes to the poorest fifth. All this makes the U.S. income inequality the greatest in the industrial world.

Critical Thinking: *Do you think people who are poor resent people who are rich? Why or why not?*

Source: Data from U.S. Census Bureau, 2003.

CRUEL CONDITIONS Karl Marx believed that capitalists sought to maximize profit by exploiting workers. He had seen the appalling working conditions in English factories in the mid nineteenth century, where women and children were employed for long hours at low pay. Conditions in the United States were not much better, as shown here in a famous photograph of child laborers taken by Lewis Hine in the early twentieth century. ■

Even so, the United States still suffers from glaring economic inequalities. According to the latest data, the richest 20 percent of the population earn nearly *48 percent* of the nation's total income. In contrast, the poorest 20 percent have *only 4.2 percent* of the national income (see Figure 7.1). In fact, the U.S. income inequality is the greatest in the industrial world (Bradsher, 1995; Wright, 1995).

■ Power

Power—the ability to control the behavior of others, even against their will—is associated with wealth. Most sociologists agree that people with more wealth tend to have more power. This is evident in the domination of top government positions by the wealthy. Higher-income persons are also more likely to feel a strong sense of power. Thus, they are more likely to be politically active, working to retain or increase their power. Meanwhile, lower-income people are more likely to feel powerless to influence major political decisions. They are therefore more indifferent to politics and less likely to participate in political activity—a reaction likely to exacerbate their lack of power.

It is clear that power is distributed unequally. To what extent? A lot? A little? Power cannot be identified and measured as easily as wealth because people with power do not always express it. As a result, sociologists disagree about how it is distributed.

Both Marxist and elite theorists argue that a very small group of people hold most of the power in the United States. According to *Marxist theorists,* that group consists of *capitalists* (or *top business leaders*). Even if they do not hold office, say Marxists, capitalists set the limits of political debate and of the government's actions, protecting their own interests. This is why large corporations, through heavy political campaign contributions and congressional lobbying, are able to hold down their taxes and avoid government regulation. According to *elite theorists,* a lot of power resides in what C. Wright Mills (1959a) called the **power elite**, a small group of top leaders not just from business corporations but also from the federal government and the military. Members of this power elite have similar backgrounds, values, and interests, and together they have enormous power to make important decisions for the nation.

In contrast to both Marxist and elite theorists, *pluralist theorists* argue that power is not tightly concentrated but widely dispersed—more or less equally distributed among various competing groups. The power of big business, for example, is balanced by that of big labor, and government actions are ultimately determined by competition and compromise among such diverse groups. Even ordinary citizens have the power to vote anyone into or out of office.

In sum, while Marxists and elitists see a great deal of inequality in power distribution, pluralists see very little. Both views may be correct. Most of the power in U.S. society is concentrated at the top, but the elite is not all-powerful. It is subject to challenge by voters from below. It is true that the general public is usually powerless—because it is not organized. But occasionally, when people feel strongly enough about an issue to make their wishes known, as they did in opposition to the Vietnam War in the 1960s, the government does change its policy to follow public opinion.

■ Prestige

A third basis of social stratification is the unequal distribution of prestige. Following Max Weber's lead, sociologists call this kind of stratification a **status system**, a system in which people are stratified according to their social prestige.

Prestige differs from wealth and power. Wealth and power are objective entities; an individual can have them regardless of what other people think of the individual. But prestige is subjective, depending on how the individual is perceived by others. If the individual is rich and powerful but is seen by others as unworthy of respect, the individual has low prestige. The boss of an organized crime syndicate may

make millions and exercise awesome power, but he will never acquire prestige because most people refuse to hold him in esteem—and they cannot be forced to do so. On the other hand, many college professors may not be rich and powerful, but they do enjoy more prestige than the crime boss. Why the difference? The answer has much to do with occupation.

myth	Given the great diversity in the U.S. population, various groups are bound to disagree on whether a particular occupation is desirable.
reality	Virtually all groups, rich and poor, rate occupations in the same way. Even people in other countries evaluate occupations in the same way.

For many years, sociologists have found that people have very definite ideas about the prestige of various occupations. In 1947, a team of sociologists asked a large random sample of the U.S. population to evaluate 90 occupations on a scale from "excellent" to "poor." Since then, similar surveys have been periodically taken using different representative samples. The result has always been the same: Occupations that require more *education* and offer higher *income* than others are generally given higher prestige scores. Figure 7.2 shows a recent occupational ranking. Almost everybody, rich or poor, has rated the occupations in the same way. Even people in many other countries—some industrialized and

HIGH AND LOW In a sexist society, women usually suffer from status inconsistency, the condition in which the same individual is given two conflicting status rankings, such as being high in occupation but low in gender. A female doctor has a high occupational status, but she may have less prestige because of prejudice against her gender. ■

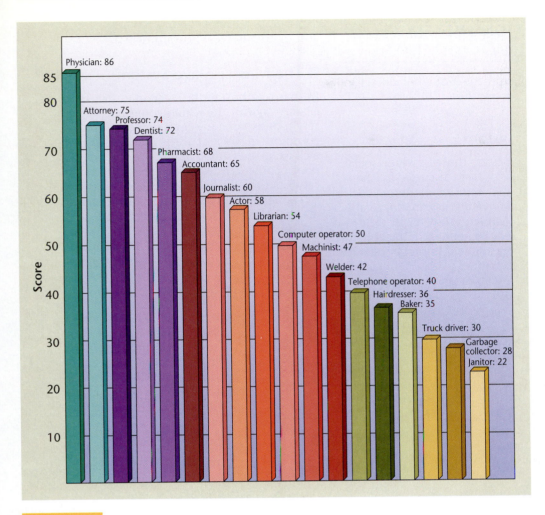

FIGURE 7.2

How Occupations Are Rated in the United States

When asked to rate the prestige of different occupations on a scale from 1 to 100, people tend to give higher scores to jobs that require more education and offer higher income, as suggested in the selected occupations here.

Critical Thinking: *Which do you value most: wealth, power, or prestige? Why?*

Source: Data from NORC, *General Social Surveys, 2001,* pp. 1391–1409.

some not—have been found to rank occupations in the same way (Treiman, 1977; Hodge et al., 1964).

Occupation is only one of a person's many statuses among those based on age, race, and gender. These statuses may create **status inconsistency**, the condition in which the same individual is given two conflicting status rankings, such as being high in occupation but low in ethnicity or gender. An African American lawyer and a female executive, for example, both have high occupational statuses, but they may have less prestige because of prejudice against their race and gender, respectively. People plagued with status inconsistency usually experience considerable stress. They resent the source of their status inconsistency. They think of themselves in terms of their higher status and expect others to do the same. But others may treat them in reference to their lower status. Consequently, people with status inconsistency are likely to support liberal and radical movements designed to change the status quo.

STRATIFICATION SYSTEMS: A GLOBAL VIEW

Stratification exists around the globe but differs in form from one society to another.

■ The Egalitarian System

The least stratified societies are those in which social inequality is minimal. As has been discussed in Chapter 2 (Society and Culture), hunting-gathering societies are the most *egalitarian*. Still, they are not totally free of inequalities. Adult men enjoy higher status than women and children. Shamans (comparable to priests) and better hunters are held in higher esteem than others. But such inequalities pale in significance when compared with those in most other societies.

Hunter-gatherers tend to be egalitarian primarily because there is hardly any opportunity in their small-scale environment for anyone to accumulate wealth. Similarly, large-scale societies without wealth-accumulating opportunities, such as communist countries, tend to be more egalitarian than capitalist societies. Deprived of those opportunities, segments of the population within a large-scale society, such as peasants, industrial workers, or pastoral laborers, are

FEUDAL TOIL Today, the feudal system persists in a few places in Latin America, such as Peru. The tenant-workers must pay for the use of land through long hours of work for the landlord. Though the landlord does pay some money for this work, the amount is small and most tenant-workers live in deep poverty. ■

also more likely than others to practice equality among themselves (Howard, 1993).

■ The Master-Slave System

In sharp contrast to the egalitarian society is the *master-slave system,* in which some people are held in servitude as someone else's property. This system was common in ancient Egypt, Rome, and Athens, as well as in the United States. Most of the slaves were poor people, ethnic groups considered inferior, war captives brought home from conquered nations, or foreigners imported for sale. They did most of the manual labor in society. The emergence of slavery has been attributed partly to the great accumulation of wealth in those ancient societies that could produce huge food surpluses with improved technology (Nolan and Lenski, 1999).

Today, slavery is outlawed in virtually all societies, but it still persists in certain areas. Some of this modern slavery is similar to the ancient form of human bondage called *chattel slavery*. It exists, for example, in the North African country of Mauritania. But most slaves today fall victim to *debt bondage,* which forces whole families to work in fruitless efforts to pay off loans. These debt slaves can be found in parts of India, Pakistan, Thailand, Peru, and Haiti.

■ The Feudal System

Compared with the master-slave system, the *feudal system* is less extreme in practicing inequality. This system was prevalent in the agrarian societies of medieval Europe, Asia, and Latin America. These societies were stratified into two groups: those who worked the land and those who appropriated some of the produce and labor of the workers. The first group is called *serfs* or *peasants,* and the second is called *lords* or *landlords.*

The feudal system emerged largely because the collapse of centralized political authority had caused considerable chaos, as well as struggles for power among warlords. To survive, various segments of the farming population were compelled to give some of their products to different lords for military protection.

Today, the feudal system persists only in a few places in Latin America. In highland Peru, the feudal system, called the *hacienda,* consists of two key groups of people: the landlord and the tenant-workers (with the administrators hired by the landlord to oversee the workers). To pay for the use of the land, tenant-workers work on the landlord's farm, work as servants in the landlord's house, do repairs on the landlord's house, or perform other services for the landlord. All this leaves tenant-workers little time to work for themselves. The landlord does pay them some money, but the amount is too small to keep them from falling into deep poverty (Howard, 1993).

The Caste System

The feudal and master-slave systems have one thing in common. Both are similar to the **caste system**, a relatively rigid stratification system in which people's positions are ascribed and fixed. Being *ascribed* means that positions in this hierarchy are primarily determined by inherited characteristics, such as one's race or sex. The positions are also fixed: People must marry within their caste, children are born into their parents' caste, and movement from one caste to another almost never occurs. Unlike the feudal and master-slave systems, though, the caste system does not necessarily involve one caste working solely for another.

A clear-cut example can be found in India, where people are stratified into five castes on the basis of occupation. The highest caste consists of (1) *Brahmins*—priests and scholars—considered the most spiritually pure. These are followed by (2) *warriors*, (3) *merchants*, (4) *artisans* and *menial workers*, and (5) *untouchables*, whose work is considered too spiritually unclean. The untouchables are, in effect, outcasts and can almost never become members of a higher caste. Members of higher castes fear that they would suffer ritual pollution if they touched an outcast or passed through the shadow of an outcast. Such fear, however, is slowly fading in the big cities, where people often rub shoulders to get by on the street. Still, the caste system continues to dominate the lives of rural people, who make up about 70 percent of India's population (Waldman, 1996).

The Indian caste system is associated with *religion*—the Hindu belief that people's castes reflect the moral quality of their actions in a previous life: The worse the actions, the lower the caste. In contrast, until recently, the caste system in South Africa has been based on *race*. Black, white, and colored groups were rigidly segregated by law as well as custom.

The Class System

Less rigidly segregated than the caste system is the **class system**, a relatively open stratification system in which people's positions are achieved and changeable. Since achieved characteristics such as education and skill can change, people can be socially mobile—moving from one position to another. The class system is the primary form of stratification in virtually all societies. But the inequality between classes varies in degree from one society to another.

The amount of social inequality in a society depends on its economic development. More precisely, a curvilinear, inverted-U relationship exists between development and inequality. As a country develops, inequality initially increases, then peaks, levels off, and finally declines (see Figure 7.3). This changing relationship between development and inequality is known as the **Kuznets curve**, named after its discoverer, Simon Kuznets.

As preindustrial societies develop, economic surplus increases, allowing some groups to accumulate more wealth than others, which spurs increases in social inequality. When these societies are in the midst of a transformation from agricultural to industrial, economic productivity and population growth surge, pushing inequality to its peak. Only when societies begin to become predominantly industrial does inequality start to decrease. Reasons include educational expansion and political democracy. As more people are educated, pressure for democracy increases, causing inequality to diminish.

However, since 1970, there have been signs of a resurgence of inequality in many industrial societies, including the United States, Canada, Sweden, Australia, and Germany. Contributing factors include increases in global competition, the shift from a

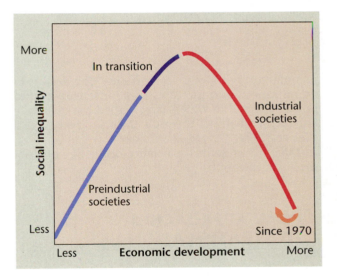

FIGURE 7.3

The Kuznets Curve

There is a curvilinear, inverted-U relationship between economic development and social inequality. As a nation develops as a preindustrial society, inequality initially increases. But as the preindustrial society becomes industrial, inequality declines. Since 1970, however, inequality has increased in many industrial societies.

Critical Thinking: *What should U.S. society do to reduce inequality?*

Source: Data from Francois Nielsen, "Income Inequality and Industrial Development: Dualism Revisited," *American Sociological Review,* 59 (October 1994), pp. 654–677.

TABLE 7.1

Types of Social Stratification

Stratification Types	Key Characteristics
Egalitarian system	Least stratified, with minimal inequality, most characteristic of hunting-gathering or other societies with too few wealth-accumulating opportunities.
Master-slave system	Most stratified, with maximum inequality, in which some people are someone else's property. Though universally outlawed, chattel slavery still exists in Mauritania. Most slaves are, however, victims of debt bondage.
Feudal system	Consists of two greatly unequal groups: farm laborers (or peasants) and farm owners (landlords), with peasants working for their landlords for extremely little pay. Known as the *hacienda* in a few places in Latin America.
Caste system	Made up of several segregated groups whose positions are ascribed and fixed, as in master-slave and feudal systems, but the lower castes are not forced to work for the higher castes, as in India.
Class system	Less rigidly segregated than the caste system, with more opportunities for moving from one class to another; the primary form of stratification in nearly all societies.

manufacturing to a service economy, the decline of unionization, and increases in poor female-headed households, all of which have caused the masses to fall further behind the rich (Morris et al., 1994; Nielsen, 1994).

Table 7.1 presents the essence of the five types of social stratification.

NEW APPROACHES TO STRATIFICATION

The study of social stratification has long excluded the experiences of women, minorities, and older people as victims of gender, ethnic, and age inequalities. Only recently have sociologists begun to take seriously the feminist and multicultural thinking that emphasizes the importance of taking women, minorities, and the elderly into account when investigating social stratification (Grusky, 2001).

■ The Feminist Perspective

The traditional study of stratification focuses on men only. Their income, occupation, and education are often used to determine not only their own social class but also that of their daughters or wives. Similarly, the income of the male head—never the female head—of a household is used to indicate the class of the family (Grusky, 2001; Szelenyi, 1994; Abbott and Wallace, 1990). All this might reflect the reality of a traditional society, in which the overwhelming majority of gainfully employed individuals are men and most of the families are headed by men. But today, especially in the United States, most women are employed. Moreover, most families are no longer headed solely by men, with Dad driving off to work and Mom tending the home and kids. Such families make up only about one-fourth of all U.S. households. The majority of families are now headed by two gainfully employed spouses or by a single mother (see Chapter 10: Families).

Focusing on men in the study of stratification also distorts the real nature of social mobility in—or openness of—the society under investigation (Berberoglu, 1994; Abbott and Wallace, 1990). With the domination of women by men removed from the picture, the society does appear more open and egalitarian than it is. Because women represent a huge portion of the population, their experiences of struggling against gender bias, if taken into account, clearly show the society to be much less open than is suggested by research on male subjects only.

WORKING WOMEN In the United States today, men are no longer the overwhelming majority of gainfully employed individuals because most women have joined the workforce. By continuing to focus on men, as in the past, we are bound to see society as more open and egalitarian than it actually is. Only by taking into account the generally lower incomes of working women in comparison to men can we realistically see society as less open and egalitarian. ■

Thus, to feminists, gender inequality should be considered a key part of a society's social stratification. A person's gender should be used, along with the traditional indicators of social class (income, occupation, and education), to determine the individual's class (Grusky, 2001; Ferree and Hall, 1996).

■ Social Diversity

Like gender, other social characteristics, particularly race and ethnicity, are important to consider when analyzing stratification in a multicultural society such as the United States. Like women, racial-ethnic minorities generally have less money, power, and prestige than the dominant group and find themselves overrepresented in the lower strata of society. This racial or ethnic inequality, like gender inequality, makes U.S. society less open than it would appear to be without it. Therefore, in addition to gender, income, occupation, and education, ethnicity can be said to determine a person's class. Similarly, age can be considered a determinant of a person's class because older retirees generally have less money and other social rewards than younger people (Anderson and Massey, 2001; Jankowski, 1995; Lieberson, 1994).

Gender, ethnic, and age stratifications have one thing in common: They are *ascribed,* providing differential opportunities, rewards, privileges, and power to individuals based on criteria (gender, ethnicity, and age) that normally cannot be altered. But these three types of ascribed stratification also differ in their impact on individuals and families. In age stratification, the *same* individuals experience within their life span both *advantages* at a younger age and *disadvantages* at an advanced age. In gender stratification, discrimination against women creates a loss for all female *individuals* but no net loss for families with an equal number of females and males. In ethnic stratification, discrimination hurts all minority individuals *and* families (Anderson and Massey, 2001; Lieberson, 1994).

The nature and consequences of these three forms of ascribed stratification are discussed in greater detail in the next four chapters. Here we focus on *achieved stratification,* better known in sociology as *social classes* or *class structure.*

THE U.S. CLASS STRUCTURE

One form of social inequality in the United States can be observed in the way the society is divided into different social classes, forming a distinctive class structure.

■ Identifying Classes

Sociologists have long defined **social class** as a category of people who have about the same amount of income, power, and prestige. But how do we know who is in which class? There are three different methods for identifying a person's class.

Reputational Method One way of finding out which classes people belong in is through the **reputational method,** identifying social classes by selecting a group of people and asking them to rank others. These selected individuals, or informants, typically have been living in the community for a long time and can rank many other residents on the basis of their reputation. If these judges are asked to rank a man whom they know to be a public drunk, they will put him in a lower-class category. If they are asked to rank a woman whom they know as a respectable banker, they will place her in an upper-class category.

The reputational method is useful for investigating the class structure of a small community where everybody knows practically everybody else. It has several disadvantages, however. First, the reputational method cannot be applied to large cities because it is impossible to find individuals who know thousands of other people. Second, it is impossible to generalize the findings from one community to another because the informants can judge only their own community. Third, it is impossible to find unanimity among the reputation judges in a community. There are always cases in which an individual is considered upper class by one judge but middle class by another.

Subjective Method   To find out the class structure of a large population, we can use the **subjective method,** identifying social classes by asking people to rank themselves.

In using this method, sociologists have long discovered that, if asked whether they are in the upper, middle, or lower class, the overwhelming majority of people will identify themselves as middle class. Both *upper class* and *lower class* have connotations offensive to democratic values. To call oneself upper class is to appear snobbish. To call oneself lower class is demeaning. As a result, many millionaires would call themselves middle class rather than upper class; meanwhile, many low-income people, such as maids and laborers, would also regard themselves as middle class. But if given *working class* as a fourth choice, many people will identify themselves as members of the working class rather than the middle class.

Thus, the weakness of the subjective method is twofold. The result depends heavily on how the question is asked, and respondents may lie about their social class. Despite these problems, the subjective method has at least two advantages. First, it can be used to investigate large cities or even an entire society. Second, it is useful for understanding and predicting behaviors that are strongly affected by attitudes. If self-employed auto mechanics, electricians, and plumbers identify themselves with the upper class, they can be expected to hold politically conservative views and to vote Republican, just as upper-class people tend to do.

Objective Method   Both subjective and reputational methods rely on people's perceptions of class. The third method depends on objective criteria, such as how much people earn annually. The **objective method** involves identifying social classes using income, occupation, and education to rank people.

Like the subjective method, the objective method is useful for identifying the classes of a large population. It has another advantage, as well: Sociologists can easily obtain the needed data on occupation, income, and education from the Bureau of the Census or by mailing questionnaires to the people themselves. Most important, the combination of occupation, income, and education, which constitutes what sociologists call *socioeconomic status (SES),* exerts a powerful influence on our lives. Not surprisingly, sociologists use the objective method of identifying classes much more often than the other two methods.

The objective method has at least one disadvantage, however. In using objective criteria, such as income and education, we can distinguish clearly between the top and the bottom of the class ladder, but it is difficult to differentiate the huge number of people in the middle. Researchers are therefore forced to establish an *arbitrary* boundary between classes—say, choosing 12 years of education rather than 11 or 13 to distinguish between the middle and working classes. As a consequence, many people who are said to be *middle* class in one study are determined to be *working* class in another.

■ Class Profiles

In the United States, very few people are either in the top, upper class or in the bottom, lower class. The majority are somewhere in the middle, and that group can be divided into the upper-middle class, the middle class, and the working class. Sociologists may disagree about the precise boundaries of these classes, but most would accept the rough estimates of their sizes based on family income (see Figure 7.4).

The Upper Class   Although it is a mere 3 percent of the population, the upper class possesses more than half of the wealth in the United States. This class consists of both the old rich and the new rich. The *old rich* are families that have been wealthy for generations—an aristocracy of birth and wealth. Examples are the Rockefellers, the Vanderbilts, and the Du Ponts. By contrast, the *new rich* have created their own wealth. They include Bill Gates of Microsoft, Michael Eisner of Disney, and TV talk show host Oprah Winfrey.

However their wealth is acquired, members of the upper class are very rich. They live in exclusive areas,

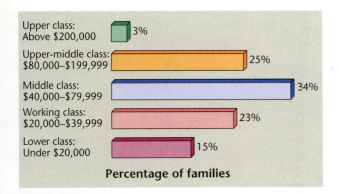

FIGURE 7.4

The U.S. Class Structure

The objective method of identifying social classes involves the use of people's income, occupation, and education. How much people make reflects the status of their occupation and the level of their education reasonably well. Thus, the distribution of annual family income in the United States can be used to show what the American class structure looks like.

Critical Thinking: *Do you expect to move up into a higher social class someday? Why or why not?*

Source: Data from U.S. Census Bureau, 2003.

belong to private social clubs, rub elbows with one another, and marry their own kind—all of which keeps them so aloof from the masses that they have been called the *out-of-sight class* (Fussell, 1992). But their lifestyles, such as wearing expensive clothes in affluent settings, are so often portrayed on TV that the masses try to emulate the rich by spending more than they can afford (Schor, 1998). More than any other class, the rich tend to be conscious of being members of a class. They also command an enormous amount of power and influence in government and business, affecting the lives of millions.

The Upper-Middle Class People in the upper-middle class are distinguished from those above them primarily by their lesser wealth and power and from those below them by their highly successful and profitable careers as doctors, lawyers, midsized business owners, and corporate executives. Many have graduated from prestigious universities and have advanced degrees. They work with unbounded enthusiasm, live comfortably with sky-high incomes, and are the envy of their professional peers.

The Middle Class The middle class constitutes the largest class in the United States and is much more diverse in occupation than the upper-middle class. It

is made up of people with college educations or at least high school diplomas. They work in low- to mid-level white-collar occupations as average professionals, small-business owners, salespersons, managers, teachers, secretaries, bank clerks, and cashiers. They have achieved the middle-class dream of owning a suburban home.

The Working Class The working class consists primarily of those who have little education and whose jobs are manual and carry little prestige. The working class is also distinguishable for having more part-time workers and union members than other classes (Heath, 1998). Some working-class people, such as construction workers, carpenters, and plumbers, are skilled workers and may make more money than some members of the middle class, such as secretaries and teachers. But their jobs are more physically demanding and, especially in the case of factory workers, more dangerous.

Other working-class people are unskilled, such as migrant workers, janitors, and dishwashers. There are also many women in this class working as domestics, cleaners, and waitresses. Because they are generally underpaid, they have to hold two jobs. Still, they find it hard just to get by, and every now and then, they are faced with a critical hardship, such as having their utilities shut off or doing without needed med-

"The Vanzeebs are old money, the Hendersons are new money, and the Gluttners are lottery money."

Source: From the *Wall Street Journal*—Permission, Cartoon Features Syndicate.

SITTING PRETTY In general, the middle class does not have inherited wealth and must earn the money to support its lifestyle. Middle-class people can be wealthy if they own successful businesses or rise to the tops of their professions. But others in the middle class are not well-off, such as teachers, church ministers, and middle-level managers. Virtually all, however, have realized the American dream of owning a suburban home.

ical care (Ehrenreich, 2001). They are thus called the *working poor.*

The working poor could escape poverty if their pay were raised significantly above the minimum wage (less than $6 an hour) to a *living wage* (above $10 an hour). However, employers are opposed to such a wage increase because it would drive up the cost of doing business. But in those cities and counties that have passed a living-wage law, the higher wages have brought about gains in productivity, lower job turnover, and greater loyalty to employers, all of which helps offset the cost (Roston et al., 2002).

The Lower Class The lower class is characterized by joblessness and poverty. It includes the chronically unemployed, welfare recipients, and the impoverished aged. These people suffer the indignity of living in rundown houses, wearing old clothes, eating cheap food, and lacking proper medical care. Very few have finished high school. They may have started out in their youth with poorly paying jobs that required little or no skill, and their earning power began to drop when they reached their late twenties. A new lower class has emerged in recent decades: people who were once skilled workers in mechanized industry but became unskilled workers in electronically run factories, where they first served as helpers, then occasional workers, and finally the hard-core unemployed.

Most members of the lower class are merely poor. But they are often stigmatized as the *underclass,* a term conjuring up images of poor people as violent criminals, drug abusers, welfare mothers who cannot stop having babies, or able-bodied men on welfare who are too lazy to work.

■ The Influence of Class

One of the most consistent findings in sociology is that people in different classes live differently. In fact, the influence of class is so great and pervasive that it is taken into account in nearly every sociological study. This is why we have discussed the impact of class on childhood socialization and mental illness in previous chapters. We will also examine class differences in religion, politics, and other human behaviors in later chapters. Here, we focus on how social class affects life chances and lifestyles.

Life Chances Obviously, the rich have better houses, food, and clothes than the middle classes, who, in turn, live in more comfortable conditions than the poor. The upper classes can also devote more money, and often more time, to nonessentials like giving lavish parties; some rich people spend more money on their pets than most people earn from their jobs. Their choices are often wider, and their opportunities greater, than those of the lower classes. Their children, for example, are more likely than lower-income children to have computers at home and in school, which enhances the opportunity for success in this technological age. In other words, the upper classes have better **life chances**—the likelihood of living a good, long, successful life.

We can see the impact of class on life chances in the *Titanic* tragedy, which took 1,500 lives in 1912. On the night the ship sank into the Atlantic Ocean, social class was a major determinant of who survived and who died. Among the females on board, 3 percent of the first-class passengers drowned, compared with 16 percent of the second-class passengers and 45 percent of the third-class passengers. All passengers in first class were given the opportunity to abandon ship, but those in third class were ordered to stay below deck, some of them at gunpoint (Hall, 1986; Lord, 1981).

Less dramatic but just as grim is the finding common to many studies that people in the lower classes generally live shorter and less healthy lives than those above them in the social hierarchy. An infant born into a poor family is much more likely to die during its first year than an infant born into a non-poor family. For adults, too, mortality rates are higher among men and women of the lower classes than among those of the higher classes. People of the lower classes are also more likely to die from syphilis, tuberculosis, stomach ulcers, diabetes, influenza, and many other diseases (Grusky, 2001; Gilbert and Kahl, 1993).

Lifestyles and Values Lifestyles—tastes, preferences, and ways of living—may appear trivial in comparison to life chances. But studying lifestyle differences among people also shows the importance of social class in our lives.

Upper- and middle-class people are likely to be active outside their homes—in parent-teacher associations, charitable organizations, and various community activities. They are also likely to make friends with professional colleagues or business contacts, with their spouses helping to cultivate the friendship. In fact, they tend to combine their social and business lives so much that friendships are no longer a personal matter but are used to promote their careers.

In contrast, working-class people tend to restrict their social life to families and relatives. Rarely do they entertain or visit their friends from work. Although male factory workers may stop off for a beer with the guys after work, the guys are seldom invited home. Many working-class men and women are also quite reluctant to form close ties with neighbors. Instead, they often visit their parents, siblings, and other relatives, which has prompted Lillian Rubin (1976) to describe the extended family as "the heart of working-class social life." Some observers believe that this type of kin-oriented sociability arises because working-class people feel less secure in social interactions, fearing or distrusting the outside world (Gilbert and Kahl, 1993).

People in different classes also tend to prefer different magazines, newspapers, books, television programs, and movies. Whereas the working class is more likely to read the *National Enquirer* and watch soap operas or professional wrestling, the middle and upper-middle classes are more likely to read *Time* or *Newsweek* and watch public television programs. The upper class does not like to watch television, tending to consider most television programs juvenile, boring, or insulting. On the other hand, working-class people are more likely to watch television, while attending fewer concerts, lectures, and theaters, and more likely to work on their cars, take car rides, play cards, and visit bars.

Social class also influences people's values in significant ways. Generally, the higher their class, the more *conservative* they are on *economic* issues but the more *liberal* they are on *social* issues. Relatively rich people, for example, are more likely to be *conservative*

DOWN AND OUT The lower class is mostly jobless and poor. It includes people who are chronically unemployed, welfare recipients, and impoverished elders. Although most members of the lower class are merely poor, they are often stigmatized as the *underclass,* a term conjuring up images of poor people as violent criminals, drug abusers, welfare mothers with too many babies, and able-bodied men too lazy to work. ■

by opposing higher corporate taxes, price or wage controls, the minimum wage, unemployment benefits, health care, and parental leave, because all these policies are seen as hurting their economic interests. Conversely, people with higher income and more education are more likely to be *liberal* by supporting abortion and gay rights or opposing capital punishment and school prayer.

POVERTY IN THE UNITED STATES

Consider an American family of four with an annual income of $18,500 in 2003. Is this family poor? The U.S. government says that it is *not* poor because its income is above the official poverty line of $18,400. But advocates for people who are needy say that the family is definitely poor. Most Americans would agree, as indicated by their responses to public opinion pollsters that a family of four is poor if it earns less than $20,000 a year. Who is right? The answer depends on which definition of *poverty* one chooses to accept.

What Is Poverty?

To determine the number of poor people, the U.S. government first defines poverty as the lack of min-

imum food and shelter necessary for maintaining life, which sociologists call **absolute poverty.** The government then decides what income is needed to sustain that minimum standard of living and determines how many people fall below it.

To find out what that income is, the government multiplies the cost of food by *3* because the average family is assumed to spend *one-third* of its income on food. Thus, for 2003, the poverty line for a four-person family was $18,400, which meant that about 12 percent of the population were considered poor (see Figure 7.5).

These figures have stirred a controversy. Conservative critics argue that the figures *overestimate* the extent of poverty because they do not count as income the many *noncash benefits,* such as food stamps, school lunches, housing subsidies, and medical assistance, that the poor receive from the government. These noncash benefits account for two-thirds of government programs for the poor. If these benefits were added to cash incomes, many people would rise above the poverty line—and hence would no longer be poor (Uchitelle, 2001; Rector, 1998).

Liberal critics, on the other hand, contend that the official rate *underestimates* the extent of poverty because it is based on the erroneous assumption that the average U.S. family today spends one-third of its income on food, as it did in the early 1960s, when the government's formula for determining poverty

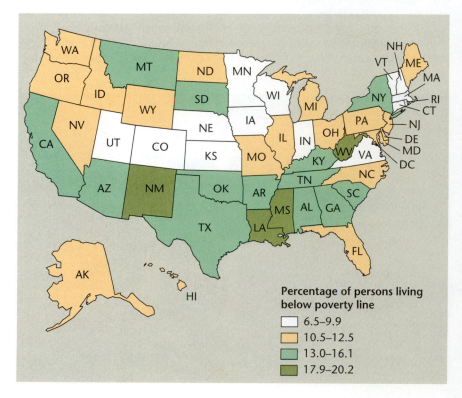

FIGURE 7.5

Poverty in the United States

According to the federal government's definition of poverty, in 2003, 12 percent of the U.S. population was poor. The poverty rate, however, varied from one state to another, with many Southern states having higher rates than the national average.

Critical Thinking: *How would you define poverty? What would you expect a poor American family to be like?*

Source: Data from U.S. Census Bureau, 2003.

Percentage of persons living below poverty line

- 6.5–9.9
- 10.5–12.5
- 13.0–16.1
- 17.9–20.2

was first used. Actually, the typical family today spends only one-fifth of its income on food, largely because of increases in *nonfood costs* such as taxes, medical expenses, and child care. In other words, the family today needs a much higher income than the family of 30 years ago in order to stay out of poverty. Failing to take this into account, the government excludes from its poverty statistics many families that are actually poor.

However, poverty experts at the National Academy of Sciences recommended to the government that both the liberal and conservative criticisms be taken into account, namely, by *deducting* nonfood costs from family income as well as *adding* noncash benefits to the income. If this recommendation were adopted, it would likely increase the official poverty rate because the nonfood costs are higher than the noncash benefits (Pear, 1995a).

Poverty can also be found to be more prevalent than officially reported if it is defined in terms of how people live relative to—that is, in comparison with—the majority of the population. According to a widely accepted *relative definition* of poverty, those who earn less than half of the nation's median income are poor because they lack what is considered to be needed by most people to live a decent life. By this definition, for more than 40 years, the percentage of the population living in poverty has usually been twice as high as what has been reported by the government. These poor people are said to live in **relative poverty**, a state of deprivation resulting from having less than the majority of the people have.

According to the preceding definitions of *poverty*, only a minority of Americans are poor in any given year. Over the last three decades, 11 to 15 percent have fallen below the poverty line and 22 to 30 percent have experienced relative poverty. But according to an analysis of American adults throughout their lifetimes, a *majority* (nearly 70 percent) will have spent at least a year being poor by the time they turn 75. This spell of poverty may result from a job loss, divorce, disability, or old age. Poverty, then, doesn't strike just a few Americans but most of them (Rank, 2003).

■ The Feminization of Poverty

Poverty affects women more than men, creating a social phenomenon that sociologists call the **feminization of poverty**, a huge number of women living in poverty, mostly as single mothers or heads of families. Compared with other industrial nations, the United States has the largest gender gap in poverty. The reason is that U.S. women are much more likely than their foreign counterparts to be both unemployed and heads of families with children (Casper et al., 1994). In fact, single mothers make up the largest proportion of the poor adult population in the United States. Thus, the feminization of poverty mostly involves poor women maintaining their own households. The problem can be attributed to several changes in U.S. society. Increases in the rates of divorce, separation, and out-of-wedlock birth have caused a growing number of women to become heads of poor households. The increase in divorced fathers not paying child support, along with the reduction in government support for welfare, also has caused many more female-headed

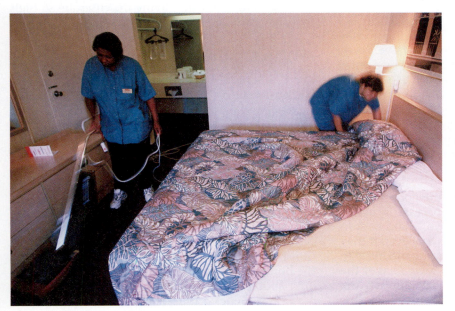

JUST GETTING BY According to feminists, women as a group are more vulnerable than men to poverty because of the sexist nature of society. Unlike men, who often can escape poverty by getting a job, women tend to remain poor even when they are employed. This is because the labor market is mostly gender segregated, with women being much more likely to work in low-paid, low-status jobs. ■

households to fall below the poverty line. The fact that women live longer than men has further contributed to a growing number of older women living alone in poverty.

Most important, however, according to feminists, women as a group are more vulnerable than men to poverty because of the sexist and patriarchal nature of the society. Unlike men, who often can escape poverty by getting a job, women tend to remain poor even when they are employed. Why? Because in the gender-segregated labor market, women are much more likely to work in low-paid, low-status jobs. By socializing women to become wives and mothers, feminist theory suggests, the patriarchal society further discourages them from developing educational and occupational skills. This is likely to cause poverty among divorced women or widows, even those from relatively affluent families.

■ Explanations of Poverty

Two kinds of theories are offered about general poverty. One essentially blames the poor for their poverty. The other is sociological in nature.

Blame-the-Poor Theories   These theories assume that there are plenty of opportunities for making it in the United States. The poor are believed to have failed to grab the opportunities by not working hard.

Attempts have long been made to find the source of this self-defeating behavior. Political scientist Edward Banfield (1974) claimed to have found it in the present-oriented outlook among the poor, who, he said, live for the moment, unconcerned about the future. Earlier, anthropologist Oscar Lewis (1961) had found about the same lifestyle among the poor families he studied. He found the poor to be fatalists, resigning themselves to being poor and seeing no way out of their poverty. They were said to have developed a "culture of poverty," characterized by a series of debilitating values and attitudes, such as a sense of hopelessness and passivity, low aspirations, feelings of powerlessness and inferiority, and present-time orientation. According to Lewis, this culture of poverty is passed on from one generation to another. All this, then, was assumed to discourage the poor from working hard, which, in turn, continues to keep them poor (Harrison, 1999; Samuelson, 1997).

But there are holes in the blame-the-poor theories. For one thing, poor people are not necessarily averse to working hard. Most are likely to work hard if given the opportunity. But the problem is that even if they have the opportunity and work, they are still likely to remain poor because of changes in such areas as the nation's economy and welfare policy. In fact, the working poor account for half of those who fall below the poverty line. Also, in fully 60 percent of all poor families, at least one person works (Ehrenreich, 2001; Roberts, 1993). Another flaw in the blame-the-poor explanation is that it confuses cause and effect. The self-defeating values that Banfield and Lewis found among the poor may well be the effect, not the cause, of poverty.

Sociological Theories   According to a functionalist theory, society creates and maintains poverty because benefits can be derived from it. Poverty is assumed to perform some positive functions for society, such as the following:

1. Poverty makes it possible for society's dirty work to be done. Many boring, underpaid, and unpleasant jobs—such as washing dishes, scrubbing floors, and hauling garbage—would be left undone if poor people did not do them.
2. By working as maids and servants, poor people make it easier for the affluent to pursue their business and professional careers.
3. Poverty creates jobs for social workers and other professionals who serve the poor. It also produces jobs for police and other law enforcers who protect other people from those who are poor (Gans, 1971).

But this functionalist theory still cannot explain how society creates poverty in the first place. Such an explanation can be found in conflict theory, which suggests that the inegalitarian nature of society makes inevitable the unequal distribution of economic opportunities. Receiving few or no opportunities, the poor are bound to be poor and to remain so. As Barbara Ehrenreich (2001) has found out, even when poor people hold two jobs, their wages are so low and their housing and other living expenses are so high that they cannot get out of poverty.

■ Who Are the Homeless?

The homeless are among the extremely poor. They are, by definition, people who sleep in streets, parks, shelters, and places not intended as dwellings, such as bus stations, lobbies, and abandoned buildings.

According to Peter Rossi's study of the Chicago homeless, most are African American men in their middle thirties with an educational level largely equivalent to that of the general population. Most have never married; if they have, their marriages have failed. Most held their last steady job more than four years earlier, and the rest have worked only occasionally at jobs involving low skills and low wages (Rossi, 1989). Other studies have shown that many of the homeless are families with children, alcohol and drug abusers, and people who are mentally ill (Kilborn, 1999; Jencks, 1994).

myth	Homelessness is a new phenomenon in the United States.
reality	There have always been homeless people in the United States.

Homelessness is not new. There have always been homeless people in the United States. But the homeless today differ in some ways from their counterparts of the 1950s and 1960s. More than 40 years ago, most of the homeless were old men, only a handful were women, and virtually no families were homeless. Today, the homeless are younger and include more women and families with young children. Today's homeless people also are more visible to the general public because they are much more likely to sleep on the streets or in other public places. In recent years, however, most cities have cracked down on the homeless, removing them from the streets (Kilborn, 1999).

Homelessness has arisen from at least three social forces. One is the increased shortage of inexpensive housing for poor families and poor unattached persons because of diminishing government subsidy of such housing. Another social force is the decreasing demand for unskilled labor that has occurred since the 1980s, which has resulted in extremely high unemployment among young men in general and African Americans in particular. A third social force is the erosion of public welfare benefits that has occurred over the last two decades. These three social forces have not directly caused homelessness. But they have enlarged the ranks of the extremely poor, thereby increasing the chances of these people becoming homeless (Snow and Anderson, 2003).

■ Welfare: Beliefs and Reforms

Contrary to popular belief, most of the poor in the United States are not on welfare. Only about one-third are. The overwhelming majority of welfare recipients are single mothers and their children. Due to the economic recession that began in 1989, the welfare roll increased sharply in the early 1990s, causing the U.S. public and government to become strongly opposed to the welfare system (Shirk, Bennett, and Aber, 1999; Bane and Ellwood, 1994).

myth	Most of the poor people in the United States are on welfare.
reality	Only one-third of the poor are on welfare.

Beliefs about Welfare In one survey, a sample of people in the United States were asked, "Do you think government spending on *welfare* should be increased, decreased, or kept about the same?" The most popular response was *decreased*. But many people did not realize that the proposed welfare cuts would affect mostly children. This is why, when asked about government spending on *poor children,* far more people said they wanted the government to *increase* it (Dowd, 1994).

The real target of public opposition to welfare is not the children but rather their single mothers. In the same survey just mentioned, a large majority (87 percent) of the general public wanted welfare recipients to be required to work. It is widely assumed that welfare encourages dependency—that most welfare recipients are so dependent on the system that they will never voluntarily leave it (Shirk, Bennett, and Aber, 1999; Toner, 1992). But the fact is that most recipients (about 70 percent) stayed on welfare for less than two years, even before 1996, when the government put a time limit on benefits (Bane and Ellwood, 1994).

Reforming Welfare In 1996, a law was passed to end welfare dependency in the United States. Its key provisions were that the head of every family on welfare must work in order for the family to receive benefits and that benefits are limited to a total of five years throughout the recipient's lifetime. Today, many welfare recipients have found employment and consequently left the welfare rolls. According to a study by economist June O'Neill (2001), the gain in employment can largely be attributed to the welfare reform. The economic boom of the late 1990s also contributed to the employment gain. But sociologists William Wilson and Andrew Cherlin (2001) have found that most of the welfare recipients who got jobs are actually *worse off* now because they are paid extremely low wages (Hofferth, 2002).

In addition to continuing the welfare reform, President Bush has tried to enlist the private sector, especially religious organizations, to fight poverty. He has proposed to Congress that federal money be given to religious groups to help the poor. But this idea has run into opposition from left and right. Liberals oppose it because it will weaken the constitutional separation between church and state, allowing religious groups to support their own religious teachings and to discriminate by hiring only those who share their faiths. On the other hand, conservatives are afraid that the religious groups receiving the federal money will be forced to compromise their religious missions by, for example, avoiding the use of spiritual activities such as prayers and rituals in helping the poor (Bruni, 2001; Wilson, 2001). It remains to be seen whether the faith-based approach to poverty will become law.

SOCIAL MOBILITY IN U.S. SOCIETY

In virtually all societies there is some **social mobility**, movement from one social standing to another. The amount of mobility, though, varies from one society to another. Generally, there is more mobility in the more industrialized societies than in the less developed societies. Sociologists long ago discovered certain patterns and causes of social mobility.

◼ Patterns: The Rich Get Richer

Social mobility can take several forms. **Vertical mobility** involves moving up or down the status ladder. Upward movement is called *upward mobility,* and downward movement is called *downward mobility.* Promotion of a teacher to the position of principal is an example of upward mobility, and demotion from principal to teacher is downward mobility. In contrast to vertical mobility, **horizontal mobility** is movement from one job to another within the same status category. If a teacher leaves one school for a similar position at another school, the teacher is experiencing horizontal mobility.

Mobility can also be intragenerational or intergenerational. When an individual moves from a low position to a higher one, it is called **intragenerational mobility** (or *career mobility*)—a change in an individual's social standing. A manager who becomes the vice president of a company illustrates intragenerational mobility. When a person from a working-class family gets a higher-status job, as in the case of a factory worker's daughter becoming company vice president, it is called **intergenerational mobility**—a change in social standing from one generation to the next.

Of these various forms of mobility, upward intergenerational mobility has attracted the most attention from sociologists. Their research has focused primarily on the question of how much such mobility exists in the United States. This interest is understandable because we revel in stories about the son of a poor person becoming president—as politicians and journalists proclaim, "Only in America." This may be an exaggeration, but it reflects the high place that upward mobility holds in U.S. values. Rags-to-riches tales make people feel good about their country, and they make interesting stories. By publicizing them, the media reinforce the vision of the United States as a land of opportunity, where through sheer hard work, the son of a janitor can become a millionaire. This view of the United States is further reinforced by the experiences of those who have achieved moderate but real upward mobility.

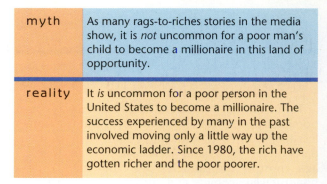

myth	As many rags-to-riches stories in the media show, it is *not* uncommon for a poor man's child to become a millionaire in this land of opportunity.
reality	It *is* uncommon for a poor person in the United States to become a millionaire. The success experienced by many in the past involved moving only a little way up the economic ladder. Since 1980, the rich have gotten richer and the poor poorer.

But is this picture accurate? Is upward mobility common? Until 1980, the answer was yes and no: Numerous people did climb a little way up the social ladder, but very few people rose from rags to riches. In the last few decades, however, the rich have gotten richer and the poor poorer. As Figure 7.6 shows, the share of national income in the hands of the

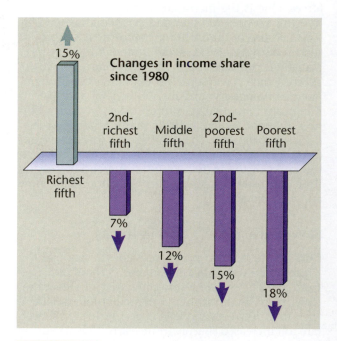

FIGURE 7.6

Richer and Poorer

Since 1980, the rich have gotten richer and the poor poorer. The share of the total national income in the hands of the richest fifth of the U.S. population has *risen* 15 percent, but the income shares of all the poorer groups have *fallen*, with the poorest fifth experiencing the largest drop of 18 percent.

Critical Thinking: *Is the United States still the land of opportunity? Why or why not?*

Source: Data from U.S. Census Bureau, 2002.

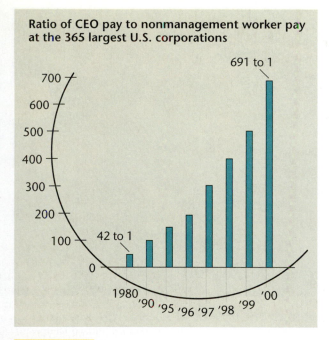

Ratio of CEO pay to nonmanagement worker pay at the 365 largest U.S. corporations

FIGURE 7.7

Sharp Increases in Pay Gap

The pay gap between U.S. company executives and their workers has gone up sharply over the last two decades. Twenty years ago, company executives' salaries were about 42 times highre than their workers', but today, they are a whopping 691 times higher.

Critical Thinking: *Do you think it's fair for executives to earn nearly 700 times more than their employees? Why or why not?*

Source: Data from U.S. Department of Labor, 2000; *U.S. News & World Report,* February 21, 2000, p. 42.

richest portion of the U.S. population has gone up, but the income shares of the poorer groups have gone down. Moreover, as Figure 7.7 shows, the earnings gap between company executives and their workers has increased sharply.

The widened disparity between rich and poor can be attributed to a number of changes in U.S. society. First, there has been a shift in the economy away from manufacturing jobs that paid high wages to low-skilled workers. Second, many industries have increased their reliance on the use of computer and computer-assisted technology, which requires higher skills and education and offers proportionately high salaries. Third, unionized and well-paid workers have become scarcer, while part-time and underpaid workers have become more prevalent. And fourth, there has been a significant increase in the number of two-career families in which both husbands and wives are well educated and highly paid (Holmes, 1996).

Sources: Societal and Individual Factors

Why, in the pursuit of the American dream, are some people upwardly mobile while others stay in the same positions or fall behind? Two major factors determine the chances for upward or downward mobility: structural changes in the society and individual characteristics (Baron, 1994).

Structural Mobility Sometimes, large changes in society enable many people to move up or down the social ladder at the same time. The result is **structural mobility**, social mobility related to societal factors—namely, changes in society. As we have suggested, much of the downward mobility of blue-collar workers over the last two decades has been due to the decline of manufacturing industries and labor unions, which have long shored up wages and benefits for workers without much education or high-level skills. As for the downward mobility of many well-educated managers and technicians in recent years, it can be attributed to the increased globalization of the U.S. economy. Pressured by international competition, many U.S. corporations have tried to be "lean and mean" by greatly reducing both size and expenses.

In the early 1900s, by contrast, most of the structural mobility was upward rather than downward. This kind of structural mobility can be traced to at least four sources. First, there was a tremendous expansion of the industrial economy. In 1900, agricultural workers made up nearly 40 percent of the labor force, but massive industrialization has reduced this proportion to only 4 percent today. At the same time, many unskilled jobs were gradually taken over by machines but were replaced by numerous higher-status jobs—clerical, service, business, and professional jobs. This created the opportunity for large numbers of people from farming and blue-collar families to enter those higher-status occupations. Moreover, soon after the end of World War II, government programs such as the GI Bill and the Land Grant College System enabled massive numbers of Americans to attend college, which created a great deal of upward mobility throughout the nation (Lipset et al., 1994; Kerckhoff et al., 1985; Blau and Duncan, 1967).

A second source of structural mobility has been the dramatic increase in the educational attainment of the population. High school enrollment exploded from a mere 7 percent of the appropriate age group in 1900 to nearly 100 percent today. College enrollment jumped from only 250,000 in 1900 to over 16 million today. Thus, more people have achieved the knowledge and skills needed to fill higher-status jobs (U.S. Census Bureau, 2003; Davis, 1982; Featherman and Hauser, 1978).

A third source of structural mobility has been the lower birth rate in the higher classes than in the lower classes. In the early 1900s, professional and other white-collar workers had relatively few children, but manual workers, especially farmers, had many. As the economy expanded, many more new professional positions were created. Because there was a shortage of higher-status people to fill all those higher-status jobs, the lower classes were provided with an opportunity to take them.

myth	Because most immigrants are poor and need financial assistance, countries with unusually large numbers of them cannot become prosperous.
reality	The world's most prosperous societies, such as the United States, Canada, Israel, and Australia, have unusually large numbers of immigrants.

A fourth source of structural mobility has been the large influx of immigrants into the United States. Immigrants traditionally took jobs as laborers on farms, in factories, and in mines, pushing many native-borns into higher-status occupations. When the children of immigrants grew up, they, too, had the opportunity, as native-borns, to become upwardly mobile. It is no accident that the world's most prosperous societies—Israel, Canada, Australia, and the United States—have had unusually large numbers of immigrants.

All in all, as a result of a rapidly industrializing economy, increasing education, lower birth rates in the higher classes, and considerable immigration, many people whose parents were factory or farm workers came to fill higher-status jobs. In today's increasingly postindustrial society, however, higher-status jobs require much more education and skill than before. This may explain why most of the people who have suffered downward mobility in recent decades are the less educated blue-collar workers (Wright, 1995).

Individual Mobility   Even when structural mobility opens up higher-status positions, some people move up and some do not. Let us take a closer look at this **individual mobility**, social mobility related to an individual's personal achievement and characteristics.

Among the characteristics that influence individual mobility are racial or ethnic background, gender, education, occupation, place of residence, and sheer luck. More specifically, white Americans and men have greater chances for upward mobility than minority Americans and women do. (In later chapters, we look at these inequalities in detail.) College gradu-

BEHIND THE POWER OF EDUCATION   Education is one of the most effective determinants of individual upward mobility. Thus, while individual upward mobility is largely due to achievement, it is also subject to the influence of ascription because the amount of education people have is related to their family background. ■

ates are much more likely than the uneducated to be upwardly mobile. White-collar workers are more likely than blue-collar workers to experience upward career mobility. People who live in urban areas have a greater chance of upward mobility than those who live in rural areas. Finally, sheer luck often acts as the force pushing a person up the status ladder.

Some personal characteristics are *achieved,* such as education, talent, motivation, and hard work. Others are *ascribed,* such as family background, race, and gender. As has been suggested, both achieved and ascribed qualities have a hand in determining who gets ahead in U.S. society. But the popular belief in equal opportunity would lead us to expect career success to be attained through achievement more than ascription. Is achievement, then, really the more powerful determining force in upward mobility?

According to most sociological studies, achievement may appear on the surface to be the predominant factor, but it is actually subject to the influence of ascription. It is well known that the more education people have, the more successful they are in their careers. But the amount of education people have is related to their family background. Thus, compared with children from blue-collar families, white-collar children can be expected to get more education—and then have a better chance for career mobility (Erickson and Jonsson, 1996; Jencks et al., 1994).

GLOBAL STRATIFICATION

Just as people in a given society can be found in different classes, so can nations, with some nations being in a higher or lower class than others in a social system called *global stratification*. The essence of global stratification, then, is inequality among nations. This inequality has serious consequences for various people in the poor countries. It also involves exploitation of the poor countries by the rich.

■ Characteristics

Global inequality appears in many different forms, the most important of which have to do with economic conditions and quality of life. By definition, economic conditions are better in relatively rich countries than in poor ones, but the disparity between rich and poor appears to be extreme. Although they constitute only about 20 percent of the world's population, richer countries have well over 85 percent of global income and other economic opportunities. These disparities reflect others, such as those in productivity, trade, savings, and investment. The richest 20 percent of the world's population have 78 percent of the world's GDP (gross domestic product—the total value of all the goods and services produced by a nation, excluding those exported). In sharp contrast, the poorest 20 percent of the world's population have only 1.4 percent of the GDP. The global inequality appears even worse in other economic indicators: The poorest fifth has less than 1 percent of world trade, domestic savings, and domestic investment, well below the over 84 percent enjoyed by the richest fifth (United Nations, 1996).

A similar gap exists in regard to the quality of life. Compared with poor developing countries, affluent industrial countries have a considerably higher income per person, far greater longevity, and a much higher rate of literacy. While the world's affluent enjoy a better life, the poor bear the cost of global inequality.

■ Consequences

The consequences of global inequality are massive and profound. We can see them in the form of widespread poverty, extensive female disadvantages, relatively prevalent child exploitation, and shockingly widespread slavery in the relatively poor countries.

Widespread Poverty Most of the world's poor live in Africa, Asia, and Latin America. The extent of poverty in the developing countries of these areas appears extremely great compared with that of industrial countries in the West. About 30 percent of the people in developing countries live in absolute poverty (unable to meet their most basic needs), in sharp contrast with only 3 percent in industrial countries. In other words, the developing countries' poverty rate is about 10 times higher than that of the industrial nations (United Nations, 1998).

Poverty is most widespread in African countries south of the Sahara, where 18 of the world's 20 poorest countries are located. Close to 50 percent of their populations are poor compared with about 30 percent for all developing countries. To understand how difficult it is for the Africans to meet their basic needs, consider this fact: The gross national product of all sub–Saharan African countries combined (excluding South Africa), home to 600 million people, is about the same as the gross national product of Belgium, which has a population of only 10 million (Crossette, 1998).

Even more tragically, when there is civil war, widespread poverty can easily turn into a massive famine, as happened over the last 10 years in such countries as Ethiopia, Sudan, and Somalia. Both government and rebel forces usually seize food supplies from civilians as well as international relief organizations as a military strategy to starve the enemy into defeat (Keen, 1994). Drought can also trigger a large-scale famine because agricultural production has plummeted over the last 20 years while population rates have soared. Even when there is no famine, the combination of food shortages and population explosion often causes malnutrition, disease, and death.

The Plight of Women Associated with widespread poverty is the prevalence of disadvantages faced by women in poor countries. According to the United Nations, women's *human development index*—a measure of the quality of life or living standard—is significantly lower in poor countries, where women face all kinds of social, cultural, legal, and economic disadvantages that men do not.

Compared to men who are equally poor, women have a much lower literacy rate. Concentrated in poor countries, women make up two-thirds of the world's illiterate population. In addition, women lag far behind in education. Their rate for having completed secondary education is only about 70 percent the male rate and for having completed a college education, only 50 percent. Enrollment of girls in primary school has increased over the last several decades, but more girls than boys are still kept out of school in many poor countries, where the prejudice persists that educating girls is a waste of time and money (see Figure 7.8, p. 200).

Women in poor countries have fewer opportunities for paid employment. There are only 58 women

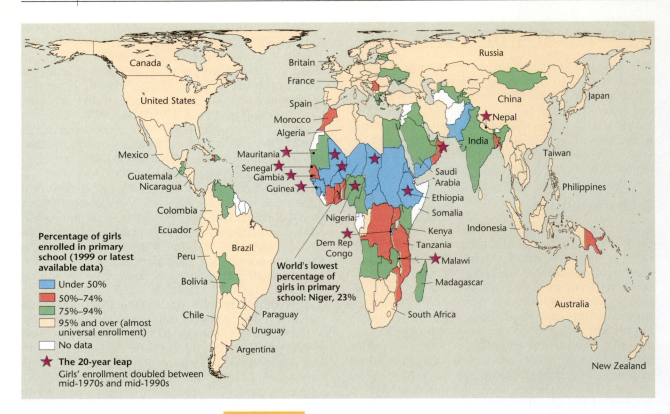

FIGURE 7.8

Making the Grade

Girls' primary school enrollment rates have increased around the world over the last 20 years. Some of these increases have been dramatic, going up as much as 100 percent. But many more girls than boys are still kept out of school, especially in poor countries, primarily because of the persistent prejudice that educating girls is not worthwhile.

Critical Thinking: *How would you propose to combat such prejudice?*

Source: From *The Penguin Atlas of Women in the World,* by Joni Seager, copyright © 1997, 2003 by Myriad Editions Ltd, maps & graphics. Used by permission of Penguin, a division of Penguin Group (USA) Inc.

employed for every 100 men, and they are paid considerably less. Women not gainfully employed are far from idle, however. In fact, they usually work an average of 12 hours a day, while men work only 8 hours. Women not only do domestic chores and care for children and the elderly but also work on farms, gather firewood, weave baskets, or engage in petty trade such as selling small quantities of produce or food (United Nations, 1996).

Women live longer than men in the United States and other industrialized countries, but in developing countries, women die sooner than men. Thus, females constitute less than 47 percent of the population in poor countries compared with more than 52 percent in rich countries. The causes include poor health care, inadequate nutrition, and outright vio-

lence against women and girls. One of the greatest health risks is childbirth. The average rate of maternal mortality in poor countries is about 400 per 100,000 live births, 40 times higher than the rate (only 10 per 100,000) in affluent societies (Seager, 2003; Dentzer, 1995).

Child Exploitation Another consequence of global inequality is the greater prevalence of child exploitation in relatively poor countries. There are three different types of child exploitation: work at home, labor outside the home, and slavery.

Children's work at home includes housekeeping, taking care of younger siblings, and helping parents with such activities as working on the farm, hawking on the street, or running errands. The child workers,

CHILD CHATTEL One of the costs of global inequality is the prevalence of child exploitation in relatively poor countries. Parents are sometimes compelled to send their children to work for pay, as shown here in Pakistan, where a young child works at making bricks. The health of child workers is often ruined, and they are also deprived of an education. Because they are paid so little, they are never able to pay off the heavy debts sometimes imposed by employers for food, housing, and the use of work tools. ■

usually aged 5 to 15, are not paid. At first glance, these children may not appear to be exploited. After all, children in the United States do all kinds of chores for their parents, who see chores as an important part of socialization—useful for teaching diligence, discipline, and other positive values that will ensure success in the child's future. This may be true for the children in affluent societies, but children's work in poor countries is vastly different. The economic well-being of most families in a rich country does not depend on children's work, but without it, many families in a poor country could hardly survive.

In poor villages around the world, children as young as 5 routinely perform such chores as babysitting, fetching water, and looking after small livestock. By the age of 8, they often contribute as much as their parents to the family's survival. They may help their parents with their occupational activities such as weaving baskets, spinning yarn, fishing, and selling fruits and vegetables (Nieuwenhuys, 1994). Thus, contrary to popular belief, children in poor countries are not their parents' dependents but *partners* in a common struggle for survival. This may partly explain why parents in poor societies want to have many children. However, since the children must work as hard as their parents, school attendance is often impossible. These children may appear to be exploited by their own parents, but they are actually victims of the stratification system of domestic and global society.

If children's work at home cannot help keep the family from starving to death, poor parents are compelled to send their children to work for pay as farmers, miners, factory workers, or domestic servants. Such child labor is widely condemned in affluent societies, though, because it is well known to be harmful to the children (Basu, 1995; Herbert, 1995). The children's health is often ruined for life, and they are deprived of education as well as robbed of the normal enjoyment of their early years.

Child labor is in great demand for several reasons. Children are more docile than adults, easier to discipline, and more often too frightened to complain. Their small frames and nimble fingers are considered an asset for certain kinds of work. Although only 7 to 10 years old, they are forced to work 12 to 14 hours a day. Most important, child labor is quite cheap; children are generally paid less than one-third of the adult wage. Not surprisingly, when children are given jobs, their parents may lose theirs (United Nations, 1996).

Some child laborers are slaves. The International Labor Organization has reported that child slavery is relatively common. In extremely poor countries in West Africa, parents sell their children to merchants for as little as $15. In Thailand, many poverty-stricken peasants sell or lease their young daughters to urban employment agencies, which in turn sell them to work in homes, restaurants, factories, and brothels (Robinson and Palus, 2001).

Adult Slavery Shocking as it may be, adult slavery is not uncommon today. According to Britain's Anti-Slavery International, the oldest human rights organization in the world, there are more than 100 million slaves. This figure includes a large number of child laborers and slaves. Still, the number of adults in servitude can safely be assumed to be several million.

Like their ancient counterparts, some of these slaves are held as someone's property. This old-fashioned human bondage, called *chattel slavery,* can be found in the North African country of Mauritania, where some 100,000 black Africans live as the property of Arab-descended Berbers. As chattel, these slaves are used for labor, sex, and breeding or can be exchanged for camels, trucks, guns, or money (Burkett, 1997; Jacobs and Athie, 1994).

Most slaves today, however, are victims of debt bondage, which forces whole families to work, sometimes for generations, in fruitless efforts to pay off loans. Typical are Sadram and his wife, who have worked in a stone quarry outside India's capital city of New Delhi for eight years. Sadram breaks large rocks into smaller ones and loads them into trucks. His wife carries soil in a basket. The couple are paid $25 a month, nearly all of which goes for food and the explosives needed for the job. In the meantime, the $46 loan they took out eight years ago has grown to $88. When they told someone that they wanted to go home without paying off the debt, four men broke into their mud house and beat them with iron bars. After recovering from their wounds, Sadram and his wife returned to work. They simply have no way out (Schemo, 1995).

The same kind of debt slavery exists in such poor countries as Pakistan, Thailand, Peru, Haiti, and the Dominican Republic (Schemo, 1995; Masland, 1992). Such human bondage will cease only if poor countries are able to achieve social mobility in the global stratification system.

■ Dependency Theory: Exploitation by Rich Nations

Using the conflict perspective, sociologists are critical of the rich and powerful for exploiting the poor and weak. Rich nations are thus blamed for the development failure of most poor nations. To conflict sociologists, rich nations may appear interested in providing poor nations with adequate assistance, but actually they are not. For evidence they point to the fact that aid to poor nations represents a negligible portion of rich nations' incomes, as shown in Figure 7.9, or *only 0.48 percent* of their combined gross national products (GNPs). Conflict sociologists suspect that rich nations are more interested in exploiting poor nations. This suspicion has led to the development of **dependency theory**, which says that rich nations exploit poor ones for power and commercial gain, thereby perpetuating poverty, underdevelopment, and dependency on rich nations. The theory suggests various ways the exploitation is carried out.

First, much of the exploitation is a legacy of colonialism. Many of today's poor nations used to be colonies of rich nations in the West. As the Western countries industrialized, they used their colonies as sources of low-priced raw materials and markets for their higher-priced manufactured goods. These colonies have been independent nations for more than three decades but are still very much under the thumb of their former masters. The control is in the form of **neocolonialism,** the economic control exercised by rich nations over their former colonies.

FIGURE 7.9

The Tiny Foreign Aid
Aid to poor countries represents only a tiny, negligible portion of rich nations' incomes—an average of less than 0.5 percent of the total value of their combined gross national products.

Critical Thinking: *How much foreign aid would you want your government to give to poor countries? Why?*

Source: Data from Joni Seager, *The Penguin Atlas of Women in the World* (New York: Penguin Group, 2003), p. 89.

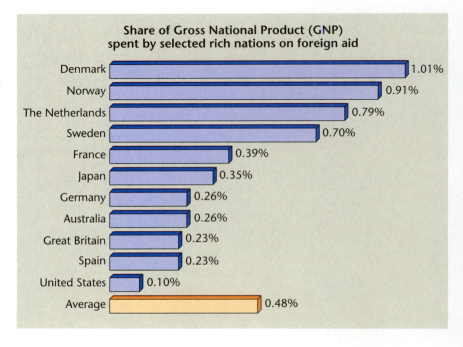

Share of Gross National Product (GNP) spent by selected rich nations on foreign aid

Nation	Percent
Denmark	1.01%
Norway	0.91%
The Netherlands	0.79%
Sweden	0.70%
France	0.39%
Japan	0.35%
Germany	0.26%
Australia	0.26%
Great Britain	0.23%
Spain	0.23%
United States	0.10%
Average	0.48%

Thus, a similar pattern of unequal trading continues to this day: The rich nations import raw materials at a low price from their former colonies and then send them manufactured goods for a large profit.

Rich nations also use their powerful banks, particularly the International Monetary Fund and the World Bank, to control the economies of poor nations. Desperate for financial aid from these banks, many poor nations are forced to accept whatever conditions the banks impose on them. Basically, they are required to practice Western-style capitalism: maximizing free-market enterprise with minimum government interference. This may stimulate production, but it imposes unbearable costs on people's lives. For example, in the African nation of Ghana, an aid recipient, gold production has tripled since 1986, but many miners skip lunch because they cannot afford it.

Foreign investors can even get farmers to switch from producing food for local consumption to producing commodities (such as coffee, sugar, fruits, and palm oil) for export. The consequence is often disastrous for local people. In Central America, for example, for the last 30 years, huge increases in the production of beef for export to the United States have sharply increased hunger by reducing production of staple foods such as corn and beans, damaged the environment by cutting and clearing millions of

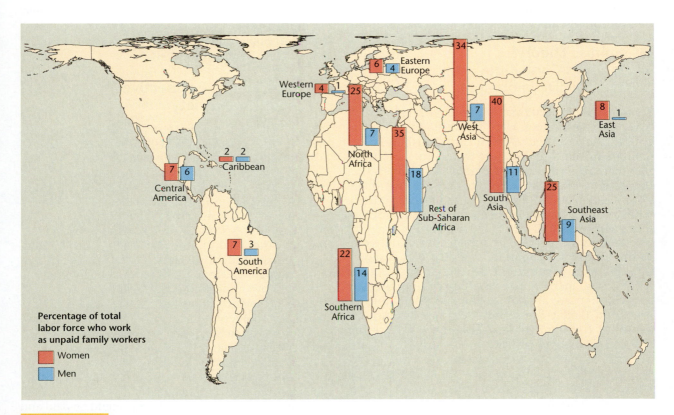

FIGURE 7.10

Housework and Economic Development

When women are heavily involved in unpaid housework, their societies tend to be relatively poor. As unpaid domestic workers, women cannot directly contribute to their nations' economies as much as men who are gainfully employed. Thus, countries in sub–Saharan Africa and Western and Southern Asia, which have much higher percentages of women doing housework than other regions, are economically underdeveloped.

Critical Thinking: *Could the women in these poor countries be free to enter the labor force as gainfully employed? Why or why not?*

Source: From *The Penguin Atlas of Women in the World,* by Joni Seager, copyright © 1997, 2003 by Myriad Editions Ltd, maps & graphics. Used by permission of Penguin, a division of Penguin Group (USA) Inc.

acres of forests for cattle to graze, and produced more poverty by forcing countryfolk onto considerably smaller pieces of land (Darnton, 1994).

Dependency theory is useful for understanding how foreign exploitation helps perpetuate poverty in many poor nations in Africa, Asia, and Latin America. But the theory ignores how the poor nations themselves also contribute to their economic deprivation. Their governments, for example, are usually corrupt, misusing public funds and spending too much on military expenditures, and their rich citizens avoid paying taxes, which could pay for basic services such as schools and clinics (Crossette, 1998). By emphasizing foreign exploitation as the perpetuator of poverty in poor nations, dependency theory also fails to explain the rapid economic ascendancy of the formerly poor East Asian societies.

■ Feminist Theory: Women's Contribution to Economic Development

Women's role in national development has a significant influence on a society's position in the global stratification system. Women can contribute to development through domestic work and gainful employment. But when women are heavily involved in domestic work, their society tends to be relatively poor (see Figure 7.10, p. 203). On the other hand, when women participate more in gainful employment, their society is likely to be wealthier.

Domestic work by women contributes indirectly to the economies of countries at all levels of development. All over the world, because of what women do at home, men are free to seek paid employment and children are able to grow up to join the labor force. But female housework does not produce income for the family. Consequently, by confining married women to unpaid housework—and shutting out of paid employment not only these married women but also many single women—a society tends to be poor. This can be seen in many developing countries in Africa, Asia, and Latin America. By contrast, a society that allows a relatively large number of women to join its labor force is usually richer, as can be seen in North America, Japan, and Western Europe.

Poor countries can therefore become better off if their women engage in paid work (Crossette, 1995). In fact, the development of the newly industrialized countries in East Asia and Latin America would not have taken place without greatly increased female participation in paid employment. In prosperous South Korea and other East Asian countries, women have taken most of the jobs in the electronics, textile, and garment industries. Women also make up the majority of the workers in the northern part of Mexico, along its border with the United States, where an industrial complex has been booming over the last three decades. Because of gender discrimination, however, these women are mostly relegated to low-wage jobs. If given the opportunity to compete with men for higher-paying employment, their contribution to national development would be greater.

SOCIOLOGICAL PERSPECTIVES ON STRATIFICATION

Social stratification is in essence social inequality, contrary to the U.S. belief in equality. Functionalists argue that it is necessary. Conflict theorists disagree. Symbolic interactionists, however, are more interested in *how* differences in status and power influence social interaction.

■ Functionalist Perspective: Benefiting Society

In the most influential tenet of the functionalist view, Kingsley Davis and Wilbert Moore (1945) said that stratification is necessary. Davis and Moore were trying to explain why stratification exists in all societies. The reason, they said, is that stratification serves a useful, positive function—in effect, a function necessary for the survival of a society.

What is this function? According to Davis and Moore, stratification motivates people to work hard by promising them such rewards as money, power, and prestige. The amount of reward depends on two things: how important a person's job is to society and how much training and skill are required to perform that job. A physician, for example, must receive more rewards than a garbage collector, not only because the physician's job is more important but also because it requires more training and skill.

Without this system of unequal rewards, many jobs important to society would never be performed. If future physicians believed they would be paid and respected just as much as garbage collectors, they would not bother to spend years studying for long hours at medical school.

In brief, stratification is necessary for society because it ensures that "the most important positions are conscientiously filled by the most qualified persons" (Davis and Moore, 1945).

■ Conflict Perspective: Harming Society

The Davis-Moore theory has encountered much criticism. Some critics argue that it is difficult to see why such large inequalities are necessary to fulfill the

theoretical thumbnail

What Stratification Does to Society

Perspective	Focus	Insights
Functionalist	How stratification benefits society	The more rewarding a position is, the more motivated people are to work hard to acquire the education and skills it requires.
Conflict	How stratification harms society	Stratification limits opportunities for the underprivileged, preserves injustices, and provokes unrest.
Symbolic interactionist	How stratification influences interactions	In their interactions, higher-status people show off their power while lower-status ones appear polite or respectful.

functions Davis and Moore described. Why is it functional, for example, to pay a corporate executive two or three times more than the president of the United States? The functionalist theory suggests that the corporate executive's job is more important. But is it really? Many people may disagree. Even the physician's job is not necessarily more important than the garbage collector's because uncollected refuse can pose a serious problem to society. The functionalist theory also fails to take into account the inherent interest of certain jobs. The intrinsic satisfaction of being a doctor far outweighs that of being a garbage collector. Why, then, should the doctor be given more rewards?

As an unfair system of differential rewards, according to Melvin Tumin (1953), stratification is dysfunctional rather than functional. First, by limiting the opportunities of those who are not in the privileged class, stratification restricts the possibility of discovering and exploiting the full range of talent in society. Thus, when some intelligent teenagers are too poor to stay in school and never develop their talents fully, society loses. Second, stratification helps maintain the status quo of social injustices, such as denying the poor, minorities, and women the opportunities for good jobs. Third, because the stratification system distributes rewards unjustly, it encourages the less privileged to become hostile, suspicious, and distrustful. The result may be social unrest and chaos.

■ Symbolic Interactionist Perspective: Influencing Interactions

According to symbolic interactionists, social inequality influences how people interact with one another. When persons of different statuses interact with each other, higher-status persons tend to show off their

power, and lower-status persons tend to appear polite or respectful.

A common example involves a higher-status person calling lower-status persons by their first names. At work, our bosses call us by our first names, but we do not call them by their first names unless we get their permission first. When we go to see a doctor, he or she calls us by our first names, but we address him or her as "doctor." By readily using lower-status persons' first names, higher-status persons apparently try to be personal, but in doing so, they disregard whether the lower-status persons may prefer to be shown respect instead (Karp and Yoels, 1998). As a result, the lower-status persons may feel humiliated or resentful.

In short, interactions between unequals tend to involve superiors using various symbols of power to put inferiors in their place and inferiors showing respect and humility to superiors.

The Theoretical Thumbnail above summarizes all three perspectives on stratification.

sociological frontiers

Stratification in Cyberspace

In the beginning of this chapter, we learned that people are divided into different classes according to how much wealth, power, and prestige they have. We have also seen through the lenses of the feminists and the multiculturalists that people are stratified on the basis of gender, race, ethnicity, and age. Now, as U.S. society continues its romance with technology, two new classes have emerged: the computer haves and the computer have-nots. But this digital divide is associated with the other determinants of stratification, especially income and race.

One survey has shown that among households with an average annual income of $75,000 or more, 68 percent have computers. By sharp contrast, among households with an average annual income of $20,000 or less, only 19 percent do. In another study, computer ownership also was found to vary by race in some ways. In households where the average annual income is less than $30,000, 34 percent of whites have computers, compared with only 19 percent of African Americans. There is virtually no racial gap at higher income levels, however. All this means that the rich are much more likely than the poor to have computers at home. And among low-income people, whites are significantly more likely than blacks to have computers (U.S. General Accounting Office, 2003; Hafner, 2000; Nussbaum, 1998).

As we observed earlier, the traditional form of stratification exerts a great influence on people's life chances. So does the stratification in cyberspace. Thus, children with computers at home generally do better in school than those without. This is because the machine has become a key communication and research tool in education. Access to a home computer also helps to improve self-esteem because peer pressure has now made it cool to have good computer skills. This makes the computer have-nots feel even more uncomfortable. Presumably, those children with home computers will enhance their chances of having successful careers and lives in the future (Hafner, 2000; Nussbaum, 1998).

 ■ For more of the latest Sociological Frontiers, look up Continuing Update at www.ablongman.com/thio6e.

using *sociology*

How to Become a Millionaire

There is a popular myth about millionaires: They are high-powered lawyers, doctors, business executives, celebrities, and others with sky-high incomes and lavish lifestyles. Their annual incomes are widely imagined to be over $1 million or at least $500,000. They are believed to live in upscale neighborhoods, drive foreign luxury cars, wear expensive clothes and watches, attend fancy parties, eat gourmet food, and join country clubs.

But the reality is just the opposite. Here are some key facts from a study about American millionaires (Stanley and Danko, 1998):

- Their annual median income is far less than $500,000. It is $131,000, equal to less than 7 percent of their total accumulated wealth.
- Two-thirds are self-employed, mostly in such dull-normal businesses as welding contracting, auctioneering, rice farming, pest control, coin and stamp dealing, and paving contracting.
- They work very hard; about two-thirds put in 45 to 55 hours a week.

- About half live in the same modest home for more than 20 years, which they bought long before they got rich.
- They live well below their means: Most wear inexpensive clothes and drive inexpensive, older-model cars.
- They are fastidious savers and investors. On average, they save nearly 20 percent of their income every year, which is mostly invested in stocks and mutual funds.

The most striking thing about millionaires is their frugality. Most lawyers, doctors, and other high-income people do not become millionaires because they live above their means with a high-consumption lifestyle. By contrast, most millionaires live far below their means by saving as much as they can. So, if you really want to get rich, start by being frugal with your money (Lee and McKenzie, 1999; Stanley and Danko, 1998).

In addition to being frugal, however, you should still consider what has been suggested earlier in this chapter: The probability of getting rich varies from one individual to another. Thus, the more favorable your *achieved* and *ascribed characteristics* are, the more likely you are to get rich. Thinking critically, which of your characteristics might boost or lessen your chances of becoming a millionaire? Why?

▮ CHAPTER REVIEW

1. *What are the bases of social stratification?* There are three: wealth, power, and prestige. The unequal distribution of these social rewards constitutes social stratification.

2. *How equal is the distribution of wealth in the United States?* It is very unequal. The richest 20 percent of the population earn nearly 48 percent of the total national income, and the poorest 20 percent earn less than 2.5 percent. *How is power distributed in the United States?* It is distributed very unequally, according to Marxist and elite theorists, who argue that power is concentrated in the hands of very few people. In contrast, pluralist theorists contend that power is widely dispersed among competing groups. *What is an important source of prestige in the United States?* Occupation is significant.

3. *How does social stratification vary from one society to another?* Different societies have different kinds of stratification, including the egalitarian, master-slave, feudal, caste, and class systems. *Why is it important to consider gender, ethnicity, and age when studying social stratification?* Without taking these issues into ac-

count, the social inequality of a society will appear to be less than it is.

4. *How do we know who is in which social class?* We may use the reputational method, asking a selected group of people to rank others; the subjective method, asking people how they rank themselves; or the objective method, ranking people according to such criteria as income, educational attainment, and occupation. *How is the U.S. population distributed into social classes?* About 3 percent are in the upper class, 25 percent in the upper-middle class, 34 percent in the middle class, 23 percent in the working class, and 15 percent in the lower class. *How does social class affect our lives?* People of different classes have different life chances, lifestyles, and values.

5. *What is poverty?* Poverty can be absolute or relative. Absolute poverty is the lack of minimum food and shelter necessary for maintaining life. Relative poverty is having less than the majority of the people have. *What is the feminization of poverty?* It refers to the huge number of women bearing the burden of poverty, mostly as single mothers. *What causes poverty?* To some social scientists, personal weaknesses and the "culture of poverty" cause people to be poor. To sociologists, however, society's need for dirty work to be done and its inegalitarian nature cause poverty.

6. *Who are the homeless, and why are they so?* Extremely poor, most are African American men in their middle thirties, but some are single mothers with children, mental patients, and alcohol or drug abusers. The social causes of homelessness include the increased shortage of inexpensive housing, declining demand for unskilled labor, and erosion of welfare. *What does the public think of the welfare system?* A large segment of the public does not like welfare because they believe it encourages dependency. *How does the federal government deal with the welfare problem?* It requires welfare recipients to work while limiting their benefits to five years.

7. *Is upward mobility common in the United States?* Before 1980, upward mobility was common but mostly within the middle segment rather than "from rags to riches." In the last few decades, however, the rich have gotten richer and the poor poorer. *What factors influence the opportunity for social mobility?* Structural factors of mobility include the decline of manufacturing industries in recent decades and an expanding economy, increasing education, low fertility among the higher classes, and massive immigration in earlier periods. Individual characteristics include social and ethnic background, gender, education, occupation, and luck.

8. *What is global inequality?* Global inequality is the extreme disparity in economic condition and life quality between rich and poor nations. *What are the consequences of global inequality?* Poor countries experience widespread poverty, extensive female disadvantages, relatively prevalent child exploitation, and shockingly widespread adult slavery. *What is dependency theory?* Derived from the conflict perspective, dependency theory is critical of rich nations, arguing that their exploitation of poor countries tends to perpetuate poverty, underdevelopment, and dependency. *According to feminist theory, how do women contribute to a society's economic development and hence its position in the global stratification system?* By participating in gainful employment, particularly if given the opportunity to compete with men for higher-paying positions.

9. *Why do functionalists think that social stratification is useful to society?* Stratification ensures that relatively important jobs are performed by competent people. *How do conflict theorists view stratification?* It is considered harmful to society—limiting opportunities for those not in the privileged class, preserving the status quo of injustices, and producing social unrest. *How do symbolic interactionists view stratification?* Stratification influences interactions between higher-status and lower-status people.

10. *How does stratification exist in cyberspace?* It consists of two classes of people: those who have home computers and those who do not. The computer haves earn much higher incomes and are much more likely to be white when compared with the computer have-nots. *Who's likely to become a millionaire?* People who have lower incomes than rich lawyers and doctors but who live far below their means and save as much as they can.

KEY TERMS

Absolute poverty The lack of minimum food and shelter necessary for maintaining life (p. 192).

Caste system A relatively rigid stratification system in which people's positions are ascribed and fixed (p. 185).

Class system A relatively open stratification system in which people's positions are achieved and changeable (p. 185).

Dependency theory The theory that rich nations exploit poor ones for power and commercial gain, thereby perpetuating poverty, underdevelopment, and dependency on rich nations (p. 202).

Feminization of poverty A huge number of women bearing the burden of poverty, mostly as single mothers or heads of families (p. 193).

Horizontal mobility Movement from one job to another within the same status category (p. 196).

Individual mobility Social mobility related to an individual's personal achievement and characteristics (p. 198).

Intergenerational mobility A change in social standing from one generation to the next (p. 196).

Intragenerational mobility A change in an individual's social standing (p. 196).

Kuznets curve The changing relationship between economic development and social inequality, named after its discoverer, Simon Kuznets (p. 185).

Life chances The likelihood of living a good, long, successful life in a society (p. 190).

Lifestyles Tastes, preferences, and ways of living (p. 191).

Neocolonialism The economic control exercised by rich nations over their former colonies (p. 202).

Objective method The method of identifying social classes using occupation, income, and education to rank people (p. 188).

Power The ability to control the behavior of others, even against their will (p. 181).

Power elite A small group of top leaders not just from business corporations but also from the federal government and the military (p. 181).

Relative poverty A state of deprivation resulting from having less than the majority of the people have (p. 193).

Reputational method The method of identifying social classes by selecting a group of people and asking them to rank others (p. 187).

Social class A category of people who have about the same amount of income, power, and prestige (p. 187).

Social mobility Movement from one social standing to another (p. 196).

Social stratification The system in which some people get more or fewer rewards than others (p. 180).

Status inconsistency The condition in which the same individual is given two conflicting status rankings (p. 183).

Status system A system in which people are stratified according to their social prestige (p. 182).

Structural mobility Social mobility related to changes in society (p. 197).

Subjective method The method of identifying social classes by asking people to rank themselves (p. 188).

Vertical mobility Moving up or down the status ladder (p. 196).

QUESTIONS FOR DISCUSSION AND REVIEW

THE BASES OF STRATIFICATION

1. What is social stratification?
2. How are economic rewards distributed in the United States?
3. In what ways is the power basis of stratification different from the system of prestige?

STRATIFICATION SYSTEMS: A GLOBAL VIEW

1. Why are hunter-gatherers and other similar groups relatively egalitarian?
2. How do the master-slave and feudal systems differ?
3. What are the differences between the caste and class systems?
4. What is the Kuznets curve?

NEW APPROACHES TO STRATIFICATION

1. Why is it important for the study of social stratification to consider gender, ethnicity, and age?

THE U.S. CLASS STRUCTURE

1. What methods can be used to study social class, and what are their strengths and weaknesses?
2. What features distinguish each of the social classes in the United States?
3. How does social class influence life chances, lifestyles, and values?

POVERTY IN THE UNITED STATES

1. How does the rate of poverty depend on its definition?
2. How do different theories explain the causes of poverty?
3. For what specific reasons do the working poor remain poor?
4. Who are the homeless?
5. What does the public think about welfare?
6. What do you think is the best idea for solving the welfare problem?

SOCIAL MOBILITY IN U.S. SOCIETY

1. What are the different patterns of mobility?
2. What structural and individual characteristics influence social mobility?

GLOBAL STRATIFICATION

1. How do economic conditions and quality of life differ among nations?
2. How poor are the countries in sub–Saharan Africa? What characteristics do they share with poor countries in other regions of the world?
3. What disadvantages do women have in the world's poor countries?
4. What is the nature of child exploitation in poor countries?
5. What kind of life do slaves have today? How have most of them become slaves in the first place?
6. How does dependency theory explain the continuing poverty of poor nations?
7. How do women influence their society's position in the global stratification system?

SOCIOLOGICAL PERSPECTIVES ON STRATIFICATION

1. How does the functionalist theory of stratification differ from the conflict approach?
2. How do status differences affect symbolic interaction?

SOCIOLOGICAL FRONTIERS/USING SOCIOLOGY

1. How does stratification exist in cyberspace?
2. What are the myths and realities about U.S. millionaires?

■ SUGGESTED READINGS

Bales, Kevin. 1999. *Disposable People: New Slavery in the Global Economy*. Berkeley: University of California Press. A critical analysis of how profound poverty and official neglect lead to slavery, in which people are forced by threat of violence to work without getting paid.

Ehrenreich, Barbara. 2001. *Nickel and Dimed: On (Not) Getting By in America*. New York: Metropolitan Books. An analysis of how the working poor struggle with their lives, based on the author's personal experiences in three different sections of the country.

Harrington, Charles C., and Susan K. Boardman. 2000. *Paths to Success: Beating the Odds in American Society*. Cambridge, MA: Harvard University Press.

A study of how people from poor families achieve economic success.

Keister, Lisa A. 2000. *Wealth in America: Trends in Wealth Inequality*. New York: Cambridge University Press. Uses many surveys and tax records to show the growing inequality in wealth over the last 40 years.

Shirk, Martha, Neil G. Bennett, and J. Lawrence Aber. 1999. *Lives on the Line: American Families and the Struggle to Make Ends Meet*. Boulder, CO: Westview Press. Shows how families below or near the federal poverty line deal with the daily problems of being poor.

■ Additional Resources

The New York Times
expect the world®
nytimes.com

Expand your knowledge of the concepts discussed in this chapter by reading the following current and historical articles from the *New York Times*. Go to the "eThemes of the Times" section of the Companion Website (www.ablongman.com/thio6e):

"In a Battered Taxi, a Nurse Goes to India's Poorest"

"Most Americans in Poverty in 2002, Census Study Says"

Research Navigator.com

Research Navigator, a research database, provides immediate access to hundreds of full-text articles from EBSCO's ContentSelect Academic Journal Database. If the Research Navigator access code was included with your textbook, go to the website www.research navigator.com and read the following articles related to this chapter by typing in the article number:

Hayaud-Din, and Mian Ahad. "The Hawallah Network: Culture and Economic Development in Afghanistan." *International Social Science Review*, 2003, Vol. 78 Issue 1/2, p21, 10p. Accession Number: 10271281. Explores the dangers that Hawallah networks pose for American efforts to reconstruct Afghanistan.

Scott, John. "Social Class and Stratification in Late Modernity." *Acta Sociologica,* 2002, Vol. 45 Issue 1, p 23, 13p. Accession Number: 6677420. Proves that far from being dead, class remains an important analytical tool.

chapter 8

Race and Ethnicity

myths & realities

myth *There are three distinct, pure races: white, Asian, and black.*

reality There are no pure races. People with the physical traits of these three groups have been interbreeding for centuries. In the United States, for example, about 70 percent of blacks have some white ancestry, and approximately 20 percent of whites have at least one black ancestor (p. 212).

myth *When people move from one country to another, their racial characteristics, such as skin color and facial features, do not change. Therefore, if African Americans go to another country, they will be considered blacks there, too, as in the United States.*

reality It is true that people's physical features do not change when they move to another country. But their racial identification may change. Most African Americans in the United States, for example, would be considered whites in many Latin American countries (p. 213).

myth *The Jews are a race.*

reality Jews do not constitute a race because throughout the centuries, Jews and non-Jews have interbred extensively so that members of both groups are often physically indistinguishable. Jews are instead an ethnic group, a collection of people sharing a distinctive cultural heritage—in this case, Judaism (p. 214).

myth *Since Jewish Americans are generally prosperous, they tend to be conservative and vote Republican, like other prosperous U.S. citizens.*

reality On the contrary, Jewish Americans tend more to be liberal, supporting welfare, civil rights, women's rights, and the like. They are also more likely to vote Democrat (p. 223).

myth *If a white person discriminates against blacks, he or she must be prejudiced.*

reality Not necessarily. Many whites discriminate without being prejudiced, primarily because of social pressure. Unprejudiced white men, for example, might not date black women for fear of being ostracized (p. 229).

f you take a walk in a typical neighborhood in Sacramento, California, you will meet people of many races and ethnicities living together. There are Tom and Debra Burruss. He is black and she is white. Living next door are Ken Wong and Binh Lam, a Vietnamese couple. Directly across the street is the home of the Cardonas, a Hispanic and white couple. If you go downtown to the elementary school, you will find 347 kids, 189 of whom speak a language other than English at home. At the mall nearby, you may find many teenage couples like Kayla and Gerald. "Personally, it doesn't matter what color you are," Kayla once said to a reporter. "I am mixed, he is mixed, and most everybody is mixed."

Indeed, Sacramento is the most integrated city in the United States. Still, there is racial and ethnic segregation. Every Sunday, for example, Russian immigrants, African Americans, and Hispanic Americans go to separate churches (Stodghill and Bower, 2002).

The segregation in Sacramento is due largely to language barriers and differences in cultural heritage, which have occurred because of the enormous increase in immigration from many countries over the last decade. Segregation driven by language and culture also exists in the rest of the United States, although to a lesser extent. More often, however, it is racial or ethnic prejudice and discrimination that divides Americans to one degree or another. In this chapter, we will analyze various aspects of this social problem throughout the world. We will also take a close look at the lives of people from various racial and ethnic groups in the United States.

SOCIOLOGICAL DEFINITIONS

People are accustomed to thinking of a *minority* as a category of people who are physically different and who make up a small percentage of the population. But this is not the way sociologists define a minority. Consider the Jews in China and the United States and the blacks in South Africa. The Jews in China do not "look Jewish"; they look like other Chinese. Similarly, the Jews in the United States do not "look Jewish"; they look like other white Americans. Jews cannot be differentiated from the dominant group on the basis of their physical characteristics, but sociologically, they are considered a minority. In South Africa, blacks are also sociologically a minority, although they make up a majority of the population. Neither physical traits nor numbers alone determine whether people constitute a minority. To understand the sociological idea of minority, we need first to look at race and ethnicity.

■ Race

As a biological concept, *race* refers to a large category of people who share certain inherited physical characteristics. These may include a particular skin color, nasal shape, or lip form. The popular classification of human races recognizes three groups: Caucasoid, Mongoloid, and Negroid. Caucasoids have light skin, Mongoloids yellowish skin, and Negroids dark skin. Other physical differences also exist among the three groups.

myth	There are three distinct, pure races: white, Asian, and black.
reality	There are no pure races. People with the physical traits of these three groups have been interbreeding for centuries. In the United States, for example, about 70 percent of blacks have some white ancestry, and approximately 20 percent of whites have at least one black ancestor.

There are at least two problems with this classification of races. First, some groups fit into none of these categories. Natives of India and Pakistan have Caucasoid facial features but dark skin. The Ainu of Japan have Mongoloid faces but white skin. The Vogul of Siberia have Caucasoid faces but yellowish skin. Some aboriginal groups in Australia have dark

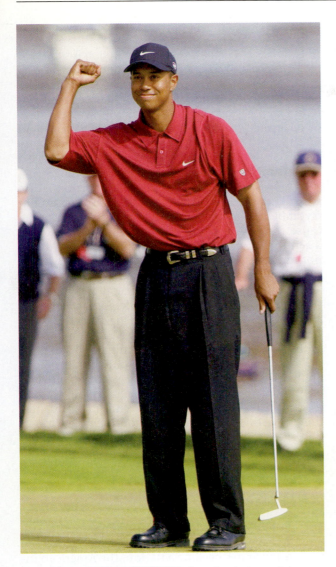

A MATTER OF PERCEPTION Race is what a society perceives it to be. Golfer Tiger Woods sees himself as a *Cablinasian,* which accurately reflects his Caucasian, African American, Native American, Thai, and Chinese ancestries. But he is widely known only as an African American because that is what U.S. society perceives him to be. ■

skin and other Negroid features but blond hair. The Polynesians of Pacific islands have a mixture of Caucasoid, Mongoloid, and Negroid characteristics (Jacquard, 1983).

Another problem with the biological classification of races is that there are no pure races. People in these groups have been interbreeding for centuries. In the United States, for example, about 70 percent of blacks have some white ancestry, and approximately 20 percent of whites have at least one black

ancestor (Kilker, 1993; Davis, 1991). Biologists have also determined that all current populations originated from one common genetic pool—one single group of humans that evolved some 100,000 years ago in Africa. Today, 99.9 percent of the DNA molecules (which make up the gene) are the same for all humans, and only the remaining 0.1 percent are responsible for all the differences in appearance (Angier, 2000; Shipman, 1994). Even these outward differences are meaningless because the differences among members of the same race are greater than the average differences between two racial groups. Some American blacks, for example, have lighter skin than many whites, and some whites are darker than many blacks.

Since there are no clear-cut biological distinctions between racial groups—in physical characteristics or genetic make-up—sociologists define race as a social rather than a biological phenomenon. Defined sociologically, a **race** is a group of people who are *perceived* by a given society to be biologically different from others. People are assigned to one race or another not necessarily on the basis of logic or fact but by public opinion, which, in turn, is molded by society's dominant group.

myth	When people move from one country to another, their racial characteristics, such as skin color and facial features, do not change. Therefore, if African Americans go to another country, they will be considered blacks there, too, as in the United States.
reality	It is true that people's physical features do not change when they move to another country. But their racial identification may change. Most African Americans in the United States, for example, would be considered whites in many Latin American countries.

Consider a boy in the United States whose father has 100 percent white ancestry and whose mother is the daughter of a white man and a black woman. This youngster is considered black in U.S. society, although he is actually more white than black, because 75 percent of his ancestry is white. In many Latin American countries, however, this same child would be considered white. In fact, according to Brazil's popular perception of a black as a person of African descent who has no white ancestry at all, about three-fourths of all U.S. blacks would *not* be considered blacks (Holmes, 2001; Fish, 1995; Denton and Massey, 1989).

The definition of race, then, varies from one society to another. Sociologists use this societal definition to identify races because it is the racial status to which people are assigned by their society, rather than their real biological characteristics, that has profound significance for their social lives. Individuals, however, do not necessarily accept the societal definition of their race. The famous golfer Tiger Woods, for example, is widely known as African American, but he sees himself as *Cablinasian,* an acronym he has crafted to reflect his one-eighth Caucasian, one-fourth African American, one-eighth Native American, one-fourth Thai, and one-fourth Chinese roots (White, 1997). Still, the societal definition of race has a powerful impact on the individual's life, as shown later in this chapter.

■ Ethnicity

The Jews have often been called a race. But they have the same racial origins as Arabs—both are Semites—and throughout the centuries, Jews and non-Jews have interbred extensively. As a result, as noted earlier, Jews are often physically indistinguishable from non-Jews. Besides, any person can become a Jew by conversion to Judaism. Thus, the Jews do not constitute a race but instead are a religious group or, more broadly, an ethnic group.

myth	The Jews are a race.
reality	Jews do not constitute a race because throughout the centuries, Jews and non-Jews have interbred extensively so that members of both groups are often physically indistinguishable. Jews are instead an ethnic group, a collection of people sharing a distinctive cultural heritage—in this case, Judaism.

Whereas race is based on popularly perceived physical traits, ethnicity is based on cultural characteristics. An **ethnic group**, then, is a collection of people who share a distinctive cultural heritage. Members of an ethnic group may share a language, religion, history, or national origin. They always share a feeling that they are a distinct people. In the United States, members of an ethnic group typically have the same national origin. As a result, they are named after the countries from which they or their ancestors came. Examples are Polish Americans, Italian Americans, and Irish Americans.

For the most part, ethnicity is culturally learned. People learn the language, values, and other characteristics of their ethnic group. Members of an ethnic group are usually born into it, but the cultural traits of the group are passed from one generation to the next.

■ Minority

A **minority** is a racial or ethnic group that is subjected to prejudice and discrimination. **Prejudice** is a negative attitude toward a certain category of people. It includes ideas and beliefs, feelings, and predispositions to act in a certain way. For example, whites prejudiced against blacks might fear meeting a black man on the street at night. They might resent blacks who are successful. They might plan to sell their house if a black family moved into the neighborhood.

Whereas prejudice is an attitude, discrimination is an act. More specifically, **discrimination** is an unfavorable action against individuals that is taken because they are members of a certain category. It is discrimination, for instance, when a landlord will not rent an apartment to a family because its members are African American or Hispanic.

A minority is not necessarily a small percentage of the population. Blacks are considered a minority in South Africa, even though they make up about 70 percent of the population, because they are the subordinate group. Similarly, the dominant group need not make up a large part of the population. People of English descent in the United States today constitute only about 13 percent of the population. But because of their continuing social and cultural influence, they are still considered the dominant group—as they were more than 200 years ago.

RACIAL AND ETHNIC DIVERSITY

The United States is a nation of immigrants, as Figure 8.1 suggests. More than 20,000 years ago, before the United States became a nation, the American Indians arrived from Asia and settled as Native Americans (Petit, 1998). Long after that time, numerous immigrants began to pour in from Europe and later from Africa, Asia, and Latin America. They came as explorers, adventurers, slaves, and refugees—most hoping to fulfill a dream of success and happiness. The English were the earliest of these immigrants and, on the whole, the most successful in fulfilling that dream. They became the dominant group. Eventually, they founded a government dedicated to the democratic ideal of equality, but they kept African Americans as slaves and discriminated against other racial and ethnic groups. This *American dilemma*—the discrepancy between the ideal of equality and the reality of discrimination—still exists, though to a lesser degree than in the past. Let us look at how the minority groups along with the dominant group have fared under the burden of the American dilemma.

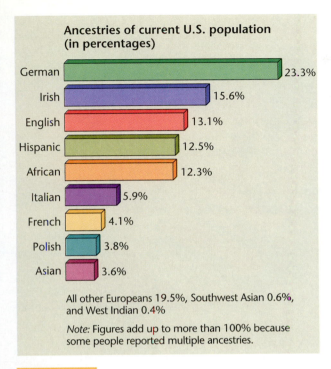

Ancestries of current U.S. population (in percentages)

German 23.3%
Irish 15.6%
English 13.1%
Hispanic 12.5%
African 12.3%
Italian 5.9%
French 4.1%
Polish 3.8%
Asian 3.6%

All other Europeans 19.5%, Southwest Asian 0.6%, and West Indian 0.4%

Note: Figures add up to more than 100% because some people reported multiple ancestries.

FIGURE 8.1

Nation of Immigrants

The United States is a nation of immigrants, who have come from all over the world. More than 20,000 years ago, the American Indians came from Asia and settled as Native Americans. Long after then, masses of immigrants began to pour in from Europe and later from Africa, Asia, and Latin America. Today, their descendants make up various proportions of the U.S. population, as we can see here.

Critical Thinking: *How does the fact that the United States is a nation of immigrants influence its relationships with other nations?*

Source: Data from U.S. Census Bureau, 2001.

■ Native Americans

Native Americans have long been called *Indians*—one result of Columbus's mistaken belief that he had landed in India. The explorer's successors passed down many other distorted descriptions of the Native Americans. They were described as savages, although it was whites who slaughtered hundreds of thousands of them. They were portrayed as scalp hunters, although it was the white government that offered large sums to whites for the scalps of natives. They were stereotyped as lazy, although it was whites who forced them to give up their traditional occupations. These false conceptions of Native Americans were reinforced by the contrasting pictures whites painted of themselves. The white settlers were known as pioneers rather than invaders and marauders; their conquest of the Native Americans' land was called homesteading, not theft.

Ironically, when Columbus discovered the land that would later become the United States, the natives he encountered around the Caribbean were very friendly. He wrote: "Of anything they have, if it be asked for, they never say no, but do rather invite the person to accept it, and show as much lovingness as though they would give their hearts" (Hraba, 1979). In North America, too, the earliest white settlers were often aided by Native Americans.

As the white settlers increased in number and moved west, however, Native Americans resisted them. But the native population was decimated by outright killing, by destruction of their food sources, and by diseases brought by the whites, such as smallpox and influenza. With their greater numbers and superior military technology, the whites prevailed. Sometimes, they took land by treaty rather than by outright force. The treaties required the U.S. government to provide Native Americans with foreign aid, such as helping them maintain a reasonable level of education and health and protecting their resources. But the treaties were often violated (Van Biema, 1995). As a result, the three-quarters of the U.S. land mass that Native Americans controlled two centuries ago has shrunk to only 2 percent today.

"You just show up here illegally and expect us to tell you about corn?"

Source: © The New Yorker Collection 1996 J. B. Handelsman from Cartoonbank.com. All Rights Reserved.

KEEPING THE PAST ALIVE
In recent years, many Native Americans, such as this Navajo grandmother, have actively sought to pass along their native languages, crafts, and ceremonies to the younger generations. At the same time, many tribes are striving to establish a viable economic base on which to build better lives for their members. ■

Native Americans have also suffered a huge loss of population, from 10 million at the time of Columbus's arrival to 2.5 million today. Slightly more than half now live on 314 reservations, mostly in the Southwest and Northwest, and the rest live in urban areas. After more than two centuries of colonial subjugation, Native Americans today find themselves at the bottom of the socioeconomic ladder—the poorest minority in the United States. Their unemployment and poverty rates are much higher than those of other Americans, and their average family income is also considerably lower (see Figure 8.2). Moreover, they have much higher rates of pneumonia, influenza, diabetes, tuberculosis, suicide, alcoholism, and car accidents compared with the general U.S. population.

Under constant pressure from Native Americans, since 1988, the U.S. government has instituted a policy "to promote tribal economic development, tribal self-sufficiency, and strong tribal government." Today, on some reservations, Native Americans are exempt from paying taxes and, further, are allowed to run highly profitable gambling operations that cater to non-Indians. At least seven tribes have recently been allowed to govern themselves virtually as sovereign nations, despite opposition from some state governments. These tribes set their own budgets and run their own programs, functions that have long been performed by the U.S. Bureau of Indian Affairs. Such self-determination has made the tribes more economically successful than they were under government control (Egan, 1998; Anderson, 1995).

All this has sparked a national movement to recapture traditions, to make Native Americans feel proud of their distinct cultural heritages. Virtually

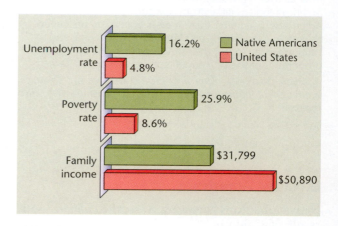

FIGURE 8.2

Native Americans as the Poorest Minority

After more than 200 years of colonial subjugation, Native Americans today find themselves at the bottom of the U.S. socioeconomic ladder. They have not only higher rates of unemployment and poverty than other Americans, as shown here, but also higher rates of pneumonia, alcoholism, and other health problems.

Critical Thinking: *Do you think these problems would be solved if more land was returned to Native Americans? Why or why not?*

Source: Data from U.S. Census Bureau, 2002.

every tribe places heavy emphasis on teaching the younger generation its native language, crafts, tribal history, and religious ceremonies. Many tribes have become more active in preserving sacred sites and demanding repatriation of sacred objects from museums (McCoy, 1996). Among the 300 tribes that lacked unity in the past, intertribal visiting and marriage are now common. Moreover, in the last 15 years, many Native American men and women have successfully established themselves in business, law, and other professions.

Of course, the majority of Native Americans still have a long way to go. Without a viable economic base, they still find themselves powerless, mired in high unemployment, deep poverty, and other prob-

lems. The change that has occurred in the last 15 years has not been enough to overcome two centuries of government oppression.

■ African Americans

There are about 36 million African Americans, constituting about 11.3 percent of the U.S. population. They are the second-largest minority in the nation, with high concentrations in the South (see Figure 8.3). In fact, there are more blacks in the United States than in any African nation except Nigeria.

Their ancestors first started coming from Africa to North America as indentured servants in 1619. Soon after, they were brought as slaves. Most lived in what

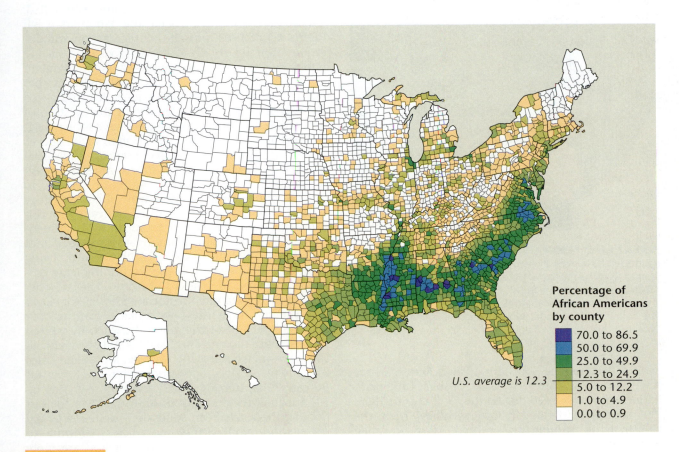

Percentage of African Americans by county

- 70.0 to 86.5
- 50.0 to 69.9
- 25.0 to 49.9
- 12.3 to 24.9
- 5.0 to 12.2
- 1.0 to 4.9
- 0.0 to 0.9

U.S. average is 12.3

FIGURE 8.3

Geographical Distribution of African Americans

African Americans are heavily concentrated in the South. Over the last two decades, the great migration from the rural South to northern cities has stopped and then reversed. Increasingly, affluent African Americans are finding the good life in southern suburbs, and lower-income African Americans are looking for a better life in southern cities.

Critical Thinking: *Why do most African Americans want to live in the South?*

Source: Data from U.S. Census Bureau, 2001.

GREAT LEAP FORWARD Since the 1960s, the Civil Rights Act has paved the way for improvement in the position of African Americans. Here, the U.S. Secretary of State, Colin Powell, greets the British Prime Minister, Tony Blair. The proportion of African Americans today contributing to the nation's cultural, educational, and political life is greater than ever before, but full equality is still far from achieved. ■

cans. Beginning in the early 1900s, as southern farms were mechanized and the demand for workers in northern industrial centers rose during the two world wars, many southern African Americans migrated north. When the wars ended and the demand for workers decreased, however, they were often the first to be fired. Even in the North, where there were no Jim Crow laws, African Americans faced discrimination and segregation.

A turning point in U.S. race relations came in 1954, when the U.S. Supreme Court ordered that the public schools be desegregated. The order gave momentum to the long-standing campaign against racial discrimination. In the late 1950s and 1960s, the civil rights movement launched marches, sit-ins, and boycotts. The price was high: Many civil rights workers were beaten and jailed; some were killed. Eventually, Congress passed the landmark Civil Rights Act of 1964, prohibiting segregation and discrimination in virtually all areas of social life, such as public facilities, schools, housing, and employment.

In the last 30-plus years, the Civil Rights Act has put an end to many forms of segregation and paved the way for some improvement in the position of African Americans. Various studies have shown a significant decline in white opposition to such issues as school integration, integrated housing, interracial marriage, and voting for an African American president. The number of African Americans elected to various public offices has sharply increased since 1980. The proportion of African Americans with college degrees has also grown significantly. An affluent middle class has emerged among African Americans.

Full equality, however, is still far from being achieved. Most evident is the continuing large economic gap between blacks and whites. The latest figures on median family income are $29,026 for blacks and $46,900 for whites—with blacks earning only about 62 percent of the amount earned by whites. Job discrimination against blacks is still prevalent, although somewhat less than before. More than twice as many blacks live in poverty as whites (U.S. Census Bureau, 2003; Herring, 2002). Even more glaring racial inequalities show up in housing. Over the last decade, there has been some decline in residential segregation. Nonetheless, most blacks continue to reside in segregated neighborhoods and are more likely than whites with similar incomes to live in overcrowded and substandard housing (U.S. Census Bureau, 2003; Farley and Frey, 1994; Massey and Denton, 1993).

In sum, progress has been significant in education and politics but not in housing and economic conditions. The economic situation is a little complicated, though. Unemployment and poverty have soared in the black working class, primarily because

would become the southern United States, where they worked on cotton, tobacco, or sugar-cane plantations. Slavery ended during the Civil War in 1865. But soon after federal troops withdrew from the South, white supremacy returned. Many so-called **Jim Crow laws** (the name was a derogatory term for blacks) were enacted to segregate blacks from whites in all kinds of public and private facilities, from restrooms to schools. A more basic control tactic was terror. If an African American man was suspected of killing a white person or of raping a white woman, he might be lynched, beaten to death, or burned at the stake.

Lynchings occurred in the North, too. Still, the North offered more opportunities for African Ameri-

of numerous plant shutdowns caused by the shift from a manufacturing to a service economy in the face of increased global competition. On the other hand, the black middle class has become more prosperous, largely because they have attained an advanced education and the skills required by the technological changes in the U.S. economy (Wilson, 1996; Takaki, 1993). Still, it is difficult for middle-class blacks to enjoy the rewards of their success. They are often outraged at being treated like the black underclass, which involves being stopped and questioned as crime suspects by police, getting bad or no service in shops and restaurants, having difficulty flagging down a taxi, and being falsely charged with shoplifting (Feagin, 1995; Close, 1993).

■ Hispanic Americans

In 1848, the United States either won in war or bought from Mexico the lands that would become Texas, California, Nevada, Utah, Arizona, New Mexico, and Colorado. Many Mexicans consequently found themselves living in U.S. territories as U.S. citizens. The vast majority of today's Mexican Americans, however, are in the United States as the result of emigration from Mexico since 1900. At first, immigrants came largely to work in the farmlands of California and to build the railroads of the Southwest. Later, a steady stream of Mexicans began to pour into the United States, driven by Mexico's population pressures and economic problems and attracted by U.S. industry's need for low-paid, unskilled labor.

In 1898, the United States added Puerto Rico to its territory by defeating Spain in the Spanish-American War. In 1917, Congress granted all Puerto Ricans citizenship, but because it is not a state, Puerto Ricans may not vote in presidential elections and are not represented in Congress. Over the years, especially since the early 1950s, many Puerto Ricans, lured by job opportunities and the cheap plane service between San Juan and New York City, have migrated to the mainland. In the last two decades, though, more have returned to Puerto Rico than have come to the United States.

Thus, a new minority group has emerged in the United States—Hispanic Americans, also called *Latinos*. Today, the category includes several groups. Besides Mexican Americans and Puerto Ricans, there are Cuban immigrants who began to flock to the Miami area when their country became communist in 1959. There are also immigrants from other Central and South American countries who have come as political refugees and job seekers. By 2003, the members of all these groups totaled about 38.8 million, constituting 12.1 percent of the U.S. population. Hispanics have just narrowly surpassed blacks as the largest minority (see Figure 8.4, p. 220).

The Spanish language is the unifying force among Hispanic Americans. Another source of their common identity is religion: At least 85 percent are Roman Catholic. There are, however, significant differences within the Hispanic community. Mexican Americans are by far the largest group, accounting for 64 percent of Hispanics. They are heavily con-

HELD TOGETHER BY LINGO AND FAITH Hispanic Americans now make up the largest minority group in the United States. The Spanish language is the unifying force among Hispanic Americans, who come from Mexico, Cuba, Puerto Rico, and Central and South American countries. Another source of common identity is religion: At least 85 percent of Hispanic Americans are Roman Catholic. ■

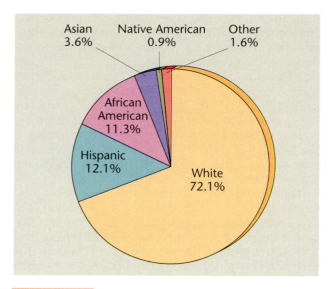

FIGURE 8.4

Hispanics Have Just Become the Largest Minority

Hispanics have narrowly surpassed African Americans to become the largest minority in the United States. Hispanics share the same language (Spanish) and religion (Catholicism) but lag behind other Americans in education, employment, and income. They are becoming a powerful force in politics, however.

Critical Thinking: *Why has the Hispanic population increased so much in the last few years?*

Source: Data from U.S. Census Bureau, 2003.

centrated in the Southwest (see Figure 8.5). Puerto Ricans make up 11 percent and live mostly in the Northeast, especially in New York City. As a group, they are the poorest among the Hispanics, which may explain why many have gone back to Puerto Rico. The Cubans, who constitute 5 percent of the U.S. Hispanic population and live mostly in Florida, are the most affluent and therefore have the greatest tendency toward integration with Anglos (white Americans). The remaining Hispanics are a diverse group from Central and South America, ranging from uneducated, unskilled laborers to highly trained professionals.

Hispanics, in general, lag behind both whites and blacks in educational attainment. Among those age 25 or older, only 9 percent have completed college compared with 25 percent of whites and 12 percent of blacks. But some Hispanic groups are more educated than others. Cubans are the best educated, primarily because most of the early refugees fleeing communist Cuba were middle-class professional people. Mexican Americans and Puerto Ricans are less educated because they consist of many recent immigrants with much less schooling. Young U.S.-born

Hispanics usually have more education. Lack of proficiency in English has slowed recent Hispanic immigrants' educational progress. As many as 25 percent of Hispanics in public schools speak little or no English, which has resulted in higher dropout rates than among non-Hispanic students (Barone, 2001; U.S. Census Bureau, 2001; Bernstein, 1990).

Hispanics are primarily clustered in lower-paying jobs, earning far less than whites. They also have higher rates of unemployment and poverty. However, the higher educational achievement of young Hispanics provides hope that more will join the higher-paid white-collar workforce in the future. Research has shown that if Hispanics speak English fluently and have at least graduated from high school, their occupational achievement is close to that of non-Hispanics with similar English fluency and schooling (Stolzenberg, 1990). Nationwide, Hispanics are also a growing force in politics, gaining representation as members of Congress, state governors, and mayors of large cities (Barone, 2001; Ayres, 1996).

■ Asian Americans

Since 1980, Asian Americans have been the fastest-growing minority, although they remain a much smaller minority—about 4 percent of the U.S. population—than Hispanics and African Americans. There is tremendous diversity among Asian Americans, whose ancestry can be traced to more than 20 different countries. The larger groups are Chinese, Japanese, Filipinos, Koreans, and Vietnamese. The first two have the longest history in the United States.

The Chinese first came in 1849 during the gold rush on the West Coast, pulled by better economic conditions in the United States and pushed by economic problems and local rebellions in China. Soon, huge numbers of Chinese were imported to work for low wages, digging mines and building railroads. After these projects were completed, jobs became scarce and white workers feared competition from the Chinese. As a result, special taxes were imposed on the Chinese, and they were prohibited from attending school, seeking employment, owning property, and bearing witness in court. In 1882, the Chinese Exclusion Act restricted immigration to the United States, and it stopped all Chinese immigration from 1904 to 1943. Many Chinese returned to their homeland (Cassel, 2001; Henry, 1990; Kitano, 1981).

Immigrants from Japan met with similar hostility. They began to come to the West Coast somewhat later than the Chinese, also in search of better economic opportunities. At first they were welcomed as a source of cheap labor. But soon they began to op-

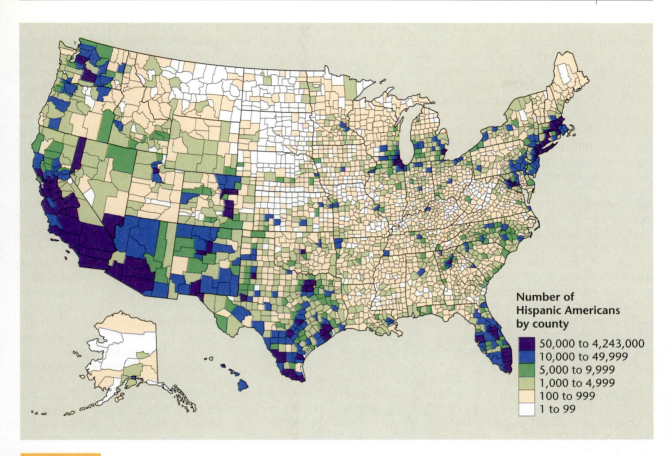

Number of
Hispanic Americans
by county

50,000 to 4,243,000
10,000 to 49,999
5,000 to 9,999
1,000 to 4,999
100 to 999
1 to 99

FIGURE 8.5

Geographical Distribution of Hispanic Americans

Among Hispanic Americans, Mexicans are the largest group and are heavily concentrated in the Southwest. Puerto Ricans live mostly in the Northeast, especially in New York City, and most Cuban Americans live in Florida.

Critical Thinking: *Can the geographical differences of these three groups weaken their common identity as Hispanics? Why or why not?*

Source: Data from U.S. Census Bureau, 2001.

erate small shops, and anti-Japanese activity grew. In 1906, San Francisco forbade Asian children to attend white schools. In response, the Japanese government negotiated an agreement whereby the Japanese agreed to stop immigrating to the United States, and President Theodore Roosevelt agreed to end harassment of the Japanese who were already here. But when the Japanese began to buy their own farms, they met new opposition. In 1913, California prohibited foreign-born Japanese from owning or leasing lands; other Western states followed suit. In 1922, the U.S. Supreme Court ruled that foreign-born Japanese could not become U.S. citizens.

Worse events occurred during World War II. All the Japanese from the West Coast—both aliens and

U.S. citizens—were rounded up and confined in concentration camps in isolated areas. They were forced to sell their homes and properties. The action was condoned even by the Supreme Court as a legitimate way of ensuring that Japanese Americans would not help Japan defeat the United States. Racism, however, was the real source of such treatment. There was no evidence of any espionage or sabotage by a Japanese American. Besides, German Americans were not sent to concentration camps, although Germany also was at war with the United States and there were instances of subversion by German Americans. In 1987, when the survivors sued the U.S. government for billions of dollars in compensation, the solicitor general acknowledged that the detention was "frankly racist" and "deplorable." And in 1988, the Senate voted overwhelmingly to give $20,000 and an apology to each of the surviving internees (Molotsky, 1988).

Despite this history of discrimination, Asians have shown signs of success in the United States today. As Figure 8.6 suggests, when compared with whites, Asians are more likely to graduate from college and have a higher family income. However, as indicated by the same figure, there is more poverty among Asians than among whites. Moreover, the higher family income among Asians is misleading for two reasons. First, the average Asian family is larger and more members of the family work, compared with the average white family. *Individual* income is actually lower for Asians than for whites. Second, most Asians live in California, Hawaii, and New York, where the cost of living is higher than the national average (Takaki, 1993). Contrary to popular belief, then, Asian Americans still have not attained real income equality with whites, even though they have more education.

Discrimination against Asians is subtle. Many well-educated Asian Americans can get work as professionals and technicians, but they rarely become officials and managers. White bosses often cite language deficiencies as an excuse for denying promotions. Privately, they stereotype Asians as weak and incapable of handling people, although Japanese-managed companies are well known for outperforming U.S. companies. It is assumed that Asian talent can flourish in the classroom or laboratory but not in senior management. The Asians are, in effect, victims of the **glass ceiling**, the prejudiced belief that keeps minority professionals from holding leadership positions. Thus, many Asian professionals are prevented from joining the top ranks of corporations.

The stereotype of Asians as a so-called model minority also hurts. It implies that virtually all Asians do well, which, of course, is not true; there is still much poverty among, for example, Filipinos and Chinatown residents. By suggesting that Asian Americans are not victims of discrimination, the model minority stereotype further shuts Asians out of affirmative action programs. The stereotype is similarly used against Hispanics and African Americans, who are told directly or indirectly that they do not need racial preferences because "the Asians have made it, so why can't you?" This provokes resentment and even hostility against Asians, as African Americans have shown at Korean stores in some cities. Finally, the model minority stereotype puts undue pressure on young Asian Americans to succeed in school, particularly in mathematics and science classes, which may lead to mental health problems (U.S. Commission on Civil Rights, 1992).

Jewish Americans

The first Jews came to the United States from Brazil in 1654; their ancestors had been expelled from Spain and Portugal. Then other Jews arrived directly from Europe. Their numbers were very small, however, until the 1880s, when large numbers of Jewish immigrants began to arrive—first from Germany and then from Russia and other Eastern European countries. In the United States, they were safe from the *pogroms* (massacres) they had faced in Europe but not from prejudice and discrimination.

During the 1870s, many colleges in the United States refused to admit Jewish Americans. At the turn of the century, Jews often encountered discrimination when they applied for white-collar jobs. During the 1920s and 1930s, they were accused of being part of an international conspiracy to take over U.S. business and government, and **anti-Semitism**—prejudice or discrimination against Jews—became more widespread and overt. The president of Harvard University proposed restrictive quotas for Jewish Americans. Large real estate companies in New Jersey, New York, Georgia, and Florida refused to sell property

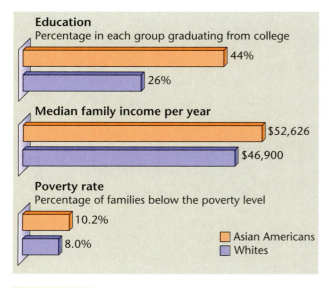

Education
Percentage in each group graduating from college

44%

26%

Median family income per year

$52,626

$46,900

Poverty rate
Percentage of families below the poverty level

10.2%

8.0%

■ Asian Americans
■ Whites

FIGURE 8.6

How Asian Americans Fare

Although Asian Americans have more education and a higher average family income than whites, they also have a higher rate of poverty. Also, family income is higher for Asians only because the average Asian family is larger and more family members work, compared with the average white family. Thus, Asian Americans do not fare as well as they appear.

Critical Thinking: *Why are Asian Americans often stereotyped as the model minority?*

Source: Data from U.S. Census Bureau, 2003.

STICKING TOGETHER Today, many Jews are successfully integrated into U.S. society—so much so that some Jewish Americans fear they are losing their traditional identity. Yet Jewish sociologists point out that Jews have been able to maintain a sense of group identity and cohesion through occupational and residential concentration. By sharing similar neighborhoods, schools, occupations, organizations, and friends, Jewish Americans have been able to maintain a higher level of cohesion than most other ethnic groups. ■

to Jews. The Chamber of Commerce of St. Petersburg, Florida, announced its intention to make St. Petersburg "a 100 percent American gentile city" (McWilliams, 1948). Many country clubs and other social and business organizations barred Jewish Americans from membership.

Anti-Semitism has declined sharply since the late 1940s, but recent years have seen an increase in anti-Semitic acts—including verbal slurs, vandalism, and physical violence. In general, though, Jewish Americans face less prejudice and discrimination than other minority groups, such as African Americans and Hispanics. In fact, Jewish Americans are widely recognized as hard working, family oriented, religious, and friendly. Their contributions to U.S. cultural life are appreciated. And a growing number of Jews are regularly elected to high public office by non-Jews (Niebuhr, 1996; Lipset and Raab, 1995).

Jewish Americans are so highly regarded largely because they have become the most successful minority. Their levels of education, occupation, and income are higher than those of any other group. Their success may stem from the emphasis Jewish culture gives to education, from a self-image as God's chosen people, and from parental pressure to succeed. Not all Jews are successful, though. There is still significant poverty in their midst. Being rich or poor has much to do with how recently they arrived in the United States. Most of the poor Jews are Orthodox, the most recent immigrants in the United States. The more successful are Conservative Jews, who have been in this country longer. The wealthiest are Reform Jews, who have been in the United States the longest.

myth	Since Jewish Americans are generally prosperous, they tend to be conservative and to vote Republican, like other prosperous U.S. citizens.
reality	On the contrary, Jewish Americans tend more to be liberal, supporting welfare, civil rights, women's rights, and the like. They are also more likely to vote Democrat.

Although Jewish Americans as a whole are prosperous, they are not conservative and inclined to vote Republican, as other prosperous U.S. citizens are. Instead, they tend to be liberal—supporting welfare, civil rights, women's rights, civil liberties, and the like—and to vote Democrat. Perhaps this reflects their ability to identify with the dispossessed and oppressed. It also reflects the impact of Jewish norms underlying *tzedakah* (pronounced *si-DOCK-ah,* meaning "righteousness"), which requires the fortunate and the well-to-do to help individuals and communities in difficulty (Lipset and Raab, 1995).

Jewish Americans, however, seem in danger of losing their traditional identity. Today, about half of all Jewish Americans are not affiliated with a synagogue, and only a small minority (about 20 percent) attend synagogue regularly. Marriage with non-Jews has increased greatly; over half of all Jewish marriages involve a non-Jew. The Jewish birth rate has also declined. All this has caused consternation among most rabbis and Jewish community leaders (Niebuhr, 2000; Dershowitz, 1997).

But Jewish sociologists point out that, despite all those changes, Jews "have been able to maintain a stronger sense of group identity than most other ethnic groups" in the United States (Waxman, 1990). A major reason is that Jewish cohesion does not derive from traditional Jewish values but rather from occupational and residential concentration. By sharing similar neighborhoods, schools, occupations, organizations, and friends, Jewish Americans have been and continue to be able to maintain the highest level of cohesion among minority groups. This cohesive community also includes the majority of the Jews' non-Jewish spouses and their biethnic children because they see themselves and are seen by others as Jewish (Goldscheider, 2003; Waxman, 1990; Zenner, 1985).

■ European Americans

Descendants of immigrants from Europe, or *European Americans,* are popularly known as whites. And despite the growing number of nonwhites who have immigrated to the United States in the last decade, whites still make up the majority—72 percent—of the total U.S. population (Patterson, 2001).

WASPs and Other Western and Northern European Americans Western and Northern European Americans make up the dominant group in the United States. This group includes WASPs (white Anglo-Saxon Protestants), Germans, Irish, and others whose ancestors came from Western and Northern Europe. Most WASPs are English, and a few are Scottish and Welsh. With the exception of Native Americans, WASPs have a longer history in the United States than any other racial or ethnic group. However, since 1990, WASPS have been outnumbered by Germans and Irish.

Still, WASPs continue to dominate U.S. society with their English language, English laws, and Protestant religion. WASPs also continue to control U.S. political and economic institutions, since most high government officials, large business owners, and corporate executives are WASPs. WASP dominance has faced vigorous challenges from other European Americans, such as the Russians, Hungarians, and Dutch, who have rapidly moved up the success ladder in education, the professions, politics, and business (see, for example, Figure 8.7). The WASP culture, into which various minorities have long been forced to assimilate, has also been under siege by multiculturalism, which emphasizes the equal importance of various minority ways of life. Many average middle-class WASPs, along with other European Americans, now feel that minorities are getting special advantages in jobs and education at their expense (Baltzell, 1994, 1991; Brookhiser, 1991).

Southern and Eastern European Americans Toward the end of the nineteenth century, a new wave

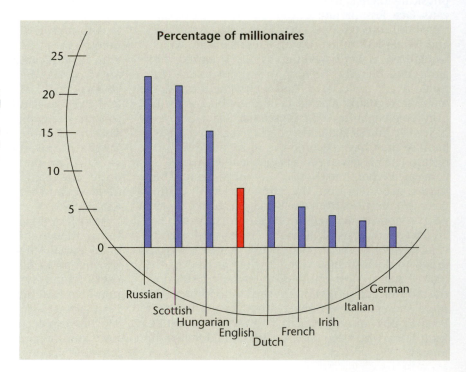

FIGURE 8.7

The Top Groups of U.S. Millionaires

WASP dominance has faced vigorous challenges from other European Americans, who have rapidly moved up the ladder of success in business and other fields. Here is how English Americans, or WASPs, compare with Americans of other European ancestries in percentage of households having a net worth of $1 million or more.

Critical Thinking: *Why are English Americans often stereotyped as the most successful ethnic group in the United States?*

Source: Data from Thomas Stanley and William Danko, *The Millionaire Next Door* (New York: Pocket Books, 1998).

Percentage of millionaires

FROM OUTSIDERS TO INSIDERS Many white ethnics, like the owners of this Greek market in Chicago, are the descendants of immigrants from Eastern and Southern Europe, who arrived in the United States at the end of the nineteenth century. Although they have worked at low-paying, manual jobs and have been subjected to discrimination, many have made their way into the middle class and become an integral part of mainstream U.S. society. ■

of immigrants came from Southern and Eastern Europe. Many native-born citizens proclaimed these new immigrants to be inferior and treated them as such. This belief was reflected in the National Origins Act of 1924, which set quotas that greatly restricted immigration from Southern and Eastern Europe—a policy that was not altered until 1965.

Today, the descendants of those immigrants have made their mark in education, business, the professions, and politics. There are more middle-class people among these white ethnics than among other minorities, and about half have attended college, the same proportion as other European Americans. According to several surveys, Southern and Eastern European Americans largely favor liberal policies, such as welfare programs, antipollution laws, and guaranteed wages. While they are sometimes depicted in the media as racists, these white ethnics are generally free of racial prejudice, perhaps because they can easily identify with African Americans who, like them, have held low-paying manual jobs and been subjected to discrimination (Feagin and Feagin, 1999; Farley, 1995).

Southern and Eastern European Americans by and large no longer speak their immigrant parents' languages, no longer live in ethnic neighborhoods, and routinely marry into the dominant group. They have become such an integral part of mainstream U.S. society that it is difficult to tell them apart. Traces of prejudice toward some white ethnics still exist, though. Italian Americans, for example, continue to be associated with organized crime, although people of Italian background make up less than 1 percent of the 500,000 individuals involved in such activities.

In general, young and highly educated white ethnics are particularly sensitive to ethnic stereotypes because they identify themselves strongly with their ethnicity (Alba, 1990; Giordano, 1987).

■ Putting It All Together

Put in perspective, the status of all American minorities is generally better today than before. Getting closest to the American dream of success are Jews, Asians, and white ethnics, followed by Hispanics and blacks. Ironically, the original owners of this land—Native Americans—have experienced the least improvement in their lives.

Of course, there is still considerable prejudice and discrimination in the United States. Americans continue to live in largely segregated neighborhoods and to commit hate crimes against minorities, especially in times of national crises—for instance, assaulting Arab Americans soon after the 2001 terrorist attacks in New York City and Washington (Schmitt, 2001a; Rodriguez, 2001). But there is less racial intolerance than before, and the intolerance is also less serious than in other countries, where a single incident of ethnic conflict often takes hundreds or thousands of lives.

Therefore, as black sociologist Orlando Patterson (1991) has noted:

The sociological truths are that America, while still flawed in its race relations, is now the least racist white-majority society in the world; has a better record of legal protection of minorities than any other society, white or black; offers more opportunities to a greater number of black persons than any other society, including all those of Africa; and has gone through a dramatic change in its attitude toward miscegenation [interracial marriage or sexual relations] over the last 25 years.

However, Americans tend to focus on current racial problems, without comparing them with how things were in the past or with similar problems in other societies. Interestingly, although the lack of historical and cross-cultural concern may limit Americans' understanding of race relations, it can intensify their impatience with their own racial inequality. This may be good for American society because it compels all individuals—especially minorities—to keep pushing for racial equality. On the other hand, the historical and cross-societal analysis in this chapter, which does reveal improvement in U.S. race relations, is also useful. It counsels against despair, encouraging Americans to be hopeful that racial equality can be achieved.

RACIAL AND ETHNIC RELATIONS

Racial and ethnic relations appear in different forms, from violent conflict to peaceful coexistence. The functionalist perspective emphasizes peaceful coexistence and other positive forms of intergroup relations because they are functional to society, contributing to social cohesion and stability. In contrast, the conflict perspective focuses on violent conflict and other negative aspects of intergroup relations, in which the powerful dominant group abuses powerless minorities. Finally, the symbolic interactionist perspective focuses on how stereotyped perceptions influence intergroup interactions and vice versa.

■ Functionalist Perspective: Cohesive Relations

According to the functionalist perspective, various racial and ethnic groups can contribute to social cohesion through assimilation, amalgamation, or cultural pluralism. **Assimilation** is the process by which a minority adopts the dominant group's culture as the culture of the larger society. **Amalgamation** is the process by which the subcultures of various groups are blended together, forming a new culture. **Cultural pluralism**, also known as *multiculturalism,* is the peaceful coexistence of various racial and ethnic groups, each retaining its own subculture.

Assimilation   Assimilation can be expressed as A + B + C = A, where minorities B and C lose their subcultural traits and become indistinguishable from the dominant group A (Newman, 1973). There are two

CULTURAL COHESION According to the functionalist perspective, various racial and ethnic groups contribute to social order through assimilation, amalgamation, and cultural pluralism. Through assimilation, a minority adopts the dominant group's culture, whereas through amalgamation, the subcultures of various groups are blended, forming a new culture. Cultural pluralism encourages minority groups to retain their cultural identities while living peacefully with others in the midst of the mainstream culture. ■

kinds of assimilation. The first is **behavioral assimilation**, the social situation in which the minority adopts the dominant group's language, values, and behavioral patterns. Behavioral assimilation, however, does not guarantee **structural assimilation**, the social condition in which the minority is accepted on equal terms with the rest of society. For instance, a white Russian immigrant who speaks halting English may find it relatively easy to become structurally assimilated in the United States, but a middle-class African American will have a more difficult time. Nevertheless, most members of disadvantaged minorities consider assimilation necessary to get ahead—economically and socially—in the United States.

Amalgamation In a society that encourages assimilation, there is little respect for the distinctive traits of minority groups. By contrast, a society that seeks amalgamation as an ideal has a greater appreciation for the equal worth of various subcultures. Amalgamation is popularly compared to a *melting pot,* in which many subcultures are blended together to produce a new culture, one that differs from any of its components. It can be described as A + B + C = D, where A, B, and C represent different groups jointly producing a new culture—D—unlike any of its original components (Newman, 1973).

More than 80 years ago, a British-Jewish dramatist portrayed the United States as an amalgamation of subcultures. "There she lies," he wrote, "the great melting pot—listen! . . . Ah, what a stirring and seething—Celt and Latin, Slav and Teuton, Greek and Syrian, Black and Yellow—Jew and Gentile" (Zangwill, 1909). Indeed, to some extent, the United States is a melting pot. Popular music and slang contain elements of many subcultures. And there has been considerable intermarriage among various ethnic groups, particularly among those of English, German, Irish, Italian, and other European backgrounds. But such amalgamation is less likely to involve white and nonwhite groups.

Cultural Pluralism Switzerland provides an example of a third way in which ethnic groups may live together. In Switzerland, three major groups—the Germans, French, and Italians—retain their own languages while living together in peace. They are neither assimilated nor amalgamated. Instead, these diverse groups retain their distinctive subcultures while coexisting peacefully. Unlike either assimilation or amalgamation, cultural pluralism encourages each group to take pride in its distinctiveness, to be conscious of its heritage, and to retain its identity. Such pluralism can be shown as A + B + C = A + B + C, where various groups continue to keep their subcultures while living together in the same society (Newman, 1973). To some extent, the United States has long been marked by cultural pluralism. This can be seen in the Chinatowns, Little Italies, and Polish neighborhoods of many U.S. cities.

■ Conflict Perspective: Abusive Relations

To conflict theorists, racial and ethnic relations can be negative, marked by **racism**, the belief that one's own race or ethnicity is superior to that of others. Racism tends to cause the dominating group to abuse minorities by *segregating, expelling,* and *exterminating* them.

Segregation Segregation means more than spatial and social separation of the dominant and minority groups. It means that minority groups, because they are believed to be inferior, are compelled to live separately and in inferior conditions. The neighborhoods, schools, and other public facilities for the dominant group are both separate from and superior to those of the minorities.

The compulsion that underlies segregation is not necessarily official or acknowledged. In the United States, for example, segregation is officially outlawed, yet it persists. In other words, **de jure segregation**—segregation sanctioned by law—is gone, but **de facto segregation**—segregation resulting from tradition and custom—remains. This is particularly the case with regard to housing for African Americans.

Like the United States, most nations no longer practice de jure segregation. Even South Africa finally ended its official policy of *apartheid*—racial separation in housing, jobs, and political opportunities—in 1992. But apartheid has become so entrenched that it will continue in the form of de facto segregation for many years to come.

Expulsion In some cases, the dominant group has expelled a minority from certain areas or even from the country entirely. During the nineteenth century, Czarist Russia drove out millions of Jews, and the U.S. government forced the Cherokee nation to travel from their homes in Georgia and the Carolinas to reservations in Oklahoma. About 4,000 Cherokee died on this "Trail of Tears." During the 1970s, Uganda expelled more than 40,000 Asians—many of them Ugandan citizens—and Vietnam forced 700,000 Chinese to leave the country (Schaefer, 2001).

Extermination The most drastic action against minorities is to kill them. **Genocide**, the wholesale killing of members of a specific racial or ethnic group, has been attempted in various countries. For instance, in the early nineteenth century, on the island of Tasmania, near Australia, British settlers killed the entire native population, whom they hunted like wild animals. From 1915 to 1923, the Turks massacred more than 1 million Armenians. Between 1933 and 1945, the Nazis systematically murdered 6 million Jews. More recently, in 1992, the Serbs in Bosnia killed and tortured numerous Muslims and Croats as part of their campaign of ethnic cleansing. From 1993 to 1996, thousands of minority members were massacred in Rwanda and eastern Zaire (Chirot and Edwards, 2003; Frantz, 2001; Purvis, 1996).

■ Symbolic Interactionist Perspective: Perception and Interaction

According to this perspective, if the dominant group perceives a minority as inferior, undesirable, or dan-

theoretical thumbnail

The Nature of Racial and Ethnic Relations

Perspective	Focus	Insights
Functionalist	Cohesive relations	Various groups can contribute to social cohesion through assimilation, amalgamation, and cultural pluralism.
Conflict	Abusive relations	The dominant group can abuse minorities by segregating, expelling, and exterminating them.
Symbolic interactionist	Perception and interaction	The way the dominant group perceives minorities shapes their interaction and vice versa.

gerous, interaction between them will be greatly affected. There is likely to be segregated interaction, with members of each group interacting mostly with others of the same group (Charon, 1992). If dominant-group members do interact with minority-group members, the interaction will likely be tense or superficial. The nature of intergroup interaction, then, can be determined by the dominant group's perception of minorities.

That perception is seldom based on reality. Instead, it is a **stereotype**, an oversimplified, inaccurate mental picture of others. Consider, for example, the stereotype of African Americans as dangerous. Many whites seem to carry this picture in their minds after having been repeatedly fed images of black violence and criminality by the media. The reality is that the vast majority of blacks are law-abiding people. Less than 23 percent fall below the poverty line, and most are far from being violent criminals; rather, they are young children and single mothers (U.S. Census Bureau, 2001). The small minority that commit violence rarely target whites; most of their victims are fellow African Americans (Harris and Meidlinger, 1995). Still, many whites are fearful of blacks.

The stereotype of them as dangerous often causes African Americans—including those who are highly successful and middle class—to suffer legal harassment at the hands of white police officers as well as other indignities, as mentioned earlier. The stereotype can also bring about grotesque consequences for whites themselves. As a white man said:

My wife was driving down the street in a black neighborhood. The people at the corners were all gesticulating at her. She was very frightened, turned up the windows, and drove determinedly. She discovered, after several blocks, she was going the wrong way on a one-way street and they were trying to help her. Her assumption was they were blacks and were out to get her. Mind you, she's a very enlightened person. You'd never associate her with racism, yet her first reaction was that they were dangerous. (Terkel, 1992)

While perception can shape intergroup interaction, interaction can also change perception. If an interaction is *cooperative,* in which two groups work or play together, negative perceptions may dissolve into positive ones, such as perceptions of African Americans as helpful and friendly. Similar positive perceptions are also likely to emerge if the interactants from different groups are of *equal status,* such as being equally well educated (Powers and Ellison, 1995; See and Wilson, 1988).

The three major perspectives on racial and ethnic relations are summarized in the Theoretical Thumbnail.

PREJUDICE AND DISCRIMINATION

Is it possible for a prejudiced person to act in a respectable, nondiscriminatory way toward a minority person? Don't prejudiced people always discriminate? In this section, we will answer these and other similar questions by analyzing the characteristics, causes, and consequences of prejudice and discrimination, as well as attempted solutions to the problem.

Characteristics

Prejudice and discrimination can be the characteristics of both individual persons and social institutions.

Individual Responses to Minorities As noted earlier, prejudice is an attitude; discrimination is an act. Robert Merton (1976) found that the two do not necessarily go hand in hand. Analyzing the possible combinations of prejudice and discrimination, Merton developed a typology of four dominant-group members on the basis of their responses to minorities (see Table 8.1).

First are the *unprejudiced nondiscriminators.* These people believe in the U.S. creed of equality and put

TABLE 8.1

A Typology of Dominant-Group Members

	Nondiscriminator	Discriminator
Unprejudiced	1. *Unprejudiced nondiscriminator* (all-weather liberal) is not prejudiced and does not discriminate, whatever the social pressure might be.	2. *Unprejudiced discriminator* (fair-weather liberal) is not prejudiced but because of social pressure, does discriminate.
Prejudiced	3. *Prejudiced nondiscriminator* (fair-weather illiberal) is prejudiced but because of social pressure, does not discriminate.	4. *Prejudiced discriminator* (all-weather illiberal) is prejudiced and does discriminate, whatever the social pressure might be.

Source: Based on Robert K. Merton, *Sociological Ambivalence and Other Essays* (New York: Free Press, 1976).

their belief into action; their attitude and behavior are consistent. Merton also calls them *all-weather liberals* because they are likely to abide by their belief regardless of where they are—even if their friends and neighbors are bigots.

myth	If a white person discriminates against blacks, he or she must be prejudiced.
reality	Not necessarily. Many whites discriminate without being prejudiced, primarily because of social pressure. Unprejudiced white men, for example, might not date black women for fear of being ostracized.

Second are the *unprejudiced discriminators*. These people's discriminatory behavior is inconsistent with their unprejudicial attitude. Although free from prejudice themselves, they practice discrimination because of social pressure. Hence, they are also called *fair-weather liberals*. Unprejudiced homeowners are fair-weather liberals if they refuse to sell their homes to minority families for fear of offending the neighbors. Unprejudiced executives may also hesitate to promote minority employees to managers lest other employees be resentful.

Third are the *prejudiced nondiscriminators,* who are afraid to express their prejudice through discrimination. Like the fair-weather liberals, these people do not practice what they believe in. They allow social pressure to keep them from doing what they want to do. But since they are prejudiced, despite their nondiscriminatory behavior, they are also called *fair-weather illiberals* rather than *liberals*. Under the pressure of antidiscrimination laws, prejudiced people will hire or work with minorities.

Finally, there are the *prejudiced discriminators,* who are deeply prejudiced against minorities and practice discrimination. Like all-weather liberals, these *all-weather illiberals* are consistent: Their actions match their beliefs. Examples include members of the Ku Klux Klan and neo-Nazis.

Institutionalized Discrimination Even if every single white person in the United States were no longer prejudiced and discriminating, discrimination would still exist for some time. Over the years, it has been built into various social institutions, so that discrimination can occur even when no one is aware of it. When blacks and whites have long lived in separate neighborhoods, neighborhood schools will remain segregated, even though no one tries to discriminate against blacks. If employers prefer to hire people who graduated from their own universities, which have long denied entrance to blacks, then blacks will not have much chance of being hired. When fire and police departments continue to use the height requirements in hiring that were originally intended for evaluating white applicants, then many otherwise qualified Mexican and Asian Americans—who are generally shorter than whites—will not get the jobs (Trond, Saporta, and Seidel, 2000).

These are all cases of **institutionalized discrimination**, the persistence of discrimination in social institutions that is not necessarily recognized by everybody as discrimination. They are traceable to the long history of discrimination by educational, economic, and other social institutions, not to individual prejudice. African Americans suffer the most from institutionalized discrimination. Long victimized by racial oppression, many African Americans lack adequate education and job skills. Many colleges and companies have therefore unintentionally practiced discrimination by denying them college admission and professional or managerial positions solely because of their inadequate scholastic and occupational performance. In doing so, these in-

INSIDE OUT Members of the Ku Klux Klan are an example of *prejudiced discriminators,* who not only harbor feelings of prejudice against minorities but also express them through acts of discrimination. Merton calls them "all-weather illiberals" because they always turn their prejudice inside out, regardless of where they are. They are thus out-and-out bigots, even ready to commit crimes of violence against minorities. ■

stitutions have failed to recognize that these are largely the effects of the long history of slavery and discrimination.

■ Causes

Prejudice and discrimination are far from unique to the United States. They are found throughout the world, and they are caused by many factors.

One cause is *social-psychological.* It involves **scapegoating,** or blaming others for one's own failure. Through prejudice and discrimination, dominant-group members who have suffered failures in life make themselves feel superior to minorities and so build up their own self-image. Hostility against minorities is likely to mount when many dominant-group members are beset with poverty, unemployment, and other problems that threaten to deflate their self-image. In the nineteenth century, mob violence against African Americans usually increased in the Deep South during an economic downturn. In the Middle Ages, when thousands of Europeans died in a plague, "rioters stormed Jewish ghettos and burned them down, believing that Jews were somehow responsible for the epidemic" (Coleman and Cressey, 1993; Beck and Tolnay, 1990).

A second cause is *sociological.* It involves socialization. If our parents, teachers, and peers are prejudiced, we are likely to follow their lead. If minorities

are often portrayed in the media as inferior or violent, we are likely to be prejudiced and to discriminate against them. Even parents opposed to racism may unknowingly plant seeds of racist thought when they select for their children popular books, such as *The Story of Little Black Sambo,* that contain disparaging images of African Americans (Madsen, 1982).

A third cause is *economic.* It involves the desire for job security and business profit. Historically, given widespread prejudice and discrimination, minorities were prevented from competing for employment, thereby helping to ensure job security for the dominant group's middle and working classes. Prejudice and discrimination also brought profits to the dominant group's upper class. Racism created a huge supply of cheap labor from among oppressed minorities and prevented much competition from minority businesses.

A fourth cause is *political.* It involves maintaining governmental power. This is why for so many years, the white regime in extremely racist South Africa denied black people the right to vote. In the United States in the past, many state and local governments used various means to keep minorities out of the political process, primarily to prevent African Americans from voting. When these efforts became unconstitutional, some states continued to discourage minorities from political participation by charging a poll tax, requiring a literacy test, or printing ballots only in English in areas where many minority people did not know the language.

■ Consequences

Prejudice and discrimination have several costly consequences for minorities.

First, minorities generally have a lower quality of life than the dominant group. As we have observed, Native Americans, African Americans, and Hispanics have lower income, more unemployment and poverty, fewer years of schooling, and lower life expectancy than whites. There are exceptions. Blacks from the West Indies—immigrants or descendants of immigrants from the Caribbean, such as Colin Powell—have suffered discrimination, but they have achieved higher educational and economic levels than the national average (Sowell, 1994; Harrison, 1992).

Second, partly because of prejudice and discrimination, the black lower class has grown larger and more desperate. Deep poverty persists from generation to generation; the rate of unemployment continues to remain distressingly high among young people; and the number of poor female-headed families is soaring. All this has, in turn, generated a dramatic rise in violent crime, especially among youths (as discussed in Chapter 6: Deviance and Control). Occasionally, riots erupt, as occurred in South-Central Los Angeles in 1992 and in Cincinnati in 2001. In many other cities, the rage of the underclass simmers just below the surface.

Third, young victims of prejudice and discrimination tend to develop a negative self-image. In 1947, Kenneth and Mamie Clark did a study that helped influence the U.S. Supreme Court to desegregate schools in 1954. In the study, 253 African American children were asked to choose between four dolls, two black and two white. Two-thirds of the children chose white dolls. In 1985, Darlene Powell-Hopson updated the Clarks' experiment and found essentially the same result: About 65 percent of the black children preferred white dolls. Powell-Hopson believes that the result would likely be the same if the study were repeated today. One reason is the pervasive real-life reminders that blacks are still regarded less highly than whites. Another reason is that television, movies, and children's books seem to link everything beautiful with whiteness. But most black parents try to shield their children from this racial bias and instill ethnic pride (White, 1993).

■ Remedy: Affirmative Action

In the 1960s, under the pressure of the civil rights movement, federal legislators passed a series of antidiscrimination laws. But because of institutional-ized discrimination, Congress further instituted the policy of **affirmative action**, which requires employers and colleges to make special efforts to recruit qualified minorities and women for jobs, promotions, and educational opportunities. Given equal qualifications, the opportunity must be given to the minority or woman. Sometimes, a less qualified black may have to be chosen over a more qualified white. President Lyndon Johnson summarized the reasoning behind special opportunities for African Americans in a 1965 speech: "You do not take a person who for years has been hobbled by chains, and liberate him, bring him up to the starting line, and then say, 'You are free to compete with all the others'" (Hacker, 1992).

Since then, affirmative action has helped many qualified African Americans to enter higher education and to gain professional and managerial positions. This has partly contributed to the rise of a significant black middle class (Bowen and Bok, 1998). Affirmative action has nonetheless sparked racial tensions. Many whites, especially conservatives, see it as a form of reverse discrimination against them. They argue that equal opportunities should be open to all people, without regard to race. Not surprisingly, as Table 8.2 shows, whites are much more likely than blacks to oppose affirmative action. But as Table 8.2 also indicates, most Americans still consider it important for a college to have a racially diverse student body.

TABLE 8.2

Americans' Views on Programs for Minorities

Do you favor or oppose affirmative action?			
	Favor	**Oppose**	**No Opinion**
Whites	44%	49%	7%
Blacks	70%	21%	9%
Hispanics	63%	28%	9%
All	49%	43%	8%

How important is it for a college to be racially diverse?	
Very important	50%
Somewhat important	30%
Not too important	10%
Not at all important	10%

Source: Data from the Gallup Poll, June 12–18, 2003. Available online: www.gallup.com/poll/topics/race3.asp.

Consistent with the popular support for diversity, the U.S. Supreme Court in 2003 ruled that it was legal for the University of Michigan's law school to achieve diversity by considering race as a factor in admissions. The Court also said that race should be only one among many factors considered, such as grades, test scores, special talents, extracurricular activities, work experiences, and family background. Liberals cheered this ruling as a victory for affirmative action.

Conservatives also applauded this ruling but for a different reason. They noted that the Court struck down the university's practice of using a point system to favor minority applicants for undergraduate admissions, such as giving 20 points for being a minority as opposed to 12 points for getting the highest SAT score. This point system was apparently considered an attempt to set a quota of admissions for minority students. Conservatives saw this decision as a victory over affirmative action.

Thus, the Supreme Court effectively sent a double message: It is legal to consider race for attaining diversity (a general mix of different races) but not for seeking a quota (a specific number of minority persons). Most colleges and corporations have already heeded that message by focusing on diversity efforts and rejecting quotas. The search for diversity includes not only considering race but also using outreach programs to find qualified minority students and workers. These diversity efforts avoid reverse discrimination and rigid quotas while considering *only* qualified minorities for college admission, employment, and promotion. In the few states that have banned affirmative action, there has been yet another attempt to achieve diversity. In Texas, for example, the top 10 percent of students from all high schools, which includes schools with mostly minority students, are automatically granted admission to the state university of their choice (Golden, 2003; Murray, 2003).

A GLOBAL ANALYSIS OF RACE AND ETHNICITY

Wherever there is a racial or ethnic minority, there is discrimination. Virtually every nation has a minority population (see Figure 8.8). Consequently, discrimination exists practically all over the world. Extremely few countries are free of discrimination. Iceland is one such country, but this is because its population is totally homogeneous in race or ethnicity. The nature or amount of racial problems around the world, however, varies from one country to another.

The Developing World

Ethnic antagonism exists in many African countries, the most violent being Rwanda, where numerous lives have been lost as a result. Similarly, many Asian countries are no stranger to racial or ethnic problems, which occasionally erupt into violent clashes. In the 1980s, for example, a full-scale civil war broke out in Sri Lanka (formerly called Ceylon) when the oppressed minority Indian Tamil population rebelled against the central government controlled by the majority Buddhist Sinhalese. Although the war ended in 2002, interethnic tension still reigns. Generally, ethnic problems seem much more severe in Africa and Asia than in other parts of the world. In the 1992 Los Angeles race riot, for example, the most destructive in recent U.S. history, 44 people died, whereas some 250,000 were killed in the ethnic conflict in Rwanda in 1994 alone (Rosenblatt, 1994).

Many Latin American scholars have argued that their societies are not racist, but the U.S. State Department has reported racial discrimination in Bolivia, Brazil, Ecuador, Guatemala, and Peru. In Brazil, for example, blacks receive less education and income than whites and experience discrimination in housing and services. In nearly all Latin American countries, the privileged classes are largely European in origin or lighter skinned than the less affluent classes. However, in these countries, "Money whitens": Darker-skinned persons who succeed economically do not encounter overt discrimination, and they often marry whites (Jalali and Lipset, 1993).

Western Europe

Before the 1960s, relatively few countries in Western Europe had serious ethnic problems. The most notorious was the genocidal slaughter of Jews by the Nazis during World War II. Several other old ethnic problems still continue. The most widely known involves the clash between the majority Protestants and the minority Catholics in Northern Ireland. The Catholics want to join the predominantly Catholic Republic of Ireland because they have long felt that they are discriminated against by the dominant Protestants, but the Protestants prefer to remain a part of predominantly Protestant Britain. Britain, in turn, seeks to suppress the nationalist aspirations of the Catholics. A similar problem has long existed in Spain, which tries to control the restless minority Basques and Catalans, and in France, which attempts to subdue the Bretons, Corsicans, and Basques (Jalali and Lipset, 1993; Stavenhagen, 1991).

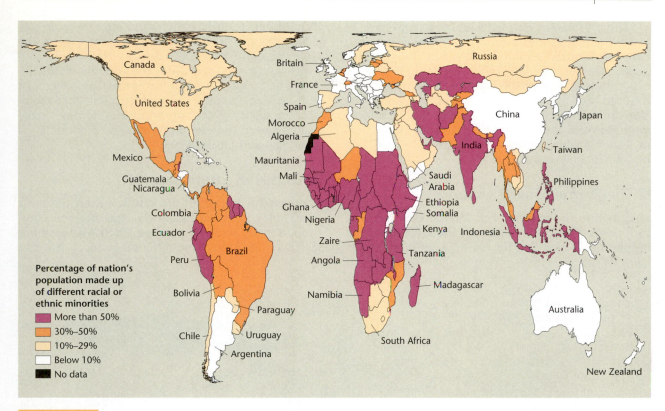

FIGURE 8.8

Global Distribution of Minorities

Virtually all nations have minority groups, but some have more than others. For example, about 31 percent of the U.S. population are members of a minority group, but everyone in Afghanistan belongs to a minority. In Afghanistan, even the Pashtun—the largest of the country's many ethnic groups—represent less than half (or 38 percent) of the whole Afghan population.

Critical Thinking: *Do you think the racial problem is more or less serious in the United States than in other parts of the world? Why?*

Source: From *The Penguin Atlas of War and Peace,* by Dan Smith, copyright © 2003 by Dan Smith. Used by permission of Penguin, a division of Penguin Group (USA) Inc.

Over the last 30 years, new sources of ethnic conflict have emerged throughout Western Europe. They have to do with the significant numbers of guest workers and immigrants pouring into virtually every Western European country from North Africa and other developing countries and most recently from Eastern Europe, as well. Racist attacks on foreign workers and their descendants occur often, and extreme right-wing political groups routinely campaign against immigrants. Such ethnic hostilities are most common in France and Germany and least common in Sweden and Luxembourg (Jalali and Lipset, 1993).

■ Eastern Europe

Ethnic problems exploded throughout Eastern Europe after the collapse of communism in the early 1990s. The most devastating conflict took place in the former Yugoslavia. Ethnic conflict split this country into five independent republics—Serbia, Bosnia, Croatia, Slovenia, and Macedonia—but all except Slovenia have remained ethnically diverse and continue to experience interethnic hostilities. Especially in Bosnia and Croatia, violence continues to break out among the Serbs, Muslims, and Croats.

Ethnic problems also led the Czechs and Slovaks to divide their former country, Czechoslovakia, into two independent republics, although they did not experience the same kind of violence as in Bosnia. In other Eastern European countries, minorities continue to face discrimination. Examples include the Hungarian minority in Romania, the Turkish minority in Bulgaria, and the Jews, Gypsies, and foreigners in other Eastern European countries (Jalali and Lipset, 1993; Williams, 1994).

■ The Former Soviet Union

Long before the demise of the Soviet Union in the early 1990s, the Russians forced various minorities to become "Russified" by, for example, sending minority children to Russian schools. Sometimes, whole ethnic groups—such as the Tartars of the Crimea, the Germans of the Volga, and the Chechens of the Caucasus—were deported. After the collapse of the Soviet Union, all the republics under the control of non-Russians became independent. But since many of these republics contain minorities, tensions have risen between the new dominant group and minorities (Jalali and Lipset, 1993).

■ Causes of Ethnic Conflict

The world is full of ethnic conflict. Even the most extreme type of conflict—war—has become common in many societies (see Figure 8.9). Various studies have suggested many different factors to explain

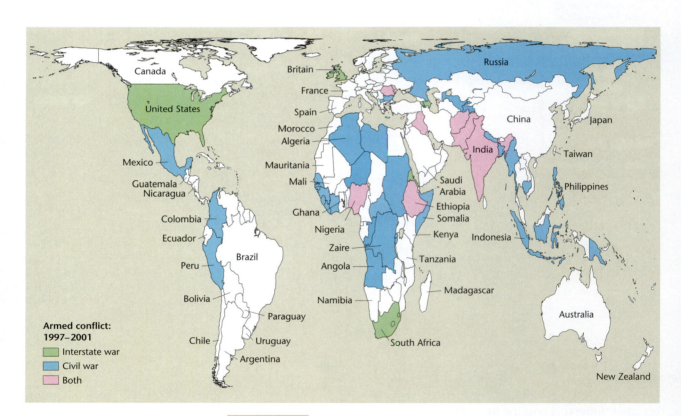

FIGURE 8.9

Ethnic Wars around the World

In recent decades, ethnic conflicts have escalated into all-out wars in many countries. Some of these armed conflicts have been civil wars, involving different ethnic groups within the same country. Others have been interstate wars, involving groups from different countries.

Critical Thinking: *How could nations avoid ethnic wars?*

Source: From *The Penguin Atlas of War and Peace,* by Dan Smith, copyright © 2003 by Dan Smith. Used by permission of Penguin, a division of Penguin Group (USA) Inc.

why ethnic conflict has increased in recent decades or why the problem is more severe in some countries than in others.

First, over the last few decades, many ethnically diverse countries have become *modernized*—industrialized and urbanized. Modernization has created more opportunities for various ethnic groups to enjoy a higher standard of living. At the same time, however, modernization has increased *economic competition* among ethnic groups, primarily for jobs and secondarily for housing and other valued resources (Jalali and Lipset, 1993).

Second, more severe ethnic problems usually exist in mostly authoritarian, nondemocratic countries that *discourage diverse ethnic expressions*. In such societies, the state is defined as the preserve of only one ethnic group, with other groups made to feel like outsiders. By contrast, ethnic tension is muted in most of the democratic countries because such countries, at least officially, encourage respect for ethnic differences while providing aggrieved minorities with legal recourse, as in the United States (Maybury-Lewis, 1994; Jalali and Lipset, 1993).

At least three other factors have been found to contribute to ethnic conflict. One is the hostile group's *excessive ethnic identity,* which usually originates in a shared history of victimization. In Rwanda, for example, the Hutus who slaughtered the Tutsis in 1994 had kept alive the memory of how Tutsis had killed some 100,000 Hutus in 1972. Another factor likely to cause ethnic strife is a nation's *enormous economic problems,* especially high rates of inflation, unemployment, and poverty. Finally, *power-hungry politicians* play a powerful role by blaming the problems on minorities and inciting destructive action against them (Lemarchand, 1994).

■ A Global Conference against Racism

In the summer of 2001, representatives of over 160 countries came together in Durban, South Africa, for the first United Nations World Conference against Racism, Racial Discrimination, Xenophobia, and Related Intolerance. The goal was to raise awareness of the plight of minorities throughout the world. Although the Israeli and U.S. delegations walked out after disagreeing with the wording of a document that compared Zionism to racism, the conference did produce some useful results.

The conference gave hope to African Brazilians that their quest for equality would be taken seriously. It prompted European countries to take a closer look at discrimination against their various minority groups, especially the gypsies. And it publicized the plights of such minorities as the Kurds in Turkey, the slaves in Niger, the untouchables in India, and the indigenous people in Australia. Thus, the conference served as the court of world opinion to encourage or pressure many countries to protect their minorities (Cose, 2001).

sociological **frontiers**

A New Theory about Child Abandonment

As we saw earlier in this chapter, African Americans continue to experience racial prejudice and discrimination today. Therefore, when faced with the fact that as many as 60 percent of African American children are abandoned by their fathers, many social scientists blame the problem solely or mainly on racial prejudice and discrimination. But according to Harvard's black sociologist Orlando Patterson (2000), the problem comes primarily from the traditional culture of slavery and only secondarily from contemporary racism.

This culture, in Patterson's view, encourages African American men to leave their children behind. It has evolved from their forefathers' lives as slaves (from about 1640 to 1865) and as poor sharecroppers (from 1880 to 1940). As slaves, the men did not have any legitimacy or authority as fathers or husbands. Moreover, most slaves—at least three-quarters of them—lived most of their lives away from stable households with children. Yet their masters encouraged them to have as many children as possible without having to provide for them. Later, as sharecroppers, African American men could survive only by putting their wives and children to work on their farms. Thus, they tended to marry young and have as many children as they could. But by exploiting their children for labor, they failed to develop a strong parent-child attachment.

African American men are further confronted with an array of contemporary problems that often affect minorities, such as poverty, unemployment, low income, and substandard housing. As a consequence, there is a high rate of paternal abandonment of children among African Americans. It should be noted, however, that the great majority of African American fathers behave responsibly toward their children. It is a minority of usually poor black men with little education who abandon their children. But because of these men's high rates of fertility, they produce many children, more than half of whom they will leave fatherless (Patterson, 2000).

■ For more of the latest Sociological Frontiers, look up Continuing Update at www.ablongman.com/thio6e.

using *sociology*

How to Achieve Diversity without Preferences

Since the inception of affirmative action in the 1960s, it has helped many African Americans to enter higher education, thereby making many universities and colleges much more racially diverse than before. But the general public, as well as the courts, have increasingly tried to get rid of affirmative action, primarily because they believe it favors minorities at the expense of whites. Black high school graduates with relatively low SAT scores, for example, may be admitted to college while their white peers with higher scores are denied admission. Since universities and colleges have been banned from giving minorities such preferences, some have experienced significant declines in minority enrollment. How, then, can these schools boost minority enrollment to achieve racial diversity without relying on preferential policies?

Sociological analysis suggests that universities and colleges should provide—or help high schools to offer—academically weak minority students a strong dose of positive learning experiences comparable to those that students with higher test scores have long received from their home and school environments. This is what West Point, the army's elite officer training academy, does for high school graduates who fail admission requirements. These graduates, including many African Americans, are put through their paces at a special preparatory school called the United States Military Academy Prep School (USMAPS).

The USMAPS program runs for 10 months, focusing on the basics: math and English. These subjects are fortified with the *student success course,* which teaches students how to learn, including how to study, take notes, set goals, manage time efficiently, and think positively. To instill positive thinking involves replacing negative, self-defeating attitudes and behaviors with positive, responsible ones. Students learn, for example, to replace the negative attitude "This always happens to me" with a positive one, such as "This happened because I didn't study enough" or "Am I doing the most effective thing I could be right now?" At the end of the program, African American students usually score high enough to get admitted to West Point. Similar prep classes are offered at many universities and colleges for the purpose of boosting rates of graduation rather than admission (Bailey, 2003; Dickerson, 1998).

This example shows how an educational institution can turn around academically weak minority students. But what about these students' families, presumably the most important socializing agent in their lives? Thinking critically, what would you recommend a family do to help a student get admitted to a university or college of his or her choice?

CHAPTER REVIEW

1. *Do racial classifications mean anything?* Biologically, they have little significance. They do not correspond to genetically distinct groups. Socially, however, racial classifications have profound meaning because people often think of themselves and respond to others in terms of race. *How does an ethnic group differ from a race?* People are categorized into races on the basis of their popularly perceived physical characteristics, whereas ethnic groups are based on shared cultural characteristics. *How do racial and ethnic groups become minorities?* They become minorities when subjected to prejudice and discrimination by the dominant group.

2. *What is the social condition of Native Americans today?* Their levels of income and health are below the national average, while their levels of unemployment and poverty are higher. But they have been recapturing their proud traditions.

3. *Have the civil rights laws of the 1960s made a difference?* Yes, but they have not ended inequality. They have helped African Americans make significant strides in education and politics, but not in housing and economic conditions.

4. *What are the origins of Hispanic Americans?* This category lumps many peoples together—from the descendants of Mexicans and Puerto Ricans, who became citizens because the United States took their lands in wars, to more recent immigrants from Cuba and other Central and South American countries. *What are their current social conditions?* Hispanics find their common identity in the Spanish language and in Roman Catholicism. They generally lag behind whites in educational and economic achievement, but they have become a significant political force in the United States.

5. *How do Asian Americans fare today?* They seem to have achieved more than other groups in education and family income. But they have a relatively high poverty rate and continue to face discrimination.

6. *What is the position of Jewish Americans today?* Their educational, occupational, and economic statuses are very high. Their affluence, however, has not weakened their traditionally liberal stand on social and political issues.

7. *Who are European Americans?* Most have their national origins in Western and Northern Europe, among whom WASPs are the dominant group. A much smaller group of European Americans are those whose ancestors emigrated from Southern and Eastern Europe. These white ethnics are successful in various arenas of U.S. life, but some still encounter traces of prejudice.

8. *What is the status of U.S. minorities today?* While still experiencing prejudice and discrimination, minorities are faring better today than before and better in the United States than in other countries.

9. *What do racial and ethnic relations look like from the three sociological perspectives?* Seen from the functionalist perspective, intergroup relations appear in the form of assimilation, amalgamation, and cultural pluralism, all of which are assumed to contribute to social cohesion. Viewed from the conflict perspective, intergroup relations appear in the form of segregation, expulsion, and extermination, all of which harm society. According to symbolic interactionists, stereotyped definitions affect intergroup relations and vice versa.

10. *Can a person be prejudiced without being discriminatory or discriminatory without being prejudiced?* Yes, because prejudice and discrimination are not the same; the first is an attitude and the second an act. Although the two are related, they do not always go together. *What is institutionalized discrimination?* It is the practice of discrimination in social institutions that is not necessarily recognized by everybody as discrimination. *What causes prejudice and discrimination?* Causes include scapegoating, socialization, and the desire for jobs, profits, and power. *What are the consequences of prejudice and discrimination?* A lower quality of life for minorities, a larger and more desperate black underclass, and a negative self-image among African American children. *What official efforts have been made in the United States to combat prejudice and discrimination?* School segregation has been outlawed, antidiscrimination laws have been enacted, and affirmative action has been instituted.

11. *What are the conditions of racial and ethnic problems in other parts of the world?* Ethnic problems seem most severe in Africa and Asia; racial discrimination exists in Latin America; Western Europe has both old and new ethnic problems; and ethnic hostilities appeared throughout Eastern Europe and the former Soviet Union after the collapse of communism. *What causes worldwide ethnic conflicts?* Causes include modernization and economic competition, the authoritarian practice of discouraging diverse ethnic expressions, and excessive ethnic identity, enormous economic problems, and power-hungry politicians. *What did the first global conference against racism accomplish?* It publicized the plight of minorities in various countries, thereby encouraging their governments to protect them.

12. *What is Orlando Patterson's theory of paternal abandonment?* It attributes the high paternal abandonment of black children primarily to the past culture of slavery and secondarily to current-day racism. *How has West Point achieved diversity without relying on admissions preferences?* Academically weak high school students are provided with a strong dose of learning experiences so that they can meet admissions standards.

▌Key terms

Affirmative action   A policy that requires employers and academic institutions to make special efforts to recruit qualified minorities for jobs, promotions, and educational opportunities (p. 231).

Amalgamation   The process by which the subcultures of various groups are blended together, forming a new culture (p. 226).

Anti-Semitism   Prejudice or discrimination against Jews (p. 222).

Assimilation   The process by which a minority adopts the dominant group's culture as the culture of the larger society (p. 226).

Behavioral assimilation   The social situation in which a minority adopts the dominant group's language, values, and behavioral patterns (p. 226).

Cultural pluralism   The peaceful coexistence of various racial and ethnic groups, each retaining its own subculture (p. 226).

De facto segregation   Segregation resulting from tradition and custom (p. 227).

De jure segregation   Segregation sanctioned by law (p. 227).

Discrimination   An unfavorable action against individuals that is taken because they are members of a certain category (p. 214).

Ethnic group   A collection of people who share a distinctive cultural heritage (p. 214).

Genocide   The wholesale killing of members of a specific racial or ethnic group (p. 227).

Glass ceiling   The prejudiced belief that keeps minority professionals from holding leadership positions in organizations (p. 222).

Institutionalized discrimination   The persistence of discrimination in social institutions that is not necessarily recognized by everybody as discrimination (p. 229).

Jim Crow laws   A set of laws that segregated African Americans from whites in all kinds of public and private facilities (p. 218).

Minority   A racial or ethnic group that is subjected to prejudice and discrimination (p. 214).

Prejudice   A negative attitude toward a certain category of people (p. 214).

Race   A group of people who are perceived by a given society to be biologically different from others (p. 213).

Racism   The belief that one's own race or ethnicity is superior to that of others (p. 227).

Scapegoating   Blaming others for one's own failure (p. 230).

Stereotype   An oversimplified, inaccurate mental picture of others (p. 228).

Structural assimilation   The social condition in which the minority is accepted on equal terms with the rest of society (p. 226).

QUESTIONS FOR DISCUSSION AND REVIEW

SOCIOLOGICAL DEFINITIONS

1. Why do sociologists define *race* as a social rather than a physical phenomenon?
2. How do various minority-group members identify themselves?
3. When does a racial or ethnic group become a minority group?

RACIAL AND ETHNIC DIVERSITY

1. Why have Native Americans become the poorest minority in the United States?
2. What is the social condition of African Americans today?
3. Who are the different groups of Hispanic Americans, and what factors unify them?
4. What is the nature of prejudice and discrimination against Asian Americans?
5. How have the experiences of Jewish Americans differed from the experiences of other white ethnic groups?
6. Do European Americans constitute a homogeneous group?

7. What is the general status of U.S. minorities as a whole?

RACIAL AND ETHNIC RELATIONS

1. What kinds of racial and ethnic relations are best explained by the functionalist and conflict perspectives?
2. How is intergroup interaction related to the dominant group's perception of a minority?

PREJUDICE AND DISCRIMINATION

1. How do dominant-group members typically react to minorities?
2. What is institutionalized discrimination?
3. What causes prejudice and discrimination?
4. What consequences do prejudice and discrimination have for minorities?
5. How well have attempts to end discrimination succeeded?

A GLOBAL ANALYSIS OF RACE AND ETHNICITY

1. How do ethnic and racial problems differ in various areas of the world?
2. What causes ethnic and racial conflicts around the globe?

SOCIOLOGICAL FRONTIERS/USING SOCIOLOGY

1. How does Patterson's theory explain the high rate of child abandonment by African American fathers?
2. How can the institution of higher education increase admission of minorities using the same criteria as for whites?

SUGGESTED READINGS

Alba, Richard, and Victor Nee. 2003. *Remaking the American Mainstream: Assimilation and Contemporary Immigration.* Cambridge: Harvard University Press. Redefines *assimilation* as *amalgamation:* a two-way street with mainstream and minority groups adapting to each other's cultures.

Berger, Maurice. 1999. *White Lies.* New York: Farrar, Straus & Giroux. An interesting memoir with a sociological insight into what it means to be white.

Freedman, Samuel G. 2000. *Jew vs. Jew: The Struggle for the Soul of American Jewry.* New York: Simon & Schuster. Analysis of how the growing power of Orthodox Jews have generated a "civil war" within Jewish American enclaves, such as between the liberals and conservatives and between traditionalists and modernists.

Wilson, William Julius. 1999. *The Bridge over the Racial Divide.* Berkeley: University of California

Press. Presents the theory that the powerful forces that limit the life chances of poor African Americans are economic and global rather than racial and local.

Zia, Helen. 2000. *Asian American Dreams: The Emergence of an American People.* New York: Farrar, Straus & Giroux. Shows what it means and takes to be an Asian American.

■ Additional Resources

The New York Times
expect the world®
nytimes.com

Expand your knowledge of the concepts discussed in this chapter by reading the following current and historical articles from the *New York Times*. Go to the "eThemes of the Times" section of the Companion Website (www.ablongman.com/thio6e):

"Racial Tensions Lead to Student Protest at Colgate"

Research Navigator.com

Research Navigator, a research database, provides immediate access to hundreds of full-text articles from EBSCO's ContentSelect Academic Journal Database. If the Research Navigator access code was included with your textbook, go to the website www.research navigator.com and read the following articles related to this chapter by typing in the article number:

Black, Amy E. African American and White Elites Confront Racial Issues. *Society*, May/Jun2002, Vol. 39 Issue 4, p39, 7p. Accession Number: 6530676. Examines two perspectives on race relations in the United States.

Kebede, Messay. "Directing Ethnicity toward Modernity." *Social Theory and Practice*, Apr2001, Vol. 27 Issue 2, p265, 20p. Accession Number: 4760077. Investigates the impact of ethnic conflict on modernization in Africa.

chapter 9

Gender and Age

241

In the African nation of Kenya, Naataosim Mako's father wanted to marry her off to a friend of his. In return for her hand in marriage, the friend was ready to give a handsome dowry: 10 cows, 4 goats, more than 200 quarts of beer, more than 6 pounds of sugar, and a sack of rice. But he was about 30 years old, and she was only 9. And so she ran away and found sanctuary in a boarding school for girls that sought to escape early marriage, an old practice that still survives among the Masai, the most traditional of the 42 tribes in Kenya (Fisher, 1999).

In Zimbabwe, another African country, Grace Ngondo wonders what happened to the good life she expected in her old age. When her late husband first retired as a farm worker, Ngondo received from her children the same support and reverence she had provided her own aging parents. But now two of her sons have died of AIDS, and a third son has moved away. She is left with more than a dozen grandchildren to support. To survive, she has to toil in the fields and then walk to the local school to sell ice cream to the departing pupils (Longman, 1999).

The experiences of these two people reflect what it is like being female and growing old around the world today. Many in the United States, for example, still experience prejudice and discrimination because of their gender, though to a lesser degree than the young Kenyan girl. The elderly in Western societies also are increasingly called upon to work much later in life and to get more involved in rearing the next generation, just like the old Zimbabwean woman. In this chapter, we take a closer look at these issues of gender and age.

GENDER ROLES

Societies expect different things of women and men. These differences are made explicit in **gender roles:** patterns of attitude and behavior that a society expects of its members because they are female or male. What is the nature of gender roles? Are they the same in other societies? Where do the roles come from? Let us analyze each of these issues.

Gender Roles in the United States

In the United States, women were traditionally assigned the role of homemaker and men the role of breadwinner. The woman's world was the home; her job was to comfort and care for her husband and children, maintain harmony, and teach her children to conform to society's norms. The man was expected to work in the outside world, competing with other men in order to provide for his family. The man's world outside the home was viewed as a harsh and heartless jungle in which men needed to be strong, ambitious, and aggressive.

This basic division of labor was accompanied by many popular stereotypes—oversimplified mental images—of what women and men are supposed to be, and to some extent, these stereotypes persist. Women are supposed to be shy, easily intimidated, and passive; men, bold, ambitious, and aggressive. Women should be weak and dainty; men, strong and athletic. It is not bad form for women, but it is for men, to worry about appearance and aging. Women are expected to be emotional, even to cry easily, but men should hold back their emotions and never cry. Women are expected to be sexually passive and naive; men, aggressive and experienced. Women are believed to be dependent, in need of male protection; men are supposed to be independent, fit to be leaders. Women are expected to be intuitive and inconsistent; men, logical, rational, and objective.

These are the traits that have long been associated with each gender in the United States. They represent both *stereotypes* about how men and women behave and *expectations* about how they should behave. Today, some groups are more likely than others to hold or reject them. Among women, those who are relatively young, not married, well educated, and gainfully employed—or who have strong feelings of personal competence—tend to reject the traditional gender-role attitudes. Among men, the working and lower classes are more traditional in gender-role outlook than are the middle and upper classes.

SHIFTING STEREOTYPES
The basic division of labor in society has been influenced by gender stereotypes about how men and women should behave and therefore what work they are best suited to do. These stereotypes gradually are giving way in U.S. society, especially among the better educated and those in the middle and upper classes. Only in the last decade or so, for example, would we not be surprised to find a female flight engineer in the cockpit. ■

myth	As a group, women are more emotional than men in every way.
reality	Women are more likely than men to express such emotions as sympathy, sadness, and distress but are more inhibited when it comes to showing anger and sexual desire.

Although people may consciously reject the traditional gender roles, they tend to behave otherwise. Research has shown that women are more likely to be passive and men aggressive in a number of ways. In interactions between the sexes, the male is more likely to initiate interactions and the female to respond. During a conversation, men tend more to touch women than vice versa. When a man opens the door for a woman, most women would say "thank you" or smile their appreciation. But men tend to look confused if a woman opens the door for them because they are not accustomed to being women's passive beneficiaries. Women are also more likely than men to express feelings of sympathy, sadness, and distress but are more inhibited in expressing anger and sexual desire (Gerstel and Gallagher, 2001; Campbell, 1993; Tannen, 1990). All these behaviors reflect the powerful influence of traditional gender roles, which make men and women behave differently.

■ Gender Roles in Other Societies

The traditional gender roles in the United States are not necessarily the same in all societies. Many years ago, anthropologist Margaret Mead (1935) found striking differences among three tribes in the Southwest Pacific island of New Guinea. Among one of them, the Arapesh, *both* women and men behaved in what many North Americans would consider a *feminine* way. They were passive, gentle, and home loving. The men were just as enthusiastic as the women about taking care of babies and bringing up children. The second tribe, the Mundugumor, were just the opposite: *Both* sexes showed what many in our society would consider *masculine* traits. Both women and men were competitive, aggressive, and violent. In the third tribe, the Tchambuli, the female and male roles were sharply different, and they were the *opposite* of those traditional in the West: Tchambuli women were the bosses at home; they were the economic providers, doing the hunting, farming, and fishing. Tchambuli men were emotional, passive, and dependent; they took care of children, did housework, and used cosmetics.

But the traditional U.S. gender roles can be found in most societies, with men assigned the primary role of breadwinner and women the secondary role of homemaker. The public world is considered a man's domain and the private world a woman's. Men's work is more highly valued than women's work. Even in most of the egalitarian hunting-gathering societies, where women often contribute more than half of the food supply by gathering nuts, fruits, and plants, men may dominate women. Thus, male dominance over females is nearly universal. As anthropologists Kay Martin and Barbara Voorhies (1975) have observed, "A survey of human societies shows that positions of authority are almost always occupied by males." Since this gender difference appears to be universal, is it biologically determined?

Biological Constraints

What makes one person female and another person male has to do with their *chromosomes,* the materials in a cell that transmit hereditary traits to the carrier from the carrier's parents. Females have two similar chromosomes, XX, one inherited from each parent. Men have two different chromosomes, XY, the X inherited from the mother and the Y from the father.

Whether a person will develop the appropriate sex characteristics—say, breasts or facial hair—depends on the proportion of female and male sex *hormones,* chemical substances that stimulate or inhibit vital biological processes. If a woman has more male than female hormones, she will have facial hair rather than breasts. If a man has more female than male hormones, he will end up with breasts instead. But in most females, the proportion of female hormones is greater, and in most men, the proportion of male hormones is greater. It is clear that women and men differ both chromosomally and hormonally.

The chromosomal and hormonal differences underlie other biological differences between the sexes. Stimulated by the greater amount of male sex hormones, men are on average bigger and stronger than women. Yet due to their lack of a second X chromosome, men are less healthy. Men are susceptible to more than 30 types of genetic defects, such as hemophilia and color blindness, which are very rare in women. At birth, males are more likely to die. Throughout life, males tend to mature more slowly. They are more physiologically vulnerable to stress. They are stricken with heart disease at a younger age. And they die sooner (Gorman, 1992; Stoll, 1978).

There are also sex differences in brain structure. Neuroscience research has long established that the left hemisphere, or half, of the brain controls speech, and the right hemisphere directs spatial tasks such as object manipulation. There is less specialization in the female's brain, so that she tends to use both hemispheres for a given task at the same time, whereas the male tends to use only one hemisphere. For example, women are more likely to listen with both ears and men with the right ear. Moreover, the female experiences greater cell growth in her language-dominated hemisphere, while the male's greater growth is in his spatial perception–dominated hemisphere (Gorman, 1992; Goy and McEwen, 1980; Restak, 1979).

The differences in brain structure and hormonal production may have contributed to some behavioral differences between the sexes. Thus, female babies are more sensitive than male babies to certain sounds, particularly their mother's voices, and are more easily startled by loud noises. Female infants are also more quiet, and males are more vigorous and inclined to explore, shout, and bang in their play. Female infants talk sooner, have larger vocabularies, and are less likely to develop speech problems. Stuttering, for example, is several times more prevalent among males. Girls are superior not only in verbal abilities but also in overall intelligence, while boys excel in spatial performances such as mental manipulation of objects and map reading. When asked how they have mentally folded an object, boys tend to say simply "I folded it in my mind," but girls are more likely to produce elaborate verbal descriptions. Women are more sensitive to touch, odor, and sound. They show greater skill in picking up peripheral information as well as nuances of facial expression and voice. They are six times more likely than men to sing in tune (Trotter, 1987; Rossi, 1984).

In sum, nature makes women and men different, but these differences do not add up to female inferiority or male superiority. On some measures—such as physical health and early verbal ability—females as a group seem superior to males, and by other measures—especially size and strength—males as a group seem superior.

The Role of Culture

The biological differences between males and females seem logically related to the division of labor between the sexes. If men are bigger and stronger, then it makes sense for them to do the work that requires strength. Likewise, assigning women the care of the home and children may be a logical extension of their biological ability to bear and nurse children.

However, there are limitations to biological constraints on gender roles. Since women generally have smaller hands and greater finger agility than men, they are logically more fit to be dentists and neurosurgeons. Yet men dominate these high-paying professions because American culture has long defined them as men's work. Indeed, the cultural definition of gender roles exercises awesome power. Because U.S. culture has defined being a physician as men's work, the majority of our doctors are males, and they are among the highest-paid professionals. By contrast, in the former Soviet Union, where medicine was a feminine profession, most of the doctors were women, and they were generally paid women's wages—less than what skilled blue-collar male workers earned.

Undeniably, biology sets females and males apart. But it can only predispose—not force—us to behave in certain ways. Society does much to accentuate gender differences. As Alice Rossi (1984) points out,

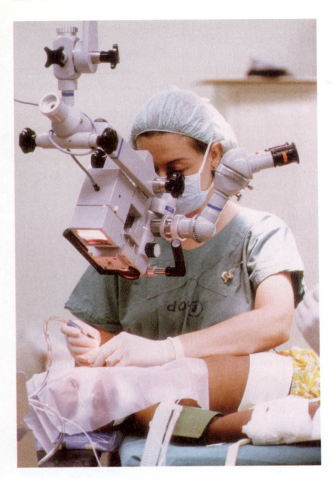

CULTURE REIGNS OVER BIOLOGY There are limits to the biological constraints on gender roles. For example, since women generally have smaller hands and greater dexterity than men, they are logically more fit—in terms of biology—to be dentists and neurosurgeons. Even so, men dominate these high-paying professions because U.S. culture has long defined them as men's work. ▪

women may have the natural tendency to handle an infant with tactile gentleness and a soothing voice, and men may have the natural tendency to play with an older child in a rough-and-tumble way, but these tendencies are often exaggerated through socialization—under the guidance of culture. Also, boys may have been born with *slightly* greater spatial ability than girls. But as adults, men can perform *much* better on spatial tasks, largely due to socialization. As Beryl Benderly (1989) explains, "Most boys, but few girls, grow up throwing baseballs, passing footballs, building models, breaking down engines—activities that teach about space." Thus, we are born female or male, but we learn to become women or men. We will take a closer look at this learning process in the next section.

GENDER SOCIALIZATION

However a society defines gender roles, its socializing agents pass that definition from generation to generation. The family, peer group, school, and mass media all teach important lessons about these roles.

▪ The Family

Newborn babies do not even know their gender, much less how to behave like girls or boys. Influenced by parents, children quickly develop a sexual identity and learn their gender roles. Right from birth, babies are usually treated according to their gender. At birth, girls tend to be wrapped in pink blankets and boys in blue ones. Baby girls are handled more gently than boys; girls are cuddled and cooed over, but boys are bounced around and lifted high in the air. Girls are given dolls, whereas boys are given action figures. Mothers tend to fuss about how pretty their little girls should look, but they are less concerned about their little boys' appearance.

When they learn to talk, children become more aware of the gender difference. They are taught to differentiate *he* and *his* from *she* and *hers*. Gender cues are also available. Both parents use more words about feelings and emotions with girls than with boys, so that by age 2, girls use more emotion words than boys do. Mothers also tend to talk more politely ("Could you turn off the TV, please?"), but fathers use more commanding or threatening language ("Turn off the TV!"). By age 4, girls and boys have learned to imitate those conversational styles: When talking among themselves, girls emphasize agreement and mutuality, and boys use more threatening, dominating language (Shapiro, 1990).

Girls are taught to be ladylike, polite, and gentle and to rely on others—especially males—for help. They are allowed to express their emotions freely. Observing their mothers' relative interest in fashion and cosmetics, they learn the importance of being pretty, and they may even learn that they must rely more on their beauty than their intelligence to attract men (Power and Shanks, 1989; Elkin and Handel, 1988).

On the other hand, boys are taught to behave like men and to avoid being sissies. They are told that boys don't cry. If they put on makeup and wear dresses, though in play, their parents are horrified. Growing up with a fear of being feminine, young men learn to maintain a macho image, as well as an exploitive attitude toward women. Boys are also encouraged to be self-reliant and assertive, to avoid being "mama's boys" (Power and Shanks, 1989; Elkin and Handel, 1988).

In recent years, though, there has been a trend toward more gender-neutral socialization. Young parents, female professionals, and well-educated parents are particularly inclined to socialize their children into egalitarian gender roles. Still, these children continue to be subjected to traditional gender-role socialization outside the home. Influenced by peers and TV commercials, most children tend to enjoy playing with gender-stereotyped toys. Girls go for Barbie and other dolls that teach the importance of dressing, grooming, and other so-called feminine activities. By contrast, boys prefer Nintendo and other action games that encourage them to be so-called masculine by being tough. Not surprisingly, youngsters of both sexes also gravitate toward gender-stereotyped games in cyberspace, as we will see in the Sociological Frontiers toward the end of this chapter.

The Peer Group

The socialization of girls and boys into their gender roles gets a boost from their same-sex peers, as Barrie Thorne (1993) found in her research. First, girls engage more often in cooperative kinds of play. They jump rope and count in unison, swing around jungle gym bars one after another, or practice dance steps in a synchronized fashion. Girls further tend more to say "Let's . . ." or "We gotta . . ." to generate collaborative action. By contrast, boys engage more in competitive rough-and-tumble play and physical fighting. Older boys like to play competitive sports. Boys also like to appear tough by issuing verbal threats: "Shut up or I'll bust your head" or "I'm gonna punch you." Such threats are sometimes made in annoyance or anger but also in a spirit of play.

Second, girls like to spend time with only one or two best friends, whereas boys tend more to hang around with a larger group of casual friends. With best friends, girls often show gestures of intimacy, such as combing each other's hair or borrowing each other's sweaters. By contrast, boys express their solidarity in a rough way—giving "high five" hand slaps, friendly teasing, or mock violence such as pushing or poking. This gender difference may explain why friendships among young women are much more likely than friendships among young men to endure far into adulthood, remaining strong more than 20 years later (Zaslow, 2003a).

Third, far from being "sugar and spice and everything nice," girls do occasionally suffer breakdowns in group harmony, experiencing considerable tension and conflict. But girls are not as direct and confrontational as boys in expressing their conflict. The offenses of others are usually talked about behind their backs rather than to their faces. A dispute among girls is consequently more protracted, much

of it carried out through reports to and by third parties (Thorne, 1993).

In short, girls are more likely than boys to learn cooperation, intimacy, and indirectness in dealing with conflict. But as Thorne cautions, these gender differences should not be exaggerated. Not all youngsters show the same gendered characteristics. These traits are less common among nonwhite and working-class youth. For example, African American girls are just as skilled in direct verbal conflict as boys, and white working-class girls value being tough as much as boys do.

The School

Until recently, schools usually segregated courses and sports on the basis of gender. Secretarial courses and home economics were for girls; business and mechanics courses were for boys. Girls played softball; boys, baseball. High school counselors were less likely to encourage girls to go on to college because they were expected to get married and stay home to raise children. If a girl was going to college, counselors tended to steer her toward traditionally feminine careers, such as teaching, nursing, and social work. While these overtly differential treatments are no longer prevalent, more subtle lessons of gender-role differences are still common (Sadker and Sadker, 1995).

myth	Boys are born to be more proficient in math than girls.
reality	Much of boys' greater proficiency in math comes from socialization. Because math is stereotyped as a male domain, boys benefit more than girls from math classes. They are spoken to more, are called on more, and receive more feedback, interaction, instruction, and encouragement.

For example, girls are often led to believe that they are not as proficient in mathematics as boys. If a gifted female student builds a robot, her achievement may be trivialized with questions like "Did you build it to do housework?" Since math is stereotyped as a male domain, boys benefit more than girls from math classes; they are spoken to more often, are called on more often, and receive more corrective feedback, social interaction, individual instruction, and encouragement. They learn more than what is in the textbook. By contrast, girls are mostly consigned to learning by rote the math in the text, with little exposure to extracurricular math and science. Not surprisingly, girls usually end up scoring lower on standardized math tests, though they may receive better grades on classroom exams—which largely require memorization of course material (Kimball, 1989).

Another subtle lesson of gender-role differences is rooted in the structure of the school. In virtually all elementary and secondary schools, men hold positions of authority (principals and superintendents) and women hold positions of subservience (teachers and aides). In such a male-dominant atmosphere, children are led to believe that women are subordinate, needing the leadership of men. As Laurel Richardson (1988) observes, "Children learn that although their teacher, usually a female, is in charge of the room, the school is run by a male without whose strength she could not cope; the principal's office is where the incorrigibles are sent."

■ The Mass Media

The media are pervasive sources of gender-role socialization. In such traditional magazines as *Good Housekeeping* and *Family Circle,* until recently, the tendency has been to talk down to women as if they were children needing endless reiterations of basics on how to take care of the family. Today, the publications are more sophisticated, but they still tend to define the female role in terms of homemaking and motherhood and to offer numerous beauty tips to help attract men or please husbands. *Cosmopolitan,* for example, recently featured such articles as "Be the Best Sex of His Life" and "Ten Make-Him-Throb Moves So Hot You'll Need a Firehose to Cool Down the Bed" (Kuczynski, 1999).

Women's magazines are not alone in perpetuating gender stereotypes. Traditionally, television commercials presented women as sex objects and as dedicated housewives. Young bikini-clad women were shown strolling on the beach in front of ogling, beer-drinking men. Housewives were shown in ecstasy over their shiny waxed floors or stricken with guilt for not using the right detergent to remove stains from their children's clothes. Prime-time television programs also often typecast women as lovers, as mothers, or as weak, passive sidekicks to powerful, effective men.

Today, the media are more likely to present the image of women as successful and able to support themselves and their families, but the traditional stereotypes of women still exist. On television and in movies, women are still too often depicted as sex objects, even when they are successful professionals. In women's as well as general-interest magazines, women are told that it's all right to be successful in the workplace but that they shouldn't forget that they must also be sexy because "looks are crucial" (Kuczynski, 1999; Sidel, 1990).

LIKE FATHER, LIKE SON According to social learning theory, children learn gender roles by imitating older people of the same sex. This leads to the development of a stable gender identity: "I do boy things like carpentry and building; therefore, I must be a boy." Parents serve as models of gender-typed behavior for their children. ■

■ The Learning Process

We may know much about what a socializing agent teaches, but we still need to understand how the child learns the gender role in the first place. According to social learning theory, such social-psychological factors as *conditioning* and *imitation* are part of the process of learning gender roles. Children are rewarded for behaving in ways that parents and others consider appropriate for their gender—and punished for not doing so—so they eventually conform to their society's gender roles. A little boy, for example, learns to hide his fears or pain because he has been praised for being brave and scolded for crying. Children also learn by imitation. They tend to imitate their same-sex parent and other adult models because these adults are powerful, nurturant, and able to reward or punish them. Through reinforcement and imitation, children engage in certain gender-typed activities that lead to the development of a stable gender identity: "I do girl things; therefore, I must be a girl."

But according to cognitive development theory, gender *identification* is the cause rather than the product of gender-role learning. Children first learn to identify themselves as a male or female from what they observe and what they are told. Then they seek to act and feel like one: "I am a boy; therefore, I want to do boy things." Thus, children are not passive objects in the acquisition of gender roles. They are active actors developing their gender identities and performing their gender roles. How clear their identities are and how well they perform their gender roles depend significantly on their *cognitive skills* as, for example, fast or slow learners.

Apparently, all the processes discussed here—conditioning, imitation, identification, and cognition—play a part in the learning of gender roles. They are also interrelated. Children cannot rely on their cognition alone to distinguish what is masculine from what is feminine. They have to depend on their parents to serve as models of masculinity and femininity. In serving as models, the parents are likely to reinforce specific gender-typed behavior. Identification with the same-sex parent may also result from—as well as influence—the parent's tendency to reinforce certain gender-typed behaviors (Basow, 1986).

SPHERES OF GENDER INEQUALITY

At one time or another, laws have denied women "the right to hold property, to vote, to go to school, to travel, to borrow money, and to enter certain occupations" (Epstein, 1976). In recent years, there has been significant movement toward gender equality, but large inequalities remain, even in the United States. They are evident in such areas of life as education, employment, politics, and religion. Underlying these inequalities is **sexism**—prejudice and discrimination based on one's gender. Sexism also involves sexual abuses against women, of which the most common is sexual harassment.

Sexism

A fundamental characteristic of sexism is the belief that women are inferior to men. Even when a male and a female have the same personalities or are equally competent in performing the same task, the woman is still likely to be considered inferior to the man. We can see this sexist attitude even in psychiatry, a profession that is supposed to be scientific and objective in analyzing human traits. Psychiatrists tend to describe normal men positively—as independent, courageous, and the like—but are more likely to describe normal women negatively as having sexual timidity and social anxiety. What if women lose their sexual timidity and become sexually active—a trait typically considered normal for men? Then they are likely to be diagnosed as abnormal (Leslie, 1996; Goleman, 1990).

This no-win attitude toward women is revealed in a study of college students asked to evaluate the so-

"I can stand the heat. I just can't stand the kitchen!"

Source: From the *Wall Street Journal*—Permission, Cartoon Features Syndicate.

cial desirability of men and women with various characteristics. Women with supposedly feminine traits, such as compassion and sensitivity to others' needs, were rated more poorly than men with supposedly masculine characteristics, such as assertiveness. But women with masculine traits were also rated less favorably than men with feminine traits (Gerber, 1989).

Sexism has long exerted a negative impact on women, tending to make them believe that they were somehow inferior to men. In the past, many women were afraid to pursue careers in competition with men because sexism had led them to believe that such competition would ruin their lives—making them unpopular, unmarriable, lonely, or otherwise miserable. This belief is far less common among educated women today, a consequence of the women's movement, which has vigorously attacked sexism since the 1960s. Nevertheless, sexism is still powerful enough to make some women reluctant to pursue careers as men do and willing to stay home to care for their families. This is because today's sexism forces women, but not men, to choose home over career (Hochschild, 1998; Faludi, 1991).

Sexism may produce inequality between the sexes in two ways. When sexism takes the active form of discrimination against women, it obviously creates inequality. At each level of occupational skill, for example, men receive higher pay than women. Sexism may also foster inequality in a less direct way. If women have been socialized to feel inferior or abnormal, they may lower their expectations, aiming to achieve less than they otherwise might. Whether through overt discrimination or traditional gender-role socialization, sexism has brought gender inequalities in education, employment, politics, and religion.

■ Education

Before the turn of the twentieth century, it was widely believed that "schoolwork would make women sick, diverting blood from their wombs to their brains" (Manegold, 1994). In general, U.S. schools began to offer elementary and high school education to girls and young women in the second half of the nineteenth century. However, women were long deprived of the opportunities for higher education. Although some women's colleges were founded in the 1800s, generally, women were barred from many colleges and universities until the mid 1900s. Many graduate and professional schools did not admit women students until the 1960s. In general, the more prestigious the educational institution, the more strongly it discriminated against women. Harvard's graduate business school, for example, was one of the last to admit women, in 1963.

In 1973, the federal government, under pressure from the women's movement, began to pass laws against sex discrimination in schools. As a result, American women have made impressive gains in ed-

ucation. As Figure 9.1 shows, more women than men are now attending and graduating from college. Women in many other rich nations are also attending universities in equal or greater numbers than men (see Figure 9.2, p. 250). In the United States, still fewer women than men receive medical and law degrees, but the proportion of women earning these degrees has increased enormously since 1970. Women are expected to equal or surpass men in receiving these and other advanced degrees in the near future. Apparently, education has become the institution in the United States with the most equal opportunity for both sexes (Glater, 2001; Holmes, 1998c).

But substantial inequality still exists in other aspects of education. From preschool through high school, girls are given less attention than boys. Teachers call on boys more often, offer boys more detailed and constructive criticism, and allow boys to shout out answers but reprimand girls for doing so, especially in math and science classes. Receiving less attention from teachers, girls further suffer a drop in self-esteem when they reach high school. At age 9, a majority of girls are confident and assertive and feel positive about themselves, but by age 14, less than one-third feel that way. Some conservatives, however, argue that boys are doing *worse* than girls in school, but feminists emphasize that this is true only in regard to reading and writing (Sommers, 2000; Sadker and Sadker, 1995).

Significant inequalities also persist on the faculties of numerous colleges and universities. Women

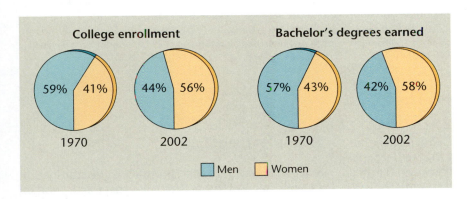

FIGURE 9.1

Progress toward Gender Equality in Education

American women have made impressive gains in education. More women than men now attend and graduate from college. Education has apparently provided more equal opportunity for young people of both sexes than any other social institution.

Critical Thinking: *Do you have the same opportunity to succeed in college as members of the opposite sex? Why or why not?*

Source: Data from U.S. Department of Education, 2003.

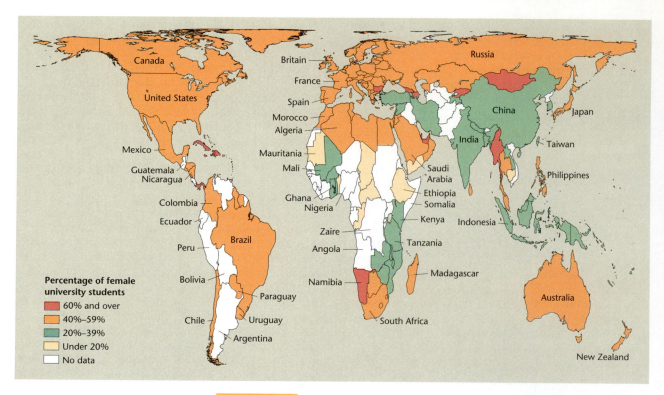

FIGURE 9.2

Women in Higher Education: A Global Perspective

Increasing numbers of women worldwide are pursuing higher education. In richer, industrialized countries, women attend universities in equal or slightly greater numbers than men. The number of women on university faculties has not grown at the same pace, however. Also, in many poorer countries, women are still much less likely than men to attend college.

Critical Thinking: *What prevents many women in Third World countries from going to college? Can those obstacles be removed? Why or why not?*

Source: From *The Penguin Atlas of Women in the World,* by Joni Seager, copyright © 1997, 2003 by Myriad Editions Ltd, maps & graphics. Used by permission of Penguin, a division of Penguin Group (USA) Inc.

make up less than 30 percent of full-time college faculty. The figures are even lower in the higher ranks of faculty and at prestigious universities. Various studies have consistently shown that compared with their male colleagues, female academics are less likely to be hired, less likely to be promoted, and more concentrated in the lower ranks of institutions. They are also paid substantially less. This treatment is attributed to gender discrimination because there is no evidence that women faculty are less competent in teaching or doing research (Koerner, 1999; Valian, 1998).

■ Employment

Since laws were passed to prohibit sex discrimination in employment more than 40 years ago, women have made certain gains in the workplace. More women are gainfully employed than before, and their pay has increased on average. Still, women are far from economically equal to men.

Women typically hold lower-status, lower-paying jobs such as nursing, public school teaching, and secretarial work. These traditionally female occupations are subordinate to positions usually held by men.

Thus, nurses are subordinate to doctors, teachers to principals, and secretaries to executives.

myth	Women receive lower pay than men simply because their jobs typically require fewer skills and less training.
reality	Sexism is a factor because even when women hold the same jobs as men, they tend to earn less.

Even when women hold the same jobs as men and have comparable skills, training, and education, they tend to earn less. Even in predominantly female occupations, such as nursing and hairdressing, women generally earn less than men (Budig, 2002). Not surprisingly, although Washington and other states have instituted the policy of *comparable worth* by paying women the same as men for doing different but equally demanding work, such as office cleaning and truck driving, the gender gap in earnings persists (see Figure 9.3).

A growing number of American women have been climbing the corporate ladder, but the glass ceiling still has kept most of them out of the top jobs. According to several studies, women represent less than half of the officials and managers in various industries as a whole. The situation is even worse in most other countries, with far fewer women in managerial positions (Jacobs, 2003; Seager, 2003).

■ Politics

Theoretically, women can acquire more political power than men. After all, female voters outnumber male voters, and most of the volunteer workers in political campaigns are women. Yet until recently, most women felt that politics was a male activity and that women should not plunge into that dirty world. Sexism also tended to trap women in a double bind to squash their political ambition: If a woman campaigned vigorously, she would likely be regarded as a neglectful wife and mother. If she was an attentive wife and mother, she was apt to be judged incapable of devoting energy to public office. But in a man, comparable qualities—a vigorous campaigner or a devoted husband and father—are considered great political assets.

myth	As a highly democratic society, the United States has proportionately more female political leaders than other nations.
reality	The United States lags behind most other industrial nations in female political leadership.

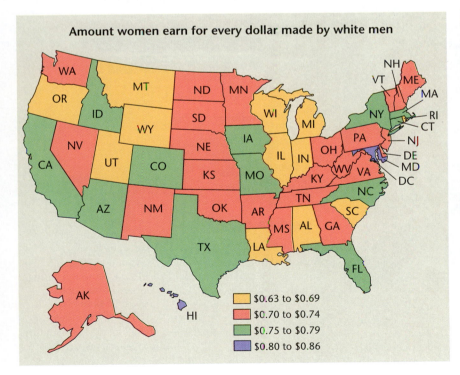

Amount women earn for every dollar made by white men

$0.63 to $0.69
$0.70 to $0.74
$0.75 to $0.79
$0.80 to $0.86

FIGURE 9.3

Women Are Paid Less Than Men

American women earn, on average, 78 cents for every dollar white men make. This gender gap in pay has narrowed, though, from 60 cents on the dollar 20 years ago. The gap has shrunk most significantly for relatively young women and men. Among people aged 27 to 33, women who have never had a child now earn about 98 cents for every dollar men earn.

Critical Thinking: *Do you think women will earn the same as men 10 years from now? Why or why not?*

Sources: Data from U.S. Census Bureau, 2003; Institute for Women's Policy Research, 2003.

In recent years, more and more women have assumed political leadership, but they still have a long way to go. Although they make up over 50 percent of the voting population in the United States, women capture no more than 5 percent of all public offices. Globally, as Figure 9.4 shows, the United States also lags behind most other industrial nations in female political leadership.

Why don't U.S. women recognize their power as a majority of the voting population and use it to elect more women candidates? A major reason, Naomi Wolf (1993) suggests, is lack of unity. According to Wolf, many women wrongly assume that in order to be feminists, they must be liberal feminists and promote abortion rights. Wolf therefore calls for a broadly inclusive "power feminism" that helps all kinds of women, whether liberal or conservative, to win more political offices. This is more likely to materialize, another feminist observes, if career women and stay-at-home mothers genuinely respect each other, knowing that "it takes guts, courage, and strength to run a household, and it takes the very same qualities to work outside the home" (Arnold, 1996).

■ Religion

Long used to justify male dominance, the sexist notion of female inferiority can be found in the sacred texts of all the world's major religions. Buddhism and Confucianism instruct wives to obey their husbands. The Muslim Koran states, "Men are superior to women on account of the qualities in which God has given them preeminence." The Christian Bible says that after Eve ate the forbidden fruit and gave it to Adam, God told her, "In pain you shall bring forth children, yet your desire shall be for your husband, and he shall rule over you" (Genesis 3:16). The daily Orthodox Jewish prayer for men includes this sentence: "I thank Thee, O Lord, that Thou has not made me a woman."

All this should *not* be taken to suggest that religion *always* puts down women. In the four Gospels of the New Testament, for example, "there is a total

BLAZING A TRAIL Traditionally, many in the United States felt that politics was a male activity. In recent years, a growing number of women, among them U.S. Senator Hillary Rodham Clinton, have assumed political leadership, though there is still some way to go before women reach parity of numbers with men in elected office. ■

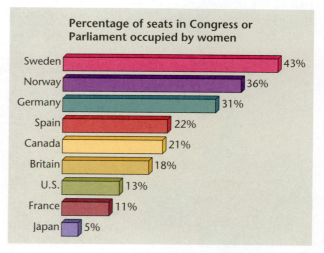

Percentage of seats in Congress or Parliament occupied by women

Country	Percentage
Sweden	43%
Norway	36%
Germany	31%
Spain	22%
Canada	21%
Britain	18%
U.S.	13%
France	11%
Japan	5%

FIGURE 9.4

The Gender Gap in Politics: A Global View

More and more U.S. women have assumed political leadership, but they still have a long way to go. Although women constitute more than 50 percent of the voting population, they usually capture less than 5 percent of all public offices. Thus, the United States lags behind most other industrial countries in female political leadership.

Critical Thinking: *Why have U.S. women achieved far less in politics than in education?*

Source: Data from United Nations, *The World's Women,* 2000.

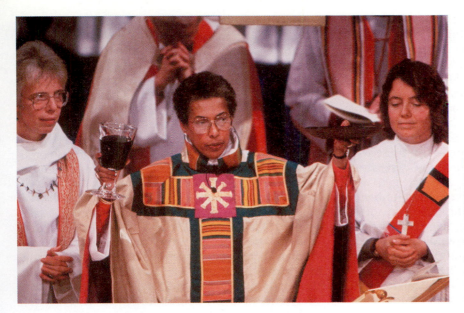

FEMINIZING FAITH Over the past 20 years, sexism in religion has been unraveling as women have questioned gender inequalities both in sacred texts and in religious organizations and practices. During this time, more women have enrolled in seminaries and become ordained clergy, but they are still a small minority and have limited career opportunities. ■

of 633 verses in which Jesus refers to women, and almost none of these is negative in tone" (van Leeuwen, 1990). But sexist ideas can be found in other parts of the Bible. Even the most central concept of religion—God—is spoken and thought of as being male. To some feminists, the notion of the Supreme Being as male is the quintessence of sexism. For this reason, some liberal church leaders have begun purging hymnals and liturgies of references to God as male (such as "God the Father") and preaching about a genderless deity (called the *Creator* or *Great Spirit*). But many bishops, pastors, and laypeople have resisted these changes (Götz, 1999; Niebuhr, 1992).

Sexism is hardly confined to sacred historical texts. It also shapes contemporary religious organizations and practices. For the past 20 years in the United States, under the increasing influence of the women's movement, more women have been enrolling in theological seminaries and becoming ordained ministers. But they are still a small minority and have limited career opportunities. Compared with their male counterparts, female clergy are more likely to be underemployed, to be paid low salaries, to serve merely as assistant or associate pastors, and to be relegated to small congregations. Moreover, Conservative and Orthodox Judaism and the Missouri Synod Lutherans are still opposed to ordaining women. The Roman Catholic and Eastern Orthodox churches, which represent over half of all Christians, also continue to prohibit ordination for women. These church hierarchies are at odds with the rank-and-file, though, as at least 60 percent of lay Catholics favor

opening the priesthood to women (Götz, 1999; Gray, 1995; Cowell, 1994; Andersen, 1993).

In sum, gender inequalities in religion can be found in both sacred texts and contemporary practices. These two subjects will continue to be a focus of debate as the world's religions confront gender-related issues.

■ Feminism

Confronted with these instances of prejudice and discrimination, many women fight back by advocating **feminism**—the belief that women and men should be equal in various aspects of their lives—and joining the social movement for gender equality. This feminist or women's movement can be divided historically into three waves. The first wave began in the midnineteenth century, developing out of the larger social movement to abolish slavery. The women who participated in the abolitionist movement came to realize that they also lacked freedom. Initially, they attempted to eradicate all forms of sexual discrimination, but gradually, they focused their attention on winning the right for women to vote. When women's suffrage finally became a reality in 1920, the feminist movement came to a complete halt (Flexner and Fitzpatrick, 1996).

But in the mid 1960s, the women's movement was revived, and thus began *the second wave* of feminism. Two factors seem to have brought it on. First, after World War II, more and more women went to college. After receiving so much education, they were unhappy only to be housewives or to hold low-status, low-paying jobs outside the home. Second, many young women participating in various social movements (including the civil rights movement, the student movement, and the anti–Vietnam War movement), supposedly fighting for the freedom of the oppressed, found themselves oppressed by the male freedom fighters. These women, wrote Annie Gottlieb (1971), "found themselves *serving* as secretary, mother and concubine, while men did all the speaking, writing, and negotiating—and these were men who professed to reject the 'oppressive' ritual machinery of their society."

Out of this background emerged a number of women-only organizations. Some were considered radical because they hated men, rejected marriage, and vowed to tear down the whole gender-role system. They gave their organizations such names as SCUM (Society for Cutting Men) and WITCH (Women's International Terrorist Conspiracy from Hell). Other feminist groups were more moderate, the most well known being NOW (National Organization for Women). NOW has been the most successful feminist organization and continues to have a strong influence on women's positions today. NOW's aim is to end sexual discrimination in education, work, politics, religion, and all other social institutions. Consequently, many states have passed laws requiring equal pay for equal work, and government departments have issued affirmative action guidelines to force universities and businesses to hire more women. Also, in many cases, court decisions have supported women's charges of sexual discrimi-

nation in hiring, pay, and promotion (Rosen, 2000; Flexner and Fitzpatrick, 1996; Whittier, 1995).

In the 1990s, a new generation of young women in their teens and twenties started *the third wave* of feminism. These women grew up taking equality for granted because of the victories their mothers had won for women's rights. Thus, the third wavers were different from their mothers. These young feminists were more inclusive, welcoming men to join them in addressing not only women's concerns but also problems that affect both sexes, such as racism, pollution, and poverty (Schrof, 1993). By being inclusive in organization and concern, these young feminists were able to achieve goals that the older generation largely ignored. Made up largely of highly educated white women, the older feminists made great strides for women in college education, professional schools, and white-collar jobs. But less attention was paid to the plight of poor and minority women, and these issues remain to be addressed by the third wavers (Rosen, 2000; Whittier, 1995; Guttman, 1994).

Today, only about one-third of young females, aged 13 to 20, consider themselves feminists, but a large majority of them embrace most of the same feminine values espoused by the women's movement of the last 40 years (see Table 9.1). But unlike their feminist ancestors of the 1960s and 1970s, who tended to say that "acting like a girl" was asking to be treated as such, most of the young women today do not see any conflict between being a feminist and being feminine. As 15-year-old Karisa Powers says, "Just because you want to be treated as equal doesn't

---

TABLE 9.1

The Feminist Views of Today's Young Women

Only about 34 percent of young females (aged 13 to 20) call themselves *feminists,* but a large majority of them agree with most of the traditional feminist values, as indicated below.

Viewpoint	Agree	Disagree
Feminists believe strongly in women's rights.	86%	3%
Feminists believe in equal rights for everyone.	59%	16%
Being a feminist is a positive thing.	56%	6%
All feminists are women.	23%	56%
Feminists aren't feminine.	12%	63%
Feminists hate men.	9%	70%
Feminists are homosexual.	6%	77%

Note: The "Agree" and "Disagree" percentages do not add up to 100 because "Neutral" responses were not included.

Source: Data from Rebecca Gardyn, "Granddaughters of Feminism," *American Demographics,* April 2001, p. 47.

mean you can't scream when you see a spider." Most of the young women in one survey also agreed that "a man should always open the door for a woman" (Gardyn, 2001b).

CONSEQUENCES OF GENDER INEQUALITY

Gender inequality hurts women in different ways. Here, we discuss various examples. One is sexual harassment. Another is the varying impact of gender inequality on women of diverse backgrounds. A third is how women of developing countries are affected by gender inequality much more than women in affluent societies.

■ Sexual Harassment

Most sociologists define **sexual harassment** as an unwelcome act of a sexual nature. In 1993, the U.S. Supreme Court provided a more precise legal definition: Sexual harassment is any sexual conduct that makes the workplace environment so hostile or abusive that people find it hard to perform their jobs.

The Supreme Court's definition came with its ruling on the suit that Teresa Harris filed against her former boss, Charles Hardy. In 1987, Harris quit her job in despair because she felt she had been sexually harassed by Hardy. According to Harris, Hardy often asked her—and other female employees—to retrieve coins from the front pockets of his pants. He once asked her to go with him to a hotel room to negotiate her raise. And he routinely made such remarks to her as "You're a woman; what do you know?" She spent six years trying to convince judges that she was sexually harassed in violation of federal law but to no avail. The judges found Hardy's conduct was not severe enough to "seriously affect her psychological well-being." But Harris persisted, and finally the Supreme Court ruled that sexual harassment does not have to inflict "severe psychological injury" on the victim. As the Court says, federal law "comes into play before the harassing conduct leads to a nervous breakdown" (Sachs, 1993).

The Harris case was the second one on sexual harassment to reach the Supreme Court. In the first, in 1986, the Court ruled that sexual harassment was a form of gender discrimination prohibited by the Civil Rights Act of 1964. Since that first ruling, the number of harassment charges has increased substantially. To avoid being sued, many companies, as well as universities and colleges, have instituted antiharassment policies, guidelines, and educational programs (Lublin and Schellhardt, 1998; Sachs, 1993).

Even today, however, it is still not easy for victims of harassment to win in court. The problem is that to many judges, there is no sexual harassment unless it occurs *repeatedly,* as happened to Teresa Harris. In 1998, for example, the judge in Paula Jones's case against former President Clinton dismissed it because Clinton allegedly asked her for oral sex *only once*—despite the fact that to most women, "even one unwelcome sexual advance is too many" (Mink, 1998). Even if the law were completely on the side of harassment victims, the problem of harassment is too prevalent to disappear. According to various studies, about half of all working women have been sexually harassed at some point in their careers. Examples of harassment range from unwanted sexual remarks to actual rape. Also, among high school and junior high school students, some 67 percent of girls and 42 percent of boys have been touched, groped, or pinched while on school grounds (AAUW, 2001; Henneberger and Marriott, 1993; Kantrowitz, 1991).

Generally, sexual harassment reflects men's attempt to preserve their traditional dominance over women. Men are therefore more likely to harass a woman if they feel threatened by her supposed invasion of their male-dominated world. This may explain why sexual harassment seems to occur most frequently in heavily male-dominated occupations such as the U.S. military. In essence, sexual harassment is an expression of power, involving a more powerful person victimizing a less powerful one. It is possible, for example, for a female boss to sexually harass a male employee. But because of the prevalence of men in positions of power over women, men are the offenders in most cases (Lewis, 2001).

■ Violence against Women

There are various instances of violence against women. The most widely known is rape. As mentioned in Chapter 6 (Deviance and Control), about 110,000 cases of rape are reported to the police every year, and according to a survey, some 22 percent of women have been forced to have sex at least once since age 13. Date or acquaintance rape is especially prevalent. More than half of all college women are sexually assaulted in some way, and about 15 percent are forcibly raped by a date at some point (Thio, 2004). Given the sexist culture that defines women as sex objects that men can exploit for their own pleasure, it should not be surprising that rape is a common problem.

Even more common is the violence against women that takes place at home. As will be discussed in Chapter 10 (Families), the family is the most violent institution in American society, except the military in time of war. The law does not adequately protect women against family violence, as many husbands who strike their wives to keep them under control are not arrested, prosecuted, or imprisoned. Nonetheless, many women continue to remain in abusive relationships because they are afraid that their husbands will stalk and kill them if they leave. Yet by staying, the abused women are likely to end up getting killed by their husbands or being forced to survive by killing their husbands. The violence against wives stems largely from the sexist, patriarchal nature of society, which treats women as if they were their husbands' property (Thio, 2004).

Social Diversity

In the multicultural U.S. society, the impact of gender inequality varies with race and class. Middle- and upper-class white women may feel oppressed by gender discrimination, but they enjoy advantages made possible by their favorable economic and racial status. Working-class white women are subject to both gender and economic exploitation. And African American, Hispanic, and other minority women face either a combination of two social injustices (gender and racial discrimination) or a convergence of all three (gender, racial, and economic oppression).

While gender inequality is burdensome to all women, it is more so to those who are already racially or economically oppressed. Most white women from affluent families traditionally raised their children and took care of their homes while their husbands went to work. By contrast, poor, African American, and Hispanic women generally had to do more than household work; they also had to work in low-paying jobs to help support their families. Since the early 1970s, because of the women's movement, many white women have entered relatively well-paying professions. Yet the poor among them, as well as minority women, are more likely to have remained at the bottom of the occupational hierarchy (Young and Dickerson, 1994).

It is not only poverty and racism that compound the effects of gender discrimination on many minority women. Culture also plays a role, especially for women in recent immigrant families. Japanese parents, for example, usually treat boys better than girls, as in the case of the mother of 6-year-old twins Peggy and Henry. Peggy is expected to be her mother's helper. If Henry leaves his sweater at school, Peggy has to go back and get it. She has to carry both her own and her brother's lunch boxes. Difficulty in treating female workers as equal to male workers is also more likely to exist in companies where managers and executives of Asian, Middle Eastern, or Latin American descent have been steeped in old-world paternalistic cultures (Dresser, 1996).

A Global Analysis

Discrimination against women is a universal problem. Every country in the world today still treats its women less well than its men. The problem seems more serious and widespread in developing countries than in industrial societies. More specifically, the gender gaps in literacy, education, employment, income, and health are significantly larger in developing than in industrial countries. Consequently, gender inequality hurts women in less affluent countries much more.

The ways these women suffer from gender inequality may appear unique to certain countries. Many women in China, for instance, are forced to undergo sterilization and abortion so that they will not have more than one child; young village girls in Thailand are sold by their parents to brothel owners; women in the Arab world are killed for sexual misconduct, such as committing adultery; and girls in some African countries are ritually subjected to female circumcision (see Figure 9.5). In China and India, the tradition of female infanticide continues in small pockets of those huge countries, and the availability of ultrasound machines that can detect the sex of a fetus has resulted in widespread abortions of female fetuses. In Russia, business etiquette often calls for female secretaries to sleep with their bosses (Jehl, 1999; Dugger, 1996b; Greenhouse, 1994; Pope, 1994). Such practices of gender discrimination continue to evoke condemnation by people around the world.

SOCIOLOGICAL PERSPECTIVES ON GENDER INEQUALITY

We have seen how gender inequality manifests itself in various facets of society. But where does it come from? Functionalists suggest that gender inequality derives from the fact that men and women have to perform different roles to help society function well. But conflict theorists argue that gender inequality stems from men's desire to exploit women economically and sexually. Symbolic interactionists contend that the interaction between men and women often sustains or reinforces gender inequality.

Functionalist Perspective: Instrumental versus Expressive Roles

According to functionalists, it is functional for society to assign different tasks to men and women. This division of labor was originally based on the physical differences between the sexes. For thousands of years when hunting-gathering societies predominated, men

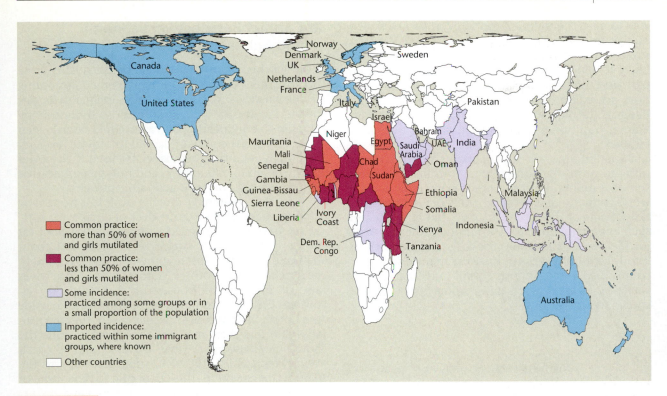

FIGURE 9.5

Global Distribution of Female Genital Cutting

Women in relatively poor countries experience much more gender inequality than their peers in affluent countries. One horrendous example is being subjected to genital cutting, also known as *female circumcision,* a cultural tradition in some developing countries. The procedure involves excision (removing the clitoris and all or part of the labia minora) or infibulation (removing the clitoris and labia and stitching together most of the vaginal opening). The purpose of the procedure is to ensure the marriageability of women by destroying their sexual responsiveness and thus presumably keeping them chaste.

Critical Thinking: *Since female genital cutting is a cultural tradition in some societies, would you condemn it? Why or why not?*

Source: From *The Penguin Atlas of Women in the World,* by Joni Seager, copyright © 1997, 2003 by Myriad Editions Ltd, maps & graphics. Used by permission of Penguin, a division of Penguin Group (USA) Inc.

were more likely to roam far from home to hunt animals because men were larger and stronger, and women were more likely to stay near home to gather plant foods, cook, and take care of children because only women could bear and nurse babies. Today, in industrial societies, muscle power is not as important as brain and machine power. Contraceptives, baby formula, child-care centers, and convenience foods further weaken the constraints that the childbearing role places on women. Yet traditional gender roles persist.

The reason for this persistence, functionalists assume, is that these roles continue to be functional to modern societies. How? Talcott Parsons and Robert Bales (1953) argued that two basic roles must be fulfilled in any group. One is the **instrumental role,** which requires performance of a task. The other is the **expressive role,** which requires taking care of personal relationships. In the modern family, the instrumental role is fulfilled by going out to work and making money; playing this role well requires competence, assertiveness, and dominance. The expressive role requires offering love and affection, as in child care, and it is best filled by someone warm, emotional, and nonassertive. When men are socialized to have the traits appropriate for the instrumental role and women are socialized to have the traits suitable for the expressive role, then the family is likely to function smoothly. Each person fits into a part, and the parts fit together. Such role differentiation, according to functionalists, holds many families together, as suggested by lower divorce rates among traditional families than among two-career families.

Functionalists are wrong about role differentiation, however. In addition to performing the expressive role more often than men, women around the world actually spend more time on instrumental tasks. Some of these tasks are paid, but most are not, such as growing food for the family, gathering wood for fuel, collecting water, cooking, and housecleaning. Taking both types of instrumental work into account, the United Nations (2000) finds that in most societies, women work more hours than men, as shown in Figure 9.6.

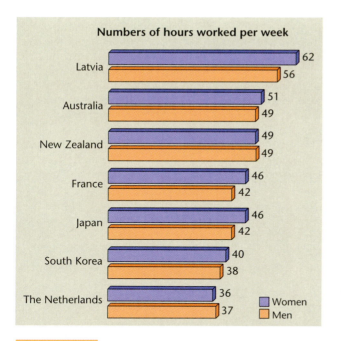

Numbers of hours worked per week

Latvia — 62 / 56
Australia — 51 / 49
New Zealand — 49 / 49
France — 46 / 42
Japan — 46 / 42
South Korea — 40 / 38
The Netherlands — 36 / 37

■ Women ■ Men

FIGURE 9.6

Women Work More Than Men

According to functionalists, in order for society to function smoothly, men have to perform instrumental tasks while women perform expressive tasks. But if both paid and unpaid instrumental tasks are taken into account, women work more hours than men in most societies.

Critical Thinking: *What tasks do the men and women in your family perform? How many hours a week do you think they each work?*

Source: Data from United Nations, *The World's Women,* 2000.

■ Conflict Perspective: Economic and Sexual Exploitation

Conflict theorists argue that gender inequality arose because men were able to exploit women. According to the classic Marxist view, gender inequality is part of the larger economic stratification. By restricting women to childbearing and household chores, men have ensured their own freedom to acquire property and amass wealth. They have also used their power over women to obtain heirs and thus guarantee their continued hold on their economic power.

Moreover, men have directly exploited women by getting them to do a great deal of work with little or no pay. Thus, married women are not paid for housework and child care, which would cost about half of most husbands' incomes if those tasks had to be purchased from others. Gainfully employed wives also do most of the housework and child care, although they work as much as their husbands outside the home. In addition, as we have seen, they are usually paid less than men for their work outside the home (Shellenbarger, 1996; Ingrassia and Wingert, 1995; Hochschild, 1989). In sum, according to the conflict perspective, the economic exploitation of women helps bring about gender inequality.

Some conflict theorists give greater weight to sexual exploitation as the source of gender inequality. Randall Collins (1975) argues that "the fundamental motive is the desire for sexual gratification, rather than for labor per se; men have appropriated women primarily for their beds rather than their kitchens and fields, although they could certainly be pressed into service in the daytime too." More recently, according to some feminists, surrogate motherhood has emerged as the ultimate exploitation of women by men because it turns women into mere breeding machines. To conflict theorists, female exploitation of one type or another contributes greatly to the development of gender inequality.

■ Symbolic Interactionist Perspective: Interaction between the Sexes

According to symbolic interactionists, interaction between the sexes often sustains or reinforces gender inequality.

When women interact with men, the interaction tends to reflect their inequality. Suppose a group of women and men discuss some issues at a meeting. Men usually talk more often than women, and they tend to interrupt women more than the other way around. Men are also more likely to boast about their accomplishments and take credit for those of others. By contrast, women tend to speak more softly and politely and to say "please," "thank you,"

theoretical thumbnail

Sources and Sustenance of Gender Inequality

Perspective	Focus	Insights
Functionalist	Role differentiation as the source of gender inequality	Men perform the instrumental role and women the expressive role so that the family (and, by extension, society) can function smoothly.
Conflict	Men's desire to exploit women as the source of gender inequality	Men's economic and sexual exploitation of women contributes greatly to gender inequality.
Symbolic interactionist	Interaction between the sexes as the sustenance of gender inequality	In intersex interaction, men tend to be more aggressive and to gain more than women, thus helping to sustain or reinforce gender inequality.

and "I'm sorry" more often. Such interaction between men and women, while reflecting gender inequality, sustains or reinforces it. Because of their verbal aggression, men are more likely to end up being considered highly competent, having their arguments and decisions accepted and getting promotions or larger salary raises. By contrast, the less verbally aggressive women tend to lose out, even if they may actually be more competent, be the ones who actually get the job done, or contribute more to the company (Tannen, 1994a).

Nonverbal interactions between the sexes also sustain or reinforce gender inequality. Women talking to men typically give such low-status signals as smiling, nodding, holding their arms to their bodies, and keeping their legs together. Men are more likely to use such high-status gestures as smiling only occasionally, holding their heads still, and standing with legs spread apart, taking up substantial space around them (as noted in Chapter 4). Because of such an unequal interaction, a mutually aggravated spiral is likely to occur: The woman's conciliatory and nonaggressive gestures lead the man to see her as weak, which makes him more overbearing and aggressive, which intimidates her so as to make her more conciliatory (Tannen, 2001; Cory, 1979). All this helps to sustain gender inequality by enhancing the man's power at the woman's expense.

For a quick review of this and the other two perspectives on gender inequality, see the Theoretical Thumbnail above.

WOMEN'S WORK Conflict theorists argue that men have directly exploited women by getting them to do a great deal of work for little or no pay. The tasks of housework and child care would cost about half of most husbands' incomes if that work had to be purchased from others. In short, the economic exploitation of women helps bring about gender inequality. ■

THE AGING PROCESS

The Heinz company once tried to market dietetic food to older persons under the name "Senior Foods." It turned out to be a flop. A perceptive observer explained, "People didn't want to be seen eating the stuff. It was labeling them old—and in our society, it is still an embarrassment to be old." Another company, Johnson & Johnson, made a similar mistake when it introduced Affinity shampoo. Its first TV commercial featured a chance meeting between a middle-aged woman and a former boyfriend. He says, "You still look great." By emphasizing age, the commercial failed to sell the product and was soon pulled off the air (Gilman, 1986).

The bottom line is that American culture is youth oriented. Even though the U.S. population is rapidly aging (see Figure 9.7), growing old bothers many older Americans. This feeling is related to the biological and psychological effects of aging. But social forces, such as society's tendency to define older persons as a national burden rather than a national treasure, play an important role, as well. These social forces can aggravate or diminish the biological and psychological effects of aging.

ARRESTING AGING Biological aging does not affect all people in the same way. Social factors and lifestyles, such as exercise, can retard aging. Those who are physically active usually look and feel younger than those who sit in lounge chairs waiting for the Grim Reaper. ■

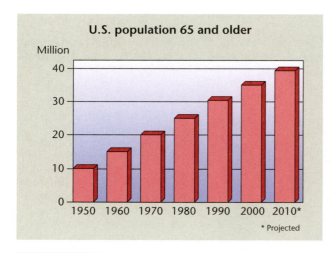

U.S. population 65 and older

FIGURE 9.7

An Aging Boom

Even though there are more and more older people in the United States, growing old still bothers many older Americans. Social forces—such as society's tendency to define the aged as a national burden rather than a national treasure—can make people feel bad about getting old.

Critical Thinking: *How can you tell if someone is prejudiced against older people? How can this problem be minimized?*

Source: Data from U.S. Census Bureau, 2003.

■ Biological Consequences of Aging

Sooner or later, we all gradually lose our energies and our ability to fight off diseases. This natural physical process of aging is called **senescence.** Biologists have been trying to crack the mystery of why it occurs but without much success. Some believe that humans are genetically programmed to age; others point to the breakdown of the body's immune system, cells, and endocrine and nervous systems. In any event, it is clear that senescence involves a decline in the body's functioning, which increases the vulnerability to death. It is a gradual process in which the changes come from within the individual, not from the environment. It is also both natural and universal, occurring in all people.

Old age has many biological consequences. The skin becomes wrinkled, rough, dry, and vulnerable to malignancies, bruises, and loss of hair. Because aging also causes the spinal disks to compress, most older persons lose 1 to 3 inches in height. Another result of aging is a loss of muscular strength. More important, blood vessels harden as people age, creating circulatory problems in the brain and heart—problems that raise the incidence of stroke and heart disease among older people. Functioning of the kidneys shows the greatest decline with advancing age. Although aging produces all of these deteriorative effects, they do not cause disability in most older persons.

Aging also affects sensory perceptions. By age 65, over 50 percent of men and 30 percent of women in the United States suffer hearing losses severe enough to hinder social interaction. Visual acuity also declines with age: 87 percent of those over age 45 wear glasses compared with only 30 percent of those under 45. For most people, though, hearing and visual problems are generally inconveniences, not disabilities (Butler, 2001; Kart, 1990).

■ Psychological Consequences of Aging

Aging affects such psychological processes as psychomotor responses, memory, and personality. Older persons tend to have slower, though more accurate, psychomotor responses—such as being able to type at lower speeds but with fewer errors—than young persons. Short-term memory—recall of recent events for a brief time—seems to decline with age, although memory of remote events does not. Old age, however, does not inevitably lead to **senility**, an abnormal condition characterized by serious memory loss, confusion, and loss of the ability to reason. Nor does aging necessarily lead to a decline in intellectual performance. In fact, **crystalline intelligence**—wisdom and insight into the human condition, as shown by one's skills in language, philosophy, music, or painting—continues to grow with age. Only **fluid intelligence**—the ability to grasp abstract relationships, as in mathematics, physics, or some other science—tends to stabilize or decline with age (Rutherford, 2000; Kart, 1990; Butler, 1984).

myth	It is natural for older people to become senile, experiencing serious memory loss, confusion, and loss of reasoning ability.
reality	Old age does not inevitably lead to senility. Senility is an abnormal condition, not a natural result of aging. The large majority of older people are not senile.

Much of the decline in psychomotor and intellectual performance amounts only to a slowing in work, not a falling off in quality. Older people may lose some mental speed, but their accumulated experience more than compensates for their loss of quick-

ness. In fact, compared with young persons, older persons may take longer to make a decision, but it is usually a better one. Therefore, contrary to the stereotyped assumption about older people automatically experiencing mental deterioration, many studies have shown the quality of job performance to improve with age. With advancing age, people also tend to change from an active to a passive orientation to their environment, becoming less inclined to bend the world to their own wishes and more likely to conform to and accommodate it (Butler, 2000, 1984).

■ Social Causes of Aging

Biological aging does not affect all people in the same way. The speed of aging, for example, varies greatly from one individual to another. Some people look 60 at age 75, and others who are 60 look 75. A number of social factors may determine the disparities. The older look, characterized by the sagging and wrinkling of the skin, may stem from too much sun exposure in earlier years, a legacy of an active, outdoor lifestyle. Lack of exercise, another lifestyle, may also speed up the aging process. Thus, those who sit in a rocking chair waiting for the Grim Reaper usually look and feel older than those who are physically active. Social isolation and powerlessness also enhance aging. These largely social and environmental factors suggest that if aging can be accelerated, it can also be retarded (Carstensen, 2001; Begley, 1990; Gelman, 1986).

Psychological aging does not affect all people in the same way, either, because of the intervention of social factors. Older persons who are well educated, and thus presumably accustomed to flexing their minds, maintain strong mental abilities. So do older persons who have complex and stimulating lifestyles. By contrast, deterioration of the intellect is more likely to occur among the lower classes and those whose lifestyle is marked by lack of mental activity, rigid adherence to routine, and low satisfaction with life.

myth	Worldwide, aging has the same impact on people's memory skills.
reality	Older people in China generally have sharper memories than their peers in the United States.

The society's definition of *aging* also influences the impact of aging on mental ability. In their cross-societal study, Becca Levy and Ellen Langer (1994) gave a memory test to comparable samples of young and old people in the United States and China. They found that the U.S. youths turned in a slightly better performance than the Chinese youths. But the older people in China were found to have sharper memories than their U.S. counterparts (see Figure 9.8). A self-fulfilling prophecy is apparently at work here: Widely respected in Chinese society for being wise, elders are often asked for advice, thus creating considerable opportunities for keeping the aging mind active and sharp. But older people in U.S. society are less respected and less often given such opportunities.

■ Age Prejudice and Discrimination

Older people can be said to be victims of *ageism,* prejudice and discrimination against older people. Like race and gender, age is frequently used as the basis for judging and reacting to people, regardless of their individual characteristics.

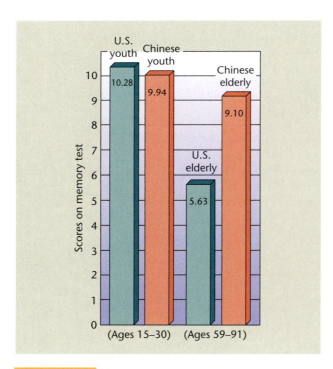

FIGURE 9.8

Societal Impact on Older People's Memory

Memory declines only slightly among older Chinese but considerably more among their American counterparts. A self-fulfilling prophecy seems to be at work there: Respected in society for being wise, Chinese elders are often asked for advice, thus creating opportunities for keeping the aging mind active and sharp. This isn't true of how American society treats its elders, thus with the reverse effect.

Critical Thinking: *When you get older, what will you do to keep your memory sharp?*

Source: Data from Becca Levy and Ellen Langer, "Aging Free from Negative Stereotypes," *Journal of Personality and Social Psychology,* 66 (June 1994), p. 994.

Prejudice against older people is often expressed in various ways. When an 82-year-old man went to visit a doctor with the complaint that his left knee was stiff and painful, the physician examined it. Then he said, "Well, what do you expect? After all, it's an 82-year-old knee." The patient retorted, "Sure it is. But my right knee is also 82, and it's not bothering me a bit" (Dychtwald, 1989). In fact, age prejudice, with its underlying stereotype of older people as frail or weak, as shown by that doctor, has become so ingrained in many people that they are unaware of its existence. Consider an AT&T commercial in which the older woman's son calls "just to say I love you, Ma." It won the hearts of many television viewers because they were apparently touched by how sweet the son was to his mother. But they did not realize that it also implied that older people waste their time doing nothing. As one older person says about the commercial, "What do you think we do—just sit around waiting for someone to call?" (Beck, 1990b).

Prejudice is also evident in the common beliefs that old people are set in their ways, old fashioned, forgetful, and spend their days dozing in a rocking chair. Some of these ageist beliefs are expressed in jokes such as "Old college presidents never die; they just lose their faculties." Prejudice can further be found in mass communication: In prime-time television shows, older people tend to be depicted as evil, unsuccessful, and unhappy. Stereotypes about older people being accident prone, rigid, dogmatic, and unproductive are often used to justify firing older workers, pressuring them to retire, or refusing to hire them (Brewer, 2000; Meer, 1986; Levin and Levin, 1980).

Discrimination against elders can be seen in mandatory retirement laws, substandard nursing homes, and the domestic neglect and abuse of elders. Older people often lose their jobs or are refused employment because they are said to be *overqualified*—a code word for "too old," or an expression of age bias (Gregory, 2001; Schellhardt, 1998). Even people who are well intentioned may unconsciously practice discrimination by patronizing older persons, treating them like children. As the famous psychologist B. F. Skinner (1983) observed from his perspective as a 79-year-old:

> Beware of those who are trying to be helpful and too readily flatter you. Second childishness brings you back within range of those kindergarten teachers who exclaim, "But *that* is very *good!*" Except that now, instead of saying, "My, you are really growing up!" they will say, "You are not really getting old!"

In some respects, though, older persons are far from oppressed. Especially in government and politics, many leaders are age 65 or older. And older people are such a powerful political force that many elected officials are afraid to anger them by cutting their Social Security payments.

Aging in Global Perspective

Older people generally enjoy higher status in traditional societies than in modern industrialized societies. Part of the reason is that it is no mean feat to live to old age in traditional societies, which typically have far fewer older persons than modern societies, as Figure 9.9 shows. Thus, by merely living to be old at a time when few survive past middle age, older persons earn a certain respect.

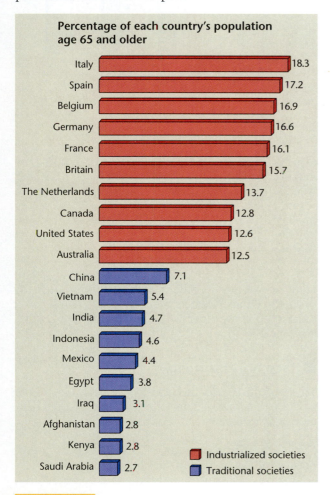

Percentage of each country's population age 65 and older

Italy	18.3
Spain	17.2
Belgium	16.9
Germany	16.6
France	16.1
Britain	15.7
The Netherlands	13.7
Canada	12.8
United States	12.6
Australia	12.5
China	7.1
Vietnam	5.4
India	4.7
Indonesia	4.6
Mexico	4.4
Egypt	3.8
Iraq	3.1
Afghanistan	2.8
Kenya	2.8
Saudi Arabia	2.7

■ Industrialized societies
■ Traditional societies

FIGURE 9.9

Fewer Older People in Traditional Societies

Older people generally enjoy higher status in traditional societies than in modern societies. One reason is that it is no small feat to live to old age in a traditional society.

Critical Thinking: *Why do traditional countries have far fewer older people?*

Source: Data from U.S. Census Bureau, 2002

In addition, because traditional societies change slowly, the knowledge and skills of older persons remain useful. Their experience is greatly valued. They are the community's experts. Not surprisingly, throughout Africa, growing old results in rising status and increased respect. For example, among the Igbo of Northwestern Africa, older people are widely regarded as wise, consulted for their wisdom, and accorded great respect. In Central and Southern Africa the male Bantu elder is known as "the Father of His People" and revered as such. In Samoa, too, old age is considered the best time of life, and elders are highly respected. Similar respect for older persons has also been observed in various other countries, from Thailand to rural Mexico (Posner, 1995; Cowgill, 1974).

In many societies, however, the norm changed with the arrival of industrialization. Older people lost their previous role and status. No longer were they regarded the storehouses of a community's knowledge or the guardians of its traditions because the knowledge important to the community changed and the traditions lost their hold. Thus, in many modern societies, older people lose status because their skills become obsolete. The loss of status can also be found in rural areas that have been touched by modernization. In a remote community in the Nepal Himalayas, for example, older people are unhappy with their lot, wishing that they were dead, complaining that their children have abandoned them, and trying to drown their sorrows in home-brewed liquor every day. The reason is that many of their young men have gone to India to work on construction projects and have brought back ideas and attitudes that have no room for the traditional value of filial devotion (Gilleard and Gurkan, 1987; Goldstein and Beall, 1982).

Modernization does not always have such adverse effects on older persons, though. Faced with an extremely high level of industrialization, Japan mostly continues to embrace its long-standing tradition of respect for old people. This tradition is derived from the Confucian principle of filial duty, which requires children to repay their parents with a debt of gratitude for bringing them up. It is further supported by a sharply inegalitarian social structure that requires inferiors, like servants, students, and children, to respect superiors, like masters, teachers, and parents (Palmore and Maeda, 1985). Nevertheless, extreme modernization has reduced the older person's status in Japan, though to a much less degree than in the United States (Kristof, 1997).

In contrast to Japan, the United States is founded on the ideology of equality and individualism. With egalitarianism opposing the traditional inequality between old and young, older people began to lose their privileged status when independence was declared in 1776. The emphasis on individualism also helped loosen the sense of obligation between young and old. Assisted by this ideological background, excessive industrialization has brought down the status of older people in the United States. Today, it sometimes seems as if older people are expected to do nothing but wait to die. Older people can be imprisoned in a **roleless role**—being assigned no role in society's division of labor.

SOCIAL DIVERSITY IN AGING

In the multicultural U.S. society, the experience of aging varies among people of different social classes, races, and ethnicities, as well as between women and men.

■ Social Class

Social class exerts a powerful influence on the lives of older people. Compared with working-class and poor persons, older persons of the middle and upper classes live better because they have greater resources—more education, more money, better health, better housing, and fewer worries. Not surprisingly, the positive aspects of aging presented earlier are often found in the higher social classes, and the problems associated with aging are concentrated among the working class and the poor (Atchley, 2000).

■ Gender

Living longer, women outnumber men in later years. Consequently, a greater number of older women live alone, without a spouse (see Figure 9.10). Older women are also more likely to suffer financially as a result of being divorced or widowed. Although gainful employment has increased significantly among women, a substantial number of older women remain completely dependent on their husbands' earnings. Even if they have been gainfully employed, most of these women have been paid much less than men, so their retirement incomes are substantially lower (Macdonald and Rich, 2001; Atchley, 2000).

Elderly women also face special issues when they divorce or remarry. If an elderly man and his longtime wife want to get a divorce, their adult children will tend to shake their heads at both of them. (This has inspired a joke about a couple in their late 90s visiting a divorce lawyer. When asked why they have waited so long, they say, "Because our children are all dead now.") But when it comes to remarriage, adult children tend to be more critical of their father's girlfriend than of their mother's boyfriend. An older woman, then, has to work harder to win approval from the man's children. Also consider that it is al-

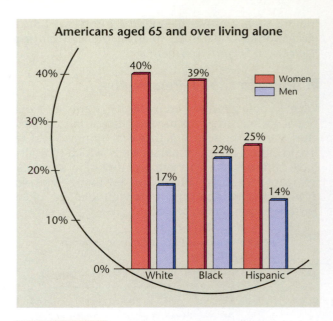

FIGURE 9.10

Gender, Old Age, and Living Alone

Because older women live longer than older men, they are more likely to end up living alone. Older women are also more likely to have limited financial resources and to find it hard to get married again.

Critical Thinking *What can be done to improve the living situation of older women?*

Source: Data from Joni Seager, *The Penguin Atlas of Women in the World* (New York: Penguin Group, 2003).

ready harder for an older woman to find a husband in the first place because there are considerably fewer older men than older women (Fram, 2003; Zaslow, 2003b).

■ Race and Ethnicity

The impact of race and ethnicity on the experience of aging can be seen in the differences in later life among various racial and ethnic groups.

Native Americans Older Native Americans are the poorest older population yet the least likely to have access to social and government services. Native Americans are also unique in their rejection of the concept of retirement; their elders continue to work in the family or community until they become physically incapable. It is a tradition among older Native Americans to help support their children and care for their grandchildren. Given the recent revitalization of their culture, the prestige of elders has risen to a point where they are now actively sought out as religious and personal counselors or as narrators of tribal traditions and folk stories. While the rates of alcoholism and suicide are very high among Native Americans as a whole, they are lower among older than younger persons. A major reason is that older Native Americans are more likely to have developed a strong tribal identity and thus avoid the stress of being caught between two cultures, unable to feel at home in either (Atchley, 2000; Markides and Mindel, 1987).

African Americans   Older African Americans experience the effects of racial discrimination to a greater degree than younger ones. In their youth, a large majority of older African Americans were relegated to low-paying jobs and substandard housing. In old age, they struggle with the problems of having lower Social Security benefits, fewer private pensions, and higher incidences of illness and disability than older whites. Older African Americans are also more likely than older whites to be forced out of the labor market early because of poor health, which helps to create great dissatisfaction with and poor adjustment to retirement. But older African Americans are more likely than older whites to receive aid from relatives because of the greater prevalence of extended families among African Americans. And older African Americans have lower suicide rates than older whites (Atchley, 2000; Markides and Mindel, 1987).

Hispanic Americans   Generally, older Hispanic Americans have better health and higher retirement incomes than either older African Americans or Native Americans, but they are less healthy and well-off than older Anglo and Asian Americans. They tend to retire because of declining health, but they usually refrain from doing so completely and permanently. Instead, they generally withdraw gradually from the labor force, with intermittent periods of unemployment. Part of the reason is a desire to contribute as long as possible to the system of mutual support among Hispanic family members, which is stronger than among Anglo and African American families. This family system, in turn, helps explain the relatively low rate of mental problems among older Hispanics because the individual is protected from outside stress. The strong family system, coupled with the Catholic background, can also explain the low incidence of suicide among older Hispanics (Atchley, 2000; Markides and Mindel, 1987).

Asian Americans   Financial situations vary among older Asian Americans, ranging from relatively high retirement incomes for the Japanese to low incomes for the Filipinos. As a group, however, older Asian Americans have lower incomes than older whites. But the Asians tend to be in better health, probably because of their lower-fat, lower-cholesterol diet (Atchley, 2000). The traditional respect accorded Asian American elders still exists, despite the eroding influence of the mainstream U.S. culture. Older Asian Americans are either equally or more likely than the general population to suffer from depression and emotional distress. Generally, those who are less assimilated into U.S. culture are more likely than others to have psychological problems (Markides and Mindel, 1987).

THE FUTURE OF AGING

What will it be like to age in the United States 20 or 30 years from now? Older people will probably have a higher overall educational level and occupational status, perhaps destroying the stereotype of doddering, senile oldsters. The divorce rate of older people will probably increase, too, because as people expect to live longer, they may demand more from their marriages. Social pressure against taking early retirement and receiving Social Security will probably increase because of the high cost of providing income to retirees. Over the last few years, there has already been a significant rise in the percentage of older Americans staying on the job (Walsh, 2001; Calmes, 1997).

The prediction that can be made with most confidence, however, is that the size of the older population will grow because older Americans are living longer and are healthier. If present trends continue, by the year 2020, older people will make up more than 20 percent of the U.S. population compared to about 12 percent today. There will be more geriatric day-care centers offering part-time supervision and care, including medical treatment, rehabilitation, and counseling. The political power of older people, already considerable, will likely increase, as well (Reuters, 1998; Thurow, 1996).

Other consequences of the growth in the older population are less certain. Some people argue that prejudice against the aged will decline with society's greater familiarity with them. But prejudice against a minority often *increases* as the size of the group grows because its members are more likely to be seen as a threat. If unemployment increases, as it did in the early 1990s, younger unemployed workers may resent older persons who hold jobs. Even those who are employed may see older high-status workers as obstacles to their own upward mobility. However, if the economy is strong, age conflict is unlikely to break out. One reason is that jobs will be abundant. Another reason is that as a result of the low birth rates during the 1960s and 1970s, labor will be scarce. Thus, employment opportunities for older people may increase, and workers young and old will enjoy greater bargaining power with their employers.

sociological frontiers

The Games Girls Like to Play in Cyberspace

As we have observed, young parents, female professionals, and well-educated parents are inclined to socialize their children into more gender-neutral roles. But social influences outside the home, such as those from peers and television commercials, continue to steer children toward gender-stereotyped games in cyberspace.

Consider what happened when Ike Onley brought home a "Star Wars" CD-ROM for his 6-year-old daughter. He had assumed that she would enjoy the shoot-em-up game. But soon after he loaded the game, his daughter lost interest. When he asked why, she said, "It's boring." Later, however, she took a liking to more female-oriented games, which centered on makeup, role-playing, and relationships.

Before the mid 1990s, few games catered to girls in cyberspace. The general view within the industry was that girls simply were not interested in computer games. Starting in November 1996, however, Mattel Media introduced "Barbie Fashion Designer," an interactive game in which girls select Barbie's dresses. The game caught on right away, selling more than 500,000 copies within a month. This popular game was soon followed by such spinoffs as "Barbie Magic Hair Styler" and "Barbie Nail Designer." For older girls, there were "Teen Digital Diva," "My Disney Kitchen," and "Secret Paths in the Forest." All have been selling fabulously because they provide, according to an industry insider, what "girls want most," such as characters "with which girls can relate and develop emotional connections."

Despite the popularity of these feminine games, some girls enjoy action games without feeling alienated. Girls who are into the shoot-'em-up game "Quake," for example, can get together at the all-female "Quake" tournaments. But such girls are a distinct minority. Most are still attracted to feminine games, while most boys continue to enjoy shooting bad guys and blowing things up in the virtual world. Such differences between girls and boys in playing computer games shows how traditional gender roles have invaded cyberspace (Gahr, 1998; Race, 1998).

 ■ For more of the latest Sociological Frontiers, look up Continuing Update at www.ablongman.com/thio6e.

using sociology

How to Reduce Gender Inequality

In this chapter, we have seen that men still typically enjoy greater rewards in the workplace, including higher salaries and better positions. Sociologists Cecilia Ridgeway and Shelley Correll (2000) have found that this inequality derives from the popular belief that men are more competent than women. So, how can this belief be eroded and gender inequality be reduced?

1. Actively recruit skilled women for valued and well-paid jobs in greater numbers than now. The presence of many competent women in the workplace will likely reduce their colleagues' competence bias against them.
2. Pay women the same as men for work of comparable worth. Because equal pay for both sexes implies equal competence, people will regard women more competent than before.
3. Make public the real distribution of pay among employees. This will create pressure for greater equality in pay, which will, in turn, undercut the biased presumptions about women being less competent than men.
4. Hold the firm accountable for equal treatment of women and men. The more accountable the company is for gender-fair evaluations, the more women will be hired and promoted into valued positions, which will reduce the competence bias against women.
5. Make the workplace more family friendly, providing child care, flexible work schedules, and other provisions for family duties. Doing so will free women to participate more fully in the workforce and to pursue more demanding jobs with greater authority and higher pay. Having more such women in the workplace will undermine the presumptions of women's lesser competence.

Thinking critically, do you agree that gender inequality can be significantly reduced by taking these five steps? Why or why not?

■ CHAPTER REVIEW

1. *What are the traditional gender roles of men and women in the United States?* Men are expected to be breadwinners, aggressive, and ambitious. Women are expected to be homemakers, passive, and dependent. Consequently, the sexes tend to behave differently. *Are these gender roles the same all over the world?* No. They are different in some societies, although similar in most other societies. *Do biological differences between the sexes make women inferior to men?* No. In some ways, women seem biologically superior and in other ways, men seem superior. *How does culture influence gender-role differences?* Culture defines what the gender differences should be, and through socialization, people develop those differences.

2. *How do we learn our gender roles?* We learn our gender roles through socialization by the family, peer group, school, and media. *What is the process by which children learn gender roles?* Gender roles are learned through conditioning, imitation, identification, and cognition.

3. *What is sexism?* It involves prejudice and discrimination against women based on the belief that they are inferior to men. *Do women today match men in educational attainment?* More women than men are now attending and graduating from college. *Have women in the workplace achieved equality with men?* No. Women still tend to hold lower-status jobs and to be paid less than men. *How have U.S. women fared in politics?* They have fared better than before, but women are still far from achieving political parity with men. *What is the nature of gender inequality in religion?* Women are generally accorded low status and are refused ordination in conservative religious organizations. *How has the women's movement changed over time?* Before 1920, the movement fought for women's right to vote. Since the 1960s, the aim has been to end all forms of gender discrimination, but the plight of poor and minority women has largely been ignored. The young feminists of today deal with such issues while inviting men to join them.

4. *What is the sociological nature of sexual harassment?* It reflects an attempt by the powerful to control the less powerful through unwelcome acts of a sexual nature. *What is the nature of the violence against women?* The most common forms of violence against women are being sexually assaulted by men, especially dates or acquaintances, and being physically beaten by husbands. *How does social diversity in U.S. society affect women's experience of gender inequality?* The experience varies with the individual's race, class, and cultural background. *How does global analysis reveal the impact of gender inequality on women?* Gender inequality affects women in developing countries much more than in affluent societies.

5. *According to functionalists, why are gender roles still functional in industrial societies?* With men playing the instrumental role and women the expressive role, the family's smooth functioning can be ensured. *How do conflict theorists explain gender inequality?* It stems from the economic and sexual exploitation of women. *How does symbolic interactionism enhance understanding of gender inequality?* It shows how interaction between women and men often sustains or reinforces gender inequality.

6. *What are the biological and psychological consequences of aging?* With age, people become more vulnerable to disease. Many more specific changes also typically accompany old age—from wrinkled skin to declining visual acuity and slowing of psychomotor responses. *How do social forces influence aging?* These forces slow down or speed up the biological and psychological processes of aging. *What is ageism?* It is prejudice and discrimination against older people. *Why are older people in traditional societies more respected than their peers in modern societies?* Few people in traditional societies survive to old age. Moreover, because their society changes slowly, older people are admired and their knowledge and skills remain useful.

7. *How do class, gender, race, and ethnicity impact the older person's life?* Older people of the higher social classes live better than those of the lower classes. Older women are more likely than older men to live alone, to have fewer financial resources, and to face more difficulties in getting married. Older members of various minority groups are poorer than their white counterparts but are more likely to receive support from their children. Among minority groups themselves, differences exist, as exemplified by the stronger support older Hispanic Americans receive from their children compared with older African Americans.

8. *What is the status of aging likely to be a few decades from now?* Older people will likely make up a larger share of the U.S. population, and their educational level and occupational status will likely be higher. But social pressure against early retirement and Social Security will likely increase unless the economy is strong.

9. *Do young girls and boys like the same kinds of computer games?* No. Most girls prefer to play fashion- and relationship-oriented games, whereas most boys prefer action-oriented games. *How can gender inequality be reduced in the workplace?* By actively recruiting skilled women, paying women the same as men, publicizing pay distribution, holding employers accountable for equal treatment of women and men, and making the workplace more family friendly.

◼ KEY TERMS

Crystalline intelligence Wisdom and insight into the human condition, as shown by one's skills in language, philosophy, music, or painting (p. 261).

Expressive role A role that requires taking care of personal relationships (p. 257).

Feminism The belief that women and men should be equal in various aspects of their lives (p. 253).

Fluid intelligence The ability to grasp abstract relationships, as in mathematics, physics, or some other science (p. 261).

Gender role The pattern of attitudes and behaviors that a society expects of its members because of their being female or male (p. 242).

Instrumental role A role that requires performance of a task (p. 257).

Roleless role Being assigned no role in society's division of labor, which is a predicament of older people in industrial society (p. 264).

Senescence The natural physical process of aging (p. 260).

Senility An abnormal condition characterized by serious memory loss, confusion, and loss of the ability to reason (p. 261).

Sexism Prejudice and discrimination based on one's gender (p. 248).

Sexual harassment An unwelcome act of a sexual nature (p. 255).

QUESTIONS FOR DISCUSSION AND REVIEW

GENDER ROLES

1. What are gender roles, and what traits does U.S. society associate with them?
2. How are gender roles different or similar in various societies?
3. How do biology and culture influence the development of gender roles?

GENDER SOCIALIZATION

1. How do the family, peer group, school, and mass media contribute to gender-role socialization?
2. How do girls and boys learn gender roles through the processes of conditioning, imitation, identification, and cognition?

SPHERES OF GENDER INEQUALITY

1. What is the nature of sexism?
2. What is the current status of women in educational institutions?
3. How have women fared in employment and politics in recent years?

4. What impact does sexism have on women in religion?
5. What is the history of the women's movement?

CONSEQUENCES OF GENDER INEQUALITY

1. How did the U.S. Supreme Court define sexual harassment, and why is harassment so common?
2. How does the social diversity of U.S. society affect the experience of gender inequality?
3. In what ways is the impact of gender inequality similar and different around the world?

SOCIOLOGICAL PERSPECTIVES ON GENDER INEQUALITY

1. According to the functionalist and conflict perspectives, what is the origin of gender inequality?
2. What insight into gender inequality can be learned from the symbolic interactionist perspective?

THE AGING PROCESS

1. What are some of the biological and psychological consequences of aging?
2. How do social factors blunt or worsen the biological and psychological effects of aging?
3. What is the nature of ageism in the United States?
4. Why are older persons more respected in traditional societies?

SOCIAL DIVERSITY IN AGING

1. How do social class and gender affect the experience of aging?
2. How do the lives of older people of various races and ethnicities differ?

THE FUTURE OF AGING

1. What kind of life do you think older people will have 20 or 30 years from now?
2. What economic factors could minimize conflict between young and old?

SOCIOLOGICAL FRONTIERS/USING SOCIOLOGY

1. What kinds of computer games do young girls like to play? Why?
2. How can gender inequality in the workplace be reduced?

SUGGESTED READINGS

Faludi, Susan. 1999. *Stiffed: The Betrayal of the American Man.* New York: William Morrow. Offers the provocative idea that the media-driven, ornamental culture of manhood, as symbolized by Calvin Klein underwear ads, has made American men more feminine—that is, more passive, less powerful, and less confident of making a living.

Pollack, William S., and Todd Shuster. 2000. *Real Boys' Voices*. New York: Random House. Analyzes how the boy culture, or "boy code," makes boys feel ashamed about expressing weakness and vulnerability.

Posner, Richard A. 1995. *Aging and Old Age*. Chicago: University of Chicago Press. Discusses the social, biological, and economic aspects of aging.

Rosen, Ruth. 2000. *The World Split Open: How the Modern Women's Movement Changed America*. New York: Viking. A greatly detailed history of the women's movement, including both its achievements and failures.

Sommers, Christina Hoff. 2000. *The War against Boys: How Misguided Feminism Is Harming Our Young Men*. New York: Simon & Schuster. A highly controversial argument that since the late 1980s, boys have been treated worse than girls and thus are doing far worse in school.

■ Additional Resources

The New York Times
expect the world®
nytimes.com

Expand your knowledge of the concepts discussed in this chapter by reading the following current and historical articles from the *New York Times*. Go to the "eThemes of the Times" section of the Companion Website (www.ablongman.com/thio6e):

"The Race for a Pill to Save Memory"

"Desire for Sons Drives Use of Prenatal Scans in China"

Research Navigator.com

Research Navigator, a research database, provides immediate access to hundreds of full-text articles from EBSCO's ContentSelect Academic Journal Database. If the Research Navigator access code was included with your textbook, go to the website www.research navigator.com and read the following articles related to this chapter by typing in the article number:

Petersen, William. "Age and Sex." *Society*, May/Jun2001, Vol. 38 Issue 4, p46, 7p. Accession Number: 4326126. Discusses the effects of age structure and sex ratio on the economy and politics of the United States.

Vincent, Susan. "Preserving Domesticity: Reading Tupperware in Women's Changing Domestic, Social and Economic Roles." *Canadian Review of Sociology and Anthropology*, May2003, Vol. 40 Issue 2, p171, 26p. Accession Number: 9935955. Explores the changing role of women through writings about Tupperware.

Families

myths & realities

myth *There is no difference between dating and marriage in the choice of partners. In both cases, people choose partners close to their own level of attractiveness.*

reality The similarity in attractiveness is greater among married couples than among dates. In marriage, people usually choose someone whose looks match theirs, but this is less true in dating (p. 279).

myth *So many American couples divorce that few people want to get married anymore.*

reality Despite high divorce rates, marriage remains popular. The United States has the highest marriage rate in the industrial world (p. 282).

myth *The traditional U.S. family, which consists of a breadwinner father and a homemaker mother, has been around since the colonial period.*

reality On the farms of colonial days, the family was, in effect, a two-career family, with the wife working side by side with her husband. Only toward the end of the nineteenth century, when industrialization was in full swing, did the wife lose her status as her husband's economic partner and acquire the subordinate position of homemaker (p. 284).

myth *Children from single-parent families are more likely than other children to have problems because their fathers are not around.*

reality It is not the absence of a father in the single-parent family that causes the problems. It is the other factors that characterize the two-parent family with problem children: low income, poor living conditions, and lack of parental supervision (p. 286).

myth *Couples who have lived together without being married are less likely to get divorced. Cohabitation works like a trial marriage and prepares the couple for marital success.*

reality There are more divorces among couples who have cohabited than among those who have not. The reason for marital failure, though, is not the prior experience of cohabitation; it is the lack of strong commitment to marriage among people who choose to cohabitate (p. 288).

An hour before dawn in Phoenix, Arizona, Rick Mauntel has already showered, dressed for work, and had coffee. At 6 A.M., he wakes up his 4-year-old son and 2-year-old daughter, dresses them, and makes them breakfast while his wife Barbara gets ready for work. Later, Rick drops off the children at the day-care center before heading for his job as a project manager at Motorola. Barbara Mauntel also works at Motorola as a payroll manager. Her turn to take care of the children starts at 6 P.M., when she leaves her office. She picks them up at day care and then goes home to feed them, bathe them, and read to them before bedtime (Shellenbarger, 1996).

The traditional image of the U.S. family shows Mom tending her two kids in a house in the suburbs while Dad drives off to work. But in reality, such a family is relatively rare today. Meanwhile, new forms of the family unit—especially two-career families, like the one just described—are fast becoming very common. In this chapter, we discuss various forms of family, not only in the United States but also around the world.

FAMILIES: A GLOBAL ANALYSIS

People who marry have, in effect, two families. One is the **family of orientation**, the family in which one grows up, made up of oneself and one's parents and siblings. The other is the **family of procreation**, which one establishes through marriage, consisting of oneself and one's spouse and children. As the abundance of jokes about mothers-in-law illustrates, the relationships between these two families can be complicated. Societies need norms that govern this relationship, as well as norms that assign roles within each family. Societies must offer the answers to questions like these: Who is part of my family? Who lives with whom? Who is an acceptable spouse? Who makes that decision?

All over the world, societies have given varied answers to these and other questions. The responses have much to do with family composition, norms of mate selection, rules of residence and descent, and rules of authority.

Family Composition

Who makes up a family? Societies' definitions of a family can be classified into two basic types. In the United States, a family has long been defined as a **nuclear family**, consisting of two parents and their unmarried children. It is also called a *conjugal family* because its members are related by virtue of the marriage between the parents. This type of family is quite common in Western industrial societies.

Another type of family is more prevalent in less industrialized societies. It includes not only the nuclear family but also grandparents, uncles, aunts, and cousins. When a nuclear family lives in close proximity to other relatives, interacting with them frequently and acting together as a unit for some purposes, it becomes an **extended family**, consisting of two parents, their unmarried children, and other relatives. This kind of family is also called a *consanguine family* because the blood tie among relatives is considered more important than the marital bond. In traditional Chinese and Japanese extended families, for example, the tie between a married man and his mother is much stronger than his bond to his wife. In fact, if a mother does not like her son's wife, she can force him to divorce the wife.

■ Mate Selection

Societies differ, too, in their norms specifying who selects marriage partners. In many traditional societies, **arranged marriages**—in which partners are selected by the couples's parents—are the rule. The young couple may not even know each other until the wedding day, but they are expected to learn to love each other during the marriage. They are considered too emotional to choose compatible mates. Usually, the parents base their choice of a husband for their daughter on how financially secure his family is, how agreeable the prospective daughter-in-law is to the young man's mother, and how compatible the couple's personalities are. In arranged marriages, the brides are usually very young, aged 15 to 19. Such marriages are most prevalent in relatively poor and traditional societies, where marrying off a young daughter often means having one fewer mouth to feed and avoiding the dishonor of her bearing illegitimate children (see Figure 10.1, p. 274). In affluent and modern societies,

ALL IN THE FAMILY An extended family includes not only the nuclear family, which consists of two parents and their unmarried children, but also grandparents, uncles, aunts, and cousins. Members of the extended family live in close proximity to one another, interacting frequently and acting together as a group. ■

such as the United States, women marry later and make their own decisions on whom to marry.

Everywhere, however, the selection of a partner depends to some degree on society's norms regarding which partners are appropriate. In most societies, people are required to practice **exogamy** (literally, "marrying outward"), the act of marrying someone from outside one's group—such as the clan, tribe, or village. Contrasted with exogamy is **endogamy** ("marrying within"), the act of marrying someone from within one's own group. Endogamy stops short, though, of violating the incest taboo because endogamous societies do not encourage marriage between close relatives.

Other norms govern the number of spouses a person may have. **Monogamy**—the marriage of one man to one woman—is the most common form in the world. But many societies, especially Muslim and small, preindustrial ones, approve of **polygamy**, the marriage of one person to two or more people of the opposite sex. It is rare for a society to allow the practice of **polyandry**, marriage of one woman to two or more men. But many societies permit **polygyny**, marriage of one man to two or more women. A new variant of polygamy has become increasingly common in the United States. Rather than have several spouses at the same time, many persons have one spouse at a time, going through a succession of marriage, divorce, and remarriage. Such practice is not really polygamy but **serial monogamy**, the marriage of one person to two or more people but only one at a time.

■ Residence and Descent

In the United States, when a couple marries, they usually establish a home of their own, away from both families of orientation. They have what is called a **neolocal residence**, a home where the married couple live by themselves, away from both the husband's and the wife's families. Although this is the most common rule of residence in the United States, it is the least common in the world. People in most societies have a **patrilocal residence**, a home where the married couple live with the husband's family. People in other societies have a **matrilocal residence**, a home where the married couple live with the wife's family.

There are similar rules about who are considered our close relatives. The most common such rule in the world is **patrilineal descent**, the norm that recognizes only the father's family as a child's close relatives. The children belong to their father's family of orientation, not that of their mother, and they adopt their father's family name. But daughters lose their family name when they marry, and their tie to their father's family is not permanent. Only sons, not daughters, may inherit property from the father in patrilineal societies. Much less common is **matrilineal descent**, the norm that recognizes only the mother's family as a child's close relatives. Even in matrilineal societies, however, daughters rarely have the right to inherit property. Usually, sons inherit property from their mother's brother.

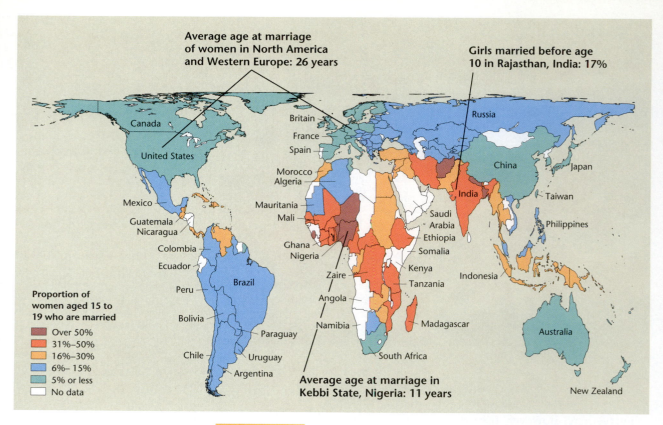

FIGURE 10.1

Where the Young Brides Are

In many relatively poor and traditional societies, women marry very young, at ages 15 to 19. Key reasons for marrying off a young daughter include having one less mouth to feed and the fear of her bearing illegitimate children and bringing dishonor to the family.

Critical Thinking: *What age do you think is too young to get married? Why?*

Source: From *The Penguin Atlas of Women in the World,* by Joni Seager, copyright © 1997, 2003 by Myriad Editions Ltd, maps & graphics. Used by permission of Penguin, a division of Penguin Group (USA) Inc.

The influence of patrilineal traditions seems to exist in U.S. society. Wives and children usually adopt only the husband's family name. But there is an observance of **bilateral descent,** the norm that recognizes both parents' families as the child's close relatives. Children feel closely related to both their father's and their mother's kin, and both sons and daughters may inherit property from their mother's and their father's families.

■ Authority

Societies differ in defining who has authority in the family. In most societies, authority rests with the oldest male. Thus, the **patriarchal family,** in which the dominant figure is the oldest male, is the most prevalent around the world. In such a family, the oldest male dominates everyone else. He allocates tasks, settles disputes, and makes other important decisions that affect family members.

Other options are a **matriarchal family,** in which the dominant figure is the oldest female, and an **egalitarian family,** in which authority is equally distributed between husband and wife. Globally, these two types of family are rare. A variant of the matriarchal family, however, has appeared in many industrial countries. In the United States, for example, many poor families are matriarchal by default. Either the father is not present or he has lost his dominant status because of chronic unemployment. Many other U.S. families, though still dominated by husbands, are also becoming increasingly egalitarian due to the women's movement.

SOCIOLOGICAL PERSPECTIVES ON THE FAMILY

The three perspectives in sociology shed light on different aspects of the family. Together, they can give us a deeper understanding of the family than each can alone.

Functionalist Perspective: Familial Functions

According to the functionalist perspective, the family performs certain functions for virtually all societies. The more important functions include sexual regulation, reproduction, socialization, economic cooperation, and emotional security.

Sexual Regulation   No society advocates total sexual freedom. Although societies have different sexual norms, all impose some control on who may have sex with whom. Even societies that encourage premarital and extramarital sex restrict and channel these activities so that they reinforce the social order. The Trobrianders of the South Pacific, for example, use premarital sex to determine whether a girl is fertile and to prepare adolescents for marriage. Traditional Inuit society condones extramarital sex but under conditions that do not disrupt family stability: As a gesture of hospitality, husbands offer their wives to overnight guests.

Traditionally, Western sexual norms have been relatively restrictive, demanding that people engage in sex only with their spouses. Tying sex to marriage seems to serve several functions. First, it helps minimize sexual competition, thereby contributing to social stability. Second, it gives people an incentive to marry. Even today, most young adults eventually feel dissatisfied with unstable, temporary sexual liaisons and find the prospect of a regular, secure sexual relationship in marriage attractive. And most divorced persons, who usually find their postmarital sex lives pleasurable, eventually remarry because sex with commitment is available in marriage. Finally, encouraging people to marry and confining sexual intercourse to those who are married tends to ensure that children will be well cared for.

Reproduction   In order to survive, a society must produce children to replace older adults who die, and practically all societies depend on the family to produce these new members. In some traditional societies, such as the Baganda in the African nation of Uganda, children are considered so precious that a marriage must be dissolved if the wife turns out to be barren. In many industrial nations, like the United States, families with children are rewarded with tax deductions.

Socialization   To replace members who pass away, a society needs not only biological reproduction but also *sociological reproduction*. It needs, in other words, to transmit its values to the new generation, to socialize them. As we saw in Chapter 3 (Socialization), the family is the most important agent of socialization. Because parents are likely to be deeply interested in their own children, they are generally more effective socializing agents than other adults.

Economic Cooperation   Besides socialization, children need physical care—food, clothing, and shelter. Fulfilling these needs is the core of the family's economic function, and it can facilitate effective social-

BLOOD THICKER THAN WATER   The family is the center of emotional life. Throughout life, the family is the most important source of primary relationships, the most likely place we turn to when we need comfort or reassurance. ■

ization. Generally, however, the family's economic role goes beyond care for children and embraces the whole family. Family members cooperate as an economic unit, working to earn income or doing household chores to minimize expenditures. Each person's economic fate rises and falls with that of the family as a whole.

Emotional Security   Finally, the family is the center of emotional life. As we saw in Chapter 3 (Socialization), the relationships we form in our families as children shape our personalities and create hard-to-break patterns for all of our relationships. Throughout life, the family is the most important source of primary relationships, the most likely group for us to turn to when we need comfort or reassurance.

■ Conflict Perspective: Violence and Exploitation

Through the functionalist perspective, we see the bright side of the family. But the family also has a dark side, as revealed by the conflict perspective.

First of all, the family, because of the strong feelings it generates, is a powerful source not just of love and care but also of pain and conflict. According to a major study, the family is the most violent institution in U.S. society, except the military in time of war (Gelles and Cornell, 1990). In most families, there are instances of conflict and violence, such as anger, physical punishment of children, and spouses poking and slapping each other. In fact, the family is one of the few groups in society empowered by law or tradition to hit its members. It is legal, for example, for parents to spank their children as a form of punishment. Moreover, many husbands who strike their wives are not arrested, prosecuted, or imprisoned (Mignon et al., 2002).

Second, as feminists emphasize, the family is a mechanism for men's exploitation of women (Delphy and Leonard, 1992; Thorne and Yalom, 1992). Homemakers and mothers have greatly contributed to the rise and maintenance of capitalism with such forms of labor as reproduction and care of children, food preparation, daily health care, and emotional support. Without this *household production*, men would not have been free to go out to work. Yet while men are paid for their work outside the home, women are not paid for their work inside the home. Ironically, women's household work is, on average, worth more than men's paid employment. If a woman were paid for her services as a mother and homemaker according to the wage scale for chauffeurs, babysitters, cooks, and therapists, she would earn more than most men do. By devaluing women's housework, however, the family serves the interests of male domination. Even in families where both spouses are gainfully employed, wives generally do most of the housework (Ingrassia and Wingert, 1995; Hochschild, 1989).

In short, according to the conflict perspective, the family is far from a "haven in a heartless world." It is seen as an extension of that world, full of violence and exploitation of women.

■ Symbolic Interactionist Perspective: Interaction and Happiness

Both the functionalist and conflict perspectives deal with the larger issue of what the family is like as a social institution. The symbolic interactionist perspective focuses on more immediate issues, such as how the interaction between husband and wife can bring marital happiness or unhappiness.

In a family, symbolic interaction occurs between husband and wife, between parent and child, between one sibling and another, and among all of these individuals. Using the symbolic interactionist perspective as a guide, researchers can focus on any of these interactions and learn how they affect the group. In his studies of marital interaction, John Gottman (2002, 1994) has observed many couples in his lab, concentrating not only on what the spouses say to each other but also on the tone of voice they use. He finds three different types of interaction. One is *validating* interaction, in which the partners compromise, showing mutual respect and accepting their differences. The second is *volatile* interaction, in which conflict erupts, resulting in a vehement, loud dispute. The third is *conflict-avoiding* interaction, in which the partners agree to disagree, making light of their differences rather than trying to confront and resolve them. The first type of interaction contributes most to marital happiness, the second type least, and the third is in between.

Gottman has also found another great contributor to marital happiness: *an excess of positive interactions over negative interactions.* Positive interactions involve acts of *thoughtful friendliness*, such as touching, smiling, and paying compliments. Negative interactions involve acts of *thoughtless nastiness,* such as ignoring, criticizing, and calling names. Among happy couples, there are at least five positive interactions for every one negative interaction, but among unhappy couples, there are less. Presumably, a similar excess of positive interactions involving others in the family, such as the parents and children, can also bring happiness to the family as a whole (Gottman, 2002, 1994; Marano, 1997).

For a quick review of the three perspectives on the family, see the Theoretical Thumbnail that follows.

Diverse Aspects of the Family

Perspective	Focus	Insights
Functionalist	Positive aspects of the family	The family is useful to society for providing sexual regulation, reproduction, socialization, economic cooperation, and emotional support.
Conflict	Negative aspects of the family	The family is full of violence and female exploitation.
Symbolic Interactionist	Interaction of happy and unhappy couples	Happy couples are more likely than unhappy ones to have more positive interactions than negative interactions.

PATTERNS OF U.S. MARRIAGES

In the United States, the family is, by and large, nuclear and monogamous and increasingly egalitarian. Its cornerstone is the relationship between husband and wife. In this section, we discuss how people prepare for marriage, how they choose a spouse, and how most U.S. couples achieve marital success.

■ Preparing for Marriage

Most people do not consciously prepare themselves for marriage or diligently seek a person to marry. Instead, they engage in activities that gradually build up a momentum that launches them into marriage. They date, they fall in love, and they decide to commit to one another. In each of these steps, they usually follow patterns set by society.

The Dating Ritual Developed largely after World War I came to an end in 1918, the U.S. custom of dating has spread to many industrial countries. It has also changed in the United States in the last three decades. Before the 1970s, dating was relatively formal. Males had to ask for a date at least several days in advance. It was usually the male who decided where to go, paid for the date, opened doors, and was supposed to be chivalrous. The couple often went to an event, such as a movie, dance, concert, or ballgame.

Today, dating has become more casual. In fact, the word *date* now sounds a bit old fashioned to many young people. Usually, no one calls and asks for a date. Things are much more spontaneous and unstructured. A young man may meet a young woman at a snack bar and strike up a brief conversation with her. If he bumps into her a day or two later, he may ask if she wants to go to the beach, to the library, or to have a hamburger.

PLAYING THE FIELD Dating is a form of entertainment. More important, it provides opportunities for learning to get along with others—to develop companionship, friendship, and intimacy. Finally, dating offers opportunities for courting and falling in love with one's future spouse. ■

Young men and women are also more likely today than in the past to hang out—socialize in unpartnered packs or get involved in a group activity—rather than pair off for secluded intimacy. Neither has the responsibility to ask the other out, which spares them much of the anxiety of formal dating. Getting together has also become less dominated by males. Females are more likely than before to ask males out, suggest activities, pay the expenses, and initiate sexual intimacies. Premarital sex has also increased, but it tends to reflect true feelings and desires rather than the need for the male to prove himself or for the female to show gratitude (Gabriel, 1997; Strong, 2001).

The functions of dating, however, have remained fairly constant. It is still a form of entertainment. More important, dating provides opportunities for learning to get along with members of the opposite sex—to develop companionship, friendship, and intimacy. Finally, it offers opportunities for courting, for falling in love with one's future spouse. "Playing the field" does not lead to a higher probability of marital success, though. Those who married their first and only sweethearts are just as likely to have enduring and satisfying marriages as those who married only after dating many people (Gallagher, 2001; Whyte, 1992).

Romantic Love   Asked why they want to get married, Americans usually say, "Because I am in love." In U.S. society, the love between husband and wife is the foundation of the nuclear family. In fact, young people are most reluctant to marry someone if they do not love the person even though the person has all the qualities they desire in a spouse (see Figure 10.2). Many people in traditional societies, though, believe that love is too irrational to form the basis for a marriage and that intense love between husband and wife may even threaten the stability of the extended family. To them, it is more rational to marry for such pragmatic reasons as economic security and good character.

But does romantic love really cause people to choose their mates irrationally? Many studies have suggested that the irrationality of love has been greatly exaggerated. An analysis of these studies led William Kephart and Davor Jedlicka (1991) to reach this conclusion: "Movies and television to the contrary, U.S. youth do not habitually fall in love with unworthy or undesirable characters. In fact, [they] normally make rather sound choices." In one study, when people in love were asked "Does your head rule your heart, or does your heart rule your head?" 60 percent answered, "The head rules." Apparently, romantic love is not the same as infatuation, which involves physical attraction to a person and a tendency

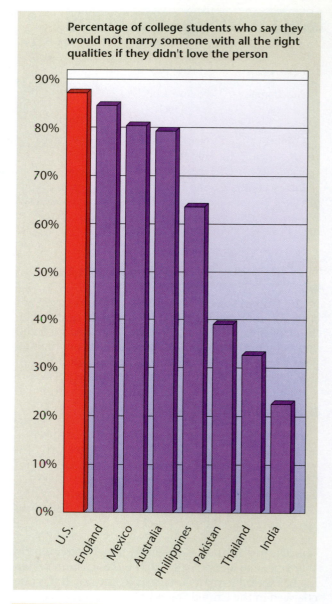

Percentage of college students who say they would not marry someone with all the right qualities if they didn't love the person

FIGURE 10.2

No Love, No Marriage

Most Americans would marry someone only if they loved that person. But people in traditional societies consider love too irrational to form a solid foundation for marriage. To them, it is more rational to marry someone who has all the qualities they desire in a spouse, even though they do not love that person.

Critical Thinking: *Do you consider romantic love to be the most important reason for marrying someone? Why or why not?*

Source: Data from Robert Levine et al., "Love and Marriage in Eleven Cultures," *Journal of Cross-Cultural Psychology,* 26 (September 1995), pp. 554–571.

to idealize that person. Romantic love is less emotionalized, but it is expected to provide intrinsic satisfactions, such as happiness, closeness, personal growth, and sexual satisfaction. These differ from the extrinsic rewards offered by a pragmatic, loveless marriage—rewards such as good earnings, a nice house, well-prepared meals, and overt respect.

In the United States over the last 40 years, the belief in romantic love as the basis for marriage has grown more fervent. In several studies in the 1960s, 1970s, 1980s, and 1990s, college men and women were asked, "If a person had all the other qualities you desired, would you marry this person if you were not in love with him/her?" Today, as opposed to in earlier decades, a greater proportion of young people say no (Levine et al., 1995; Simpson et al., 1986).

Marriage Choices

Romantic love is far from blind, but it does not develop in a social vacuum. It depends heavily on the partners' support from others, particularly family and friends. Such support is usually available if the couple believes in **homogamy**, marrying someone with social characteristics similar to one's own.

Most marriages occur between people within the same social class because of shared values, expectations, tastes, goals, and occupations. People also tend to choose mates of the same religious faith. The more cohesive and smaller the group is in a community, the more homogamous it is. Jews are therefore more likely to marry Jews than Catholics are to marry Catholics. Most marriages also involve members of the same race, as well (Gardyn, 2002).

There is also a tendency to marry people very close to one's own age. Most couples are only 2 years apart. But most men who marry at 25 have a wife who is 3 years younger; at 37, most men marry a woman 6 years younger. A major reason that older men tend to marry much younger women is that men generally place greater importance than women on physical attractiveness. But the age difference between brides and grooms increases only until the men reach age 50. After this time, most men marry women close to their own age again (Benokraitis, 2002; Mensch, 1986; Schulz, 1982).

Since people of similar race, religion, and class are likely to live close to one another, there also is a strong tendency to marry someone who lives nearby. This tendency may be weakening as cars and airplanes continue to increase mobility, yet most couples still come from the same city, town, or even neighborhood. According to many studies, there is more than a 50–50 chance that one's future spouse lives within walking distance (Kephart and Jedlicka, 1991). As James Bossard (1932) said, "Cupid may

have wings, but apparently they are not adapted for long flights."

We have seen how homogamy applies to the *social* characteristics of couples. What about their individual characteristics, such as aggressive personalities and talkativeness? Do they also follow the same pattern? According to Robert Winch's (1971) well-known theory of complementary needs, the answer is no. Winch argues that people with *different* personality traits are attracted to each other if these traits complement each other. This theory resembles the popular belief that opposites attract. Thus, aggressive men tend to marry passive women; weak men like strong women; talkative women go for quiet men; emotional men find rational women attractive; and so on. Winch's own research has supported this theory, but more recent studies by other investigators have backed the social-psychological version of homogamy—the theory that people with *similar* traits are attracted to each other (Benokraitis, 2002; Morell et al., 1989; Wilson, 1989). Perhaps, given the increase in gender equality in recent decades, men and women have become more alike. For example, men now seem more sensitive and women, more assertive.

myth	There is no difference between dating and marriage in the choice of partners. In both cases, people choose partners close to their own level of attractiveness.
reality	The similarity in attractiveness is greater among married couples than among dates. In marriage, people usually choose someone whose looks match theirs, but this is less true in dating.

Homogamy also reigns in regard to physical attractiveness. Everybody hopes for the person of their dreams, but most people end up marrying someone close to their own level of attractiveness. Interestingly, the similarity in attractiveness is greater among deeply committed couples than among casual ones. When people are playing the field, their looks may not match their dates'. But they are more likely to get serious with the dates who have about the same level of attractiveness (Stevens et al., 1990; Kalick and Hamilton, 1986).

Marital Happiness

With time, both the physical attraction and the idealization of romantic love are likely to fade, so that marital love involves mostly commitment. Love may be less exciting after marriage, but as William

KEY TO WINNING WEDLOCK The success of marriages depends on how we define *successful*. If the criterion is how people themselves rate their own marriages, then most U.S. marriages can be judged successful. Studies have shown that the majority of people say they are either "very happy" or "pretty happy" in their marriages. Regarding one's spouse as a friend is one of the characteristics found to be associated with a happy marriage. ◼

Kephart and Devor Jedlicka (1991) observe, it "provides the individual with an emotional insight and a sense of self-sacrifice not otherwise attainable," qualities that may be keys to marital success.

How successful are U.S. marriages? The answer obviously depends on how we define *successful*. Gerald Leslie and Sheila Korman (1989) suggest that in a successful marriage, the couple have few conflicts, basically agree on major issues, enjoy the same interests during their leisure time, and show confidence in and affection for each other. To others, this sounds like a static, spiritless relationship. Instead, some argue, a successful marriage is one that is zestful and provides opportunity for personal growth. Such disagreement among scholars suggests that a successful marriage is basically a value judgment, not an objective fact (Strong, 2001).

It is, therefore, best simply to look at whether people consider their own marriages successful, however experts might judge them. By this standard, most U.S. marriages are successful. Several studies have shown that the overwhelming majority (over 90 per-

cent) of people say they are either "very happy" or "pretty happy" with their marriages. In fact, married couples are much more likely than single people to say that they are happy, whether it is about love, sex, personal growth, or even job satisfaction (Strong, 2001; Waite, 1995; NORC, 1994). Marriage, however, rather than parenthood, is the focal point of marital happiness. As research has suggested, the presence of children often detracts from marital happiness because the couple see their relationship less as a romance and more as a working partnership. In fact, these working partners often find parenting so stressful that they feel relieved or happy after their children reach adulthood and leave home (White and Edwards, 1990).

What makes for marital happiness? By comparing happily married with unhappily married couples, researchers have come up with a long list of characteristics associated with happy marriages. Among these are having happily married parents; knowing the prospective spouse for at least two years; being engaged for at least two years; getting married at an age above the national average (about 27 for men and 25 for women); being religious or adhering to traditional values; regarding one's spouse as a friend; being of the same religion and race; having the same level of education; and having good health, a happy childhood, emotional stability, parental approval of the marriage, and an adaptable personality (Kephart and Jedlicka, 1991; Hatch et al., 1986). But why are couples with these characteristics likely to be happy? Perhaps they engage in positive interactions far more often than negative interactions (Gottman, 2002, 1994), as discussed earlier.

PROBLEMS OF U.S. FAMILIES

While most American couples are happy with their marriages, many do have problems. Two of the most prevalent are violence and divorce.

Violence

Family violence is relatively common in the United States. Its exact incidence is hard to pin down because various researchers do not define family violence in the same way. There is, of course, little disagreement about extreme cases, in which one family member is killed or seriously injured by another. But there is disagreement over what kinds of behavior are acceptable for disciplining children and dealing with spousal conflict. Some researchers consider spanking, for example, an act of violence, whereas others do not. Thus, there have been different estimates of the extent of family violence in the

United States. The estimates on the proportion of families in which violence occurs at least once in a year range from 10 to 20 percent, and anywhere between 25 and 50 percent of all couples have been estimated to experience serious family violence at least once during the course of their marriage (Waltermaurer, Ortega, and McNutt, 2003; Straus, 1995; Gelles and Cornell, 1990). All this may make family violence appear to be an enormous problem because the family is supposed to be a source of love and support.

Why does family violence occur? A major reason is stress. Research shows that the incidence of violence is highest among groups most likely to feel stressed, such as the urban poor, families with a jobless husband, and those with four to six children. Stress by itself, however, does not necessarily cause violence. People would not resort to violence as a way of relieving stress if they were not culturally encouraged to do so. There seems to be a culturally recognized script for behavior under stress in U.S. society. The violence on television, corporal punishment in schools, and the death penalty, for example, all convey the idea that violence is an acceptable solution to problems. Research further suggests that the tendency for marital violence is transmitted from one generation to another. It has been found that most violent married individuals have, as children, seen their parents hit each other (Linsky, 1995; Straus, 1995; Kalmuss, 1984).

Ironically, though, many women who have been abused do not leave their husbands. Why? One reason is that they are *the most socially and economically isolated* of all women because they have too little education and are not able to earn enough to support themselves or their children. Another reason is the victims' *fear that their husbands will retaliate* by stalking them to inflict more serious violence if they leave. By staying, however, these women are more likely to end up getting killed or to struggle desperately to survive by killing their husbands (Anderson et al., 2003; Mann, 1996; Goetting, 1995).

■ Divorce

Divorce is common the United States. About half of the Americans who marry now will eventually get a divorce. The U.S. divorce rate is the second highest in the world (see Figure 10.3).

Why do so many marriages end in divorce? Numerous studies have compared divorced couples with nondivorced couples and found a number of personal problems and social characteristics to be associated with divorce: infidelity, incompatibility, financial difficulties, lower socioeconomic status, marrying too young, and parents' unhappy marriage

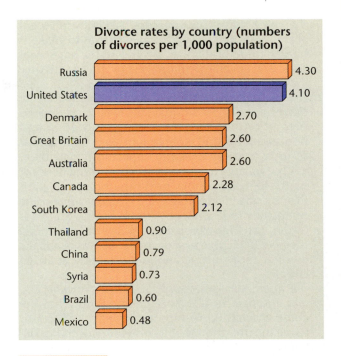

Divorce rates by country (numbers of divorces per 1,000 population)

Russia	4.30
United States	4.10
Denmark	2.70
Great Britain	2.60
Australia	2.60
Canada	2.28
South Korea	2.12
Thailand	0.90
China	0.79
Syria	0.73
Brazil	0.60
Mexico	0.48

FIGURE 10.3

Higher Rates of Divorce in Industrial Societies

As a leading industrial society, the United States has the second-highest divorce rate in the world. Generally, divorce occurs more frequently in modern Western countries than in traditional developing countries. A comparative analysis of these two types of societies can reveal the social forces behind the higher divorce rates in the West, as discussed in the text.

Critical Thinking: *Do you think a high divorce rate has a positive or negative impact on society? Explain your answer.*

Source: Data from Heritage Foundation, 2002.

or divorce (Strong, 2001; Wallerstein et al., 2000; Goode, 1993). But these data cannot explain why industrial Western societies have higher divorce rates than less individualized traditional societies or why the U.S. divorce rate today is far higher than it was a century ago. A cross-cultural analysis suggests at least five larger social forces behind the current high divorce rate in U.S. society:

1. *Decreased social disapproval of divorce.* In many traditional societies, unhappily married couples stay married because of the stigma attached to divorce. In the United States, there is virtually no stigma anymore. Divorce has gained wide acceptance as a solution to marital unhappiness, and it has become easier to obtain from the courts. Under the no-fault divorce law, anybody may end a marriage without getting their spouse's consent (M. Gallagher, 1996). In fact, it has become so easy to get

a divorce that it has caused a backlash, in recent years, with many Americans wanting to make it harder to get a divorce. Several states have even passed a covenant marriage law to bar divorce (Schemo, 2001).

2. *Greater availability of services and opportunities for the divorced.* In traditional societies, men depend heavily on marriage for sexual gratification and housekeeping, and women look to it for financial security. Such services and opportunities are more easily available to U.S. adults without the need for marriage. For example, men can find sexual gratification outside marriage, and women can become financially independent without husbands. In addition, the high divorce rate today has expanded the pool of eligible new partners. All this can make divorce more attractive to unhappily married couples.

3. *The family's increased specialization in providing love and affection.* In U.S. society, the family has become specialized in offering love and affection, while the importance of its other functions has declined. When love and affection are gone, a couple are likely to break up their empty marriage. By contrast, in traditional societies with low divorce rates, the family's other functions—especially socializing children and providing economic security—remain highly important. Thus, even when love has disappeared from marriage, there are still other reasons for keeping the family together (Kristof, 1996b).

4. *High expectations about the quality of the marital relationship.* Young people in traditional societies do not expect exciting romantic experiences with their spouses, especially if their marriages are arranged by their parents. But young people in the United States expect a lot, including an intense love relationship. These expectations are difficult to fulfill year after year, and the chances of disillusionment with the partner are therefore great. Since young people have higher expectations than older ones, it is not surprising that most divorces occur within the first four years of marriage (Krasnow, 2001; Cherlin, 1992).

5. *Increased individualism.* The rights of individuals are considered far more important in the United States than in traditional societies. Individualism encourages people to put their own needs and privileges ahead of those of others, including their spouses, and to feel that if they want a divorce, they are entitled to get one. In traditional societies, people are more likely to subordinate their needs to those of the kinship group and thus to feel that they have no right to seek a divorce (Kramer, 1997).

myth	So many American couples divorce that few people want to get married anymore.
reality	Despite high divorce rates, marriage remains popular. The United States has the highest marriage rate in the industrial world.

The current high divorce rate in the United States does not mean, as common sense would suggest, that the institution of marriage is unpopular. On the contrary, people seem to love marriage too much, as suggested by several pieces of evidence. First, U.S. society has the highest rate of marriage in the industrial world despite having one of the highest rates of divorce (see Figure 10.4). Second, in the United States, most of the Southern, Southwestern, and Western states have higher divorce rates than the national av-

FIGURE 10.4

Marriage Rates in the Industrial World
Although the United States has one of the highest divorce rates in the world, Americans are more likely to marry than people in other industrial societies. Apparently, the prevalence of divorce in the United States does not discourage Americans from marrying.

Critical Thinking: *What would make you want to get married? And if you were divorced, what would make you want to remarry?*

Source: Data from *Infoplease,* 2004.

erage, but they also tend to have higher marriage rates. Third, the majority of those who divorce eventually remarry (Cherlin, 1992). Why don't they behave like Mark Twain's cat, who after having been burned by a hot stove would not go near *any* stove? Apparently, divorce in U.S. society does not represent the rejection of marriage, only the rejection of a specific partner.

CHANGES IN THE U.S. FAMILY

The traditional nuclear family, which consists of two parents living with children, has not been the typical U.S. family for some time now. As far back as 1970, the proportion of traditional families had already declined to 40 percent. By 2000, it was only 23.5 percent (see Figure 10.5). Increasingly, people are choosing new patterns of family life. To see how much the family has changed, let us first take a quick tour of its past.

■ Historical Background

Before the industrialization of the United States in the nineteenth century, the family had long consisted of a husband, wife, and children, with no other relatives. One reason for the popularity of the nuclear family in those days was that few people lived long enough to form an extended three-generation family. Another reason was that *impartible* inheritance practices—which allow only one heir to inherit all the property—forced sons who did not inherit their families' farm to leave and set up their own households (Cherlin, 1983).

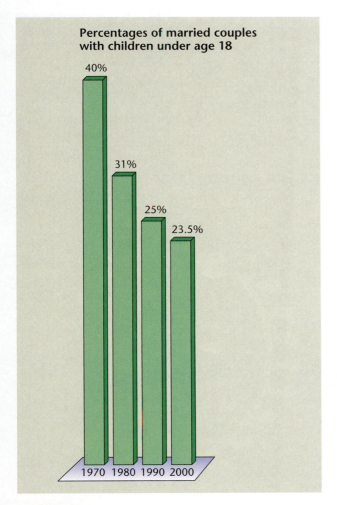

Percentages of married couples with children under age 18

40% — 1970
31% — 1980
25% — 1990
23.5% — 2000

FIGURE 10.5

Traditional Nuclear Families: A Shrinking Minority

The traditional nuclear family, which consists of two parents living with their children, has not been the typical American family for some time. Some 30 years ago, the proportion of traditional families had already dropped to 40 percent. Today, it has dwindled down to less than one-quarter of all families.

Critical Thinking: *Do you think the nuclear family is the best setting in which to raise children? Why or why not?*

Source: Data from U.S. Census Bureau, 2001.

PULLING HER WEIGHT In colonial America, the wife was typically an essential economic partner with her husband. If they had a craft, she would work with her husband as a skilled craftsperson. In the case of the husband being a weaver, for instance, the wife would shear the sheep and spin and dye the yarn. ■

myth	The traditional U.S. family, which consists of a breadwinner father and a homemaker mother, has been around since the colonial period.
reality	On the farms of colonial days, the family was, in effect, a two-career family, with the wife working side by side with her husband. Only toward the end of the nineteenth century, when industrialization was in full swing, did the wife lose her status as her husband's economic partner and acquire the subordinate position of homemaker.

On colonial farms, men, women, and children helped produce the family's livelihood. The wife was typically an essential economic partner to the husband. If her husband was a farmer, she would run the household; make the clothes; raise cows, pigs, and poultry; tend a garden; and sell milk, vegetables, chickens, and eggs. If her husband was a skilled craftsman, she would work with him. Thus, weavers' wives spun yarn, cutlers' wives polished metal, tailors' wives sewed buttonholes, and shoemakers' wives waxed shoes (Tilly and Scott, 1978).

But as the United States became industrialized in the nineteenth century, the "household ceased to be a center of production and devoted itself to child rearing instead" (Lasch, 1979). Industrialization took production out of the home. Initially husbands, wives, and children worked for wages in factories and workshops to contribute to the common family budget. But due to the difficulty of combining paid employment with the domestic tasks imposed on them, married women tended to work for wages irregularly. As wages rose, growing numbers of families could earn enough without the wife's paid work. Then, increasingly, the home was seen as the emotional center of life and a private refuge from the competitive public world. The woman's role became emotional and moral rather than economic. Women were expected to rear their children and comfort their husbands. This became the stereotype of a typical and ideal U.S. family.

Thus, after industrialization was in full swing, women lost their status as their husbands' economic partners and acquired a subordinate status as homemakers (Cherlin, 1983). But over the last few decades, there have been significant increases in gender equality, female independence through paid employment, and personal freedom for everybody. As a result, a diversity of family types has emerged, causing the traditional nuclear family to become less common. Some of these new family types are discussed in the following sections.

■ Two-Career Families

Today in the United States, it is more likely in a traditional family (one with a married couple and children) to find both parents working rather than just one (see Figure 10.6). More married women than ever have entered the workforce, doubling in number since 1970. Their employment has made it difficult, if not impossible, for them to care for their children while going out to work. They have solved the problem by turning to others, which has spawned a huge industry for child care (see Figure 10.7). More important, the employment of married women has also increased family income significantly. The income of two-career families is now much higher than the income for one-career families. According to the latest statistics, the average two-career family earns $63,816 a year, compared with $34,423 for the average one-career family (U.S. Census Bureau, 2002).

Does this economic gain bring marital happiness? Apparently, it does for *most* two-career couples. Such couples have also been found to be happier than couples in one-career families (Barnett and Rivers, 1996).

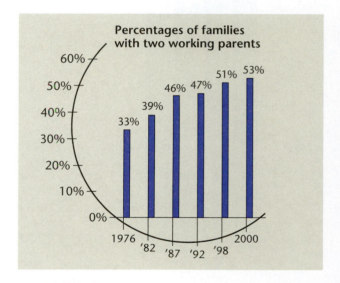

Percentages of families with two working parents

FIGURE 10.6

Two-Career Families: A Majority Since 1998

Today, the majority of traditional families with married couples and children have both parents working outside the home. This has resulted from a great surge of married women entering the labor force over the last three decades. The employment of two parents has boosted the average family income, which, in turn, has brought marital happiness for most two-career families.

Critical Thinking: *Would you foresee any problems raising the kids if both you and your spouse worked? Why or why not?*

Source: Data from U.S. Census Bureau, 2001.

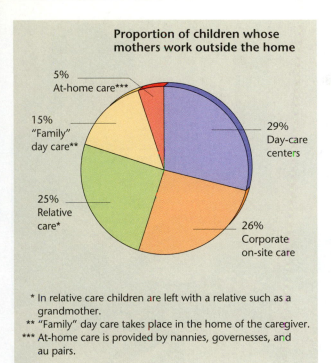

Proportion of children whose mothers work outside the home

5%
At-home care***

15%
"Family"
day care**

25%
Relative
care*

29%
Day-care
centers

26%
Corporate
on-site care

* In relative care children are left with a relative such as a grandmother.
** "Family" day care takes place in the home of the caregiver.
*** At-home care is provided by nannies, governesses, and au pairs.

"It was a purely professional decision, Harris. I hope my firing you won't affect our marriage in any way."

Source: From the *Wall Street Journal*—Permission, Cartoon Features Syndicate.

FIGURE 10.7

Child-Care Industry

The enormous surge in the gainful employment of mothers with young children has spawned a huge industry for child care. Most of this care is provided by professionals at day-care centers and corporate onsite care facilities. Studies have shown children who attend day care to be more aggressive, disobedient, and antisocial but to have better language skills when compared with their peers in home-based care (Belsky, 2003).

Critical Thinking: *If you were a working parent, would you send your child to a day-care center? Why or why not?*

Source: Data from Andrew J. Cherlin, "By the Numbers," *New York Times Magazine,* April 5, 1998, p. 41.

There is, however, more strain in a two-career marriage if the wife is still expected to be a homemaker rather than a career seeker. The strain is much heavier for the employed wife than for her husband because she does most of the housework and child care. The resulting fatigue of the overworked wife has helped create a new demographic group, DINS (dual-income, no-sex couples), who actually still have sex but only about once a month or less (Deveny, 2003; Hochschild, 1997, 1989; Skinner, 1980).

The effect of a wife's employment seems to depend on how much support she gets from her husband. Some husbands still find it difficult to render total support to their wives' careers, particularly if their wives earn more than they do. Consequently, in cases where the wife outperforms the husband in earnings, sex lives are more likely to suffer, feelings of love are more likely to diminish, and marriages are more likely to end in divorce (Rubenstein, 1982). On the other hand, in cases where the husbands fully support their wives' employment by doing their share of house cleaning and child care, the couples head off marital stress and achieve marital happiness (Cooper et al., 1986). Generally, supportive husbands have long been exposed to egalitarian ideologies and lifestyles. They have accepted the value of gender equality. They have also seen their mothers as competent and influential individuals who shared equal status with their fathers (Barnett and Rivers, 1996; Rosin, 1990).

Interestingly, as sociologist Arlie Hochschild (1997) has found out, more married career women today are discovering the "great male secret" that work can be an escape from the pressures of home life. Thus, they enjoy working in the male world of work much more than in the female world of home and children. This is especially true today because the work environment has become more employee friendly and the home life more hectic. As a result, according to Hochschild, many working women choose to work long hours, as their husbands do. Unfortunately, this makes it difficult for both parents to spend enough time with their children.

MOM ALONE Compared with parents in two-parent families, single mothers are more likely to experience social and psychological stress because they more often have severely limited financial resources. Children of these families often have a larger share of problems, such as truancy and delinquency, but these problems stem from factors that can also be found in two-parent families, such as low income, poor living conditions, and lack of parental supervision. ■

■ Single-Parent Families

With the increased frequency of divorce and out-of-wedlock births, there has been a steep rise in the number of American children growing up in households with just one parent—from about 3 million in 1970 to 12 million in 2000. A large majority (83 percent) of such families are headed by women. About one-quarter of the children today will live for some time in female-headed families. It has been estimated that more than half of all children born in the 1990s will live with their mothers alone before they reach age 18 (U.S. Census Bureau, 2001).

The majority of unmarried women are 20 and older rather than teenagers. They have been divorced, separated, widowed, or abandoned by their husbands (Usdansky, 1996; Lewin, 1992). Most of these families live below or near the poverty level. Among these families, African American mothers are more likely to reside with the children's grandmothers, who provide free child care. But they are far from well prepared to cope with the challenges of single parenthood (Coontz, 1997; Hogan et al., 1990).

Since the early 1980s, there has been a significant increase in *never-married* women having children. The most dramatic increase is among women in managerial and professional jobs, whites, and college graduates. This increase may be attributed to the growing middle-class acceptance of unwed mother-

hood, women's rising earning power, and women's higher standards for choosing husbands (Seligmann, 1993). Nevertheless, these affluent unmarried mothers are still far fewer in number than their lower-income peers.

Since the early 1990s, the number of unmarried *teenage* mothers has declined sharply, thanks to an increase in birth control and a reduction in sexual activity. But states with higher poverty rates, such as those in the South, continue to have higher teenage birth rates than other states (see Figure 10.8). Also, since the early 1990s, teen birth rates have plummeted the most among African Americans, but due to their higher poverty rates, African American teens are still much more likely than whites to have babies (Lewin, 1998).

myth	Children from single-parent families are more likely than other children to have problems because their fathers are not around.
reality	It is not the absence of a father in the single-parent family that causes the problems. It is the other factors that characterize the two-parent family with problem children: low income, poor living conditions, and lack of parental supervision.

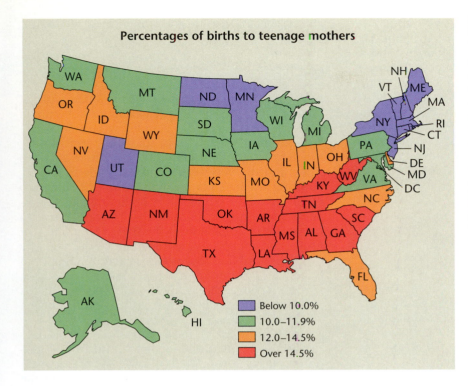

Percentages of births to teenage mothers

Below 10.0%
10.0–11.9%
12.0–14.5%
Over 14.5%

FIGURE 10.8

Teenage Birth Rates

Over the last 10 years, the number of unmarried teenage mothers has gone down sharply (by 30 percent), due to an increase in the use of birth control and a reduction in sexual activity. But in states with higher poverty rates, such as those in the South, more babies continue to be born to teenage girls than occurs in other states.

Critical Thinking: *What would you recommend families and schools do to reduce teen pregnancy?*

Source: Data from National Center for Health Statistics, 2003.

Compared with two-parent families, female-headed families are more likely to experience social and psychological stress, such as unemployment, job change, lack of social support, negative self-image, and pessimism about the future. Children from single-parent families also have a larger share of such problems as juvenile delinquency, truancy, and poor schoolwork. Whatever problems these children may have, however, they do not result directly from the absence of a father in a female-headed home, as is popularly believed, but from other factors that characterize the two-parent family with problem children, such as low income, poor living conditions, and lack of parental supervision. Remove these factors and the majority of children from single-parent families do just fine (Kantrowitz and Wingert, 2001; Cherlin, 1992; Cherlin and Furstenberg, 1983).

■ Blended Families

Given the high rates of divorce and remarriage, blended families (or stepfamilies) have become quite common. About one-third of all Americans are members of some type of blended family. Because women usually get custody of children in divorce cases, most blended families consist of mothers, their biological children, and stepfathers. Nine out of ten stepchildren live with their biological mothers and stepfathers (U.S. Census Bureau, 2001).

The happiness of blended families depends largely on how well the stepfather gets along with the children. It is extremely difficult to be a stepfather. Society has not yet provided a script for performing the stepfather role, as it has for the father role. Thus, it is much more difficult for stepfathers to develop intimate and durable bonds with their stepchildren than for other fathers to do so with their biological children (Coontz, 1997; Cherlin and Furstenberg, 1994).

Accustomed to living with their biological fathers, children tend to regard their stepfathers as interlopers or as distant, unwanted relatives overstaying their visits. They may resent having to change their lifestyle. As a 15-year-old girl sobbed to her mother, "I can't stand it. I have to put on my bathrobe at 10 o'clock at night in 'our' own house to go downstairs to get an apple from the refrigerator because he's there in 'our' living room." Aside from running into such conflicts over territoriality, stepfathers are likely to have problems with discipline. If they tell a 13-year-old stepson that he should not watch an R-rated cable movie, he may retort, "My dad lets me watch them. Besides, it's Mom's television set" (Herbert, 1999b; Nordheimer, 1990).

Conflicts over territoriality and discipline are most likely to erupt with teenagers. Young children can quickly accept a stepfather's love and discipline because of their physical and emotional dependence on adults. But teenagers are striving to break free of adult authority, as they are preoccupied with schoolwork, friends, sports, and their developing sexuality. They accept parental discipline only out of love and respect, which the stepfather initially does not or may never have. During an argument, they are likely to shout at their stepfathers, "You're not my real father!" It is even harder to be a stepmother because the children's bond with their biological mother is very powerful.

Not surprisingly, the presence of stepchildren has been found to be a major reason why second marriages fail at a higher rate than first marriages. Nevertheless, most blended families are relatively free of serious trouble and conflict (Strong, 2001; Herbert, 1999b; Nordheimer, 1990).

OTHER LIFESTYLES

A certain number of people will reject conventional family life and pursue different lifestyles. Some of these lifestyles have become more popular in recent decades.

■ Staying Single

Of the various lifestyles that are different from conventional marriage, staying single is by far the most common. In 2000, adults who lived alone accounted for 26 percent of all U.S. households. Many of these individuals are in their thirties and forties, but most are younger adults who postpone marriage into their late twenties. More significant, a growing number of young adults live with their parents and stay single for some time (U.S. Census Bureau, 2003).

Most singles are not actually opposed to marriage and do expect to be married sooner or later. One reason they often give for their current singlehood is that they have not met the right person. But increasing numbers of men and women choose to stay single. Some studies have found them to be happier than their married counterparts. They are also more likely to see themselves as very romantic. If asked why they are single, they are likely to say that "Marriage entails too much commitment and responsibility" or "I prefer the lifestyle" (Janus and Janus, 1993; Harayda, 1986; Simenauer and Carroll, 1982). There are, however, two sociological reasons for the increase in committed singlehood.

First, the social pressure to get married has declined. This is particularly true for city dwellers, who face far less pressure to marry than small-town residents. Second, the opportunity for singles to have a good life has expanded. This is especially true for women. As educational and career opportunities open up for them, along with the freedom to choose to be a single mother, marriage is no longer the only avenue to economic security, emotional support, so-

cial respectability, and meaningful work (Edwards, 2000).

■ Living Together

In the past, very few couples lived together without having a formal wedding ceremony or obtaining a marriage license. These couples were said to be "shacking up" or "living in sin." They were mostly the very rich, who could afford to ignore society's rules, and the very poor, who had little to lose by ignoring them. Today, cohabitation has spread to other sectors of U.S. society, including college students and young working adults. The result is a dramatic rise in cohabitation. In 1970, the number of unmarried couples living together was only slightly over half a million, but it had soared to 5.5 million by 2000. Social disapproval has vastly diminished, and courts have stepped in to protect couples' rights as if they were legally married (U.S. Census Bureau, 2001; Smock, 2000).

Because the incidence of cohabitation continues to rise, some fear that it may undermine the institution of marriage. In Sweden, however, where cohabitation is already four times as prevalent as in the United States, living together has not posed a threat to marriage at all. Most cohabitants live like married couples and intend to marry eventually. The situation in the United States is similar. Often called *common-law marriage,* cohabitation as a permanent alternative to marriage is relatively rare today; it occurs mostly among the very poor. For most cohabitants, living together is a temporary arrangement that usually lasts for less than 5 years. Although it does not imply a commitment to marry later, cohabitation often leads to marriage. In fact, 55 percent of cohabiting couples eventually marry. Thus, it is a modern extension of the courtship process, comparable to the traditional custom of going steady (Smock, 2000).

myth	Couples who have lived together without being married are less likely to get divorced. Cohabitation works like a trial marriage and prepares the couple for marital success.
reality	There are more divorces among couples who have cohabited than among those who have not. The reason for marital failure, though, is not the prior experience of cohabitation; it is the lack of strong commitment to marriage among people who choose to cohabit.

Does living together lead to more marital happiness than traditional courtship? Couples who live together often argue that cohabitation works like a trial marriage, preparing them for marital success. But research has mostly shown less marital satisfaction as well as more divorces among couples who have cohabited than among those who have not. The reason for marital failure, however, is not the prior experience of cohabitation. It is the lack of strong commitment to marriage, which often exists among couples who have lived together (Amato et al., 2003; Smock, 2000).

■ Gay and Lesbian Marriages

More gay men and lesbians live together today than ever before. Gay marriages have recently been legalized in only a few countries, such as Canada, Belgium, and the Netherlands. But they are not legally recognized in the United States, where gay couples do not have the same legal protections and financial benefits as heterosexual couples, such as tax exemptions and deductions or Social Security survivor's benefits.

In recent years, though, a number of cities have granted unmarried couples, no matter what their

GOING MAINSTREAM Like their heterosexual counterparts, many gay and lesbian couples have children. Most of these children come from earlier heterosexual relationships, but a growing number are adopted or born through artificial insemination. Many gay families have eased into suburban life, well accepted by their predominantly heterosexual communities, but the level of acceptance varies from one state to another. ■

sexual orientation, a legal document called a *domestic partnership agreement*. Some gay couples have used it to gain family benefits from employers, insurance companies, health clubs, and other commercial establishments. Furthermore, the overturning of a Texas antisodomy law by the U.S. Supreme Court in 2003 has stirred hope that gay marriage will soon become legal. Although a small majority of Americans are still opposed to gay marriage, the opposition has declined since 1996. A significant majority of young adults are already in favor of legalizing gay marriage (see Figure 10.9, p. 290).

Like heterosexuals, most gay men and lesbians want to get married when they are in love. Even though they are denied the legal right to marry, they tie the knot in about the same way as their heterosexual counterparts. Gay weddings range from simply exchanging rings in private to having an elaborate ceremony. In sociological terms, the wedding serves to strengthen the couple's relationship. By expressing their vows and love for each other in the presence of their significant others, the partners in a same-sex couple tend to feel a stronger sense of commitment and security.

Also, like their heterosexual counterparts, many gay and lesbian couples have children. Most of these children come from earlier heterosexual relationships. But an increasing number of the children are adopted or born through artificial insemination. Many of these gay families have eased into suburban life, well accepted by their predominantly heterosexual communities (Dunlap, 1996). The American Academy of Pediatrics (AAP) has found that children who grow up with homosexual parents fare as well in emotional, cognitive, social, and sexual functioning as do children with heterosexual parents. The key to children's optimal development, the AAP has further noted, is the quality of parental care, rather than whether the parents are gay or straight (Robison, 2003).

Gay and lesbian couples are generally far more egalitarian in their relationships than heterosexual couples. Heterosexual men and women usually have been socialized to play different gender roles, with the husband expected to do masculine things, such as fixing the family car, and the wife feminine things, such as preparing the family meals. Such gender-role differences often make men dominant over women. By contrast, gay partners have been socialized to the same gender role, so that they tend to have an egalitarian relationship. If both partners in a gay or lesbian couple work—as most do—both do about the same amount of housework. One does not do more housework than the other, as is often the case with heterosexual couples (see Chapter 9: Gender and Age).

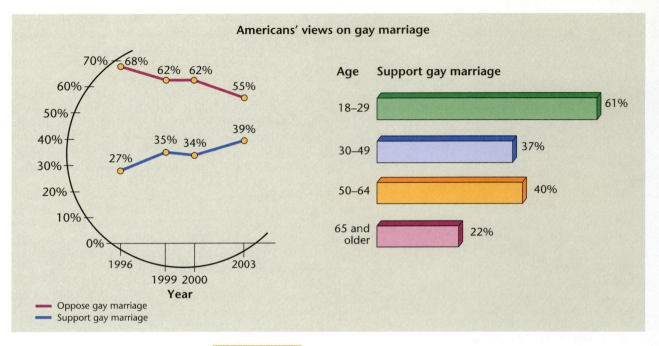

FIGURE 10.9

Attitudes toward Gay Marriage

A small majority of Americans are still opposed to the legalization of gay marriage, but the opposition has declined: from 68 percent in 1996 to 55 percent in 2003. More significant, a majority of young adults, who will soon exercise huge influence on society, are already in favor of legalizing gay marriage.

Critical Thinking: *Do you support or oppose gay marriage? Why?*

Source: Data from Linda Lyons, "U.S. Next Down the Aisle toward Gay Marriage," *Gallup Poll Tuesday Briefing*, 2003. Available online: www.gallup.com.

SOCIAL DIVERSITY OF U.S. FAMILIES

The discussion so far has been based mostly on studies of European American families. Now, let's focus on families with other ethnicities.

■ Native American Families

Before the emergence of the United States as a nation, some Native American tribes were patrilineal but most were matrilineal, including the better-known tribes like the Zuni and Hopi in the Southwest and the Iroquois in the Northeast. Despite their tribal differences, various Native American families shared certain characteristics. Infants were born in special birth huts. During the years of breastfeeding, mothers refrained from sexual intercourse. Physical punishment was rarely used to discipline children, who were taught instead by example. Children learned

adult roles at an early age, so that most girls were married between ages 12 and 15 and boys between ages 15 and 20. Most tribes were monogamous. Only a few allowed men to have two wives or engage in extramarital sex when their wives were pregnant or breastfeeding. Extended family networks predominated, and kinship ties and obligations to relatives flourished (Strong, 2001; Wilkinson, 1993).

Today, this traditional family life has disappeared among many Native Americans. Between 1870 and 1930, the U.S. government embarked on a program of destroying the Native American culture. It involved assimilating Native Americans into the white culture by, among other things, sending their children to white-run boarding schools. Today, only a small minority of Native Americans have successfully resisted assimilation and kept alive their traditional values, particularly the importance of kinship ties and obligations. The rest, including the one-third of all Native Americans who marry outside their ethnic group, have adopted either white values completely or a mixture of white and traditional values. Compared with other ethnic groups, Native Americans have higher rates of poverty, alcoholism, suicide, and other problems, all of which create severe difficulties for many Native American families (Strong, 2001; Harjo, 1993).

■ African American Families

When they were slaves, African Americans were prohibited from legally marrying. Nonetheless, they created their own marriages, developing strong family ties similar to those in the traditional extended African family. These emotional bonds helped African Americans cope with the daily indignities of servitude. Still, slavery made it difficult for many African American families to be stable because family members were often sold. After slavery was abolished, African Americans continued to suffer, this time due to racism and poverty. Throughout their travails, however, *the mutual aid and emotional support* that characterized the early family system has survived (Strong, 2001; Wilkinson, 1993).

Since the early 1970s, many African American families have been dealt a devastating blow from deindustrialization and the resulting massive loss of blue-collar jobs from many U.S. cities to labor-cheap countries. One consequence has been rampant unemployment among African Americans in inner cities. As their poverty rate soared, the traditional African American family declined sharply. In 2001, about 61 percent of African American families had only one parent, usually a single mother, and 69 percent of African American babies were born to unmarried women (U.S. Census Bureau, 2001).

It has been observed that, ironically, "the traditional family system that slavery could not destroy during 200 years may be dismantled in a few short years by the modern industrial transition" (Billingsley, 1993). Still, the African American family continues to survive because it continues to draw its strength from the legacy of mutual assistance among relatives, friends, neighbors, and church members.

■ Hispanic American Families

Most Hispanic families are nuclear, with only parents and children living together, but they do have the characteristics of an extended family. Strong kinship ties exist, as various relatives live close to one another and often exchange visits, emotional support, and economic assistance (Vega, 1992).

Hispanic families tend to have large numbers of children, generally more than families of other ethnicities. Children typically occupy the center of family life. They are taught to respect their elders, to appreciate family unity, and to assume family responsibilities. The father tends to be very affectionate and easygoing toward younger children but becomes more authoritarian and strict as they grow older. His role as the head of the family is often described as *machismo,* being manly in protecting and providing for the family, exercising authority fairly, and respecting the role of his wife (Becerra, 1988). The wife is in charge of the day-to-day matters of childrearing and homemaking. Gender equality increases with the length of residence in the United States; families started by younger generations tend to be more egalitarian than families of older generations (Chilman, 1993; Wilkinson, 1993).

Imbued with strong family values, Hispanics generally have lower divorce rates than Anglos. The exception is Puerto Ricans, who have a much higher divorce rate as a result of a greater prevalence of poverty. Hispanics are also likely to marry outside their group, especially among those with a higher socioeconomic status. Generally, the longer their families have been in the United States, the higher their rates of interethnic marriage (Wilkinson, 1993).

■ Asian American Families

Compared with other U.S. families, Asian American families—particularly Chinese, Japanese, Korean, and Vietnamese—generally are more stable, having lower divorce rates, fewer female-headed households, fewer problems with childrearing, greater family solidarity, and stronger kinship associations (Wilkinson, 1993).

These qualities are often attributed to the Asians' Buddhist or Confucian culture, which emphasizes the subordination of the individual to the family. Instead of stressing the importance of the individual's independence and autonomy, Confucianism emphasizes the individual's obligation to the family. The nature of the obligation varies with the status of each family member. The father is the head of the family and thus must provide for the economic welfare of his family. The mother is expected to be the nurturant caretaker of both her husband and children. And the children are supposed to practice *hsiao,* or filial piety. This essentially involves showing gratitude toward parents by performing two tasks: (1) providing parents with economic and emotional support, such as aid, comfort, or affection, especially in their old age, and (2) bringing parents reflected glory by achieving success in educational and occupational activities (Hwang, 1998; Lin and Liu, 1993; Shon and Ja, 1992).

The influence of this traditional culture declines with succeeding generations of Asian Americans. Thus, among the third or fourth generation, the family has fewer children, the father is less authoritarian, the mother is more likely to be gainfully employed, interracial marriage has increased significantly, and

FAMILY FIRST Asian cultures, particularly Buddhist and Confucian cultures, typically emphasize subordination of the individual to the kinship group. Although such traditions tend to decline over succeeding generations of Asian Americans, the residual effect is to make their families more stable than many U.S. families from other backgrounds. ■

divorce is more common. But the Confucian culture still has a residual effect on many Asian American families, making them more stable than other U.S. families (Lin and Liu, 1993; Wilkinson, 1993).

THE FUTURE OF THE FAMILY

The death of the family has been predicted for decades. In 1949, Carle Zimmerman concluded from his study on the family, "We must look upon the present confusion of family values as the beginning of violent breaking up of a system." By the "confusion of family values," Zimmerman referred to the threat that individualism presented to the tradition of paternalistic authority and filial duty. He assumed that individualism would eventually do in the family. Today, many continue to predict the demise of the family, pointing out as evidence the increases in divorce, out-of-wedlock births, cohabitation, and singlehood.

However, the family is alive and well. The flaw in the gloomy forecast is that it confuses change with breakdown. Many traditional families—with husbands as breadwinners and wives as homemakers—have merely changed into two-career families, which still stay together as nuclear families rather than disintegrate. Despite the increased number of people

staying single, the majority of those who now live alone will eventually marry. Although the divorce rate has doubled over the last two decades, three out of four divorced people remarry, most within three years of their marital breakup. Likewise, most young adults who live together before marriage eventually marry. It is true that being part of a single-parent family, especially from an out-of-wedlock birth, is a problem for many mothers and their children. But the problem stems more from economic deprivation than from single parenthood as a new form of family.

What will the U.S. family be like in the next 20 years? It will be much the same as it is today: maintaining *diversity* without destroying the basic family values. The vast majority of young people still value marriage, parenthood, and family life. They plan to marry, have children, and be successful in marriage. Even if they stay single, it will usually be because they care too much about marriage, not too little. They want to get it right by finding "the perfect soulmate of their dreams" (Edwards, 2000).

sociological frontiers

The Revival of Covenant Marriage

As we have observed, it is extremely easy to get a divorce in the United States. Now, there is a movement underway to make getting a divorce more difficult by bringing back the old-style *covenant marriage*. Reflecting the biblical teachings about the sanctity of marriage, a covenant marriage bars divorce except under extreme circumstances, such as adultery, abandonment, and life-threatening abuse. So far, three states—Arizona, Louisiana, and Arkansas—have passed laws providing for covenant marriage, and 20 more states have proposed or are considering adoption of similar laws. Generally, such laws require that couples who want a covenant marriage seek counseling before taking marital vows or before breaking those vows through divorce, for which they must wait up to two and a half years.

Sociologist Steven Nock and two colleagues at the University of Central Florida have been conducting a five-year study on covenant marriages. So far, they have found a number of significant differences between couples in covenant marriages and those in standard marriages. Compared to standard couples, covenant couples have more education and higher incomes, are more deeply connected to their churches, and have approached courtship and marriage in a more serious, traditional way. They also have brought fewer unresolved problems to marriage: Fewer bridegrooms are in debt, and virtually all couples have discussed children before marriage (something only one-third of standard couples have done). Most important, covenant couples are much less likely to divorce (Schemo, 2001).

Consider what a typical covenant couple is like: Christian Lesher, 27, and Samantha Myers, 24, recently wed. They dated for six years and were engaged for over a year. Before marriage, they spent hours in counseling, discussing their experiences, expectations, attitudes, and foibles. And they never allowed themselves physical intimacy. They like the restrictions imposed by covenant marriage. As Myers said, "This is insurance that we're not going to make a decision that we'll regret because we hit a valley in our marriage" (Schemo, 2001).

 ■ For more of the latest Sociological Frontiers, look up Continuing Update at www.ablongman.com/thio6e.

using *sociology*

How to Solve Marital Problems

Twice as many couples seek marriage counseling today as 20 years ago. And to meet this increase, the number of licensed counselors has grown dramatically, from 9,000 in 1982 to more than 50,000 in 2001.

For many years, however, these counselors were not very successful: Only half of their clients reported significant increases in marital happiness. The problem was that counselors focused on *changing behavior.* Suppose a couple had reached an impasse because she couldn't get him to do any housework and he couldn't get her to make time for just the two of them. Faced with this problem, the counselor usually would try to change the behavior of both the husband and wife. Thus, the counselor would advise the husband to agree to do some housework, the wife to agree to one night out per month, and both to agree to stop yelling at each other. But this effort at change was much easier said than done. After all, agreeing to change is one thing, but actually doing it is another.

Recently, two researchers at the University of Washington have developed a new and better approach to marriage counseling called *acceptance therapy* (Christensen and Jacobson, 2000). The goal is for spouses to stop trying to change the annoying things about each other that most likely cannot be changed. Instead, the couple should learn to tolerate and live with those annoyances, much in the same way one learns to live with a bad back. This is similar to what other researchers have called the *marital endurance ethic.* That is, couples do not have to solve their problems; they only need to endure and outlast them (Zaslow, 2003c).

A pilot study of 20 unhappy couples has found that after six months of acceptance therapy, 90 percent reported dramatic increases in satisfaction. One of these couples had come for therapy because the wife complained of recurrent bouts of stomach pain after three decades of being constantly criticized by her husband.

Now, after one year of acceptance therapy, the couple say they are happier than ever. "I still tell her it's ridiculous to spend $500 on a coat that's really just a scarf," the husband says, but his anger about her overspending is gone. And pleased with her new cashmere stole, the wife says that she has learned not to be bothered by his criticism (Schrof, 1998a).

Thinking critically about your future spouse, what bad habits of his or hers could you learn to accept, and what bad habits of your own would you want him or her to accept?

▌CHAPTER REVIEW

1. *In what ways does the family vary from one society to another?* Key variations occur in the definition of who makes up the family, in norms regarding who selects a marriage partner and who is an appropriate partner, and in rules of residence, descent, inheritance, and authority.

2. *What is the family like, as seen through the three sociological perspectives?* From the functionalist perspective, the family is functional for society by providing sexual regulation, reproduction, socialization, economic cooperation, and emotional security. Seen through the conflict perspective, the family is full of violence and female exploitation. Symbolic interactionism focuses on how certain interactions between a couple lead to marital happiness.

3. *How do people in the United States prepare for marriage?* Usually, they do not prepare for marriage intentionally, but dating, falling in love, and making a commitment are the traditional preparatory steps in the United States. *Is there any truth to the saying that opposites attract?* Winch believes so, but most studies support the contrary view. The theory that people with similar personality traits are attracted to each other gains further support from the norm of homogamy—namely, that a person is likely to marry someone of the same class, race, religion, and other social characteristics. *Are most marriages successful?* An overwhelming majority of individuals say that they are very happy or pretty happy with their marriages.

4. *What causes family violence?* One reason is the popular acceptance of violence as a solution to problems. Another reason is a history of violence in the offender's family of orientation. *Why is the divorce rate so high in the United States?* Among the likely social causes are (1) decreased social disapproval of divorce, (2) greater availability of services and opportunities for the divorced, (3) increased specialization of the family in providing love and affection, (4) higher expectations about the quality of marital relationships, and (5) increased individualism.

5. *What changes have taken place in the U.S. family in recent decades?* The family has taken on diverse forms, such as two-career families, single-parent families, blended families, cohabitation, singlehood, and gay and lesbian families. *How is social diversity revealed among U.S. families?* The families of Native Americans, African Americans, Hispanic Americans, and Asian Americans are basically alike in emphasizing the importance of kinship ties, which contrasts with European American families' emphasis on individual independence. But differences in history and culture bring about different types of family life.

6. *What is the future of the U.S. family?* The diversity of family forms will continue, and the basic family values, such as marrying and having children, will remain very much alive.

7. *How can covenant marriage laws make divorce less likely?* Under such laws, couples must seek counseling before marriage, and if they later want a divorce, they must wait for a number of years and go through more counseling. *How does the new method of marriage counseling differ from the traditional one?* The traditional method focused on *changing* spouses' annoying behavior, but the new approach encourages the couple to tolerate and live with one another's annoyances.

▌KEY TERMS

Arranged marriage   A marriage in which partners are selected by the couple's parents (p. 272).

Bilateral descent   The norm that recognizes both parents' families as the child's close relatives (p. 274).

Egalitarian family   The family in which authority is equally distributed between husband and wife (p. 274).

Endogamy   Literally, "marrying within," the act of marrying someone from one's own group (p. 273).

Exogamy   Literally, "marrying outward," the act of marrying someone from outside one's group—such as the clan, tribe, or village (p. 273).

Extended family   The family that consists of two parents, their unmarried children, and other relatives (p. 272).

Family of orientation   The family in which one grows up, consisting of oneself and one's parents and siblings (p. 272).

Family of procreation   The family that one establishes through marriage, consisting of oneself and one's spouse and children (p. 272).

Homogamy   Marrying someone with social characteristics similar to one's own (p. 279).

Matriarchal family   The family in which the dominant figure is the oldest female (p. 274).

Matrilineal descent   The norm that recognizes only the mother's family as a child's close relatives (p. 273).

Matrilocal residence   The home where the married couple lives with the wife's family (p. 273).

Monogamy   The marriage of one man to one woman (p. 273).

Neolocal residence   The home where the married couple live by themselves, away from both the husband's and the wife's families (p. 273).

Nuclear family   The family that consists of two parents and their unmarried children (p. 272).

Patriarchal family   The family in which the dominant figure is the oldest male (p. 274).

Patrilineal descent   The norm that recognizes only the father's family as a child's close relatives (p. 273).

Patrilocal residence   The home where the married couple live with the husband's family (p. 273).

Polyandry   The marriage of one woman to two or more men (p. 273).

Polygamy   The marriage of one person to two or more people of the opposite sex (p. 273).

Polygyny   The marriage of one man to two or more women (p. 273).

Serial monogamy   The marriage of one person to two or more people but one at a time (p. 273).

▌QUESTIONS FOR DISCUSSION AND REVIEW

FAMILIES: A GLOBAL ANALYSIS

1. How do family composition and mate selection differ among societies?
2. How do the world's families differ in regard to residence, descent, and authority?

SOCIOLOGICAL PERSPECTIVES ON THE FAMILY

1. What functions does the family perform for society?
2. How does the family appear from the conflict perspective?

3. How can the symbolic interactionist perspective be used to understand the quality of family life?

PATTERNS OF U.S. MARRIAGES

1. What roles do dating and romantic love play in preparing individuals for marriage?
2. What are the distinguishing characteristics of homogamy?
3. What accounts for marital happiness?

PROBLEMS OF U.S. FAMILIES

1. What causes family violence?
2. What are the social causes of divorce?

CHANGES IN THE U.S. FAMILY

1. Why did the traditional nuclear family—made up of the breadwinner husband and homemaker wife—emerge in the nineteenth century?
2. How has the entry of large numbers of married women into the labor force changed the family?
3. What special problems do single mothers and stepfathers face in raising children?

OTHER LIFESTYLES

1. Why do some people stay single?
2. Does the great increase in cohabitation threaten the institution of marriage? Why or why not?
3. In what ways are gay and lesbian families similar to and different from heterosexual families?

SOCIAL DIVERSITY OF U.S. FAMILIES

1. What are the similarities among Native American, African American, Hispanic American, and Asian American families?
2. What are the differences?

THE FUTURE OF THE FAMILY

1. What will the U.S. family be like in the future?

SOCIOLOGICAL FRONTIERS/USING SOCIOLOGY

1. What do covenant marriage laws require of couples?
2. What is the nature of acceptance therapy?

■ SUGGESTED READINGS

Hackstaff, Karla B. 1999. *Marriage in a Culture of Divorce*. Philadelphia: Temple University Press. A study of how the divorce culture influences married couples over such issues as whether to seek a divorce or who should get what in the marriage.

Hetherington, E. Mavis, and John Kelly. 2002. *For Better or For Worse*. New York: Norton. A survey of 1,400 families and more than 2,500 children,

showing how a majority (75 to 80 percent) function well after divorce.

Waite, Linda J., and Maggie Gallagher. 2000. *The Case for Marriage: Why Married People Are Happier, Healthier, and Better Off Financially*. New York: Doubleday. A data-packed analysis of the positive things that marriage can do for people.

Wallerstein, Judith, Julia Lewis, and Sandra Blakeslee. 2000. *The Unexpected Legacy of Divorce: A 25 Year Landmark Study*. New York: Hyperion. A case study of how the negative impact of divorce on children continues to affect them as they grow into adulthood.

■ Additional Resources

The New York Times
expect the world®
nytimes.com

Expand your knowledge of the concepts discussed in this chapter by reading the following current and historical articles from the *New York Times*. Go to the "eThemes of the Times" section of the Companion Website (www.ablongman.com/thio6e):

"Gay Wedding Bells: Why No Hubbub? It's Canada"

"Staking Out a Place in a House Divided"

Research Navigator.com

Research Navigator, a research database, provides immediate access to hundreds of full-text articles from EBSCO's ContentSelect Academic Journal Database. If the Research Navigator access code was included with your textbook, go to the website www.research navigator.com and read the following articles related to this chapter by typing in the article number:

Astone, Nan Marie, Kendra Rothert, Nicola J. Standish, and Young J. Kim. "Women's Employment, Marital Happiness, and Divorce." *Social Forces*, Dec2002, Vol. 81 Issue 2, p643, 20p. Accession Number: 8593918. Examines the controversial relationship between women's employment and the risk of divorce.

Raffaelli, Marcela, and Lenna L. Ontai. "'She's 16 Years Old and There's Boys Calling over to the House': An Exploratory Study of Sexual Socialization in Latino Families." *Culture, Health and Sexuality*, Jul2001, Vol. 3 Issue 3. Accession Number: 5171836. Explores the role of cultural beliefs and values in sexual socialization.

chapter 11

Education and Religion

myths & realities

myth *Because college education provides abstract knowledge rather than practical training, college graduates find it increasingly difficult to find well-paid work in today's highly competitive economy.*

reality Due to the increasing reliance of modern industries on highly educated workers, the value of a college education has risen dramatically. In 1980, college graduates earned about 32 percent more than high school graduates, but by 2002, the earnings difference had increased to 91 percent (p. 298).

myth *A major function of schools is to teach children only the truth about their country.*

reality A major function of schools is to foster national unity. Therefore, the nation's glorious achievements are played up, but its shameful acts are often watered down or left out (p. 299).

myth *Japanese schools are so much better than American schools that U.S. society would benefit if its educators emulated the Japanese.*

reality Japanese schools are not necessarily better. They may even be worse: By emphasizing extreme conformity, they tend to stifle individuality and creativity, qualities that U.S. schools cultivate (p. 304).

myth *It is beneficial to society for the faithful to identify as strongly as possible with their religions.*

reality History has shown that when people identify too strongly with their religions, they tend to end up believing that there is only one true religion— namely, their own. Consequently, they are likely to be intolerant of others' religions, which they consider false. The result is often social conflict or intergroup violence (p. 312).

myth *Most of the immigrants from predominantly Muslim Arab countries are Muslims, so that a majority of Arab Americans are Muslims.*

reality Most Arab Americans are Christians because Christians from those Arab countries are much more likely to immigrate to the United States (p. 319).

297

n August 2001, J. C. Penney started selling T-shirts showing a picture of a trailer home along with the caption "Home Skooled." Enraged families of homeschooled children quickly protested, threatening a boycott, and within a week, Penney's had removed the T-shirts from its shelves. Why the fuss? Penney's had not realized that the number of homeschoolers in the United States has grown dramatically in recent years from a mere 0.3 million in 1990 to 1.7 million today. On top of this, research has shown that homeschooled children are academically superior to their public school peers and that the parents of homeschoolers are better educated than the parents of public schoolchildren (Cloud and Morse, 2001).

Similarly, a new kind of faith has flourished in the U.S. religious landscape. At a modern mosque with twin minarets towering over the cornfields in Toledo, Ohio, hundreds of families get together to worship Allah. These worshipers represent the fast-growing population of American Muslims, whose numbers have soared from only 0.5 million in 1970 to 7 million today, more than twice the number of Episcopalians (Sheler, 2001b). In this chapter, we will analyze homeschooling, American Islam, and other new and important facets of education and religion.

SOCIOLOGICAL PERSPECTIVES ON EDUCATION

From the three sociological perspectives, we can see various aspects of education. One is the positive side of education, another is the negative side, and the third is the teacher–student interaction.

■ Functionalist Perspective: Positive Functions of Education

According to the functionalist perspective, education performs many functions for society. Here, we discuss only the most important: teaching knowledge and skills, enhancing social mobility, promoting national unity, and providing custodial care.

Teaching Knowledge and Skills   The most obvious function of education is to provide a new generation with the knowledge and skills necessary to maintain the society. Of course, family background does have an impact on student learning. Given their greater learning resources—such as a daily newspaper, dictionary, and encyclopedia in their homes—upper- and middle-class students do have higher educational attainment than their lower-class peers. Nevertheless, when researchers take family background into account, they still find that schools make a difference in how much their students learn. Students from lower-income families attending

good high schools, for example, have been found to learn more and have a better chance of going to college than other lower-income students attending bad high schools. Moreover, studies conducted during summer months and teacher strikes have shown that inner-city and minority youngsters are most likely to suffer sharp drops in learning skills and knowledge when not in school. Studies in developing countries, where schooling is not available to all children, have also shown that whether or not children attend school has a significant impact on their cognitive development. In fact, an extensive review of relevant studies concludes that schools can and do make a big difference in transmitting knowledge and skills to students (McMahon, 2002; Griffith et al., 1989; Mortimore, 1988; Rutter, 1983).

myth	Because college education provides abstract knowledge rather than practical training, college graduates find it increasingly difficult to find well-paid work in today's highly competitive economy.
reality	Due to the increasing reliance of modern industries on highly educated workers, the value of a college education has risen dramatically. In 1980, college graduates earned about 32 percent more than high school graduates, but by 2002, the earnings difference had increased to 91 percent.

Enhancing Social Mobility Most people value the knowledge and skills transmitted by the schools because they hope to translate those skills into good jobs and money. Does education really enhance the opportunity for social mobility? The answer is apparently yes. As Figure 11.1 shows, the more education people get, the higher their incomes are. In the past, even a high school dropout could find a job that paid well enough to support a family. That kind of job has all but disappeared today due to the greatly increased reliance of modern industries on highly educated workers. Thus, the value of a college education has risen dramatically. In 1980, college graduates earned about 32 percent more than high school graduates, but by 2002, the earnings difference had soared to 91 percent (U.S. Census Bureau, 2003; Kosters, 1990).

Education also makes social mobility available throughout the society by stimulating economic growth. Pamela Walters and Richard Rubinson (1983) have found that the expansion of education in the United States since 1933 has boosted the nation's economy by increasing worker productivity, developing more productive and labor-saving technology, and creating a stable political climate. Studies in other industrial societies, as well as in developing countries, have further shown that mass schooling contributes to modernization (McMahon, 2002; Ramirez and Meyer, 1980).

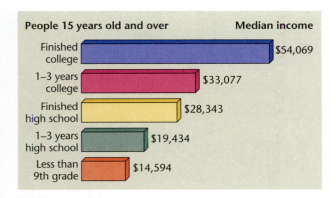

FIGURE 11.1

How Education Raises Income

The knowledge and intellectual skills learned in school can be translated into good jobs and money. Not surprisingly, then, the more education people have, the bigger their earnings. The value of college education, in particular, has risen dramatically. Today, college graduates can earn 91 percent more than high school graduates, compared to 32 percent more in 1980.

Critical Thinking: *Do you expect to earn more than your parents? Why or why not?*

Source: Data from U.S. Census Bureau, 2003.

Promoting National Unity To foster national unity, schools—especially primary and secondary schools rather than colleges and universities—play an important role in transmitting the culture to a new generation. Students are taught to become good citizens, to love their country, to cherish their cultural values, and to be proud of their nation. Teaching good citizenship may involve the performance of rituals. In the United States, for example, schoolchildren are taught to recite the Pledge of Allegiance to the flag and to stand at attention for the playing of "The Star-Spangled Banner" before an assembly or sporting event.

myth	A major function of schools is to teach children only the truth about their country.
reality	A major function of schools is to foster national unity. Therefore, the nation's glorious achievements are played up, but its shameful acts are often watered down or left out.

Schools also plant seeds of patriotism in their young charges by teaching civics, history, and other social studies. In these courses, glorious national achievements are played up but shameful acts are often watered down or left out for fear of a negative effect on children. Thus, U.S. children are taught that their European ancestors came to this country as heroic pioneers; they are less likely to learn that those pioneers slaughtered massive numbers of Native Americans and stole their lands. In Japan, school textbooks do not contain information or pictures showing Japanese wartime atrocities in China, such as massacring 200,000 civilians in the city of Nanjing, bayoneting civilians for practice, and burying civilians alive (French, 2001; Kristof, 1995a; Sayle, 1982).

Providing Custodial Care Another major but latent function of schooling is to offer custodial care of children—providing a place for them and someone to watch them. Schools keep children off the streets and presumably out of trouble. The importance of this function has increased as the number of two-career and single-parent households has grown.

Schools have traditionally been effective in performing their custodial role. In the past, many schools were run under strict discipline, with teachers diligently enforcing rules and regulations and students obeying without question. But since the mid twentieth century, a growing number of schools seem to have turned into "blackboard jungles," where violence and drug use are rampant. In the 1990s, school violence even spread from large cities to small towns and rural areas. Nevertheless, an orderly routine still prevails in most schools (Arnette and Walsleben, 1998; Blank et al., 1998; Applebome, 1996).

The custodial function of schools is important for yet another reason: It keeps the young out of the job market. The U.S. unemployment rate would shoot up dangerously if there was no compulsory school attendance. The need to keep young people out of the job market, though, requires that they spend more years in school than are necessary for acquiring basic knowledge and skills. Thus, most students take 12 years—from grades 1 through 12—to acquire basic reading and mathematical skills that could be attained in about 3 years of intensive training between ages 15 and 18 (White, 1977). Given the enormous amount of time left over after these basic skills are learned, how can students be kept so long in school without getting too restless? They are given ample opportunities for recreational, extracurricular, and nonacademic activities. In fact, the schools play their custodial role so well that many students end up considering games, sports, and friends—not books, classes, and teachers—the most important features of their school experience (Goodlad, 1984).

■ Conflict Perspective: Inequality and Cultural Imperialism

While the functionalist perspective focuses on how education benefits society, the conflict perspective is more critical, revealing how education can harm society.

Reinforcing Social Inequality Functionalists assume that schools serve to reduce social inequality in the larger society by improving the life chances of the poor and minorities. But conflict theorists argue just the opposite—that schools reinforce the existing social structure of inequality.

Education in the United States is therefore seen as supporting the capitalist system by producing an array of skills and attitudes appropriate for maintaining social inequality. In elementary and secondary schools, lower-class children are trained to respect authority and obey orders—characteristics that employers like in manual laborers. In high school, higher-income youths are usually channeled into college preparatory courses, and thus eventually into higher-status jobs, while lower-income students are typically guided into vocational courses, which lead to lower-status jobs. After graduating from high school, higher-income students are more likely to attend college than are lower-income students. Those in elite universities learn independent thinking and decision-making skills, which are useful for leader-

PREP VERSUS SHOP In high school, youths from the upper and middle classes are usually channeled into college-preparatory courses, but students from lower classes are more likely to end up in vocational, or shop, courses, which lead to lower-status jobs. ■

ship positions. Meanwhile, in average universities and colleges, middle-class youths are taught responsibility, dependability, and the ability to work without close supervision—qualities that are needed for middle-level professions and occupations. In short, according to the conflict perspective, education teaches youths to know their place and to fill it (Lee and Smith, 2001; Weis, 1988; Bowles and Gintis, 1976).

There is evidence to support the conflict argument. In the United States, a majority of elementary and secondary schools practice **tracking**, the system of sorting students into different groups according to past academic achievement (Strum, 1993). In his study of nearly 900 high school classes throughout the United States, John Goodlad (1984) found that higher-income students tend to be in higher-track (higher-ability) classes and lower-class and minority students in lower-track classes. Goodlad further discovered that higher-track students were taught "a more independent type of thinking—self-direction, creativity, critical thinking, pursuing individual assignments, and

SINK OR SWIM To functionalists, schools play an important role in the Americanization of young people, enabling the nation to enhance its unity and helping minorities to improve their life chances. But conflict theorists see Americanization as a threat to the cultural heritages of minorities. The resulting loss of ethnic pride is assumed to bring down self-esteem and grades, creating a bleak future for minority youth. ■

active involvement in the process of learning." By contrast, lower-track students were taught "a more conforming type of classroom behavior—working quietly, punctuality, cooperation, improving study habits, conforming to rules and expectations, and getting along with others." Higher-income students were, in effect, taught to be high-paid professionals, while lower-class and minority students were taught to become low-paid manual workers.

Education as Cultural Imperialism Like other societies, the United States has long recognized the importance of using education to unify its people by teaching history from its own viewpoint. School-children can therefore be "Americanized," thinking of themselves as U.S. citizens, supporting the American democratic ideal, and becoming assimilated into the mainstream of U.S. culture.

Seen from the functionalist perspective, Americanization is not only necessary for the nation as a whole, it is also useful to immigrants and minorities. It enables minorities to improve their life chances and the nation to enhance its unity. Viewed from the conflict perspective, however, Americanization looks like **cultural imperialism**, the practice of making minorities accept the dominant group's culture. It involves forcibly imposing much of the WASP (White Anglo-Saxon Protestant) culture on U.S. citizens of other cultural backgrounds. The typical U.S. history textbook is written from the WASP's point of view so that it presents mostly whites as heroes—and very few heroes from minority groups. Americanization also forces minority children to give up their cultural heritage, such as the Spanish language, and to be taught in English only. Thus, so-called Americanization not only threatens to destroy minority cultures but also encourages teachers to stereotype minority students as culturally deprived.

■ Symbolic Interactionist Perspective: The Power of Teacher Expectations

According to a key tenet of symbolic interactionism, in social interaction, we tend to behave in accordance with how we think others see us. Thus, in classroom interaction, how the teacher defines a student can have powerful consequences for the student's academic performance. If a student is viewed as intelligent, the student will likely perform well. If another student is considered less intelligent, that student will likely perform less well. Such power held by the teacher reflects the **Pygmalion effect**, the impact of a teacher's expectations on student performance.

The Pygmalion Effect In Greek mythology, Pygmalion was a sculptor who created Galatea, an ivory statue of a beautiful woman. Pygmalion fell in love with his creation and prayed to the goddess of love, who brought the statue of Galatea to life. In a sense, teachers can be compared to Pygmalion and their students to Galatea: Teachers can bring their expectations to life. If a teacher expects certain students to fail, they are likely to do so. If a teacher expects them to succeed, then they are likely to succeed. Thus, the Pygmalion effect is an example of a *self-fulfilling prophecy*. Robert Rosenthal (1973) and numerous other researchers have demonstrated the Pygmalion effect in a series of

theoretical thumbnail

The Influences of Education

Perspective	Focus	Insights
Functionalist	Positive functions of education	Schools teach knowledge and skills, enhance social mobility, promote national unity, and provide custodial care of children.
Conflict	Social inequality and cultural imperialism	Schools reinforce the existing inequality in society and impose the dominant group's culture on minorities.
Symbolic interactionist	The power of teacher expectations	Whether teachers expect students to do well or to do poorly, students will likely perform accordingly.

experiments, one of which was described briefly in Chapter 1 (The Essence of Sociology).

How does the Pygmalion effect work? The teacher's expectations do not affect the student's performance directly, but they do influence the teacher's behavior, which in turn directly affects the student's performance. Teachers tend to give attention, praise, and encouragement to students they consider bright. If the students fail to perform as well as expected, the teachers work extra hard to help them live up to expectations. But teachers tend to be uninterested in, critical toward, and even impatient with those they expect to do poorly in school. When these students have some difficulty, teachers are likely to think it would be a waste of time trying to help them. As a result of this differential treatment, the differences in students' performances tend to match teachers' expectations: The presumably bright students do better than the presumably poor ones (Harris and Rosenthal, 1985; Rosenthal, 1973).

The Tracking Effect   In view of the Pygmalion effect, it is not surprising that school tracking generally benefits higher-track students more than lower-track students. Tracking raises teacher expectations for higher-track students and lowers them for lower-track students.

This may explain why, as research by John Goodlad (1984) indicates, teachers in higher-track classes spend more time on instruction, expect students to study more at home, and are seen by students as more enthusiastic about teaching, more concerned about them, and less punitive toward them compared with teachers in lower-track classes. Thus, the good students tend to get better and the weak students weaker. As many studies have shown, higher-track students are more likely to go to college, and lower-track students are more likely to have low self-esteem, drop out of school, and become delinquents (Strum, 1993; Goodlad, 1984; Alexander and Cook, 1982).

For a quick review of the three perspectives on education, see the Theoretical Thumbnail above.

EDUCATION IN THE UNITED STATES

For some time, many of the critiques of education in the United States have documented a decline in educational standards and achievement compared with the past and with other countries. Scores on Scholastic Aptitude Tests (SATs) taken by college-bound high school seniors fell sharply and continuously from the 1960s to the 1980s. Although SAT scores have inched upward since 1990, they still remain far below those in the 1960s (see Figure 11.2). Compared with their counterparts in such countries as Singapore, South Korea, Japan, and the Czech Republic, U.S. high school students also score lower on math and science tests. As a result, the media, as well as many national task forces on education, have raised the alarm about a crisis in U.S. schools said to threaten the very future of the United States and its people (Feller, 2003; Hinds, 2000; Kronholz, 1998). Is U.S. education really in a state of crisis? If we put the discouraging data in proper perspective, the answer is probably no.

Problems in Perspective

First, the decline of SAT scores may have resulted partly from the increasing democratization of U.S. education. In contrast to the continued elitism of foreign educational systems, the U.S. system has included growing numbers of poor, minority, and immigrant students. Because of inadequate academic preparation or the tests' cultural bias or both, the socially disadvantaged students do not do as well on the SAT as the socially advantaged, helping to bring down the average score for the entire group. But the investment in equal education has begun to pay off.

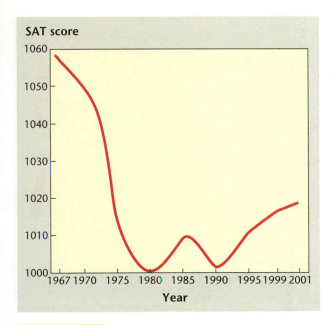

"I wasn't playing hooky—I was fleeing the deteriorating public school system."

Source: From the *Wall Street Journal*—Permission, Cartoon Features Syndicate.

FIGURE 11.2

Declining SAT Scores

The SAT scores of college-bound high school seniors fell significantly and continuously from the 1960s to the 1980s. The scores started to rise around 1990, but they are still far below those of the 1960s. This has raised concerns about the quality of American schools and the future of the United States as a nation and a people.

Critical Thinking: *Do you feel you received a good education in high school? Why or why not?*

Source: Data from U.S. Census Bureau, 2002.

Since 1999, national SAT averages have been rising, partly as a result of the steady improvement in test scores among African American, Hispanic, and other minority students.

Second, the United States is not alone in having educational problems. Japan, which is often touted as being a world leader in science and technology, has serious problems with its higher education. Although Japanese schoolchildren are under enormous pressure to study hard, university students are allowed to take it easy, as if to be rewarded for having worked so hard before college. As Robert Christopher (1983) has observed, "The great majority of Japanese universities are extraordinarily permissive: once you get into one, it takes real effort to get kicked out. . . . Japanese university authorities do not regard a student's failure to attend classes or even to pass courses as a ground for dismissal." Moreover, Japanese leaders have grown concerned that their schools' emphasis on conformity, such as finding the single right answer to a problem, is depriving their society of much needed creativity, especially in the current age of rapid change (Fiske, 1987).

Third, U.S. schools are not entirely to blame for the lower achievement of their students compared with the Japanese. For one thing, U.S. schools are expected to dilute their teaching resources by dealing with such social problems as alcohol and drug abuse and teenage pregnancy, which Japanese schools do not have. Also, given the high rates of divorce, single parenthood, and two-career couples, U.S. parents are often too stressed, tired, or self-absorbed to do what Japanese mothers do—help with their children's homework and make sure they study for three or four hours a night. Moreover, many U.S. teenagers hold part-time jobs, significantly reducing their ability to hit the books after school. By contrast, working during the schoolyear is virtually unheard of in Japan. In addition, U.S. teenagers are under great pressure from their peers to look good, drink, socialize, date, and even have sex. In contrast, the Japanese adolescent peer culture pressures teenagers to study hard. Japanese students like to say, though a little facetiously, "Four you score; five you die," meaning "If you sleep five hours a night instead of four, you won't pass the exams." In short, it is largely social problems, the lack of support from parents, and the adolescent subculture that make it hard for U.S. schools to compete with their Japanese counterparts (Morse, 2001b; Steinberg et al., 1996; Steinberg, 1987).

Finally, while many problems can be found in U.S. schools, there is a lot of good in them, as well, particularly in their mission of providing quality with equality. Although education researcher and

NOSES TO GRINDSTONE Japanese society offers a school setting for children that is different from that in the United States. Unlike U.S. schools, Japanese schools do not spend time dealing with such problems as alcohol and drug abuse or teen pregnancy. Japanese mothers make sure their children study three to four hours a night, and Japanese adolescent peer culture pressures teenagers to study hard. ■

reformer Theodore Sizer (1984) has criticized the nation's high schools for being rigid and impersonal, he has still found that "they are, on the whole, happy places, settings that most adolescents find inviting, staffed by adults who genuinely care for youngsters."

myth	Japanese schools are so much better than American schools that U.S. society would benefit if its educators emulated the Japanese.
reality	Japanese schools are not necessarily better. They may even be worse: By emphasizing extreme conformity, they tend to stifle individuality and creativity, qualities that U.S. schools cultivate.

In contrast, most Japanese students do not enjoy their school experience because they feel like robots or prisoners in a rigidly controlled environment. Moreover, Japanese students are not as creative as their U.S. counterparts (Tharp, 1987). Like Japanese society, Japanese schools stress extreme conformity, pressuring students to do what everybody else is doing while discouraging them from standing out by taking risks. By contrast, U.S. schools, like U.S. society, place a high premium on individuality and creativity, prodding students to think for themselves in innovative ways. Otherwise, the United States would not have become the world's most technologically advanced nation today (Elliott, 1998).

Nonetheless, efforts are always being made to improve U.S. education. In the next few sections, we

will look at some reforms, as well as trends that have emerged over the last three decades and still continue today: Head Start, school choice, homeschooling, and lifelong learning.

■ Head Start

Sociologists in the 1960s often found that trying to equalize the quality of the nation's schools and educational opportunities did not produce educational equality because some children's family backgrounds handicapped them from the very start of school. Some youngsters never saw a book at home and were never encouraged to do well at school. There seemed to be a need for **compensatory education**, a school program intended to improve the academic performance of socially and educationally disadvantaged children. So in the mid 1960s, the federal government began funding Head Start, a compensatory education program for disadvantaged preschoolers across the nation. It was run mostly by pediatricians and child psychologists working for poverty agencies. The aim was to prepare poor children ages 3 and 4 for kindergarten. These children were taught the skills and vocabulary that many of their middle-class peers absorb at home. Their parents were also brought in to learn about child care, health care, and nutrition.

Early studies of the results were not encouraging. They showed that although the training did raise children's IQ scores and scholastic achievement, the benefits were temporary. In the first grade, disadvantaged pupils who had had preschool training might perform better than those who had not, but by the third grade this difference tended to disappear, and both disadvantaged groups were equally likely to fall behind their grade level (Stearns, 1971). This is the kind of evidence that conservative politicians in the 1990s often pointed to in their call for the elimination of Head Start.

Why did the benefits disappear, and why did students not respond better to remedial programs? In the 1970s, researchers were unable to find a definitive answer. Most argued that the continuing influence of a poor family environment was the answer because it simply overwhelmed the influence that any educational program could have. Others contended that the preschool programs had been doomed to failure because of inadequate funding. A few argued that they had been unfairly evaluated before they had time to prove their effectiveness. The last argument turns out to be the one that hit the nail on the head.

In the 1980s and 1990s, many studies showed that the preschool programs do benefit low-income students in the long run. When poor youngsters who were in the preschool programs reach ages 9 to 19, they do better in school than peers who were not. They have higher reading scores, are less likely to be held back a grade, and are more likely to graduate from high school, attend college, and have higher rates of employment. They are also less likely to go on welfare or get involved in delinquency and crime (Zigler, 2000; Svestka, 1996; Barnett, 1995; Yoshikawa, 1995).

In short, among poor children, those who attend Head Start will more likely succeed in school and life than those who do not. But lower-income children as a whole still lag behind their peers from higher-income families in reading and math skills. To close this learning gap, the Bush administration wants Head Start to focus more on teaching the alphabet, vocabulary, and numbers. Such a strict emphasis on academics worries some early education experts, though, because it may cause a decline in children's social and emotional development, such as learning to get along and to pay attention (McGrath, 2003).

■ School Choice

In the late 1960s, a new idea began to receive considerable publicity. It was vintage American: If there were more competition among the schools, perhaps the schools would be better. After all, people were entitled to more freedom in choosing where their children would be educated. This idea inspired proposals for voucher plans. Public schools have a virtual monopoly on public funds for education, and which school children attend depends, for the most part, on where they live. A voucher plan could change this situation. Parents, not schools, would receive public money in the form of a *voucher,* which they would use to pay for their children's attendance at the schools of their choice. The schools would receive money from the government in return for the vouchers. The greater the number of parents who chose a particular school, the more money it would receive. The idea is to force the public schools to compete with each other, and with private and parochial schools, for customers. Presumably, good schools would attract plenty of students, and poor schools would be forced to improve in order to compete effectively.

But the majority of teachers and their unions oppose vouchers for several reasons. First, vouchers would encourage white parents to choose schools on the basis of racial or ethnic prejudice. They would thus promote racial segregation and, eventually, greater divisiveness in U.S. society generally. Second, by taking government money away from poor schools, the voucher plan would make the schools worse because they desperately need the money to improve. Third, because the voucher program would mean giving government funds to religious schools, many worry that it would violate the principle of separation of church and state required by the Constitution (Doerr et al., 1996; Hegedus, 1976).

In the 1990s, popular support for vouchers grew significantly because many schools continued to face such problems as overcrowding, violence, and poor test scores. The voucher program was particularly popular among poor parents because they were anxious to pull their children out of failing public schools and put them in better schools. In 1998, the U.S. Supreme Court even upheld a Wisconsin law that provides low-income students with public money to attend private or parochial schools.

Then, in 2002, the U.S. Supreme Court ruled that the voucher program in Cleveland did not violate the constitutional separation of church and state, even though most of the parents who received the tax dollars chose to send their children to religious schools. The key reason the Court cited for its decision was that the program provided a "true private choice," letting the individual decide where the public money should go, without the government promoting one religion over another (Tomsho, 2003; Greenhouse, 2002).

But will vouchers greatly improve poor schools, as its advocates believe? So far, the evidence is inconclusive: Some studies have shown higher test scores among voucher students than among their public school peers, but other studies have found no such differences between the two groups (Greene, 2003; Lord, 2002; Toch and Cohen, 1998).

Another form of school choice involves the establishment of *charter schools* outside the regular school system. Such schools are supported by public funds, but they are operated like private schools because they do not have to answer to the local school board, as public schools do. Like vouchers, charter schools have become increasingly popular (see Figure 11.3). The growing popularity of both vouchers and charters has begun to compel their strongest opponents, the teachers' unions, to improve the regular public schools. As the president of the National Education Association said, "We must revitalize our public schools from within or they will be dismantled from without" (Toch and Cohen, 1998). Certain reforms have thus been instituted. An important example is the *peer review* program, which places both new teachers and experienced but failing teachers under the guidance of mentor teachers. While helping their charges become better teachers, the mentors are given the power to recommend removing underperformers from the classroom.

■ Homeschooling

There has been phenomenal growth in the number of children who receive their formal education at home, from only 0.3 million in 1990 to 1.7 million today, compared to only 0.5 million in charter schools. Before 1994, most homeschooling parents were fundamentalist Christians who believed that religion was either abused or ignored in the public school. But today, three-quarters of homeschooling families reject public education for secular reasons: poor teaching, crowded classrooms, and lack of safety. Many of the older children, though, enroll in public schools part time, for a math class or a chemistry lab, or for after-school activities, such as football or volleyball. Compared to parents whose children attend public schools, homeschooling parents are more likely to be white and college educated (Cloud and Morse, 2001; Steven, 2001).

There are different kinds of home-based curricula. One is the *back-to-basics* approach, which emphasizes the three Rs, patriotism, and Bible studies. It is free of sex education, drug abuse programs, AIDS education, self-esteem exercises, and other nonacademic programs that are often provided in public schools. Most back-to-basics programs teach reading phonetically; use fact-rich history, geography, and science texts; and emphasize simple repetition and drill methods.

Another type of home teaching is the *unschooling* approach, which offers children the freedom to pursue their interests but with parental guidance. The parent provides various educational resources such as encyclopedias, dictionaries, atlases, and computers—supported by the Internet and new educational

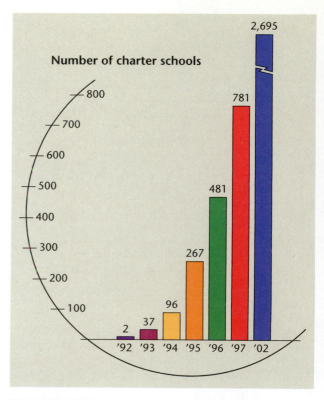

FIGURE 11.3

The Fast-Growing Popularity of Charter Schools

Charter schools, like public schools, are supported by public funds, but they are operated like private schools for not having to answer to the local school board. The fast-growing popularity of charters has forced their staunchest opponents—teachers unions—to improve the regular public schools through such means as placing new teachers and incompetent teachers under the guidance of mentor teachers.

Critical Thinking: *Why have charter schools become so popular?*

Source: Data from Center for Education Reform, 1998, 2003.

software. The parent also teaches concepts related to the activities the children have chosen (Kilborn, 2000).

A third type of home curriculum emphasizes *classical learning*. Children are taught to read great books, to memorize important facts, and to think logically and express their ideas effectively. They study not only classical literature but also history, geography, and Latin or some other foreign language in the early grades. This kind of curriculum has long been popular with missionary and diplomatic families stationed abroad. Famous figures of the past such as Abraham Lincoln, Thomas Edison, Leo Tolstoy, and John Stuart Mill had this kind of homeschooling during childhood (Seuffert, 1990).

Homeschooling has been criticized for depriving children of the opportunity to interact with their peers. Such criticism is based on the popular assumption that children need to socialize with their peers in order to learn how to get along with people. But many homeschoolers are taught to develop social skills by associating with people of different ages and backgrounds rather than mostly with their peers (Seuffert, 1990). Moreover, homeschool children are not isolated at home all day. They get involved in various outside activities, including Scouting, ballet, church activities, sports, and 4-H clubs (Farris, 1997).

What about the quality of home education? There is some evidence that compared to students in public schools, homeschoolers score much higher on standardized tests and have a better chance of getting admitted to top universities. Undoubtedly, some homeschools turn out to be disasters, but their advocates argue that public schools are no better; they already are disasters (Cloud and Morse, 2001; Hawkins, 1996; McArdle, 1994; Allis, 1990).

■ Lifelong Learning

Yet another trend in education involves not children and adolescents but adults who have been out of school for some time. The appeal of *lifelong learning* has led many adults to return to the classroom, often for formal college credits. Most of these lifelong learners are enrolled in two-year community colleges. But seeing the popularity of adult education in community colleges and facing declining enrollments of traditional students, many four-year colleges and universities have offered their own continuing education programs. Today, adults aged 35 and older make up over 21 percent of total enrollment, nearly twice the figure of 20 years ago (see Figure 11.4, p. 308) (U.S. Census Bureau, 2003; Levine, 1993).

The remarkable growth of continuing education owes much to changing economic forces, such as the loss of blue-collar jobs that paid middle-class wages and the demands imposed on workers by new technology. Not surprisingly, many nontraditional students are adult workers seeking retraining, additional training, or new careers. But there are others: homemakers preparing to enter the job market at middle age; retired people seeking to pursue interests postponed or dormant during their working years; and people who want to enrich the quality of their personal, family, and social lives. Most of these adults are serious students; they are much more likely than younger students to earn A's and B's (Francese, 2002; Rimer, 2000).

To accommodate their students' diverse responsibilities and interests, continuing education courses tend to be flexible. The courses are usually offered in the evenings or on weekends, and sometimes outside conventional classrooms, in various community facilities such as libraries. Their requirements are flexible, too. Some programs allow students to earn college credits without taking a course, by passing an examination, or by proving their competency through their job, hobby, writing, and so on. Students can even take courses via the Internet (Newman, 1996). Many courses offered on the campus are shorter and more focused than typical college courses. Although most of the students are over age 35 and are working full time, most of the courses

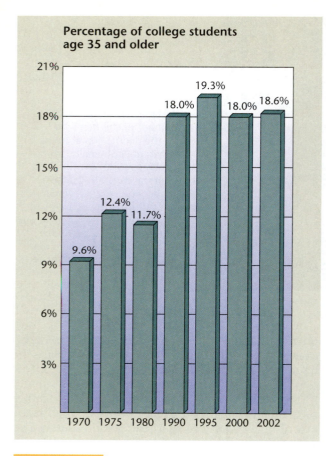

Percentage of college students age 35 and older

- 1970: 9.6%
- 1975: 12.4%
- 1980: 11.7%
- 1990: 18.0%
- 1995: 19.3%
- 2000: 18.0%
- 2002: 18.6%

FIGURE 11.4

Older Students on Campus

The remarkable increase of older students in college has resulted from changing economic forces, such as the loss of high-paid blue-collar jobs and the rising demand for new technological skills. But there are also other reasons for attending college after age 35, including the desire to enrich the quality of personal, family, and social lives.

Critical Thinking: *Would you return to college after 35? Why or why not?*

Source: Data from National Center for Education Statistics, 2003.

currently designed for lifelong learners may well become the standard curricula at most colleges and universities (Rimer, 2000; Johnson, 1995).

SOCIAL DIVERSITY IN U.S. EDUCATION

In the United States, various ethnic groups do not receive the same kind or amount of education. Whites generally have better or more education than non-whites. As a result, educational attainment is higher among whites than among most minority groups. But differences in attainment and other educational experiences also exist among minority groups themselves.

■ Native American Education

For over 100 years, Native American children were subjected to forced assimilation into the European American culture. They were sent away to boarding schools that the U.S. government's Bureau of Indian Affairs (BIA) operated with the intent to supposedly civilize the "wild Indians." At these schools, the children were forbidden to speak their native languages, indoctrinated with white values, and compelled to dress and act like whites. But since the 1960s, Native Americans have often pressed for the inclusion in BIA-operated schools of classes in native languages, art, and other aspects of Native American cultures. Many of these schools have consequently included Native American cultures in the curriculum. Even so, they generally have very low academic standards and poorly trained teachers.

Most Native American children are enrolled in local public schools, which usually fail to meet these students' needs. The problem stems from the absence of a Native American perspective in the curricula, the loss of native language ability, the abandonment of native spiritual values, and the racism of white teachers and administrators (Feagin and Feagin, 1999).

Whether in reservation or public schools, Native American students have more problems than their peers of any other ethnic group. As the director of the Native American Scholarship Fund has said, "We got the worst of everything: the lowest test scores, lowest rate of reading books, highest dropout rate, and lowest rate of entering college" (Belluck, 2000b). Apparently, students have little incentive to become educated, as they find themselves surrounded by widespread signs of poverty, unemployment, and alcoholism (Eig, 2002).

Of the better students who go on to college, most are enrolled in the same schools as other citizens around the country. A few—about 13 percent—attend tribal colleges, where students can reclaim their native identity while simultaneously learning to function well in the larger society. Most of these tribal colleges, however, are small, poorly financed two-year institutions that stress vocational education (Feagin and Feagin, 1999; Simpson, 1995).

■ African American Education

From the late nineteenth century to the mid twentieth century, black and white children attended separate schools, with the former receiving inferior education. This prompted the U.S. Supreme Court in 1954 to declare segregated public schools unconstitutional and to order them desegregated "with all deliberate speed." But the attempt to achieve integration ran into the roadblock of residential segregation: Because they lived in different neighborhoods, black and white children typically went to different schools. Thus, the courts ordered that pupils be bused to schools away from their own neighborhoods. In the 1980s and 1990s, most white parents did not want their children transported to predominantly black schools, but many black parents agreed to let their children be bused to mostly white schools. As a result, the level of school integration has improved, so that today, both white and black children throughout the United States are more likely to attend integrated schools than before. In fact, the schools in the South, which were once the most segregated in the country, are now the most integrated (Pinkney, 1993).

But mandatory, court-ordered busing has also led to some "white flight" from the cities (where many African Americans live) to the suburbs (where there are fewer African Americans). To lure white families back, city schools that need to be integrated have been turned into *magnet schools,* which offer special science labs, language classes, and superior teaching. Most of these schools have become popular, but there are not enough of them to admit all applicants. Only about one-third of the school districts are able to get government funds to open magnet schools (Kunen, 1996; Wells, 1991).

Still, even before forced busing, many whites had already moved from the city to the suburbs. Due to this residential segregation, schools in the central city have become predominantly black while those in the suburban periphery have become mostly white. Moreover, since 1989, the courts have helped slow school integration by rescinding some mandatory busing and other past desegregation orders. Even a growing number of African Americans have come to support the dismantling of mandatory desegregation. One reason is that court-ordered busing programs often involve forcing African American children to travel long distances to schools where they may not be welcome. A second reason is that some African Americans consider it better to focus on improving inner-city schools with whatever resources, such as millions of dollars in transportation money, are available. A third reason is an increased concern among some African Americans that forced integration can result in a loss of their identity and community (Fineman, 1996).

At the college level, most black students attend predominantly white institutions. But there is no real integration on such campuses, where African American students usually establish their own social networks, separate from white networks, because they do not feel part of the white campus life. Historically, black colleges, where the majority of black faculty members teach, are more hospitable to black students. As a consequence, African American students are more likely to succeed in earning a bachelor's degree at a black college than at a white school (Feagin and Feagin, 1999; Pinkney, 1993).

■ Hispanic American Education

Educational attainment is lower among Hispanic Americans than among most other groups. Hispanic

THUMBS DOWN ON WHAT WORKS Research has generally shown that Hispanic children with limited English proficiency, such as these fourth-grade students in a bilingual classroom in Texas, learn English faster and get better grades when taught academic subjects in their native language for several years while gradually learning English as a second language. But many schools do not have such bilingual classes, as nearly half of the U.S. population are opposed to bilingual schooling. This is especially true among conservative politicians. ■

students are also much more likely than most other groups to drop out of school. Their higher poverty rate is a major factor, but there are at least two school-related factors that contribute more directly to the problem (Headden, 1998).

First is a lack of multicultural sensitivity on the part of school administrators and teachers. Most Hispanic American children attend predominantly minority schools in the city, whose educational resources are generally less adequate than those of white suburban schools. Although the majority of the students in these schools are Hispanic, most teachers and administrators are European Americans, and they tend to be insensitive to Hispanic history and culture. Not surprisingly, European American teachers treat Hispanic students less well than their white peers: Hispanics are praised less often, are asked fewer questions, and have their ideas used less frequently. All this contributes to their lower academic achievement and higher dropout rate (Feagin and Feagin, 1999).

Another contributor to the problem is the lack of bilingual programs for many Hispanic children with limited English proficiency. Research has generally suggested that children learn English faster and get better grades when taught academic subjects in their native language for several years while gradually learning English as a second language. But many schools do not have bilingual classes. In fact, nearly half of the U.S. population, especially conservative politicians, are opposed to bilingual schooling. When instructed entirely in English, however, many Hispanic pupils with limited English proficiency become discouraged, feel less self-confident, and fall behind their English-speaking peers. But opponents of bilingual education argue that instruction in English only will raise their test scores for reading and math (Portes, 2002; Wildavsky, 2000; Feagin and Feagin, 1999).

■ Asian American Education

Asian Americans have the highest educational attainment of any group. Especially at the top U.S. universities, Asian Americans are overrepresented, composing more than 10 percent of the freshman classes, although they constitute only about 3 percent of the U.S. college-age population. This seems to have led such universities as Harvard, MIT, and Stanford to discriminate against Asian Americans, as suggested by the lower proportion of admissions for Asian applicants than for whites, despite comparable or higher academic qualifications. The universities often prejudicially consider Asian students with high academic achievement to be too narrowly focused and therefore use the so-called *academic-plus factor* (demonstration of interest in sports, music, and other nonacademic activities) to deny them admis-

sion (Kitano and Daniels, 1995; U.S. Commission on Civil Rights, 1992). Critics suggest that some universities are apparently fearful of being swamped by Asian American students. This prejudice-driven fear recalls the past fear about African Americans taking over professional sports. But perhaps the increasing support for multiculturalism will eventually make the common sight of Asian American students on campus as acceptable as that of professional African American athletes in sports arenas today.

In high school, Asian Americans are also overrepresented among students who excel in math and science, particularly as winners of the annual national science competition, the Westinghouse Science Talent Search. This has served to reinforce the popular stereotype of Asian Americans as naturally gifted in science. The fact is that not all Asians are scientifically competent. Many Asian Americans, especially immigrants not proficient in English, often have low grades and high dropout rates. Another fact is that the Asians who score high on math and science tests do so because of hard work rather than natural talent. Some even attend after-school or weekend classes to ensure academic success.

SOCIOLOGICAL PERSPECTIVES ON RELIGION

Like education, religion is an important social institution. Not surprisingly, some form of religious belief exists all over the world. Some people may see religion as a carryover from the superstitious past, and hence as important only for supposedly primitive or backward societies. Actually, religion is also very much a part of modern social life. Although the United States is one of the world's most scientifically and technologically advanced societies, it is also one of the most religious. Why does religion seem so important to many people? What can religion do for or to society? Various answers to such questions can be found in the three sociological perspectives.

■ Functionalist Perspective: Religion as a Positive Force

According to the functionalist perspective, religion is a positive force to society and in the lives of individuals. Exactly why is religion so important? One answer can be found in Durkheim's classical functionalist theory and another in modern sociologists' functionalist analyses.

Society as Representation of God Émile Durkheim presented his functionalist view of religion in *The*

Elementary Forms of Religious Life, first published in 1912. It was Durkheim's aim to refute the popular view that God—or whatever is worshiped as sacred—is merely an illusion, a figment of human imagination. According to Durkheim, if religion were an illusion, it would have disappeared in rational modern societies. But it has not. "It is inadmissible," said Durkheim, "that systems of ideas like religion, which have held so considerable a place in history, and to which people have turned in all ages for the energy they need to live, should be mere tissues of illusion." If God were merely a product of the individual's imagination, Durkheim also argued, God would occupy the same status as any other idea—a part of the profane world incapable of inspiring reverence, awe, and worship. Instead, God must be sacred and far above humans, as demonstrated by the fact that the deity is widely worshiped.

If this revered entity is both real and superior to us, then what is God? Durkheim's answer: society. Society is more powerful than any of us and beyond our personal control. It is separate from us, yet we are part of it, and it is part of our consciousness. It outlives each of us and even our children. We are dependent on it, and it demands our obedience. It is neither a person nor a thing, yet we feel and know its reality. These attributes of society are also characteristics of the sacred—in Western religions, of God. In short, the sacred, according to Durkheim, is the symbolic representation of society. By worshiping God, we are, in effect, worshiping society.

Such a view of religion led Durkheim to emphasize that religion functions to preserve social order. Every religion, he argued, possesses both rituals and moral norms. Through their religion's rituals, people sanctify and renew their bonds to one another. Their belief in the sacred and their acceptance of common norms are strengthened. Thus, religion binds the society and helps maintain it.

While Durkheim made the general statement that religion helps to preserve social order, today's functionalist sociologists are more specific on the functions of religion. They also find a paradox in each of these functions: If religion is too successful in carrying out a positive function, it may produce negative results for society (O'Dea and Aviad, 1983).

Supportive Function Religion often performs a supportive function by providing consolation, reconciliation, and relief from anxiety. By praying, believers may become less anxious about losing their jobs or about old age and death. Faith may console those who have lost a loved one or are beset by illness, loneliness, disappointment, frustration, or sorrow. Religion can reconcile people to the sinfulness of others, the hostility of enemies, the injustices of society, and other unpleasant aspects of this world. Not surprisingly, as research has shown, actively religious people are healthier and happier than those who are not religious (Sheler, 2001a; Myers, 1993).

However, if the faithful receive *too much* support and consolation, religion can impede useful social change. Many religions urge their believers to see all worldly things as trivial compared with the life of the spirit. Others perceive this world as a mere waystation, or a "vale of tears" that is meant to be a test of love and faith or even as an illusion. All these beliefs can encourage the faithful not only to be consoled but also to endure their suffering docilely. Thus, religions can discourage people from confronting the sources of their suffering or from joining a social or revolutionary movement that may help to alleviate their suffering.

Social Control Function Religion performs a social control function by strengthening conformity to society's norms in at least two ways. First, religion helps to *sacralize* (make sacred) the norms and values of established society with such commandments as "Thou shalt not kill" and "Thou shalt not steal." Thus, religious people are less likely to violate the laws of the state because these laws are taken to be the laws of God. Not surprisingly, as over 50 research studies have shown, religious participation inhibits crime, delinquency, and deviant behavior in general (Ellis, 1985; Peek, Curry, and Chalfont, 1985). Second, religion encourages good, friendly, and cooperative behavior, as illustrated by the story of the Good Samaritan, the maxim "Do unto others as you would have others do unto you," and similar teachings. As a result, as research has indicated, religious people seem more friendly and cooperative—more likely to stop and comfort a crying child, to be good listeners, and even to get along with loud-mouthed, obnoxious people (Morgan, 1984, 1983).

However, religion's power to reinforce social control may set up yet another roadblock to useful change. Some of the state's laws and values sacralized by religion are unjust and harmful, such as those supporting racial or gender inequality. But the extremely faithful may consider them too sacred to question or change, perhaps saying, for example, "It is God's will that women should stay home and be only wives and mothers."

Prophetic Function Acting as a source of social change, religion may perform a prophetic function. It does this through some leaders who, like the ancient Jewish prophets, challenge the unjust political authorities of their day in order to bring a better life to the people. In the 1950s and 1960s, for example, Dr. Martin Luther King, Jr., led the fight against racial discrimination in the United States. During the 1980s, Anglican Archbishop Desmond Tutu played an important role in blacks' struggle against the white racist government in South Africa. Similarly, the leader of the Roman Catholic Church in the Philippines, Jaime Cardinal Sin, helped bring down President Ferdinand Marcos's repressive government.

Sometimes, however, prophetic calls for reform may produce violent fanaticism. During the seventeenth century, some 20,000 peasants in Russia were inspired to burn themselves as a way of protesting liturgical reforms in the Russian Orthodox Church. In 1420, the Adamites, a religious cult of Bohemians in Europe, set about making holy war to kill the unholy. They believed that they had to continue killing until they could make the blood fill the world to "the height of a horse's head" (Morrow, 1978). Today, Muslim terrorists are also waging a holy war against what they consider to be the infidels—including the United States.

Identity Function Religion may perform the identity function by enabling individuals to know who they are, what they are, and what the purpose of their lives is. In modern societies marked by impersonal relations and a confusing variety of values and norms, this function of providing self-identity may be especially important to individuals. Without their own identities, people may fall into an existential vacuum, finding life meaningless and merely muddling through.

myth	It is beneficial to society for the faithful to identify as strongly as possible with their religions.
reality	History has shown that when people identify too strongly with their religions, they tend to end up believing that there is only one true religion—namely, their own. Consequently, they are likely to be intolerant of others' religions, which they consider false. The result is often social conflict or intergroup violence.

Intense social conflict, however, is likely to erupt if people identify too strongly with their own religions. Such people tend to believe that there is only one true religion—their own—and become intolerant of all other, presumably false religions. Indeed, history is filled with persecutions and wars related to religious differences. Consider the medieval Christian Crusades against the Muslim heathens, the Thirty Years' War between the Catholics and Protestants in seventeenth-century Europe, the persecution and slaughter of the Mormons in the United States dur-

ing the nineteenth century, the Hindu–Muslim conflicts that resulted in the creation of mostly Hindu India and a separate Islamic Republic of Pakistan in 1947, the strife between the Protestants and Catholics in Northern Ireland, and the clash between the Buddhists and Hindus that plagues the Asian nation of Sri Lanka today.

■ Conflict Perspective: Religion as an Oppressive Illusion

While Durkheim assumed that religious beliefs are based on reality, Marx considered them to be mere illusions. More important, Marx believed these illusions to be an oppressive force in society.

A Supporter of the Ruling Class Marx presented the conflict theory that in a society divided into classes, the dominant religion usually represents the interests of the ruling class. The religion, however, disguises and justifies the power of that class. The deception is not deliberate. The ruling class is not conscious of its religion as illusory but believes it to be real. Yet religion, argued Marx, is nonetheless an oppressive illusion, one that helps the ruling class perpetuate its domination of the masses. In medieval Europe, the Roman Catholic Church bolstered the feudal system by promoting the notion that kings ruled by divine right. In India, for thousands of years, the Hindu religion has provided religious justification for the caste system. Religion supports the ruling class by justifying existing inequalities.

The Opium of the Masses If religion is merely an oppressive illusion, why would the masses support and even cling to it? The reason, according to Marx, is the prevailing social inequality and oppression, which drive the masses to seek solace somewhere. "Religion," Marx declared, "is the sigh of the oppressed creature, the heart of a heartless world, the soul of soulless circumstances. It is the opium of the people" (Acton, 1967). Opium offers relief and escape, and it drains people's will to find the source of their problems. Similarly, religion brings relief to oppressed workers, dulls their sensitivity to suffering, and diverts them from attacking the root of their pain—their exploitation by the wealthy and powerful. Religion accomplishes all this, argued Marx, by emphasizing the superiority of spiritual over earthly matters or by promising eternal bliss in the afterlife with such doctrines as "Blessed are the poor." As a result, religion ends up alienating workers from themselves by acquiring a harmful power over them—causing them to develop a false consciousness, an acceptance of the dominance of their oppressors.

theoretical thumbnail

The Characteristics of Religion

Perspective	Focus	Insights
Functionalist	Religion as a positive force	By making society a symbol of God, religion maintains social order with social support, control, reform, and identity, but these positive functions, if carried too far, may turn negative.
Conflict	Religion as an oppressive illusion	Religion supports the ruling class by justifying inequalities, which, in turn, encourages the oppressed masses to seek solace from religion.
Symbolic interactionist	Religion as an ironic belief	By suggesting that worldly success provided assurance of going to heaven, Calvinism encouraged the accumulation of wealth that led to the development of capitalism.

Many studies have supported Marx's assumption that poverty or oppression tends to make people embrace religion for consolation (Wimberley, 1984). This serves as a useful counterbalance against the functionalist analysis. But as discussed earlier, sometimes religion does fight oppression through its prophetic function.

■ Symbolic Interactionist Perspective: Religion as an Ironic Belief

Marx's analysis suggests that religion in general induces passive resignation to poverty. But Max Weber saw that at least one religion—Protestantism—promoted active pursuit of wealth, which is ironic because religion is supposed to be concerned with spiritual matters, not material things.

A Powerful Interpretation of the World As a symbolic interactionist, Weber regarded religion as people's interpretation of the world around them that powerfully influences their behavior toward that world. He noticed that the early Protestants in Europe, especially those of the Calvinist sect, had a unique belief. The belief was that long before they were born, God had predestined them to either salvation in heaven or damnation in hell. But they could not know which would be their eternal destiny. This generated a great deal of anxiety. To relieve anxiety, the Calvinists turned to constant self-control and work. They further believed that whether saved or damned, the faithful must work hard for the glory of God so as to establish God's kingdom on earth. Work came to be seen as a calling from God, and the worldly success that work brought came to be interpreted as a sign of election to heaven. Inevitably, the Calvinists worked extremely hard.

The Rise of Capitalism The Calvinists also had a unique definition of hard work. To them, the purpose of hard work was to glorify God, not to produce wealth. Thus, the Calvinists believed that they should not spend their wealth on worldly pleasures. Instead, they invested and reinvested their profits to make their businesses grow. The constant accumulation of wealth—the continual investment of profit—laid a foundation on which capitalism could emerge in Protestant societies.

Weber further argued that capitalism did not emerge in the predominantly Catholic countries or in China or India because their worldviews differed from what he called the *Protestant ethic*. Catholicism does not teach predestination. It encourages people to seek their rewards in heaven, and it does not view earthly success as a sign of God's favor. Confucianism values social harmony, not individualist strivings. Taoism teaches acceptance of the world as it is and withdrawal from it. Buddhism views worldly things as illusory and encourages escape from them through meditation. Hinduism requires its believers to endure the hardships of life and fulfill the obligations of their respective castes. These religions, Weber argued, did not offer ideas and habits favorable to the development of capitalist industrialism, as Calvinist Protestantism did.

But it is difficult to see how Weber's theory can be valid today. Catholics in the United States are now economically better off than many Protestants. Capitalism is also booming in such non-Protestant countries as Japan, South Korea, and Taiwan. Even so, Weber's theory seems convincing in explaining the *emergence* of capitalism in Europe.

For a quick review of the three perspectives on religion, see the Theoretical Thumbnail above.

RELIGION IN THE UNITED STATES

As early as 1835, French historian and political philosopher Alexis de Tocqueville observed that "there is no country in the world in which the Christian religion retains a greater influence over the souls of men" than the United States. Even today, religion is pervasive in American society. According to several surveys, about 95 percent of U.S. adults believe in God, 90 percent pray, and 88 percent believe that God loves them. Some 57 percent also consider religion "very important" in their lives (Gallup, 2001; NORC, 2001).

Just what do all these Americans believe? There is an amazing diversity of religions in the United States. While most Americans are still Christians, the last three decades of increased immigration from the Third World has helped establish Muslim, Buddhist, and Hindu communities, making the United States the most religiously diverse society in the world. But this diversity reflects more than differences in religious affiliation. It also reflects differences in social characteristics such as social class, age, and gender, as we will see in this section.

■ Religious Affiliation

There are more than 280 religious denominations in the United States, but a few large churches have the allegiance of most people. The Protestants constitute the largest group, although the Catholics outnumber the largest Protestant denomination—the Baptists. According to the latest survey, 91 percent of the U.S. adult population has a specific religious preference, with nearly 60 percent saying they are Protestants, 26 percent Catholics, and 2 percent Jews (see Figure 11.5).

The correlation between affiliation with an organized religion and religious belief and practice is far from perfect. Although a large majority (91 percent) of the U.S. population claim to have a religious preference, only a small minority (about 20 percent of Protestants and 28 percent of Catholics) attend religious services regularly (Hadaway et al., 1993). Among those who do go to church, very few do so for strictly religious reasons, such as worshiping God. Apparently, for most Americans, having a religious affiliation reflects something besides religious belief and practice. Belonging to a church can also provide a way of enjoying fellowship within a community of faith or conforming to social norms to gain respectability.

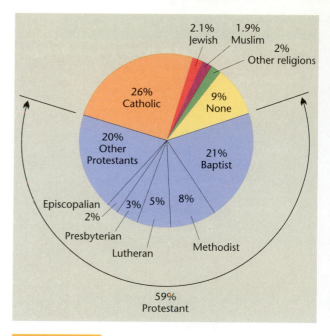

FIGURE 11.5

Religious Affiliations in the United States

An overwhelming majority of Americans belong to a religious organization. But only a small minority attend religious services regularly. Even among those who go to church regularly, very few do so for strictly religious reasons, such as worshiping God. Most attend church in order to enjoy fellowship and to gain social respectability.

Critical Thinking: *What do you expect to get out of attending a religious service?*

Sources: Data from U.S. Census Bureau, 2000; *Britannica Book of the Year 2003.*

■ Social Diversity

People of different social classes, ages, genders, and ethnicities have their own ways of getting involved in religion. Class, age, gender, and ethnicity can therefore help explain certain religious beliefs and practices.

Class Differences Although they may consider themselves equal before God, various religious groups are far from equal socioeconomically. They have different statuses, and they tend to attract people from different educational and income levels. Usually, Jews, Episcopalians, and Presbyterians top the status hierarchy. Next come Catholics and Methodists and then Baptists and Pentecostals.

Social class also influences people's religious participation. In general, the higher their class, the more likely people are to attend church regularly, to join

BACK TO THE FOLD Active church involvement generally increases for adults above age 24. Many parents feel the desire to baptize their infants and to offer their children the religious training they received. In addition to their return to organized religion, young families tend to reach out to various social organizations as they seek to establish a sense of community in which to raise their children. ■

Bible study groups, and to provide their children with religious education. Moreover, people of higher classes hold most of the leadership positions, such as membership on a church's board of trustees. But these facts do not mean that higher-income people have a stronger faith in God. In fact, belief in God is more widespread among the poor than among the rich. The lower classes are also more likely to believe in a literal interpretation of the Bible, to believe in a personal God, and to be emotionally involved in religion. The higher rate of participation by higher-income people seems to reflect a greater inclination to participate in *all* kinds of voluntary organizations. For many higher-income people, religious participation appears to be a public activity required for social respectability (Johnston, 1996; Hargrove, 1989).

Age Differences Adults above age 24 are more active in their churches than younger people. Religious involvement normally begins to escalate by age 25, first with marriage and then with parenthood. Adults are also more involved in a variety of social, political, and charitable activities—more likely, for example, to be registered to vote. Church involvement, then, reflects a broader pattern of social involvement (Gallup and Castelli, 1989).

The same age factor in religious involvement was found in a study of baby-boomers, most of whom are now in their forties. During their teens or early twenties, two-thirds dropped out of their churches and synagogues. Later, by the 1990s, nearly 40 percent of these dropouts had returned to religious practice. Why did they return to organized religion? One rea-

son was their feeling that religion is important for bringing up children. Another was their personal quest for meaning, triggered by feelings of emptiness and loneliness. A third reason was their need to belong to a community—to be with others, share faith, and do things together (Roof, 1993). In short, religious involvement tends to increase with age.

Gender Differences In Chapter 9, we discussed gender inequalities in the church, such as the prohibition of ordination of women as priests. Here, we focus on gender differences in religious experiences. Sociologists have long known that women are generally more religious than men, attending church more often, praying more, and reading the Bible more. But some studies have revealed many other gender differences.

In one study by Edward Lehman (1994), gender difference exists in ministry style: Among whites, women pastors tend more to give power away by striving to enhance the power the church members have over their individual and collective lives. Male pastors, however, tend more to seek power over the congregation, "lording it over" the lay members. Another study, by Lynn Davidman and Arthur Greil (1994), suggests that women are more likely than men to be converted to a religion through personal contacts, such as encouragement from friends and relatives. By contrast, men tend more to be active in seeking knowledge of the faith on their own.

Ethnic Differences African Americans are more likely than whites to be church members, with the large majority being either Baptist or Methodist. Most of the churches to which they belong are predominantly or entirely African American. Compared with their white counterparts, African American ministers and congregations tend to express religious emotions more openly during church services. Most significant, African American churches still serve, as they have historically, as an important community center for various social and civic activities including meetings of outside organizations, social events, concerts, and mass meetings. They also continue to play a key role in the civil rights movement, as movement leaders are typically church ministers (Pinkney, 1993).

Native American nations have their own religions. In general, these traditional religions teach respect for the land and nature as well as strong support for the community. Christianity is thus often seen as a crude religion that emphasizes blood, crucifixion, and organized charity rather than true sharing with and compassion for others. Although many Native Americans have been converted to Christianity, they continue to embrace their traditional religions, as well (Feagin and Feagin, 1999).

Hispanic Americans have long been mostly Catholics. They look to their church as an important place not only for Sunday mass but also for holiday celebrations and community gatherings. In recent years, however, a growing number of Hispanics have joined Protestant churches, especially conservative ones such as the Evangelicals, Pentecostals, and Jehovah's Witnesses, which are known to welcome new immigrants and make them feel like part of a family (Gardyn, 2001; Feagin and Feagin, 1999).

Asians usually brought Buddhism with them when they immigrated to the United States. Today, many among the older generations of Asian Americans still consider themselves Buddhists and participate in the celebration of Buddhist festivals. But most among the younger generations are Christian, with some, such as Vietnamese and Filipino Americans, being predominantly Catholic and others, such as Japanese and Chinese Americans, being Presbyterian and Methodist (Feagin and Feagin, 1999).

Fundamentalist Revival

Although religious membership throughout the United States remains high, the growth in church membership has not kept pace with the growth of the general population. Since the early 1970s, the U.S. population has grown by over 12 percent, but religious institutions have expanded by only 4 percent. Some churches have actually lost members. Others, however, have gained many members (Cook, 2000; Naisbitt and Aburdene, 1990).

Generally, the large, mainline churches—Episcopal, Methodist, Presbyterian, and Congregational—have lost many members. Those churches that have registered large gains tend to be smaller and less-established religious groups. They are also more conservative. Among them are various fundamentalists, such as Southern Baptists, Pentecostals, and Mormons. In contrast to mainline Protestants, fundamentalists emphasize a literal interpretation of the Bible. Evangelical, born-again Christians also stress emotional demonstrativeness rather than quiet, inward devotion at church services. Through the experience of being born again, they believe that their lives have been dramatically changed. Some of these groups also speak in tongues, utter prophecies, and heal the sick (Paul, 2003; Fogel, 2000).

Southern Baptists, Jehovah's Witnesses, Mormons, members of the Church of God, and Catholic Pentecostals are among the groups participating in this revival. In the past, fundamentalist and evangelical Christianity was associated with the poor and uneducated. Today, however, its appeal has spread to higher social classes, and business executives and prominent politicians can be found among its advocates. The evangelical boom has also spawned most of the megachurches (churches with more than 2,000 worshippers every Sunday), whose number has skyrocketed from about 10 to 500 over the last 20 years. These churches are located mostly in the South and the highly populated Northern states (see Figure 11.6).

The fundamentalist revival is a reflection of the conservative trend in American society. It is also a culmination of a number of factors. First is the aggressive, skillful use of television or other modern marketing techniques, as illustrated by the popularity of such fundamentalist preachers as Jerry Falwell and Pat Robertson. A second factor is the social changes of the last three decades that generally trouble conservatives. These changes have involved the women's movement, the gay rights movement, the growing number of unmarried mothers, the legalization of abortion, and court decisions against school prayer, all of which have driven many conservative people into fundamentalist churches. A third factor is the highly personal style of worship in fundamentalist churches, which tends to attract people who are casualties of this fast-changing, high-tech age—those who are socially isolated, alienated, and dehumanized by modern society. A final factor is that compared with mainstream Christians, fundamentalists have more children, which obviously enlarges the size of their denomination (Hout, Greeley, and Wilde, 2001; Fogel, 2000; Marty and Appleby, 1992).

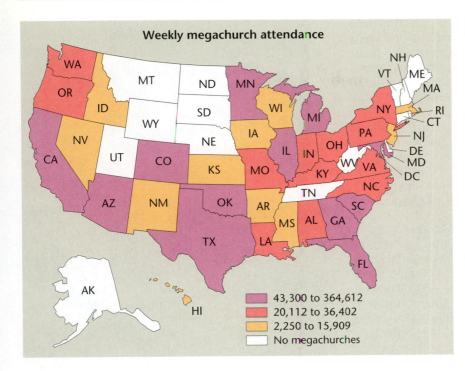

Weekly megachurch attendance

43,300 to 364,612
20,112 to 36,402
2,250 to 15,909
No megachurches

FIGURE 11.6

Megachurch Attendance

The fundamentalist, evangelical boom that has occurred in the United States over the last two decades has skyrocketed the number of megachurches from only about 10 to 500 today. These churches serve more than 2,000 worshippers every Sunday. They are located mostly in the South, where fundamentalism has long prevailed, and in highly populated northern states, where fundamentalism has spread to include people from higher social classes among its followers.

Critical Thinking: *What about a megachurch would make you want to join it or reject it? Why?*

Source: Data from John Vaughan, *Church Growth Today,* 2001.

■ Proliferation of Cults

A **cult** is a religious group that professes a new belief system, rejects society, and consists of members with extreme devotion to their leader. Like evangelical groups, U.S. cults have been growing. Today, there are about 3,000 cults. But most are very small, with memberships numbering only a few dozen (Kleiner, 2000).

An example of these smaller cults is Heaven's Gate, whose 39 members shocked the world in 1997 when they committed mass suicide. By doing so, they believed that they—or, more precisely, their souls—were leaving their bodies, which they called "human containers" or "vehicles," in order to board the spaceship believed to follow the Hale-Bopp comet that was close to Earth at the time. The spacecraft was expected to take them to God's Heavenly Kingdom. They regarded their leader, Marshall Herff Applewhite, who "took the journey"—that is, died—with them, as the modern-day Christ. According to Applewhite, two millennia ago, Jesus was sent to Earth as God's representative to collect disciples and take them to the Father's mansion among the stars. And with the year 2000 approaching, Applewhite taught, he was chosen to do what Jesus did. To prepare for the journey, cult members had shed their humanness by giving up sex, drugs, and alcohol, as well as renouncing their families.

An example of a much larger and more successful cult is the Unification Church. Its founder, Sun Myung Moon, a South Korean businessman, has de-

clared himself to be the New Messiah. He says that Jesus appeared to him, telling him that he has been chosen by God to complete the mission that Jesus could not finish because of the crucifixion. Moon's mission is to combine all the world's religions and nations into one, to be headed by Moon himself. Members of the cult, most of whom are young, must break all ties with their families, work 18 hours a day soliciting donations, and give all their possessions to the church. All the while, Moon lives in splendor on a huge estate, owns several yachts, and controls an enormous business empire.

A cultist's life is not at all easy. Why, then, would anyone want to join a cult? Contrary to popular belief, the young people who join cults are mostly normal and come from stable, religious families that uphold traditional values of family life and morality. Most have maintained good relationships with their parents and have done particularly well in school. Indeed, their warm, concerned parents have given them every material, social, and intellectual benefit (Galanter, 1999; Wright and Piper, 1986; Barker, 1984). What possible rewards can *they* find from joining a cult?

In his classic study of at least 100 cults, in which more than 1,000 individual members were interviewed, Saul Levine (1984) concluded that the cults provide young people with "desperate detours to growing up." Like most of their peers, the youthful joiners must grow up to be free and independent by leaving their parents. But *lacking the skills, confi-*

dence, or courage to strike out on their own, they find it too painful to leave their families. For these youngsters, a cult provides separation without the accompanying pain because the communal group typically operates like an exaggerated and idealized family that offers an enormous amount of love and care. For the same reason, a cult is very appealing to older adults when they are *going through a difficult period in their lives* such as having a divorce, business failure, or job loss (Kisser, 1997; Conway and Siegelman, 1995).

Serving as a halfway house between the parental home and the outside world, the cult enables its young joiners to pick up skills for living independent lives. Once they have learned to take care of themselves, they usually leave the group. So do older members when they get over their personal problems. In fact, more than 90 percent of cult joiners return home within two years (Levine, 1984). This may partly explain why Heaven's Gate finally had only 39 members, a far cry from the 200 to 1,000 people who had joined the cult at one time or another (Gleick, 1997). A few members, however, will never leave their cult because they have lost their sense of self and cannot live without the group (Kisser, 1997; Conway and Siegelman, 1995).

■ New Age Movement

A new religious phenomenon that has attracted a great deal of attention is known as the *New Age movement.* In every major city, its devotees can be seen seeking insight or personal growth with spiritual teachers, at bookstores specializing in metaphysics, or at educational centers. But only about 28,000 people regard themselves as New Agers. Despite their small number, they have been given far more attention than any other new group on the U.S. religious landscape because they are affluent, well-educated, successful individuals (Gumbel, 2002; Goldman, 1991). The New Age has also become a subject of enormous interest to the general public, as shown by the great popularity of James Redfield's 1993 novel about the new spirituality, *The Celestine Prophecy,* and its 1996 sequel, *The Tenth Insight.*

New Agers are without an organization like the United Methodist Church or the Southern Baptist Convention. They do not have a coherent philosophy or dogma either. But many do believe in a number of phenomena, two of which have been widely publicized as the major characteristics of the New Age. One is the belief in *reincarnation*—rebirth after death in a new body or life form. The other is *channeling*—using one's body and voice as a vehicle for some person from the great beyond (Anderson and Whitehouse, 1995).

WE'RE DIVINE Followers of the New Age movement believe that the divine resides in humanity. This is similar to the Christian belief that people are made in the image and likeness of God and therefore possess a divine spark. But New Agers commune with God in their own way, such as through meditation, rather than with the help of an organized Western religion. They seek to realize the limitless potential of humanity for themselves, not to try to change the world. ■

Running throughout these beliefs is a strong sense that the divine resides in humanity. Thus, New Agers seek to realize the limitless potential of humanity for themselves. They are not interested in transforming the world, only themselves. Many New Agers were once Christians who attended church regularly but were left spiritually hungry. "They wanted God, not to hear God," as a Harvard theologian said. In the New Age movement, they find God within themselves (Gumbel, 2002; Bloom, 1992; Hoyt, 1987).

Some Christians say that the notion of a person being God is blasphemous. They believe that only through Christ can humanity be *united* with the divine; humanity alone cannot *be* divine. Actually, the New Age movement's concept of human divinity is similar to the Christian belief that people are made in the image and likeness of God and therefore possess a divine spark. But New Agers prefer to seek God in their own way, such as through meditation, rather than with the help of an organized Western religion.

They regard Jesus as an enlightened teacher like Buddha, Muhammad, or Gandhi rather than as the only savior of humanity (Gumbel, 2002; Bloom, 1992; Naisbitt and Aburdene, 1990).

■ American Islam

Contrary to popular belief, most U.S. Muslims are not of Arab origin. Arab Muslims make up only about 12 percent of all Muslims in the United States, being far outnumbered by African American Muslims and even Muslims from South Asian countries such as Pakistan and Bangladesh. In fact, most Arab Americans are Christian because immigrants from Arab countries are mostly Christian rather than Muslim. Only 23 percent of Arab Americans are Muslim (see Figure 11.7).

myth	Most of the immigrants from predominantly Muslim Arab countries are Muslims, so that a majority of Arab Americans are Muslims.
reality	Most Arab Americans are Christians because Christians from those Arab countries are much more likely to immigrate to the United States.

Also, contrary to popular belief, most African American Muslims do not follow Minister Louis Farrakhan, well known for his inflammatory racial comments. His followers constitute only 2 or 3 percent of all African American Muslims. The overwhelming majority of African American Muslims are moderates who have left behind the militant, antiwhite, and separatist philosophy and now essentially embrace orthodox, mainstream Islam. Taken together, U.S. Muslims are one of the fastest-growing religious groups in the United States (van Biema, 2001; Blank, 1998).

Muslims follow a strict code of ethics and diet. They cannot consume alcohol, illicit drugs, or pork. They must refrain from premarital and extramarital sex and dating. They are forbidden to gamble and to pay or accept interest on loans or savings accounts. These religious rules bring Muslims into conflict with the dominant U.S. culture, which is based largely on credit purchases and payment of interest for such activities as buying homes and cars. Devout Muslims find U.S. society shockingly permissive, riddled with what they consider moral problems such as sexual freedom, drug use, crime, and lack of respect for authority. Immigrant parents often clash with their teenage children over dating and drinking (Tolson, 2001; Blank, 1998; Sheler, 1990).

The conflict between the Islamic and Western cultures may ultimately produce a brand of Islam

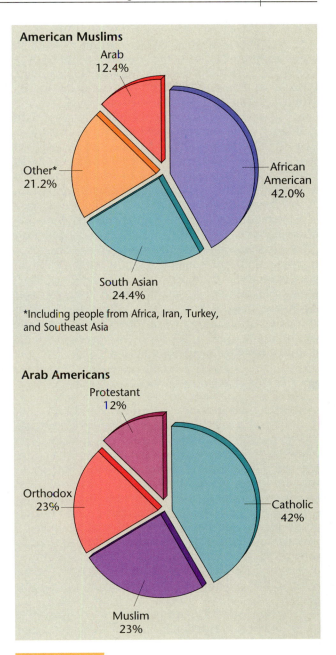

*Including people from Africa, Iran, Turkey, and Southeast Asia

FIGURE 11.7

American Muslims and Arab Americans

Contrary to popular belief, most U.S. Muslims are not of Arab origin. Arab Muslims constitute only 12 percent of all Muslims in the United States, being far outnumbered by African American Muslims and even Muslims from South Asian countries such as Pakistan and Bangladesh. In fact, a large majority of Arab Americans are Christian.

Critical Thinking: *Why do so many Americans believe that all Muslims are Arabs? How might this perception be harmful?*

Sources: Data from American Muslim Council, 1998; Arab American Institute Foundation, 2001.

that is distinctively American. In many ways, some U.S. mosques already function more like Christian churches than traditional mosques in Islamic countries. The Toledo Center—the largest U.S. mosque, located in Perrysburg, Ohio—has 22 nationality groups among its members. Weddings and funerals are held in the mosque. There are Sunday classes for children and teenagers as well as lectures for adults. After the afternoon prayer service, the faithful get together for a meal in a lower-level dining room. In contrast, traditional mosques in Islamic countries are more likely to be used only for praying and other strictly religious activities.

Also distinctively American is the fact that U.S. Muslims are generally more tolerant of religious differences, more resistant to fundamentalism, more at home in a secular society, and more ethnically diverse than their counterparts in other societies. Black Muslims even refer to their American-born founder as the prophet and messenger of Allah, while in other countries, only Muhammad, who founded Islam 13 centuries ago in Saudi Arabia, is recognized as Allah's prophet (Sheler, 2001b; Lincoln, 1994).

■ The Promise Keepers

A new religious movement started by and for American men who call themselves the *Promise Keepers* has grown phenomenally (see Figure 11.8). They stage men-only rallies in sports stadiums across the country, where they listen to sermons about Bible-based rules for living, along with rock-and-roll hymns, and engage in spiritual catharsis by praying out loud, confessing sins, crying, and hugging one another while asking for forgiveness and professing love. Afterward, these people return home to form men's support ministries in their local churches that number over 20,000 throughout the United States (Clarke, 1998; Goodstein, 1997; Ross and Cokorinos, 1996).

The Promise Keepers vow to honor their promises to be devoted Christians, faithful husbands, and good fathers. They further seek to unite Christian men of all races, cultures, and denominations. But they also regard abortion and homosexuality as sins comparable to adultery. Most controversially, they believe that men should take leadership over their wives. This has caused some 60 liberal religious leaders to warn the nation's churches that the Promise Keepers' movement threatens the modern egalitarian family system. Similarly, the National Organization for Women, a leading feminist group, denounces the Promise Keepers for posing a great danger to women's rights. The Promise Keepers, however, insist that their concept of a man's leadership over his wife actually translates into servant-

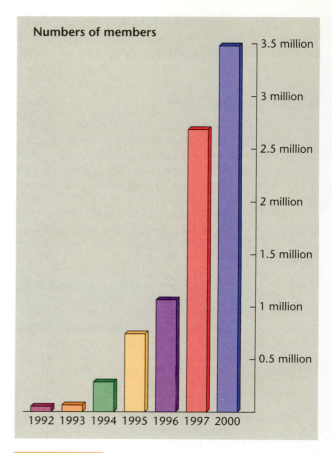

Numbers of members

1992 1993 1994 1995 1996 1997 2000

FIGURE 11.8

The Promise Keepers: Phenomenal Growth

As a new religious movement founded by and for men, the Promise Keepers have grown phenomenally, from only 72 participants in 1990 to 3.5 million today. They vow to honor their promises to be devoted Christians, faithful husbands, and good fathers, and they have succeeded in strengthening the American family. But they have stirred controversy for advocating husbands' leadership over their wives.

Critical Thinking: *Would you join the Promise Keepers? Why or why not?*

Source: Data from the Promise Keepers, 2001.

hood rather than domination. As the founder of the group explains, "You know what a woman is told in the Bible? Respect your husband . . . and he in turn would lay down his life. He would serve her, affectionately and tenderly serve her" (Stodghill, 1997).

Understandably, many conservative women give their support to Promise Keepers, but additional support comes from other sources, as well—some quite surprising. Hillary Clinton, a liberal senator, praises Promise Keepers in her book *It Takes a Village*. A major reason is that the men's crusade has been able to strengthen the family, even accomplishing what feminists try to achieve. As sociologist Robert Wuthnow says, "Contrary to what some of the critics say—that Promise Keepers is turning them into real macho men—it's domesticating them. I think it's a new model of manhood for our times" (McDonald, 1997). The wives of many Promise Keepers have further reported positive results, such as husbands becoming more attentive and affectionate and fathers spending more time with children (Stodghill, 1997).

FACING THE SECULAR WORLD: CONFRONTATION OR COMPROMISE?

A religion is concerned with the sacred, but it exists in this world, an earthly rather than a heavenly society. It must stand in some relation to that society—in harmony or disharmony, as an integral part of other institutions or apart from them, or in some position between these extremes. Within Christianity, as in any other religion, there have established different relations to society.

Church and Sect

Christian organizations can be divided into two categories: churches and sects. Churches compromise with society; sects confront it. Many groups do not fit into either of these extreme categories, but we can think of mainline Protestant groups, such as the Episcopal and Presbyterian churches, as examples of churches, whereas Pentecostals and Jehovah's Witnesses are examples of sects.

A **church** is a relatively large, well-established religious organization that is integrated into the society and does not make strict demands on its members. It has a formalized structure of belief, ritual, and authority. It is also an inclusive organization, welcoming members from a wide spectrum of social backgrounds. Thus, members often have little but their religion in common, and they may hardly know one another. Members tend to be born into the church, and the church sets up few if any requirements for membership. Its demands, on both its members and society, are far from exacting. Over the years, the church has learned to take a relatively tolerant attitude toward its members' failings. It has learned to reconcile itself to the institutions of the society, coexisting in relative peace with society's secular values.

The church's compromises do not satisfy the **sect**, a relatively small religious group that sets itself apart from society and makes heavy demands on its members. It begins with a relatively small religious movement that has broken away from an established church. Time and again, groups have split off from Christian churches because some members believed the church had become too worldly. The sect that results holds itself separate from society, and it demands from its members a deep religious experience, strong loyalty to the group, and rejection of the larger society and its values. The sect is a tightly knit community offering close personal relations among its members.

Dilemmas of Success

Most pure sects do not last long. They either fail to maintain their membership and disappear, or they undergo change. Consider Methodism, which was founded in opposition to the Church of England. At first, it was a sect that sought to correct social injustices and to aid the poor. Then Irish immigrants brought it to the United States, where it was initially associated with the lower classes. But it has become a highly institutionalized religion today—successful, respectable, middle class, and less demanding of its members than it originally was.

A paradoxical relation exists between religiosity and success. The more successful a religion is (in the sense of being more popular and more respectable in society, as well as having more members), the less religious its members tend to be (in the sense of spending less time reading the Bible, praying, or engaging in other spiritual activities). Established churches, such as the Episcopal, Methodist, and Catholic churches, are more successful than sects, such as the Amish and Jehovah's Witnesses. But members of sects tend to be more religious, devoting more of their time to such religious matters as reading the Bible, praying, and door-to-door evangelizing. They may show greater willingness to suffer or even die for their beliefs, as did their ancient counterparts such as Jesus, his disciples, and early Christians. Success presents a religion with at least five dilemmas (O'Dea and Aviad, 1983):

1. *The dilemma of mixed motivation.* The success of a church offers its leaders new, self-centered motives for their careers—motives such as power and prestige. A similar change may occur among the rank-and-file members. Once a religion is institutionalized, its members may be born into the church rather than converted to it. The security, friendship, and prestige that the church offers may become a more important motive for membership than religious conviction. These motives may be useful for ensuring the success of a church, but they are basically secular and opposed to the religious doctrines that stress single-minded devotion to God, reflecting God-centered rather than human-centered needs.

2. *The dilemma of administrative order.* The organization that emerges with institutionalization brings another problem as well: bureaucracy. The Roman Catholic Church, for example, has a vast bureaucracy, with an elaborate hierarchy including the pope, cardinals, archbishops, bishops, monsignors, and priests—plus many other ranks and lines of authority. Such an administrative order is necessary for maintaining the success of the church. But its hierarchy of positions—which is essentially a practice of social inequality—is contrary to the religious idea that all people are equal before God and should be treated as such.

3. *The symbolic dilemma.* At the heart of religions are symbolic expressions of the sacred. They are necessary for ensuring the success of a church because they can make profound, complex religious ideas comprehensible and help people relate to God more effectively. But people may end up misusing the symbols and missing the message behind them. The cross, for example, is a Christian symbol of God's love for humanity, which should cause Christians to accept and worship Christ with fervor. But illiterate Christians in traditional societies may be so awed by the cross that they worship it as an idol or use it as a charm to ward off evil spirits. Better-educated Christians in traditional and industrial countries may find the cross so beautiful that they use it as a mere ornament. In short, the sacred symbols of a popular religion can lead to such irreligious behaviors as idolatry and vulgarization of God.

4. *The dilemma of oversimplification.* This is similar to the symbolic dilemma. In order to ensure the success of its religion, the institutionalized church oversimplifies its teachings to make them easily comprehensible. To make people understand how much God still loves them even though they are sinful or worthless, Christian preachers may tell the story about the prodigal son or about the lost sheep. God is compared to the prodigal son's father, who still loves the son despite his sins, or God is portrayed as the shepherd who is still looking everywhere for his one lost sheep, though he still has many sheep left. Just as symbols may be transformed into idols, however, the stories, parables, fables, and other preaching techniques of oversimplification may become mere objects of admiration and awe, causing the faithful to miss the message behind the stories. For example, some Christians may say, "Oh, how moving the prodigal son story is!" but they continue to sin.

5. *The dilemma of power.* In societies where there is no separation of religion and state, religious organizations use the state to enforce religious conformity and, in turn, lend their authority to sanctify what the state does. Coercion may replace faith. In many places in the past, heresy was punished by torture and even death. All this may ensure the success of the church, but it is basically irreligious because the church is supposed to show compassion, love, and forgiveness.

Today, a more subtle form of power, gained through media such as radio and television, is employed to capture the souls of prospective followers. Preachers with easy access to the media are more successful than others. But their success is usually bought at the price of irreligiosity. TV evangelists tend to sell God like household goods, transforming the holy into the profane. Urging his viewers to send in money ("donation") to buy his product (God), televangelist Richard Roberts once asked them to "sow a seed on your MasterCard, your Visa, or your American Express, and then when you do, expect God to open the windows of heaven and pour you out a blessing" (Woodward, 1987).

■ Church and State

In 1978, when the whole world was shocked by the Jonestown bloodbath, in which over 900 U.S. cult members committed suicide, President Jimmy Carter commented, "I don't think we ought to have an overreaction because of the Jonestown tragedy by injecting government into trying to control people's religious beliefs." This is testimony to the unusually high degree of religious tolerance in the United States. Without this tolerance, the diversity of U.S. religions would not be possible.

This diversity would have appalled some of the earliest settlers of this country. They came to the New World in order to establish a holy commonwealth, a community that would be ruled by church officials. In the Puritans' republic, "theology was wedded to politics and politics to the progress of the kingdom of God" (Bercovitch, 1978). Even after independence was won, some of the states had official religions. But the U.S. Constitution guarantees religious freedom by forbidding government interference in religious activities. Eventually, the courts interpreted this guarantee to mean that church and state must be kept separate and that the government, including state governments, must refrain from promoting religion.

Thus, the United States has no official religion. But in practice, the separation of church and state is far from complete. In a sense, the U.S. government does support religion in general by exempting religious organizations from taxation. Every day in public schools, students salute the flag with the affirmation of "one nation, *under God.*" Even at the opening of legislative sessions, presidential inaugurations, and other public ceremonial occasions, ministers, priests, and rabbis offer religious invocations or benedictions. The state occasionally even intervenes in religious affairs. Thus, church activities are investigated if a church is suspected of abusing its tax-exempt privileges or otherwise violating the law. The government has even acted on issues that some groups consider religious, such as prohibiting Mormons from practicing polygamy and forcing Christian Scientists to accept medical treatment.

There is, then, no strict separation between church and state in American society. According to a poll, only slightly more than half of U.S. adults agree with the statement that "We have to keep church and state completely separate" (Sheler, 1994). Other surveys show that most people do not object to the inclusion of religion in the public realm as long as the religion involved represents all faiths rather than one particular faith. In times of national crisis, even public school officials are free to conduct prayer meetings, as they did soon after the terrorist attacks on September 11, 2001. And when it comes to President Bush's idea of the government funding religious groups' charitable activities, many more Americans support it than oppose it. In short, the separation between church and state is more often fiction than reality (Goodstein, 2001; Morse, 2001a).

■ Civil Religion

Rather than a formal separation of church and state, sociologists see full integration of the two in the form of **civil religion,** a collection of beliefs, symbols, and rituals that sanctify the dominant values of a society. The civil religion is a hybrid of religion and politics. The state takes up certain religious ideas and symbols, and religion sacralizes certain political principles, backing up the government's claim to a right to rule with its own moral authority. Thus, a civil religion can unify the citizens of a country by heightening their sense of patriotism.

The U.S. civil religion includes faith in what is popularly known as the American way of life, with freedom, democracy, equality, individualism, efficiency, and other typically U.S. values as its creeds. The "American way of life," said Will Herberg (1983), is the common religion of U.S. society by which Americans define themselves and establish their unity. Protestantism, Catholicism, and Judaism are its "subfaiths."

God plays an important role in this civil religion. God is cited on coins ("In God We Trust") and in national hymns ("God Bless America"). References to God are made in all oaths of office, in courtroom procedures, at political conventions, in the inaugural ad-

GOD BLESS AMERICA Sociologists see an integration of church and state in the form of civil religion, which intermixes religion and politics. God, though not the deity of any particular church, is invoked on ceremonial occasions, such as when the president takes the oath of office. The civil religion also includes faith in the U.S. way of life. ■

dress of every president, and on practically all formal public occasions.

But the God of U.S. civil religion is not the god of any particular church. Adherence to U.S. civil religion requires only people's belief in God, however they choose to define the deity—as a personal god, an impersonal force, a supreme power, an ideal, or any other form. Americans do not have to believe in Moses, Jesus, the Bible, heaven and hell, or any other doctrine of a particular religion. They are instead exhorted to go to any church of their choice. As President Eisenhower said, "Our government makes no sense, unless it is founded on a deeply felt religious faith—*and I don't care what it is.*" The civil religion does not favor one particular church but, rather, religion in general. Everyone is expected to pay at least lip service to religious principles, if not to join a church, synagogue, or mosque. It is considered un-American to be godless or, worse, to attack religion.

Like a genuine religion, U.S. civil religion contains symbols, rituals, and scriptures. Its sacred writings are the Declaration of Independence and the Constitution. George Washington is seen as the Moses who led his people out of the hands of tyranny. Abraham Lincoln, the martyred president, is seen as the crucified Jesus and his Gettysburg Address as a New Testament. The civil religion's holy days are the Fourth of July, Thanksgiving, Memorial Day, and Veterans Day, when Americans sing sacred hymns such as

"The Star-Spangled Banner" and "America the Beautiful," invoke the name of God, listen to sermonlike speeches, and watch ritualistic parades. The U.S. flag, like the Christian cross, is supposed to inspire devotion.

A GLOBAL ANALYSIS OF RELIGION

There are various forms of religion around the world, as shown in Figure 11.9. They can be classified into three broad categories: **theism**, the type of religion that centers on the worship of a god or gods; **ethi-**

calism, the type of religion that emphasizes moral principles as guides for living a righteous life; and **animism**, the belief in spirits capable of helping or harming people.

■ Theism

Theistic religions define the sacred as one or more supernatural beings. These religions center on the worship of a god or gods. There are two subtypes of theism: **monotheism**, or belief in one god, and **polytheism**, belief in more than one god.

Christianity, Islam, Judaism, and Zoroastrianism are all monotheistic. With 2 billion followers, Chris-

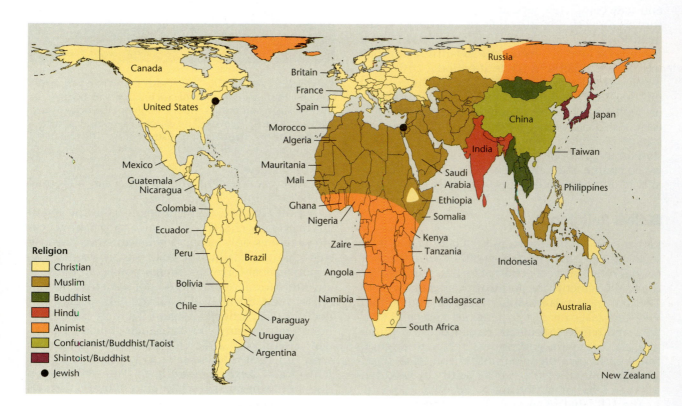

Religion

- Christian
- Muslim
- Buddhist
- Hindu
- Animist
- Confucianist/Buddhist/Taoist
- Shintoist/Buddhist
- ● Jewish

FIGURE 11.9

Religions around the Globe

Religion takes different forms around the world. One is *theism,* which centers on the worship of a deity, such as Christianity, Islam, and Judaism. Another form of religion is *ethicalism,* which emphasizes moral principles as a guide for living a righteous life, as do Buddhism, Confucianism, and Shintoism. And finally there is *animism,* the belief in spirits capable of helping or harming people, as exemplified by shamanism and totemism.

Critical Thinking: *Do you think people generally choose their religion or are born into it? Why?*

Sources: Data largely from Gerard Chaliand and Jean-Pierre Rageau, *Strategic Atlas,* 3rd ed. (New York: HarperCollins, 1992); and *Encyclopaedia Britannica Yearbook,* 2003.

tianity is the world's largest religion. It is split into three principal groups—Roman Catholic, Protestant, and Eastern Orthodox—but all three share a belief in God as the creator of the world and in Jesus as its savior. Islam, the world's second-largest religion, with 1.2 billion devotees, was established by the prophet Muhammad in the seventh century A.D. It emphasizes that believers must surrender totally to the will of Allah (God), the creator, sustainer, and restorer of the world. Judaism worships Yahweh, the God of the Old Testament, as the creator of the universe and teaches that He chose the people of Israel as witness to His presence. Zoroastrianism is an ancient pre-Christian religion that still has 250,000 followers, known as Parsees, in India. Parsees believe in one supreme God whose omnipotence is temporarily limited by an ongoing battle with evil—although God is ensured of eventual victory. The faithful join forces with God by keeping themselves pure through ablution, penance, and prayers.

The best-known polytheistic faith is Hinduism. In small villages throughout India, where the majority of Hindus live, countless gods are worshiped, each believed to have a specific sphere of influence, such as childbirth, sickness, the harvest, or rain. These local deities are often looked on as manifestations of higher gods. Hinduism also teaches that we are *reincarnated*—born and reborn again and again—into new human or animal bodies. People may escape the cycle of reincarnation and achieve salvation by practicing mystical contemplation and steadfast endurance and by following traditional rules of conduct for their castes, families, and occupations.

■ Ethicalism

Some religions do not focus on supernatural beings. Instead, these *ethicalist religions* ascribe sacredness to moral principles. The heart of these religions is a set of principles that serve as guides for a righteous life. The best examples are Buddhism, Confucianism, Taoism, and Shintoism.

Buddhism was founded in India in the sixth century B.C. by Gautama, who is known as the Buddha ("enlightened one"). Today, it is the largest ethical religion. According to Buddhism, there is no independent, unchanging self and no physical world—both are illusions. Belief in their reality, attachment to them, and the craving for human pleasures are, according to Buddhism, the source of human misery. To escape this misery is to attain *nirvana* (salvation). It requires meditation—freeing one's mind from all worldly desires and ideas—and right thinking, right speech, right action, and the right mode of living. Buddhism is widely practiced in many Asian societies.

Confucianism was founded by Confucius (551–479 B.C.) in China. For over 2,000 years, it was practically the state religion of China. Confucianism stresses personal cultivation through learning and self-examination, so that the individual becomes imbued with confidence and serenity. It also urges harmony between individuals. Confucius described proper social conduct as reciprocity, which means, in his words, "Do not do to others what you would not want others to do to you."

Like Confucianism, Taoism has shaped the Chinese character for more than 2,000 years, but today, it has a much smaller following. Whereas Confucianism compels its adherents to be austere and duty conscious, Taoism encourages joyful, carefree quietism, nonintervention, or "not overdoing." According to Taoism, every deliberate intervention in the natural course of events sooner or later turns into the opposite of what was intended. In essence, in a mystical manner, Taoism tells people to yield totally to the *Tao* ("the Way"), accepting what is natural and spontaneous in people. Actually, Taoism and Confucianism pursue the same goal—the subordination of individuals to groups, such as families and society. They differ only in the means of achieving that goal. While Confucianism urges *activism* through performance of one's social duties, such as obeying one's parents and being polite to others, Taoism teaches *passivity* through avoidance of self-indulgence, power seeking, and self-aggrandizement.

Shintoism has always been a part of Japanese culture. It teaches that people should strive for *magokoro*—a "bright and pure mind" and "truthfulness, sincerity, or uprightness." This means that individuals must be sincerely interested in doing their best in whatever work they choose, and they must be truthful in their relationships with others. Purification, physical and spiritual, is the path to these goals. To remove the "dust" of humans' wickedness believed to cover their divine nature, purification rites are performed at Shinto shrines.

■ Animism

Animists believe that spirits, whether helpful or harmful to people, may reside in humans, animals, plants, rivers, or winds. They are not gods to be worshiped but supernatural forces that can be manipulated to serve human ends. Rituals such as feasting, dancing, fasting, and cleansing are often performed to appease the spirits so that crops can be harvested, fish caught, illness cured, or danger averted. Animism is prevalent in sub–Saharan Africa.

SPIRITUALLY SPEAKING Among Native Americans, a common type of animism is called *shamanism,* the belief that a spiritual leader can communicate with the spirits by acting as their mouthpiece or letting the soul leave the leader's body and enter the spiritual world. Here, a shaman performs at a Ute ceremony in Utah. ■

Among indigenous peoples in North and South America, a common type of animism is called **shamanism**, the belief that a spiritual leader can communicate with the spirits by acting as their mouthpiece or by letting the soul leave the leader's body and enter the spiritual world. The spirits, in effect, live in the shaman ("one who knows"). By communicating with them, the shaman heals the sick, discovers lost animals, sees events in distant places, foresees those in the future, and forecasts prospects for farming, fishing, and hunting.

Another form of animism, popular among native peoples of Australia and some Pacific islands, is **totemism**, the belief that kinship exists between humans and an animal (or, less commonly, a plant). The animal, called a *totem,* represents a human family, a clan, or a group of ancestors. It is thought of as a person—but a person with superhuman power—and it must be treated with respect, awe, and fear. Killing, eating, touching, and even seeing the animal

are often prohibited. The totem is relied on as a helper and protector, but it also punishes those who breach a taboo.

■ Global Religion Today

Although religion appears in different forms, it is universal, existing in every society. But religion does not attract people all over the world to the same degree. Generally, the more wealthy a country is, the less religious its people are. Thus, people in the developed countries of North America, Western Europe, and Japan are less religious than people in the developing countries of Latin America, Asia, and Africa (see Figure 11.10). What explains this trend? Apparently, the people in affluent societies are not as heavily burdened with the travails and adversities of day-to-day life as the people in poor societies, so that the wealthy may not feel as strong a need as the poor for consolation and the other positive functions of religion that we observed earlier.

Among wealthy nations, however, the United States is the most religious. When asked in a global survey if religion plays a very important role in their lives, only a minority of Western Europeans, Canadians, and Japanese said yes, but a majority of Americans answered affirmatively (see Figure 11.10). Americans are also far more likely than people in other affluent countries to attend religious services at least once a month (Chaves, 2002). Why are Americans more religious? One likely reason is that the population of the United States is much more diverse than the populations of other affluent societies. Thus, Americans are more likely to use their religion in the same way as their gender, sexual orientation, or ethnicity to identify themselves as different from members of other groups. Another reason for the United States being the most religious among affluent societies is the surge of immigrants from Third World countries; these new Americans are far more religious than native-born Americans.

The relative lack of religiosity in the affluent West reflects a diminishing interest in Christianity. But Christianity, which has been long been known as the primary Western religion, has now become an essentially non-Western, Third World religion. For hundreds of years, most of the world's Christians were either Europeans or North Americans, but since 2000, the majority (over 60 percent) of Christians have been non-Westerners in Latin America, Africa, and Asia. These mostly poor Third World people are attracted to Christianity because, ironically, they see it as the religion of the modern, successful West, which they aspire to be like (Woodward, 2002).

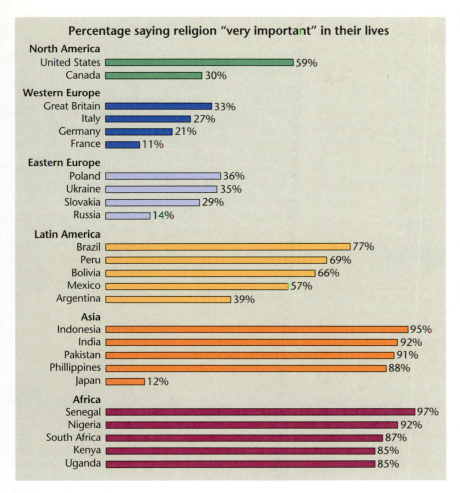

Percentage saying religion "very important" in their lives

North America
- United States 59%
- Canada 30%

Western Europe
- Great Britain 33%
- Italy 27%
- Germany 21%
- France 11%

Eastern Europe
- Poland 36%
- Ukraine 35%
- Slovakia 29%
- Russia 14%

Latin America
- Brazil 77%
- Peru 69%
- Bolivia 66%
- Mexico 57%
- Argentina 39%

Asia
- Indonesia 95%
- India 92%
- Pakistan 91%
- Phillipines 88%
- Japan 12%

Africa
- Senegal 97%
- Nigeria 92%
- South Africa 87%
- Kenya 85%
- Uganda 85%

FIGURE 11.10

Global Attitudes toward Religion

The people in wealthy countries are less religious than those in poor countries, presumably because their lives are more pleasant and they feel less need for comfort and the other benefits brought by religion. Among wealthy nations, though, the United States is the most religious. This is probably because given the diversity of society, Americans use religion to identify themselves as distinct from other groups. In addition, most of the immigrants in the United States have come from the developing world, where people are more religious than native-born Americans.

Critical Thinking: *Will Americans follow Europeans in becoming less religious about 20 years from now? If so, why? If not, why not?*

Source: Data from Pew Research Center, December 19, 2002.

sociological frontiers

Religious Fanaticism and Terrorism

As we have seen in this chapter, the functionalist perspective views religion as a positive force in society, one that serves various useful functions for its followers. But religion can also be turned into a negative force in the form of violent fanaticism.

In 1420, as noted earlier, a religious cult of Bohemians in Europe called the Adamites declared a holy war against those whom they felt were unholy and went about killing them until, they hoped, the blood would "flood the world to the height of a horse's head." The Adamites were, however, eventually exterminated after committing uncounted murders (Morrow, 1978). A similar kind of religious fanaticism was carried out on an immensely larger scale on September 11, 2001, when Muslim terrorists hijacked planes and crashed them into the World Trade Center in New York City and the Pentagon in Washington, DC. Like the Adamites in 1420,

the terrorists in 2001 believed they were waging a holy war against the unholy, or the infidels, calling the United States "the Great Satan."

According to their leader, Osama bin Laden, the U.S. culture of secularism, materialism, and free immorality threatens the traditional Islamic way of life. Moreover, U.S. foreign policy—including support for Israel and the occupation of Iraq—is seen as destroying Muslims' lives and wounding their dignity as the proud inheritors of a great religion. To redress these perceived wrongs, bin Laden encourages his followers to engage in a holy war against the United States. He further mesmerizes them with the seductive message that should they die as martyrs, they will go to heaven, where they will be rewarded with the affections of virgins (MacFarquhar, 2001). Yet when some of bin Laden's followers attacked New York and Washington, DC, killing over 3,000 innocent people, they horrified and outraged the whole world, including the vast majority of Muslims.

Bin Laden and his terrorist followers obviously do not represent Islam as a peaceful religion. The very word

Islam is related to the Arabic word *salam,* which means "peace." And *jihad,* a word that the terrorists like to use, does not mean "holy war" but "struggle," which refers to the difficult effort needed to put God's will into practice. In Islam's holy scripture, the Koran, warfare is always evil, unless it is one of self-defense. By killing innocent civilians, then, the terrorists effectively violate this sacred precept. In short, bin Laden, along with his terrorist followers, is far from being a true representative of Islam (Armstrong, 2001).

 ■ For more of the latest Sociological Frontiers, look up Continuing Update at www.ablongman.com/thio6e.

u s i n g *sociology*

How to Make It in College

After 10 years of interviewing 1,600 Harvard students, the university's Professor Richard Light (2001) discovered the following secrets of what makes a student successful and happy:

1. *Find a faculty mentor.* At the beginning of each semester or quarter, get to know one professor reasonably well and get that professor to know you reasonably well. If you do that, at the end of four years, you will have 8 or 12 professors to choose from to write recommendation letters for you when you apply for jobs. Even more important than this practical, opportunistic reason for seeking out faculty mentors, you will do better academically. In Light's study, those freshmen who asked for help with academic problems improved their grades but those who did not got worse.
2. *Take a smorgasbord of courses.* Your well-meaning parents may have told you to take required courses during the first year, to choose a major during the second, to take advanced courses for your major during the third, and to save fun electives for the last. But Light advises that you avoid taking only required courses during the early years. Instead, you should *also* take a variety of other courses that seem interesting to you. Afterward, you will know for sure what you really want to major in or whether your chosen major really interests you as much as expected.
3. *Manage your time effectively.* Don't study the way you might have in high school, squeezing in 25 minutes in study hall, 35 minutes after some social or physical activity, and 45 minutes after dinner. Rather than study in short bursts like these, set aside a long uninterrupted block of several hours. You will accomplish much more.
4. *Study in groups.* It's important to do homework, but make sure you do it in a way that helps you under-

stand the material. Thus, after studying on your own, discuss your work with a group of four to six classmates. By doing so even just once a week, you will comprehend the material better and feel more engaged with your classes. This is particularly true with science courses, which have complicated concepts and require a great deal of solitary study.
5. *Engage in extracurriculars.* According to Light, students who have worked hard to get into college tend to say, "Academic work is my priority, and doing other things will hurt that." But Light's research found otherwise: Students who worked long hours at jobs had the same grades as those who worked a few hours or not at all. More important, students who worked or got involved in extracurricular activities, such as athletics, band, or volunteer work, were the happiest on campus.

Thinking critically, what advice seems most useful to you and what seems least useful? Why?

■ **CHAPTER REVIEW**

1. *According to the functionalist perspective, what are the functions of education?* The main functions are teaching knowledge and skills, enhancing social mobility, promoting national unity, and providing custodial care. *Viewed from the conflict perspective, what does education do for society?* Education reinforces inequality by channeling students of different socioeconomic backgrounds into different classes and colleges. Education also imposes much of the dominant WASP culture on U.S. minorities. *According to symbolic interactionism, how does the Pygmalion effect work?* By having certain expectations about students, teachers behave in particular ways that cause students to live up to what their teachers expect of them. *What does the Pygmalion effect have to do with school tracking?* Because of tracking, students who are perceived positively or negatively are treated accordingly; thus, they end up doing well or poorly in school, as expected.

2. *Does the decline in standardized test scores mean that there is a crisis in U.S. education?* Not necessarily. The drop in test scores may reflect the opening up of educational opportunities for the poor and minorities. Lower achievement scores in the United States, compared to other industrialized countries, may also reflect the impact of democratization. The United States is not the only country having some problems with its schools. Thus, U.S. education is not as bad as it appears, though it always needs improvement.

3. *What is the nature of each of these four programs: Head Start, school choice, homeschooling, and lifelong learning?* Head Start is designed to help young disadvantaged children become better students. School choice reflects an effort to improve schools by establishing competition among them for students. Homeschooling involves parents teaching their own children at home. Lifelong learning involves adults who want to continue their education by attending college.

4. *How is social diversity reflected in U.S. education?* Whites have better or more education than most minority groups. Native Americans have more problems in school than the members of any other ethnic group due to widespread poverty. More African Americans attend integrated public schools than before, and most are enrolled in predominantly white colleges, but a great deal of segregated education still exists for African American students. Hispanic Americans have lower educational attainment than most other groups, which can be attributed not only to a high poverty rate but also to the schools' lack of multicultural sensitivity and effective bilingual programs. Asian Americans have the highest educational attainment of any group, but they are stereotyped as naturally gifted in math and science, while, in fact, there are many who do not do well in school.

5. *According to Durkheim, what is God?* Durkheim argued that God is a symbolic representation of society. By their worship, members of society strengthen their bonds to each other and their acceptance of the society's norms. Thus, religion helps preserve social order. *What other functions does religion serve?* Religion supports people, provides social control, stimulates social change, and provides individuals with a sense of identity. If these functions are carried too far, however, religion can become dysfunctional. *How did Marx view religion?* To Marx, religion is an oppressive illusion that helps the rich and powerful to perpetuate their domination of the masses. He argued that religion justifies society's inequalities and gives solace to the masses, diverting their attention from the source of their oppression. *According to Weber, how did Calvinist Protestantism help develop capitalism?* It helped by encouraging believers to work hard and accumulate money.

6. *What is the distinguishing characteristic of religion in the United States?* Diversity of religion exists in the United States, reflecting different religious affiliations. *How are class, age, gender, and ethnicity related to religion?* People with different educational and income levels tend to join different religious groups and participate in different religious activities. Older

persons are more religiously active than younger ones. Compared with men, women are more religious, less interested in power as pastors, and more likely to become converted through personal contacts. African Americans and other ethnic minorities tend to have different religions and practice their religion differently than whites. *What has happened to fundamentalist churches, religious cults, the New Age movement, and Islam in the United States?* Fundamentalist churches have grown larger, while mainline churches have suffered a decline. Religious cults, the New Age movement, and Islam have also surged in numbers, size, and influence. *Who are the Promise Keepers?* They are American men who get together to help each other become devoted Christians, faithful husbands, and good fathers, but they have been criticized for supporting gender inequality.

7. *What is the basic difference between a church and a sect?* A church is well integrated into society, but a sect sets itself apart from society. *How can success be harmful to religion?* The success of a religion tends to make its followers become less religious. *How are church and state related in the United States?* There is no official church, and freedom of religion is guaranteed by the Constitution, but the separation of church and state is not absolute. *What is the U.S. civil religion?* It includes belief in God, support for religion in general—but not for any particular religion—and celebration of the American way of life.

8. *What kinds of religions can be found around the world?* They appear in three different forms: theism, which worships a god or gods; ethicalism, which provides a guide for living a righteous life; and animism, which believes in spirits capable of helping or harming people. *What is the state of global religion today?* Affluent societies are less religious than poor ones. Among rich countries, the United States is the most religious. And Christianity, long known as the primary Western religion, is now essentially a non-Western faith.

9. *How is religious fanaticism related to the terrorist attacks on the United States on September 11, 2001?* Osama bin Laden condemned the United States as "the great Satan" for what he believed to be its negative influence on Islam and its policies in the Middle East and encouraged his Muslim followers to embark on a holy war.

10. *What are the secrets of being a successful and happy college student?* The secrets include finding a faculty mentor, taking a smorgasbord of courses, managing time effectively, studying in groups, and engaging in extracurricular activities.

KEY TERMS

Animism   The belief in spirits capable of helping or harming people (p. 324).

Church   A relatively large, well-established religious organization that is integrated into the society and does not make strict demands on its members (p. 321).

Civil religion   A collection of beliefs, symbols, and rituals that sanctify the dominant values of a society (p. 323).

Compensatory education   A school program intended to improve the academic performance of socially and educationally disadvantaged children (p. 304).

Cult   A religious group that professes a new religious belief, totally rejects society, and consists of members with extreme devotion to their leader (p. 317).

Cultural imperialism   The practice of making minorities accept the dominant group's culture (p. 301).

Ethicalism   The type of religion that emphasizes moral principles as guides for living a righteous life (p. 324).

Monotheism   The belief in one god (p. 324).

Polytheism   The belief in more than one god (p. 324).

Pygmalion effect   The impact of a teacher's expectations on student performance (p. 301).

Sect   A relatively small religious group that sets itself apart from society and makes heavy demands on its members (p. 321).

Shamanism   The belief that a spiritual leader can communicate with the spirits by acting as their mouthpiece or letting the soul leave the leader's body and enter the spiritual world (p. 326).

Theism   The type of religion that centers on the worship of a god or gods (p. 324).

Totemism   The belief that a kinship exists between humans and an animal—or, less commonly, a plant (p. 326).

Tracking   The system of sorting students into different groups according to past academic achievement (p. 300).

QUESTIONS FOR DISCUSSION AND REVIEW

SOCIOLOGICAL PERSPECTIVES ON EDUCATION

1. How does education promote social mobility and national unity?
2. What benefits does society gain from having schools provide custodial care?
3. How does the conflict perspective on education differ specifically from the functionalist perspective?
4. What is the *Pygmalion effect?*
5. What is the connection between the Pygmalion effect and school tracking?

EDUCATION IN THE UNITED STATES

1. What educational problems do U.S. schools face?
2. How can Head Start improve children's academic performance?
3. What is school choice, and why do many teachers and some civil rights groups oppose this kind of educational reform?
4. Can homeschooling eventually replace the existing public school system? Why or why not?
5. How have community college and continuing education programs tried to meet the educational needs of adults?

SOCIAL DIVERSITY IN U.S. EDUCATION

1. How do the educational experiences of Native Americans, African Americans, Hispanic Americans, and Asian Americans differ?

SOCIOLOGICAL PERSPECTIVES ON RELIGION

1. Why did Émile Durkheim argue that society is a representation of God?
2. How can positive functions of religion turn into negative forces in society?
3. According to Karl Marx, how does religion support the ruling class?
4. What did Marx mean when he wrote that religion is "the opium of the masses"?
5. How did the early Protestants in Europe interpret the world, and how did this interpretation help develop capitalism?

RELIGION IN THE UNITED STATES

1. What are the traditional religious affiliations in the United States?
2. How are social class, age, gender, and ethnicity related to religion?
3. What does the current fundamentalist religious revival have in common with the upsurge in cults,

and how do these two types of religious movements differ?

4. Who are the New Agers and the Muslims in the United States? What is the nature of each of these religions?

5. Who are the Promise Keepers, and why do some find them controversial?

FACING THE SECULAR WORLD: CONFRONTATION OR COMPROMISE?

1. What is the difference between a *church* and a *sect?*

2. What problems are likely to occur when a church becomes highly successful?

3. Do you support the separation of church and state? Why or why not?

4. What is the nature of the U.S. civil religion?

A GLOBAL ANALYSIS OF RELIGION

1. What are the differences among theism, ethicalism, and animism?

2. How can peace be promoted among different religions in the world?

3. What is the nature of religion in today's world?

SOCIOLOGICAL FRONTIERS/USING SOCIOLOGY

1. How did religious fanaticism lead to the recent terrorist attacks on the United States?

2. How can students become successful and happy in college?

SUGGESTED READINGS

Greeley, Andrew M. 2000. *The Catholic Imagination.* Berkeley: University of California Press. An analysis of how Catholic art reflects the imaginations of ordinary Catholics.

Light, Richard J. 2001. *Making the Most of College: Students Speak Their Minds.* Cambridge, MA: Harvard University Press. Offers useful advice to parents, college administrators, and especially students.

Mathews, Jay. 1998. *Class Struggle: What's Wrong (and Right) with America's Best Public High Schools.* New York: Random House. Shows how the nation's best public schools turn out a high proportion of excellent students but at the expense of lower-track students.

Smith, Christian. 2000. *Christian America? What Evangelicals Really Want.* Berkeley: University of California Press. Shows how ordinary evangelical Christians are generally far from intolerant and in many other ways different from popular perception.

Smith, Jane I. 1999. *Islam in America.* New York: Columbia University Press. A scholarly but easily readable analysis of the origins, history, and development of the Muslim community in the United States.

■ Additional Resources

The New York Times
expect the world®
nytimes.com

Expand your knowledge of the concepts discussed in this chapter by reading the following current and historical articles from the *New York Times.* Go to the "eThemes of the Times" section of the Companion Website (www.ablongman.com/thio6e):

"For These Believers, The Visions Endure"
"24 Win MacArthur 'Genius Awards' of $500,000"

Research Navigator.com

Research Navigator, a research database, provides immediate access to hundreds of full-text articles from EBSCO's ContentSelect Academic Journal Database. If the Research Navigator access code was included with your textbook, go to the website www.research navigator.com and read the following articles related to this chapter by typing in the article number:

Dirksen, Hans Hermann. "Jehovah's Witnesses under Communist Regimes." *Religion, State and Society*, Sep2002, Vol. 30 Issue 3, p229, 10p. Accession Number: 7411885. Discusses the persecution of the Jehovah's Witnesses under communist regimes.

Selwyn, Neil. "Schooling the Mobile Generation: The Future for Schools in the Mobile-Networked Society." *British Journal of Sociology of Education*, Apr2003, Vol. 24 Issue 2, p131, 14p. Accession Number: 10005016. Examines the implications of mobile technologies such as cell phones for schools.

chapter 12

The Economy and Politics

myths & realities

myth *In the United States and Japan, two of the world's most capitalist societies, the governments pursue a strict laissez-faire, free-enterprise policy by not interfering in economic affairs at all.*

reality Governments in even the most capitalist societies do not follow a strict laissez-faire policy. They often step in to regulate business (p. 339).

myth *In the United States, most workers would rather pursue leisure than work.*

reality Most workers are satisfied with their jobs. Even if they inherited enough money to live comfortably without working, most would still want to work (p. 347).

myth *The most successful Asian Americans in the United States are those of Japanese, Chinese, and Korean descent.*

reality The most successful are probably Asian Americans from India. Having by far the largest proportion (over 50 percent) of college graduates, the majority of Asian Indians are professionals and businesspeople. Constituting less than 1 percent of the U.S. population, they own about 26 percent of all the nation's hotels (p. 350).

myth *Many conservatives dislike big government and want to "get government off our backs," especially in our private lives.*

reality Many conservatives are ideologically opposed to government intervention in people's private lives, but at the same time, they support school prayer and antiabortion laws, which, in effect, represent government intervention in private lives (p. 353).

myth *In the 2000 presidential election, George W. Bush received 48 percent of the popular vote—from about 48 percent of all U.S. citizens who were eligible to vote.*

reality Only about 24 percent of all eligible voters voted for Bush because nearly half did not even register to vote (p. 354).

myth *Poverty is the breeding ground for revolution and terrorism. Revolutionary and terrorist leaders are therefore mostly poor.*

reality Most revolutionary and terrorist leaders come from relatively affluent families (p. 361).

333

n 1998, right in the American heartland, far away from Asia, Dave Trench could feel the impact of the economic problems in the Pacific Rim countries. Fifty-seven years old, Trench had long worked for Harnischfeger Industries in St. Francis, Wisconsin. Harnischfeger was a proud company that built mining equipment and huge machines that produced 70 percent of the world's printing paper. Yet the company saw its sales to Singapore and other financially troubled Asian countries plummet from $600 million a year to nearly zero. As a result, the company laid off some 3,000 employees—one-fifth of its workforce. Trench was not one of the casualties, but he feared he would be if there were another round of dismissals.

Luckily, the Asian economy soon recovered, thanks, in large part, to its ability to export a huge quantity of products to the United States. This allowed the Asian countries to resume buying U.S. goods, which, in turn, helped the United States to prosper. By 2001, however, because of the collapse of the dot.com industry, the U.S. economy went weak again, decreasing the demand for computers and other electronic goods from Asia. Consequently, a recession hit the Asian countries, threatening the jobs of many of their workers (Omestad, 2001; Gwynne, 1998).

This demonstrates that people everywhere are affected by the economy not only in their own society but also in faraway lands. The economy is important in people's lives because they have to work to fulfill even their simplest needs. Beyond the basic needs of survival, people have formed countless others—for clothing, housing, schooling, medical care, entertainment, and innumerable other goods and services. To meet these needs, society develops an **economic institution**, a system for producing and distributing goods and services.

In studying this institution, economists tend to focus on impersonal things such as productivity, wages, prices, and profits. Sociologists, however, are more interested in people, such as Trench and other workers around the world, and how the economy affects their work and lives. Sociologists are further interested in how the economy relates to other aspects of society, especially **politics**—the type of human interaction that involves some people acquiring and exercising power over others. We will therefore analyze both the economic and the political institutions in this chapter.

THE ECONOMY IN PERSPECTIVE

To understand the economic world today, we need to look back at least to the eighteenth century, when a momentous event took hold in England. It was the **Industrial Revolution**, the drastic economic change brought about by the introduction of machines into the work process about 200 years ago. The revolution transformed the world's economies and its societies, and in recent decades it has been succeeded by the **postindustrial revolution**, the change of an economy into one dominated by high technology. While these revolutions have changed the nature of economic production, an economic system called *capitalism* has thrived, and many more women have entered the workforce. Let us take a look at these issues from various perspectives.

■ The Historical Perspective: From Industrial to Postindustrial World

For 98 percent of the last 10,000 years, the pattern of economic life changed rather little. Practically all of our ancestors eked out a mere subsistence living from relatively simple economies such as hunting and gathering (see Chapter 2: Society and Culture). Dur-

FIRST FACTORIES The Industrial Revolution began in England around 1760, sparked by the invention of spinning jennies and other machines that made mass production possible. Here, workers spin wool and cotton into thread in an early U.S. textile mill in 1820. The Industrial Revolution brought tremendous wealth to the West, while changing work patterns, the distribution of population, human relations, and social values. But it also brought about global inequality. ■

ing all those years, as sociologists Raymond Mack and Calvin Bradford (1979) pointed out, "The whole economic process was wrapped up in the individual." This was particularly true for crafts workers: They owned their own tools, secured their own raw materials, worked in their own homes, set their own working hours, and found their own markets for finished products.

But gradually, as the population grew and the demand for goods increased, individual crafts workers became more and more dependent on intermediaries to find raw materials and to sell their finished products. Some of these intermediaries took over the economic process, telling crafts workers what and how much to produce. In essence, these intermediaries became capitalists, and the formerly independent crafts workers became employees. Crafts workers, however, still worked separately in their own homes, forming what is called a *cottage industry*.

Characteristics   As the Industrial Revolution was about to dawn in England, the cottage industry began to give way to the *factory system*. Capitalists found it more economical to hire people to work together in one building than to collect goods from many scattered cottages. They began to own every part of the manufacturing process: the factory, the tools, the raw materials, and the finished products. In effect, they even owned the landless workers, who had only their labor to sell in order to survive. To make the process more efficient, capitalists increased

the division of labor. Some individuals were hired to spin thread, others to weave cloth, and one person to oversee all the workers as their supervisor.

Then, with the invention of steam engines, spinning jennies, and other machines, mass production became possible, and the Industrial Revolution was underway. It began in England around 1760, and during the following century, it profoundly changed the economic structure of Western Europe and North America. The Industrial Revolution substituted machines for human labor to perform many tasks, greatly improved the getting and working of raw materials, developed widespread railroad and steamship systems to transport huge quantities of raw materials and manufactured goods, and moved labor and resources from agriculture to industry. All this created tremendous wealth. At the same time, small machines were replaced by large ones, little mills became giant factories, and modest partnerships changed into large corporations.

Consequences   Industrialization has a number of far-reaching results:

1. *It changes the nature of work.* The mechanization of agriculture calls for few operators, leading most farmers into industrial work. Bigger and better machines in the factory, in the mines, and at construction sites also require fewer workers, reducing the number of blue-collar jobs. But because technology is highly productive, it brings prosperity,

which increases the demand for all kinds of services, from education and health to entertainment and money management. Thus, white-collar occupations proliferate. Even in manufacturing companies, white-collar workers outnumber blue-collar ones. The General Electric Company, for example, produces numerous different items from turbines to light bulbs, but the majority of its employees provide white-collar services from accounting to marketing.

2. *Industrialization brings about demographic changes—changes in the characteristics of a population.* In general, as a society industrializes, cities grow and fewer people live on farms, but the population as a whole increases. Once a society has developed an industrialized economy, population growth tends to slow, and the percentage of elderly people in the population rises.

3. *Industrialization changes human relations.* In industrial societies, people usually spend much of their time in huge bureaucratic organizations. They interact with a broad range of people, but their relationships with these people tend to be formal, fragmentary, and superficial. Ties to primary groups loosen. Industrialization alters other institutions as well: Formal schooling tends to become more important, and functions once served by the family are taken over by other institutions, such as business and government. According to a study of 50 countries, industrialization also creates global inequality, with highly industrialized nations enjoying higher status and more power than the less industrialized, thereby threatening world peace (Rau and Roncek, 1987).

4. *Industrialization changes the values of a society.* Many of the traditional values and ways of living are discredited. People learn to view change as natural and to hope for a better future. Thus, industrialization brings a dynamism into society. It produces greater energy and open-mindedness but also restlessness and discontent. This problem may be related to the relentless pursuit of material things in the industrial world.

Toward a Postindustrial World   Many developing countries have been trying to achieve in a few years the industrialization that took the West over 200 years to develop. Thus, they can realize modernization only partially. These countries have imported Western technology that has lowered death rates but not birth rates, with the result that population growth has eaten up or outstripped any gains in income. They have instituted Western-style education, enough to let people dream of a better life but not enough to create and operate a modern economy. They have seen the rewards of an industrial technol-

ogy—and developed a craving for what they believe to be a material paradise—but they do not have the means to satisfy that appetite. As a result, widespread poverty, high unemployment, and other social problems tend to ensue.

Meanwhile, the developed countries continue to industrialize and to take the process a step further. During industrialization, machines take over tasks from humans and people control the machines. Increasingly, the task of controlling the machines is given over to computers. A growing number of factory workers sit at computer terminals in clean, quiet offices, monitoring tireless, precise robots doing the kind of work that assembly-line workers used to do with dirty, noisy machines. Along with computers, other related technological breakthroughs such as electronics, microchips, and integrated circuits are ushering in a postindustrial age.

Postindustrialism has brought many developed countries a high degree of affluence and leisure. It has also made it possible for anyone on earth to be in instant communication with anyone else. Consequently, the spread of high technology throughout the world will likely mean greater output per worker and a higher standard of living in more and more societies. Instant communication, especially through the Internet and e-mail, may further undermine authoritarian controls, as it has in Eastern Europe, and keep democratic governments on their toes with a new degree of scrutiny. In short, we are likely to see more economic wealth and political freedom in the postindustrial world.

■ The Three Sociological Perspectives: The Nature and Origin of Capitalism

No factory functions on its own. It must buy raw materials and sell its products. It is enmeshed in a complicated network of exchanges. This network must be organized in some way. One way is through markets. A market economy is driven by the countless decisions individuals make to buy and sell. This is how capitalism works.

Capitalism is an economic system based on private ownership of property and competition in producing and selling goods and services. To functionalists, capitalism brings about a prosperous and stable social order. But to conflict theorists, capitalism threatens society by allowing a powerful wealthy class to exploit a weak lower class. Finally, the symbolic interactionists focus on how people's definition of their world creates or supports capitalism.

Functionalist Perspective: How Capitalism Benefits Society   Functionalist ideas about the contributions of capitalism to a prosperous society can be traced to Adam Smith (1732–1790). Although Smith was an economist, his theory of capitalism has become part of economic sociology. At the core of the theory lies a belief about the psychology of human beings: We are inherently selfish and act to serve our own interests. Capitalism works by allowing this pursuit of self-interest to flourish. It does so through two key characteristics: (1) *private ownership* of property and (2) *free competition* in buying and selling goods and services. Without these characteristics, capitalism does not exist.

Private ownership is considered functional for society's economic health because it motivates people to be efficient and productive. This may explain why, for example, Federal Express and other private delivery companies in the United States are generally more financially successful than the U.S. Postal Service. Private ownership may also explain why private lands in China are far more productive than state-owned farms. In that country, the private plots once constituted only 4 percent of all cultivated land, but they produced some 33 percent of the country's meat and dairy products and 50 percent of its potatoes (Naisbitt and Aburdene, 1990).

Free competition is also considered beneficial to society's economic health because it compels businesses to make the most efficient use of resources, to produce the best possible goods and services, and to sell them at the lowest price possible. Only by doing so can businesses expect to beat their competitors. Competition, then, acts—in Smith's terminology—as an "invisible hand," bringing profits to the efficient producers and putting the inefficient ones out of business.

Doesn't the pursuit of self-interest reduce society to a jungle and harm the public good? On the contrary, Smith argued, because of free competition the self-serving decisions of individuals to buy and sell end up promoting the public good. Competition forces people to take account of others' interests in order to serve their own. If Apple Computer does not meet your needs, you can buy a product from IBM or Gateway—and Apple knows it. It is in *their* interest to serve *your* interests. Because many businesses strive to serve their own interests by serving those of the public, the whole society will benefit. There will be an abundance of high-quality, low-priced goods and services, which will entice many people to buy. Businesses will then produce more to meet consumers' increased demand, which will create more jobs and raise wages. The result will be a prosperous economy for the society as a whole (Dougherty, 2002).

Conflict Perspective: How Capitalism Harms Society

The conflict ideas about the harmfulness of capital-ism can be traced to Karl Marx (1818–1883). He saw as inevitable private property owners' exploitation of their laborers by paying them as little as possible. Marx also disagreed with Smith on the specialized division of labor in industrial capitalism. To Smith, specialization *enhances efficiency* in the generation of wealth. But when Marx looked at specialization, he saw **alienation of labor,** laborers' loss of control over their work process. Because workers own neither their tools nor the products they make, and because they cannot exercise all their capacities as they choose but are forced to perform an isolated, specific task, their work is no longer their own. Instead, Marx contended, it becomes a separate, alien thing.

Marx further saw severe contradictions within the capitalist system, contradictions that would serve as "its own gravediggers." One such contradiction grows from capitalism's devotion to individualism. As Robert Heilbroner (1972) said, "*Capitalism* had become so complex that it needed direction, but *capitalists* insisted on a ruinous freedom." Marx saw another contradiction, as well: Capitalists depend on profit, but their profit comes from the fact that workers put more value into products than they are given in the form of wages. To increase their profits, capitalists often hold down wages and, whenever possible, also substitute machines for human labor. As a result, the poor get poorer from lower wages or job loss. This, in turn, reduces the demand for the capitalists' products, thereby decreasing their profits. The economy can work itself out of this crisis, but such crises will recur, argued Marx, with each one getting worse until the workers revolt.

Ultimately, Marx believed, the contradictions of capitalism would lead to **communism,** a classless society that operates on the principle of "from each according to his ability to each according to his needs." In this society, the state would wither away. First, however, the destruction of capitalism would be followed by a temporary era of **socialism,** an economic system based on public ownership and government control of the economy.

No state, including so-called communist countries such as the former Soviet Union and China, has ever reached full-blown communism, but many, such as these two countries, have tried socialism. In a socialist economy, the state owns and operates the means of production and distribution, such as land, factories, railroads, airlines, banks, and stores. It determines what the nation's economic needs are and develops plans to meet those needs. It also sets wages and prices. Individual interests are subordinate to those of society. Some of these socialist practices can also be found in the United States, as we will discuss later.

theoretical thumbnail

The Nature and Origin of Capitalism

Perspective	Focus	Insights
Functionalist	How capitalism benefits society	Capitalism brings prosperity to society as whole.
Conflict	How capitalism harms society	Capitalism enables the rich to exploit the poor.
Symbolic interactionist	How shared beliefs create capitalism	Capitalism was created and is sustained by the early Protestants' belief that to live a hard-working and responsible life is God's command.

Symbolic Interactionist Perspective: How Shared Beliefs Create Capitalism As a symbolic interactionist, Max Weber (1864–1920) concentrated on how subjective meanings affect economic action. To Weber, subjective meanings involve "taking into account the behavior of others," which, in turn, leads the individual to engage in certain activities (Weber, 1968). As suggested in Chapter 11 (Education and Religion), Weber saw how the early Protestants in Europe acquired from their interactions with each other some shared beliefs that gave rise to capitalism.

First, the Protestants defined hard work as a sign that God would send them to heaven rather than hell. In effect, they equated toil with God's work. By working hard, they were able to produce wealth. Second, they defined play as the devil's temptation. They were thus afraid to spend the fruit of their labor on amusements and other worldly pleasures (Biggart, 1994). The wealth, then, was used as capital to be put into business. The continuing accumulation of capital and the growth of business led to the development of capitalism.

After capitalism emerged, it continued to operate for a long time because the early Protestants learned to behave in a rational or responsible manner. Early Protestantism helped discipline an unruly working class, restraining its members from consuming alcohol, from engaging in disorderly conduct, and even from taking breaks or walking off their jobs, thus turning them into a docile labor force (Wuthnow, 1994). Simultaneously, the same religion encouraged the capitalist class to run its businesses rationally. As a result, these capitalists developed bureaucracy as a rational form of organization to perpetuate capitalism.

In short, the meanings imputed by the Protestants to hard work and play helped create capitalism. Moreover, the continuing existence of capitalism is further supported by the Protestant values of self-restraint and rationality.

For a review of the three sociological perspectives on capitalism, see the Theoretical Thumbnail above.

■ The Feminist Perspective: Women's Economic Status

One of the most notable economic trends of the last half century has been the sharp increase in the number of women in paid employment. About 60 percent of women are in the labor force today. This trend is popularly attributed to two factors. One is the liberation of women from their traditional role of homemaker, made possible by smaller family size and labor-saving household devices. Another factor is the job market's increased demand for women, who find the wages significantly higher than necessary for paying the costs of child care and other household chores (U.S. Census Bureau, 2001; Peterson, 1994).

Seen from the feminist perspective, however, most women are not truly liberated from traditional housework. Even those who work full time outside the home still perform most of the childrearing and other household tasks. Feminist theorists also view the increased female participation in the labor force not as a reflection of increased economic opportunities but as a sign of declining living standards and increasing economic need. Due to a decline in real incomes, many families now need two incomes to maintain the standard of living previously achieved by one—usually male—breadwinner. In addition, a growing number of women enter the labor force not because they choose to but because they are forced to as unmarried heads of families (Peterson, 1994).

Feminist theorists further observe that women workers are concentrated in lower-paid, lower-status jobs with minimal benefits and few opportunities for advancement. The reason, according to feminist theorists, can be found in the exploitive and oppressive nature of capitalism and patriarchy. Under capitalism, employers seek greater profit by paying women workers less than their male counterparts or by using cheap female labor to replace expensive male labor. And under patriarchy, men seek to dominate women by either relegating them to low-paid jobs or keeping them at home with the discouraging prospect of paid employment offering no better conditions than housework. Thus, the feminist theorists see little to cheer about in the economic status of U.S. women (Peterson, 1994; Abbott and Wallace, 1990).

THE WORLD'S ECONOMIC SYSTEMS

Economic systems vary from one society to another. Some are mainly capitalist or free and others socialist or unfree, but they all are **mixed economies**, having elements of both capitalism and socialism. They differ only in degree, ranging on a continuum from the most capitalist to the most socialist. Table 12.1 shows examples of the countries with different degrees of economic freedom.

The Economic Continuum

The United States and Japan are widely known to be among the world's most capitalist societies. Yet the U.S. government manages the economy by, for example, levying taxes and controlling the supply of money. In Japan, the government takes a leading role in planning investment for the future and in turning corporations toward industries that are likely to grow.

myth	In the United States and Japan, two of the world's most capitalist societies, the governments pursue a strict laissez-faire, free-enterprise policy by not interfering in economic affairs at all.
reality	Governments in even the most capitalist societies do not follow a strict laissez-faire policy. They often step in to regulate business.

Ranging along the middle of the continuum are the European democracies. From time to time, several of these democracies have had socialist governments. In general, these nations have combined capitalist enterprise with wide-ranging government control—and high taxes. They tend to set stricter controls on business and offer more extensive social services than the United States. All these states, for example, provide a national system of health insurance. Over the years, their governments have owned and managed many industries. In Great Britain, for example, the coal, steel, automobile, and television industries have been under government control at various times. Even before France elected a socialist government in 1981, its government had created subway and aerospace industries. Nevertheless, these European democracies are so much more capitalist than socialist that they are usually considered capitalist.

TABLE 12.1

Societies Ranked in Order of Economic Freedom (from most free to most repressed)

Most Free	Mostly Free	Mostly Unfree	Most Repressed
1. Hong Kong	18. Canada	68. Saudi Arabia	*135. Russia
2. Singapore	19. Germany	72. Brazil	*135. Vietnam
3. New Zealand	27. Taiwan	85. Kenya	143. Syria
5. Ireland	*29. Italy	94. Lebanon	146. Iran
*6. Denmark	*29. Spain	99. Pakistan	148. Burma
*6. United States	35. Japan	104. Egypt	151. Libya
*9. Australia	40. France	113. Ghana	*153. Laos
*9. Great Britain	44. Costa Rica	118. Ecuador	*153. Zimbabwe
11. Sweden	*56. Greece	119. Turkey	155. Cuba
15. Switzerland	*56. Mexico	127. China	156. North Korea

*Two or more nations tied for this ranking.

Source: Data from *Index of Economic Freedom,* 2003.

LOOSENING IT At the socialist end of the economic continuum are countries such as Vietnam, North Korea, China, and Cuba, whose governments largely control their economies by restricting free enterprise and private ownership of property. But some, such as Vietnam and China, have recently loosened government control. Here, Vietnamese women practice free enterprise by selling goods in a market stall in Ho Chi Minh City. ■

At the socialist end of the continuum, we find so-called communist countries such as North Korea, Vietnam, China, and Cuba. These countries are basically economically unfree; their governments control their economies by restricting free enterprise and private ownership of property. Some communist countries, however, have recently tried to introduce a new economic arrangement in which centralized direction of the economy by the government is reduced. China, for example, has adopted some free enterprise practices, granted state-owned enterprises wide autonomy in running their businesses, and opened up some industries to foreign investors. Still, the economies of China and other officially socialist countries remain mostly unfree.

Also economically unfree are a number of countries whose governments do not consider themselves socialist, such as Kenya and Sudan in Africa, Pakistan and India in Asia, and Colombia and Peru in Latin America. These countries do not restrict private ownership and free enterprise in the same way as their socialist counterparts. But their governments do severely control their economies by imposing heavy taxes, setting wages and prices, and excessively regulating various industries (O'Driscoll et al., 2002).

■ Economic Performance

Socialist or unfree economies have a decidedly mixed record. Their total wealth is generally far below that of capitalist or economically free countries. True, under socialism, nations such as Cuba and China have improved the standard of living for vast numbers of people who had been destitute. In general, socialist nations have reduced the extremes of poverty, inflation, and unemployment that occasionally hit capitalist states. But the central planning of socialist states often creates inefficiencies, causing, among other things, severe shortages of food and products. Similar problems also plague a number of countries in Africa, Asia, and Latin America that are not socialist but are economically unfree.

In the meantime, capitalist economies in the West have little trouble producing ample quantities of goods, although they have faced periodic bouts of extreme inflation and unemployment, as in the late 1970s and early 1980s. Moreover, their social peace has depended to a great extent on economic growth, which gives even the poor some hope of improving their standard of living. Their ability to sustain this growth may not be certain all the time. Around 1980, the U.S. economy, for example, seemed to get stuck, unable to continue up the spiral that Adam Smith predicted would generate more productivity and more wealth. In fact, its productivity went down, increasing unemployment as well as inflation. But in 1983, the U.S. economy began to make a dramatic comeback, showing a substantial growth in productivity and a decline in unemployment and inflation. The economies in Canada and Western Europe also rebounded. In 1991 and 2001, another worldwide economic recession hit these capitalist countries, but once again, recovery followed sooner or later.

Despite the ups and downs of economic conditions, capitalist countries tend to remain considerably more productive than their socialist counterparts—as well as many nonsocialist but economically unfree countries (see Figure 12.1). The capitalist system is much more efficient because it allows the freedom to pursue personal gain and minimizes government control of the economy. In fact, a study of some 156

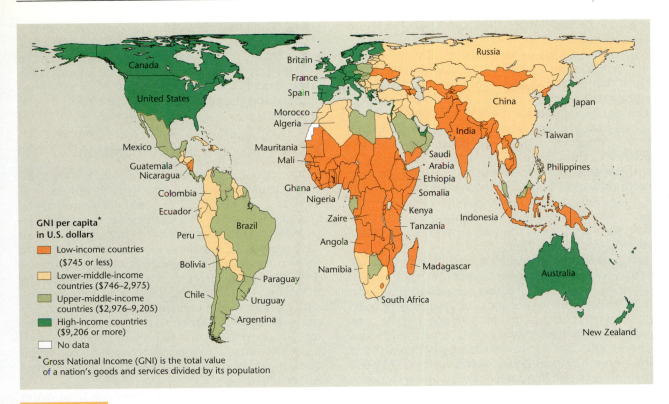

GNI per capita*
in U.S. dollars

- Low-income countries ($745 or less)
- Lower-middle-income countries ($746–2,975)
- Upper-middle-income countries ($2,976–9,205)
- High-income countries ($9,206 or more)
- No data

*Gross National Income (GNI) is the total value of a nation's goods and services divided by its population

FIGURE 12.1

Economic Performance around the World

Socialist economies, such as those of China, the former Soviet Union (including Russia), and Eastern Europe, are generally poor. So are other economically unfree countries, such as many African nations, though their governments do not declare themselves to be socialist. The free, capitalist economies, such as those of the United States, Western Europe, and Japan, are considerably more prosperous.

Critical Thinking: *Are people in economically free countries generally happier? Why or why not?*

Source: World Bank Atlas, 2003.

countries shows that those with more economic freedom are generally more prosperous than those with less freedom. Economic freedom, then, is the key to prosperity (O'Driscoll et al., 2002).

■ The Global Economy

Modern transportation and communication have created a *global economy,* in which many countries trade with each other. In the past, most countries had self-contained economies, with international trade confined to the importing of raw materials such as food, fuels, and minerals from poor countries and a few industrial products such as clothes and shoes from rich countries. Today, all kinds of products and services, as well as stocks, bonds, and other investments, flow from one country to another. Over

the last decade, world trade in goods has doubled in value to $6.4 trillion today, which is about equal to one-fourth of the value of all the nations' goods and services (Samuelson, 2003b; Kurlantzick and Allen, 2002).

The global economy seems to work relatively well. Some poor countries sell inexpensive labor-intensive products (such as clothes, shoes, and toys) to rich nations and buy from rich nations sophisticated knowledge-intensive goods and services (such as jets, pharmaceuticals, banking, and insurance). In rich countries, importing this low-cost merchandise enables consumers to live better. While low-wage workers may temporarily lose their jobs, they will eventually get re-employed in trade-competitive industries. The international trade, in turn, helps those in poor countries to prosper (Samuelson, 2003a).

The world economy is not completely free, however. There are limits to international trade. Rich countries control international organizations such as the World Bank and the International Monetary Fund, which allows them to keep out developing countries' exports of textiles, agricultural products, and steel. Of the three groups of developing countries today, the poorest and the richest do not threaten the economies of developed countries. The poorest cannot create strong companies to compete with those in developed countries because they are preoccupied with trying to alleviate poverty. The richest group, which includes only a few countries, such as South Korea and Taiwan, is now able to compete with developed countries without considerable subsidy from government.

It is the great majority of developing countries, which occupy a middle ground between the poorest and the richest, that give developed countries pause. In these developing countries, the government heavily supports businesses by, for example, having state-owned banks lend them money at extremely low interest rates. Such government support has alarmed the United States and other rich countries. They fear that given the huge number of developing countries with government-subsidized companies, the rich countries will be swamped with supercheap imports, which will bankrupt many of their own companies and cause a widespread loss of jobs. Rich countries have therefore demanded "a level playing field," pressuring this group of developing countries to abandon government support if they want to join the international trading system. Of course, complying with this demand will effectively dash these countries' hope of becoming prosperous (Amsden, 2002, 2001).

THE DOMINANCE OF BIG CORPORATIONS

There is an inherent contradiction in the competitive market system: The more efficient it is, the more it threatens to destroy itself. Through free competition, the best producers gain more resources, which gives them an edge on their competitors. They may use this edge to drive their competitors out of business or to buy them out and prevent other potential producers from entering the market. Eventually, just one firm might dominate production of a product, achieving a **monopoly**—the situation in which one firm controls the output of an industry. It is far more likely that a handful of firms will control a certain market, forming an **oligopoly**—the situation in which a very few companies control the output of an industry. Indeed,

today, a small number of big corporations dominate the economy in many countries. In the United States, for example, 2,000 corporations, which represent only 0.1 percent of all companies in the country, own 40 percent of all company assets and 88 percent of all business income (U.S. Census Bureau, 1998; Useem, 1980).

■ The Nature of Big Corporations

A big corporation does not have a single owner. Instead, it may have thousands or even hundreds of thousands of *stockholders,* who own shares in the firm and its profits. Stockholders do not communicate with one another, much less organize to control the corporation. But they can exercise their right to vote, usually to elect a board of directors to run the corporation. The directors make overall plans for the company. They may decide how to raise money, how to expand the company, and what dividends are to be paid to shareholders. The directors also appoint the president, vice president, and other officers to conduct the company's day-to-day operations. In corporations, then, ownership and control are separated.

The big corporation is a far cry from what Adam Smith expected. To him, a typical company would be small, started by one or a few individuals with their personal savings. These entrepreneurs would personally manage the company and reap the profits or suffer the losses, depending on how well they performed in a competitive market. Thus, the rise of giant corporations today can have serious consequences that Smith did not anticipate.

First, the few dominant companies, relatively free from competitive challenges, can force consumers to pay high prices for their products. They may slow down production and then increase the prices for their supposedly scarce goods. This is what the oil, steel, and other mining and manufacturing companies did in the 1970s. Price hikes can generate inflation, and production slowdowns can cause unemployment, both of which can throw society into an economic crisis.

Moreover, given their control over large shares of the market, giant corporations may *not* feel competitive. Thus, they have little incentive to build new plants, increase research and development of new products, make themselves more efficient, and offer consumers better goods and services. This may partly explain why, in recent decades, some giant U.S. companies—especially in the car and steel industries—sat back and did not compete with Japanese and other foreign firms until shrinking market share and falling profits spurred them back into action.

But big corporations also contribute to the well-being of society. By combining the capital of millions of investors and the talents of numerous workers, giant corporations make it possible for many to enjoy a relatively high standard of living. Large corporations also contribute heavily to universities and colleges, charitable organizations, and public service projects. Corporate philanthropy may be intended to stimulate sales by generating good will, but it does help improve the nation's health, education, and welfare (Levy, 1999; Burt, 1983). Since corporations are considered vitally important, they receive a great deal of help from the government, as we will see in the next section.

■ Welfare for the Rich

There are two welfare systems in the United States. One is the well-known welfare system for the poor, and the other is that for the rich. Government help for wealthy individuals and big corporations may be in the form of *special tax breaks* called *tax credits* or *deductions* or other loopholes in the tax law. Some of the government help for corporations may also be in the form of direct payments or loans, usually called not welfare but *subsidies*. Welfare for rich individuals and big corporations is far more generous than welfare for the poor.

Big corporations seem to get the greatest amount of government benefits. The income taxes that are paid by corporations have always been proportionately smaller than those paid by individuals. Over the last 30 years, the corporate income tax as a fraction of federal government revenue has steadily declined, from over 20 percent in the 1960s to less than 10 percent today (Barlett and Steele, 1998; Auerbach, 1983). The government also supplies big business with more dollars in direct loans and loan guarantees than all the commercial and industrial loans provided by private banks. Every year, the government further pays an enormous sum for research and development projects in areas such as the military, space exploration, and atomic energy. After developing the technology at taxpayers' expense, corporations are allowed to use it to earn a profit. The government even gives annually about $100 million to food and beverage companies to advertise their products abroad, such as Miller beer, Campbell's soup, and McDonald's burgers (Nader and Weissman, 2001; Rosenbaum, 1997b).

■ Corporate Corruption

Given these tax breaks and other favors from the government, corporate executives are tempted to seek more easy money by engaging in illegal business practices. One notorious example is the executives at Enron, a huge energy-trading company, who plunged the company into bankruptcy by pocketing millions of dollars from defrauding investors, employees, and pensioners. Another example involved two executives of WorldCom, a global communications corporation, who masterminded a $7.2 billion securities fraud by pumping up the company's earnings to keep its stock price high. Some have suggested that these executives became corrupt because they were paid much more than their law-abiding peers at other companies. Apparently, then, receiving sky-high compensation tends to make executives feel that they (unlike their lowly and dispensable workers) are above the law (Backover and Dugas, 2002; Klinger and Sklar, 2002).

Perhaps more important, however, others have attributed corporate corruption to the business deregulation that has run amok for more than two decades. This may explain why the corrupt activities are not much different from the legal business practices at many U.S. corporations that have been liberated by the government's hands-off policy. These legal practices include (1) moving the corporate headquarters without its people to Bermuda and other foreign places to evade paying U.S. taxes; (2) overpaying executives and granting them huge stock options and interest-free loans, even when they do their jobs poorly and cause their companies to lose money; (3) stacking the board of directors with insiders and friends, who will shower lavish compensation on executives and turn a blind eye to their wrongdoing; and (4) giving campaign contributions to candidates from *both* major parties to ensure a receipt of government subsidies, tax breaks, and other favors (Lavelle and Prasso, 2002).

■ Multinational Corporations

In many big corporate mergers, a corporation buys others that operate different kinds of business to form a **conglomerate**, a corporation that owns companies in various unrelated industries. An example is International Telephone and Telegraph Corporation (ITT), which, over the years, has bought a long string of companies that had nothing to do with telephones and telegraphs, such as hotels, insurance companies, and bakeries.

Most of these conglomerates have further expanded by becoming **multinational corporations**, with subsidiaries in many countries. Many multinationals have more economic power than a medium-sized nation. One way to measure their power is to compare the annual sales of a corporation with the gross national product of a nation. By this standard, General Motors is more powerful than Ireland, Greece, Pakistan, and Nicaragua combined, and Exxon is more powerful than Israel, Jordan, the Philippines, and Guatemala (Chimerine, 1995).

In search of lower labor costs, lower taxes, and larger markets, many multinational corporations have shifted their assets out of their industrialized birthplaces into the developing world. From these foreign investments, U.S. corporations can earn as much as 70 percent of their total profits. For these profits, multinational corporations pay very little in taxes because of the much lower tax rates in foreign countries. In recent years, the growing affluence of many developing countries has led multinational corporations to change from the pursuit of cheap labor to the direct selling of U.S. consumer goods (Benjamin, 2003; Tolentino, 2000; Zachary, 1996).

Multinational corporations can have far-reaching effects on developing nations. They can promote social conflict by bringing in elements of a foreign culture. They can promote dangerous practices such as smoking. They can control a small nation's most important industry such as copper production. Despite these dangers, most developing countries still welcome multinationals. They often try to attract more foreign investment with a wide array of incentives, ranging from extensive tax benefits to subsidized labor, including the elimination of trade unions. Apparently, they appreciate the fact that multinationals usually create many badly needed jobs, transfer modern technology to them, and stimulate their economic growth (Luo, 2000; Gibbs, 1996; Brauchli and Biers, 1995).

WORK IN THE UNITED STATES

When we meet a stranger, one of our first questions is likely to be "What do you do?" The person might answer "I'm a salesperson" or "I'm a cabdriver" or a doctor or lawyer. Work is not just a way to make enough money to pay the bills. For many of us, work helps define our identity and our sense of self-worth.

Just what it is that we are able to do for a living, however, depends to a great extent on the economic institutions we have described. As we will see in the following sections, the kinds of workers needed by the complex U.S. economy have implications for job satisfaction and the workplace.

■ Occupations

With the industrialization of farming—a process that accelerated greatly after World War II—the stage was set for the appearance of today's labor force. Thanks to technological innovations ranging from new machinery to new fertilizers to new breeding techniques, agricultural productivity soared during the twentieth century. In 1900, one U.S. farmer on average produced enough food to support 7 other people.

" 'Chicken Vindaloo for the Hindu Soul' is but the tip of the iceberg in our initial strategy of global expansion."

Source: © The New Yorker Collection 1998 Jack Ziegler from Cartoonbank.com. All Rights Reserved.

Now, one farmer produces enough for more than 60 people.

This increasing agricultural productivity pushed many workers off the farm. Today, only about 1 percent of the U.S. labor force works on the farm compared with nearly 60 percent in 1870 and 30.2 percent in 1920. The continuing exodus also reflects the failure of many small family farms to survive. Government subsidies and other "save the family farm" programs, such as crop insurance and production control, have largely come to naught. What remains is an increasingly smaller number of highly efficient farms that need only a few workers to produce enough food for the whole nation (Robbins, 1990).

Many of those who left the farm in earlier decades went to work in manufacturing industries producing clothes, furniture, and cars. But major changes were underway in manufacturing, as well. Just as in agriculture, new machines decreased the number of people needed to produce things. Since World War II, the share of jobs in manufacturing held by white-collar workers—managers, professionals, clerical workers, salespersons—has increased greatly. Before 1945, blue-collar workers had long outnumbered white-collar workers, but then the number of white-collar workers began to grow so fast that today they are three times as numerous as blue-collar workers in manufacturing companies (U.S. Census Bureau, 2001; Rosecrance, 1990).

Meanwhile, the growth of jobs in manufacturing and other goods-producing industries has slowed, but jobs in service industries—education, health care, tourism, banking, real estate, insurance—have increased. In the 1990s, the rapid growth in the service

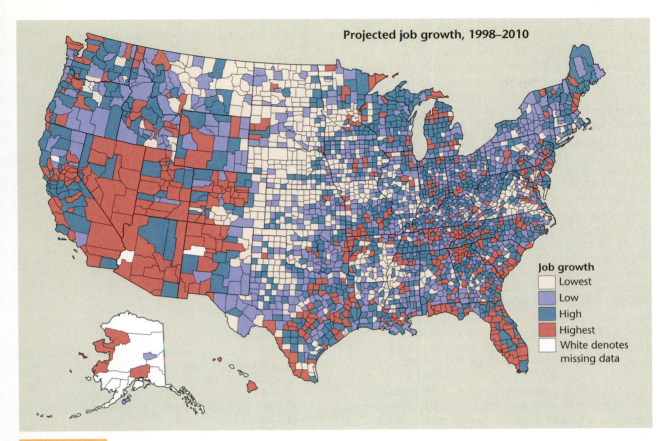

Projected job growth, 1998–2010

Job growth
- Lowest
- Low
- High
- Highest
- White denotes missing data

FIGURE 12.2

Where the Jobs Are in 1998–2010

The number of U.S. jobs is projected to increase by an average of 12.7 percent between 1998 and 2010. The greatest job growth will likely take place in the Southwest and, to a lesser extent, the Southeast.

Critical Thinking: *Would you be willing to move to find a job in either of these regions? Why or why not?*

Source: From *American Demographics,* May 1998. Copyright 1998 PRIMEDIA Business Magazines & Media Inc. All rights reserved.

sector as a whole resulted largely from an increased demand for health care, entertainment, and business and financial services. The highest job growth in recent years has taken place in the Southwest and Southeast and is expected to continue in these areas for the next 10 years or so (see Figure 12.2).

■ Workers

The composition of the U.S. labor force has changed, too. The most dramatic change is that today, about 60 percent of U.S. women are in the labor force compared with just 43 percent in 1970. Women accounted for about two-thirds of the entire labor force growth between 1982 and 1995, and the number of women workers is expected to continue rising (U.S. Census Bureau, 2001). By publicizing and legitimizing the rights of women and their need to earn enough money to support themselves and contribute to total family income, the feminist movement has largely aided the increase. This, in turn, has brought about some *feminization of the workplace,* the prevalence of the younger generation of women showing their femininity by dressing attractively, teasing, bantering, and flirting and thereby bringing down the traditional barrier between social and work lives (Pollock, 2000).

Important changes have also occurred in the age and racial composition of the workforce. In the 1980s and 1990s, the employment rate for men older than 65 declined significantly. Age discrimination, as well as retirement programs such as Social Security and private pension plans, has probably played a part in this decline. But in recent years, a growing industrial demand for cheaper labor—stimulated by global competition—has fueled a dramatic increase in labor force participation among minorities and immigrants. These groups accounted for most of the workforce growth in the 1990s.

These breakdowns by gender, race, and age do not tell much about what is actually going on in the U.S. economy. It is a **dual economy** that comprises a *core* of large corporations dominating the market and a *periphery* of small firms competing for the remaining smaller shares of business. In addition, there is a *third sector,* consisting of various government agencies. About 30 percent of the U.S. labor force works in the third, state sector, and the rest are employed in the private core and the peripheral sector. Contrary to popular belief, most privately employed individuals do not work in the core's large companies (more than 1,000 employees each); only 30 to 40 percent do so. Most work in the peripheral sector, especially in small firms with fewer than 100 employees (U.S. Census Bureau, 2001; Granovetter, 1984).

Whatever sector they work in, U.S. workers are now better educated than ever before. In 1940, most workers had slightly more than a grade school education. Today, nearly 30 percent have some college education, and two-thirds are high school graduates (U.S. Census Bureau, 2001; Granovetter, 1984). Unfortunately, U.S. workers today are faced with problems that did not exist before.

In today's fiercely competitive global economy, many U.S. companies have begun to minimize production costs by paying their employees low wages, comparable to those received by skilled but low-paid workers in the fast-developing economies of Asia and Eastern Europe. A popular way to keep payroll costs low involves hiring temporary, contingent, part-time, and contract workers. In fact, since 1982, temporary employment has soared by nearly 250 percent compared with less than a 20 percent increase in all employment. Temporary workers now compose at least one-third of the U.S. labor force, and their ranks are still growing (Kadlec, 2003; Thottam, 2003; Larson, 1996).

Temporary workers normally do not join labor unions, but some full-timers do in order to get higher pay and better working conditions. Over the last two decades, however, the proportion of the workers in unions has declined continuously, from about 20 percent in 1983 to nearly 13 percent in 2003 (see Figure 12.3). One reason for the decline is the loss of unionized jobs in the manufacturing industry to

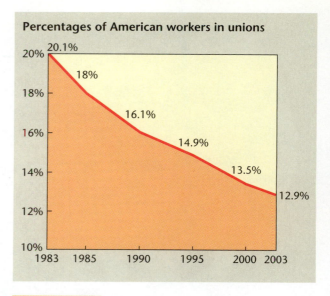

Percentages of American workers in unions

20.1% (1983)
18% (1985)
16.1% (1990)
14.9% (1995)
13.5% (2000)
12.9% (2003)

FIGURE 12.3

Labor Unions in Decline

Over the last 20 years, union membership among Americans has been declining continuously. One reason is the loss of unionized manufacturing jobs to labor-cheap countries. Another is the lack of union appeal to relatively well-educated employees in fast-growing service and high-tech industries.

Critical Thinking: *When you pursue a career, will you be willing to join a union? Why or why not?*

Source: Data from U.S. Bureau of Labor Statistics, 2004.

lower-paid workers in labor-cheap countries. Another reason is the lack of union appeal in fast-growing service and technological industries, where employees are relatively well educated.

■ Job Satisfaction

It may be extremely important to have a job, but does it bring happiness? Are U.S. workers really happy with their jobs? In many studies during the 1980s and 1990s, representative samples of workers were asked whether they would continue to work if they inherited enough money to live comfortably without working. More than 70 percent replied that they would continue working. Asked how satisfied they were with their jobs, even more—85 percent—replied that they were very or fairly satisfied. And in another survey, nearly 70 percent said that they would "decide without hesitation to take the same job again"; fewer than 10 percent would do something else (Zuckerman, 2003; Bowman, 2001; NORC, 1994). In short, most people like their work.

myth	In the United States, most workers would rather pursue leisure than work.
reality	Most workers are satisfied with their jobs. Even if they inherited enough money to live comfortably without working, most would still want to work.

Job satisfaction varies from one group to another. Generally, older workers are more satisfied with their jobs than younger ones. One reason is that older workers, being more advanced in their careers, have better jobs. Another is that younger workers are more likely to expect their jobs to be highly interesting and stimulating and hence are more likely to be disillusioned because of the difficulty in realizing their high aspirations (Bowman, 2001).

White-collar workers, especially professionals and businesspeople, are also more likely than blue-collar workers to feel genuinely satisfied with their jobs. Among blue-collar workers, union members report significantly *less* job satisfaction than nonmembers, which may reflect job dissatisfaction as the primary reason for joining unions in the first place. As a likely cause of job dissatisfaction, feeling stressed on the job is more prevalent in the South, which has a higher percentage of blue-collar workers than other regions (see Figure 12.4, p. 348).

Generally paid less and having less prestigious jobs than men, women may be expected to be less satisfied with their work. But research has shown just the opposite: Women are equally or more satisfied when compared with men. Why? One reason is that because of gender discrimination, women expect less than men from the job market and so can more easily fulfill their lower expectations. If they get jobs that are as good as men's, going beyond their expectations, they are likely to express more satisfaction than men (Weaver and Matthews, 1990; Hodson, 1989).

■ The Changing Workplace

The traditional work ethic among U.S. workers has been imbued with the early Protestant belief in work as a moral duty—a way of sacrificing for others. Thus, until recently, most have believed that a man with a family has a responsibility to choose the job that pays the most, rather than one that is more satisfying but pays less. Workers labored hard to support their families, disregarding how unpleasant and boring their work might be. But today, a majority reject that view and attitude. Most are more interested in jobs that allow for personal growth, self-fulfillment, and other nonmaterialist values. Thus, a shift has occurred in the work ethic, from an emphasis on self-sacrifice to a stress on self-development as the primary motive for hard work (Katzenbach, 2003; Bowman, 2001; Auerbach, 1996).

How has this new ethic come about? As we have observed, the number of white-collar workers and the amount of the average worker's education have increased substantially over the last several decades. It is these better-educated and white-collar workers who value autonomy and personal growth at work.

As a result, attempts have been made to reorganize the workplace. They have usually included offering

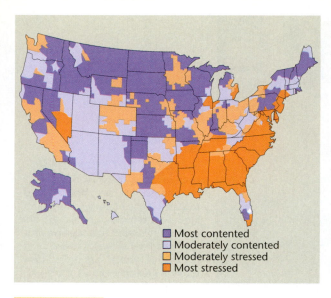

FIGURE 12.4

Where Workers Are Most Stressed

Compared with their white-collar peers, blue-collar workers are more likely to find their jobs stressful. And workers in the South are more likely to be stressed by their jobs than those in other regions.

Critical Thinking: *What will you do if you find your work stressful?*

Source: Data from *Newsweek,* May 11, 1998, p. 6.

workers more interesting jobs, more autonomy, and increased participation in decision making. A growing number of companies have given workers some freedom to set their own working hours within specified limits. Some have introduced procedures that allow workers to take part in decisions about production methods, promotions, hiring, and firing. Some companies have even raised wages by sharing profits with workers. After a decade of widespread corporate downsizings, a growing number of companies have begun to ease employee anxiety by guaranteeing job security. All these efforts have significantly boosted productivity. Apparently, workers are more productive when management treats them as equal partners (Gardyn, 2000a; White and Lublin, 1996; Wartzman, 1992).

SOCIAL DIVERSITY IN THE U.S. ECONOMY

Economic inequality exists in the United States, with whites generally occupying higher positions in the economy than minority groups. At the same time, however, economic diversity also exists among the minorities themselves.

■ Native Americans

Before being driven onto reservations, Native Americans had a self-sustaining, land-based economy, whose form ranged from farming in the Southwest to hunting on the Plains to a varying mix of farming and hunting across the continent. The loss of land to white settlers resulted in the destruction of these traditional economies.

Today, Native Americans on most reservations find themselves in the worst economic straits of any ethnic group, as indicated by an average income that is the lowest in the United States. But most Native Americans have moved to the cities, where they work largely in low-wage, blue-collar occupations. In recent decades, a growing number of these workers have obtained better jobs through increased work experience and education. Also in recent years, prosperity has come to some reservations through their operation of casinos and other gambling facilities (Feagin and Feagin, 1999; Nies, 1996; Viola, 1996).

■ African Americans

In the 1800s, after having been freed from slavery, most African Americans continued to live in the South, where they struggled to eke out a living as sharecroppers or tenant farmers. Beginning in 1900, however, wave after wave of African Americans moved to the industrial North, where the slowing of massive foreign immigration created a huge demand for laborers. But most ended up getting relatively unskilled jobs, such as working as truck drivers or maids. A few pursued business and professional careers as store owners, teachers, ministers, and physicians, but they served mostly their own communities (Feagin and Feagin, 1999; Turner et al., 1991).

After the Civil Rights Act of 1964 prohibited discrimination in employment, the number of African Americans in better-paying job categories grew significantly for the next 16 years or so. But the growth slowed in the 1980s and 1990s. Today, the proportions of African American men and women in professional, managerial, and other better-paying positions continue to lag behind those of their white peers. Meanwhile, African Americans are still far more likely than whites to hold lower-paying, blue-collar jobs and to be unemployed (Feagin and Feagin, 1999; Turner et al., 1991).

A key obstacle to black advancement in employment has been the persistence of *discrimination,* aided by a change in how the Supreme Court defined this term. Before 1980, discrimination was defined quite simply as white employer practices that put African American employees at a disadvantage. But since 1980, an employer who practices discrimination can

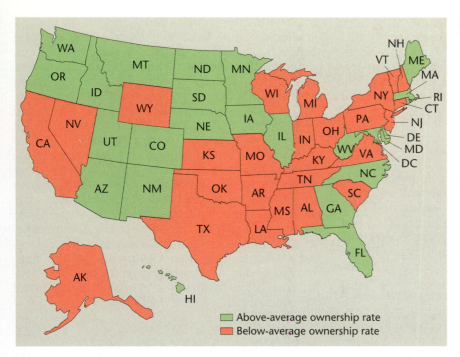

FIGURE 12.5

African American Entrepreneurs

African Americans are starting business enterprises at a higher rate than most other groups in the United States. Most of these entrepreneurs are young—in their thirties and forties—and well educated, and they generally live in those states that have more African Americans with these demographics.

Critical Thinking: *What would you need to start a business and be successful at it?*

Source: From *American Demographics,* June 1996. Copyright 1996 PRIMEDIA Business Magazines & Media Inc. All rights reserved.

□ Above-average ownership rate
□ Below-average ownership rate

---

be found guilty only if there is an *intent* to discriminate, which is difficult to prove (Feagin and Feagin, 1999; Turner et al., 1991).

The civil rights movement, however, has spurred an entrepreneurial spirit among a growing number of African Americans. To start and maintain a business, they usually rely on a self-help network of family, friends, and voluntary associations, with additional capital from the government and the general business community. The number of black-owned businesses has gone up 170 percent over the last 25 years. In fact, African Americans are starting business enterprises at a greater rate than whites and most other groups in the United States. Most of these entrepreneurs are young—in their thirties and forties—and well educated, which may explain why there are many more black-owned businesses in states that have a higher proportion of young and well-educated African Americans (see Figure 12.5).

■ Hispanic Americans

Despite the civil rights laws, discrimination has long kept most Mexican Americans in low-wage jobs as farm workers, urban laborers, and service workers. To increase profits from hiring these workers, many Anglo-owned companies have moved their garment factories, food-processing plants, and other labor-intensive facilities from higher-wage regions to many Southwestern cities where Mexican Americans live. Many employers in the Sun Belt also tend to seek un-

documented workers who can be exploited more easily than their U.S. peers. These workers are often paid less than the minimum wage, and they dare not protest oppressive working conditions for fear of being turned in to the immigration authorities. Like African Americans, Mexican Americans as a group are saddled with a high rate of unemployment, twice that of white Americans (Feagin and Feagin, 1999; Camarillo, 1996; Perlo, 1996).

Puerto Rican immigrants have brought their various occupational and professional skills to New York City and neighboring areas, but most have faced limited choices for employment. They have thus worked mostly as busboys, janitors, garment workers, and in other low-level jobs in factories, restaurants, and sweatshops. Many may also be haunted by recurring unemployment. Today, many Puerto Ricans continue to toil in low-wage jobs with a high risk of being laid off. The few who hold professional and other white-collar positions usually have lower-paid jobs as, for example, teachers, librarians, and nurses. As a group, Puerto Ricans have become the poorest minority, second only to Native Americans (Feagin and Feagin, 1999).

When they began to arrive in southern Florida in the 1960s, many Cuban immigrants with business and professional skills were forced to take far less prestigious, lower-paying jobs. Unemployment among the immigrants was also rampant. But today, of all the Hispanic American groups, Cuban Americans have achieved the greatest upward mobility, with the highest levels of education and income. They have helped bring an economic boom to southern Florida and have turned Miami into the "capital of Latin America," where numerous international corporations have set up their headquarters for doing business with Latin American countries (Feagin and Feagin, 1999).

■ Asian Americans

The first generation of Japanese Americans was mostly self-employed, with the majority engaging in gardening businesses. But the second and later generations gradually moved into professional and other white-collar jobs. Today, a larger proportion of Japanese Americans than the general U.S. population hold white-collar positions. Still, Japanese Americans, along with Chinese and other Asian Americans, are less likely than whites with comparable education and experience to hold managerial and executive positions. They are often stereotyped as being good scientific and technical workers but not corporate executives (Feagin and Feagin, 1999).

Chinese Americans are also heavily concentrated in white-collar jobs. The more recent immigrants, however, tend to work long hours for little pay in restaurants, garment factories, and other service jobs in the Chinatowns of large cities (Feagin and Feagin, 1999; Thomas, 1995).

Korean American immigrants are more likely than other Asians to own and run small grocery and other retail stores, often in African American and Hispanic American neighborhoods. Most held white-collar professional jobs in Korea but were forced into self-employment by limited English proficiency and discrimination in the job market. They work incredibly long hours so that their children can have a good education and a bright future. Already successful, some have dispersed to the suburbs and beyond to open bigger stores (Feagin and Feagin, 1999; McDowell, 1996; Thomas, 1995).

myth	The most successful Asian Americans in the United States are those of Japanese, Chinese, and Korean descent.
reality	The most successful are probably Asian Americans from India. Having by far the largest proportion (over 50 percent) of college graduates, the majority of Asian Indians are professionals and business-people. Constituting less than 1 percent of the U.S. population, they own about 26 percent of all the nation's hotels.

The most successful Asian Americans in the U.S. economy are probably the Asian Americans from India. They represent less than 1 percent of the U.S. population but are widely dispersed across the nation. Having by far the largest proportion (over 50 percent) of college graduates of any group in the United States, the majority of Asian Indians are professionals and businesspeople. They have carved out a huge share of the hotel industry, now owning more than 12,000 hotels in the United States, about 26 percent of the nation's total lodgings. Even more remarkably, they own 46 percent of all economy hotels, such as Days Inn, Econo Lodge, and Rodeway. Their success has stemmed from a willingness to invest years of long, hard work as well as from strong family ties and close-knit communities. To start or expand a hotel business, Asian-Indians often get financial backing from their extended families or borrow from fellow Asian-Indians, often with only a handshake as collateral (Feagin and Feagin, 1999; McDowell, 1996).

■ POWER AND AUTHORITY

People everywhere are political animals. Because valued resources such as jobs and money are scarce rather than boundless, people feel compelled to play politics to determine who gets what, when, and how. Politics, as previously noted, is the type of human interaction that involves some people acquiring and exercising power over others. In most societies, the government steps in to regulate conflict and allocate resources among the citizens because it commands a tremendous amount of power and authority.

■ The Nature of Power

In some societies, the government has the power to tell citizens what work they will do and what god, if any, they can worship. Governments take their citizens' money and spend it to educate children, overthrow a foreign government, or do many other things. What, then, is power?

Power is the ability to control the behavior of others, even against their will. If a robber forces us to hand over our wallet, that is an example of power. If our friends convince us to cancel a dinner and help them move, that is power. Power is at work when we pay taxes. Power is an aspect of all kinds of social interaction, but obviously, there are important differences in the types of power people can exercise.

The most basic difference is between illegitimate and legitimate power. *Illegitimate power* is control that is exercised over people who do not recognize the right of those exercising the power to do so. Weber (1957) referred to the use of such power as

coercion, the illegitimate use of force or the threat of force to compel obedience. In contrast, *legitimate power* is control that is exercised over people with their consent; they believe that those exercising power have the right to do so.

Exercising power through coercion requires constant vigilance. If coercion is their only source of power, leaders are not likely to be able to sustain their power for long. In contrast, legitimate power can often be exercised with little effort, and it can be very stable. Employers, for example, often need to do little more than circulate a memo to control their employees' behavior. A memo goes out telling workers to stop making personal telephone calls or to request vacations in writing a month in advance, and, at least for a while, workers are likely to obey.

There are at least two kinds of legitimate power. One is **influence**, the ability to control others' behavior through persuasion rather than coercion or authority. Frequently, those who wield other types of power also exercise influence. They may acquire influence because of wealth, fame, charm, knowledge, persuasiveness, or any other admired quality. Business executives may use their wealth to achieve influence over politicians through campaign contributions. Television reporters may acquire the ability to influence public opinion because of their personal attractiveness or journalistic skill. In general, influence is less formal and direct, and more subtle, than other forms of power. A second type of legitimate power is **authority**, which is institutionalized in organizations. When authority exists, people grant others the right to power because they believe that those in power have the right to command and that they themselves have a duty to obey. Authority is essential to the government.

■ Types of Authority

What is the source of the government's authority? For an answer, we turn to Weber (1957). He described three possible sources of the right to command, which produce what he called *traditional* authority, *charismatic* authority, and *legal* authority.

Traditional Authority   In many societies, people have obeyed those in power because, in essence, that is the way it has always been. Thus, kings, queens, feudal lords, and tribal chiefs did not need written rules in order to govern. Their authority was based on long-standing custom and handed down from parent to child so that it was maintained from one generation to the next. Often, traditional authority has been justified by religious tradition. For example, medieval European kings were said to rule by divine

THAT'S THE WAY IT IS   In many societies, people have obeyed their leaders because that is the way it has always been. Examples of these leaders are kings, queens, feudal lords, and tribal chiefs, such as the African chief shown here. These leaders' authority, called *traditional authority,* derives from long-standing custom. It is handed down from parent to child, so that it is maintained from one generation to the next. Often, some religious belief is called upon to justify traditional authority. Thus, medieval European kings were said to rule by divine right and Japanese emperors were considered the embodiment of heaven. ■

right, and Japanese emperors were considered the embodiment of heaven.

Charismatic Authority   People may also submit to authority because of the extraordinary attraction of an individual. Napoleon, Gandhi, and Mao Zedong all illustrate authority that derives its legitimacy from **charisma**—an exceptional personal quality popularly attributed to certain individuals. Their followers see charismatic leaders as persons of destiny endowed with remarkable vision, the power of a savior, or the grace of God. Charismatic authority is inherently un-

LEADING WITH CHARM In some societies, people have obeyed those in power for their extraordinary attraction. Such leaders are said to hold *charismatic authority* because their legitimacy to rule comes from charisma—an exceptional personal quality popularly attributed to certain individuals. Their followers see them as persons of destiny endowed with remarkable vision, the power of a savior, or God's grace. Examples of these charismatic leaders include Napoleon, Mao Zedong, and the Indian nationalistic leader Mahatma Gandhi, shown here. Charismatic authority is inherently unstable; it will collapse when the leader dies or change into another type of authority. ■

stable; it cannot be transferred to another person. If a political system is based on charismatic authority, it will collapse when the leader dies. Otherwise, it will go through a process of *routinization,* in which the followers switch from personal attachment to organizational commitment, with their personal devotion to a leader being replaced by formal commitment to a political system (Madsen and Snow, 1983). In essence, charismatic authority is thus transformed into legal authority.

Legal Authority The political systems of industrial states are based largely on a third type of authority: legal authority, which Weber (1957) also called *rational authority*. These systems derive legitimacy from an explicit set of rules and procedures that spell out the ruler's rights and duties. Typically, the rules and procedures are put in writing. The people grant their obedience to the law. It specifies procedures by which certain individuals hold offices of power, such as governor or president or prime minister. But the authority is vested in those offices, not in the individuals who temporarily hold the offices. Thus, a political system based on legal authority is often called a "government of laws, not of men." Individuals come and go, as U.S. presidents have come and gone, but the office, the presidency, remains. If individual officeholders overstep their authority, they may be forced out of office and replaced.

In practice, these three types of authority occur in combinations. The U.S. presidency, for example, is based on legal authority, but the office also has con-

RULING BY RULES In industrial societies, people usually obey leaders for their *legal authority*. This authority derives from an explicit set of rules and procedures that spell out the ruler's rights and duties. The people in effect grant their obedience to the law. It specifies procedures by which certain individuals hold offices of power as, for example, president, prime minister, or governor, as illustrated here by Arnold Schwarzenegger, the governor of California. ■

siderable traditional authority. Executive privilege, whereby a president can keep certain documents secret, even from Congress, acquired its force from tradition, not through the Constitution or laws. Some presidents—such as Abraham Lincoln, Franklin Roosevelt, and John F. Kennedy—have also possessed charismatic authority. Still, the primary basis of the power of the president is legal authority. In general, when societies industrialize, traditional and charismatic authority tend to give way and legal authority becomes dominant, as in the United States. But the legal authority of the U.S. president is not absolute, as we will see in the next section.

THE WORLD OF U.S. POLITICS

The U.S. government consists of three branches: the executive (including the president), the legislative (Congress), and the judiciary (the Supreme Court). The three check and balance each other so that no one can become too powerful. Thus, gross abuse of power can be avoided and democracy preserved. But how all this happens depends on several aspects of American politics.

■ Political Socialization

As in other spheres of life, socialization is one key to behavior in politics. **Political socialization** is a learning process by which individuals acquire political knowledge, beliefs, and attitudes. It begins at a young age, when the family is the major socializing agent. As children grow up, the schools, peer groups, and media also become important agents of political socialization.

What is it that children learn? Before they are 10 years old, most know who the U.S. president is and are aware of the Democratic and Republican parties. Childhood socialization also appears to shape several important political attitudes. Schools and parents begin to influence children's sense of political efficacy—their belief that they can participate in politics and that their participation can make a difference. In addition, parents often transmit their party identification (their support of a political party) to their children. If both of their parents support the same party, children are likely to support that party. With age, however, their identification with their parents' party tends to decline. Parental influence is generally stronger among conservative Republicans than among liberal Democrats. As explained by sociologist Fredrick Koenig (1982), conservative children feel more strongly about preserving traditions across generations and have greater respect for authority figures like parents.

Socialization continues in adulthood because our social environment can affect our political beliefs. Our neighborhood, for example, tends to influence our choice of a political party. Thus, people who live in predominantly Democratic neighborhoods are mostly Democrats themselves, but the likelihood of their becoming Republicans increases significantly if they move into Republican neighborhoods. Also, the conservative nature of today's political climate has made many people more conservative than before—more likely to oppose welfare and other government programs that help the poor and other less fortunate individuals (Taylor et al., 1997).

■ Political Attitudes

Social class seems to play a leading role in shaping attitudes toward government and its policies. Members of the working class tend to be economic liberals and social conservatives. They are likely, for example, to support intervention in the economy by the government but to oppose gay rights. In contrast, higher-income groups tend to be economic conservatives, opposing government intervention, and social liberals, supporting gay rights (Lipset, 1996, 1981).

There is more consensus in public opinion, however, than these statements may suggest. Surveys have found wide support among all social classes for government spending to clean up the environment, improve the nation's health, combat crime, strengthen the educational system, improve the situation of minorities, and provide medical care and legal assistance for the poor. But while citizens support all these government services, they are highly critical of the government itself, which they believe has become too powerful, too intrusive, and too wasteful—spending too much of taxpayers' money (NORC, 1994; Lipset and Schneider, 1983).

myth	Many conservatives dislike big government and want to "get government off our backs," especially in our private lives.
reality	Many conservatives are ideologically opposed to government intervention in people's private lives, but at the same time, they support school prayer and antiabortion laws, which, in effect, represent government intervention in private lives.

In short, most citizens are angry over big government, yet they support it by demanding more services. This inconsistency reflects a uniquely U.S. political character. There is a strong tendency for Americans to be **ideological conservatives**, who, in theory, are opposed to big government because of their belief in free enterprise, rugged individualism, and capitalism. Simultaneously, the same individuals tend to be **operational liberals,** who, in effect, support big government by backing government programs that render services to the public. Such mixed, ambivalent attitudes pertain not only to economic issues but also to social issues. Many conservatives, for example, want to "get government off our backs," but at the same time, they support school prayer and antiabortion laws, which, in effect, represent government intervention in private lives (Lakoff, 2002; Ladd, 1983).

■ Political Participation

Individuals can participate in government and politics in numerous ways. They can attend a rally or run for office, form an interest group or send money to a candidate, write to their representatives or work for their opponents. But few U.S. citizens choose to take an active role in their government, even when it comes to the easiest form of political participation—voting.

myth	In the 2000 presidential election, George W. Bush received 48 percent of the popular vote—from about 48 percent of all U.S. citizens who were eligible to vote.
reality	Only about 24 percent of all eligible voters voted for Bush because nearly half did not even register to vote.

The percentage of people who vote is lower in the United States than in nearly any other Western nation. Usually, only about half of all eligible voters in the United States go to the polls compared with over 75 percent in other countries. As a consequence, U.S. officials are routinely put into office by a minority of citizens. In the 2000 presidential election, George W. Bush was widely reported to have won 48 percent of the votes cast, but actually, only 24 percent of the eligible electorate voted for him because close to half didn't bother to register to vote. In the 1980 presidential election, Ronald Reagan's victory was often called a landslide because he beat Jimmy Carter by a wide margin. But most eligible voters did not vote and only about 20 percent voted for Reagan (Ranney, 1983).

What explains these low turnouts? There are many reasons. First, numerous U.S. citizens simply get tired of voting because many more elections are held here than in other countries. Second, many regard political campaigns as mean spirited and lacking in substance. The profusion of negative political advertising launched by two candidates against each other makes *both* look like liars and crooks. Third, even in regard to substantive issues such as jobs and taxes, voters see little or no difference between candidates, who are equally inclined to promise the same things that voters like to hear. Fourth, the long-standing political stability of the United States makes it seem unnecessary to vote, so Americans can usually forget about politics and focus on the serious business of living—education, jobs, families, and the like. Finally, poverty, youth, and lack of education tend to discourage people from voting. This may explain why voter apathy is more common in the South, which has a higher rate of poverty than other regions of the United States (see Figure 12.6).

Does the low voter turnout pose a threat to democracy? Most political scientists say yes. They assume that a true democracy requires citizens' full participation because the people are supposed to rule. Without adequate support from its citizens, the government lacks legitimacy and therefore tends to be unstable. The government is also likely to ride roughshod over the people. But there is a contrary view: The low voter turnout means that people are relatively contented with their lives. They "see politics as quite marginal to their lives, as neither salvation nor ruin" (Krauthammer, 1990). Nonvoting, then, reflects a preference against politics, which is assumed to be healthy because it reminds politicians that the United States was founded on the belief that the government is best when it governs least.

■ Social Diversity

Whites dominate politics in the United States, as reflected by their overrepresentation in various branches of government. Minority groups, while suffering a similar lack of power, differ from each other in their political experiences.

Native Americans are the only ethnic group that has been kept on reservations, with their lives directly controlled by the federal government through its Bureau of Indian Affairs. For many years, they could not vote outside reservations because they were not considered U.S. citizens. Only after being granted citizenship in 1924 did they begin to participate in off-reservation politics. Today, Native Americans can be found serving in several state legislatures as well as in the U.S. Congress. They are most interested in seeking government aid for education and health care, but their political influence is limited.

African Americans were long prevented from voting, especially in the South. But with passage of various civil rights laws, including those that ensured voting rights in the 1960s, participation of African Americans as voters and public office seekers rose dramatically. As a result, the nation's total number of

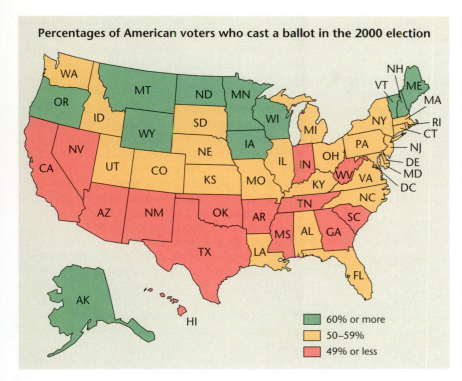

Percentages of American voters who cast a ballot in the 2000 election

- 60% or more
- 50–59%
- 49% or less

FIGURE 12.6

More Voter Apathy in the South

In general, Americans who are poorer, younger, or less educated are less likely to vote in political elections. This may explain why voter apathy is generally more common in the South, where the poverty rate is higher, than in other regions.

Critical Thinking: *Will you vote in the next presidential election? Why or why not?*

Source: Data from Federal Election Commission, 2001.

African American elected officials has soared from only a few hundred in the 1960s to over 8,000 today. Of all the minority groups, African Americans can thus be said to be the most successful politically. Nevertheless, they still hold only about 2 percent of the nation's total elective and appointive offices—far less than 11 percent, their share of the U.S. population (Feagin and Feagin, 1999; Pinkney, 1993).

Mexican Americans and Puerto Ricans, like most other minority groups, are largely Democrats, consistently voting for more liberal or progressive candidates at the national, state, and local levels. In the 1990s, they became more politically organized, focusing most of their efforts on voter registration. Cuban Americans are more politically active than other Hispanic groups, holding many public offices as mayors, public school superintendents, state legislators, and members of Congress. Also, unlike other Hispanics, Cuban Americans tend to identify with the conservative Republican party, which they consider more anti-Castro, like themselves, than with the Democratic party (Feagin and Feagin, 1999).

Asian Americans have traditionally shied away from politics. In the 1990s, however, their significant population growth led to an increase in political organization and activity. To further enhance their political clout, various Asian American groups joined forces to form pan-Asian organizations such as the Asian-American Voters Coalition. They seek better representation at all levels of government while trying to protect the civil rights of all Asian Americans and fight anti-Asian laws, distorted media images of Asians, anti-Asian violence, and employment discrimination against Asians. By 1998, the number of elected officials of Asian descent had grown to 2,000 in 33 states, including the governor of Washington (Feagin and Feagin, 1999; Ratnesar, 1998).

Asian Americans, however, are often confused in the minds of the general public with Asians who are not U.S. citizens. Thus, after some Asian businessmen were discovered to have donated money to former President Clinton's reelection campaign in 1996, which is illegal, the Democratic party interrogated U.S. donors with Asian last names, sparking outrage from Asian Americans (Glastris and Auster, 1997). For many, this incident brought to mind how Japanese Americans felt during World War II when they were treated as Japanese and sent to concentration camps.

■ Political Parties

A **political party** is a group organized for the purpose of gaining government offices. In seeking this goal for themselves, political parties also perform several functions vital to the operation of a democracy. First, parties recruit adherents, nominate candidates, and raise campaign money to support their choices for public office. Without the parties, the process of electing officials would be chaotic; hundreds of people might offer themselves as candidates for each office. Second, parties formulate and promote policies. The desire to seek voters' support ensures that these policies reflect public opinion. This is one way in which the parties serve as a link between the people and their government. Finally, the parties help organize the main institutions of government. Leadership positions in the legislature and its committees are parceled out on the basis of which party holds the allegiance of most members of Congress.

The Two-Party System   In the United States, there are only two major parties. For more than a century, the Democratic and Republican parties have held unquestioned dominance over the political system. Of course, there are many other parties, which are collectively called *third parties*. Occasionally, a third-party candidate wins a local or even a state election, as some Socialist party candidates have done. But no third party has had much of a chance of winning the presidency. No third party has any influence in Congress, either.

Generally, the Republicans are more conservative than the Democrats. The Republicans tend to advocate tax breaks for the wealthy, reduction in government spending, more local control, and less government interference with the economy. Consequently, the Republican party usually gets more support from the economically advantaged, whites, members of major Protestant churches, and suburban and small-town residents. The Democrats, on the other hand, are inclined to emphasize the government's role in promoting social welfare, and they institute programs to combat unemployment and relieve poverty. Therefore, the Democratic party tends to gain more support from the economically disadvantaged, minority groups, and residents of the central-city areas in large metropolitan regions.

The two-party system requires that each party represent as many citizens as possible if it is to win election or reelection. Thus, both parties usually aim for the center of political opinion, trying to appeal to everyone and offend no one. They represent a broad coalition of politicians with many viewpoints. We can find such "strange bedfellows" as conservatives and liberals in each party. When it's time to nominate presidential candidates, each party usually looks to its party's center. This has led to the charge that there is "not a dime's worth of difference" between them. Yet if the Republican party overemphasizes its conservatism and the Democratic party its liberalism, either is certain to turn off many voters and get a severe beating at the polls. This is what happened when the conservative wing seized control of the Re-

publican party and nominated ultraconservative Barry Goldwater for president in 1964; Democratic liberals did the same with ultraliberal George McGovern in 1972. Both choices led to landslide defeats in the general election.

Declining Party Influence   For more than 25 years, U.S. political parties have suffered a decline in influence. More and more voters identify themselves as "independent" than as Democrat or Republican (U.S. Census Bureau, 2001). Even those who say they are Democrats or Republicans often split their vote, choosing some candidates from one party and some from the other. Most politicians still call themselves Democrats or Republicans, but they often act like independents, refusing to follow the direction of party leaders in Congress or even the president from their party. A number of forces seem to have caused this decline (Coleman, 1996).

Two such forces are television and, increasingly, the Internet, which enable candidates to reach voters directly rather than through an organized army of volunteers and party activists knocking on doors. A third force is the spread of party primaries, which increasingly put the choice of candidates in the hands of voters rather than party leaders and activists. A fourth factor is the increasing cost of elections and the rise of political action committees (PACs) as a big source of campaign money. PACs are political organizations that funnel money from business, labor, and other special-interest groups into election campaigns to help elect or defeat candidates. PACs act independently of the parties, so party leaders can no longer keep straying members in line by threatening to cut off their campaign funds. Finally, politicians have increasingly turned to pollsters and political consultants rather than local or state party leaders for data on what the public is thinking and feeling.

In short, whatever the parties can offer, politicians can find elsewhere. The parties have fewer carrots and sticks to control politicians. But if politicians do not follow a party's position, then the party labels mean less and less, and voters have little reason to pay attention to them.

■ Interest Groups

For those people who find neither party to be an effective representative of their concerns, there is another alternative: interest groups. An **interest group** is an organized collection of people who attempt to influence government policies. If you are a hog farmer interested in keeping the price of hogs high, there is a group for you. If you are a hunter interested in preventing the regulation of firearms or a baseball bat manufacturer interested in breaking into the Japanese market, there are groups for you, too. There are business groups like the U.S. Chamber of Commerce and the National Association of Manufacturers; labor groups like the AFL-CIO; professional groups like the American Medical Association; and civil rights groups, civil liberties groups, environmental groups, consumer groups, religious groups, and more.

All of these groups use the same basic methods in trying to influence the government's policies. First, they try to influence public opinion. They advertise in the media, collect petitions, and send out letters urging people to write or call their legislators. Second, they help elect sympathetic candidates by endorsing them, urging their members to support those candidates, and donating money to their campaigns. Third, interest groups frequently file lawsuits to further their goals. Finally, interest groups hire lobbyists, people who deal directly with government officials and attempt to influence them on behalf of the groups. There are more than 31,000 lobbyists in Washington, which averages out to nearly 62 lobbyists working on each member of Congress for his or her votes (Abramson, 1998; Evans, 1996; Birnbaum, 1993).

Interest groups serve some useful functions. First, they provide a way for millions of citizens to make their voices heard. Civil rights, environmental issues, and term limits for political officeholders are but a few examples of issues that were first put on the political agenda by interest groups. To the political parties and those in office, these issues were either unimportant or too controversial to warrant action until interest groups forced the politicians to address them. Second, interest groups inform and advise lawmakers. Being masters of their subject, lobbyists, in effect, become technical advisers to legislators and their staffs, supplying them with information vital to wise decision making and to the writing of workable laws. Of course, lobbyists are likely to slant the information they present to favor their interest group. But one hopes that lawmakers rely on a multitude of lobbyists with different views that balance one another.

If interest groups appear so useful, why do so many people fear and criticize them? Why do Democrats and Republicans, along with the general public, rail against special interests? One concern is that through relentless pursuit of their narrow goals, some interest groups are thwarting the will of the majority and harming the public good. Although polls have consistently shown broad support for gun control, for example, the National Rifle Association (NRA) has often successfully persuaded Congress to reject gun-control bills. Another concern is that as the power of interest groups grows, the government may end up being for sale to whatever group has the most money to contribute. Federal tax policy, for example, favors business more than labor because business donates much more money to legislators (see Figure 12.7). To stop this kind of monetary influence on government policy, Congress passed a law banning unregulated, unlimited contributions to political parties (Rogers, 2001).

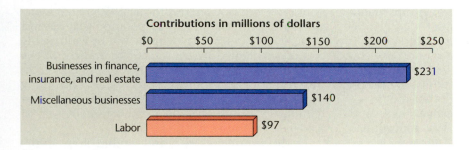

Contributions in millions of dollars

Businesses in finance, insurance, and real estate: $231
Miscellaneous businesses: $140
Labor: $97

FIGURE 12.7

Political Campaign Contributions

Compared to labor unions, business corporations in the United States donate much more money to politicians who later become legislators. This may explain why tax policies often favor business more than labor. To stop money from influencing government policy, Congress has tried to pass a law banning unlimited political contributions from business, labor, and wealthy individuals.

Critical Thinking: *What would be the best way to finance political campaigns? Why?*

Source: Data from Center for Responsive Politics, 2004.

WHO REALLY GOVERNS IN U.S. SOCIETY?

The emergence of political parties and interest groups in the United States has brought Americans a long way from the government envisioned by James Madison, U.S. president from 1809 to 1817. It was his hope to exclude interests and factions from the government. Legislators were to represent and vote for the public good, not one interest or another.

Where has this evolution brought U.S. government? Are the interest groups and political parties mechanisms through which the people gain more effective control of government, or have the people lost control? Who, in fact, has **political power**, the capacity to use the government to make decisions that affect the whole society?

■ The Pluralist View: Diverse Interest Groups

A pluralist looking at the U.S. government sees many centers of power as well as many competing interest groups. Government reflects the outcome of their conflict. In this view, the interest groups are central to U.S. democracy. Together, they create a mutually restraining influence. No one group can always prevail. Thus, through their competition, the interests of the public are reflected in government policy.

But as we have seen in Chapter 7 (U.S. and Global Stratification), there are large inequalities of wealth, power, and prestige. How, in the face of such inequalities, can pluralism be maintained? Cannot one group marshal its resources to dominate others? Why doesn't one group or one coalition of groups gradually achieve a concentration of power?

The reason, according to Robert Dahl (1981), is that inequalities are *dispersed,* not cumulative. Inequalities would be cumulative if a group rich in one resource (wealth, for example) were also better off than other groups in almost every other resource— political power, social standing, prestige, legitimacy, knowledge, and control over religious, educational, and other institutions. In the United States, however, one group may hold most of one of these resources, but other groups may have the lion's share of the others. What the upper-middle class lacks in wealth, for example, it makes up for in knowledge and legitimacy. Power over economic institutions may be concentrated in the hands of corporations, but U.S. religious institutions elude their grasp.

This dispersal of power in U.S. society is reflected in a dispersal of political clout. The country's many competing groups vie for control over government policy and end up dominating different spheres.

POWER PLAY According to the pluralist view, various interest groups constitute veto groups that have enough power to block each other's actions. In order to get anything done, these groups must seek support from the unorganized public. Thus, there is much lobbying and jockeying for position among various veto groups, such as the American Association of Retired Persons (AARP) and the National Rifle Association (NRA). ■

Corporations may dominate the government's decisions on taxes but not on crime. Even tax policy is not dictated solely by corporations because labor unions and other groups fight with the corporations for influence on politicians and voters. The structure of the government, with its separation of powers, promotes this pluralism. What civil rights groups could not win in Congress in the 1950s, they sometimes won in the courts. A corporation that has lost a battle in Congress may win the war by influencing regulations issued by the executive branch. In the end, in Dahl's view, competing groups usually compromise and share power. Thus, there is no ruling group in the United States. It is instead a pluralist democracy dominated by many different sets of leaders.

David Riesman (1950) and Arnold Rose (1967) have developed a somewhat different analysis. In their views, the United States has become so pluralistic that various interest groups constitute *veto groups,* which are powerful enough to block each other's actions. To get anything done, the veto groups must seek support from the unorganized public. The masses, then, have the ultimate power to ensure that their interests and concerns will be protected. The bottom line is that the overall leadership is weak, stalemate is frequent, and no single elite can emerge to dominate the others.

■ The Elitist View: Rule by a Few

It is true that there are many competing groups in the United States. But does their competition actually determine how policy is made? Is the government merely the neutral arbitrator among these conflicting interests? According to power-elite theorists, the answer is no.

Many years ago, Italian sociologists Vilfredo Pareto (1848–1923) and Gaetano Mosca (1858–1941) argued that a small elite has governed the masses in all societies. Why should this be so? If a nation is set up along truly democratic lines, isn't control by an elite avoidable? According to German sociologist Robert Michels (1915), there is an "iron law of oligarchy" by which even a democracy inevitably degenerates into an *oligarchy*—rule by a few. A democracy is an organization, and according to Michels, "whoever says organization says oligarchy."

In Michels's view, three characteristics of organizations eventually produce rule by the elite. First, to work efficiently, even a democratic organization must allow a few leaders to make the decisions. Second, through their positions of leadership, the leaders accumulate skills and knowledge that make them indispensable to the rank-and-file. Third, the rank-and-file lack the time, inclination, and knowledge to master the complex tasks of government, and they become politically apathetic. Thus, in time, even a democracy yields to rule by an elite.

How does this view apply to the United States? According to C. Wright Mills (1916–1962), there are three levels of power in this country. At the bottom are ordinary people—powerless, unorganized, fragmented, and manipulated by the mass media into believing in democracy. In the middle are Congress, political parties, and interest groups as well as most political leaders. At this level, pluralism reigns. The middle groups form "a drifting set of stalemated, balancing forces" (Mills, 1959a). Above them, however, ignored by pluralist theorists, is an elite—what Mills called the *power elite*—that makes the most important decisions. This elite consists of the top leaders in three institutions—the federal government, the military, and the large corporations. These leaders cooperate with one another in controlling the nation. Government leaders can allocate billions of dollars to defense to strengthen the military and enrich the corporations from which the weapons are purchased. Big business can support political leaders with campaign money. The politicians can aid business with favorable legislation.

If Mills is correct, all the hoopla of political campaigns and debates is but so much sound and fury because the power elite determines who gets elected and how the government is run. There is some evidence to support Mills's view that a cohesive elite exists. Time and again, researchers have found, for example, that top officials in both Democratic and Republican administrations previously held high positions in corporations, that they return to those corporations after leaving the government, and that leaders come disproportionately from upper-class backgrounds (Abramson, 1998; Barlett and Steele, 1992; Domhoff, 1983, 1978).

■ The Marxist View: Dominance by the Capitalist Class

According to the Marxist view, Mills's analysis confuses the issue. Marxists argue that his political and military elites are not free to act in their own interests; they are merely agents of the corporate elite. What we have are not three elites that come together but one ruling class.

Marxist sociologist Albert Szymanski (1978) provides an example of this approach. He suggests that there are four classes in the United States. The first is the *capitalist class,* which owns and controls the major means of production and is commonly known as *big business.* The second is the *petit bourgeoisie,* which includes professionals, small-business people, and independent farmers. Some of these people own the means of production, but they must work with it themselves. The third class is the *working class,* including industrial, white-collar, and rural workers; they must sell their physical or mental labor to live. The fourth is the *lumpenproletariat,* which consists of the unemployed, welfare recipients, criminals, and down-and-outs. Szymanski argues that the capitalist class uses the state as an instrument for exploiting the other three economically subordinate classes.

To control the state, capitalists may use the same methods employed by interest groups, such as lobbying and supporting sympathetic candidates. In using these tools, however, the capitalist class has a great advantage over the run-of-the-mill interest group: It has more money. The capitalist class also uses the media, schools, churches, and other institutions to permeate society with its values, such as free enterprise, economic growth, and competition. Violations of these capitalist values are often taken to be un-American, giving capitalist interests a potent weapon against unsympathetic politicians. Understandably, few U.S. politicians want to be branded antigrowth, antibusiness, or socialist. In addition, if the government acts against the capitalists' interests, big business can refuse to put its capital to work. The corporations may close plants or stop investing or send their money abroad (Greider, 1992). As a result, "business can extort favors, virtually without limit, from the political authorities" (Walzer, 1978).

Thus, politicians of all stripes have often talked about molding an economic policy that would "send a message" to "reassure Wall Street." In state after state in recent years, gubernatorial and mayoral campaigns have been fought over the issue of whether a particular candidate will create a good or bad business climate—that is, which candidate has the best plan of subsidies and tax breaks to lure business into the city or state. The public interest is identified with business interests, and political choices thus become hostages to the decisions of capitalists.

■ Putting It Together

The issue of who really governs in U.S. society boils down to three questions: Which group holds the most power? Where does it get the power? And what role do the masses play in the government?

The three views that we have discussed are different in some respects and similar in others. Both elitists and Marxists see power concentrated in the hands of a small group and hardly any influence by the masses on the government. These theorists differ, however, in regard to the key source of power. To elitists, the ruling elite's power comes from its leadership in business, government, and the military, whereas to Marxists, the ruling class gets its power from controlling the economy. The pluralists disagree with both. They argue that political leaders ultimately derive their power from the citizenry, and they must compete among themselves to stay at the top. Table 12.2 summarizes these three views of power.

Which view, then, most accurately represents the reality of the U.S. government? It is difficult, if not impossible, to answer the question because relevant data are unavailable. But it seems obvious that each of the three views captures only a small portion, rather than the complex whole, of the political reality. Pluralists are most likely to hit the bull's eye in regard to most domestic issues, such as jobs and inflation, about which the public feels strongly. In these cases, the government tries to do what the people want. Elitists and Marxists are more likely to be correct on most foreign and military policy matters, about which the masses are less concerned and knowledgeable. This explains why defense contractors are able to sell the U.S. government far more arms than are needed. The three views may be simplistic and one sided, but they are basically complementary, helping to enlarge our understanding of the complex, shifting nature of political power.

A GLOBAL ANALYSIS OF POLITICAL VIOLENCE

Throughout U.S. history, various groups that believed the government would not respond to their needs have resorted to some form of violence. Analyzing 53 U.S. protest movements, William Gamson (1975) found that 75 percent of the groups that used violence got what they wanted compared with only 53 percent of those that were nonviolent. Violence, it seems, can pay off.

But much of the violence in U.S. history has taken the form of riots or brief seizures of property for limited aims, inspired by specific grievances. Violent as U.S. history is, it has included little of the two forms of political violence—revolution and terrorism—aimed more broadly at overthrowing the government.

■ Causes of Revolution

If a protest movement turns to violence, it may produce a **revolution**—a movement aimed at the violent overthrow of the existing government. Numerous studies on revolutions in many different societies differ in explaining the causes of revolution, but they all suggest, in one way or another, that a revolution is likely to occur if the following conditions are met (Doyle, 1998; Devlin, 1995; Echikson, 1990):

TABLE 12.2

Who Really Governs?

Issue	Pluralist View	Elitist View	Marxist View
1. Who holds the most power?	Various competing groups	Top leaders in business, government, and military	Capitalists; top leaders of the corporate world
2. Where does the power come from?	The authority vested in elected officials	Key positions in business, government, and military	The control of the nation's economy
3. What role do the masses play?	Choose political leaders in competitive elections	Are exploited or manipulated by the power elite	Are exploited or manipulated by the capitalists

1. *A group of well-off, well-educated individuals is extremely dissatisfied with the society.* They may be intellectuals or opinion leaders such as journalists, poets, playwrights, teachers, clergy, and lawyers. These people withdraw support from the government, criticize it, and demand reforms. Discontent may also exist within such elites as wealthy landowners, industrialists, leading bureaucrats, and military officials. It is from among all these groups that most revolutionary leaders emerge.

2. *Revolutionary leaders rely on the masses' rising expectations to convince them that they can end their oppression by bringing down the existing government.* By itself, poverty does not produce revolution. Most of the world, after all, is poor. When people have long lived with misery, they may become fatalists, resigned to their suffering. They may starve without raising a fist or even uttering a whimper against the government. But if their living conditions improve, fatalism may give way to hope. They may *expect* a better life. It is in times of such rising expectations that revolutionary leaders may succeed in attracting mass support.

3. *A deepening economic crisis triggers peasant revolts and urban uprisings.* In a social climate of rising expectations, large masses of peasants and workers tend to respond explosively to serious economic problems. When the state raises taxes too high and landlords, in turn, raise the dues of tenant farmers or take over their lands, the peasants will likely revolt. When the cost of food and the rate of un-employment soar, food riots and large-scale anti-government protests tend to erupt in the cities.

4. *The existing government is weak.* Usually, before a government is overthrown, it has failed to resolve one problem after another and has gradually lost legitimacy. As the crisis mounts, the government often tries to initiate reforms but usually too little or too late. This only reinforces people's conviction that the regime is flawed and encourages demands for even bigger reforms. All this can quicken the government's downfall. As Niccolò Machiavelli (1469–1527) said in his warning to rulers, "If the necessity for [reforms] comes in troubled times, you are too late for harsh measures. Mild ones will not help you, for they will be considered as forced from you, and no one will be under obligation to you" (Goldstone, 1994).

myth	Poverty is the breeding ground for revolution and terrorism. Revolutionary and terrorist leaders are therefore mostly poor.
reality	Most revolutionary and terrorist leaders come from relatively affluent families.

■ Terrorism

What if the masses do not support a revolutionary movement and the government is not vulnerable? In that case, a violent protest is likely to produce not

MONSTROUS MASSACRE
While some terrorists are powerless individuals futilely fighting their own government, others are international terrorists who leave their country to attack a foreign government. One example of international terrorists is the Islamic extremists who crashed hijacked planes into the twin buildings of the World Trade Center in New York on September 11, 2001. ■

revolution but **terrorism**—the use of violence to express dissatisfaction with a government. The would-be leaders of a revolution become terrorists, trying on their own to destabilize, if not topple, the government through violence. Their methods include bombing, kidnapping, airplane hijacking, and armed assault. Terrorist groups include Palestinian extremists in Israel, neo-Nazi extremists in Germany, right-wing extremists in the United States, and anti-American Muslim militants in various countries. Most terrorist leaders are in their early twenties and have attended college. They usually come from affluent or middle-class rather than poor families. In short, their backgrounds resemble those of leaders of revolutions—but the terrorists are self-styled leaders without widespread public support.

These terrorists are basically powerless individuals futilely fighting a government. Some are international terrorists who leave their country to attack a foreign government. An example is the group of Islamic radicals from the Middle East who attacked the World Trade Center and the Pentagon on September 11, 2001. Other international terrorists, however, carry out the policies of their own governments. Examples of such governments are the militant regimes in Iran and North Korea—referrred to by President Bush as "the Axis of Evil"—which have sent terrorists to foreign countries to assassinate their opponents. Other terrorists fight their own governments. Examples of these domestic terrorists include the bombers of the Murrah federal office building in Oklahoma City in 1995.

sociological frontiers

Politics Going Online

As we observed earlier, political parties have lost much of their influence on American voters in today's information age. People running for office no longer urgently need their parties to provide them with an organized army of volunteers and party activists knocking on doors. Both television and the Internet make it possible to reach massive numbers of voters directly. While television still exerts a far greater influence on voters, the Internet is fast becoming an important mass medium in U.S. politics.

The proportion of Americans going online for election news has increased from only 4 percent during the 1996 presidential campaign to nearly 20 percent in the 2000 campaign and to 49 percent in 2004. In 1996, most online users said they turned to the net because other media didn't provide enough news, but in 2000 and 2004, most said going online was a *more convenient* way to get the information. Typical of these "wired voters" is Terry Rolland, a 45-year-old federal government employee in California. She researched candidates

and ballot measures on the Internet, which played a crucial role in her voting decisions (Carlson, 2004; CNN, 2000; Raney, 1998).

Consequently, all the candidates running for high office today use this new campaign medium. Some campaigns are still producing dull websites with only the candidates' pictures and biographies, but most use flashy sites to promote themselves, get their message out, and raise funds. The spirit of innovation is also flourishing. A new, effective tactic that is becoming popular is the electronic newsletter. Campaigners attract subscribers on their websites, who are then e-mailed weekly updates that keep the candidates' names in the minds of voters. Other innovations are the "blog," short for "web log," the daily updating of information with pictures from the campaign trail, along with the chat room, where people voice opinions and ask questions. These online strategies are particularly important to presidential candidates because of the public's constant demand for news about them and their handlers' need to control their campaign appearances (Carlson, 2004; Lilleston, 2000; Raney, 1998).

Another powerful trend is to use the Internet for voting. Given its convenience, online voting may reduce the problem of low voter turnout. It can also increase the accuracy and speed of counting ballots, thereby solving the problems created by the conventional method of using paper and pencil. Even so, there are concerns about how to prevent voters from committing fraud on the Internet as well as how to stop hackers from manipulating the voting. Understandably, most Americans still oppose Internet voting. Once the security issues are resolved, though, online voting may well replace conventional voting (McGuire, 2001).

 ■ For more of the latest Sociological Frontiers, look up Continuing Update at www.ablongman.com/thio6e.

using sociology

How to Stop Terrorists

What can the United States do to stop terrorists, such as those who attacked New York City and Washington, DC, on September 11, 2001? Efforts can be made on three fronts: military, political, and cultural (Zakaria, 2001).

On the military front, the goal should be the total destruction of terrorist organizations such as al Qaida, which was responsible for the September 11 attacks. The U.S. military must track down and bring to justice any person who plans or helps in a terrorist operation. Even the government of a country that harbors terrorists must be brought down militarily with international support, so that it will be easier to find and capture the terrorists and their leaders.

On the political front, the United States should seek cooperation from around the world to fight terrorism. This will involve getting other governments to make arrests, destroy hideouts, close bank accounts, and share intelligence. To avoid arousing envy, anger, or opposition because of the United States' position as the world's superpower, it should refrain from taking over a country after a military victory but instead work with other nations to help the local people form their own government. The United States should further provide whatever aid is needed to turn a war-devastated country around, so that goodwill toward Americans can blossom in the Arab world. As for the conflict between the Israelis and Palestinians, the United States should take a more balanced approach to encourage both sides to work for peace.

On the cultural front, the United States should reduce the rage that has fueled terrorist strikes by correcting Arab misperception of U.S. society. To refute the popular Arab belief that U.S. foreign policy places little value on Muslim lives and priorities, for example, it should be pointed out how the United States has sent soldiers to protect the Muslims in Kuwait, Bosnia, and Kosovo. Messages such as this could be broadcast over the radio and other U.S. media. More American officials should appear on Arab media to counter the anti-American bias in its news and views. The cultural exchange programs that link U.S. students, government officials, and entrepreneurs with their counterparts in the Arab world should be increased. Finally, the American embassies in Arab countries should work with the local education ministries to ensure that teachers and textbooks present a fair view of the United States (Kinzer, 2001).

Since the terrorist attacks in late 2001, the Bush administration has fought the war against the terrorists on these three fronts. The Taliban rulers of Afghanistan, who used to provide sanctuary to the Islamic fundamentalist terrorists, have been eliminated. And with cooperation from other governments, the United States has "hacked" into foreign banks' computer systems to find people who finance terrorist activities. The Americans also have obtained assistance from friendly Muslim intelligence services in tracking down terrorists. While some of the captured terrorists are imprisoned at the U.S. naval base in Guantanamo, Cuba, others have been sent to secret prisons overseas, including those in friendly Muslim countries that do not shy away from using torture as an interrogative aid. On the cultural front, however, not enough has been done to counter the Arab extremist groups' distortion of American actions and intentions. Although over half of al Qaida's key operational leaders have been killed or captured, along with some 3,000 of their associates, the terrorist organization still exists, with hundreds of operatives and would-be martyrs spread around the globe (Kaplan, 2003; Gilgoff and Tolson, 2003).

Thinking critically, would you advocate the continued use of these three strategies in fighting terrorism? Why or why not?

CHAPTER REVIEW

1. *How did the Industrial Revolution change the economic process?* Machines replaced much human labor, mass production in factories displaced cottage industry, and agriculture lost ground to industry. *What are some effects of industrialization?* Industrialization speeds up production, shrinking blue-collar employment and enlarging white-collar work. It further changes demographic features, human relations, and the values of society. *What are the major sociological perspectives on capitalism as an economic system?* To functionalists, capitalism serves a useful function by bringing about a prosperous and stable society. To conflict theorists, capitalism threatens society by allowing the rich to exploit the poor. Symbolic interactionists focus on how people's definition of their world creates or supports capitalism. *According to feminist theorists, what causes the increased female participation in the labor force?* The causes are declining living standards and rising economic need. *How do feminists explain the concentration of women workers in lower-paid jobs?* Women's low economic status is ascribed to the exploitiveness and oppressiveness of capitalism and patriarchy toward women.

2. *What kinds of economic systems exist around the globe?* Some are primarily capitalist and others are socialist, but they are all mixed economies, with elements of both capitalism and socialism. They differ only in degree, ranging from the most capitalist to the most socialist. *Which economic system is generally more productive?* Capitalist economies are more productive than socialist or unfree ones. *What is the global economy like today?* There is enough free trade to benefit both developing and developed countries, but government support of companies in numerous developing countries has led rich nations to demand that such support be abandoned.

3. *How does a big corporation work?* The numerous shareholders who own the corporation do not run it. A small group of directors and managers do. Owners and managers may profit from the corporation's assets but may not be held responsible for its liabilities. Corporations tend to grow into giants through mergers and acquisitions. The rise of giant corporations has both positive and negative consequences for the economy and society. *What is wel-*

fare for the rich? The government provides special tax breaks for rich individuals and big corporations as well as direct payments to big corporations. *What causes corporate corruption?* The causes include excessive pay for executives and business deregulation. *What are some characteristics of multinational corporations?* They reap huge profits from abroad, are more powerful than some governments, and can create problems for some peoples. But they are still welcomed in many developing countries.

4. *How has the U.S. labor force changed in recent years?* The number of jobs in agriculture has dropped sharply, the number of jobs in service industries has risen, and the population of white-collar workers has expanded. Meanwhile, the employment rates for women, African Americans, and other minorities have increased, while the rate for older men has declined significantly. At the same time, temporary employment has increased sharply. *What groups are more likely to be satisfied with their work?* Older and white-collar workers are generally the most satisfied. Given the same kinds of jobs, women are happier than men. *How has the U.S. workplace changed?* Workers today are less willing to accept unpleasant jobs and more likely to expect meaningful ones. Thus, efforts have been made to give employees more interesting jobs, more freedom, and more power in the workplace.

5. *What do the economic conditions of various U.S. minority groups have in common, and how do they differ?* Most minority groups share the experience of discrimination, which makes them less economically successful than whites. But economic diversity does exist among them: Native Americans generally have the worst economic condition of any ethnic group. African Americans found increasing opportunities for better-paying jobs in the 1960s and 1970s but a setback in the 1980s and 1990s. Mexican Americans and Puerto Ricans generally find themselves in low-wage, blue-collar jobs, while Cuban Americans have achieved a great deal of economic success. Japanese and Chinese Americans are heavily concentrated in white-collar jobs but often are denied top executive positions. Korean and Asian-Indian Americans generally circumvent discrimination by being self-employed, with the Koreans opening small retail stores and the Indians buying hotels.

6. *How is legitimate power different from illegitimate power?* When power is exercised over people with their consent, the power is called legitimate; other-

wise, it is illegitimate. The legitimate power institutionalized in the state is called authority. *Where does authority come from?* It may be derived from tradition, from the charisma of a leader, or from a set of legal rules.

7. *What is the nature of political socialization during childhood?* Children acquire both political information and political attitudes from their families, schools, peers, and the media. *How are political attitudes in the United States divided?* Attitudes are divided along class lines. People of the higher classes are generally more conservative on economic issues and more liberal on social issues. But there is wide support among all social classes for a great variety of government programs—and widespread opposition to big government. Thus, there is a tendency, across class lines, for U.S. citizens to be ideological conservatives but operational liberals. *Are U.S. citizens active participants in their government?* No. Many limit their participation to voting, and the percentage of those who bother to vote has been low.

8. *What are the distinctive political experiences of various minority groups?* Native Americans have a history of being denied voting rights outside their reservations, but today, they have gained some, though limited, political influence. African Americans have achieved remarkable political success in recent decades. Mexican Americans and Puerto Ricans are mostly Democrats, while Cuban Americans are largely Republicans. Asian Americans have recently become more politically active and have tried to enhance their political influence by working together as Asians, rather than separately as Japanese, Chinese, or Koreans. *What is the nature of the U.S. political parties?* Two parties dominate national politics, and each usually avoids adhering to an extreme ideology because both want to appeal to people with a wide range of interests and opinions. But the two parties have suffered a decline in influence, challenged by independent voters and politicians. *How do interest groups influence the government?* They try to sway public opinion, support sympathetic candidates, and hire lobbyists to deal personally with government officials.

9. *According to pluralist theory, who really governs in the United States?* Diverse interest groups share power in the United States. *Who controls the government, according to C. Wright Mills?* Control is held by a power elite made up of those who hold top positions in the federal government, the military, and corporations. *According to Marxists, what is wrong with Mills's power-elite theory?* Mills' theory does not

recognize that the power elite serves as the agent for the capitalist class. In Marxists' view, capitalists use the state to maintain their dominance over the other classes.

10. *What conditions make revolution likely?* There are four: (1) some disgruntled, well-off, and well-educated individuals; (2) the masses' rising expectations; (3) a sudden economic crisis; and (4) weak government. *When is terrorism likely to occur?* It is likely to occur when the would-be leader of a revolution does not have the support of the masses against a strong government.

11. *How does the Internet influence U.S. politics?* American politicians have been increasingly going online to woo voters, and there is some trend toward using the Internet to vote. *How can terrorists be stopped?* A successful plan must include military, political, and cultural actions.

◾ KEY TERMS

Alienation of labor   Marx's term for laborers' loss of control over their work process (p. 337).

Authority   Legitimate power institutionalized in organizations (p. 351).

Capitalism   An economic system based on private ownership of property and competition in producing and selling goods and services (p. 336).

Charisma   An exceptional personal quality popularly attributed to certain individuals (p. 351).

Coercion   The illegitimate use of force or threat of force to compel obedience (p. 351).

Communism   A classless society that operates on the principle of "from each according to his ability to each according to his needs" (p. 337).

Conglomerate   A corporation that owns companies in various unrelated industries (p. 343).

Dual economy   An economy that comprises a *core* of giant corporations dominating the market and a *periphery* of small firms competing for the remaining, smaller shares of business (p. 346).

Economic institution   A system for producing and distributing goods and services (p. 334).

Ideological conservatives   U.S. citizens who, in theory, are opposed to big government because of

their belief in free enterprise, rugged individualism, and capitalism (p. 353).

Industrial Revolution   The dramatic economic change brought about by the introduction of machines into the work process about 200 years ago (p. 334).

Influence   The ability to control others' behavior through persuasion rather than coercion or authority (p. 351).

Interest group   An organized collection of people who attempt to influence government policies (p. 356).

Mixed economy   An economic system that contains elements of both capitalism and socialism (p. 339).

Monopoly   The situation in which one firm controls the output of an industry (p. 342).

Multinational corporations   Corporations that have subsidiaries in many countries (p. 343).

Oligopoly   The situation in which a very few companies control the output of an industry (p. 342).

Operational liberals   U.S. citizens who, in effect, support big government by backing government programs that render services to the public (p. 354).

Political party   A group organized for the purpose of gaining government offices (p. 355).

Political power   The capacity to use the government to make decisions that affect the whole society (p. 358).

Political socialization   A learning process by which individuals acquire political knowledge, beliefs, and attitudes (p. 353).

Politics   The type of human interaction that involves some people acquiring and exercising power over others (p. 334).

Postindustrial revolution   The change of an economy into one dominated by high technology (p. 334).

Power   The ability to control the behavior of others, even against their will (p. 350).

Revolution   The movement aimed at the violent overthrow of the existing government (p. 360).

Socialism   An economic system based on public ownership and government control of the economy (p. 337).

Terrorism   The use of violence to express dissatisfaction with a government (p. 362).

QUESTIONS FOR DISCUSSION AND REVIEW

THE ECONOMY IN PERSPECTIVE

1. How did the Industrial Revolution change economic institutions and societies?
2. What is the nature of capitalism as seen from the functionalist and conflict perspectives?
3. According to the symbolic interactionist perspective, how did early Protestantism produce and support capitalism?
4. How do feminist theorists explain the increase in female paid employment and the concentration of women workers in lower-paid jobs?

THE WORLD'S ECONOMIC SYSTEMS

1. How can the world's economies be classified?
2. How well has each type of economic system performed in recent history?
3. How can free trade both benefit and harm rich countries?

THE DOMINANCE OF BIG CORPORATIONS

1. How can a competitive market system lead to oligopoly or monopoly?
2. What are the characteristics of big corporations?
3. What is welfare for the rich?
4. How much should executives be paid?
5. How do multinational corporations earn profits?

WORK IN THE UNITED STATES

1. What occupations make up the U.S. labor force today, and what kinds of people fill these positions?
2. What kinds of people are most satisfied with their jobs and why?
3. How and why has the U.S. work ethic changed?

SOCIAL DIVERSITY IN THE U.S. ECONOMY

1. What are the economic differences among Native Americans, African Americans, Hispanic Americans, and Asian Americans?

POWER AND AUTHORITY

1. How does legitimate power differ from illegitimate power?
2. What are the differences among traditional, charismatic, and legal authorities?

THE WORLD OF U.S. POLITICS

1. What is political socialization?
2. How are U.S. citizens' attitudes toward their government contradictory?

3. Does low voter turnout threaten democracy? Why or why not?
4. What are the different political experiences of Native, African, Hispanic, and Asian Americans?
5. What is the nature of the U.S. political parties today?
6. What are the functions and dysfunctions of interest groups?

WHO REALLY GOVERNS IN U.S. SOCIETY?

1. How does the elitist view of who exercises political power differ from the pluralist view?
2. According to the Marxist view, which elite makes the most important decisions, and how does this elite exercise power?

A GLOBAL ANALYSIS OF POLITICAL VIOLENCE

1. What social conditions usually exist before a revolution occurs?
2. Who are terrorists, and what are they trying to do?

SOCIOLOGICAL FRONTIERS/USING SOCIOLOGY

1. How does the Internet influence U.S. politics and voting?
2. How can international terrorists be stopped?

SUGGESTED READINGS

Kuttner, Robert. 1977. *Everything for Sale: The Virtues and Limits of Markets.* New York: Knopf. Shows the importance of government's role in solving the problems created or neglected by free markets.

Lipset, Seymour Martin, and Gary Marks. 2000. *It Didn't Happen Here: Why Socialism Failed in the United States.* New York: W. W. Norton. A careful, clear analysis of how certain social, cultural, and other forces prevented the United States from becoming a socialist state.

Patterson, Thomas E. 2002. *The Vanishing Voter: Public Involvement in an Age of Uncertainty.* New York: Knopf. An analysis of voter apathy in the United States, showing what it is like, why it is prevalent, and how it can be reduced.

Pillar, Paul R. 2001. *Terrorism and U.S. Foreign Policy.* Washington, DC: Brookings Institution Press. Shows the nature of terrorism as well as how terrorism can be managed and reduced but not permanently eradicated.

Underhill, Paco. 1999. *Why We Buy: The Science of Shopping.* New York: Simon & Schuster. An interesting study of the world of shopping, examining not only why shoppers buy but also how retailers sell.

■ Additional Resources

The New York Times
expect the world®

nytimes.com

Expand your knowledge of the concepts discussed in this chapter by reading the following current and historical articles from the *New York Times*. Go to the "eThemes of the Times" section of the Companion Website (www.ablongman.com/thio6e):

> "California Insurrection Puts Other Politicians on Notice"

Research Navigator.com

Research Navigator, a research database, provides immediate access to hundreds of full-text articles from EBSCO's ContentSelect Academic Journal Database. If the Research Navigator access code was included with your textbook, go to the website www.research navigator.com and read the following articles related to this chapter by typing in the article number:

Etzioni, Amitai. "Decriminalizing Politics." *Society*, Mar/Apr2001, Vol. 38 Issue 3, p43, 7p. Accession Number: 4098139. Shows how the United States can protect the integrity of public office when elected officials face criminal charges.

Hazan, Miryam. "The Structure of Mexican Elites: An Enduring Puzzle." *International Review of Sociology*, Jul2001, Vol. 11 Issue 2, p217, 13p. Accession Number: 4781165. Focuses on the social structure of elites in Mexico.

chapter 13

Health and Population

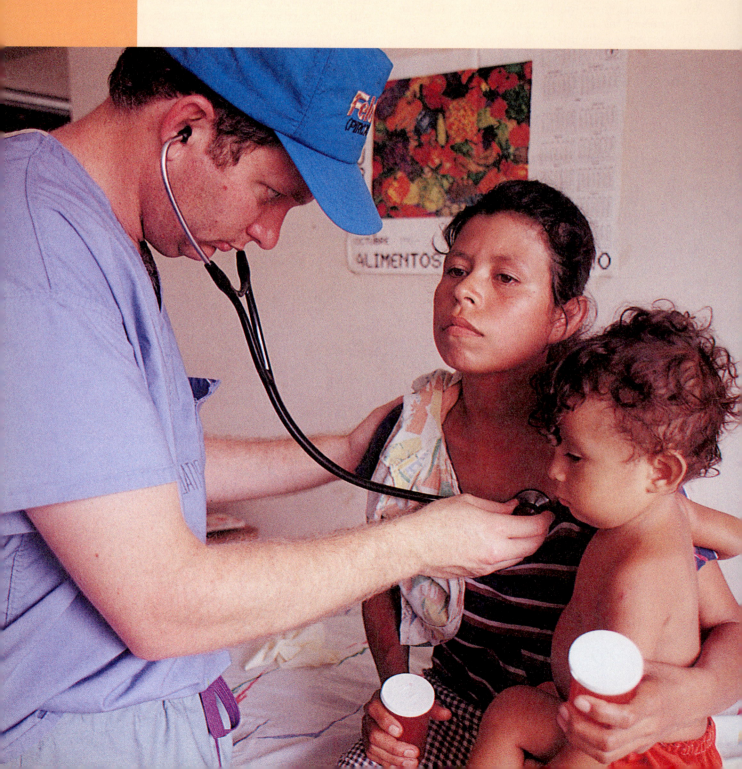

myths & realities

myth *Living in one of the richest countries in the world, Americans have the highest life expectancy.*

reality While living longer than people in poor countries, Americans have a lower life expectancy than people in nearly all other industrial societies (p. 370).

myth *Older people are more vulnerable than younger people to nearly all kinds of illness.*

reality While they are more likely to suffer from such chronic illnesses as arthritis, heart disease, and cancer, older people are less susceptible to acute and infectious illnesses, such as measles and pneumonia (p. 371).

myth *Compassionate and sensitive, most doctors listen to their patients' complaints with great attentiveness and understanding.*

reality Most doctors tend to interact poorly with patients. Consequently, about 60 percent of patients fail to adequately understand instructions about their medications (p. 384).

myth *The world's large population reflects steady growth over thousands of years.*

reality Most of the world's population growth has occurred in the relatively recent past. Before the modern era began (in 1600), the global population had reached only about half a billion in more than 500,000 years. Since then, in less than 400 years, world population has skyrocketed to more than 6.4 billion (p. 386).

myth *The fact that poor countries have high birth rates is virtually the only reason for their tremendous population growth.*

reality Modern medicine, along with better hygiene and sanitation, also contributes to population growth by sharply reducing death rates (p. 390).

myth *Population growth is inevitable; the population of every country continues to grow.*

reality While poor countries continue to experience population growth, rich countries, such as those in Western Europe, are close to having or already have *zero population growth*, a situation in which the population stops growing (p. 390).

t was a hot day in Bardera, a small town in southern Somalia in Africa. A crowd of starving, emaciated people gathered at a United Nations feeding center. They were waiting for a meal of brown gruel. A 5-year-old boy passed out. Two relief workers rushed over, picked him up, and put him down under a shade tree. The child was suffering from severe dehydration. A nurse quickly inserted an intravenous tube, hooking the bottle to a branch. But it was too late. The boy's eyes rolled back beneath his quivering eyelids, which an older woman gently shut with her fingers. The boy had come from a village 34 miles away, where both of his parents and eight brothers and sisters had also died from starvation in the past six months. Weak and hungry, the boy had walked for four days to this town with his last relative, an older brother. Now, his sibling was rocking and weeping quietly by his lifeless body. In another African country, Sudan, hundreds of thousands of children—and adults—also have starved to death in the same way (Nelan, 1998; Purvis, 1992).

The mass starvation in Somalia, Sudan, and other African countries, though often triggered by drought or civil war, can be traced partly to the population explosion. Even hard-won advances in food production cannot catch up with the continuing enormous growth in population. Increased population pressure has made many of Africa's farms and fields barren through overuse. The resulting famine inevitably threatens human health and even causes death. In this chapter, we first discuss various social aspects of health and then population.

HEALTH AND SOCIETY

As a social phenomenon, health varies from one society to another and from one group to another within the same society. From these variations, we can see how social factors affect health and what consequences an outbreak of illness has for society. We can also track down the origin of a disease by examining all of its victims for something that they have in common as a social group.

A Global Analysis of Health

People in the United States are much healthier than ever before. Since 1900, their life expectancy has increased by more than 50 percent, from about 49 years in 1900 to 77 today. At birth, they can expect to live 28 more years than did their counterparts in 1900—more than one and a half times as long as they did then. Another indicator of health, the infant mortality rate, has shown even more dramatic improvement: About 15 percent of all U.S. babies died during the first year of life at the turn of the twentieth century, but less than 1 percent do today (U.S. Census Bureau, 2002). All this can be chalked up to healthier living conditions, better diet, immunization against various diseases, and penicillin and other antibiotics.

myth	Living in one of the richest countries in the world, Americans have the highest life expectancy.
reality	While living longer than people in poor countries, Americans have a lower life expectancy than people in nearly all other industrial societies.

But Americans' increased life expectancy loses its impressiveness when compared with the life expectancies of people in other industrial countries. As Table 13.1 shows, people in nearly all other industrialized countries live longer than Americans do. Their standing in regard to infant mortality is the same: Proportionately more babies die in the United States. This seems ironic because Americans spend much more money on health care than the people in any of these nations.

The lower rate of health in the United States can be attributed to its being less egalitarian than other

TABLE 13.1

Health among Industrial Countries

The United States usually has the lowest life expectancy and the highest infant mortality in the industrial world.

Country	Life Expectancy*	Country	Infant Mortality Rate**
1. Japan	80.8	1. United States	6.8
2. Australia	79.8	2. Italy	5.8
3. Canada	79.6	3. Britain	5.5
4. Italy	79.1	4. Canada	5.0
5. Spain	78.9	5. Australia	5.0
6. France	78.9	6. Spain	4.9
7. Netherlands	78.4	7. Germany	4.7
8. Britain	77.8	8. France	4.5
9. Germany	77.6	9. Netherlands	4.4
10. United States	77.3	10. Japan	3.9

*Number of years an infant at birth can expect to live
**Number of infant deaths per 1,000 live births

Source: Data from U.S. Census Bureau, 2002.

industrialized countries. This is because in a less egalitarian society, relatively few people are at the top, enjoying power or domination over others and therefore having better health. But many more people are at the bottom, feeling resigned, resentful, or submissive and therefore unhealthy. By contrast, in a more egalitarian society, most people experience feelings that contribute to good health, such as support, friendship, cooperation, and sociability (Bezruchka, 2001, 1997). All this may also explain why the United States has a much higher life expectancy (see Figure 13.1, p. 372) and a considerably lower infant mortality rate than many poor, developing countries, which are generally less egalitarian.

■ Social Diversity in U.S. Health

In the United States, older people are less likely than young people to suffer from acute and infectious illnesses, such as measles and pneumonia. But older people are more susceptible to chronic illnesses such as arthritis, heart disease, and cancer. Cancer deaths, in particular, have been climbing steeply and steadily among people aged 55 and older (U.S. Census Bureau, 2003).

Health also varies with gender. Women live longer than men—generally, five years longer. Part of the reason is biological, as evidenced by, for example, the

fact that women's sex hormones protect them from the risk of cardiovascular disease up to the time of menopause. Most of the reason, however, is sociological, as reflected in the cultural belief that taking risks is a badge of masculine toughness. Thus, men are more likely than women to put their health at risk by smoking, drinking excessively, abusing drugs, and driving without wearing a seatbelt. Further, when sick, men are less likely than women to see a doctor (Williams, 2003; Verbrugge, 1985).

myth	Older people are more vulnerable than younger people to nearly all kinds of illness.
reality	While they are more likely to suffer from such chronic illnesses as arthritis, heart disease, and cancer, older people are less susceptible to acute and infectious illnesses, such as measles and pneumonia.

Race and ethnicity are also correlated with health. African Americans, Hispanic Americans, and Native Americans all have shorter life expectancies than whites. Minorities are far more likely to suffer or die from many diseases, such as influenza, pneumonia, and AIDS (see Figure 13.2, p. 373). Both Hispanic Americans and Native Americans, however, are less likely than whites to die from heart disease and can-

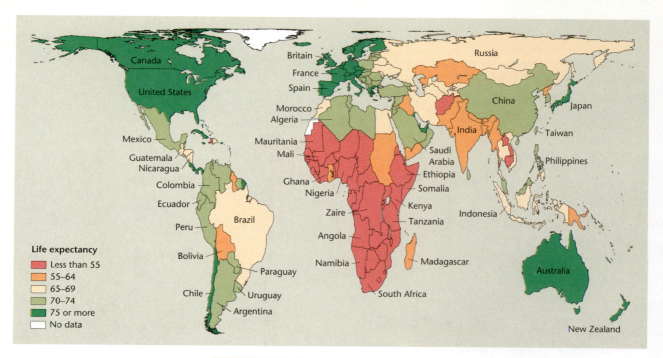

Life expectancy

- ■ Less than 55
- ■ 55–64
- ■ 65–69
- ■ 70–74
- ■ 75 or more
- □ No data

FIGURE 13.1

Life Expectancies around the World

Although Americans have the lowest life expectancy in the industrial world, they do have a much better outlook than people in poor, developing countries. Generally, the more egalitarian a society is, the healthier it is. Thus, Americans are less healthy than the Europeans and Japanese because U.S. society is less egalitarian, but Americans are more healthy than people in developing countries because U.S. society is more egalitarian.

Critical Thinking: *What are the social implications of egalitarianism, and how could you use them to improve your health and others'?*

Source: World Bank Atlas, 2003.

IN SICKNESS AND HEALTH

Social factors figure strongly in sickness. Poverty can aggravate the hypertension suffered by minorities, and various other acute and infectious diseases are more common among people in the lower social classes. Reasons include unhygienic environment, stress due to job loss or divorce, poor medical care, and unhealthy eating habits. ■

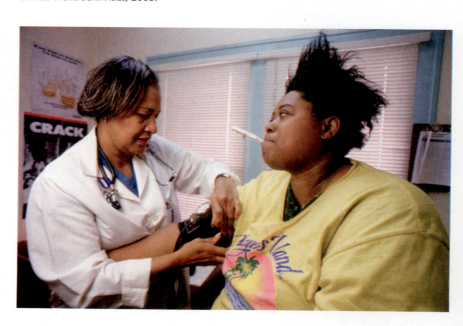

cer, partly because whites live longer and the odds of developing these chronic illnesses typically increase with age (Cockerham, 2001; Johnson et al., 1991).

These racial and ethnic differences may reflect another social factor that influences health: social class. The diseases that hit minority groups the hardest are those associated with poverty. In particular, acute and infectious diseases, such as influenza and tuberculosis, are more prevalent among the lower social classes. Researchers have attributed the higher rates of disease among the lower classes to several related factors: toxic, hazardous, and unhygienic environments; stress resulting from life changes, such as job loss and divorce; and inadequate medical care (Shweder, 1997; Syme and Berkman, 1987). Many researchers have also found another problem: unhealthy eating habits. Poor people are much more likely than others to eat high-sugar, high-salt, and high-fat food (Freedman, 1990). Poverty can also aggravate the problem of hypertension suffered by minorities. Because they may be less able to deal with the sociopsychological stress induced by racism in the United States, poor African Americans are signif-

icantly more likely than middle-class African Americans to have high blood pressure (Klag et al., 1991).

■ Epidemiology

In analyzing the social forces behind illness, sociologists can help physicians and public health workers track down the causes of diseases. This task requires a kind of detective work called **epidemiology**, the study of the origin and spread of disease in a given population. In their role as epidemiologists, sociologists and medical scientists first seek out all the people who already have the disease. Then, they ask the victims where they were and what they did before they got sick. Epidemiologists also collect data on the victims' age, gender, marital status, occupation, and other characteristics. The aim is to find out what all the victims have in common besides the disease so that its cause can be identified and eliminated. Usually, the common factor that ties all the victims together provides the essential clue.

Epidemiology emerged as an applied science in 1854, when the English physician John Snow dis-

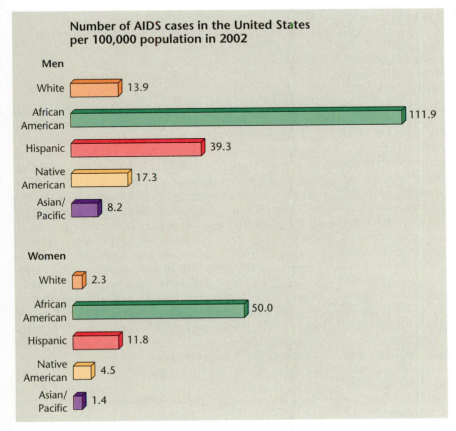

Number of AIDS cases in the United States per 100,000 population in 2002

Men

White — 13.9
African American — 111.9
Hispanic — 39.3
Native American — 17.3
Asian/Pacific — 8.2

Women

White — 2.3
African American — 50.0
Hispanic — 11.8
Native American — 4.5
Asian/Pacific — 1.4

FIGURE 13.2

Social Diversity in AIDS

Health is related to race and ethnicity. Generally, racial and ethnic minorities are far more likely than the dominant group to suffer from many diseases, including AIDS. One reason for this is the higher poverty rate among minorities.

Critical Thinking: *If you were poor, what would you do to resist behaviors that may cause AIDS?*

Source: Data from Centers for Disease Control, 2003.

covered the source of one of London's periodic cholera epidemics. He had gone to the neighborhoods where the patients lived and asked them what they did every day, where they worked, what they ate and drank, and many other questions about their lives and activities. Finally, after sifting through a huge pile of information, Snow hit upon the clue to the origin of the disease. He found that they all had one thing in common: They had drunk water from a particular pump on Broad Street. Snow simply shut off the pump and, with that single act, stopped the epidemic in its tracks. Not until many years later, with the discovery of germs, could anyone explain why shutting down the pump was effective: Dr. Snow had removed the source of the cholera bacterium (Cockerham, 2001).

Since then, epidemiology has been used to trace the origins of many different diseases such as cancer and heart disease. In investigating heart disease, for example, epidemiologists have discovered that the majority of victims have eaten high-cholesterol foods, smoked or drunk heavily, and failed to get enough exercise. Thus, avoiding these habits can reduce the risk of heart disease.

■ AIDS

Directly caused by a virus called *human immunodeficiency virus (HIV),* acquired immune deficiency syndrome (AIDS) is a deadly disease that destroys the body's immune system, leaving the victim defenseless against other diseases. The disease first came to the attention of U.S. physicians in early 1981. Since then, it has spread rapidly.

Social Causes   In searching for the cause of AIDS, epidemiologists have found clues in the social characteristics and behaviors of the victims. So far, in the United States, the largest group of victims are gay men. The second largest group consists of intravenous drug users. The rest are non-drug-using heterosexuals. Most of them have caught the virus through sex, and a few have been infected through blood transfusions or by being born to mothers with HIV or AIDS (see Figure 13.3).

New cases of HIV and AIDS among gay men declined in the late 1980s and the 1990s because of the increasing practice of safe sex. But now, both are on the rise again among gay men, a result of the return to unsafe sex (Cloud, 2001). HIV and AIDS have also increased among non-drug-using heterosexuals as well as intravenous drug users. These drug users are mostly poor, African American, and Hispanic American heterosexuals in the inner city. They often share contaminated needles when shooting drugs, thus passing the virus that causes AIDS from one to another.

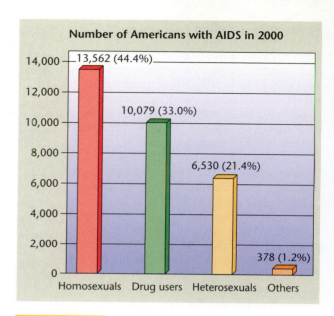

FIGURE 13.3

People with AIDS in the United States
Knowing the social characteristics of people with AIDS, epidemiologists can get clues on what causes the disease. They have thus discovered that most people with AIDS got the disease by engaging in unprotected sex or shooting drugs with contaminated needles.
Critical Thinking: *How would you help high schoolers avoid getting AIDS?*
Source: Data from Centers for Disease Control, 2001.

All these epidemiological facts clearly suggest that HIV spreads mostly through sexual intercourse with an infected person and through the sharing of a hypodermic needle that has been contaminated with the virus. Studies in other societies can also be useful. For example, epidemiologists have discovered some similarities and differences between Africans with AIDS and their U.S. counterparts. Unlike U.S. citizens with AIDS, those in Africa do not have histories of intravenous drug use, homosexuality, or blood transfusion. But like American gays with AIDS, African heterosexuals with the disease mostly live in large cities and have had sex with many different partners. Thus, AIDS has spread among Africans in the same way it has among gays in the United States: through sex with multiple partners. By itself, though, promiscuity is not the source of the AIDS virus. Rather, *unprotected sex* is what increases the risk of infection (Altman, 1998; Rushing, 1995).

Social Consequences   Unlike such familiar killers as cancer and heart disease, AIDS is mysterious and has had an unusual impact on U.S. society. As we have seen, the disease is not only lethal but can be transmitted through life's most basic human interaction—sex and procreation. Understandably, the general public is gripped with the fear of contagion. The initial appearance of AIDS among two groups of which the larger society disapproves—gays and drug addicts—has added to the fear because prejudice discourages understanding of "their" disease.

According to a series of surveys by the U.S. Public Health Service, a growing number of people have quickly learned the risk factors for HIV and AIDS, but misinformation about the virus's transmission remains a problem. Many still fear that they can get HIV by donating blood or through casual contact with an infected person. Such fears are particularly rampant in small towns and rural areas (Belluck, 1998). And while the fears are groundless, they have spawned strange, sad, and sometimes hostile actions against people with HIV and AIDS.

Many parents, for example, have demanded the mandatory testing of schoolchildren and segregation of those with HIV and AIDS. There have also been many instances in which people with HIV and AIDS have been prevented from keeping jobs or getting housing, insurance coverage, and medical care. Such acts of discrimination sometimes are directed against those who are not already infected with HIV but are only perceived to be at risk for the disease. Those who care for AIDS patients are also likely to encounter discrimination.

Many states, however, have passed laws to protect the general public against HIV. These laws seek to identify certain people with the virus, to notify partners, and, in some cases, even to punish those who intentionally transmit the virus to others. Thus, doctors are required to report to authorities the names of HIV-positive people so that their partners can be notified of potential exposure. An increasing number of states also mandate HIV testing for specific segments of the population, such as prisoners and pregnant women (Richardson, 1998).

■ Smoking

While many people die of AIDS because they engage in unsafe sex and intravenous drug use, far more die from lung cancer, heart disease, and other cardiovascular illnesses because they smoke cigarettes. Every year since 1990, about 33,000 Americans have died from AIDS. However, at least 13 times that many—over 430,000—have died of illnesses resulting from smoking, which gives the United States one of the highest rates of tobacco-related deaths in the world (see Figure 13.4, p. 376). Moreover, every year, anywhere from 37,000 to 40,000 nonsmokers who are exposed to tobacco smoke die from cardiovascular diseases (Holmes, 1998a; AHA, 1998).

Nonetheless, too many Americans continue to smoke regularly; smokers still make up about one-quarter of the U.S. population. Worse, in any given month, more than one-third of high school students smoke. Most of these young smokers are very likely to continue smoking in their adult lives because research has shown that 75 percent of adult smokers started before age 18.

As teenagers, whites are much more likely than African Americans to smoke. Among adults, however, African Americans are more likely to smoke. Of

DYING TO LIGHT UP While many people die of AIDS because they engage in unsafe sex and intravenous drug use, far more die of other diseases because they smoke cigarettes. Too many Americans continue to smoke regularly. In any given month, more than one-third of high school students smoke, and among them, there are proportionately many more whites than African Americans. ■

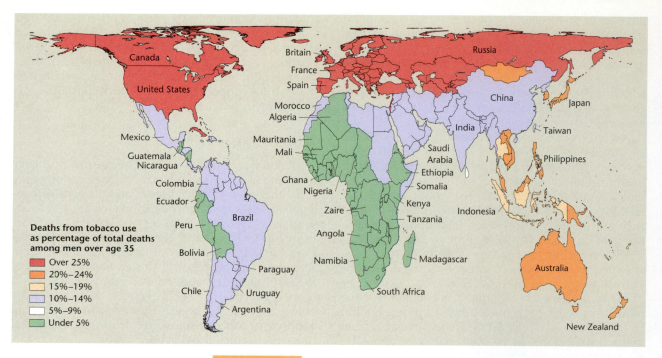

FIGURE 13.4

Deaths around the World from Smoking

Tobacco use is a relatively common cause of death in the United States. In fact, the United States, like other industrial nations, leads the world in smoking-related deaths, not only for men but also women. (To save space, only the data on men are presented here. Fewer American women die from smoking than men do.)

Critical Thinking: *Knowing the hazards of smoking could hardly persuade people who like to take risks to avoid smoking. What, then, can be done to effectively discourage them from smoking?*

Source: Data from Judith MacKay and Michael Eriksen, *The Tobacco Atlas* (Geneva, Switzerland: World Health Organization, 2002), p. 37.

various racial and ethnic groups, Native Americans have the highest percentage of smokers and Asian Americans have the lowest. These racial and ethnic differences in smoking may have something to do with education. As many studies have shown, the prevalence of smoking is three times higher among people with less than 12 years of education compared to those with more than 16 years of education. Those groups with less education are thus more likely than other groups to smoke. There is also a gender factor in smoking: Within most ethnic groups, there are many more male smokers than female smokers, the exception being that among white teenagers, females are more likely to smoke (SAMHSA, 2002; AHA, 1998).

Given the terrible health hazards of smoking, why do smokers continue to smoke? Are they irrational, or do they fail to appreciate the hazards of smoking?

Many smokers have become addicted, so that they cannot quit. But others continue to smoke even if they can quit because to them, the benefits of smoking outweigh the costs. The benefits include releasing tension, feeling relaxed, and enjoying quiet companionship and lively conversation. It is, however, more than these benefits that cause smokers to continue smoking. Smokers are simply much less risk averse than nonsmokers (Emmons et al., 2004). Contrary to popular belief, smokers are acutely aware of the hazards of smoking. In fact, they tend to greatly overrate the risks of smoking. In one study, for example, smokers placed the risk of lung cancer at 38 percent, while a more realistic risk is less than 10 percent (Viscusi, 1992).

Whatever benefits smokers claim to enjoy from their tobacco use, nonsmokers can still assert their right to be protected from harmful secondhand

"It's the only place they're allowed to advertise anymore."

Source: From the *Wall Street Journal*—Permission, Cartoon Features Syndicate.

smoke. But smokers can claim their right to risk their own health by smoking. Faced with this conflict between smokers and nonsmokers, the government has tried to bring about a smoke-free society but one in which only smoking in public is prohibited, not smoking per se.

MEDICAL CARE

Before 1870, doctoring was a lowly profession. Many doctors were more like quacks than true medical scientists. They had little knowledge of how the various body systems worked and of how diseases developed. In the face of such ignorance, doctors could be a menace. For numerous ailments, they bled patients profusely; evacuated their bowels, often until they passed out; stuffed them with dangerous drugs; and tormented them with various ghastly appliances. One treatment for syphilis involved roasting the patient in an oven. Sometimes, the patients survived despite all this "assistance," but more often, they died. Either way, the doctors learned a great deal from them. In time, they developed a store of knowledge that eventually enabled them to practice a highly respectable profession (Blundell, 1987).

■ The Changing Medical Profession

Over the last 20 years, significant changes have occurred in the medical profession. Today, doctors often find their autonomy eroded, their prestige reduced, and their competence challenged by everyone from insurance companies to patients.

Before 1980, most doctors practiced alone. By 1983, the share of doctors in solo practice had already decreased to only 41 percent, and later it fell even further—to 26 percent by 1997. Today, a large majority of doctors are salaried employees, working in group practices, health maintenance organizations (HMOs), and other health-care companies. One reason is that the cost of starting a private practice is too high for most young doctors, whose medical training has left them deeply in debt. Another reason is that doctors get most of their payments from the government and insurance companies, not from patients, as they did in the past. To be paid, doctors must fill out numerous forms to justify their fees, which often proves too burdensome for a private doctor to handle (Stolberg, 1998a).

Efforts by employers, insurance companies, and the government to control rising medical costs have caused many doctors to complain about losing their professional autonomy. Physicians must seek permission from outside regulators, such as agencies and insurance companies, for major but nonemergency hospitalization and surgeries. If the regulators do not approve a case in advance, they will not pay the cost of treatment. They occasionally refuse to authorize a treatment that they consider too costly or unnecessary. While chafing at these outside regulators, doctors also complain of internal controls from their employers. HMOs routinely pass around lists ranking their physicians on the time spent with patients. This is intended to give the doctors the subtle but clear message that those highest on the list cause a financial drain on the organization (Gorman, 1998; Belkin, 1990).

The general public also seems to hold doctors in less esteem than before. According to a Gallup poll, a majority (57 to 75 percent) of the people questioned agreed with these statements: "Doctors don't care about people as much as they used to," "Doctors are too interested in making money," and "Doctors keep patients waiting too long." Another Gallup poll showed that only 44 percent of Americans have "a great deal" or "quite a lot" of confidence in the medical system. Not fully trusting their doctors, people who are better educated often feel obliged to become as informed as possible about their illness so that they can get the best treatment. This has led many doctors to complain that some patients challenge their expertise after learning about medical advances only from television or newspapers and magazines (Mallory, 2003; Gorman, 1998; Altman, 1990).

For a while, before the late 1990s, the growing discontent among doctors discouraged many college students from pursuing a medical career. But today, numerous students are eager to become doctors, with significant increases in the numbers of women and minority-group members. These demographic changes will make the medical profession more representative of and responsive to an increasingly diverse society. Moreover, today's medical students of diverse backgrounds have a lower income expectation and a greater sense of public duty than their elders, which should help them meet the increasingly cost-conscious need for health care more effectively in the near future. More important, patients are likely to see them as less authoritarian and more patient friendly than the traditional doctors of past years (Eisenberg, 1999; AAMC, 1998; Rosenthal, 1995; Altman, 1990).

■ Sexism in Medical Research

With more women entering the medical profession, more attention is being given to women's health issues. Indeed, researchers have found that some well-accepted treatments may actually be dangerous to

SQUEAKY WHEEL GETS GREASED Gender bias in medical research has resulted in a lack of research on women's health problems. However, mounting pressure from women's groups has helped bring this research bias into the open and has begun to increase the amount of research money devoted to women's health issues. ■

women patients because they are based on research on men only.

In 1988, the medical profession, along with the general public, was informed that aspirin reduces the risk of heart attacks. This conclusion was based on a study of 22,071 men. Because the study did not include women, nobody knows whether aspirin also benefits women. If it does not, women with heart disease who rely on aspirin for treatment could be in trouble. In 1990, a similar study showed that heavy coffee intake did not increase the risk of heart attacks or strokes. Is it safe, then, for women with heart problems to drink coffee heavily? Not necessarily, because the 45,589 subjects of the study, aged 40 to 75, were all men (Ames, 1990; Purvis, 1990).

It is not necessary to include women in a study on heart disease if their hearts do not differ from men's. But they do. For example, cardiovascular disease strikes women later in life, and they are much more likely to die after undergoing heart-bypass surgery. Another issue is that blood cholesterol levels seem to affect female patients differently. Women seem less vulnerable than men to high levels of LDL (low density lipoprotein—the so-called bad cholesterol) but more vulnerable to low levels of HDL (high density lipoprotein—the good cholesterol). Diets that reduce *both* levels, as promoted by the American Heart Association, may end up harming women (Gorman, 2003; Ames, 1990; Purvis, 1990).

The bias against women further shows up in the lack of research on health problems that affect women only. The medical profession therefore knows very little about how any of the 19 million women with osteoporosis could have prevented the bone-breaking condition. Doctors also do not know for sure whether it is wise to supply women with replacement hormones when they go through menopause. There is also a serious lack of knowledge about breast cancer, which kills about 44,000 women *every year*. (By comparison, the Vietnam War, which lasted *for more than 10 years,* took 58,000 U.S. lives.) Still, research institutes have not studied these female diseases as much as they have studied diseases that also afflict men (Beck, 1990a; Silberner, 1990).

However, increased awareness of the medical research bias against women, coupled with mounting pressure from various women's health groups, has begun to produce positive results. The National Institutes of Health, for example, has issued new guidelines stipulating that applications for research grants should include women as subjects. Likewise, the National Academy of Sciences has urged researchers to focus more on how women are uniquely affected by certain diseases and various treatments for diseases (Pear, 2001; Silberner, 1990).

ANCIENT ALTERNATIVES Some ethnic groups turn first for medical care to ancient systems of herbal or folk medicine. Such systems of alternative medicine have worked for thousands of years yet are largely unknown in Western medical systems. Among Mexican Americans, for example, relatives, friends, neighbors, and *curanderos* (folk healers) often provide patients with certain patent medicines, herbs, and teas. Here, an *herbolaria* in a Mexican American community sells traditional herbal medicines and potions. ■

■ Social Diversity in Seeking Medical Care

When people feel sick, they obviously want to get well again, but not everyone automatically goes to see a doctor. Some may simply shrug off their illness, thinking that it's not serious enough. But more than the severity of illness motivates people to seek medical care. Social factors such as age, gender, ethnicity, and class, which reflect the social diversity in the United States, are also involved. They help determine who is likely to visit a doctor and who is not.

It is common knowledge that older people are ill more often than younger people are. It is therefore not surprising that the elderly are the most likely age group to seek medical care.

Women are more likely than men to use health services, but women are less likely to obtain proper care. Under the influence of sexual prejudice, doctors tend to dismiss women's complaints with such comments as "Overstress," "Back strain," "Could be just the heat," or "Nothing to worry about." Even when a patient complains of chest pains and other symptoms of heart disease, the doctor is less likely to take the complaints seriously when they come from a woman. For example, doctors are twice as likely to label women's chest pains as a psychiatric complaint or something other than a sign of heart disease. Among those who suffer from kidney failure, women are also less likely than men to receive kidney transplants. Nevertheless, when they feel ill, women are more likely than men to consult doctors (Jauhar, 2001; Blakeslee, 1989; Tobin et al., 1987).

Some ethnic groups tend to visit doctors less often than others. When ill, Mexican Americans often see the doctor as a last resort, preferring to try Mexican folk medicine first. Their relatives, friends, neighbors, and *curanderos* (folk healers) are generally ready to provide certain patent medicines, herbs, and teas along with the performance of religious rituals. Native Americans have a similar system of folk medicine, which they believe to be capable of restoring health by restoring a harmonious balance among various biological and spiritual forces in the sick person's life. Similar principles of harmonious balance can be found in traditional Chinese medicine, which is popular with residents in America's Chinatowns. According to the Chinese, illness results from an imbalance between *yin* (the female, cold force) and *yang* (the male, hot force). If illness results from an excess of (cold) yin over (hot) yang, certain herbs and foods that are classified as hot should be taken to bring back the balance between yin and yang—and hence health. If illness results from too much (hot) yang, cold herbs and foods should be taken (Cockerham, 2001).

African Americans, who lack the systems of folk medicine available to other minorities, are nearly as likely as whites to visit physicians. But the quality of the health care they receive tends to be lower. Blacks are also more likely than whites to receive treatment in hospital outpatient clinics and emergency rooms, which are more often public than private. Whites are more likely to go to a private doctor's office. This difference is largely because a greater proportion of African Americans are poor. The poor are, indeed, more likely than the rich to get medical treatment in public clinics and emergency rooms (Blizzard, 2003b; Cockerham, 2001; Dutton, 1978).

But poor blacks are apparently more reluctant than poor whites to seek treatment for AIDS and HIV because they distrust the government. This has resulted partly from the infamous Tuskegee experiments conducted by the U.S. government for 40 years (from 1932 to 1972). For the experiments, 399 poor black men were recruited and led to believe that they would receive free medical treatment for what they called "bad blood," while, in fact, they were left untreated for syphilis so that government health researchers could study the impact of the disease on them. To restore government trust among African Americans, former President Clinton publicly apologized to the few remaining survivors and to relatives of the 399 victims (Stolberg, 1998b; Mitchell, 1997).

■ The U.S. Health Care System

Americans seem overwhelmingly dissatisfied with the U.S. health care system. In 2003, a Gallup poll asked whether U.S. health care was in a state of crisis, having major problems, having minor problems, or not having any problems. Only 2 percent said "no problems," with 8 percent mentioning "crisis," 50 percent "major problems," and 39 percent "minor problems." The problems that most Americans complain about all relate to the high cost of health care (Blizzard, 2003a).

High Cost In the last 30 years, health care costs in the United States have gone up faster than the rate of inflation for other goods and services. Now, the national yearly medical expenditure amounts to over 10 percent of GNI (gross national income)—more than any other nation spends on medical care. That translates into about $1.42 trillion, which is greater than the economy of France (Wessel, 2003; Cockerham, 2001).

Why have health care costs escalated so rapidly? The aging of the U.S. population is one contributing factor, and proliferation of expensive medical technology is another. Significant advances also have been made in keeping coma and stroke victims alive, but these patients sometimes require extremely expensive medical care for years. Perhaps most important, Americans now visit doctors more often, spend more days in hospitals, swallow more pills, and seek ever more costly treatments and prescription drugs (Wessel, 2003).

More generally, the high cost of health care in the United States stems from the fact that medical care is organized as a business that is quite different from other businesses. For instance, medical customers do

"I don't use chemical anesthetics anymore. I just give them an estimate of their hospital bill."

Source: Harley Schwadron.

not have much say about what they buy because they usually cannot judge what they need. They rely on doctors to tell them what they need and how much they must pay. Meanwhile, consumers have few incentives to keep prices down. They pay only a small share (about one-third) of the cost directly. Most of it is passed on to third parties, including insurance companies, employers, and the government.

Since the early 1990s, however, these third parties have tried to reduce costs through managed health care: putting a squeeze on doctors' incomes, requiring patients to pay a larger share of the cost, and cutting back on treatment and hospital stays. But these efforts to cut costs may have forced doctors to be too stingy with care, causing many patients to complain and some to sue the managed care companies. Moreover, the cost of prescription drugs has gone up so much that some Americans are buying cheaper drugs in Mexico and Canada (Martinez, 2003; Cowley and Turque, 1999; Freudenheim, 1996).

Payment System Reflecting the historical opposition to big government in favor of greater personal liberty, the United States stands alone among rich industrialized societies for not having government-paid universal health insurance for all its citizens. There is instead a fee-for-service system, which requires patients to pay directly for the services they receive from doctors and hospitals. But as has been suggested, most Americans pay a portion rather than the entirety of the fees, with the rest paid by a third party—typically, an employer, insurance company, or the government.

A majority (about 60 percent) of Americans have private medical insurance. Most of them share the cost of that insurance with their employer, and about half receive their medical care from an HMO (health maintenance organization) for a fixed fee. Another 25 percent of Americans are covered by one of two types of public, government-paid insurance: *Medicare,* which pays most of the medical bills for older, retired people, and *Medicaid,* which pays all of the medical expenses of the poor and the disabled. But about 15 percent of the population, or 43 million Americans (12 million more than the entire population of Canada), are left high and dry, without any insurance to protect them in the case of illness or death (Gallup, 2003).

According to a recent Gallup poll, however, a large majority (82 percent) of Americans with either private or public insurance are satisfied with the quality of the medical care they receive. They are critical, though, of the U.S. health care system in general, largely because the media present many more stories of patient dissatisfaction than satisfaction (Gallup, 2003; Chambers, 2000).

■ Facing Death

Advanced medical technology can prolong life. But, ironically, the same technology can also prolong the agony of dying for the hopelessly ill—and the suffering of the families who have to live with their loved one's living death. Today, about 10,000 patients lie irreversibly comatose in hospital beds across the United States, kept alive by machines such as respirators and feeding tubes.

Since the U.S. Supreme Court ruled in 1990 that Nancy Cruzan's parents had the right to remove the feeding tube that kept their comatose daughter alive, a growing number of Americans have come to believe that there is no virtue in heroically prolonging life against the patient's wishes. In fact, most Americans believe that terminally ill patients should be allowed to die with dignity rather than live in a deathlike, vegetative state. In response to this development, all states have passed laws giving patients the right to control their treatment through **living wills**—advance instructions about what they want their doctors to do in the event of a terminal illness. This, in effect, allows patients to die by refusing life-sustaining treatments.

Exercising the right to die, however, is different from carrying out a doctor-assisted suicide, in which the doctor *helps* the patient die by prescribing a deadly drug overdose or providing a suicide machine like the one made by Dr. Jack Kevorkian. In every state except Oregon, it is still a crime for a doctor to assist a patient in committing suicide (Ray, 2003).

DOCTOR DEATH Dr. Jack Kevorkian is currently serving a 10- to 25-year sentence for second-degree murder after giving a lethal injection to a patient suffering from Lou Gehrig's disease. In most states, it is a crime for a doctor to assist a patient in committing suicide. ■

Nevertheless, according to various surveys, anywhere from 7 to 20 percent of U.S. doctors have helped patients end their lives (Lemonick, 1996; Gibbs, 1995). Still, the large majority of U.S. doctors are reluctant to assist suicide, probably because they have been trained to save lives rather than end them or because they are afraid to break the law.

Doctors would not have to face the issue of assisted suicide if they could help patients die more comfortably. Nearly half of U.S. patients die in pain. If the medical profession could eliminate the pain, the terminally ill would stop requesting assisted suicide. But most doctors flinch at using stronger pain medications because of the harsh antidrug laws in the United States. Thus, they use weaker medications on a regular basis even though stronger ones are safe and appropriate. Many physicians also erroneously worry that they will addict or even kill their patients. To solve this problem, medical schools started in 2000 to offer courses in managing pain and other symptoms of the dying. Hopefully, managing pain better will give patients more comfortable deaths (Cloud, 2000).

SOCIOLOGICAL PERSPECTIVES ON HEALTH AND MEDICAL CARE

From the functionalist perspective, we can see the positive aspects of medical care and even the positive functions of sickness for society. In contrast, the conflict perspective directs our attention to the negative side of health and medical care. While these two perspectives deal with the larger issues of health, symbolic interactionism focuses on the direct interaction between doctor and patient.

■ Functionalist Perspective: The Functions of Sick and Healing Roles

According to functionalists, both physicians and patients play roles that contribute to social order. Patients must play the **sick role,** a set of social expectations regarding how an ill person should behave. As discussed in Chapter 2, a role is associated with a status, which, in turn, presents the person with a set of rights and obligations. In his classic definition of the *sick role,* Talcott Parsons (1964) essentially laid out what rights the sick can claim and what obligations they should discharge.

First, their rights:

1. The sick have the right to be taken care of by others because they do not choose to be sick and thus should not be blamed for their illness.
2. They have the right to be exempted from certain social duties. They should not be forced to go to work. Students should be allowed to miss an exam and take it later.

Now, their obligations:

1. The sick are obligated to want to get well. They should not expect to remain ill and use the illness to take advantage of others' love, concern, and care for them or to shirk their work and other social responsibilities.
2. They are obligated to seek technically competent help. In seeing a doctor, they must cooperate to help ensure their recovery.

Doctors have their own rights and obligations in playing the **healing role,** a set of social expectations regarding how a doctor should behave. Basically, doctors are obligated to help the sick get well, as required by the Hippocratic oath, which they take

when beginning their medical careers. At the same time, they have the right to receive appropriate compensation for their work. Because their work is widely regarded as highly important, they may expect to make a great deal of money and enjoy considerable prestige.

Seen from the functionalist perspective, both the sick and the healing roles serve a social control function. They help to prevent illnesses from disrupting economic production, family relations, and social activities. Moreover, the functionalist perspective suggests that the system of medical care helps to maintain the health of society. Thus, functionalists tend to attribute an improvement in the nation's health to medicine, the physician, the medical profession, or some new technology of treatment. Medical discoveries such as the germ theory and medical interventions such as vaccines and drugs are credited for the great victory over infectious diseases. All this, however, is a myth to conflict theorists.

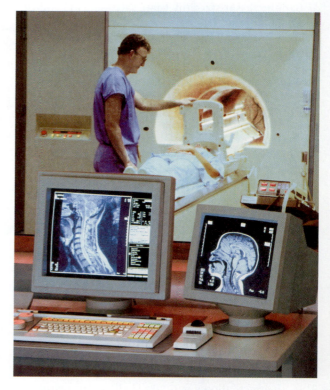

MEDICAL HIT AND MISS Expensive medical advances, such as this MRI (magnetic resonance imaging) machine, have become so popular that they can now be found in most of the hospitals in the United States. According to the conflict perspective, the profit motive has driven corporations to oversell many expensive technological advances, even though they have benefited only a limited number of patients and have not significantly improved the health of the nation as a whole. ■

■ Conflict Perspective: The Negative Aspects of Medical Care

According to conflict theorists, improvements in the social environment contribute far more than medical interventions to the reduction of illness and mortality. As one study has shown, only about 3.5 percent of the total decline in mortality from five infectious diseases (influenza, pneumonia, diphtheria, whooping cough, and poliomyelitis) since 1900 can be attributed to medical measures. In many instances, the new measures to combat those diseases were introduced several decades *after* a substantial decline in mortality from the diseases had occurred (McKinlay and McKinlay, 1987). According to the conflict perspective, this decline in mortality has been brought about mostly by several social and environmental factors: (1) a rising standard of living, (2) better sanitation and hygiene, and (3) improved housing and nutrition (Conrad, 2001).

Conflict theorists, however, do not mean to suggest that modern clinical medicine does not alleviate pain or cure disease in *some individuals*. Their point is that the medical institution fails to bring about significant improvements in the health of *the population as a whole*. Why, then, does U.S. society continue to spend such vast sums of money on medical care? This, according to conflict theorists, has much to do with the pursuit of private profit in a capitalist society.

In his Marxist analysis of coronary care technology, for example, Howard Waitzkin (1987) found that soon after their introduction in the 1960s, the expensive coronary care units became so popular that they could be found in half of all acute-care hospitals in the United States. But the intensive care provided by that medical technology had not been proven to be more effective than simple rest at home. Waitzkin argued that the proliferation of this expensive but relatively ineffective form of treatment could be traced to the profit motive. He found that corporations such as Warner-Lambert Pharmaceutical and Hewlett-Packard had participated in every phase of the research, development, promotion, and dissemination of coronary care technology, which ultimately produced huge profits for them. Waitzkin also noted that the same profit motive had driven corporations to oversell many other expensive technological advances, such as computed tomography and fetal monitoring devices, even though they had not significantly improved the nation's health; they benefited only a limited number of patients.

The conflict perspective further suggests that the unequal distribution of health and medical care reflects the larger social inequality. The poor have higher rates of most diseases than do the rich. The poor are also more likely to receive inadequate or no medical care.

■ Symbolic Interactionist Perspective: The Importance of Doctor–Patient Interaction

An important aspect of medical practice is the symbolic interaction between doctor and patient. As research has suggested, patients tend to evaluate warm, friendly doctors favorably even when these doctors have not provided successful treatment. By contrast, patients are most likely to sue for malpractice those physicians who are the most highly trained and who practice in the most sophisticated hospitals. Although these physicians are not intentionally negligent, they are most likely to be viewed by their patients in general—not just the ones who sue them—as cold and bureaucratic (Twaddle and Hessler, 1987). It is the friendly doctor's affiliative style of communication that enhances patient satisfaction, and it is the highly competent but bureaucratic doctor's dominant style that alienates patients. *Affiliative style* involves behaviors that show honesty, compassion, humor, and a nonjudgmental attitude. *Dominant style* involves the manifestation of power, authority, professional detachment, and status in the physician's interaction with the patient (Buller and Buller, 1987).

Why does the doctor's communication style affect patient satisfaction? From the symbolic interactionist perspective, we can assume that in interacting with patients, friendly doctors are more likely than dominant doctors to take into account the views, feelings, and expectations the patients have about themselves, their illnesses, and their doctors. To the patients, illness is unusual, as it does not happen to them every day, and their suffering is a highly intimate, emotional reality. Thus, they expect their doctors to show a great deal of concern. They obviously want a cure, but they also crave emotional support. If doctors attune themselves to these expectations, they can develop warm relationships with their patients. But this is no easy task because physicians have been trained to take an objective, dispassionate approach to disease. They have learned to view patients unemotionally, especially when performing surgery, which involves inserting their hands in diseased strangers without flinching or losing their nerve (Konner, 2001; Easterbrook, 1987).

Such emotional detachment often intrudes into the medical interview, as well. In a typical doctor–patient encounter, the doctor tends to dominate with questions based on his or her technical understanding of the cause and treatment of the illness, thereby failing to pay attention to the patient's very

theoretical thumbnail

The Nature of Health and Medical Care

Perspective	Focus	Insights
Functionalist	The positivity of sickness and healing	Both sickness and healing, and thus the medical care system, contribute to social order and better health.
Conflict	The negativity of medical care	Providing a better social environment reduces mortality more than medicine does; medical care reflects the profit motive and social inequality.
Symbolic interactionist	The interaction between doctor and patient	Patients are more satisfied with medical treatment if their doctors interact positively with them.

personal sense of the illness. More specifically, after asking a patient "What brings you here today?" the doctor usually interrupts the reply within just 18 seconds. Many doctors also intimidate patients into being silent by, for example, tapping a pencil impatiently or keeping one hand on the door handle. If patients are allowed to speak freely, physicians often respond merely with an "um hum," which indicates only minimal interest (Schrof, 1998b).

myth	Compassionate and sensitive, most doctors listen to their patients' complaints with great attentiveness and understanding.
reality	Most doctors tend to interact poorly with patients. Consequently, about 60 percent of patients fail to adequately understand instructions about their medications.

This detached professionalism tends to exact a price by alienating patients, making them feel that they are being treated as mere cases of disease rather than as people. Such patients are also likely to suffer other consequences. For example, as many as 60 percent of patients leave their doctors' offices confused about medication instructions, and more than half of new prescriptions are taken improperly or not at all (Schrof, 1998b; Nazario, 1992; Winslow, 1989).

For a quick review of the three sociological perspectives on health and medical care, see the Theoretical Thumbnail above.

A GLOBAL ANALYSIS OF POPULATION

The scientific study of population is called **demography.** More than any other area of sociology, demography is based on a large body of reasonably accurate data. Most of these data come from vital statistics and censuses. **Vital statistics** consist of information about births, marriages, deaths, and migrations into and out of a country. Since 1933, the U.S. government has required all states to record these data. The other source of population information, the **census,** is a periodic head count of the entire population of a country. It includes a wealth of data, such as age, sex, education, occupation, and residence.

■ How the Census Is Taken

Census taking has been with us for a long time. As early as 3000 B.C., China conducted a census in some parts of the country for tax purposes. And in biblical times, after the Israelites escaped from Egypt, they listed all men aged 20 and older to assess their military strength. These and other ancient censuses were intended to control particular categories of people—to identify who should be taxed, drafted into military service, or forced to work on certain government projects, such as building the Great Wall in China. Early censuses did not seek to count the entire population—only such categories of people as family heads or males of military age.

By contrast, the modern census, which began to develop in the seventeenth century, is designed to count all people within a country for governmental, scientific, and commercial purposes. A good example is the U.S. census, which has been taken every 10 years since 1790. It is used for determining the number of congressional seats for each state and allocating federal and state funds to local governments. It is also used for scientific analyses of the nation's demographic traits and trends, economic development, and business cycles. Moreover, businesses find useful information in the census data. Orthodontists, for example, can learn where there are many teenagers in high-income households and then establish a business in that area.

EVERYONE COUNTS In taking a census, efforts are made to count everyone. Even so, there is a tendency to miss people who are poor, homeless, and nonwhite, who, if counted, would stand to benefit the most from receiving government funds. Census takers have thus made an extra effort to reach these individuals and with increasing success. In the latest census, only 1.2 percent of the entire U.S. population was missed, compared with 1.6 percent 10 years earlier. ■

But how is a census taken in a huge, complex society like the United States? Taking the latest U.S. census, in 2000, was a massive task. It required the delivery of more than 100 million forms to people throughout the United States, Puerto Rico, Guam, the U.S. Virgin Islands, Samoa, and other U.S.-held Pacific locales. Using a decentralized approach, the U.S. Bureau of the Census, which is part of the Department of Commerce, set up numerous computer-equipped district offices in various parts of the country, hiring mainly local people with a wide variety of backgrounds. Most of the census takers worked part time only, but they all received special training. Their jobs ranged from office managers, data-entry people, and payroll clerks to regular enumerators and Special Place enumerators (who went to such places as bus depots and abandoned buildings to count the homeless). These workers compiled and checked address lists, marked census questionnaires, followed up on nonrespondents, and reported results.

In all of these operations, however, there is a tendency to miss the poor, the homeless, and the nonwhites, who, if counted, would stand to benefit the most from receiving government funds. Thus, the U.S. Census Bureau has made an extra effort to reach these individuals and with increasing success. The latest head count showed that only 1.2 percent of the entire U.S. population had been missed, compared with 1.6 percent in 1990. The 2000 census was also the first in which Americans could identify themselves as having more than one race or ethnicity, but only 2.4 percent of the population did so (Schmitt, 2002; Kulish, 2001; Thornton, 2001).

The 2000 census put the U.S. population at 281 million—an increase of more than 32 million people, or 13 percent, over the 1990 total. Is this number, along with the numbers delineating various subgroups, accurate? The 2000 census was not perfect, but it can be considered highly accurate. It was at least more accurate than any of the past censuses. For instance, in the 1890 census, families were asked if they had any "idiots" and whether their heads were larger or smaller than average. The 1910 census missed most of the numerous immigrants in Chicago, who hid from the counters for fear of being deported. And the 1960 and 1970 censuses seriously undercounted people in many cities, despite the great migration from rural to urban areas that had begun 20 and 30 years earlier (Schmitt, 2002; Anderson and Fienberg, 1999; Roberts, 1990).

Using today's considerably more accurate census data, demographers can tell a great deal about the characteristics of a population. Those characteristics, however, vary from one society to another, influenced by certain social forces, as we will see in the following sections.

■ Population Growth

The world's population is increasing enormously. Nearly 100 million new babies are born every year, a number equal to the size of Mexico's population. Moreover, given the same yearly growth rate, population does not increase *linearly*, with the same number of people added annually. Instead, it grows *exponentially*, with an increasingly larger number of new people appearing in each succeeding year. It works like a savings account, which earns an increasingly larger amount of interest, rather than the same interest, in each succeeding year because it builds on a larger base (the previous year's savings *plus* that year's interest) each year.

Increases in population are therefore far more dramatic in modern times, with large populations, than in ancient times, with small populations. Before the year 1600, it took more than 500,000 years for the human population to reach about half a billion. Thereafter, the population skyrocketed to 6.4 billion in less than 400 years. Today, it takes only 5 or 6 years (in contrast to the 500,000 years before 1600) for the world to produce 500 million people. Figure 13.5 shows the remarkable rate of population growth in the modern era.

myth	The world's large population reflects steady growth over thousands of years.
reality	Most of the world's population growth has occurred in the relatively recent past. Before the modern era began (in 1600), the global population had reached only about half a billion in more than 500,000 years. Since then, in less than 400 years, world population has skyrocketed to more than 6.4 billion.

In general, populations are growing much faster in poor, developing countries than in rich, developed ones. As Figure 13.6 shows, rich nations generally have an annual growth rate of less than 1 percent, but poor nations typically grow at a rate of more than 2 percent. The growth of a nation's population is determined by the number of births minus the number of deaths plus the *net immigration rate*—the excess of people moving into a country (*immigrants*) over those leaving it (*emigrants*). Let us take a closer look at these three determinants of population growth.

■ Birth Rate

The **birth rate** is the number of babies born in a year for every 1,000 members of a population:

$$\frac{\text{Births}}{\text{Total population}} \times 1,000$$

For many years, the birth rates of most industrialized nations have been far below 20 per 1,000 population, whereas those of most agricultural countries have far exceeded 30 per 1,000.

Indeed, people in poor countries tend to have larger families, an average of four or more children,

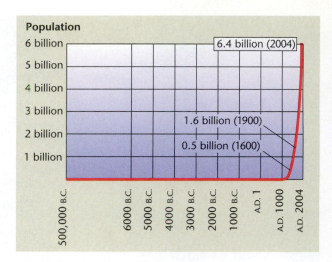

FIGURE 13.5

How the World's Population Grows

In recent history, the world's population has experienced exponential growth. Before the modern era began in 1600, it had taken more than 500,000 years for global population to reach only about half a billion. But since then, it has taken fewer than 400 years for the population to skyrocket to more than 6.4 billion today.

Critical Thinking: *Will the world's remarkable population growth affect your life 10 or 20 years from now? Why or why not?*

Source: Data from Population Reference Bureau, 2004. Available online: www.ibiblio.org/lunarbin/worldpop.

than people in rich countries, who have an average of about two children per family. Because of high birth rates in past years, poor countries also have very large numbers of women entering their childbearing years. As a result, even if these women average fewer children than their mothers did, their nations' birth rates will remain high. Meanwhile, developed countries are close to or already experiencing *zero population growth*, a situation in which the population stops growing. Consequently, well over 90 percent of the world's population increase in coming decades will occur in the poorest nations.

Why do people in rich nations have fewer babies? One reason is access to effective and convenient methods of birth control. Another is the nuclear family system. Unlike a married couple in an extended family, who have many relatives to help raise their children, couples in nuclear families must assume all the responsibility for their children's care. More fundamental than these two reasons is a third—industrialization. In agricultural societies, children are economic assets; they can help with the farmwork. In industrialized societies, however, children are eco-

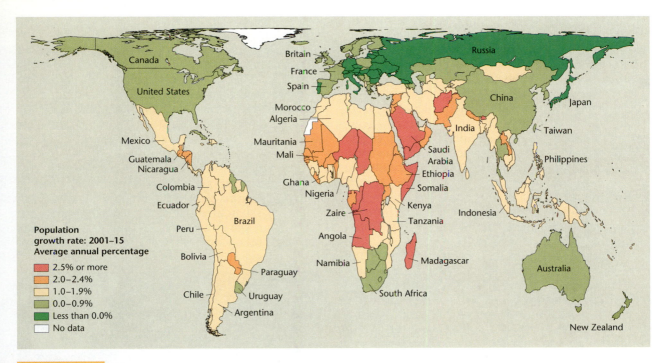

Population
growth rate: 2001–15
Average annual percentage

■ 2.5% or more
■ 2.0–2.4%
□ 1.0–1.9%
■ 0.0–0.9%
■ Less than 0.0%
□ No data

FIGURE 13.6

Population Growth around the Globe

Generally, the population of a poor country grows much more than the population of a rich country. This is largely due to the poor country's much higher birth rate.

Critical Thinking: *Other than practicing birth control, what would you recommend people in poor countries do to reduce the birth rate?*

Source: *World Bank Atlas,* 2003.

nomic liabilities. They depend on their families for financial support, but they cannot contribute significantly to their families' incomes. Industrialization is also associated with two other related factors that hold down fertility: the entrance of women into the workforce and a preference for small families. If women join the workforce, they may find the prospect of raising children too difficult. A preference for small families is then more likely to take hold.

■ Death Rate

The **death rate** is the number of deaths in a year for every 1,000 members of a population. Rich nations have an average of 10 deaths per 1,000 population, and poor nations average 13. The difference is surprisingly small. In fact, death rates obscure the large gap between rich and poor nations in health and living conditions. Because the percentage of young people is much higher in developing countries than in developed ones and the percentage of old people is much lower, the death rates in both kinds of nations are more similar than we might expect.

To compare the health and living conditions of nations, demographers therefore use refined rates, especially the **infant mortality rate**, which shows the number of deaths among infants less than 1 year old for every 1,000 live births. The average infant mortality rate is 6 in developed countries but 49 in developing countries. Another indicator of health conditions is **life expectancy**, the average number of years that a group of people can expect to live. If the group being considered is a nation's newborn infants, then the average life expectancy in developing nations is 64 compared with 78 for industrialized nations (World Bank, 2001).

At least two factors shape death rates and life expectancies. One is medical practice. Immunization of children, for example, has greatly reduced the number of deaths resulting from infectious diseases, and death rates in many poor nations today are being reduced because modern medical practices have been brought there. But early in the twentieth century, U.S. life expectancy improved *before* modern medicine could make a substantial contribution to health. The improvement resulted from a second factor that often leads to better health: wealth. As living standards rose, nutrition and sanitation improved, and the life expectancy in the United States rose as a result.

■ International Migration

International migration—movement of people from one country to another—obviously does not increase or decrease the world's population, but it may greatly alter the population of a specific country. Israel is a case in point. For several years after it was established in 1948, Israel experienced a tremendous annual population growth of 24 percent. Ninety percent of this growth was a result of immigration by European Jews. Another notable example is the United States. Between 1880 and 1910, more than 28 million European immigrants settled in the United States. In the last 30 years, the United States has further attracted millions of immigrants from Latin America and Asia (Schmitt, 2001c; Wrong, 1990).

The effect of immigration goes beyond the immediate addition to the population. Most immigrants are young adults from lower-class families—categories with relatively high fertility rates. As a result, through their children and grandchildren, the immigrants multiply population growth, producing an effect that echoes throughout the years.

Both *pushes* and *pulls* stimulate international migrations. The push typically comes from economic hardship, which compels people to leave their country; the pull comes from economic opportunity elsewhere. A hundred years ago, nearly half of Ireland's population was pushed out of the country by its great potato famine and pulled into the United States by the country's reputation for providing economic opportunity. Today, there is a worldwide mass movement of people from various poor countries to more prosperous ones. Why is this happening now? After all, poverty has existed from time immemorial. The answer is that we have had two revolutions. One is the information revolution, which enables people, even the very poor, to know what life is like in other parts of the world. Another is the transportation revolution, which makes it much easier than before for people to travel long distances.

Economics, however, is not behind all migrations. Political and religious oppression have motivated many people to brave the uncertainties of a new land. Some 70 years ago, millions of Jews fled persecution in Nazi Germany. More recently, hundreds of thousands of Vietnamese and Cubans escaped communist oppression in their homelands. In the 1990s, many Jews left behind their oppressive lives in the former Soviet Union, immigrating to Israel and the United States. Similarly, since 1990, hostility toward ethnic minorities throughout Eastern Europe and other poor countries has spurred migration to rich countries.

But since the early 2000s, sentiment against immigrants has grown sharply. Today, most of the rich countries in the world have toughened their anti-immigration policies by tightening border controls and detaining or repatriating immigrants (Birrell, 2003).

■ Age, Gender, and Marriage

Other characteristics of a population also influence its growth. Among the most important factors are the age structure, sex ratio, and marriage rate.

The **age structure**—the pattern of the proportions of different age groups within a population—shapes the birth rate. Compared with industrialized coun-

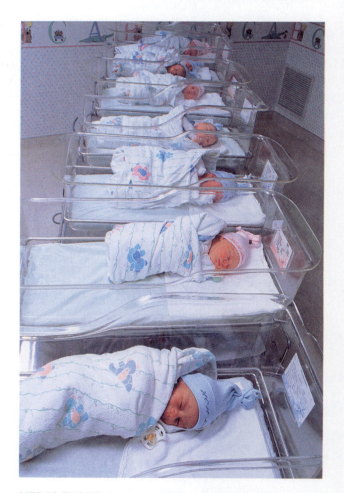

LIFE IS SHORT In most societies, slightly more boys are born than girls, but males have higher death rates. As a result, females outnumber males in the population as a whole. In the United States, about 105 boys are born for every 100 girls each year, but because males die sooner than females, the sex ratio for the entire population is 95 rather than 105. ■

tries, developing countries generally have very low percentages of old people and high percentages of children. Since the current large numbers of children will grow up to produce children themselves, future birth rates in these nations are likely to be high. The age structure also affects the death rate. If two nations have equally healthy populations and living conditions, the country with the higher percentage of older people will have a higher death rate.

The **sex ratio** indicates the number of males per 100 females. A sex ratio of more than 100 means that there are more males than females. If the sex ratio is 100, the number of males equals the number of females. In most societies, slightly more boys are born than girls, but males have higher death rates. As a result, females outnumber males in the population as a whole. The sex ratio for young adults is about even in normal times, but it falls in wartime because wars are fought mostly by men. In the United States, about 105 males are born for every 100 females each year (representing a sex ratio of 105), but because males die sooner than females, the sex ratio for the entire population is 97 (U.S. Census Bureau, 2003).

If the sex ratio is close to 100, then the **marriage rate**—the number of marriages in a given year for every 1,000 people—is likely to be high. Because more babies are born to married than to unmarried couples, a high marriage rate will likely bring a high birth rate. When soldiers came home from World War II, for example, the U.S. marriage rate went up and the baby boom followed. Since 1960, the numbers of unmarried adults, late marriages, and divorces in the United States have all increased, partly helping to bring down the birth rate.

PATTERNS OF POPULATION CHANGE

Demographers can tell us a great deal about how populations are changing. The most influential explanations of population change are the Malthusian theory and the theory of demographic transition. Demographers also can offer insight into the actual consequences of population change.

■ Malthusian Theory

In 1798, English clergyman and economist Thomas Malthus (1766–1834) published a truly dismal portrait of population dynamics in *An Essay on the Principles of Population*. He argued that population grows much faster than the production of food supplies because a population *multiplies* but food production increases only by *addition*—through the cultivation of land. Thus, population typically in-

creases geometrically (2, 4, 8, 16, . . .), but food supplies increase only arithmetically (2, 3, 4, 5, . . .). As a population outstrips its food supply, it will be afflicted by war, disease, and poverty. Eventually, population growth will stop.

People could bring a stop to this growth through what Malthus called "preventive checks"—that is, late marriage and sexual restraint, which would reduce the birth rate. But Malthus doubted that people, especially the lower classes, had the will to exercise such restraint. Instead, he argued, population growth would eventually be stopped by nature. Its tools would be what Malthus called "positive checks"—disease and famine.

Malthus failed to foresee three revolutions that undermined his theory: the revolutions in contraception, agricultural technology, and medicine. He did not anticipate the development of effective and convenient contraceptives such as the pill and the IUD (intrauterine contraceptive device), nor did he expect birth control to become widespread. In the West, especially, the use of contraceptives has helped bring birth rates down to a point lower than Malthus thought possible. Meanwhile, the technological revolution has allowed farmers to increase food production by raising the yield of their land, not just by adding farmland. Finally, medical advances have given us an arsenal of effective weapons against the contagious diseases that Malthus expected would devastate overpopulated nations.

As a result, disease and famine have not decimated the world's population, including most of the overpopulated nations in Asia, Latin America, and Africa. It can thus be concluded that the awful fate Malthus predicted has not come to pass for most of the world. But his prediction is coming true for some countries in Africa, where famine is common and AIDS is killing over one-third of the population (see Figure 13.7, p. 390). Moreover, Malthus's theory serves as a valuable warning to all nations that populations cannot expand indefinitely; natural resources are finite.

■ The Demographic Transition

Most demographers subscribe to the **demographic transition** theory, which states that human populations tend to go through specific demographic stages and that these stages are tied to economic development. This theory is based on the population changes that have occurred in Western Europe during the past 200 years. According to the theory, there are four demographic stages, as shown in Figure 13.8 (p. 391).

In the first stage, both birth rates and death rates are high. Because the two rates more or less balance each other, the population is fairly stable, neither growing nor declining rapidly. This was the stage of

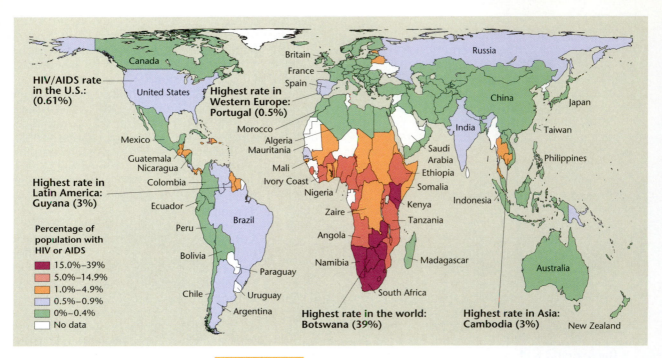

FIGURE 13.7

Global Distribution of HIV/AIDS

The Malthusian theory predicts that because human population grows faster than the food supply, famine and disease will occur and decimate the population. This prediction has not come true for most overpopulated countries, but it seems likely for some African nations, where AIDS is killing over one-third of the population.

Critical Thinking: *Could the Malthusian nightmare ever happen in the United States? Why or why not?*

Source: Data from UNAIDS, Joint United Nations Programme on HIV/AIDS, 2003.

the populations in Western Europe in 1650, before industrialization.

myth	The fact that poor countries have high birth rates is virtually the only reason for their tremendous population growth.
reality	Modern medicine, along with better hygiene and sanitation, also contributes to population growth by sharply reducing death rates.

During the second stage, the birth rate remains high but the death rate declines sharply. This stage occurred in Western Europe after it became industrialized, and it is occurring today in many developing nations. The introduction of modern medicine, along with better hygiene and sanitation, has decreased the death rates in developing countries. But the economies and values of these countries are still essentially traditional, so their birth rates remain high. As a result, their populations grow rapidly.

During the third stage, both birth rates and death rates decline. Western countries found themselves in this stage after they reached a rather high level of industrialization. Today, Taiwan, South Korea, and Argentina are among the developing nations that have reached this stage. The birth rates in these countries have declined significantly. In this stage, the population still grows because the birth rate continues to exceed the death rate, but growth is slower than during the second stage.

myth	Population growth is inevitable; the population of every country continues to grow.
reality	While poor countries continue to experience population growth, rich countries, such as those in Western Europe, are close to having or already have *zero population growth*, a situation in which the population stops growing.

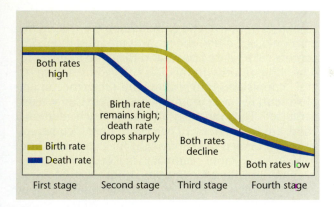

First stage — Both rates high

Second stage — Birth rate remains high; death rate drops sharply

Third stage — Both rates decline

Fourth stage — Both rates low

■ Birth rate
■ Death rate

FIGURE 13.8

The Demographic Transition

According to the demographic transition theory, human populations tend to go through four stages, each of which is tied to a specific condition of society. In the last (fourth) stage, for example, both the birth and death rates are low, which is characteristic of today's highly industrialized societies, such as Germany and other European countries.

Critical Thinking: *Will the U.S. population shrink like the German population because of a falling birth rate? Why or why not?*

The fourth stage is marked by a low birth rate and a low death rate. Only the most industrialized nations of Western Europe, the United States, and Japan have reached this stage. They have fairly stable populations and are moving close to zero population growth. At least 40 countries, such as Italy, Spain, and Germany, have already fallen below zero growth, with birth rates lower than death rates; in other words, the fertility rate is less than the replacement level.

To proponents of the demographic transition theory, the future of human populations looks bright. They believe that developing countries will eventually join the industrialized world and have stable populations. To critics of the theory, the future is far less certain. There is at least one major difference between the developing countries of today and the European nations of 200 years ago: Thanks to modern medicine, death rates in developing countries have declined far more rapidly than they did in nineteenth-century Europe. While it took Europe 200 years to lower its mortality, it takes developing countries today only a year or so. At the same time, their birth rates remain high. As a result, the population is exploding in the developing world today, a condition that did not occur in nineteenth-century Europe.

■ Demographic Fallout

The fallout from the population explosion can be seen in the oppressive poverty of many developing nations. Their cities are filled with people who live in overcrowded shacks and with others who must live on the streets, sidewalks, vacant lots, rooftops, and cemeteries. In these poor countries, most people are undernourished, and malnutrition is devastating 163 million children under age 5, weakening their bodies and minds. Some 11 million children die of starvation every year (United Nations, 2001; Ehrlich, 1984).

The rapidly growing populations of developing nations seriously complicate their efforts to fight poverty. Instead of climbing up the economic ladder, these nations are on a treadmill, constantly in danger of slipping backward into Malthusian famine. Economic investment can barely keep up with the rapid population growth. More than half of Africa's economic expansion, for example, has been used just to maintain the expanding population at a subsistence level. More than 40 percent of Africa's population is already living below the region's poverty line. Some African countries, such as Ethiopia, Somalia, and the Sudan, have experienced and will continue to face massive starvation. Other developing countries in Asia and Latin America, though, have made significant progress against poverty by slowing population growth and hastening economic growth.

COMBATING POPULATION GROWTH

Individuals have practiced birth control of various types for thousands of years. But many nations, at various times in their histories, have sought to *increase* their populations because they have associated a large population with great military power and national security. Religious, medical, and political authorities have often argued against birth control. For more than a century, the United States even had laws that prohibited the mailing of birth control information and devices.

During the 1950s and 1960s, however, many governments began to see population growth as a social problem. By 1984, most countries, representing about 95 percent of the world's population, had formulated official policies to combat population growth (Russell, 1984; Davis, 1976). These policies can be classified into two types: encouragement of voluntary family planning and compulsory population control.

■ Voluntary Family Planning

Some countries make contraceptives available to anyone who wants them. They encourage birth control, but they do not try to impose a limit on how many children a couple may have. For this voluntary family planning to work, however, people must prefer small families to large ones; otherwise, they will not use birth control.

This is the heart of the problem with family planning. Family-planning programs have reduced birth rates significantly in advanced developing countries such as Taiwan and South Korea because these societies value small families. Family planning is even more successful in the more industrialized nations of the West, where the preference for small families is strong. However, many less advanced developing countries, such as those in sub–Saharan Africa, retain the preference for large families typical of agricultural societies. In these societies, having many children is a status enhancer, particularly for the less educated. Children are also considered a form of old-age pension because there are no social welfare systems like the ones available in the United States. Because many children die young, parents are even more anxious to have large families to increase their chances of being looked after in their senior years.

As a result, voluntary planning programs in these poor societies have failed to reduce birth rates significantly. This has led the governments of some countries to resort to compulsory programs.

■ Compulsory Population Control

In the early 1970s, India forced those government employees who had more than two children to undergo sterilization. With the encouragement of the central government, some states in India also forced men to be sterilized after their second child was born. If the men refused, they could be fined $250 and imprisoned for up to a year. In some villages, overzealous government officials rounded up and sterilized all the men without checking how many children they had. The program stirred up widespread opposition. Sociologist Frank Notestein predicted in 1971 that if a developing country tried to force its people to practice birth control, it "would be more likely to bring down the government than the birth rate." Indeed, the sterilization program apparently contributed to the fall of Prime Minister Indira Gandhi's government in 1977.

Since then, India has returned to a voluntary program. But it has been difficult to control the relentless population growth because of low literacy and a dearth of sustained family-planning information and services. Thus, in 2001, the government began once again to encourage the use of sterilization, but this time resorting to incentives rather than coercion. Poor people who are sterilized can now expect to get such benefits as houses, plots of land, wells, and loans. This has helped reduce India's fertility rate from five children per woman in the 1980s to three today (Naik et al., 2003; Dugger, 2001).

China has had more success with a program that combines rewards and punishments. For a couple with only one child, the rewards are substantial. The parents get a salary bonus, and the child receives free schooling, priority in medical care, admission to the best schools and universities, and preference in employment. By contrast, multichild parents are severely penalized. They must pay all costs for each additional child, are taxed about 10 percent of their income, and are often denied job promotion for two years. Since this one-child family campaign began in 1979, China has sharply reduced its fertility, from six children per woman to only two today, a record unmatched by any other developing nation (Chang, 2001).

Beginning in 1986, however, the government relaxed its one-child policy—by allowing rural couples to have a second baby if their firstborn was a girl. One reason for the relaxation has been the increasing prosperity among the Chinese, many of whom are willing to pay the fines for having more than one child. Another reason is the international criticism that China has received for pressuring women to abort fetuses even late in pregnancy. A third reason is that the one-child policy has encouraged, albeit unintentionally, the killing of female infants by parents who hope to have sons. Nevertheless, China continues to exhort couples to have only one child, though it now focuses on persuasion, education, and publicity campaigns rather than coercion and penalties. This has been quite successful with urban couples, though it tends to fall on deaf ears with rural couples, who generally have two children (Chang, 2001; Rosenthal, 1998b).

■ U.S. Population Policy

In the 1960s, the U.S. government began to recognize global population growth as a potential problem; by 1968, it had spent several hundred million dollars to help developing countries. During the conservative Reagan and Bush administrations in the 1980s and early 1990s, however, the U.S. government suspended aid to countries that advocated abortion as a family-planning operation. The more liberal Clinton administration restored the aid. But the current Bush administration refuses to support family-planning programs here and abroad that include the use of abortion (Purdum, 2002).

Birth Control The federal government has been spending over $100 million a year to assist family-planning centers. But the U.S. population growth has slowed primarily because of social and economic factors, not government action. In fact, family planning has become the norm rather than the exception. Even the majority of U.S. Catholics practice forms of birth

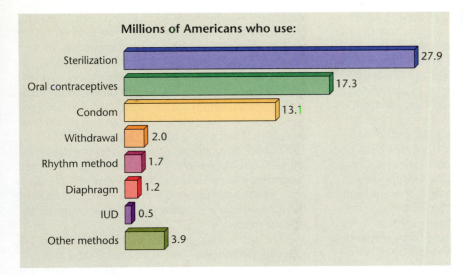

Millions of Americans who use:

- Sterilization — 27.9
- Oral contraceptives — 17.3
- Condom — 13.1
- Withdrawal — 2.0
- Rhythm method — 1.7
- Diaphragm — 1.2
- IUD — 0.5
- Other methods — 3.9

FIGURE 13.9

Contraceptive Choices in the United States

Family planning has become the norm rather than the exception. Even the majority of American Catholics practice forms of birth control frowned on by their church. The uses of sterilization and condoms have increased the most because of concern over the side effects of the pill and IUD.

Critical Thinking: *Which method of contraception would you use to prevent pregnancy and why?*

Source: Data from U.S. Census Bureau, 2003.

control forbidden by their church. Today, sterilization is the most popular type of birth control in the United States, followed by the pill and the condom (see Figure 13.9). The use of sterilization and the condom has increased faster than most other methods because of concern and controversy over the side effects of the pill and the IUD (Ingrassia, 1995).

All these contraceptives are antiquated; the pill and the IUD, for example, were introduced 40 years ago. In 1990, a more convenient and effective contraceptive called Norplant was approved for use in the United States. First introduced in Europe 30 years ago, Norplant, which is implanted in the woman's upper arm, can protect against pregnancy for 5 years. In 1997, the French abortion pill RU-486 was officially approved as a safe and effective alternative to surgical abortion for U.S. women.

The use of more traditional contraception and abortion is already prevalent. If the new options become popular, the U.S. birth rate may soon drop to below the replacement rate, and the nation will rely increasingly on immigration to stop its population from declining.

Immigration   Today, both legal and illegal immigration account for about 26 percent of the nation's population growth. But that proportion is expected to rise to 50 percent in the first half of the twenty-first century, and then immigration will comprise the bulk of the nation's population growth in the second half of that century (U.S. Census Bureau, 2003). History has shown how immigration has contributed to the prosperity of this country. Hoping to benefit the U.S. economy more quickly, Congress has passed a law to admit larger numbers of highly educated and skilled immigrants, such as scientists, engineers, and medical technicians, as Canada and Australia have done for years (Pear, 1997).

But opposition to the admission of poor and unskilled immigrants, especially illegals, has sharply increased over the last decade. In 1994, California began to deny illegal immigrants most government services, and in 1996, the U.S. government began to stop providing legal immigrants with most federal benefits, such as food stamps and cash assistance for the poor and disabled. Throughout the nation today, there is widespread fear that immigrants take jobs from U.S. workers, particularly low-skilled workers. But supporters of immigration suspect racism because most of the immigrants come from nonwhite countries rather than Europe. Besides, Americans would not do the menial work that's done by most immigrants (O'Grady, 2003; Jacoby, 2002).

sociological frontiers

Societal Reactions to Stem Cell Research

In recent years, medical researchers have sought cures for many serious illnesses, including diabetes, multiple sclerosis, paralysis, Alzheimer's, Parkinson's, and heart disease. Since each of these illnesses involves cell death as a causal factor, researchers have tried to study new, healthy *stem cells* with the hope of using them to effect a cure. These new cells are so far available from four sources.

First, there are the existing cell lines, which are estimated to number about 60 from fertility clinics all over the world, according to the Bush administration's scientists. These cell lines are clumps of stem cells that have already been harvested from leftover embryos created for reproduction. (Couples whose eggs and sperm are used to create these embryos through in-vitro fertilization normally use just one and donate the rest to researchers.) Second, there are still thousands of other leftover embryos in fertility labs that are waiting to be donated, adopted by infertile couples, or discarded. Third, sperm and egg can be combined in petri dishes to create embryos for research rather than reproduction. And fourth, a human embryo could be cloned from inserting a patient's cell (such as from the skin) into a woman's egg. The stem cells from this cloned embryo could produce a specific tissue for curing the patient's illness. Because the new cloned tissue would be a perfect genetic match for the patient, there would be no rejection problems like those faced by patients who receive new tissues from noncloned embryos.

The Bush administration has decided to use federal funds to support research *only* on the existing cell lines. It opposes the other three methods of producing and harvesting stem cells because they eventually cause the embryos to die, which to some is the same as destroying human lives. Most Americans (60 percent) approve this decision, while 34 percent disapprove and 6 percent have no opinion. Most Republicans (79 percent) also approve of the Bush administration's decision, but 52 percent of Democrats disapprove (Jones, 2001). Even more scientists disapprove, considering the policy too restrictive. To them, if the thousands of other surplus embryos are made available for research, the chances of finding the cures for those illnesses—and quickly—will be greatly enhanced.

The lack of societal support for medical innovations is not new. Vaccines were initially found objectionable because they were believed to interfere with God's plan for who should get sick. In vitro fertilization was condemned in the 1970s for the possibility of creating monsters in the same way that therapeutic human cloning is today. And recombinant DNA technology for creating synthetic genes was banned from universities for years because it was feared capable of producing horrible and dangerous creatures (Fischer, 2001).

 ■ For more of the latest Sociological Frontiers, look up Continuing Update at www.ablongman.com/thio6e.

using *sociology*

How to Be a Savvy E-Patient

Cyberspace is full of health sites and data. Here are some good ways to use them to become better acquainted with your illnesses and to help your doctors treat them effectively (Landro, 2001, 2003):

1. *Consider joining an online support group.* You will likely feel comfortable sharing even your intimate concerns with people who have the same disease, and you may learn how to deal with your illness in ways that you cannot pick up from your closest friends and family members.

2. *Double-check the information you find online.* To guard against inaccurate, misleading, or outdated information, check several sites to ensure they all give the same or similar information. You can also e-mail your questions to an online health professional.

3. *Use the net to supplement your face-to-face doctor visits, not to replace them.* Once you get a confirmed diagnosis, you can research your illness and the available treatments. But you will still need professional help to develop a treatment plan tailored specifically to your needs.

4. *Use the web to help evaluate the information and advice your doctor gives you.* If you have doubts about your care, ask your online support group or other online patients to assess your treatment. In most cases, you will find it appropriate and customary. If doubts persist, use the net to explore alternatives.

5. *Tell your doctor what you have found online.* Be an assertive, not aggressive, patient. Express your feelings and views honestly and openly while showing respect for your doctor. Your doctor will then be better able to understand and respond to your needs.

6. *Go online to get referrals to the best doctors and treatment centers you can find.* In the old, pre-Internet days, most patients had no other option than to accept whatever their doctors told them. Now, patients can play a much more active role in diagnosing their ailments and choosing the appropriate treatment and doctor.

7. *Try to understand your doctors if they are not ready to become net friendly.* Don't be pushy with them. They may already be overwhelmed by their clinical responsibilities. Besides, they may feel uneasy at having their opinions questioned or uncomfortable with their own patients consulting other sources for information and advice.

Thinking critically, what would you do if you discovered your doctor to be net unfriendly, aside from showing understanding?

■ CHAPTER REVIEW

1. *How does the health of U.S. residents compare with that of residents of other industrial nations?* Americans have lower life expectancy and higher infant mortality. *What social factors influence health?* One factor is age: Older people are more likely to suffer from chronic illnesses. Another factor is gender: Women live longer than men for biological and sociological reasons. African, Hispanic, and Native Americans

also have lower life expectancies and higher illness rates than whites. Low-income people, too, are more likely than higher-income people to become ill.

2. *Can epidemiology track down the social causes of diseases?* Yes. It can do so by finding out who has the disease and what all the victims have in common. *How has HIV/AIDS spread?* It has spread mostly through unprotected sex and intravenous drug use. *What are the social consequences of the AIDS epidemic?* There is a lot of fear about the disease and discrimination against people with AIDS. *What is the nature of smoking?* Although smoking can cause serious illnesses, more than one-fourth of Americans smoke regularly, primarily because they believe that the benefits of smoking outweigh the costs.

3. *How did the medical profession change in the 1990s?* Doctors' autonomy eroded, their prestige declined, and their competence was more open to challenge by laypersons. *How does gender bias in medical research affect women?* Because medical knowledge is derived from studies of men only, the treatment based on this knowledge can be inappropriate and dangerous to women. The lack of research on women's diseases further prolongs their suffering.

4. *Who is likely to seek medical care when ill?* Those who visit physicians more often are the elderly, women, African Americans, and whites. Mexican Americans, Native Americans, and the residents of Chinatowns are more likely to rely on folk medicine and less likely to visit physicians. The poor are more likely than others to go to public clinics and emergency rooms.

5. *What is wrong with the U.S. health care system?* The primary problem is the high cost of health care; another issue is the lack of health insurance for many Americans. Most Americans are satisfied with the quality of the medical care they get, however. *Do terminally ill patients have the right to die?* Yes, but they may exercise the right to die only by refusing life-sustaining treatments. In most states, doctors may not help patients commit suicide, though support for such suicide is growing.

6. *How do functionalists and conflict theorists view health and medical care?* To functionalists, the sick role and the healing role contribute to social order, and the system of medical care significantly maintains health or reduces illness. But to conflict theorists, a better social environment reduces mortality from diseases much more than medicine does. In this view, medical care and technology reflect the pursuit of private profit and the practice of social inequality

in a capitalist society. *How can symbolic interactionism shed light on the doctor–patient relationship?* If doctors take into account patients' own views about themselves, their illnesses, and their doctors, patients are likely to be happy with the medical treatment they receive.

7. *Why is the modern census better than the earlier ones?* The modern census seeks to achieve its governmental, scientific, and commercial objectives by employing an enormous number of trained census takers and by making extra efforts to reach typically hard-to-reach people, such as the poor.

8. *What determines a nation's growth rate?* It is the birth rate plus the net immigration rate minus the death rate. *What social factors hold down the birth rate?* Access to effective birth control methods, substitution of nuclear families for extended families, industrialization, movement of women into the labor force, and a preference for small families are all significant factors. *What social factors lower the death rate?* The availability of modern medicine and wealth or high living standards lower the death rate. *What motivates migrations?* The push of deprivation and oppression and the pull of opportunity and freedom elsewhere are often the key motives. *What other factors influence population growth?* The age structure, sex ratio, and marriage rate are all influential.

9. *What are two prominent theories regarding population patterns?* According to the Malthusian theory, human populations tend to grow faster than food supplies. As a population outstrips its supply of food, it is afflicted by war, disease, poverty, and even famine, which eventually stop population growth. Malthus's predictions have been derailed by contraceptive, technological, and medical revolutions. According to the theory of demographic transition, human populations go through four specific stages, which are tied to economic development.

10. *How can governments control population growth?* They can do so by encouraging voluntary family planning and setting up compulsory population programs. But family-planning programs work only if people prefer to have small families, and compulsory programs may meet stiff opposition. China, however, has reduced its birth rate through a basically compulsory program that combines rewards for small families and punishments for large families. *Does the U.S. government control population growth?* No, but it does give some aid to family-planning centers. Social and economic factors, not government action, keep birth rates low, whereas immigration helps contribute to population growth.

11. *How do Americans feel about stem cell research?* Most Americans—especially Republicans—support the limited use of stem cells for research, while most Democrats and scientists favor greater access to stem cells. *How can we use the Internet to improve the health care we receive?* We can, among other things, join an online support group, use the net to evaluate our doctor's advice, and surf the net to find the best treatments and doctors.

KEY TERMS

Age structure   The pattern of the proportions of different age groups within a population (p. 388).

Birth rate   The number of babies born in a year for every 1,000 members of a given population (p. 386).

Census   A periodic head count of the entire population of a country (p. 384).

Death rate   The number of deaths in a year for every 1,000 members of a population (p. 387).

Demographic transition   The theory that human populations tend to go through specific demographic stages and that these stages are tied to a society's economic development (p. 389).

Demography   The scientific study of population (p. 384).

Epidemiology   The study of the origin and spread of disease within a population (p. 373).

Healing role   A set of social expectations regarding how a doctor should behave (p. 382).

Infant mortality rate   The number of deaths among infants less than 1 year old for every 1,000 live births (p. 387).

Life expectancy   The average number of years that a group of people can expect to live (p. 387).

Living will   Advance instructions about what someone wants doctors to do in the event of a terminal illness (p. 381).

Marriage rate   The number of marriages in a given year for every 1,000 people (p. 389).

Sex ratio   The number of males per 100 females (p. 389).

Sick role   A set of social expectations regarding how an ill person should behave (p. 382).

Vital statistics   Information about births, marriages, deaths, and migrations into and out of a country (p. 384).

QUESTIONS FOR DISCUSSION AND REVIEW

HEALTH AND SOCIETY

1. How does health in the United States compare with that in other countries?
2. What is the nature of the social diversity in U.S. health?
3. What is epidemiology, and how does it help doctors locate the causes of disease?
4. What are the sources of HIV/AIDS, and how does society respond to its victims?
5. Who is most likely to smoke, and why do they smoke?

MEDICAL CARE

1. What are some recent changes in the medical profession?
2. How is sexism reflected in medical research?
3. How do social factors determine who might seek medical care?
4. Why has the cost of health care risen so dramatically over the last 30 years?
5. Should doctor-assisted suicide be allowed? Why or why not?

SOCIOLOGICAL PERSPECTIVES ON HEALTH AND MEDICAL CARE

1. How do the roles played by patients and physicians contribute to the social order?
2. What facts about U.S. health care do conflict theorists emphasize?
3. What is the nature of the doctor–patient relationship?

A GLOBAL ANALYSIS OF POPULATION

1. What is demography?
2. How are demographic data collected?
3. What influences birth rates, death rates, and international migration?
4. What are the age structure, sex ratio, and marriage rate of a population?

PATTERNS OF POPULATION CHANGE

1. How would a Malthusian theorist's view of current world population patterns differ from that of a demographic transitionist?
2. What is the demographic fallout of a population explosion?

COMBATING POPULATION GROWTH

1. How does family planning differ from population control?

2. What has been the result of compulsory birth control programs in overpopulated countries such as India and China?
3. What kinds of contraceptives are commonly used to keep the birth rate low in the United States?
4. How has the U.S. government dealt with the immigration issue?

SOCIOLOGICAL FRONTIERS/USING SOCIOLOGY

1. What kinds of stem cell research does the Bush administration support and oppose?
2. How can we use the Internet to understand and manage our health better?

SUGGESTED READINGS

Anderson, Margo J., and Stephen E. Fienberg. 1999. *Who Counts? The Politics of Census-Taking in Contemporary America*. New York: Russell Sage Foundation. Presents an interesting history of the census and a detailed discussion of current key issues, especially the problem of undercounting.

Evans, Robert G., Morris L. Barer, and Theodore R. Marmor (eds.). 1994. *Why Are Some People Healthy and Others Not?* New York: Aldine de Gruyter. A collection of articles on the social causes of health.

Petersen, William. 2000. *From Birth to Death: A Consumer's Guide to Population Studies*. New Brunswick, NJ: Transaction. A highly readable and stimulating presentation of many demographic subjects, ranging from fertility and mortality to the use of contraceptives and Malthusian theory.

Rose, Peter I. 1997. *Tempest-Tost: Race, Immigration, and the Dilemmas of Diversity*. New York: Oxford University Press. A collection of highly readable articles about how U.S. society has changed as a result of the massive immigration of various racial and ethnic groups.

Sullivan, Deborah A. 2001. *Cosmetic Surgery: The Cutting Edge of Commercial Medicine in America*. New Brunswick, NJ: Rutgers University Press. Shows how cosmetic surgery has become the most commercialized form of medicine, with surgeons frequently resorting to blatant advertising to drum up business.

■ Additional Resources

The New York Times
expect the world®
nytimes.com

Expand your knowledge of the concepts discussed in this chapter by reading the following current and historical articles from the *New York Times*. Go to the "eThemes of the Times" section of the Companion Website (www.ablongman.com/thio6e):

"Big Increase Seen in People Lacking Health Insurance"

"WHO Declaring Crisis, Plans a Big Push with AIDS Drug"

Research Navigator.com

Research Navigator, a research database, provides immediate access to hundreds of full-text articles from EBSCO's ContentSelect Academic Journal Database. If the Research Navigator access code was included with your textbook, go to the website www.researchnavigator.com and read the following articles related to this chapter by typing in the article number:

Barber, Jennifer S., Lisa D. Pearce, Indra Chaudhury, and Susan Gurung. "Voluntary Associations and Fertility Limitation." *Social Forces*, Jun2002, Vol. 80 Issue 4, p1369, 33p. Accession Number: 6767704. Investigates how participation in and exposure to voluntary associations influences fertility-limiting behavior.

Wells, N. Ree, and Norman A. Dolch, "Medical Sociology—Issues for the New Millenium." *Sociological Spectrum*, Jul2001, Vol. 21 Issue 3, p237, 9p. Accession Number: 4974777. Reviews the growth of medical sociology as a branch of sociology.

chapter 14

Environment and Urbanization

myths & realities

myth *The U.S. environment is worse today than ever before.*

reality The environment is now mostly better, thanks to various efforts since 1970 to protect it (p. 404).

myth *Most of the world's large cities—such as New York and Tokyo—are in prosperous, industrialized countries.*

reality Generally, the poorer the country, the faster its urban growth. As a result, more than half of the world's megacities are now in developing countries (p. 408).

myth *Suburbs mostly continue to be so-called bedroom communities—places where people live but from which they commute to the nearby large cities to work.*

reality Today, many suburbs have become cities in their own right, where new office buildings, factories, and warehouses have sprung up alongside residential homes and shopping malls (p. 410).

myth *All suburbs are basically alike. If you've seen one, you've seen them all.*

reality Many suburbs are affluent, but increasing numbers are not. The suburbs in Los Angeles and Pittsburgh, for example, have more poor families and substandard housing than the cities (p. 411).

myth *Living in an impersonal world of strangers, city dwellers are more lonely than rural and small-town people.*

reality Those who live in the city are no more lonely than those who live in small towns and rural areas. Urbanites visit friends and relatives as often as do rural people (p. 416).

myth *New York City is well known for its crime, poverty, homelessness, racial tension, exorbitant rents, and official corruption. It is no wonder that most New Yorkers dislike living in their city.*

reality Most New Yorkers are ambivalent about their city. On the one hand, they are fully aware of its problems; on the other hand, they very much like what the city has to offer (p. 417).

399

Julie Haley, age 39, moved with her husband and two small children to a subdivision in Alpharetta, Georgia, five years ago when the neighborhood was mostly horse farms and trees. But today, she says, "People who visited us five years ago now say, 'I couldn't find your house.' The roads have all gotten wider, they've knocked down all the trees, and there's a million shopping centers." Both of her children have developed asthma, and she attributes it to the air pollution caused by cars, which have multiplied in number partly because so many residents commute to work in Atlanta (Pedersen et al., 1999).

Like Haley, millions of Americans have moved to a quiet countryside only to see it turn into a noisy city. Such transformation of rural areas into cities, which sociologists call **urbanization**, inevitably affects the environment. By bringing in large numbers of people, urbanization causes the traffic to become congested, the air polluted, the noise level higher, the landscape fragmented, and the wildlife disrupted (Firestone, 2001a; Pedersen et al., 1999). In this chapter, we will take a closer look at both urbanization and the environment.

ENVIRONMENT

To understand how the growth of population can damage the environment and thus endanger life on earth, we look to **ecology**, the study of the interactions among organisms and between organisms and their physical environment.

■ Elements of Ecology

Like all organisms, humans exist within the **biosphere**—a thin layer of air, soil, and water surrounding the earth. Within the biosphere, we can isolate countless **ecosystems**, self-sufficient communities of organisms depending for survival on one another and on the environment. An ecosystem may be as small as a puddle in a forest or as large as the biosphere itself. But whatever ecosystem we choose to look at, we find that the organisms within it depend on one another and on the physical environment for their survival. They are bound together by mutual interdependence. Energy and matter are constantly being transformed and transferred by the components of an ecosystem, providing the organisms with the essentials of life. Plants, for example, take in carbon dioxide and give off oxygen, which humans and other animals require for survival, and animals exhale carbon dioxide. Plants, in turn, use carbon dioxide in photosynthesis, the process by which they convert solar energy into carbohydrates and become food for animals. When animals die, their decom-

posed bodies provide nutrients to the soil, which plants then use.

By analyzing ecosystems, we can isolate two simple ecological principles. First, natural resources are finite. Every ecosystem therefore has a limited *carrying capacity*, a limited number of living things that it can support. Second, all our actions have related consequences. If we try to alter one aspect of an ecosystem, we end up changing others, as well. When farmers used DDT, a toxic pesticide, for example, they meant merely to kill pests. But DDT also got into the soil and water, from there into plankton, into fish that ate plankton, and into birds that ate the fish. The chemical also found its way into our food.

Despite all the amazing things humans have managed to do, we are still limited by these ecological principles. We are still living organisms, dependent like other organisms on ecosystems. But we have tried to ignore that dependence and acted in defiance of nature's limits. Two environmental problems have resulted: depletion of natural resources and environmental pollution.

■ Diminishing Resources

Although they make up only about 4 percent of the world's population, people in the United States consume about 30 percent of the world's energy and raw materials each year. If this high level of consumption continues, the world will soon run out of resources.

According to most environmentalists, the world's reserves of lead, silver, tungsten, mercury, and other precious resources will be depleted within 40 years. Even if new discoveries increase oil reserves fivefold, the global supply of oil will last for only 50 years. Poor nations fear that by the time they become fully industrialized, the resources they hope to enjoy will be gone (Myerson, 1998; Wald, 1990). In short, we are fast running out of natural resources.

Economist Julian Simon (1990), however, disagrees. He argues that the future is likely to be better "because our powers to manage our environment have been increasing throughout human history." To Simon, if nonrenewable resources such as minerals, metals, coal, and oil are used up, substitutes will be found through technology. Solar energy can be captured to replace coal and oil. We can also find substitutes for metals, such as plastics and aluminum for tin cans, and we can use satellites and fiberoptic lines instead of copper telephone wires. A few environmentalists, such as Bjorn Lomborg (2001), have offered evidence that energy and other natural resources are more abundant today than they were in the past.

■ Environmental Pollution

To consume more, we must produce more and thereby create more waste. The by-products of our consumption must go somewhere. Nature has many cycles for transforming waste to be used in some other form, but we are overtaxing nature's recycling capacity. We put too much waste, such as automobile emissions, in one place at the same time, and we have created new toxic substances, such as dioxin, that cannot be recycled safely. The result is pollution.

Pollution of the air has many sources. Throughout the world, power-generating plants, oil refineries, chemical plants, steel mills, and the like spew about 140 million tons of pollutants into the air every year. The heaviest polluter is the automobile, which accounts for at least 80 percent of air pollution. The pollutants irritate our eyes, noses, and throats; damage buildings; lower the productivity of the soil; and may cause serious illnesses, such as bronchitis, emphysema, and lung cancer. Air pollution is especially bad in Eastern Europe. As many as 10 percent of the deaths in Hungary are attributed directly to air pollution; the problem is even worse in parts of the former Czechoslovakia, Poland, and the former East Germany (Jacobson, 2002; Nelson, 1990).

Throughout the world, the constant burning of coal, oil, and wood releases more and more industrial gases, (such as carbon dioxide) into the atmosphere; the gases, in turn, trap an increasing amount

PAYING THE PIPER To consume more, we must produce more and thereby create more waste. Nature has many cycles for transforming waste into some other form, but nature's recycling capacity is overtaxed. We have thus created new toxic substances that cannot be recycled safely. ■

of heat from the sun. This has significantly raised temperatures around the world, such that the 1990s was the hottest decade on record. This *global warming* has, in turn, caused glaciers to melt, oceans to rise, floods and hurricanes to multiply, people to die from heat shock, and crops to wither. Moreover, some of the industrial gases—especially chlorofluorocarbons, used in refrigeration and air conditioning—have already weakened the ozone layer in many areas of the globe, thereby letting in more of the sun's ultraviolet light, which may cause skin cancer, harm the human immune system, and damage some crops and wild plants (Lemonick, 2001, 1995, 1992; Stevens, 1995).

Another kind of air pollution, called *acid rain,* has also aroused concern. When sulfur and nitrogen compounds are emitted by factories and automobiles, chemical reactions in the atmosphere may convert them to acidic compounds that can be carried hundreds of miles and then fall to the earth in rain and snow. Rain as acidic as vinegar has been recorded. This acid rain can kill fish and aquatic vegetation. It damages forests, crops, and soils. It corrodes buildings, water pipes, and tanks because it can erode limestone, marble, and even metal surfaces. Because of acid rain, thousands of lakes and rivers in North America and Europe are now dead, unable to support fish and plant life. Even worst is the acid rain in Russia's Siberia, which has ruined more than 1,500 square miles of timber, an area half as large as Rhode Island (Jacobson, 2002; Turco, 2002; Feshbach and Friendly, 1992).

■ A Primary Cause

Polluting the environment and depleting its natural resources may amount to a slow form of suicide. Sometimes, the cause is ignorance; sometimes, it is poverty. In many developing nations, rivers and streams are polluted by human wastes. Poor people desperate for fuel in developing countries have stripped mountainsides of trees, clearing the way for massive erosion. Overgrazing is expanding the deserts of Africa.

Neither ignorance nor poverty, however, can explain much of the environmental damage now being done around the world. After all, affluent societies consume many more resources than poor nations. Although U.S. inhabitants make up only about 4 percent of the world's population, they consume more than 30 percent of the world's energy and raw material. By burning far more fossil fuel in power plants, factories, and family cars, each U.S. resident contributes to air pollution 15 times as much as does the average African (see Figure 14.1).

A primary source of environmental problems is the fact that clean air, clean rivers, and other environmental resources are *public,* not private, *goods.* In Aristotle's words, "What is common to the greatest number gets the least amount of care." Garrett Hardin (1993) has used a parable called the "Tragedy of the Commons" to illustrate why this is so and how damage to the environment results. Suppose you are raising sheep, and you and your neighbors

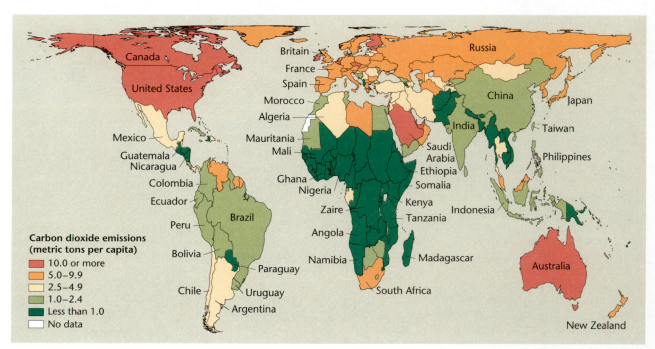

Carbon dioxide emissions
(metric tons per capita)
- 10.0 or more
- 5.0–9.9
- 2.5–4.9
- 1.0–2.4
- Less than 1.0
- No data

FIGURE 14.1

Air Pollution around the World

By burning far more fossil fuel in power plants, factories, and family cars, each resident in a rich country, such as the United States, contributes much more to air pollution than the average person in a poor country, such as Uganda and others in Africa.

Critical Thinking: *What can you do to help reduce air pollution?*

Source: World Bank Atlas, 2003.

share a commons, a common piece of land for grazing. To increase your income, you want to raise more sheep and graze them on the commons. If you do, you may damage the commons by overgrazing, but you will gain the entire benefit of raising additional sheep and share only part of the cost of the damage done to the commons. So you add another sheep to your herd and then perhaps another. Everyone else using the commons makes the same calculation, however, and in their own self-interest, they add to their herds. Eventually, overgrazing is severe enough to destroy the commons.

Without government intervention, the physical environment is much like this grazing commons. Individuals gain by using it, even polluting it, but society as a whole bears the cost of the damage. When people act on the basis of their individual self-interests, they end up degrading the environment. How, then, can the environment be saved?

■ Saving the Environment

In the last two decades, a number of methods have been used to bring environmental problems under control in the United States.

First, various antipollution laws have been passed. Initially, industry tended to resist them because of their expense. Unions sometimes opposed them because of fear that jobs would be lost as a result of the cost to industry. Some consumers objected to the laws because they feared prices would rise too high if industry was forced to reduce pollution. Therefore, state governments were often reluctant to make or enforce their own pollution-control laws for fear that companies would move their businesses elsewhere. But as pollution has continued to worsen, popular support for the laws has increased significantly. In fact, most Americans today would support antipollution laws, as Figure 14.2 suggests. And the enforcement of such laws has greatly improved air quality throughout the United States (Pianin, 2003).

Conservation provides a second method of reducing the negative impact on the environment. During the late 1970s, the federal and state governments took many steps to encourage the conservation of energy. People were urged to insulate their homes, turn down the thermostat in cold months, drive smaller cars at slower speeds, and ride buses and trains. The government began to offer tax credits and direct subsidies to encourage energy conservation. Americans were reminded that most European countries use far less energy than the United States while maintaining a high standard of living. Conservation efforts combined with rising energy prices and economic recession to produce a drop in energy use from 1979 to

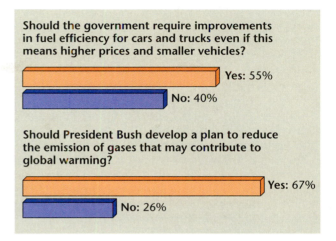

FIGURE 14.2

Public Support for Protecting the Environment

Most Americans today would support antipollution laws, such as those that require automakers to increase the fuel efficiency of their products. Even more people want their government to find a plan to reduce global warming. But support for these policies is strong only if the price is not too high. When asked if they would be willing to support tough government actions to reduce global warming that would increase unemployment or cause their utility bills to go up, less than half of Americans (38 to 47 percent) said yes.

Critical Thinking: *What do you do to conserve energy and recycle materials?*

Source: Data from poll taken for TIME/CNN by Yankelovich Partners, Inc./Harris, as published in *Time*, April 9, 2001.

1982 that was greater than experts had thought possible. Recycling, aside from combating pollution, provided another means of conserving energy and raw materials. Today, conservation has become popular. Most Americans are willing to separate their trash for recycling, to give up plastic containers and superfluous packaging to reduce waste, and to favor a ban on disposable diapers.

A third approach to dealing with environmental problems focuses on the development of new, alternative technology that is efficient, safe, and clean. Changes in automobiles illustrate this approach. Since the early 1970s, the fuel efficiency of cars has been increased and their polluting emissions have been reduced. Especially in the 1990s, the widespread use of catalytic converters in cars has greatly reduced two types of pollutants emitted by tailpipes: carbon monoxide and nitrogen oxide. Industrial scrubbers have also been used to remove much of the sulfur dioxide—the major ingredient of acid rain—from the process of producing energy from coal. More recently, the introduction of hybrid gas-electric cars can greatly boost mileage and cut pollution, and the use of wind power can generate not just energy but profits (Lemonick, 2001).

Limiting both population and economic growth is a fourth way of solving environmental problems. As John Firor (1990) has observed, nearly every environmental problem—be it acid rain, global warming, or ozone depletion—is first driven and then made worse by growth in the world's population. Stemming population growth will go a long way toward reducing environmental pollution and resource depletion. Rich countries have done much better than poor countries in curbing population growth. This is achieved primarily by abandoning the traditional value that favors having many children.

But most countries, rich or poor, have not abandoned the traditional value that favors economic growth with little regard to its *environmental* cost. Gross national product (GNP) is still measured the old-fashioned way: by adding the total value of goods and services *without* subtracting the value of clean air, water, ground, trees, fish, animals, human health, and other ecological elements that have been harmed by the production process—as if these were free goods rather than assets that are being lost. Thus, without taking into account the environmental impact of economic production, large economic growth measured as a great increase in GNP does not *truly* represent a country's wealth, the welfare of its citizens, or the value of its goods and services. Environmentalists have therefore called on governments and industries to stop pursuing this traditional kind of economic growth, which harms the environment, and to start seeking a "green," ecologically safe economic growth (Passell, 1995; Commoner, 1990; Simon, 1990).

myth	The U.S. environment is worse today than ever before.
reality	The environment is now mostly better, thanks to various efforts since 1970 to protect it.

The U.S. environment is, for the most part, better today than when the first Earth Day was celebrated 30 years ago (Easterbrook, 2003; Lomborg, 2001). But there are still problems. A major one is global warming. In the late 1990s, many nations signed the Kyoto agreement to cut carbon dioxide emissions in order to reduce global warming. But the United States—which is home to only 4 percent of the world's population but produces 25 percent of its carbon dioxide emissions—has, so far, rejected the agreement. The Bush administration has argued that it is unfair for Kyoto to require only the United States and other industrialized countries to reduce their levels of air pollution, thereby exempting China, India, and other developing countries. Environmentalists, however, have attributed the Bush rejection to political pressure from the oil and coal industries—the major sources of the fossil fuels that contribute to global warming through their greenhouse gases (Kluger, 2001a).

■ The Feminist Perspective

As feminists see it, the domination of nature by humans goes hand in hand with the domination of women by men. According to this perspective, called *ecofeminism,* the development of Western industrial civilization through the exploitation of nature reinforces the subjugation of women because women are widely considered closer to nature for bringing forth life from their bodies (Jagtenberg and McKie, 1997; Orenstein and Zemp, 1994). The assault on the environment, ecofeminists argue, often turns into a direct assault on women's bodies. By polluting the environment, radioactivity from power plants, toxic chemicals, pesticides, and nuclear and other hazardous wastes, for example, can damage women's reproductive organs and cause birth defects in their children. Therefore, seeking freedom from exploitation and pollution for the environment means doing the same for women and vice versa (Merchant,

IN ECOFEMINIST EYES *Ecofeminism* views the assault on the environment as an assault on women's bodies and their reproductive capacities. Indeed, many see phenomena among women comparable to deformed frogs found in Minnesota, Wisconsin, South Dakota, Vermont, and Quebec as evidence of the hazards of environmental pollution on physical development. Scientists are not sure, though, how pollution could cause the deformities, which include frogs with stumps for legs and others with as many as four hind legs. ■

1995). Various groups of ecofeminists pursue that goal differently, however.

Liberal ecofeminists see the source of environmental problems in governmental failure to regulate the development of natural resources and the discharge of pollutants. The liberals therefore seek to protect the environment from within the existing political system, namely, through the passage of new laws and regulations.

Cultural ecofeminists blame environmental problems on the Western culture of patriarchy, which is said to produce the largely male-developed and male-controlled technology, science, and industry for exploiting "mother earth." The by-products of this exploitation, such as the spraying of pesticides and herbicides on crops and forests, may harm women's reproductive organs and bring about miscarriages and birth defects. To combat these problems, culturalists favor direct political action to arouse public awareness of the environmental threats to women. Thus, they would, for example, protest against nuclear power plants and organize citizens to demand toxic clean-ups.

Socialist ecofeminists attribute environmental problems to capitalism. To socialists, the single-minded focus of capitalism on economic production has resulted in the pollution of the environment, thereby threatening the ability of women to reproduce healthy human lives. Socialists seek to reverse the priorities of capitalism by making production subordinate to reproduction—that is, ensuring that production always be environmentally sound (Merchant, 1995; Orenstein and Zemp, 1994).

A GLOBAL ANALYSIS OF URBANIZATION

In 1693, William Penn wrote that "the country life is to be preferred for there we see the works of God, but in cities little else than the work of man." Most people at the time probably agreed with him. Less than 2 percent of the world's population then were urban dwellers. But in 1998, about 44 percent of the world's population lived in urban areas, and more than 50 percent will do so by the end of 2010 (Haub, 1999; Linden, 1993; Fischer, 1984).

While urban populations have grown, cities themselves have changed. We can identify three periods in their history: the preindustrial, industrial, and metropolitan-megalopolitan stages.

■ The Preindustrial City

For more than 99 percent of the time that we humans have been on Earth, our ancestors have roamed about in search of food. They have hunted, fished, and gathered edible plants, but they have never found enough food in one place to sustain them for very long. They have had to move on, traveling in small bands from one place to another.

Then, about 10,000 years ago, technological advances allowed people to stop their wandering. This was the dawn of what is called the *Neolithic period.* People now had the simple tools and the know-how to cultivate plants and domesticate animals. They could produce their food supplies in one locale, and they settled down and built villages. The villages were very small—with only about 200 to 400 residents each. For the next 5,000 years, villagers produced just enough food to feed themselves.

About 5,000 years ago, humans developed more powerful technologies. Thanks to innovations like the ox-drawn plow, irrigation, and metallurgy, farmers could produce more food than they needed to sustain themselves and their families. Because of this food surplus, some people abandoned agriculture and made their living by weaving, making pottery, and practicing other specialized crafts. Methods of transporting and storing food were also improved. The result was the emergence of cities.

Cities first arose on the fertile banks of such rivers as the Nile of Egypt, the Euphrates and Tigris in the Middle East, the Indus in Pakistan, and the Yellow River in China. Similar urban settlements later appeared in other parts of the world. These *preindustrial cities* were small compared with the cities of today. Most had populations of 5,000 to 10,000 people. Only a few cities had more than 100,000 people, and even Rome never had more than several hundred thousand.

Several factors prevented expansion of the preindustrial city. By modern standards, agricultural techniques were still primitive. It took at least 75 farmers to produce enough of a surplus to support just one city dweller. For transportation, people had to depend on their own muscle power or that of animals. It was difficult to carry food supplies from farms to cities and even more difficult to transport heavy materials for construction in the cities. Poor sanitation, lack of sewer facilities, and ineffective medicine kept the death rate high. Epidemics regularly killed as much as half of a city's population. Moreover, families still had a strong attachment to the land, which discouraged immigration to the cities. All these characteristics of preindustrial society kept the cities small (Davis, 1955).

The Industrial City

For almost 5,000 years, cities changed little. Then their growth, in size and number, was so rapid that it has been called an *urban revolution* or *urban explosion*. In 1700, less than 2 percent of the population of Great Britain lived in cities, but by 1900, the majority of the British did so. Other European countries and the United States soon achieved the same level of urbanization in an even shorter period. Today, these and other Western countries are among the most urbanized in the world, along with many Latin American countries, which have become mostly urbanized in more recent years (see Figure 14.3).

The major stimulus to the urban explosion was the Industrial Revolution. It triggered a series of related events, identified by sociologist Philip Hauser (1981) as population explosion, followed by population displosion and population implosion, and then by technoplosion. Industrialization first causes a rise in production growth, and the mechanization of farming brings about an agricultural surplus. Fewer farmers can support more people—and thus larger urban populations *(population explosion)*. Workers no longer needed on the farms move to the city. There is, then, displacement of people from rural to urban areas *(population displosion)* and a greater concentration of people in a limited area *(population implosion)*. The development of other new technologies *(technoplosion)* spurs on urbanization. Improved transportation, for example, speeds the movement of food and other materials to urban centers.

The outcome of these events was the *industrial city*. Compared with the preindustrial city, the industrial city was larger, more densely settled, and more diverse. It was a place where large numbers of people—with a wide range of skills, interests, and cultural backgrounds—could live and work together in a limited space. Also, unlike the preindustrial city, which had served primarily as a religious or governmental center, the industrial city was a commercial hub. In fact, its abundant job opportunities attracted so many rural migrants that migration accounted for the largest share of its population growth. Without these migrants, cities would not have grown at all because of the high mortality rate brought about by extremely poor sanitary conditions.

Metropolis and Megalopolis

Early in this century, the large cities of the industrialized nations began to spread outward. They formed **metropolises**, large urban areas that include a city and its surrounding suburbs. Some of these suburbs are politically separate from their central cities, but socially, economically, and geographically, the suburbs and the city are tied together. The U.S. Census Bureau recognizes this unity by defining what is called a *Standard Metropolitan Statistical Area,* which cuts across political boundaries. Since 1990, most U.S. residents have been living in metropolitan areas with 1 million residents or more (Suro, 1991).

In the United States, the upper and middle classes have usually sparked the expansion of cities outward. Typically, as migrants from rural areas moved into the central city, the wealthier classes moved to the suburbs. The automobile greatly facilitated this development. It encouraged people to leave the crowded inner city for the more comfortable life of

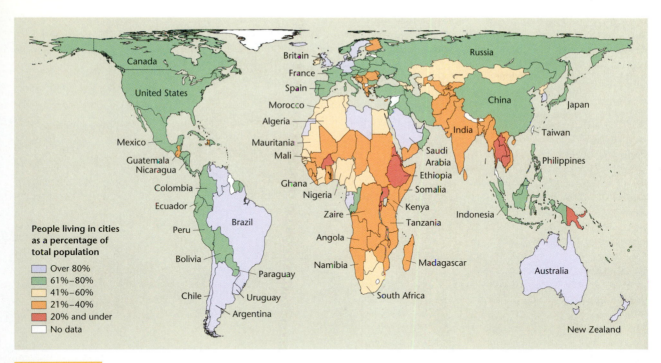

FIGURE 14.3

Countries at Various Levels of Urbanization

Western countries, such as the United States and European nations, are among the most urbanized in the world today. More recently, though, many Latin American countries have also become mostly urbanized.

Critical Thinking: *Is urbanization good for a country? Why or why not?*

Source: From *The Penguin State of the World Atlas,* by Dan Smith, copyright © 2003 by Dan Smith. Illustrations © 2003 by Myriad Editions Ltd. Used by permission of Penguin, a division of Penguin Group (USA) Inc.

the suburbs, if they could afford it. As the number of cars increased, so did the size of suburbs and metropolises. In 1900, there were only 8,000 cars in the United States; by 1930, the number had soared to more than 26 million. Meanwhile, the proportion of the U.S. population living in the suburbs grew from only 15.7 percent in 1910 to 48.6 percent in 1950 (Glaab and Brown, 1983).

Since 1950, virtually all the growth in metropolitan areas has occurred in the suburbs. During the 1960s, U.S. suburbs grew four times faster than inner cities, and stores and entertainment facilities followed the people there. Suburban jobs increased 44 percent, while inner-city employment dropped 7 percent. This pattern of suburban growth at the expense of the urban core continued in the 1970s and 1980s. Today, suburbanites outnumber city residents three to two (U.S. Census Bureau, 2003; Gottdiener, 1983; Jaret, 1983).

As suburbs expand, they sometimes combine with the suburbs of adjacent metropolitan areas to form a **megalopolis,** a vast area in which many metropolises merge. For hundreds of miles from one major city to the next, suburbs and cities have merged with one another to form a continuous region in which distinctions between suburban, urban, and rural areas are blurred. The hundreds of miles from Boston to Washington, DC, form one such megalopolis; another stretches from Detroit through Chicago to Milwaukee in the Midwest; and a third goes from San Francisco to San Diego.

■ The World's Megacities

The world's urban population has grown so fast that today, there are about 40 **megacities**—cities with populations of 5 million or more. Generally, the poorer the country, the faster its urban growth. Thus, today, only three of the world's megacities are in the United States, and more than half are in developing countries (see Figure 14.4, p. 408). Many more cities in the developing world will soon become megacities.

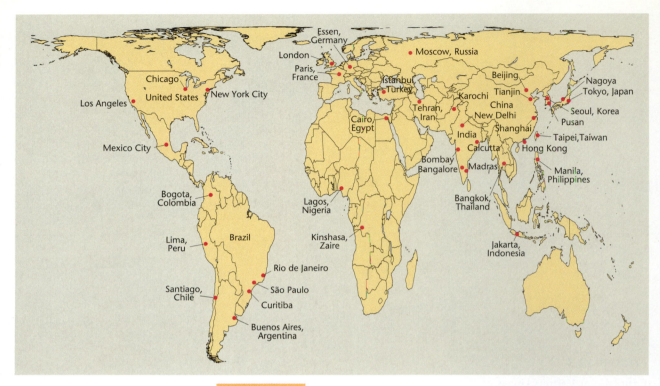

FIGURE 14.4

Megacities around the World

Generally, the poorer the country, the faster its urban growth. Today, more than half of the world's megacities (cities with 5 million or more people) are in developing countries.

Critical Thinking: *Why do poor countries have more megacities than rich countries?*

Source: Data from U.S. Census Bureau, 2000.

myth	Most of the world's large cities—such as New York and Tokyo—are in prosperous, industrialized countries.
reality	Generally, the poorer the country, the faster its urban growth. As a result, more than half of the world's megacities are now in developing countries.

Since the emergence of the preindustrial city 5,000 years ago, great cities have risen and fallen. The same is true today. One city that is collapsing is Kinshasa, the capital of Zaire. Although the country is endowed with abundant natural resources, such as gold, diamonds, copper, and rich agricultural land, Kinshasa has produced massive miseries under the corrupt 30-year-reign of former President Sese Mobutu. Government officials have routinely looted manufactured goods, fuel, food, and medical supplies, even most of the emergency food aid sent by foreign countries. As a result, the annual inflation rate has often soared to more than 3,000 percent and the jobless rate to 80 percent, posing serious threats of starvation and epidemics. In contrast, the city of Curitiba in Brazil is a success story. The city is not rich, but its government makes the most of its resources. One example is recycling: Parks are lit with lamps made from soda bottles, and some government offices were built in part with old telephone poles. The city also delivers excellent services, including a highly efficient bus system and well-constructed housing projects for the poor (Zwingle, 2002; Linden, 1993).

Most megacities fit between these two contrasting types. They are saddled with serious problems but manage to cope reasonably well, usually in ways that reflect the nature of their societies. Consider Tokyo, for example—the world's most densely populated metropolis. It faces enormous problems, such as overwhelming amounts of waste, traffic-choked streets, and sky-high housing costs. But the technologically advanced Japanese have, among other things, developed an urban heat system that extracts heat from sewage, which is then used to regulate the temperature in several of Tokyo's buildings. To reduce traffic jams, the city has used wireless communication to show drivers whose cars have a computerized navigation system where the congested streets are. And to lower housing costs, Tokyo has started planning to build an underground city (Kuchment, 2003; Wehrfritz and Itoi, 2003; Linden, 1993).

CITIES IN THE UNITED STATES

Cities around the world are similar in some ways, such as being overcrowded, polluted, and in need of ways to solve their problems. But cities also vary from one society to another. Here, we focus on the cities in the United States.

■ A Demographic Profile

In general, the poor and minority groups concentrate in the inner cities, and more affluent people live in the suburbs. A closer look, however, led sociologist Herbert Gans (1968) to find five types of people in many cities:

1. Cosmopolites—artists, intellectuals, professionals
2. Unmarried individuals and childless couples
3. Ethnic villagers—immigrants from other countries
4. The deprived—the poor, including many African Americans and other minorities
5. The trapped—poor older people

These groups are not likely to feel strong ties to each other or to the city as a whole. The deprived and the trapped are too poor to move; they live in the city by necessity, not by choice. The ethnic villagers are likely to be strongly tied only to fellow immigrants in their neighborhoods. The unmarried and childless have ties mostly to those who share their lifestyles. Cosmopolites associate primarily with those who share their interests.

The movement of African Americans into the central city has been especially striking. Just 50 years ago, less than half of the African American population was urban. Today, a large majority live in urban areas, and most of these are in the inner cities. Several large cities, such as Detroit, Baltimore, and Atlanta, are already predominantly black. For years, African Americans entering the city came from the rural South, but now, most of these migrants come from other urban areas. Compared with the inner-city natives, these later migrants rank higher in education and employment and have lower rates of crime. Some middle-class African Americans have joined the exodus to the suburbs, but they move mostly to African American suburbs.

The number of cosmopolites, young professionals, adult singles, and childless couples in the inner city has also grown significantly. Increasing numbers of these affluent people now choose to remain in the

NEW KIDS ON THE BLOCK
The movement of affluent people into poor urban neighborhoods is known as *gentrification*. Many intellectuals, artists, young professionals, adult singles, and childless couples in the inner city buy rundown buildings, such as these in a Boston neighborhood, and renovate them into elegant townhouses and expensive condominiums. ■

inner city, especially given the sharp drop in violent crime and drug gangs in recent years. They buy run-down buildings and renovate them into elegant town-houses and expensive condominiums. This urban revival is called **gentrification**, the movement of affluent people into poor urban neighborhoods. It has transformed poor neighborhoods into such stylish enclaves as Capitol Hill in Washington, Philadelphia's Queen Village, Boston's South End, Cincinnati's Mount Adams, and Chicago's New Town. To a large extent, urban rehabilitation programs have stimulated gentrification by selling abandoned homes and stores for a few dollars and offering low-interest mortgage loans. Ironically, though, gentrification tends to drive up rents and property taxes, forcing poor and elderly residents to give up their homes to the well-off gentrifiers (Waldie, 2001; Belluck, 2000a).

■ Suburbs as Edge Cities

Most suburbs still offer better schools, more living space, less pollution, and less crime than the central city, so people continue to "vote with their feet" and head for suburbia (see Figure 14.5). In the 1970s, most suburbs were largely bedroom communities; their residents commuted to the nearby cities to work. But since then, a new kind of suburbanization has taken place—involving not only people and homes but also offices and jobs—that has transformed many suburbs into economic centers.

myth	Suburbs mostly continue to be so-called bedroom communities—places where people live but from which they commute to the nearby large cities to work.
reality	Today, many suburbs have become cities in their own right, where new office buildings, factories, and warehouses have sprung up alongside residential homes and shopping malls.

In these suburbs, new office buildings, factories, and warehouses have sprung up alongside the housing subdivisions and shopping malls. Developers have already created vast clusters of big buildings, people, and cars. Thus, many suburbs, in effect, have become cities in their own right. Unlike the traditional U.S. city, where diverse businesses operate, the new suburban cities, also popularly called *edge cities,* are typically focused on a principal activity, such as a collection of computer companies, a large regional medical center, or a sports or recreation complex. The growth of edge cities, therefore, has taken away many jobs from the urban cores.

By turning into edge cities, many suburbs are now less suburban and more urban, faced with problems once considered the special burden of cities. Particularly in the larger, sprawling suburbs, the way of life has become much less centered on community and much more on work, entrepreneurship, and private

SURUBURBAN SPRAWL A recent phenomenon in the growth and spatial patterns of U.S. cities has been the growth of office complexes in suburbs, taking away many jobs from the urban centers. This dispersal has been supported by truck and auto transport, along with such technological developments as cellular telephones, personal computers, and fax machines. The office park or corporate campus, like the one shown here, is now a common sight along arterial roads in many suburbs. ■

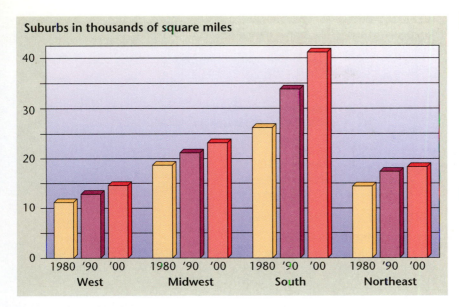

Suburbs in thousands of square miles

West: 1980, '90, '00
Midwest: 1980, '90, '00
South: 1980, '90, '00
Northeast: 1980, '90, '00

FIGURE 14.5

The Continuing Lure of the Suburbs

Most suburbs still offer better schools, more living space, less pollution, and less crime than the central city, so people continue to move to suburbia. But increasingly, suburbs soon turn into edge cities, extensions of the urban core, with the same problems that the surbanites tried to escape in the first place.

Critical Thinking: *How has your hometown changed in the past 15 years? Do you like the changes? Why or why not?*

Source: Data from U.S. Census Bureau, 2001.

life, with neighborhood grocers and gathering spots giving way to superstores and fast-food franchises. The potential for being lonely and friendless is therefore considerably greater (Firestone, 2001a; Peterson, 1999; Palen, 1995).

myth	All suburbs are basically alike. If you've seen one, you've seen them all.
reality	Many suburbs are affluent, but increasing numbers are not. The suburbs in Los Angeles and Pittsburgh, for example, have more poor families and substandard housing than the cities.

Many suburbs have also developed other characteristically urban problems, such as congestion, pollution, and crime. Rapid, unregulated growth has created some of these problems. When industry and stores move to the suburbs to be near people's homes, they often bring with them traffic, noise, and air and water pollution, not to mention landscape pollution. Although many suburbs are prosperous, increasing numbers are not. The Los Angeles suburbs have more poor families than the city, and there is more substandard housing in the suburbs of Pittsburgh than in the city itself (Firestone, 2001a; Palen, 1995; McCormick and McKillop, 1989).

Given these problems, at least 11 states have initiated the smart-growth policy of discouraging the development of suburbs while revitalizing the inner cities. As such, these states would refrain from funding the construction of infrastructure (such as water lines and highways) for the development of new edge cities. But they would subsidize the building of affordable homes for low- and moderate-income households in the urban core while enticing the middle class to the inner city with improved school quality and public safety (Cohen, 2002).

■ Recent Trends

The latest U.S. census, conducted in 2000, revealed a number of significant changes in American cities over the last decade (U.S. Census Bureau, 2001):

1. Most cities have grown rapidly, with those in the West and South expanding the most. Fueling this growth were the booming economy, the influx of immigrants, and the sharp decline in crime in the 1990s.

2. Immigration has served as a brake against population decline in some major cities such as New York and Miami. With a large influx of immigrants from countries such as India, China, the Philippines, and the Dominican Republic, these cities have registered population gains rather than losses.

3. Cities that have highly educated residents—such as Madison, Wisconsin, and Columbus, Ohio, both university towns—have gained in population. By contrast, cities with large numbers of poor people, such as St. Louis, have lost.

4. Most state capitals have grown, even though the states themselves have stagnated. North Dakota, for example, has shrunk a little, but its capital, Bismarck, has grown.

5. For the first time in U.S. history, nearly half of the 100 largest cities have more African Americans, Hispanics, Asians, and other minorities than whites. Of the total population of the 100 largest

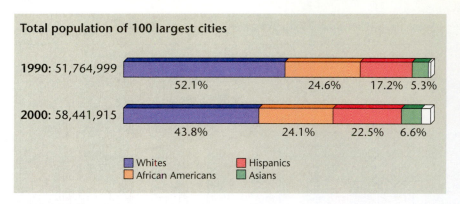

Total population of 100 largest cities

1990: 51,764,999 — 52.1% / 24.6% / 17.2% / 5.3%

2000: 58,441,915 — 43.8% / 24.1% / 22.5% / 6.6%

- Whites
- African Americans
- Hispanics
- Asians

FIGURE 14.6

More Minorities in the Cities

From 1990 to 2000, the percentage of minorities in the United States grew significantly because of increased immigration and higher birth rates among the foreign born, particularly Hispanics. During the same period, the white share of the city population declined because many whites moved out of the cities. As a result, minorities now make up a larger proportion (53.2 percent) of the total population of the 100 largest cities than do whites (43.8 percent).

Critical Thinking: *Would you consider raising a family in a big city? Why or why not?*

Sources: Data from U.S. Census Bureau, 2001; Brookings Institution, 2001.

cities, the minorities outnumber the whites because of increased immigration and higher birth rates among the foreign born as well as white flight from the cities (see Figure 14.6).

THE URBAN ENVIRONMENT

As we observed earlier, ecologists study the natural world to see how everything in it relates to everything else. Organisms affect other organisms, and they all affect the environment, which in turn affects them. During the 1920s and 1930s, some sociologists at the University of Chicago began to look at the urban world in a similar way. They initiated a new approach to the study of cities called **urban ecology**, the study of the relationship between people and their urban environment.

■ Spatial Patterns

Like a natural environment, the urban environment is not a random arrangement of elements. Walking around a city, we rarely see a mansion next to a poor neighborhood or an apartment next to a factory. Different areas tend to be used for different purposes. As a result, the people, activities, and buildings within a city are distributed in certain patterns. The urban ecologists have tried to describe these patterns and how

they arose. Three classical theories and a new one have come out of their efforts, as shown in Figure 14.7.

Concentric-Zone Theory In the 1920s, Ernest Burgess presented the **concentric-zone theory**, the model of land use in which the city spreads out from the center in a series of concentric zones, each used for a particular kind of activity. The heart of the city is the central business district. This innermost zone is occupied by shops, banks, offices, hotels, and government buildings. The next zone is the transition zone, characterized by shabby rooming houses, deteriorating apartments, and high crime rates. The third zone is in better shape. It is made up of working people's homes. Beyond it is a zone that houses mostly middle-class people, and beyond that is the commuters' zone, with large homes and plenty of open space. The rich live here and commute to the city to work (Burgess, 1967).

According to this theory, social class has a lot to do with spatial distribution: The farther a piece of land is from the center of the city, the higher the status of those using it. However, land values tend to *drop* with distance from the center of the city. Thus, the pattern of land use has a rather perverse result: The poor live on expensive land and the rich on relatively cheap land (Alonso, 1964).

The concentric-zone theory describes some U.S. cities fairly well, especially those such as Chicago and

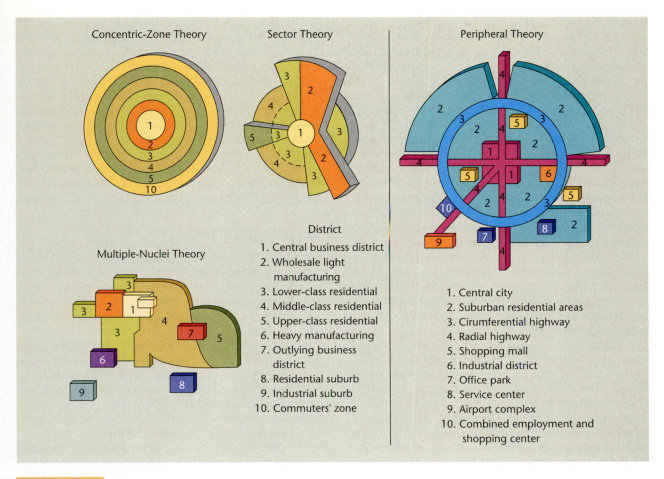

Concentric-Zone Theory

Sector Theory

Peripheral Theory

Multiple-Nuclei Theory

District
1. Central business district
2. Wholesale light manufacturing
3. Lower-class residential
4. Middle-class residential
5. Upper-class residential
6. Heavy manufacturing
7. Outlying business district
8. Residential suburb
9. Industrial suburb
10. Commuters' zone

1. Central city
2. Suburban residential areas
3. Cirumferential highway
4. Radial highway
5. Shopping mall
6. Industrial district
7. Office park
8. Service center
9. Airport complex
10. Combined employment and shopping center

FIGURE 14.7

Theories of Cities' Spatial Patterns

The elements of an urban environment are not arranged randomly. Thus, a mansion is rarely found next to a poor neighborhood or an apartment next to a factory. Instead, the houses, buildings, people, and activities within a city are usually distributed in certain patterns, which differ from one city to another. These different patterns are described in the theories depicted above.

Critical Thinking: *Which type of city would you prefer to live in and why?*

Sources: Lefthand section: From Chauncy D. Harris and Edward L. Ullman, "The Nature of Cities," *Annals of the American Academy of Political and Social Sciences,* Nov. 1945, p. 13. © 1945. Reprinted by permission. *Righthand section:* Reprinted with permission from *Urban Geography,* Vol. 18, No. 1, 1997, pp. 15–35. © V. H. Winston & Son, Inc. 360 South Ocean Blvd., Palm Beach, FL 33480. All rights reserved.

St. Louis, which grew rapidly early in the twentieth century under the stimulus of intense industrialization and the automobile. But many cities do not have concentric zones.

Sector Theory Henry Hoyt, in the late 1930s, proposed the **sector theory,** the model of land use in which a city grows outward in wedge-shaped sectors from the center. Hoyt agreed with concentric-zone theorists that a city grows outward from the center and that the center is occupied by the central business district. But, Hoyt said, growth occurs in wedge-shaped sectors that extend outward from the city, not in concentric circles. As a result, low-class housing occurs not just close to the business district but in a band extending from the center outward, perhaps to the rim of the city. The key to the extension of a sector is transportation. If, say, warehouses are built along a railroad line, they tend to expand along the length of the railroad line toward the periphery of the city. Similarly, a retail district might expand along a highway. The poor tend to live along transportation lines near factories, whereas the rich tend to choose areas that are on the fastest lines of transportation and occupy high ground, safe from floods and offering beautiful views (Hoyt, 1943). San Francisco and Minneapolis illustrate the sector pattern.

Multiple-Nuclei Theory   Boston is one of many cities that do not have either wedge-shaped sectors or concentric zones. It seems to be described better by yet a third theory, which was proposed by Chauncy Harris and Edward Ullman in the 1940s. Unlike the concentric-zone and sector theories, which suggest that each city is built around one center, Harris and Ullman's **multiple-nuclei theory** describes a model of land use in which a city is built around many discrete nuclei, each being the center of some specialized activity. There are centers of finance and commerce, which are separate from the political center, which in turn is separate from the center of heavy industries, and so on.

These separate nuclei, according to Harris and Ullman, arise as a result of at least three factors. First, some activities require specialized facilities. For instance, manufacturing districts must be located on large blocks of land with easy connections to railroads or water transportation; a port district must be attached to a suitable waterfront. Second, similar activities often profit from being grouped together. If retail stores are concentrated in one district, they all profit from an increased number of potential customers, who are usually attracted by the chance to compare the offerings of various stores. Third, putting dissimilar activities together in one location often harms them. Factories and homes do not mix well. Wholesale districts, which require street loading and rail facilities, stay away from retail districts, which need many pedestrians, cars, and buses (Harris and Ullman, 1945).

Peripheral Theory   Even though these three theories were developed more than half a century ago, they are still valuable for depicting the major patterns of some American cities, such as Chicago, San Francisco, and Boston. But many cities have changed in ways unanticipated by the three classic theories. In the past, the seaport, railroad, and huge factory complex encouraged *concentration* within the urban center. Today, truck transport and the automobile, along with such technological developments as cellular telephones, personal computers, and fax machines, have supported *dispersal* (Rybczynski, 1995).

Thus, most of the middle and white working classes no longer live within the city but in suburbs.

As has been discussed, many factories, office complexes, wholesale and retail trade, and jobs involving people (retail sales, medical services, food service) have also moved out of the urban center and into the suburbs called edge cities or suburban cities. To take into account all these new developments, Chauncy Harris (1997) has developed, as a supplement to the concentric-zone, sector, and multiple-nuclei theories, the **peripheral theory**, the model of land use in which suburban cities grow around the central city. Combined with a classic theory, the peripheral theory effectively portrays the spatial pattern of many metropolitan areas in the United States.

■ Ecological Processes

How do these urban spatial patterns come about? Nowadays, city governments often use zoning laws and building codes to determine the patterns of land use and to segregate activities. But many patterns arose without any planning, forming what are called *natural areas* of segregated activities. Urban ecologists believed that two forms of human behavior are most important in shaping the urban environment: dominance and competition. A group of people typically concentrates in a particular area of the city for a specific purpose, dominating that area. Businesses, for example, usually dominate the center of U.S. cities. Sometimes, a group achieves dominance only after competing with others to determine how the land will be used. Businesses and residents often clash over land use in a city. Businesses can usually win by buying out the land at a high price, forcing residents to move. Universities often engage in similar competition with residents. Thus, the use of land in a city is determined directly by *dominance* and indirectly by *competition*.

The city, however, is not static. Instead, over time a new group or type of land use will move into an established area, a process called *invasion*. If the new group forces others out, *succession* has occurred. The process of gentrification discussed earlier is an example: Young professionals invade an urban neighborhood, raising land values and rents, and eventually they push out its lower-income residents, who can no longer afford the neighborhood. This reverses the traditional pattern of succession that shaped many U.S. cities. As industries, immigrants, and minorities moved into the cities, those who were better off moved out to the suburbs, and their neighborhoods filtered down to the lower class.

Dominance, competition, invasion, and succession constitute what are called the **urban ecological processes**, in which people compete for certain land use, one group dominates another, and a particular group moves into an area and takes it over from others.

THE NATURE OF CITY LIFE

In 1964, people were horrified by a story that many considered typical of life in New York City—or any large city. A young woman named Kitty Genovese was walking home from work in the early morning hours when she was attacked. Her murderer stabbed her repeatedly for more than half an hour. Thirty-eight neighbors heard her screams or witnessed the attack, but no one helped or even called the police. Most of the neighbors later explained that they did not want to get involved. A similar incident took place in Detroit in 1995: Dozens of bystanders did nothing to prevent a young woman from being violently assaulted by a man, and some onlookers even cheered as the woman jumped off a bridge to escape her attacker and fell to her death (Stokes, 1995).

What could cause such cold-bloodedness? Many commentators blamed the city. Living in a city, they believed, changes people for the worse. This charge echoed what some sociologists had long been saying. Louis Wirth, for example, contended in the 1930s that the conditions of the city produce a distinctive way of life, *urbanism,* and that the urban environment harms the people who live there. His analysis represented the ecological approach of the Chicago school.

Since Wirth's time, some sociologists have supported his view. Richard Sennett (1991), for example, has criticized city life for insulating people from others who are racially, socially, or economically different. But many other sociologists have rejected Wirth's view. Some have argued that the city does not make much difference in people's lives, and others contend that the urban environment enriches people's lives by creating and strengthening subcultures. These three theories about the nature of urban life, summarized in Table 14.1, are called *urban anomie theory, compositional theory,* and *subcultural theory.*

◼ Urban Anomie Theory

In 1938, Louis Wirth presented his **urban anomie theory,** arguing that city people have a unique way of life characterized by alienation, impersonal relations, and stress. According to Wirth, the urban environment has three distinctive features: huge population size, high population density, and great social diversity. These characteristics, Wirth argued, have both a sociological and a psychological impact, producing social and personality disorders.

In the city, people are physically close but socially distant. Every day, they encounter strangers. They become accustomed to dealing with people only in terms of their roles. Their relationships tend to be impersonal. That is, much of their lives are filled not with primary relations with neighbors, who are also relatives and friends, but with secondary relations. Moreover, these people are separated by diverse religious, ethnic, and racial backgrounds. It is difficult, argued Wirth, for people in the city to form friendships across these lines or to develop a moral consensus. Under these circumstances, people can no longer ensure social order by relying on informal controls such as tradition and gossip. Instead, they turn to formal controls such as the police. Rather than talk to a young troublemaker's parents, they call the police. But formal controls, Wirth contended, are less effective than informal controls, so crimes and other forms of deviance are more frequent in the city than in the countryside.

The size, density, and diversity of the city, according to Wirth, also damage the psychological health of its residents by making life stressful. Much of the stress comes from being bombarded with various kinds of stimuli. Sights, sounds, and smells assault urbanites virtually every minute of their waking hours. Wherever they turn, they must contend with

TABLE 14.1

Theories about the Nature of City Life

Theory	Focus
Urban anomie theory	City people have a unique way of life characterized by alienation, impersonal relations, and stress.
Compositional theory	City dwellers are as involved with small groups of friends, relatives, and neighbors as are noncity people.
Subcultural theory	The city enriches people's lives by offering diverse opportunities and developing various subcultures.

the actions of others. They are jostled on the street and in the elevator. They wake to the sound of their neighbor's radio and fall asleep despite screaming sirens. Panhandlers, staggering inebriates, and soliloquizing mental patients are a common sight. All of this may make people feel irritable, nervous, and anxious. The result, Wirth claimed, is that mental disorders are more common among city dwellers than among people in rural areas.

■ Compositional Theory

Wirth's description of the urban environment and its effects sounds reasonable. But is it accurate? Many empirical studies of cities have shown that his portrait amounts to an overdrawn stereotype. Some sociologists have instead proposed a **compositional theory**, arguing that city dwellers are as involved with small groups of friends, relatives, and neighbors as are noncity people.

Perhaps the crucial difference between the urban anomie and compositional theorists concerns the influence of the urban environment on primary relations. Wirth argued that city life is impersonal, that the city erodes primary relations. But compositional theorists contend that no matter how big, how dense, how diverse the city is, people continue to be deeply involved with a small circle of friends and relatives and others who have similar lifestyles, backgrounds, and personalities. In this small social world, they find protection from the harsher impersonal world of strangers.

myth	Living in an impersonal world of strangers, city dwellers are more lonely than rural and small-town people.
reality	Those who live in the city are no more lonely than those who live in small towns and rural areas. Urbanites visit friends and relatives as often as do rural people.

Many studies show that there is, indeed, a significant amount of social cohesion within cities, as compositional theorists contend. Herbert Gans (1982), for example, has found that people in ethnic neighborhoods of large cities have a strong sense of community loyalty. He found the solidarity in these neighborhoods impressive enough to call them *ethnic villages*. Other researchers have also found that city residents carry on their personal lives much as people in rural areas do, such as visiting relatives at least once a week (Palisi and Canning, 1983).

What about studies that show higher rates of crime and mental illness in urban than in rural areas? According to compositional theorists, these disorders are not *created* by the urban environment itself. Instead, they result from the demographic makeup of the city—from the fact that the urban population includes a high percentage of those categories of people likely to suffer from social and mental disorders. Two examples are young unmarried individuals and the lower classes.

■ Subcultural Theory

Claude Fischer (1984) presented a **subcultural theory** of urban life, arguing that the city enriches people's lives by offering diverse opportunities and developing various subcultures. While urban anomie

FRIENDLY CITY According to compositional theory, no matter how big, how dense, or how diverse a city is, the people who live in it continue to be deeply involved with a network of friends, relatives, and others who have similar backgrounds and lifestyles (such as the group of New Yorkers shown here). ■

theorists emphasize the negative impact of city life, Fischer stresses the positive. In his view, the urban environment creates and strengthens various groups of people. These groups are, in effect, *subcultures*— culturally distinctive groups, such as college students, African Americans, artists, corporate executives, and so forth. These subcultures are able to emerge because of the great population size, density, and diversity of the city, and the clash of subcultures within a city may strengthen each of them. When people come in contact with individuals from other subcultures, Fischer (1984) wrote, they

> sometimes rub against one another only to recoil, with sparks flying. . . . People from one subculture often find people in another subculture threatening, offensive, or both. A common reaction is to embrace one's own social world all the more firmly, thus contributing to its further intensification.

"I like New York, but I miss having a screen door."

Source: © The New Yorker Collection 1997 Robert Weber from Cartoonbank.com. All Rights Reserved.

Fischer has also argued that the urban experience brings some personal benefits to city dwellers. For example, urban housing, compared to rural housing, generally has better plumbing facilities and is less crowded. Compared with people in the country, city people have access to far more facilities, services, and opportunities. As Harvey Cox (1966) noted:

> Residents of a city of 10,000 may be limited to one or two theaters, while people who live in a city of a million can choose among perhaps 50 films on a given night. The same principle holds for restaurants, schools, and even in some measure for job opportunities or prospective marriage partners.

■ Critical Analysis

Each of the three theories presents only a partial truth about city life. As urban anomie theory suggests, residents of large cities are usually much less satisfied with their neighborhoods than are their counterparts in small towns (Lee and Guest, 1983). At the same time, city life is not as bad as is popularly believed. People do lead normal, pleasant lives in the city with friends and subcultural groups, as compositional and subcultural theories suggest.

myth	New York City is well known for its crime, poverty, homelessness, racial tension, exorbitant rents, and official corruption. It is no wonder that most New Yorkers dislike living in their city.
reality	Most New Yorkers are ambivalent about their city. On the one hand, they are fully aware of its problems; on the other hand, they very much like what the city has to offer.

But all the theories fail to capture the ambivalence people feel toward cities. For a long time, most New Yorkers have considered their city an unpleasant place to live, with all its crime, poverty, homelessness, racial tension, heavy taxes, high rents, filth, and official corruption. Still, they very much like living in the "Big Apple." To them, "the pulse and pace and convenient, go-all-night action of the city, its rich ethnic and cultural stew, still outweigh its horrors" (Blundell, 1986). Indeed, many urbanites throughout the United States seem to consider the urban problems a fair price for the freedom of expression they enjoy in the city (Lapham, 1992). A more important reason for living in the city, though, is that it is where their jobs are (see Figure 14.8, p. 418).

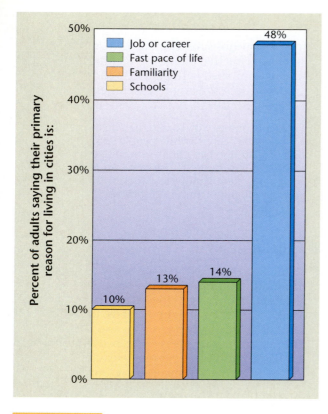

FIGURE 14.8

Why They Live in the City

Most urbanites are ambivalent about their city. They consider it unpleasant because of all its problems, such as crime, poverty, and high rents, but they nonetheless like to live in it because of its rich culture, the freedom and fast pace of life it provides, and, most important, the opportunity it offers for having a good job or career.

Critical Thinking: *If you lived in a large city, what would cause you to live there permanently or to leave? Why?*

Source: Data from National Housing Survey, Fannie Mae, Washington, DC, 1997.

CAUSES OF URBAN PROBLEMS

Almost every problem in U.S. society—drug abuse and crime, racism and poverty, poor education and environmental pollution—seems more severe in the cities, particularly in the older and more congested ones. Even as newer cities grow and age, their problems will probably become more severe. The difficulties that cities face and their ability to deal with them are shaped to a great extent by the intertwining effects of various social forces. We discuss some of them here.

Population Decline

In the last 10 years, Detroit, Buffalo, Pittsburgh, St. Louis, and other big cities have lost population. On the face of it, this may look like good news for these cities' finances: Fewer people should mean less demand for, and less spending on, police protection, fire protection, education, and other public services. In reality, however, population decreases have created serious problems.

As the years go by, a city must spend more to maintain its road, sewer, and water networks, even if it has fewer residents to pay for those services. Similarly, when families abandon the central city, the need for police and fire protection increases because abandoned homes can become magnets for vandalism and crime. They become fire hazards and finally must be torn down at the city's expense. Furthermore, behind the statistics of declining populations lies the fact that those who move out of the cities are largely middle-class whites, and with them go many businesses. Thus, the cities have fewer private-sector jobs and declining revenues. Those who are left behind in the city are typically less educated, poorer, and older—the people most in need of government spending for education, housing, health services, and welfare (Rybczynski, 1995; Gottdiener, 1994). In recent years, some efforts have been made to revitalize many cities by attracting tourists to spend money in the city, but more still needs to be done (Waldie, 2001; Kotkin, 2001).

Fiscal Squeeze

Urban problems stem largely from the inability of city governments to generate sufficient income to provide various kinds of services to the public. Cities get most of their revenues from taxes on property, income, sales, and corporations. Some money comes from charging fees for services. But all these sources of revenue have shrunk over the last decade: The suburbs have drained off much of the cities' tax base by attracting industries and stores, as well as middle- and upper-class people.

There are other potential sources of revenue, but cities generally cannot tap them. In many states, cities are prohibited from raising as much in taxes as they wish. Cities are also deprived of other revenue-producing opportunities. When federal and state governments use city property, they are exempted from paying city taxes totaling billions of dollars. Suburbanites come into town, adding to traffic congestion, garbage, and wear and tear on roads and parks, while benefiting from police protection and other urban resources. But they pay no taxes to the city for these services.

WORLDS APART Both economics and racial discrimination are factors in housing segregation. Because African Americans tend to have lower incomes, they often live in neighborhoods with older, less expensive homes. And though it is illegal to do so, some realtors also tend to steer potential black buyers away from more affluent white neighborhoods, further perpetuating segregation. ■

Consequently, since the 1960s, cities have come to depend increasingly on the state and federal governments to help pay their bills. But since the late 1980s, the federal government has not been helpful after it was forced by stringent budget cuts to end the revenue-sharing program (Gottdiener, 1994; Schwab, 1992).

■ Political Dilemma

Part of the cities' fiscal problem originates with elected officials' unwillingness to raise taxes even if they have the power to do so and their citizens have the ability to pay. Given the unpopularity of tax increases, politicians tend to avoid risking taxpayers' anger, even when taxes are low and necessary. But this political dilemma seems to have forced the cities to rely increasingly on private enterprise to tackle urban problems.

With their eyes on economic development, cities compete with one another to keep or attract businesses and industries. Low taxes and tax exemptions are used as lures. Although this may undermine the current tax base, the cities hope to build a larger tax base, through an increase in jobs, for the future.

Cities also set up **empowerment zones** (also known as *enterprise zones*), economically depressed urban areas that businesses, with the help of government grants, low-interest loans, and tax breaks, try to revive by creating jobs. In these special zones, thousands of jobs have been created for poor residents. A similar effort to solve public ills with private cures has appeared in another way. Grass-roots entrepreneurs

known as *community development corporations* have rehabilitated abandoned homes, creating commercial enterprises and organizing social services in various large cities. Their objective is to succeed where governments have failed—by reclaiming city streets from crime and economic decline (Stout, 1996; Carlson, 1991; *New York Times,* 1991).

■ Housing Segregation

Every year, billions of dollars are spent on housing in the United States. The government helps out by granting billions of dollars in tax deductions to landlords and homeowners. As a result, Americans are among the best-housed people in the world, with most families owning their own homes. But it is difficult financially for minorities to own or rent a home. For one thing, minorities, especially African Americans, make up a high percentage of the population of the inner cities, where good housing at reasonable prices is scarce. While most African Americans living in metropolitan areas are concentrated in the inner cities, most of the metropolitan whites are spread out in the surrounding suburbs. In both the inner cities and the suburbs, African Americans are frequently segregated from whites and relegated to inferior housing.

Economics may be a factor in housing segregation. Because African Americans tend to have lower incomes, they often cannot afford to move into more expensive white neighborhoods. But racial discrimination is an even bigger factor. Real estate agents tend to steer potential African American buyers and renters away from white neighborhoods, perpetuating segregation, although this is an illegal practice. Banks are often more cautious in granting loans to African Americans than to whites, making it difficult for them to own or rehabilitate homes and thus encouraging the deterioration of African American neighborhoods. Many African Americans will not move into white neighborhoods because they want to avoid rejection by whites (Krysan and Farley, 2002; Coulibaly, Green, and James, 1998).

SOCIOLOGICAL PERSPECTIVES ON URBANIZATION AND CITY LIFE

Both the functionalist and conflict perspectives can be used to explain the forces behind the urbanization of U.S. society. To functionalists, the masses of ordinary people seek and benefit from urbanization as a way of adapting to their changing environment. To conflict theorists, the driving force and beneficiary of urbanization is really big business. Symbolic interactionists, however, are more interested in explaining city life by focusing on how people interact with one another in the city.

■ Functionalist Perspective: Urbanization Driven by the Masses

According to the functionalist perspective, the masses of ordinary people are the primary driving force behind urbanization, or urbanization reflects what the masses want when faced with changes in their environment (Rybczynski, 1995). Let's take a close look at the role of the masses in urbanization.

First, technology increases agricultural production so much that considerably fewer people are needed to work on farms. So, seeking better job opportunities, throngs of people leave the farms for the cities, which leads to explosive urban growth. Since these former farmers are mostly manual laborers, their influx to the cities helps to expand the manufacturing industry, allowing the mass production of everything from shoes to clothes to cars and computers. Next, as cities become crowded, increasing numbers of people move to the outskirts to live. They can continue to work in the inner cities, however, thanks to the mass production of cars. Then, as the suburbs become increasingly populated, various businesses emerge to cater to the shopping needs of suburbanites, eventually leading to the proliferation of shopping malls. Finally, a cornucopia of jobs is created in the suburbs, so that suburbanites do not need to commute to the central cities to work. At this late stage of urbaniza-

tion, metropolises and megalopolises begin to emerge. Functionalists assume that all these social changes brought about by urbanization and suburbanization reflect what the masses need and seek to have a comfortable life.

■ Conflict Perspective: Urbanization Fueled by Big Business

The conflict perspective provides a different picture of urbanization, one that stresses the role played by big business in the growth and expansion of cities (Gottdiener, 1994, 1985).

First, in the pursuit of profit, large corporations bought up huge tracts of farmland and mass-produced food, driving many small family farms into bankruptcy and forcing huge numbers of farmers to leave for the city. In doing so, big business received considerable assistance from big government as a partner of the ruling elite. The assistance included direct subsidies to businesses, grants for research and development, low-interest loans, and support of farm-related education.

Second, the expansion of cities into suburbs has resulted from big business making a killing in the real estate, construction, and banking industries. Again, with considerable government subsidies and tax deductions, numerous single-family homes were built in the suburbs in the 1950s and 1960s. To induce people to buy these houses, the government guaranteed mortgages and provided tax deductions for interest payments. The result was massive suburbanization.

Third, from the 1970s to today, large corporations have helped turn many suburbs into edge cities by moving their businesses and factories there from central cities. This move has been motivated by profit. By building new plants in the suburbs, corporations have intended to avoid problems in central cities such as labor unrest, high city taxes, and other financial costs—or have expected to receive such benefits from the suburbs as cheap land, lower taxes, a local industry-friendly government, and the lack of organized labor.

■ Symbolic Interactionist Perspective: How Urbanites Interact

We can learn much from symbolic interactionists about how strangers interact in cities (Karp et al., 1991).

First, city people tend to interact with one another in a superficial, impersonal way. Given the density of the urban population and hence the huge number of potential interpersonal contacts, urbanites have learned to protect themselves from *psychic overload*

theoretical thumbnail

Urbanization and City Life

Perspective	Focus	Insights
Functionalist	How the masses drive urbanization	People leave farms to seek better opportunities and lives in the cities and then the suburbs.
Conflict	How big business fuels urbanization	Large corporations pursue profit by starting agribusiness that forces farmers to leave for the cities and then building homes, factories, and businesses in urban and suburban areas.
Symbolic interactionist	How city people interact	City people tend to interact superficially, with civil inattention but with tolerance for others' lifestyles.

by shutting out as many sensations as possible, maybe even the call of a neighbor for help. Thus, most interactions with strangers are brief. An example is one person asking another for a street direction and the second person responding by pointing at a street and saying "over there."

Second, city people tend to interact through *civil inattention* as a way of respecting others' desire for privacy in public places. This involves avoiding eye or physical contact in an elevator, a bus, or some other public place. Conversations with strangers do occur but often under unusual circumstances, as when people are stuck in a stalled elevator or a traffic jam.

Third, city people tend to be tolerant of others' lifestyles, such as different sexual orientations and religious practices. When such people interact, they usually refrain from imposing their values on others or showing disapproval of others' behavior.

For a quick review of the three sociological perspectives on urbanization and city life, see the Theoretical Thumbnail above.

sociological frontiers

The Future of U.S. Cities

For the foreseeable future—a least 10 years down the road—many U.S. cities, particularly those in the Northeast and Midwest, will continue to lose population to the suburbs and the countryside. This will even be more true of large cities that see themselves as likely targets of terrorist attacks. Most migrants from the city are white and middle class, which means the people left behind in the inner cities are large concentrations of African Americans, poor, and elderly people. These inner cities, however, will become cheaper places to live and will thus continue to attract more immigrants, Hispanics, and Asians, making them predominantly nonwhite. The

trend will continue toward racially separate communities, with more whites in the suburbs and edge cities and more minorities in the central cities.

The central cities will suffer more than just the loss of the white and affluent population, however. As the nation's economy continues to shift from manufacturing to service, informational, and high-tech industries, businesses will build their plants in suburban cities, where most white-collar workers live. But if enterprise zones and other urban-renewal programs in the central cities succeed, the loss of blue-collar jobs will stop and unemployment and poverty will decline.

Finally, the federal government will continue to cut its financial support for the cities. Having faced severe budget cuts since the early 1980s, the government can hardly be expected at this point to pump much money into urban programs. On the other hand, the federal government cannot leave the cities out in the cold. There will always be tension between the conservative goal of local control and the liberal tendency toward federal intervention. And the federal government will probably continue to tackle problems that are essentially national in scope, including welfare, Medicaid, and long-term health care. Programs that are local in nature will probably be returned to state and local governments, including community-development block grants, mass transit, rural wastewater grants, and vocational education.

■ For more of the latest Sociological Frontiers, look up Continuing Update at www.ablongman.com/thio6e.

using sociology

How to Revitalize the City

As the middle class has continued to migrate to the suburbs, many large cities have become poorer and more economically and physically isolated. Their governments have thus expended a great deal of energy and money to revitalize them. Consider downtown Cleveland, once a dead zone of vacant lots. It's come alive as the home to a new baseball stadium and the Rock-and-Roll Hall of Fame and Museum. Newark, too, has built its splendid New Jersey Performing Arts Center as a symbol of urban resurgence.

But cities should do more than simply transform themselves into entertainment satellites for tourists, conventioneers, and suburbanites—none of whom reside there. Specifically, cities should increase their efforts to attract more of the people who have traditionally found city life exciting—creative individuals, the young and single, childless couples, lovers of the arts, and enterprising immigrants. To do so, cities must offer what matters most to this demographic, including cultural amenities, lower taxes, greater public safety, and clean streets. Even more important, cities should also try to attract average families with children. Currently, many such families move to the suburbs primarily for the presumed superiority of the schools there. The challenge for cities, then, is to substantially improve their own schools (Jackson, 2001; Kotkin, 2001; Bissinger, 1997).

Thinking critically, how would you make people want to work and live in a large city?

CHAPTER REVIEW

1. *Why are sociologists interested in ecology?* Humans, like other organisms, live within ecosystems, dependent on other organisms and on the physical environment. Thus, we are limited by two ecological principles: One, natural resources are finite. Two, if we alter one aspect of our environment, we end up changing others, as well. *What are the basic environmental problems?* The depletion of natural resources and pollution are the basic problems. *How is pollution related to consumption?* To consume, we must produce, and both production and consumption create waste materials that must go somewhere. When our creation of wastes exceeds nature's capacity to recycle the material, pollution results.

2. *What are the main causes of environmental problems?* Poverty, ignorance, and overconsumption are the main causes. *What are the main methods of saving the environment?* The main methods include antipollution laws; conservation; development of more efficient, less polluting technology; and a slowing of traditional economic and population growth.

3. *What is the feminist perspective on the environment?* This perspective suggests that Western industrial civilization has developed through the exploitation of nature, which, in turn, has reinforced the subjugation of women because women are popularly considered closer to nature than are men.

4. *What are the main stages in the history of cities?* They are preindustrial, industrial, and metropolitan-megalopolitan. Preindustrial cities began developing about 5,000 years ago. They were very small, and people lived where they worked. The industrial city developed when the Industrial Revolution triggered urbanization. During the twentieth century, the industrial city spread outward, and the city and its suburbs became interdependent, forming a metropolis and a megalopolis. *What is the condition of megacities around the earth?* Megacities have grown faster in the developing world than in the developed world. All of them are faced with problems, but most are able to solve the problems in ways that reflect the nature of their societies.

5. *Who usually lives in the city versus the suburbs?* Generally, more affluent people live in the suburbs. The poor and minority groups tend to concentrate in central cities. But typical urban residents also include immigrants, professionals, unmarried individuals, and childless couples. *How have the suburbs changed in recent years?* Many suburbs have changed from residential communities to edge cities, economic centers that are like central cities. At the same time, the suburbs are facing typically urban problems such as congestion, pollution, and crime. *What changes have occurred in U.S. cities over the last 10 years?* Most cities have grown rapidly, fueled by the booming economy, the influx of immigrants, and the sharp drop in crime. Without immigrants, some major cities would lose in population. Cities with more well-educated residents have grown larger, while cities with more poor people have become smaller. Most state capitals have also grown, and many more of the largest 100 cities have greater numbers of minorities than whites.

6. *Is there a pattern behind land use in a city?* Three classic theories and a new one explain the patterns found in many U.S. cities. According to the concentric-zone theory, cities spread outward from a central business district, forming a series of concentric zones. According to the sector theory, cities expand from a central business district, not in concentric circles but in wedge-shaped sectors. By contrast, the multiple-nuclei theory holds that a city is not built around one center but around discrete nuclei, each of which is the center of specialized activities. A new theory, the peripheral theory, depicts the recent development of suburban cities around the central city. *What determines the spatial pattern of a city?* Dominance, competition, invasion, and succession determine the pattern.

7. *Does the urban environment make city people different from other people?* Three theories offer different answers. According to the urban anomie theory, city life is characterized by alienation, impersonal relations, and reliance on formal social control, as well as emotional stress and mental disorders. By contrast, the compositional theory argues that city dwellers' social lives, centered in small groups of friends, relatives, and neighbors, are much like those of people outside the city. The subcultural theory contends that the city enriches people's lives by offering them diverse opportunities and by promoting the development of subcultures.

8. *If some large U.S. cities have been losing in population, why have their budgets increased?* The costs of maintaining streets, sewers, public buildings, and so on have risen as the cities have aged. Many of those who remain in the city are the ones who depend most on its services to survive. *Why is it difficult for a city to be financially independent?* One reason is that a city often receives no tax revenues from suburbanites and other nonresidents who use its services. *What is the political dilemma in running a city?* Elected officials are not willing to raise taxes for fear of antagonizing voters. *Why has housing remained segregated?* Reasons include lower minority income, racial prejudice in white neighborhoods, and racial discrimination among real estate agents and banks.

9. *What insight do the three sociological perspectives provide about urban growth and city life?* According to functionalists, ordinary people contribute to and seek to benefit from urbanization. But to conflict theorists, big business, with help from big government, is the driving force behind urban expansion. Symbolic interactionists focus on how strangers interact in the city.

10. *What does the future hold for U.S. cities?* Many cities will continue to lose whites and the middle class, along with higher-paid service jobs, to the suburbs, leaving the urban core to minorities and the poor. The federal government will also continue to cut its financial support for the cities. *How can the city be revitalized?* The city needs to attract more of the people who have traditionally found city life exciting and also lure back the average families with children that have left for the suburbs.

KEY TERMS

Biosphere A thin layer of air, water, and soil surrounding the earth (p. 400).

Compositional theory The theory that city dwellers are as involved with small groups of friends, relatives, and neighbors as are noncity people (p. 416).

Concentric-zone theory The model of land use in which the city spreads out from the center in a series of concentric zones, each used for a particular kind of activity (p. 412).

Ecology A study of the interactions among organisms and between organisms and their physical environment (p. 400).

Ecosystem A self-sufficient community of organisms depending for survival on one another and on the environment (p. 400).

Empowerment zones The economically depressed urban areas that businesses, with the help of government grants, low-interest loans, and tax breaks, try to revive by creating jobs; also known as enterprise zones (p. 419).

Gentrification The movement of affluent people into poor urban neighborhoods (p. 410).

Megacity A city with a population of 5 million or more (p. 407).

Megalopolis A vast area in which many metropolises merge (p. 407).

Metropolis A large urban area that includes a city and its surrounding suburbs (p. 406).

Multiple-nuclei theory The model of land use in which a city is built around many discrete nuclei, each being the center of some specialized activity (p. 414).

Peripheral theory The model of land use in which suburban cities grow around the central city (p. 414).

Sector theory The model of land use in which a city grows outward in wedge-shaped sectors from the center (p. 413).

Subcultural theory The theory that the city enriches people's lives by offering diverse opportunities and developing various subcultures (p. 416).

Urban anomie theory The theory that city people have a unique way of life characterized by alienation, impersonal relations, and stress (p. 415).

Urban ecological processes Processes in which people compete for certain land use, one group dominates another, and a particular group moves into an area and takes it over from others (p. 414).

Urban ecology The study of the relationship between people and their urban environment (p. 412).

Urbanization The transformation of rural areas into cities (p. 400).

QUESTIONS FOR DISCUSSION AND REVIEW

ENVIRONMENT

1. What major environmental problems now challenge the ecosystems of modern industrial societies?
2. Why can't technology solve all the problems of diminishing resources and environmental pollution?
3. How does the "Tragedy of the Commons" help explain environmental destruction?
4. How can environmental destruction be brought under control?
5. What can we learn about environmental problems from the feminist perspective?

A GLOBAL ANALYSIS OF URBANIZATION

1. What accounted for the emergence of the preindustrial city?
2. How does the industrial city differ from the preindustrial city?
3. What forces have led to the development of suburbs, metropolises, and, finally, megalopolises?
4. What problems do megacities have, and how are these problems being tackled?

CITIES IN THE UNITED STATES

1. What kinds of people are most likely to live in U.S. cities?
2. How have U.S. cities changed over the last decade?
3. How have suburbs changed into edge cities?

THE URBAN ENVIRONMENT

1. According to the three theories of land use, what do cities look like?
2. How do urban ecological processes shape a city?

THE NATURE OF CITY LIFE

1. According to urban anomie theory, how does the city affect people's lives?
2. In what ways are compositional and subcultural theories similar, and in what ways are they different?

CAUSES OF URBAN PROBLEMS

1. What impact does population decline have on a city?
2. Why do many cities have serious financial problems?
3. How have cities dealt with the political dilemma of raising taxes?
4. What factors contribute to housing segregation?

SOCIOLOGICAL PERSPECTIVES ON URBANIZATION AND CITY LIFE

1. How do the functionalist and conflict perspectives differ in explaining urbanization?
2. According to symbolic interactionism, how do strangers in the city interact?

SOCIOLOGICAL FRONTIERS/USING SOCIOLOGY

1. What kind of future will U.S. cities have?
2. How can the city be revitalized?

SUGGESTED READINGS

Baxandall, Rosalyn, and Elizabeth Ewen. 2000. *Picture Windows: How the Suburbs Happened.* New York: Basic Books. A study of how government policy, along with the society's broader social ideology, created suburbs in the United States.

Gottdiener, Mark, Claudia C. Collins, and David R. Dickens. 1999. *Las Vegas: The Social Production of an All-American City.* Malden, MA: Blackwell. Offers the theory that Las Vegas is becoming a more typical American city while the rest of the nation's cities are changing to be more like Las Vegas.

Grogan, Paul, and Tony Proscio. 2000. *Comeback Cities: A Blueprint for Urban Neighborhood Revival.* Boulder, CO: Westview. Describes the remarkable improvements of previously devastated neighborhoods in New York, Cleveland, and other big cities in the United States.

Lomborg, Bjorn. 2001. *The Skeptical Environmentalist: Measuring the Real State of the World.* New York: Cambridge University Press. Presents considerable data to show that the environment is in much better shape than popularly believed.

Rybczynski, Witold. 1995. *City Life: Urban Expectations in a New World.* New York: Scribner's. Shows how U.S. cities largely reflect the needs and ideas of ordinary people rather than the aesthetic visions of planning elites, as in European societies.

■ Additional Resources

The New York Times
expect the world®

nytimes.com

Expand your knowledge of the concepts discussed in this chapter by reading the following current and historical articles from the *New York Times*. Go to the "eThemes of the Times" section of the Companion Website (www.ablongman.com/thio6e):

"Chinese Will Move Waters to Quench Thirst of Cities"

Research Navigator.com

Research Navigator, a research database, provides immediate access to hundreds of full-text articles from EBSCO's ContentSelect Academic Journal Database. If the Research Navigator access code was included with your textbook, go to the website www.research navigator.com and read the following articles related to this chapter by typing in the article number:

Lansing, Michael. "Environmental Ethics, Green Politics and the History of Predator Biology." *Ethics, Place and Environment*, Mar2002, Vol. 5 Issue 1, p43, 7p. Accession Number: 6978224. Presents the ethics and politics of environmentalism.

Wright, James D. "Small Towns, Mass Society, and the 21st Century." *Society*, Nov/Dec2000, Vol. 38 Issue 1, p3, 8p. Accession Number: 3716461. Focuses on the disappearance of small towns in the United States.

Collective Behavior, Social Movements, and Social Change

myths & realities

myth *If you are watching a humorous movie in a theater, how often you laugh depends solely on how funny you think the movie is.*

reality The size of the audience also has a significant impact. The larger the audience, the more frequent your laughter will be (p. 433).

myth *Violence in most riots is contagious; virtually all participants will get involved.*

reality Not all participants in riots engage in violence. Many simply watch others commit the violence (p. 433).

myth *It's better not to listen to rumors because they are always false.*

reality Rumors are not necessarily false; they may turn out to be true. They are merely unverified stories spread from one person to another—unverified because people do not bother to check them against facts (p. 435).

myth *Discontent, if deep enough, can bring about a social movement by itself.*

reality Discontent alone does not spark a movement; resources also must be available for mobilization, such as strong organization, effective leadership, money, and media access (p. 439).

myth *Modernization always threatens or destroys tradition.*

reality Tradition and modernization can coexist and even reinforce each other (p. 440).

myth *Since 1990, the gap between rich and poor in the United States has narrowed as a result of increasing economic growth.*

reality Since the economic boom has mostly benefited the rich, the gap between them and the poor has widened, forming a smaller middle class and larger upper and lower classes (p. 446).

myth *Americans are less healthy today than a decade ago because their lives are now more hectic and stressful.*

reality Americans are healthier today. Life expectancy has gone up, and the percentage of smokers has gone down, accompanied by lower rates of death from heart disease and car accidents. Infant mortality has also declined sharply (p. 447).

427

n 1995, Jeff Bezos, an employee of a financial management company in New York City, read a research report estimating that Internet use among Americans would grow annually by 2,300 percent. Bezos double-checked the figure to make sure he had read it correctly. Then he quit his job, packed his bags, and drove all the way to Seattle. While his wife was driving, he was busy typing out a business plan on his laptop. He would open the nation's first bookstore in cyberspace with a simple idea: Customers would be invited to type in a book's title, the author's name, or just a general subject, and the site would show a list of all the books matching the information given. Then the buyers would choose their book, type in its title, and their address and credit-card number. Bezos would have his employees find the order and mail it to the customer within a day or two—and at a hefty discount. Soon after arriving in Seattle, Bezos launched Amazon.com. Only three years later, in 1998, the online bookstore had more than 2 million customers, making Bezos a multimillionaire (Time.com, 1998).

Bezos's dazzling success reflects how much computer technology has changed our lives. In addition to buying books over the Internet, a fast-growing number of Americans have been shopping online for many other products, with sales expected to soar from $707 million in 1996 to over $37 billion in 2002 (Kelley, 1998). Only a decade ago, nobody could imagine shopping at the world's largest mall—the virtual mall—through cyberspace. Also, less than 10 years ago, hardly anybody had access to e-mail; a few technological pacesetters did, but they had almost no one to send messages to. Now e-mail has become so common that by 1998, everyone understood the meaning of the movie title *You've Got Mail* (Cook, 1998/1999).

These are only a few examples of the recent changes that have taken place in our lives. But **social change**—the alteration of society over time—is nothing new. Not long before the Internet revolution, we had already seen social change in the emergence of space travel, heart transplants, computers, fax machines, cellular phones, large shopping malls, the increased gap between rich and poor, widespread homelessness, and the many great events that made U.S. society different from what it was a decade or two earlier. Where will all this social change take us? Is there some general pattern behind the way societies change? Where can we expect future changes to come from, and do we have any control over them?

To understand these issues better, we look in this chapter at several theories of social change. We will also examine *modernization*—a particular type of social change that shaped many features of U.S. society and is now reshaping societies around the world. But let us first take a look at collective behavior, which can be an impetus to social change.

THE STUDY OF COLLECTIVE BEHAVIOR

Collective behavior is relatively spontaneous, un-organized, and unpredictable social behavior. It can be contrasted with *institutionalized behavior,* which is well-organized and rather predictable. Institutional-ized behavior is frequent and routine. Every weekday, masses of people hurry to work. On every campus, groups of students walk to classes. These predictable patterns of group action are basically governed by so-cial norms and are the bedrock of social order. Col-lective behavior, however, operates largely outside the confines of these norms.

Source: © Reprinted with special permission of King Features Syndicate.

General Characteristics

Sociologists who study collective behavior face a problem: Whereas scientific analysis seeks out pre-dictable, regular patterns, collective behavior is rela-tively unstructured, spontaneous, and unpredictable. Nevertheless, sociological analysis of collective be-havior has been fruitful. Although collective behav-ior is relatively unstructured, it does have a structure that sociologists have been able to illuminate. Even rumor, for example, includes a structural division of labor: Some people are messengers, while others are interpreters, skeptics, or merely an audience.

The difference between institutionalized and col-lective behavior is not absolute. Instead, the behav-iors can be classified according to the relative degree of control exercised by traditional norms. Thus, we can arrange social behaviors on a continuum like that shown in Figure 15.1. As we move from left to right in the figure, the behavior noted is increasingly subject to traditional norms. Thus, institutionalized behavior is at the far right of the continuum and col-lective behavior lies to the left.

Only the main forms of collective behavior are shown on the continuum. At the far left, for exam-ple, is *panic,* the least structured, most transitory, and rarest form of mass action. When people in a burning theater rush to the same exit, losing their capacity to cooperate and reducing their chance of escape, that is a panic. Next on the continuum are *crowds,* which are somewhat more structured than panics and more subject to the influence of social norms. As a result, members of a crowd can be per-suaded to work toward a common goal. Moving fur-

Degrees of normative regulation							
Collective behavior						**Institutionalized behavior**	
Panics	Crowds	Fashions	Rumors	Public opinion	Social movements	Small groups	Large organizations
Behavior less regulated by traditional norms						Behavior more regulated by traditional norms	

FIGURE 15.1

A Continuum of Normative Regulation

There are two kinds of social behavior—collective and institutionalized. The difference between them is not absolute but relative to normative regulation. Collective behav-ior is less strongly controlled by traditional norms. Collective behavior may be further divided into different forms, which vary in the degree to which they are regulated by traditional norms.

Critical Thinking: *Which type of collective behavior have you participated in? What drew you in, and how did it affect you?*

RECIPE FOR RUMBLE Despite their diversity, all forms of collective behavior are basically attempts to deal with a stressful situation, such as social injustice or an unacceptable status quo. Collective behavior, such as this riot in Cincinnati in 2001, occurs under six conditions: structural conduciveness, social strain, the growth and spread of a generalized belief, a precipitating factor, the mobilization of participants for action, and inadequate social control. ■

ther to the right on the continuum, we see that *social movements* are even more structured than crowds; their members consciously work together to achieve a common objective.

■ Social Factors

Despite the diversity among forms of collective behavior, each is basically an attempt to deal with a stressful situation, such as danger to life, threatened loss of money, social injustice, or an unacceptable status quo. The specific form such behavior takes depends largely on how the people involved define the problem. If they see it as a simple matter, they are likely to engage in such clumsy or primitive behavior as a panic or riot. If they believe the problem is complex enough to require an elaborate analysis, they are more prone to respond through a social movement. Thus, the more complex the situation of strain is believed to be, the more structured the collective behavior.

Whatever the form of the collective behavior, according to Neil Smelser (1971), six factors are necessary to produce the behavior. None of these factors by itself can generate collective behavior. Only the *combination of all six factors,* occurring *in sequence,* creates the conditions necessary for any kind of collective behavior to occur. Let us examine these six factors, illustrated by some facts about the 1992 riot in South-Central Los Angeles:

1. *Structural conduciveness.* Individuals by themselves cannot start a collective action; some aspect of so-

cial organization permits collective action to occur. Before people can take part in collective behavior, some condition, such as living in the same neighborhood, must exist in order for them to assemble and communicate with each other. In South-Central Los Angeles, the African American residents who joined the riot were brought together by media reports that a nearly all-white jury had found four white policemen not guilty of savagely beating African American motorist Rodney King.

2. *Social strain.* The strain may arise from a conflict between different groups, from the failure of a government to meet citizens' needs, or from the society's inability to solve a social problem. The strain that existed in the African American community stemmed from many cases of police brutality against African Americans.

3. *The growth and spread of a generalized belief.* Participants in a collective action come to share some belief about the social strain. The rioters in South-Central Los Angeles shared the belief that the local police had often brutalized and mistreated African Americans.

4. *A precipitating factor.* Some event brings the social strain to a high pitch and confirms the generalized belief about it. The King verdict clearly touched off the riot.

5. *The mobilization of participants for action.* Leaders emerge to move people to take a specific action. Some leaders in the Los Angeles riot urged people on the street to follow them, saying something like "Come with us. Let's burn." Others set an ex-

ample for the crowd by initiating the burning or looting of stores.

6. *Inadequate social control.* Agents of control, such as the police, fail to prevent the collective action. The Los Angeles police department was slow to respond to the riot. The police were virtually absent in the early hours of rioting, allowing many looters to smash storefronts and burn buildings with impunity.

If we look at other riots, such as those in Cincinnati in 2001, in the Liberty City section of Miami in 1980, and in the Overtown section of Miami in 1982, we find a similar sequence of events (Monroe, 2001; Porter and Dunn, 1984).

FORMS OF
COLLECTIVE BEHAVIOR

The *general* analyses of collective behavior that we have just discussed assume that all forms of collective behavior are in some way similar to one another. But each form is also *unique* in some other ways, as we will see in this section.

■ Panics

On a December afternoon in 1903, a fire broke out in Chicago's Iroquois Theater. According to an eyewitness:

> Somebody had yelled "Fire!" . . . The horror in the auditorium was beyond all description. . . . The fire-escape ladders could not accommodate the crowd, and many fell or jumped to death on the pavement below. Some were not killed only because they landed on the cushion of bodies of those who had gone before. But it was inside the house that the greatest loss of life occurred, especially on the stairways. Here most of the dead were trampled or smothered, though many jumped or fell to the floor. In places on the stairways, particularly where a turn caused a jam, bodies were piled seven or eight feet deep. . . . An occasional living person was found in the heap, but most of these were terribly injured. The heel prints on the dead faces mutely testified to the cruel fact that human animals stricken by terror are as mad and ruthless as stampeding cattle. (Schultz, 1964)

The theater did not burn down. Firefighters arrived quickly after the alarm went off and extinguished the flames so promptly that no more than the seats' upholstery was burned. But 602 people died, and many more were injured. Panic, not the fire itself, largely accounted for the tragedy. Similarly, on a July morning in 1990 in the holy city of Mecca, Saudi Arabia, when the lights accidentally went out in a 600-yard-long tunnel through which thousands of Muslim pilgrims were walking, panic triggered a stampede, killing 1,426 people.

The people in the Iroquois Theater and the Mecca tunnel behaved as people sometimes do when faced with unexpected threats such as fires, earthquakes, floods, and other disasters: They exhibited panic behavior. A **panic** is a type of collective behavior characterized by a maladaptive, fruitless response to a serious threat. That response generally involves flight, but it is a special kind of flight. In many situations, flight is a rational, adaptive response: It is perfectly sensible to flee a burning house or an oncoming car. In these cases, flight is the only appropriate way of achieving a goal—successful escape from danger. In panic behavior, however, the flight is irrational and uncooperative. It follows a loss of self-control, and it increases, rather than reduces, the danger to oneself and others. If people in a burning theater panic, they stampede each other, rather than filing out in an orderly way, and produce the kind of unnecessary loss of life that occurred in the Iroquois Theater and the Mecca tunnel.

Preconditions About 40 years ago, during a performance of the play *Long Day's Journey into Night* in Boston, word spread through the audience that there was a fire. But the audience did not stampede to the exits. One of the actors "stepped to the footlights and calmly said, 'Please be seated, ladies and gentlemen, nothing serious has happened. Just a little accident with a cigarette. . . . The fire is out now and if you will sit down again we can resume.'" The audience laughed and sat down (Brown, 1965). In this case, as in the Iroquois fire, the audience had an impulse to flee for their lives. But because the crisis was defused, a contradictory impulse—to follow the norms of polite society and remain calm and quiet—won out. In short, the existence of a crowd and a threat does not ensure that people will panic. Several social-psychological preconditions must be met for the development of a panic.

First, there must be a *perception* that a crisis exists. Second, there must be *intense fear* of the perceived danger. This fear is typically compounded by a feeling of *possible* entrapment. If people believed they are *certainly* trapped, as in the case of prisoners who are about to be executed by a firing squad, they will give in to calm resignation rather than wild panic. Third, there must be some *panic-prone individuals.* Typically, they are overly self-centered persons whose frantic desire to save themselves makes them oblivious to the fate of others and to the self-destructive consequences of their panic. Fourth, there must be *mutual emotional facilitation.* The people in the crowd must spread and enhance each other's terror. Finally, there must be a *lack of cooperation* among people (Johnson, 1987; Schultz, 1964).

Most crowds, however, are made up of many small primary groups of relatives or friends rather than strangers. Constrained by the bonds of these primary groups, members of crowds usually do not panic and stampede each other to death. More generally, as social animals, people have a certain sense of responsibility to one another as relatives, friends, and even total strangers. When faced with a disaster, they tend not to panic but to help each other to safety in a calm and orderly manner. This may explain why the overwhelming majority (90 percent) of the people in the World Trade Center were able to come out alive from the inferno on September 11, 2001 (Clarke, 2002).

Mass Hysteria   Panic sometimes takes the form of **mass hysteria**, in which numerous people engage in frenzied activity without bothering to check the source of their fear. A classic case occurred in 1938, when the play *War of the Worlds* was broadcast on the radio. Many people thought that they were hearing a news report. Tuned in to music on the radio, they suddenly heard an announcement that Martians had invaded the earth:

> Ladies and gentlemen, I have a grave announcement to make. Incredible as it may seem, both the observations of science and the evidence of our eyes lead to the inescapable assumption that those strange beings who landed in the New Jersey farmlands tonight are the vanguard of an invading army from the planet Mars. The battle which took place tonight . . . has ended in one of the most startling defeats ever suffered by an army in modern times; seven thousand men armed with rifles and machine guns pitted against a single fighting machine of the invaders from Mars. One hundred and twenty known survivors. The rest strewn over the battle area . . . and trampled to death under the metal feet of the monster, or burned to cinders by its heat ray. (Cantril, 1982)

Long before the broadcast ended, at least 1 million of the 6 million listeners had been swept away by panic. Many prayed, cried, or fled, frantic to escape death from the Martians. Some hid in cellars. Young men tried to rescue girlfriends. Parents woke their sleeping children. People telephoned friends to share the bad news or to say goodbye. Many called hospitals for ambulances; others tried to summon police cars.

But not everyone panicked. Hadley Cantril directed a study to find out who panicked, who didn't, and why. Those who did not were found to have what Cantril called *critical ability*. Some of these people found the broadcast simply too fantastic to believe. As

one of them reported, "I heard the announcer say that he saw a Martian standing in the middle of Times Square and he was as tall as a skyscraper. *That's all I had to hear*—just the word Martian was enough even without the fantastic and incredible description." Others with critical ability had sufficient specific knowledge to recognize the broadcast as a play. They were familiar with Orson Welles's story or recognized that he was acting the role of Professor Pierson. Still others tried to check the accuracy of the broadcast by looking up newspaper listings of radio schedules and programs. These people, on the whole, had more years of education than those who did panic. The less educated, aside from lacking critical ability, were found to have a feeling of personal inadequacy and emotional insecurity (Cantril, 1982).

■ Crowds

A **crowd** is a collection of people temporarily doing something while in proximity to one another. They may be gathered on a street corner watching a fire. They may be in a theater watching an opera. They may be on a street throwing rocks at the police.

Common Traits   Nearly all crowds share a few traits. One is *uncertainty:* The participants do not share clear expectations about how to behave or about the outcome of their collective behavior. Another element common to most crowds is a *sense of urgency*. The people in the crowd feel that something must be done right away to solve a common problem. The third characteristic of crowds is the *communication* of mood, attitude, and idea among the members, which pressures them to conform. Crowds are also marked by *heightened suggestibility*. Those in a crowd tend to respond uncritically to the suggestions of others and to go along impulsively with their actions. Finally, crowds are characterized by *permissiveness,* freedom from the constraint of conventional norms. Thus, people tend to express feelings and take actions that they would suppress under ordinary circumstances (Turner and Killian, 1987).

Social Contagion   Sometimes, crowds are irrational or destructive. Consider the lynch mobs in the United States before 1900. Thousands of whites and African Americans were lynched. The number of lynchings dropped during the twentieth century, but still, between 1900 and 1950, there were more than 3,000 victims, nearly all of them African American. The alleged crimes of the African American victims were often trivial, such as "trying to act like a white man," making boastful remarks, winking at a white man's wife, or being too ambitious (Raper, 1970). Why did the members of lynch mobs behave so irra-

FOLLOW THE CROWD A crowd seems to have a collective mind, with all its members thinking, feeling, and acting alike. This mind, according to nineteenth-century social psychologist Gustave Le Bon, is emotional, irrational, and uncivilized. But to most sociologists today, routine and orderly behavior prevails in most crowds, as can be seen in this throng of people peacefully walking across the Brooklyn Bridge during a massive blackout on August 14, 2003, in New York City. ■

tionally and destructively? In particular, why did otherwise civilized whites act like beasts as members of a lynch mob?

According to French social psychologist Gustave Le Bon (1841–1931), a crowd is homogeneous in thought and action. All the people in a crowd think, feel, and act alike. As a crowd, they possess a *collective mind*. This mind is emotional and irrational, stripped bare of all civilizing restraints. Beneath those restraints, Le Bon believed, hides a barbarian. All the members of a crowd bring to the situation this hiding barbarian with its primitive instincts. Normally, they suppress these instincts, wearing the mask of civilized behavior. But a crowd provides them with a different sort of mask: The large number of people gives individuals a cloak of anonymity that weakens

their restraining sense of responsibility and releases primitive emotions.

myth	If you are watching a humorous movie in a theater, how often you laugh depends solely on how funny you think the movie is.
reality	The size of the audience also has a significant impact. The larger the audience, the more frequent your laughter will be.

But why do individuals give up their individuality and let themselves become part of a collective mind? The reason, in Le Bon's view, is **social contagion**—the spreading of a certain emotion and action from one member of the crowd to another. Research has uncovered factors that can facilitate contagion, including *crowd size* and *noise*. When people are viewing a humorous movie in a theater, the larger the audience, the more frequent the laughter. If a person coughs in a room full of people, others are more likely to cough than if only a few people are around. Watching a videotaped arm-wrestling match, the subjects' tendency to imitate the wrestlers increases with higher levels of audience noise (Markovsky and Berger, 1983; Pennebaker, 1980; Levy and Fenley, 1979).

The Emergent Norm   To most sociologists today, Le Bon's notion of a collective mind is valid only as a loose metaphor for what happens in crowds. Members of a crowd may appear homogeneous. They may seem to have given up their individuality and become absorbed in a collective mind. But beneath these appearances, the members of a crowd are basically just individuals engaged in a particular kind of interaction. Whereas Le Bon set the behavior of crowds apart from normal social interaction as a sort of bizarre regression to almost subhuman behavior, other sociologists have found that routine and orderly behavior prevails in most crowds (McPhail and Wohlstein, 1983).

myth	Violence in most riots is contagious; virtually all participants will get involved.
reality	Not all participants in riots engage in violence. Many simply watch others commit the violence.

Two U.S. sociologists, Ralph Turner and Lewis Killian (1987), for example, accept Le Bon's fundamental idea that a crowd appears to act as a homogeneous group, but they argue that Le Bon exaggerated its homogeneity. In a lynch mob, for example, not all the members think or act in the same way. Some individuals storm the jail, others drag out the prisoner, others bring ropes, others hang the victim, and some just stand by and watch. Even those engaged in the same act may have different feelings, attitudes, or beliefs, and they participate because of diverse motives. How, then, does the apparent unanimity among the participants develop?

The answer can be found in Turner and Killian's **emergent-norm theory**, the theory that members of a crowd develop, through interaction, a new norm to deal with the unconventional situation facing them. Because of the norm, people feel pressed to conform to the crowd's outward behavior, even if they disagree with the action. The result is the *appearance* of unanimity, which may be more illusion than reality. Indeed, many studies have found the illusion of unanimity in most crowds (McPhail and Wohlstein, 1983).

■ Fashions

Compared with crowds, fashions are more subject to traditional norms. Practically all aspects of human life—clothes, hairstyles, architecture, philosophy, and the arts—are influenced by fashions. A **fashion** is a great, though brief, enthusiasm among a relatively large number of people for a particular innovation. But because their novelty tends to wear off quickly, fashions are usually short lived. Most are related to the latest in clothes. In the aftermath of the September 11, 2001, terrorist attacks, for example, it was suddenly fashionable to wear red, white, and blue clothes or the logo "I Love New York." As long as there is something new that strikes many people's fancy, it can become a fashion (see Figure 15.2).

Sources of Fashions Why do fashions occur in the first place? One reason is that some cultures, like that of the United States, *value change:* What is new is good. And so, in many modern societies, clothing styles change yearly, while people in traditional societies may wear the same style for generations. A second reason is that many industries *promote* quick changes in fashions to increase sales. A third reason is that fashions usually *trickle down from the top.* A new style may occasionally originate from lower-

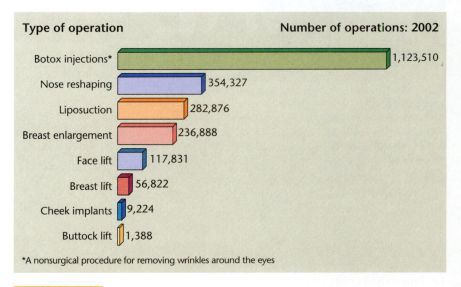

Type of operation	Number of operations: 2002
Botox injections*	1,123,510
Nose reshaping	354,327
Liposuction	282,876
Breast enlargement	236,888
Face lift	117,831
Breast lift	56,822
Cheek implants	9,224
Buttock lift	1,388

*A nonsurgical procedure for removing wrinkles around the eyes

FIGURE 15.2

Cosmetic Surgery as a Fashion

Just as "the latest" in clothes can become a fashion, so can "the latest" in cosmetic surgery. Both have the same purpose: to improve physical appearance. Cosmetic surgery has become relatively popular in the United States because of the constant pressure from the media and other aspects of society and culture to look beautiful. In fact, cosmetic surgery has become a multi-billion-dollar industry. The latest fashion favors some parts of the body more than others.

Critical Thinking: *Do any of these types of surgeries interest you or people you know? Why or why not?*

Source: Data from American Society of Plastic Surgeons, 2003.

EASY COME, EASY GO Fads and crazes are temporary enthusiasms for certain innovations. They are relatively short lived. While crazes have serious consequences, fads, like the recent popularity of scooters, are basically trivial. A fad often serves to identify those who are "with it" from others who are not, until the fad becomes widely dispersed and replaced by enthusiasm for something else. ■

status groups, as blue jeans did. But most fashions come from upper-class people, who like to adopt some style or artifact as a badge of their status. They cannot monopolize most status symbols for long, however. Their style is adopted by the middle class and may be copied or modified for use by lower-status groups, offering many people the prestige of possessing a high-status symbol (Turner and Killian, 1987).

Fads and Crazes Similar to fashions but less predictable and shorter-lived are fads and crazes. A **fad** is a temporary enthusiasm for an innovation less respectable than a fashion, while a **craze** is a fad with serious consequences. Examples of fads include Air Jordans, the *macarena*, hula hoops, telephone booth

stuffing, and streaking. If these mean nothing to you, it is testimony to how quickly the magic of fads can fade. Fads are basically trivial, but they can be *a source of status* to some people. Carrying a beeper, for example, is a status symbol for teenagers in some U.S. cities. So is wearing a Von Dutch trucker hat, as seen on the heads of Britney Spears, Justin Timberlake, and Carmen Electra (Kang, 2003). Fads also enable people to get a comfortable sense of *being part of a group* by imitating others, such as wearing ripped jeans or attending a rock concert.

More bizarre and harmful than fads, crazes are a kind of contagious folly with serious consequences. Usually, crazes are economic in nature, including a *boom,* in which many people frantically try to buy something of wildly exaggerated value, and a *bust,* in which many frantically try to sell a worthless thing. The most famous craze is probably the tulip mania that swept Holland in 1634. For some unknown reason, the Dutch developed a passion for tulips. Eventually, one bulb cost as much as a large house. Soon, the Dutch were more interested in making a fortune out of tulips than in growing them. People bought bulbs only to sell them for a huge profit. They were astonished when people who returned from long trips abroad did not share this appreciation of the bulbs at all. It was widely known that a sailor mistook a valuable bulb for an onion and ate it with his herring. Eventually, people began to realize that the price of tulips could not keep rising forever. Thus, the boom was broken and the price of tulips fell sharply, bankrupting thousands.

■ Rumors

On the face of it, a rumor may appear as unreal as a craze. But it is not necessarily false.

myth	It's better not to listen to rumors because they are always false.
reality	Rumors are not necessarily false; they may turn out to be true. They are merely unverified stories spread from one person to another—unverified because people do not bother to check them against facts.

Characteristics A **rumor** is an unverified story that spreads from one person to another. As the story circulates, each person distorts the account by dropping some items and adding his or her own interpretation. But a rumor is not necessarily false: It may turn out to be true. It is unverified *not* because it is necessarily a distortion but because people do not bother to check it against facts.

Every day, we all act on the basis of unverified reports. Sociologists therefore view rumors as a normal form of communication. According to Tamotsu Shibutani (1966), for example, rumor is a communication people use in an effort to comprehend what is going on in a situation where information is lacking. Rumor, then, is a process in which many individuals—both spreaders and receivers of rumors—try together to construct a definition of an ambiguous situation. What if a rumor is later proved to be false? People still tend to believe it to some degree because of the popular assumption that "Where there's smoke, there's fire" (Tannen, 1990).

Contributing Factors   A rumor is likely to develop and circulate if people's demand for news about an ambiguous situation is not met by institutionalized channels of communication, such as newspapers, government announcements, and television and radio newscasts. The more ambiguous a situation, the greater the chance that a rumor will develop. Thus, rumor is much more a part of interpersonal communications in police states and totalitarian societies, where people do not trust the media because they are controlled by the government.

Anxiety also plays a significant role. Not long ago, widespread anxiety over economic problems made U.S. businesses ripe for the rumor mill. People who had lost or were afraid of losing their jobs were especially likely to believe or pass on damaging rumors about big companies. Seeing a corporate giant in trouble seemed to make them feel better.

This provided fertile ground for the growth of the rumor in 1978 that McDonald's added earthworms to its hamburgers. In 1982, another rumor had it that Procter & Gamble's logo, showing 13 stars and a man in the moon, was a sign of devil worship. In 1991, it was rumored that Liz Claiborne, the clothing company, gave 30 percent of its profits to the Church of Satan. Right after the terrorist attacks in late 2001, many rumors sprang up, including the story that a 70-year-old man surfed the debris down 80 flights in one of the World Trade towers, emerging safely (Tyrangiel, 2001; Goleman, 1991; Koenig, 1982). Although *all these rumors were false,* they spread like prairie fires.

■ Public Opinion

When we talk about "the public," we usually mean the population at large. In sociology, however, the term is more precise: A **public** is a dispersed collection of people who share a particular interest or concern. The interest may involve environmental issues, civil rights, or outlawing pornography. Thus, there are a great many publics within the population at large.

Whenever a public comes into being, it forms an opinion. **Public opinion** is the collection of ideas and attitudes shared by the members of a particular public. As measured by polls and surveys, public opinion often seems fickle, changing easily even as values appear constant. This fickleness may reflect the difference between private and public opinion. "What a person says only to his wife, himself, or in his sleep," wrote Turner and Killian (1987), "constitutes his private opinion. What he will say to a stranger is public opinion." In private, many people will express doubts about an opinion, which might change a public opinion.

Propaganda   Politicians want to win our hearts and minds, and businesses want to win our dollars. Both use the media to try to gain mass support by manipulating public opinion. In other words, they generate **propaganda**—communication tailored to influence opinion. Propaganda may be true or false. What sets it apart from other communications is the intent to change opinion. In their classic study of the subject, Alfred and Elizabeth Lee (1979) identified a number of methods for swaying public opinion. The most frequently used are as follow:

1. *Name calling,* or giving something a negative label. This method is designed to make the audience reject an idea, a person, or a product without analysis. If a candidate is "ultraconservative," "ultraliberal," "flaky," or a "big spender," why bother to consider his or her qualifications seriously? If abortion is "murder," who can support its legalization?
2. *Glittering generality,* the opposite of name calling. An idea or a product is associated with a general, ambiguous, but extremely popular concept or belief. If a war represents "the defense of democracy and freedom," who can oppose it?
3. *Transfer,* or associating an idea or product with something else that is widely respected, admired, or desired. Beautiful, scantily clad actresses sell cars and mattresses on television commercials. Presidents give television speeches with the U.S. flag prominently displayed behind them.
4. *Testimonial,* or having a famous person endorse or oppose some idea or product. Top athletes tell us to use a certain shampoo or shaving cream. Famous politicians travel to towns they never heard of to urge people to vote for obscure candidates.

Media Influence   Despite those manipulations, the effect of propaganda, like the effect of any communication, is limited. Because we are not computers to be programmed or clay to be molded, neither propagandists nor the media can simply insert opinions into our heads or erase previously held beliefs.

POWER OF THE PRESS
Although there are limitations on what the U.S. media can do, they do have the power to influence public opinion. This power comes largely from the media's role as gatekeepers—determining what information will be passed on to large numbers of readers, listeners, and viewers. ■

In general, at least three factors limit the influence of the media on public opinion. First, in free countries, a multitude of independent organizations *present diverse viewpoints,* canceling each other's impact on the audience. Second, because most of the media are interested in making a profit, they often *present what the audience wants to see or hear.* Third, communication frequently occurs through the *two-step flow* of influence: We may hear an analysis of an issue on television (the first step), but we often accept or reject it after *being influenced by our* **opinion leaders** (the second step), individuals whose opinion is respected by others and influences them (Turner and Killian, 1987).

The media do influence public opinion to some degree. Their power comes largely from their role as gatekeepers—determining what information will be passed on to large numbers of people. There are at least four ways in which the media affect opinion.

First, they *authenticate* information, making it more credible to the audience. A news item reported in the mass media often seems more believable than one passed by word of mouth. Second, the media *validate* private opinions, preferences, and values. If a famous commentator offers a view similar to our own, we are likely to feel more confident of our own opinion. Third, the media *legitimize* unconventional viewpoints. The wildest idea may eventually sound reasonable, or at least worth considering, if we read it repeatedly on the editorial pages of newspapers or hear it on the evening news. Fourth, the mass media *concretize* free-floating anxieties and ill-defined preferences. By supplying such labels as "population explosion," "the crime wave," and "the great racial divide," the media in effect create a world of objects against which feelings can be specifically expressed (Turner and Killian, 1987).

What has been discussed holds true largely in democratic societies such as the United States and Canada, where the media and the public are relatively free to express their opinions. These concepts are less likely to be true in many other, less democratic countries, particularly those in the developing world, where the government takes stronger measures to censor public opinion. These countries are shown in Figure 15.3 (p. 438).

■ Social Movements

In the early 1900s, women in the United States could not vote. Until the 1950s, paid vacations for workers were almost unheard of. In the 1960s, when George Wallace was governor of Alabama, he declared "Segregation now, segregation tomorrow, segregation forever." These issues in U.S. society were transformed through **social movements,** conscious efforts to bring about or prevent change.

Compared with the forms of collective behavior we have discussed so far, social movements are far more purposive. A stock market crash, for example, unfolds without plan, but a social movement develops as a result of purposeful effort. Social movements are also far more structured than other forms of collective behavior, even if they are not centrally coordinated. A lynch mob may develop a division of labor, but it is an informal division with a very short life. By contrast, the civil rights movement has within it numerous organizations, recognized leaders, and sets of roles and statuses. Finally, a social movement

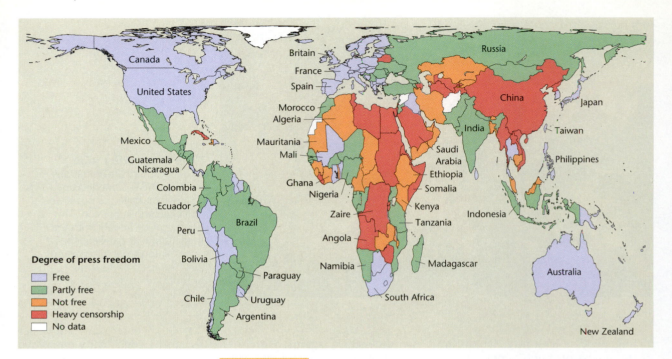

FIGURE 15.3

Freedom of the Press

In democratic societies, such as the United States and Canada, the media and the public are relatively free to express their opinions. But in many less democratic countries, especially in the developing world, the government tends to censor public opinion.

Critical Thinking: *If you were a journalist in one of those developing countries, how would you go about finding the news?*

Source: From *The Penguin State of the World Atlas,* by Dan Smith, copyright © 2003 by Dan Smith. Illustrations © 2003 by Myriad Editions Ltd. Used by permission of Penguin, a division of Penguin Group (USA) Inc.

is more enduring than other forms of collective behavior. A crowd may stay together for a few hours, but a movement may endure for years. These characteristics give social movements the potential to build a membership in the thousands or even millions.

Types   Most social movements aim to change society, but they seek varying degrees of change. They can be classified into four types on the basis of their goals:

1. *Revolutionary movements* seek total, radical change in society. Their goal is to overthrow the existing form of government and replace it with a new one. Revolutionary movements typically resort to violence or some other illegal action. Examples include the revolution for independence in the United States, the Bolshevik revolution in Russia,

the Chinese Communist revolution, and the Castro-led revolution in Cuba.

2. *Reform movements* seek only a partial change in society. They support the existing social system as a whole and want to preserve it, but they aim to improve it by removing its blemishes, typically through legal methods. Each reform movement usually focuses on just one issue. The civil rights movement seeks to rid society of racial discrimination. The women's movement seeks to eliminate gender inequality. The ecology movement seeks to put a stop to environmental pollution.

3. *Resistance movements* seek to preserve an existing system by resisting social change. The Ku Klux Klan and the U.S. Nazi party, for example, try to stop racial integration. In Muslim countries, the Islamic revolution seeks to protect the traditional Islamic way of life against Western influences.

4. *Expressive movements* seek to change the individual, not society. Many are religious, aimed at converting individuals to a particular faith. These movements enable their members to express their sense of guilt, their joy of redemption, and their devotion to their religion. Examples include the Moonies, Hare Krishnas, and other sects.

Causes   We can do so many things in this world: spend our time making money, or fishing, or whatever. Why would people instead spend their time promoting a social movement? According to Eric Hoffer's (1966) **frustration theory**, those who participate in social movements are frustrated and troubled. They use social movements as a diversion, which enables them to hide from themselves their personal problems, such as a sense of inadequacy and inferiority. Furthermore, through a social movement, they can gain a sense of being noble and magnanimous as they fight a good cause beyond their own self-interest. A social movement can also provide a sense of belonging and a way of identifying oneself. Members are therefore, in Hoffer's view, strongly dedicated to their movement's objective, following their leaders blindly as true believers.

There are, however, some holes in the frustration theory. The most important is that it effectively blames movement participants rather than society for their frustration. In fact, it is often unpleasant social conditions, such as social injustice or racial discrimination, that have brought about the discontent in the first place, as is obvious in the case of the civil rights movement. Thus, a number of sociologists have developed the **breakdown-frustration theory**, contending that a social breakdown in the form of, say, racial strife, widespread unemployment, or environmental pollution can cause a social movement by creating frustration among masses of people (Oberschall, 1992; Turner and Killian, 1987).

myth	Discontent, if deep enough, can bring about a social movement by itself.
reality	Discontent alone does not spark a movement; resources also must be available for mobilization, such as strong organization, effective leadership, money, and media access.

Other sociologists have proposed the **resource mobilization theory**, arguing that social movements result from the availability of resources for mobilization. According to this theory, what sparks a movement is not breakdown-frustration but the availability of such mobilization resources as strong organization, effective leadership, money, and media access. But this theory

has, in turn, been criticized for virtually ignoring the place of frustration in social movements (Mayer, 1995; Piven and Cloward, 1995; Oberschall, 1992).

In fact, both resource mobilization and breakdown frustration can be found in practically all social movements. The importance of each varies from one movement to another. As Harold Kerbo (1982) has noted, frustration plays a larger role in *crisis movements* involving African Americans, the unemployed, and poor people, while resource mobilization figures more in *affluence movements,* such as environmental, abortion-rights, and antiwar movements, which involve mostly affluent Americans.

Consequences   Social movements often fail to achieve their immediate goals. The antiwar protests in 2003, for example, failed to stop the U.S. government from waging war on Iraq. Nonetheless, social movements can have powerful and long-lasting consequences for society and the participants themselves (Meyer, 2003).

More specifically, social movements can influence public policy. The antiwar movement in the late 1960s and early 1970s, for example, helped to hasten the end of the Vietnam War and to abolish the draft and institute an all-volunteer armed forces. Social movements can also lead to the creation of new institutions, such as the U.S. Department of Labor, the Environmental Protection Agency, the Consumer Product Safety Commission, and the National Council on Disability. Finally, social movements can make the participants more knowledgeable about various societal problems and more active in dealing with them. Thus, those who demonstrated against the war on Iraq were likely to have participated in other demonstrations relating to such issues as globalization, the environment, and animal rights (Meyer, 2003).

A GLOBAL ANALYSIS OF SOCIAL CHANGE

Social change takes place around the world. In some respects, social change differs from one society to another, and in other respects, it does not. Sociologists therefore question whether diverse societies are converging into one world or diverging into separate worlds.

■ Tradition and Modernization

Modernization is the form of social change that involves the transformation of an agricultural society into an industrial one. Contrary to popular belief, such social change does not inevitably destroy tradition. In many instances, modernization reinforces tradition or vice versa (Hirschman and Nguyen, 2002).

myth	Modernization always threatens or destroys tradition.
reality	Tradition and modernization can coexist and even reinforce each other.

In India, for example, modernization reinforces tradition. When Indians of middle and lower levels seek upward mobility, they do so by "becoming more devoutly Hinduistic," by being as traditionally Indian as possible. Even among very Westernized elites, the native culture still exerts a powerful influence. Nearly all highly modernized Indian intellectuals speak a regional language as their mother tongue, are steeped in classical Sanskrit literature, are strongly tied to an extended family, and are likely to find a spouse through parental arrangements.

We can also see the positive impact of tradition on modernization in Japan. Without its traditional culture, Japan would not have become an industrial giant. The Japanese culture emphasizes the importance of social relations and collective welfare. It encourages consensus rather than conflict, deference to rather than disrespect for authority, and paternalism rather than indifference by those in authority. These cultural values saturate Japan's economic system. A business enterprise, no matter how large, is run like a household, with the accompanying interdependence and loyalty characteristic of the family. Because the company takes care of its workers by giving them lifetime employment, workers tend to identify strongly with employers and work as hard as they can. Moreover, the traditional emphasis on collective welfare does more than enhance productivity through cooperation between managers and workers. It also causes society to favor business and industry at the expense of individuals, transferring funds and wealth from individuals to industries. This can be seen in the fact that factories and company apartments are mostly grand and imposing, whereas private homes are cramped, though highly expensive.

■ Convergence and Divergence

Through modernization, many non-Western societies such as India and Japan are becoming technologically more like Western societies. At the same time, though, both types of societies are growing apart culturally, with one valuing tradition more than the other. These opposite trends have led to the development of two contrasting theories about the changing global society.

According to **convergence theory**, modernization will bring the West and non-West together by breaking down cultural barriers to produce a global society. It is assumed that being exposed to supersonic aircraft, satellite communication, the information superhighway, and multinational companies will make non-Western societies adopt Western ways of living and virtually all Western values. Under the influence of modernization, technocrats and leaders in Asia, Africa, and South America will become a cosmopolitan elite. They will abandon their own traditional cultures, thereby dissolving the cultural differences between their countries and the West (Barnet and Cavanagh, 1994).

Countering this view is **divergence theory**, which emphasizes the growing separation between Western and non-Western cultures. Especially in many Asian and Muslim societies, the tides of cultural nationalism are rising, rejecting Western culture. Saudi Arabia and other Middle Eastern countries, for example, preserve their traditional Islamic way of life despite their embrace of modernization. Thus, in Saudi Arabia, gambling, movies, and dancing are forbidden, and Western videos, books, and publications are heavily censored. Islamic laws are also strictly enforced: thieves' hands are chopped off, adulterers are stoned to death, murderers and rapists are beheaded, and lesser offenders are flogged. All such punishments are carried out in the city squares for the public to see (Barber, 1995; Beyer, 1990).

■ Is the United States in Decline?

The convergence and divergence theories essentially deal with the issue of whether non-Western societies are more like or unlike Western societies. Now, let us examine the same issue from the standpoint of the West: Is the United States, widely seen as the epitome of all that is Western, becoming more like the developing countries by losing its status as the world's leader?

According to Paul Kennedy (1991, 1988), the United States has not actually suffered a serious decline. But he warns that "if the trends in national indebtedness, inadequate productivity increases, mediocre educational performance, and decaying social fabric in the United States are allowed to continue at the same time that massive U.S. commitments of men, money and materials are made in different parts of the globe" in order to maintain our international status as the foremost military power, we will lose that very power in a decade or so. Kennedy is concerned that the United States does

SPEAK SOFTLY, CARRY A BIG STICK The United States has a great deal of so-called hard and soft power. *Hard power* derives from the country's economic and military strength. The United States's *soft power* is in its ability to persuade rather than command, as shown by the worldwide popularity of U.S. brand names. ■

not have the financial resources to solve its economic problems, improve its public education, and eliminate its social problems, such as crime, drugs, and homelessness. He believes that all these problems are capable of turning the United States into a poor developing nation.

Other social scientists are more optimistic. They agree with Kennedy that the United States will decline if its domestic issues are not soundly addressed, but they have faith in the country's ability to deal with these problems. One reason is that the United

States, for all of its problems, continues to be the world's largest economy, with the highest level of absolute productivity, and it now dominates the new international economy. A second reason is that the United States is still the world's greatest military power. A third reason is that the democracy of the United States remains widely admired and emulated; it is now the best example of the political system sweeping the globe (Zakaria, 1998).

In other words, the United States has a great deal of what Joseph Nye (1990) calls "hard" and "soft" power to lead the world. *Hard power* is economic and military strength. *Soft power* is the ability to persuade rather than command, which comes from intangible sources, such as the worldwide popularity of U.S. movies and the admiration and goodwill that U.S. citizens often enjoy abroad. The 1991 Gulf War showed that the United States possesses these two kinds of power. It succeeded in using its military's hard power to defeat Iraq swiftly and with remarkably few U.S. casualties. It succeeded in using its soft power to persuade the United Nations to pass resolutions demanding that Iraq withdraw from Kuwait, and it further used its soft power to mobilize an international coalition to wage war against Iraq. The United States also used both its hard and soft powers to defeat the Taliban in Afghanistan in late 2001. In 2003, however, the United States defeated Iraq militarily without adequate support from the international community—and consequently had a hard time securing peace in the conquered nation. Increasingly, soft noncoercive power will be more effective than hard military power in leading the world, and here Nye believes the United States has a clear edge over all other nations.

FUNCTIONALIST PERSPECTIVE: GRADUAL CHANGE

Modern sociology was born in a period of great social tumult, and its founders developed many of their ideas as a result of trying to understand the vast social changes of their time. Anthropologists and historians, too, were intrigued by the question of how societies change. Most of them were basically functionalists. To some, human society seemed like a well-functioning one-way train headed toward eventual Utopia. To others, it was like a healthy human body growing from innocent childhood to old age. To yet others, it was like an ocean tide, rising and falling and then rising again. To more recent sociologists, it was a social system, with its different parts cooperating to make it function properly. All these social scientists explicitly or implicitly suggested that society takes its time to change and changes gradually.

■ Evolutionary Theory

Human horizons expanded greatly during the nineteenth century as Europeans discovered and studied peoples of other lands and of the distant past. The early anthropologists believed that these peoples offered a portrait of their own ancestors. Most agreed that all societies progressed, or evolved, through three stages of development: savagery, barbarism, and civilization. Western societies, of course, were

deemed civilized; all other peoples were considered savages or barbarians.

This was the origin of **evolutionary theory**, the theory that societies change gradually from simple to complex forms. One of its early exponents was functionalist Herbert Spencer (1820–1903). He believed that all societies followed uniform, natural laws of evolution. These laws decreed survival of the fittest: Those aspects of society that worked well would survive; those that did not would die out. Thus, over time, societies would naturally and inevitably improve. Behind this theory were several questionable assumptions, including the extremely ethnocentric belief that Western culture represents the height of human civilization.

Modern evolutionary theorists have discarded several of these assumptions. In general, they argue that societies tend to change gradually from simple to complex forms. Pastoral societies may be considered simple; modern industrial societies, complex. But evolutionary theorists no longer imply that the change represents an improvement (Lenski et al., 1995). Evolving complexity can be found in the change Durkheim described from mechanical solidarity to organic solidarity (see Chapter 1: The Essence of Sociology). But organic solidarity is not necessarily better than mechanical solidarity. A modern lifestyle is not always an improvement over a traditional one.

■ Cyclical Theory

Evolutionists assume that social change has only one direction. They believe that when societies change they, in effect, burn their bridges behind them; they cannot return to their previous states. In contrast, proponents of **cyclical theory** believe that societies move forward and backward, up and down, in an endless series of cycles.

Spengler's "Majestic Cycles"   German historian Oswald Spengler (1880–1936) was the first to make the cyclical assumption explicit. He wrote in 1918 that Western civilization was headed downhill and would soon die out, just as the Greek and Egyptian civilizations had. "The great cultures," he explained, "accomplish their majestic wave cycles. They appear suddenly, swell in splendid lines, flatten again, and vanish, and the face of the waters is once more a sleeping waste." More often, Spengler likened a culture to an organism. Like any living thing, a culture went through a life cycle of birth, youth, maturity, old age, and death. Western civilization, as he saw it, had reached old age and was tottering toward death.

Spengler's theory was very popular for a time. But to modern sociologists, there is too much poetry and too little science in his argument, and the analogy between societies and biological organisms is more misleading than useful. Nevertheless, Spengler's basic idea that social change is cyclical has influenced social science. Arnold Toynbee and Pitirim Sorokin, for example, offered famous theories based on this view.

Toynbee's "Challenge" and "Response" Like Spengler, British historian Arnold Toynbee (1889–1975) believed that all civilizations rise and fall. But in his view, the rise and fall do not result from some inevitable, biologically determined life cycle. Instead, they depend both on human beings and on their environments. Environments present "challenges," and humans choose "responses" to those challenges. The fate of a civilization, according to Toynbee, depends on both the challenges presented to a civilization and the responses it devises.

The *challenge* may come from the natural environment or from human sources. Barren land, a frigid climate, and war, for example, all represent challenges. A civilization declines if the challenge it faces is either too weak or too severe. Suppose food is extremely abundant; people may become lazy, and their civilization will decline. But if food is very scarce, starvation may kill the people and their civilization, as well. A moderate challenge is likely to stimulate a civilization to grow and flourish. The relatively large population and relatively scarce natural resources of Japan, for example, might represent a moderate challenge.

The fate of a civilization, however, depends not just on the challenge from the environment but also on the people's *response*. Whether a successful response comes about usually hinges on the actions of a creative minority, which involve developing new ideas and leading the masses to meet the challenge. Without such leaders, the civilization will decline.

Toynbee's theory provides an interesting way of looking at the history of civilizations, but it does not give us a means of predicting how societies will change. What, after all, is a severe challenge? Will the depletion of oil and minerals represent a moderate or an overly severe challenge for Western civilization? We know the answer *only after the fact*. If a civilization falls, we may assume that the challenge was too severe and the response inadequate. *Before* a civilization rises or falls, we have no way of testing Toynbee's theory. But it still can be considered a useful theory. According to French sociologist Raymond Boudon (1983a, 1983b), social change is so complex that the best we can expect from a theory is whether it can help explain what has happened rather than predict what will happen. That's what Toynbee's theory does.

Sorokin's Principle of Immanent Change According to Pitirim Sorokin (1889–1968), a Russian American sociologist, societies fluctuate between two extreme forms of culture, which he called ideational and sensate. **Ideational culture** emphasizes faith or religion as the key to knowledge and encourages people to value spiritual life. **Sensate culture** stresses em-

BODY AND SOUL According to Sorokin, societies fluctuate between two extreme forms of culture, which he called *ideational* and *sensate*. Ideational culture encourages people to value spiritual life, whereas sensate culture urges people to favor a practical, materialistic, and hedonistic way of life. Sorokin's principle of immanent change proposed that a society eventually reacts against one extreme form of culture and swings to the other. ◼

pirical evidence or science as the path to knowledge and urges people to favor a practical, materialistic, and hedonistic way of life.

External forces, such as international conflict and contact with another culture, may force change on a society, but Sorokin believed in the **principle of immanent change**, the notion that social change is the product of the social forces that exist *within* a society. When the time has come for a society's "inwardly ordained change," all the main aspects of the culture change. Thus, society eventually reacts against one extreme form of culture and swings to the other extreme. Sorokin regarded the Western culture of his time, for example, as sensate and, like Spengler, thought it was declining. In the widespread pursuit of pleasure, proliferation of fraud and crime, and deterioration of the family, Sorokin saw signs that Western culture was "overripe" and ready to swing to the other extreme—ideational culture.

To most sociologists today, Sorokin's theory is too speculative, impossible to test scientifically. Although Sorokin supported his theory with a mountain of historical data, he seems to have selected those facts that supported his view and ignored those that did not. Nevertheless, Sorokin's theory, like Toynbee's, can help explain certain changes in our history, such as the rise of fundamentalist religion in the last decade (see Chapter 11: Education and Religion). Changes in society today can be interpreted as a reflection of the shift from a sensate to an ideational culture.

■ Equilibrium Theory

U.S. sociologist Talcott Parsons (1902–1979) developed yet another theory of social change, one that remains influential today. According to his **equilibrium theory,** all the parts of society serve some function and are interdependent. As a result, a change in one part produces compensatory changes elsewhere. It has recently become necessary, for example, for both parents to work in order to earn enough income to support a family. But if both parents must leave the home, who will care for their children? Society has responded with an increased availability of day-care services. Such changes keep the various parts of the social system in balance, ensuring social order and stability.

In this view of society, social change triggers the social system to make adjustments. If there is a change in one part of society, other parts will change to keep society functioning smoothly. To Parsons, social change is not the overthrow of the old and the creation of something wholly new. Instead, new elements are integrated with aspects of the old society through a *moving equilibrium,* or movement toward a new harmonious system.

Parsons's theory is useful for describing gradual change. According to its critics, though, it fails to explain *why* social change occurs, does not deal with revolutionary change, and portrays societies as far more stable and harmonious than they are.

CONFLICT PERSPECTIVE: REVOLUTIONARY CHANGE

Seen through conflict perspective, society can change swiftly and radically as a result of conflict between two sharply opposed forces. Most representative of this view is Karl Marx's (1818–1883) famous theory that society is always marked by conflict and that conflict is the key to revolutionary change. We have discussed aspects of his work in previous chapters, especially his prediction of the downfall of capitalism.

According to Marx, a capitalist society includes two classes: the owners of the means of production (the bourgeoisie or capitalists) and those who must sell their labor (the proletariat or workers). These classes are in constant conflict with each other. The capitalists want to keep wages low in order to maximize their profits, and the workers resist this exploitation. The capitalists have the upper hand, Marx argued, but they unwittingly sow the seeds of their own destruction. By exploiting workers, capitalists fuel rage and resentment among workers and lead them to feel that they have nothing to gain from the present system. Through factories and improved transportation and communication, the capitalist society brings workers together. As they share their sufferings with one another, the workers develop a consciousness of themselves as a class. According to Marx, the alienation, resentment, and class consciousness eventually lead workers to revolt against capitalist society by changing it into a communist one.

History has not fulfilled these predictions. Marx failed to anticipate the emergence of a large middle class, made up largely of white-collar workers. He also failed to see that governments might respond to social conflict by improving the condition of workers. In fact, Marx's dire predictions about the future of capitalism helped spur governments to ease the suffering of workers. In a sense, by predicting that capitalism carried the seeds of its destruction, Marx sowed seeds that would help destroy his own prediction. Through the emergence of the welfare state as well as the growth of the middle class, workers in capitalist societies have grown richer, not poorer as Marx predicted. They have thus gained a stake in the

theoretical thumbnail

The Nature of Social Change

Perspective	Focus	Insights
Functionalist	How society changes gradually	Society becomes increasingly complex, goes forward and backward, and works toward equilibrium and order.
Conflict	How society changes swiftly	Society undergoes a radical, revolutionary change as a result of social conflict.
Symbolic interactionist	How social interaction changes with society	The way a society changes, as from traditional to modern, shapes the individual's self-perception and interaction with others.

system and are not likely to overthrow it by supporting revolution.

Other aspects of Marx's work have stood up better against the test of time. For instance, he accurately predicted the rise of large-scale industry, the emergence of multinational corporations, and the continuous squeeze of technology on employees. His analysis further predicted the concentration of capital in a few giant corporations, which is evident today. Moreover, many social scientists agree with Marx that material conditions—economic production in particular—shape intellectual, political, and social life. They also accept his view that "the innermost nature of things" is dynamic and filled with conflict (Heilbroner, 1980).

SYMBOLIC INTERACTIONIST PERSPECTIVE: CHANGING INTERACTION

According to symbolic interactionism, human beings actively interpret the world around them and then act—or interact with others—in accordance with the interpretation. Embedded in this interpretation is how the individuals see themselves and want others to see them, which also influences the social interaction. Thus, when society changes to create a new social life, people will define their world differently than they have in the past. If the individuals are young and therefore familiar only with the current world, their worldview will differ from their parents' view of the earlier world. Therefore, through the symbolic interactionist perspective, we can gain insight into how social change shapes our definition of the world, ourselves, and our interactions with others.

There seem to be two major types of social change around the globe today. In most societies, the change has involved modernization, transforming society

from agricultural to industrial. In industrial societies, the modernization has transformed society from industrial to postindustrial. Both types of social change have a great impact on the individual's worldview, self-perception, and social interactions. This point can be illustrated with just two examples.

First, people in relatively traditional societies have a fairly clear concept of who they are because their social statuses have been familiar to them since childhood. They thus know themselves as farmers, carpenters, and the like—just like their parents—which determines how they interact with others. Their interactions are therefore likely to be natural and smooth, as if the individuals involved had interacted since childhood, which in fact is often the case. Such interactions are comparable to those between members of a primary group (see Chapter 5: Groups and Organizations).

By contrast, people in more modern societies tend to achieve their statuses as teachers, lawyers, businesspersons, and so on, which they have not learned to live with since childhood. As a result, people in modern societies tend to be less self-confident and more anxious. Social interactions are therefore more likely to be problematic. The individuals often have to size each other up and act as if they were learning for the first time how to interact. This is, in fact, often the case, given the fast pace of change in the increasingly postindustrial society.

A similar example of how social change influences social interaction is that people in traditional societies tend to define themselves as an integral part of a group and seek happiness from developing close relationships with others. In these kinds of societies, primary relations are prevalent, causing people to interact with genuine interest in the interaction itself. By contrast, people in modern societies tend to define themselves as being free and independent of others, appreciative of their individual rights and privacy. They are thus more likely to be guarded and afraid to give themselves away, reluctant to be open and trusting with others, with the result that they tend more to engage in superficial interactions. This is why Americans, for example, do not dare ask mere acquaintances how much money they make, although people in traditional societies think nothing of doing so.

For a review of this and the other two sociological perspectives on social change, see the Theoretical Thumbnail on the preceding page.

How U.S. SOCIETY HAS CHANGED

Since the early 1970s, there have been many significant changes in U.S. society, some for the worse but most for the better. Let's take a closer look at these changes.

myth	Since 1990, the gap between rich and poor in the United States has narrowed as a result of increasing economic growth.
reality	Since the economic boom has mostly benefited the rich, the gap between them and the poor has widened, forming a smaller middle class and larger upper and lower classes.

The U.S. economy is more prosperous than before. The average family's income has gone up, but this is because many women have joined their husbands in the labor force. In fact, many families today are more likely to rely on two spouses to earn as much as one spouse did in the past. Women workers are now better paid than before, but their earnings continue to lag behind those of their male peers. Largely due to shrinking wages, young families find it harder than those of the past to buy a new home and car. Probably most significant is the increased gap between rich and poor, forming a smaller middle class and larger upper and lower classes (Schmitt, 2001b).

Nevertheless, the living standard has risen. Today, Americans seem to live better, enjoying more goods and services than before. An increased percentage of families now own more than two TV sets, two cars, and a computer. More significantly, the numbers of airline passengers and those traveling to Europe every year have increased greatly. How can Americans manage to buy so much in the face of declining wages or purchasing power? Apparently, by saving less and borrowing more. The savings rate has gone down while consumer debt has gone up, increasing the number of bankruptcies, as shown in Figure 15.4.

People today are better educated. The percentage of the U.S. population graduating from college has increased. Women now outnumber men in earning bachelor's degrees, and more significantly, women's share of doctorates has soared. But the cost of education has also increased a great deal.

FIGURE 15.4

More Bankruptcies Now Than Before

Since 1990, many significant changes have occurred in U.S. society, most for the better but a few for the worse. One of the negative changes is the decline of savings and the rise of consumer debt, causing more people to go bankrupt.

Critical Thinking: *What would you do to avoid bankruptcy?*

Source: Data from American Bankruptcy Institute, 2003.

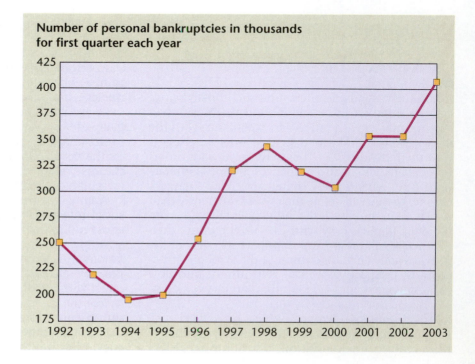

Number of personal bankruptcies in thousands for first quarter each year

GOING SOLO *Demassification* is a social change in which society becomes more individualistic and less cohesive. Technological changes have already begun to dismantle the principle of mass production aimed at a mass society. Here, Sony launches its new Digital Studio computer with CD-ROM, personal video recorder, and DVD-RW. ■

The U.S. family has gown stronger, as the rates of divorce and abortion have both gone down. Crime rates have also gone down, and Americans have become much more racially and ethnically diverse due to a significant increase in immigration. And the terrorist attacks on the United States have made Americans pull together and become more patriotic.

myth	Americans are less healthy today than a decade ago because their lives are now more hectic and stressful.
reality	Americans are healthier today. Life expectancy has gone up, and the percentage of smokers has gone down, accompanied by lower rates of death from heart disease and car accidents. Infant mortality has also declined sharply.

Americans are healthier. Life expectancy has gone up, and the percentage of smokers has gone down, accompanied by lower rates of death from heart disease and car accidents. Infant mortality has also declined sharply (U.S. Census Bureau, 2003).

sociological **frontiers**

What the Future Will Be Like

What is in store for Americans in the next 10 years? The changes that occurred over the last decade will probably continue. Even so, predicting the future is always risky: It may turn out to be different! Yet we may want to take that risk by extrapolating from what is happening today to what may likely happen in the future.

Sometime within this decade, U.S. society will take on a new demographic face. The baby-boom generation, born between 1946 and 1966, will soon reach retirement age, but unlike members of prior generations, the boomers will delay their retirement, in the same way they have delayed getting married and having children. In addition, there will be many more jobs requiring intellectual than physical skills, and consequently, many more high school graduates, especially women, will attend college.

Given that immigration has accounted for 40 percent of the U.S. population growth over the last decade, most new Americans will have come from foreign countries, rather than having been native born. The majority of these immigrants will originate from Latin America, mostly because of its proximity and the youthfulness of its population. Hispanic Americans, already the largest minority group in the United States, will continue to increase in number—likely to one-third of the U.S. population. The pattern of social diversity will turn more nonwhite than white, as is already the case with schoolchildren in California, Texas, and Florida (Francese, 2003).

Due largely to technology, the United States has already entered the postindustrial age, which seems as momentous as the Industrial Revolution. Dominated by computers and other high-tech machines, a postindustrial society is largely based on services, particularly information-related services. Today, more than two-thirds of the U.S. labor force works in information-related service industries such as health care, retail trade, and financial services. More information-related industries will open up and employ even more people.

Computer-driven technologies have also begun to dismantle the traditional industrial principle of mass production aimed at a mass society. By using computers, companies are increasingly customizing their goods and services for niche markets. The new technologies are also making local production as competitive as that on the national level. Many supermarkets not only sell national brands of bread but have begun to bake their own. Photos, which used to be sent to Rochester, New York, to be processed centrally by Kodak, can now be developed and printed anywhere in the United States. The same *demassification* process has taken away much of the audience from the three giant TV networks, as cable channels and other media have proliferated to serve new niche markets.

With demassification, however, U.S. society will become more individualistic, more fragmented, and less cohesive. There are already signs of how demassification has made Americans more aware of their individual rights. Society is now awash with almost as many different types of rights as there are individuals. There are criminals' rights, victims' rights, animal rights, housing rights, privacy rights, a damaged fetus's right not to be born, and airline pilots' right not to be randomly tested for alcohol. With many different groups all demanding that only *their* rights be protected, social responsibility and civic obligation will likely decline, and it will be harder to sustain a national consensus. Thus, more social conflict will occur and much of it will take place in the courts, given the fact that the United States has the largest number of lawyers of any country in the world.

Finally, as a result of the shocking terrorist attacks on September 11, 2001, Americans will no longer take their security for granted. Moreover, they will learn to get used to the inconvenience of longer security checks at the airport and other places. They will also tend to look the other way if the government occasionally fails to respect the civil rights of suspected terrorists in its zealous campaign against terrorism (Cannon, 2003). Nevertheless, terrorist attacks of some kind will probably take place again in the United States. Contrary to popular belief, however, there won't be many. According to the U.S. State Department, between 1995 and 2000, there were more than 2,100 international terrorist attacks but only 15 of them occurred in North America (Ferguson, 2001). Given the greatly increased vigilance following September 11, 2001, the United States will probably have many fewer than 15 terrorist attacks—and even possibly none—within the next 10 years. But if an attack does occur, Americans are a tough and resilient people and will only become stronger, as they did after 9-11.

 ■ For more of the latest Sociological Frontiers, look up Continuing Update at www.ablongman.com/thio6e.

using *sociology*

How to Use Cell Phones Properly

As we have observed from the symbolic interactionist perspective on social change, social interactions tend to be problematic in the fast-changing, postindustrial U.S. society because they are relatively new. They have not become part of the social repertoire people have picked up since childhood. An example of these problematic interactions involves the use of cell phones, which are must-have gadgets for a fast-growing number of Americans today.

If a cell phone rings in a social situation, it can be annoying, embarrassing, or worse. Imagine how mourners at a funeral would feel upon hearing the tune "When the Saints Go Marching In" come from a cell phone while they are standing around the deceased's casket. It would be an appalling disruption of a very solemn moment. Unfortunately, because cell phones can go anywhere, they often end up ringing in the wrong place at the wrong time. Thus, many concert halls and theaters prelude their programs by reminding patrons to turn off their cell phones. Some restaurants ban their use completely or require that they be checked at the door.

Etiquette experts suggest that cell phone users follow a simple rule: "Be sensitive to the effects of your actions on others." This is effectively what the symbolic interactionists would recommend. More specific suggestions include the following (Jason, 2001):

1. Treat your cell phone like a portable public phone. Not only do public phones give callers privacy, but they also protect the general public from callers and their phone calls. So, when your cell phone rings, take it to the area where a public phone booth is available.
2. If you can't find a public phone booth and must use your cell phone, talk in a normal speaking voice. Avoid talking loudly. Remember that you are not only speaking to the person on the line but also to everybody around you.
3. Turn off your cell phone in such places as symphony halls, movie theaters, and churches, where it is inappropriate to chat with friends, whether in person or on the phone.

Thinking critically, what else would you recommend cell phone users do to avoid disturbing those around them?

CHAPTER REVIEW

1. *According to Smelser, what preconditions must be met for the appearance of collective behavior?* Six conditions must be met, in this sequence: (1) structural conduciveness, (2) social strain, (3) the spread of a generalized belief, (4) a precipitating factor, (5) mobilization of participants, and (6) inadequate social control.

2. *What conditions create a panic?* There must be a perception of a crisis, intense fear of possible entrapment, some panic-prone individuals, mutual emotional facilitation, and a lack of cooperation among people. *What type of people are most likely to succumb to mass hysteria?* People with little critical ability and little education are most likely to succumb.

3. *Why do crowds sometimes act irrationally, even violently?* Le Bon argued that as a result of the anonymity of a crowd, people give up their individuality and release their primitive instincts. Then, as a result of social contagion, they become part of a collective mind that is irrational. Many sociologists today believe that Le Bon's collective mind is a fiction and that crowds are not as homogeneous as they appear to be. Instead, as Turner and Killian have argued, crowds seem to be homogeneous because they conform to a new norm that emerges to deal with the unconventional situation in which the crowd finds itself.

4. *How do fashions, fads, and crazes differ?* Fashions occur more predictably, last longer, and are more socially respectable than fads and crazes. Fads are less outrageous and less harmful than crazes.

5. *Are rumors always distortions?* No. They are merely unverified. They, or parts of them, may turn out to be true. *When are rumors likely to develop?* If a situation is ambiguous and institutionalized channels of communication do not satisfy the demand for news about it, then a rumor is likely to emerge.

6. *How can propaganda influence opinion?* Methods of influencing opinion include name calling, glittering generality, transfer, and testimonial. *Why is the influence of the U.S. media limited?* There are several reasons: the multitude of viewpoints the media present; the tendency to tell people what they want to hear; and the frequency with which communication occurs by a two-step flow—from the media to opinion leaders and only then to the public. *What influence do the media have?* They frequently authenticate information; validate private opinions, preferences, and values; legitimize unconventional viewpoints and behavior; and concretize ill-defined anxieties and preferences.

7. *What are the aims of social movements?* In general, they seek some sort of change. Revolutionary movements seek a total, radical change of society. Reform movements seek partial change. Resistance movements try to turn back some ongoing social change. Expressive movements seek to change individuals, not society. *What are the social causes of social movements?* According to breakdown-frustration theory, some social breakdown can cause a social movement by creating frustration among masses of people. But resource mobilization theory emphasizes the importance of the availability of certain resources more than frustration as the cause. *What are the consequences of social movements?* The consequences include influencing social policy, creating new institutions, and making participants more active in tackling social problems.

8. *Does modernization necessarily destroy tradition?* No. It may even reinforce tradition. *Will modernization unify Western and non-Western societies?* Not necessarily. Modernization of non-Western countries may increase their cultural differences with the West. *Is the United States really in decline?* Not really, but if its various problems remain unsolved, decline can be expected.

9. *How do modern evolutionary theorists describe social change?* They argue that societies tend to change gradually from simple to complex forms. *What is a primary difference between evolutionary and cyclical theorists?* Evolutionary theorists see social change as moving in one principal direction: toward increased complexity. Cyclical theorists portray social change as reversible: Societies may move forward and backward; they may rise and fall, in cycles. *What is equilibrium theory?* It holds that the various parts of society are all interdependent and that a change in any one part stimulates compensatory changes in other parts of the system. *What does conflict theory say about social change?* Social change stems from conflict, which always characterizes societies. *What does symbolic interactionism reveal about social change?* Social change shapes the individual's self-perception and interactions with others.

10. *In what ways has U.S. society changed since 1970?* The economy is generally better, but many families have to rely on two spouses rather than one spouse to earn a living. The gap between rich and poor has increased, although the living standard has risen. People are better educated and healthier, families are stronger, and crime has dropped. The terrorist attacks have also made Americans more patriotic.

11. *What will the future be like?* U.S. society will have many more people working into old age, attending college, immigrating from abroad, and being non-white than white. Computer technology will produce goods and services more efficiently, but its tendency to demassify production for individual needs will encourage more social conflict. Given the terrorist attacks, Americans will also feel less secure, get used to longer security checks, and support government action against terrorism, while increased vigilance will radically reduce the likelihood of terrorist attacks. *How can cell phone users avoid disturbing others?* They can be sensitive to the effects of their usage on others, treating their cell phone like a portable public phone, talking on it in a normal voice, and turning it off in certain public places.

KEY TERMS

Breakdown-frustration theory   The theory that a social breakdown can cause a social movement by creating frustration among masses of people (p. 439).

Collective behavior   Relatively spontaneous, unorganized, and unpredictable social behavior (p. 429).

Convergence theory   The theory that modernization will bring the West and non-West together by breaking down cultural barriers to produce a global society (p. 440).

Craze   A fad with serious consequences (p. 435).

Crowd   A collection of people temporarily doing something while in proximity to one another (p. 432).

Cyclical theory   The theory that societies move forward and backward, up and down, in an endless series of cycles (p. 442).

Divergence theory   The theory that emphasizes the growing separation between Western and non-Western cultures (p. 440).

Emergent-norm theory   The theory that members of a crowd develop, through interaction, a new norm to deal with the unconventional situation facing them (p. 434).

Equilibrium theory   The theory that all the parts of society serve some function and are interdependent, so that a change in one part produces compensatory changes elsewhere (p. 444).

Evolutionary theory   The theory that societies change gradually from simple to complex forms (p. 442).

Fad   A temporary enthusiasm for an innovation less respectable than a fashion (p. 435).

Fashion   A great though brief enthusiasm among a relatively large number of people for a particular innovation (p. 434).

Frustration theory   The theory that individuals who participate in social movements are frustrated and troubled (p. 439).

Ideational culture   Sorokin's term for the culture that emphasizes faith or religion as the key to knowledge and encourages people to value spiritual life (p. 443).

Mass hysteria   A form of collective behavior in which numerous people engage in a frenzied activity without checking the source of their fear (p. 432).

Modernization   The form of social change that involves the transformation of an agricultural society into an industrial one (p. 439).

Opinion leader   A person whose opinion is respected by others and influences them (p. 437).

Panic   A type of collective behavior characterized by a maladaptive, fruitless response to a serious threat (p. 431).

Principle of immanent change   The notion that social change is the product of the social forces that exist within a society (p. 444).

Propaganda   Communication tailored to influence opinion (p. 436).

Public   A dispersed collection of people who share a particular interest or concern (p. 436).

Public opinion   The collection of ideas and attitudes shared by the members of a particular public (p. 436).

Resource mobilization theory   The theory that social movements result from the availability of resources for mobilization (p. 439).

Rumor   An unverified story that is spread from one person to another (p. 435).

Sensate culture   Sorokin's term for the culture that stresses empirical evidence or science as the key to knowledge and urges people to favor a practical, materialistic, and hedonistic way of life (p. 443).

Social change   The alteration of society over time (p. 428).

Social contagion   The spreading of a certain emotion and action from one member of a crowd to another (p. 433).

Social movement   A conscious effort to bring about or prevent change (p. 437).

QUESTIONS FOR DISCUSSION AND REVIEW

THE STUDY OF COLLECTIVE BEHAVIOR

1. What makes collective behavior different from institutionalized behavior, and why is it difficult to study?
2. According to Smelser, what six factors together generate collective behavior?

FORMS OF COLLECTIVE BEHAVIOR

1. What preconditions usually exist before a panic occurs?
2. Why do individuals in a crowd tend to lose their individuality and act irrationally?
3. Where do fashions come from?
4. What is the nature of rumor, and what causes it to emerge?
5. How do people use propaganda and the media to mold public opinion?
6. What causes social movements?

A GLOBAL ANALYSIS OF SOCIAL CHANGE

1. How are tradition and modernization related in India and Japan?
2. Are various societies converging to form one world?
3. Is the United States in danger of joining the developing world?

FUNCTIONALIST PERSPECTIVE: GRADUAL CHANGE

1. How does today's evolutionary theory differ from the older one?
2. How do the separate versions of cyclical theory differ from each other, and how does each contribute to sociology's understanding of social change?
3. What is the equilibrium theory of social change?

CONFLICT PERSPECTIVE: REVOLUTIONARY CHANGE

1. What are the strengths and weaknesses of Marx's approach to social change?

SYMBOLIC INTERACTIONIST PERSPECTIVE: CHANGING INTERACTION

1. According to symbolic interactionism, how does social change influence our personal lives?

HOW U.S. SOCIETY HAS CHANGED

1. What significant changes have occurred in the United States over the last decade?

SOCIOLOGICAL FRONTIERS/USING SOCIOLOGY

1. What will our lives be like 10 years from now?
2. How can people use cell phones without disturbing others?

SUGGESTED READINGS

Falk, Gerhard. 1998. *Sex, Gender, and Social Change: The Great Revolution.* Lanham, MD: University Press of America. Shows how changes in many areas of U.S. life since the 1960s have led to changes in gender roles and statuses and how these changes, in turn, have affected many aspects of society.

Manning, Chris, and Peter Van Diermen (eds.). 2000. *Indonesia in Transition: Social Aspects of Reformasi and Crisis.* New York: Zed Books. A set of 23 articles analyzing the changes in various aspects of Indonesian society after President Suharto ended his 32-year authoritarian rule in May 1998.

Rubin, Beth A. 1996. *Shifts in the Social Contract: Understanding Change in American Society.* Thousand Oaks, CA: Pine Forge. An analysis of how long-term, stable relationships are changing into short-term, temporary ones in U.S. society.

Toffler, Alvin, and Heidi Toffler. 1995. *Creating a New Civilization.* Atlanta, GA: Turner. Discusses how the world is becoming information driven and globally integrated, impacting everything from family life to political institutions.

Veltmeyer, Henry, and James Petras. 2000. *The Dynamics of Social Change in Latin America.* A critical, Marxist analysis of the spread of political democracy and market-oriented reforms in Latin America.

■ Additional Resources

The New York Times
expect the world®
nytimes.com

Expand your knowledge of the concepts discussed in this chapter by reading the following current and historical articles from the *New York Times*. Go to the "eThemes of the Times" section of the Companion Website (www.ablongman.com/thio6e):

> "President Urging Wider U.S. Powers in Terrorism Law"

Research Navigator.com

Research Navigator, a research database, provides immediate access to hundreds of full-text articles from EBSCO's ContentSelect Academic Journal Database. If the Research Navigator access code was included with your textbook, go to the website www.research navigator.com and read the following articles related to this chapter by typing in the article number:

Bell, Wendell. "The Sociology of the Future and the Future of Sociology." *International Review of Sociology*, Nov99, Vol. 9 Issue 3, p295, 16p. Accession Number: 2721294. Focuses on the sociological study of the future.

Tindall, David B. "Social Networks, Identification and Participation in an Environmental Movement: Low–Medium Cost Activism within the British Columbia Wilderness Preservation Movement." *Canadian Review of Sociology & Anthropology*, Nov2002, Vol. 39 Issue 4, p413, 40p. Accession Number: 8695425. Shows how the structure of social networks is related to the participation of individuals in a social movement.

Glossary

Absolute poverty   The lack of minimum food and shelter necessary for maintaining life.

Achieved status   A status that is attained through an individual's own actions.

Affirmative action   A policy that requires employers and academic institutions to make special efforts to recruit qualified minorities for jobs, promotions, and educational opportunities.

Afrocentrism   The view of the world from the standpoint of African culture.

Age structure   The pattern of the proportions of different age groups within a population.

Agricultural society   A society that produces food primarily by using plows and draft animals on the farm.

Alienation of labor   Marx's term for laborers' loss of control over their work process.

Amalgamation   The process by which the subcultures of various groups are blended together, forming a new culture.

Animism   The belief in spirits capable of helping or harming people.

Anomie   A social condition in which norms are absent, weak, or in conflict.

Anti-Semitism   Prejudice or discrimination against Jews.

Anticipatory socialization   The process by which an individual learns to assume a role in the future.

Aptitude   The capacity for developing physical or social skills.

Arranged marriage   A marriage in which partners are selected by the couple's parents.

Ascribed status   A status that one has no control over, such as status based on race, gender, or age.

Assimilation   The process by which a minority adopts the dominant group's culture as the culture of the larger society.

Authority   Legitimate power institutionalized in organizations.

Behavioral assimilation   The social situation in which a minority adopts the dominant group's language, values, and behavioral patterns.

Belief   An idea that is relatively subjective, unreliable, or unverifiable.

Bilateral descent   The norm that recognizes both parents' families as the child's close relatives.

Biosphere   A thin layer of air, water, and soil surrounding the earth.

Birth rate   The number of babies born in a year for every 1,000 members of a given population.

Breakdown-frustration theory   The theory that a social breakdown can cause a social movement by creating frustration among masses of people.

Bureaucracy   A modern Western organization defined by Max Weber as being rational in achieving its goal efficiently.

Capitalism   An economic system based on private ownership of property and competition in producing and selling goods and services.

Caste system   A relatively rigid stratification system in which people's positions are ascribed and fixed.

Census   A periodic head count of the entire population of a country.

Charisma   An exceptional personal quality popularly attributed to certain individuals.

Church   A relatively large, well-established religious organization that is integrated into the society and does not make strict demands on its members.

Civil religion   A collection of beliefs, symbols, and rituals that sanctify the dominant values of a society.

Class conflict   Marx's term for the struggle between the capitalists, who own the means of production, and the proletariat, who do not.

453

Class system   A relatively open stratification system in which people's positions are achieved and changeable.

Coercion   The illegitimate use of force or threat of force to compel obedience.

Collective behavior   Relatively spontaneous, unorganized, and unpredictable social behavior.

Communism   A classless society that operates on the principle of "from each according to his ability to each according to his needs."

Compensatory education   A school program intended to improve the academic performance of socially and educationally disadvantaged children.

Competition   An interaction in which two individuals follow mutually accepted rules, each trying to achieve the same goal before the other does.

Compositional theory   The theory that city dwellers are as involved with small groups of friends, relatives, and neighbors as are noncity people.

Concentric-zone theory   The model of land use in which the city spreads out from the center in a series of concentric zones, each used for a particular kind of activity.

Conflict   An interaction in which two individuals disregard any rules, each trying to achieve his or her own goal by defeating the other.

Conflict perspective   A theoretical perspective that portrays society as always changing and always marked by conflict.

Conglomerate   A corporation that owns companies in various unrelated industries.

Content analysis   Searching for specific words or ideas and then turning them into numbers.

Control group   The subjects in an experiment who are not exposed to the independent variable.

Conventional morality   Kohlberg's term for the practice of defining right and wrong according to the motive of the action being judged.

Convergence theory   The theory that modernization will bring the West and non-West together by breaking down cultural barriers to produce a global society.

Cooperation   An interaction in which two or more individuals work together to achieve a common goal.

Craze   A fad with serious consequences.

Crowd   A collection of people temporarily doing something while in proximity to one another.

Crystalline intelligence   Wisdom and insight into the human condition, as shown by one's skills in language, philosophy, music, or painting.

Cult   A religious group that professes a new religious belief, totally rejects society, and consists of members with extreme devotion to their leader.

Cultural imperialism   The practice of making minorities accept the dominant group's culture.

Cultural integration   The joining of various values into a coherent whole.

Cultural pluralism   The peaceful coexistence of various racial and ethnic groups, each retaining its own subculture.

Cultural relativism   The belief that a culture must be understood on its own terms.

Cultural universals   Practices found in all cultures as the means for meeting the same human needs.

Culture   A design for living or a complex whole consisting of objects, values, and other characteristics that people acquire as members of society.

Cyclical theory   The theory that societies move forward and backward, up and down, in an endless series of cycles.

De facto segregation   Segregation resulting from tradition and custom.

De jure segregation   Segregation sanctioned by law.

Death rate   The number of deaths in a year for every 1,000 members of a population.

Deconstructionism   The idea that to understand society, we should deconstruct it, or take it apart, along with anything associated with it.

Demographic transition   The theory that human populations tend to go through specific demographic stages and that these stages are tied to a society's economic development.

Demography   The scientific study of population.

Dependency theory   The theory that rich nations exploit poor ones for power and commercial gain, thereby perpetuating poverty, underdevelopment, and dependency on rich nations.

Detached observation   A method of observation in which the researcher observes as an outsider, from a distance, without getting involved.

Developmental socialization   The process by which people learn to be more competent in playing their currently assumed roles.

Deviance An act that is considered by public consensus, or by the powerful at a given place and time, to be a violation of some social rule.

Differential association The process of acquiring, through interaction with others, "an excess of definitions favorable to violation of law over definitions unfavorable to violation of law."

Discrimination An unfavorable action against individuals that is taken because they are members of a certain category.

Disintegrative shaming The process by which the wrongdoer is punished in such a way as to be stigmatized, rejected, or ostracized.

Divergence theory The theory that emphasizes the growing separation between Western and non-Western cultures.

Dramaturgy A method of analyzing social interaction as if the participants were performing on a stage.

Dual economy An economy that comprises a core of giant corporations dominating the market and a periphery of small firms competing for the remaining, smaller shares of business.

Ecology A study of the interactions among organisms and between organisms and their physical environment.

Economic globalization The interrelationship among the world's economies.

Economic institution A system for producing and distributing goods and services.

Ecosystem A self-sufficient community of organisms depending for survival on one another and on the environment.

Egalitarian family The family in which authority is equally distributed between husband and wife.

Ego Freud's term for the part of personality that is rational, dealing with the world logically and realistically.

Emergent-norm theory The theory that members of a crowd develop, through interaction, a new norm to deal with the unconventional situation facing them.

Empowerment zones The economically depressed urban areas that businesses, with the help of government grants, low-interest loans, and tax breaks, try to revive by creating jobs; also known as enterprise zones.

Endogamy Literally, "marrying within," the act of marrying someone from one's own group.

Epidemiology The study of the origin and spread of disease within a population.

Equilibrium theory The theory that all the parts of society serve some function and are interdependent, so that a change in one part produces compensatory changes elsewhere.

Ethicalism The type of religion that emphasizes moral principles as guides for living a righteous life.

Ethnic group A collection of people who share a distinctive cultural heritage.

Ethnocentrism The attitude that one's own culture is superior to those of other peoples.

Ethnography An analysis of people's lives from their own perspectives.

Ethnomethodology The analysis of how people define the world in which they live.

Eurocentrism A view of the world from the standpoint of European culture.

Evolutionary theory The theory that societies change gradually from simple to complex forms.

Exchange An interaction in which two individuals offer each other something in order to obtain a reward in return.

Exogamy Literally, "marrying outward," the act of marrying someone from outside one's group—such as the clan, tribe, or village.

Experiment A research operation in which the researcher manipulates variables so that their influence can be determined.

Experimental group The group that is exposed to the independent variable.

Expressive leaders Leaders who achieve group harmony by making others feel good.

Expressive role A role that requires taking care of personal relationships.

Extended family The family that consists of two parents, their unmarried children, and other relatives.

Fad A temporary enthusiasm for an innovation less respectable than a fashion.

Family of orientation The family in which one grows up, consisting of oneself and one's parents and siblings.

Family of procreation The family that one establishes through marriage, consisting of oneself and one's spouse and children.

Fashion A great though brief enthusiasm among a relatively large number of people for a particular innovation.

Feminism The belief that women and men should be equal in various aspects of their lives.

Feminist theory　A form of conflict theory that explains human life in terms of the experiences of women.

Feminization of poverty　A huge number of women bearing the burden of poverty, mostly as single mothers or heads of families.

Fluid intelligence　The ability to grasp abstract relationships, as in mathematics, physics, or some other science.

Folkways　Weak norms that specify expectations about proper behavior.

Formal organization　A group whose activities are rationally designed to achieve specific goals.

Frustration theory　The theory that individuals who participate in social movements are frustrated and troubled.

Functionalist perspective　A theoretical perspective that focuses on social order.

Gender identity　People's images of what they are socially expected to be and do on the basis of their sex.

Gender role　The pattern of attitudes and behaviors that a society expects of its members because of their being female or male.

Genderlects　Linguistic styles that reflect the different worlds of women and men.

Generalized others　Mead's term for people who do not have close ties to a child but who do influence the child's internalization of society's values.

Genocide　The wholesale killing of members of a specific racial or ethnic group.

Gentrification　The movement of affluent people into poor urban neighborhoods.

Glass ceiling　The prejudiced belief that keeps minority professionals from holding leadership positions in organizations.

Global village　A closely knit community of all the world's societies.

Groupthink　The tendency for members of a cohesive group to maintain a consensus to the extent of ignoring the truth.

Healing role　A set of social expectations regarding how a doctor should behave.

Homogamy　Marrying someone with social characteristics similar to one's own.

Horizontal mobility　Movement from one job to another within the same status category.

Horticultural society　A society that produces food primarily by growing plants in small gardens.

Humorology　The study or practice of humor.

Hunting-gathering society　A society that hunts animals and gathers plants as its primary means for survival.

Hypothesis　A tentative statement about how various events are related to one another.

Id　Freud's term for the part of personality that is irrational, concerned only with seeking pleasure.

Ideational culture　Sorokin's term for the culture that emphasizes faith or religion as the key to knowledge and encourages people to value spiritual life.

Ideological conservatives　U.S. citizens who, in theory, are opposed to big government because of their belief in free enterprise, rugged individualism, and capitalism.

Idiosyncrasy credit　The privilege that allows leaders to deviate from their group's norms.

In-group　The group to which an individual is strongly tied as a member.

Individual mobility　Social mobility related to an individual's personal achievement and characteristics.

Industrial Revolution　The dramatic economic change brought about by the introduction of machines into the work process about 200 years ago.

Industrial society　A society that produces food for its subsistence primarily by using machinery.

Infant mortality rate　The number of deaths among infants less than 1 year old for every 1,000 live births.

Influence　The ability to control others' behavior through persuasion rather than coercion or authority.

Informal organization　A group formed by the informal relationships among members of an organization—based on personal interactions, not on any plan by the organization.

Institutionalized discrimination　The persistence of discrimination in social institutions that is not necessarily recognized by everybody as discrimination.

Instrumental leaders　Leaders who achieve their group's goal by getting others to focus on task performance.

Instrumental role　A role that requires performance of a task.

Intelligence　The capacity for mental or intellectual achievement.

Interaction ritual　A form of interaction in which the participants perform certain acts to show reverence to each other.

Interest group   An organized collection of people who attempt to influence government policies.

Intergenerational mobility   A change in social standing from one generation to the next.

Intragenerational mobility   A change in an individual's social standing.

Jim Crow laws   A set of laws that segregated African Americans from whites in all kinds of public and private facilities.

Kinesics   The use of body movements as a means of communication; also called *body language*.

Knowledge   A collection of relatively objective ideas and facts about the physical and social worlds.

Kuznets curve   The changing relationship between economic development and social inequality, named after its discoverer, Simon Kuznets.

Laissez-faire leaders   Leaders who let others do their work more or less on their own.

Latent function   A function that is unintended and often unrecognized.

Laws   Norms that are specified formally in writing and backed by the power of the state.

Life chances   The likelihood of living a good, long, successful life in a society.

Life expectancy   The average number of years that a group of people can expect to live.

Lifestyles   Tastes, preferences, and ways of living.

Living will   Advance instructions about what someone wants doctors to do in the event of a terminal illness.

Looking-glass self   Cooley's term for the self-image that we develop from the way others treat us.

Macro view   A view that focuses on the large social phenomena of society, such as social institutions and inequality.

Manifest function   A function that is intended and seems obvious.

Marginal surplus population   Marxist term for unemployed workers who are superfluous or useless to the economy.

Marriage rate   The number of marriages in a given year for every 1,000 people.

Mass hysteria   A form of collective behavior in which numerous people engage in a frenzied activity without checking the source of their fear.

Master status   A status that dominates a relationship.

Material culture   Every conceivable kind of physical object produced by humans.

Matriarchal family   The family in which the dominant figure is the oldest female.

Matrilineal descent   The norm that recognizes only the mother's family as a child's close relatives.

Matrilocal residence   The home where the married couple lives with the wife's family.

Mechanical solidarity   A form of social cohesion that develops when people do similar work and have similar beliefs and values.

Medicalization of deviance   Diagnosing and treating deviant behavior as a disease.

Megacity   A city with a population of 5 million or more.

Megalopolis   A vast area in which many metropolises merge.

Metropolis   A large urban area that includes a city and its surrounding suburbs.

Micro view   A view that focuses on the immediate social situations in which people interact with one another.

Minority   A racial or ethnic group that is subjected to prejudice and discrimination.

Mixed economy   An economic system that contains elements of both capitalism and socialism.

Modernization   The form of social change that involves the transformation of an agricultural society into an industrial one.

Monogamy   The marriage of one man to one woman.

Monopoly   The situation in which one firm controls the output of an industry.

Monotheism   The belief in one god.

Mores   Strong norms that specify normal behavior and constitute demands, not just expectations.

Multiculturalism   A state in which all subcultures in the same society are equal to one another.

Multinational corporations   Corporations that have subsidiaries in many countries.

Multiple-nuclei theory   The model of land use in which a city is built around many discrete nuclei, each being the center of some specialized activity.

Neocolonialism   The economic control exercised by rich nations over their former colonies.

Neolocal residence   The home where the married couple live by themselves, away from both the husband's and the wife's families.

Neurosis   The mental problem characterized by a persistent fear, anxiety, or worry about trivial matters.

Nonmaterial culture   The intangible aspect of culture.

Norm   A social rule that specifies how people should behave.

Normative theories   Theories that suggest what we should do to achieve our goals.

Nuclear family   The family that consists of two parents and their unmarried children.

Objective method   The method of identifying social classes using occupation, income, and education to rank people.

Oligopoly   The situation in which a very few companies control the output of an industry.

Operational liberals   U.S. citizens who, in effect, support big government by backing government programs that render services to the public.

Opinion leader   A person whose opinion is respected by others and influences them.

Oppositional interaction   An interaction in which the participants treat each other as competitors or enemies.

Organic solidarity   A type of social cohesion that arises when people in a society perform a wide variety of specialized jobs and therefore have to depend on one another.

Out-group   A group of which an individual is not a member.

Outsourcing   The practice of producing inexpensive products by building factories and hiring workers abroad.

Panic   A type of collective behavior characterized by a maladaptive, fruitless response to a serious threat.

Parkinson's law   The observation that "Work expands to fill the time available for its completion."

Participant observation   A method of observation in which the researcher takes part in the activities of the group being studied.

Pastoral society   A society that domesticates and herds animals as its primary source of food.

Patriarchal family   The family in which the dominant figure is the oldest male.

Patriarchy   A system of domination in which men exercise power over women.

Patrilineal descent   The norm that recognizes only the father's family as a child's close relatives.

Patrilocal residence   The home where the married couple live with the husband's family.

Peer group   A group whose members are about the same age and have similar interests.

Peripheral theory   The model of land use in which suburban cities grow around the central city.

Personality   A fairly stable configuration of feelings, attitudes, ideas, and behaviors that characterizes an individual.

Peter principle   The observation that "In every hierarchy, every employee tends to rise to his or her level of incompetence."

Political party   A group organized for the purpose of gaining government offices.

Political power   The capacity to use the government to make decisions that affect the whole society.

Political socialization   A learning process by which individuals acquire political knowledge, beliefs, and attitudes.

Politics   The type of human interaction that involves some people acquiring and exercising power over others.

Polyandry   The marriage of one woman to two or more men.

Polygamy   The marriage of one person to two or more people of the opposite sex.

Polygyny   The marriage of one man to two or more women.

Polytheism   The belief in more than one god.

Popular culture   A collection of relatively unsophisticated artistic creations that appeal to a mass audience.

Population   The entire group of people to be studied.

Postconventional morality   Kohlberg's term for the practice of judging actions by taking into account the importance of conflicting norms.

Postindustrial revolution   The change of an economy into one dominated by high technology.

Postindustrial society   A society that produces food so efficiently that high technology and service industry dominate it.

Power   The ability to control the behavior of others, even against their will.

Power elite   A small group of top leaders not just from business corporations but also from the federal government and the military.

Preconventional morality   Kohlberg's term for the practice of defining right and wrong according to the consequence of the action being judged.

Prejudice   A negative attitude toward a certain category of people.

Prescribed role The expectation held by society regarding how an individual with a particular status should behave.

Primary deviance Norm violations that a person commits for the first time and without considering them deviant.

Primary group A group whose members interact informally, relate to each other as whole persons, and enjoy their relationship for its own sake.

Principle of immanent change The notion that social change is the product of the social forces that exist within a society.

Propaganda Communication tailored to influence opinion.

Proxemics The use of space as a means of communication.

Psychosis The mental problem typified by loss of touch with reality.

Public A dispersed collection of people who share a particular interest or concern.

Public opinion The collection of ideas and attitudes shared by the members of a particular public.

Pygmalion effect The impact of a teacher's expectations on student performance.

Race A group of people who are perceived by a given society to be biologically different from others.

Racism The belief that one's own race or ethnicity is superior to that of others.

Random sample A sample drawn in such a way that all members of the population have an equal chance of being selected.

Rape The use of force to get a woman to do something sexual against her will.

Rationalization Max Weber's term for the process of replacing subjective, spontaneous, informal, and diverse ways of doing things with a planned, objective, formally unified method based on abstract rules.

Reference group A group that is used as the frame of reference for evaluating one's own behavior.

Reintegrative shaming Making wrongdoers feel guilty while showing them understanding, forgiveness, or even respect.

Relative deprivation Feeling unable to achieve relatively high aspirations.

Relative poverty A state of deprivation resulting from having less than the majority of the people have.

Reputational method The method of identifying social classes by selecting a group of people and asking them to rank others.

Resocialization The process by which people are forced to abandon their old selves and to develop new ones.

Resource mobilization theory The theory that social movements result from the availability of resources for mobilization.

Revolution The movement aimed at the violent overthrow of the existing government.

Role A set of expectations of what individuals should do in accordance with a particular status that they hold.

Role conflict Conflict between the roles of two different statuses being played simultaneously.

Role distance Separating role-playing as outward performance from the inner self.

Role performance Actual performance of a role.

Role set An array of roles attached to one particular status.

Role strain Stress caused by incompatible demands from the roles of a single status.

Roleless role Being assigned no role in society's division of labor, which is a predicament of older people in industrial society.

Rumor An unverified story that is spread from one person to another.

Sample A relatively small number of people selected from a larger population.

Sanction A reward for conformity to norms or punishment for violation of norms.

Scapegoating Blaming others for one's own failure.

Secondary analysis Searching for new knowledge in the data collected earlier by another researcher or a public agency.

Secondary deviance Repeated norm violations that the violators themselves recognize as deviant.

Secondary group A group whose members interact formally, relate to each other as players of particular roles, and expect to profit from each other.

Sect A relatively small religious group that sets itself apart from society and makes heavy demands on its members.

Sector theory The model of land use in which a city grows outward in wedge-shaped sectors from the center.

Senescence The natural physical process of aging.

Senility An abnormal condition characterized by serious memory loss, confusion, and loss of the ability to reason.

Sensate culture Sorokin's term for the culture that stresses empirical evidence or science as the key to knowledge and urges people to favor a practical, materialistic, and hedonistic way of life.

Serial monogamy The marriage of one person to two or more people but one at a time.

Sex ratio The number of males per 100 females.

Sexism Prejudice and discrimination based on one's gender.

Sexual harassment An unwelcome act of a sexual nature.

Shamanism The belief that a spiritual leader can communicate with the spirits by acting as their mouthpiece or letting the soul leave the leader's body and enter the spiritual world.

Sick role A set of social expectations regarding how an ill person should behave.

Significant others Mead's term for people who have close ties to a child and exert a strong influence on the child.

Social aggregate A number of people who happen to be in one place but do not interact with one another.

Social category A number of people who have something in common but who neither interact with one another nor gather in one place

Social change The alteration of society over time.

Social class A category of people who have about the same amount of income, power, and prestige.

Social consensus A condition in which most members of society agree on what is good for everybody to have and cooperate to achieve it.

Social construction of reality The process by which people create through social interaction a certain idea, feeling, or belief about their environment.

Social contagion The spreading of a certain emotion and action from one member of a crowd to another.

Social forces Forces that arise from the society of which we are a part.

Social group A collection of people who interact with one another and have a certain feeling of unity.

Social institution A set of widely shared beliefs, norms, and procedures necessary for meeting the basic needs of a society.

Social integration The degree to which people are tied to a social group.

Social interaction The process by which individuals act toward and react to others.

Social marginality Being excluded from mainstream society.

Social mobility Movement from one social standing to another.

Social movement A conscious effort to bring about or prevent change.

Social network A web of social relationships that link individuals or groups to one another.

Social stratification The system in which some people get more or fewer rewards than others.

Socialism An economic system based on public ownership and government control of the economy.

Socialization The process by which a society transmits its cultural values to its members.

Society A collection of interacting individuals sharing the same way of life and living in the same territory.

Sociobiology A new Darwinian theory that human behavior is genetically determined.

Sociocultural evolution The process of changing from a technologically simple society to a more complex one, with significant consequences for social and cultural life.

Sociological imagination Mills's term for the ability to see the impact of social forces on individuals, especially on their private lives.

Sociology The systematic, scientific study of human society.

Status A position in a group or society.

Status inconsistency The condition in which the same individual is given two conflicting status rankings.

Status system A system in which people are stratified according to their social prestige.

Stereotype An oversimplified, inaccurate mental picture of others.

Stratified sampling The process of drawing a random sample in which various categories of people are represented in proportions equal to their presence in the population.

Structural assimilation The social condition in which the minority is accepted on equal terms with the rest of society.

Structural mobility Social mobility related to changes in society.

Structured interview An interview in which the researcher asks standardized questions that require respondents to choose from among several standardized answers.

Subcultural theory The theory that the city enriches people's lives by offering diverse opportunities and developing various subcultures.

Subjective method The method of identifying social classes by asking people to rank themselves.

Subordinate status A status that does not dominate a relationship; the opposite of master status.

Superego Freud's term for the part of personality that is moral; popularly known as conscience.

Supportive interaction An interaction in which the participants treat each other as supporters or friends.

Survey A research method that involves asking questions about opinions, beliefs, or behaviors.

Symbol A word, gesture, music, or anything that stands for some other thing.

Symbolic interaction An interaction in which people actively interpret each other's actions and reactions and behave in accordance with the interpretation.

Symbolic interactionist perspective A theoretical perspective that directs our attention to the details of a specific situation and of the interaction between individuals in that situation.

Systematic sampling The process of drawing a random sample systematically rather than haphazardly.

Terrorism The use of violence to express dissatisfaction with a government.

Theism The type of religion that centers on the worship of a god or gods.

Theoretical perspective A set of general assumptions about the nature of society.

Theory A set of logically related hypotheses that explains the relationship among various phenomena.

Thomas theorem Sociologist W. I. Thomas's famous pronouncement that "If people define situations as real, they are real in their consequences."

Total institutions Places where people are not only cut off from the larger society but also rigidly controlled by the administrators.

Totemism The belief that a kinship exists between humans and an animal—or, less commonly, a plant.

Tracking The system of sorting students into different groups according to past academic achievement.

Unstructured interview An interview in which open-ended questions are asked and the respondent is allowed to answer freely in his or her own words.

Urban anomie theory The theory that city people have a unique way of life characterized by alienation, impersonal relations, and stress.

Urban ecological processes Processes in which people compete for certain land use, one group dominates another, and a particular group moves into an area and takes it over from others.

Urban ecology The study of the relationship between people and their urban environment.

Urbanization The transformation of rural areas into cities.

Value A socially shared idea about what is good, desirable, or important.

Verstehen Weber's term for empathetic understanding of the subjects studied by sociologists.

Vertical mobility Moving up or down the status ladder.

Vital statistics Information about births, marriages, deaths, and migrations into and out of a country.

References

AAMC (Association of American Medical Colleges). 1998. Available online: www.aamc.org.

AAUW (American Association of University Women). 2001. *Hostile Hallways: Bullying, Teasing, and Sexual Harassment.* Washington, DC: AAUW Educational Foundation.

Abbott, Pamela, and Claire Wallace. 1990. *An Introduction to Sociology: Feminist Perspectives.* London, England: Routledge.

Abramson, Jeffrey. 1995. "Making the law colorblind." *New York Times,* October 16, p. A11.

Abramson, Jill. 1998. "The business of persuasion thrives in nation's capital." *New York Times,* September 29, pp. A1, A22.

Acton, H. B. 1967. *What Marx Really Said.* New York: Schocken.

AHA (American Heart Association). 1998. "Tobacco smoke biostatistical fact sheet." Available online: www.amhrt.org.

Alba, Richard D. 1990. *Ethnic Identity: The Transformation of White America.* New Haven, CT: Yale University Press.

Aldrich, Howard E. 1992. "Incommensurable paradigms? Vital signs from three perspectives." In Michael Reed and Michael Hughes (eds.), *Rethinking Organization: New Directions in Organization Theory and Analysis.* Newbury Park, CA: Sage.

Alexander, Karl L., and Martha A. Cook. 1982. "Curricula and coursework: A surprise ending to a familiar story." *American Sociological Review,* 47, pp. 626–640.

Allis, Sam. 1990. "Schooling kids at home." *Time,* October 22, pp. 84–86.

Alonso, William. 1964. "The historic and the structural theories of urban form: Their implications for urban renewal." *Journal of Land Economics,* 40, pp. 227–231.

Alter, Jonathan. 1998. "It's 4:00 p.m.: Do you know where your children are?" *Newsweek,* April 27, pp. 28–33.

Altman, Lawrence K. 1990. "Changes in medicine bring pain to healing profession." *New York Times,* February 18, pp. 1, 20–21.

Amato, Paul R., et al. 2003. "Continuity and change in marital quality between 1980 and 2000." *Journal of Marriage and the Family,* 65, pp. 1–22.

Ames, Katrine. 1990. "Our bodies, their selves." *Newsweek,* December 17, p. 60.

Amsden, Alice H. 2002. "Why are globalizers so provincial?" *New York Times,* January 31, p. A27.

Amsden, Alice H. 2001. *The Rise of "the Rest": Challenges to the West from Late-Industrializing Economies.* New York: Oxford University Press.

Andersen, Margaret L. 1993. *Thinking about Women,* 3rd ed. New York: Macmillan.

Anderson, C. Alan, and Deborah G. Whitehouse. 1995. *New Thought: A Practical American Spirituality.* New York: Crossroad.

Anderson, Curt. 2003. "States face growing prison population." July 27. Available online: www.story.news.yahoo.com.

Anderson, David C. 1998. *Sensible Justice: Alternatives to Prison.* New York: New Press.

Anderson, David C. 1994. "The crime funnel." *New York Times Magazine,* June 12, pp. 57–58.

Anderson, Elijah, and Douglas S. Massey. 2001. *Problem of the Century: Racial Stratification in the United States.* New York: Russell Sage Foundation.

Anderson, Margo J., and Stephen E. Fienberg. 1999. *Who Counts? The Politics of Census-Taking in Contemporary America.* New York: Russell Sage Foundation.

Anderson, Michael, et al. 2003. "'Why doesn't she just leave?' A descriptive study of victim reported impediments to her safety." *Journal of Family Violence,* 18, pp. 151–154.

Anderson, Terry L. 1995. *Sovereign Nations or Reservations? An Economic History of American Indians.* San Francisco: Pacific Research Institute for Public Policy.

Angier, Natalie. 2000. "Do races differ? Not really, genes show." *New York Times,* August 22, pp. D1, D6.

Applebome, Peter. 1996. "Shootings at schools prompt new concerns about violence." *New York Times,* March 3, p. 8.

Archer, Dane, and Rosemary Gartner. 1984. *Violence and Crime in Cross-National Perspective.* New Haven, CT: Yale University Press.

Armstrong, Karen. 2001. "The true, peaceful face of Islam." *Time,* October 1, p. 48.

Armstrong, Louise. 1993. *And They Call It Help: The Psychiatric Policing of America's Children.* Reading, MA: Addison-Wesley.

Arnette, June L., and Marjorie C. Walsleben. 1998. "Combating fear and restoring safety in schools." *Juvenile Justice Bulletin,* April. Washington, DC: U.S. Department of Justice.

Arnold, Elizabeth A. 1996. "A new feminist agenda." *Wall Street Journal,* July 11, p. A16.

Asch, Solomon E. 1955. "Opinions and social pressure." *Scientific American,* 193, pp. 31–35.

Atchley, Robert C. 2000. *Social Forces and Aging,* 9th ed. Belmont, CA: Wadsworth.

Auerbach, Alan J. 1996. *The World of Work.* Madison, WI: Brown & Benchmark.

Auerbach, Alan J. 1983. "Welfare aspects of current U.S. corporate taxation." *American Economic Review Papers and Proceedings,* 73, pp. 76–81.

Axtell, Roger E. 1991. *Gestures: The Do's and Taboos of Body Language around the World.* New York: Wiley.

Ayres, B. Drummond, Jr. 1996. "The expanding Hispanic vote shakes Republican strongholds." *New York Times,* November 10, pp. 1, 18.

Azmitia, Margarita. 1988. "Peer interaction and problem solving: When are two hands better than one?" *Child Development,* 59, pp. 87–96.

Backover, Andrew, and Christine Dugas. 2002. "WorldCom plea could help feds' case." September 27. Available online: www.USAToday.com.

Bader, Chris, Paul J. Becker, and Scott Desmond. 1996. "Reclaiming deviance as a unique course from criminology." *Teaching Sociology,* 24, pp. 316–320.

Baehr, Helen, and Ann Gray (eds.). 1996. *Turning It On: A Reader in Women and Media.* New York: St. Martin's.

Bailey, Kenneth D. 1994. *Methods of Social Research,* 4th ed. New York: Free Press.

Bailey, Peter. 2003. "A campus head start." *Newsweek,* August 4, p. 53.

Balkan, Sheila, Ronald J. Berger, and Janet Schmidt. 1980. *Crime and Deviance in America: A Critical Approach.* Belmont, CA: Wadsworth.

Baltzell, E. Digby. 1994. *Judgment and Sensibility: Religion and Stratification.* New Brunswick, NJ: Transaction.

Baltzell, E. Digby. 1991. *The Protestant Establishment Revisited.* New Brunswick, NJ: Transaction.

Bane, Mary Jo, and David T. Ellwood. 1994. *Welfare Realities: From Rhetoric to Reform.* Cambridge, MA: Harvard University Press.

Banfield, Edward C. 1974. *The Unheavenly City Revisited.* Boston: Little, Brown.

Barber, Benjamin R. 1995. *Jihad vs. McWorld.* New York: Times Books.

Barker, Eileen. 1984. *The Making of a Moonie.* New York: Basil Blackwell.

Barlett, Donald L., and James B. Steele. 1992. *America: What Went Wrong?* Kansas City: Andrews and McMeel.

Barnet, Richard J., and John Cavanagh. 1994. *Global Dreams: Imperial Corporations and the New World Order.* New York: Simon & Schuster.

Barnett, Rosalind C., and Caryl Rivers. 1996. *She Works/He Works: How Two-Income Families Are Happier, Healthier, and Better-Off.* San Francisco: HarperCollins.

Barnett, W. Steven. 1995. "Long-term effects of early childhood programs on cognitive and school outcomes." *Future of Children,* 5, Winter, pp. 25–50.

Baron, James N. 1994. "Reflections on recent generations of mobility research." In David B. Grusky (ed.), *Social Stratification: Class, Race, and Gender in Sociological Perspective.* Boulder, CO: Westview.

Barone, Michael. 2001. "The many faces of America." *U.S. News & World Report,* March 19, pp. 18–20.

Bart, Pauline B. 1991. "Feminist theories." In Henry Etzkowitz and Ronald M. Glassman (eds.), *The Renascence of Sociological Theory.* Itasca, IL: Peacock.

Basow, Susan A. 1986. *Sex-Role Stereotypes.* Monterey, CA: Brooks/Cole.

Basu, Kaushik. 1995. "The poor need child labor." *New York Times,* November 20, p. A17.

Beagan, Brenda L. 2001. "'Even if I don't know what I'm doing I can make it look like I know what I'm doing': Becoming a doctor in the 1990s." *Canadian Review of Sociology and Anthropology,* 38, pp. 275–293.

Becerra, Rosina. 1988. "The Mexican American family." In Charles Mindel et al. (eds.), *Ethnic Families in America: Patterns and Variations,* 3rd ed. New York: Elsevier.

Beck, E. M., and Stewart E. Tolnay. 1990. "The killing fields of the Deep South: The market for cotton and the lynching of blacks, 1882–1930." *American Sociological Review,* 55, pp. 526–539.

Beck, Melinda. 1990a. "Trading places." *Newsweek,* July 16, pp. 48–54.

Beck, Melinda. 1990b. "The politics of cancer." *Newsweek,* December 10, pp. 62–65.

Becker, Howard S. 1982. "Culture: A sociological view." *Yale Review,* 71, pp. 513–527.

Becker, Howard S. 1963. *Outsiders.* New York: Free Press.

Begley, Sharon. 1990. "The search for the fountain of youth." *Newsweek,* March 5, pp. 44–48.

Beirne, Piers, and James Messerschmidt. 2000. *Criminology,* 3rd ed. Boulder, CO: Westview.

Beirne, Piers, and James Messerschmidt. 1995. *Criminology,* 2nd ed. San Diego: Harcourt Brace Jovanovich.

Belkin, Lisa. 1990. "Many in medicine are calling rules a professional malaise." *New York Times,* February 19, pp. A1, A9.

Bellah, Robert N., et al. 1986. *Habits of the Heart: Individualism and Commitment in American Life.* New York: Harper & Row.

Belluck, Pam. 2000a. "Blighted areas are revived as crime rate falls in cities." *New York Times,* May 29, pp. A1, A12.

Belluck, Pam. 2000b. "Indian schools, long failing, press for money and quality." *New York Times,* May 18, pp. A1, A22.

Belluck, Pam. 1998. "In small town, U.S.A., AIDS presents new set of hardships." *New York Times,* October 12, pp. A1, A13.

Belsky, Jay. 2003. "The dangers of day care." *Wall Street Journal,* July 16, p. A14.

Benderly, Beryl Lieff. 1989. "Don't believe everything you read." *Psychology Today,* November, pp. 67–69.

Bendix, Reinhard. 1962. *Max Weber: An Intellectual Portrait.* Garden City, NY: Anchor.

Benjamin, Matthew. 2003. "China conundrum." *U.S. News & World Report,* September 15, pp. 37–38.

Bennett, William J. 2001. "The drug war worked once. It can again." *Wall Street Journal,* May 15, p. A26.

Bennett, William J. 1989. "A response to Milton Friedman." *Wall Street Journal,* September 19, p. A32.

Bennis, Warren. 1989. "The dilemma at the top." *New York Times,* December 31, p. F3.

Benokraitis, Nijole V. 2002. *Marriages and Families: Changes, Choices, and Constraints.* Upper Saddle River, NJ: Prentice Hall.

Benson, Michael L. 1985. "Denying the guilty mind: Accounting for involvement in a white-collar crime." *Criminology,* 23, p. 594.

Berberoglu, Berch. 1994. *Class Structure and Social Transformation.* Westport, CT: Praeger.

Bercovitch, Sarcan. 1978. *The American Jeremiad.* Madison: University of Wisconsin Press.

Berger, Peter L. 1992. "Sociology: A disinvitation?" *Society*, November/December, pp. 12–18.

Berliner, David C., and Bruce J. Biddle. 1995. *The Manufactured Crisis: Myths, Fraud, and the Attack on America's Public Schools*. Reading, MA: Addison-Wesley.

Berns, Roberta M. 1993. *Child, Family, Community*, 3rd ed. New York: Holt, Rinehart and Winston.

Bernstein, Richard. 2001. "Counterpoint to unity: Dissent." *New York Times*, October 6, pp. A13, A15.

Bernstein, Richard. 1990. "In U.S. schools a war of words." *New York Times Magazine*, October 14, pp. 34, 48–52.

Berreby, David. 1995. "Unabsolute truths: Clifford Geertz." *New York Times Magazine*, April 9, pp. 44–47.

Berthelsen, Christian. 1999. "Women are speaking out to heal trauma of rape." *New York Times*, April 4, p. 17.

Beyer, Lisa. 1990. "Lifting the veil." *Time*, September 24, pp. 38–44.

Bezruchka, Stephen. 2001. "Is our society making you sick?" *Newsweek*, February 26, p. 14.

Bezruchka, Stephen. 1997. "Unhealthy societies: The afflictions of inequality." *New England Journal of Medicine*, 336, pp. 1616–1617.

Bickerton, Derek. 1995. *Language and Human Behavior*. Seattle: University of Washington Press.

Bielby, Denise D., and William T. Bielby. 2002. "Hollywood dreams, harsh realities: Writing for film and television." *Contexts*, Fall/Winter, pp. 21–27.

Biggart, Nicole Woolsey. 1994. "Labor and leisure." In Neil J. Smelser and Richard Swedberg (eds.), *The Handbook of Economic Sociology*. Princeton, NJ: Princeton University Press.

Bilheimer, Robert S. (ed.). 1983. *Faith and Ferment: An Interdisciplinary Study of Christian Beliefs and Practices*. Minneapolis: Augsburg.

Billingsley, Andrew. 1993. *Climbing Jacob's Ladder: The Enduring Legacy of African-American Families*. New York: Simon & Schuster.

Birnbaum, Jeffrey. 1993. *The Lobbyists: How Influence Peddlers Work Their Way in Washington*. New York: Times Books.

Birrell, Bob. 2003. "Strangers at the gate: The immigration backlash." *Britannica Book of the Year*, pp. 396–394.

Bissinger, Buzz. 1997. *A Prayer for the City*. New York: Random House.

Blakeslee, Sandra. 1989. "Race and sex are found to affect access to kidney transplants." *New York Times*, January 24, pp. 19, 23.

Blank, Jonah. 1998. "The Muslim mainstream." *U.S. News & World Report*, July 20, pp. 22–25.

Blank, Jonah, Jason Vest, and Suzie Parker. 1998. "The children of Jonesboro." *U.S. News & World Report*, April 6, pp. 16–22.

Blau, Peter M., and Otis Dudley Duncan. 1967. *The American Occupational Structure*. New York: Wiley.

Blizzard, Rick. 2003a. "Boomers especially sour on U.S. healthcare." June 24. Available online: www.gallup.com.

Blizzard, Rick. 2003b. "Minorities lag in satisfaction with health status." September 30. Available online: www.gallup.com.

Bloom, Harold. 1992. *The American Religion: The Emergence of the Post-Christian Nation*. New York: Simon & Schuster.

Blumer, Herbert. 1978. "Elementary collective groupings." In Louis E. Genevie (ed.), *Collective Behavior and Social Movements*. Itasca, IL: Peacock.

Blumstein, Alfred, and Richard Rosenfeld. 1998. "Assessing the recent ups and downs in U.S. homicide rates." *National Institute of Justice Journal*, October, pp. 8–11.

Blundell, William E. 1987. "When the patient takes charge." *Wall Street Journal*, April 24, pp. 5D–6D.

Blundell, William E. 1986. "Gripe session." *Wall Street Journal*, May 9, pp. 1, 9.

Bornstein, Marc H., et al. 1991. "Parenting in cross-cultural perspective: The United States, France, and Japan." In Marc H. Bornstein (ed.), *Cultural Approaches to Parenting*. Hillsdale, NJ: Erlbaum.

Bossard, James. 1932. "Residential propinquity as a factor in marriage selection." *American Journal of Sociology*, 38, pp. 219–244.

Boudon, Raymond. 1983a. "Individual action and social change: A no-theory of social change." *British Journal of Sociology*, 34, pp. 1–18.

Boudon, Raymond. 1983b. "Why theories of social change fail: Some methodological thoughts." *Public Opinion Quarterly*, 47, pp. 143–160.

Bourassa, Kevin, and Joe Varnell. 2002. *Just Married: Gay Marriage and the Expansion of Human Rights*. Madison: University of Wisconsin Press.

Bowen, William G., and Derek Bok. 1998. *The Shape of the River: Long-Term Consequences of Considering Race in College and University Admissions*. Princeton, NJ: Princeton University Press.

Bowles, Samuel, and Herbert Gintis. 1976. *Schooling in Capitalist America*. New York: Basic Books.

Bowman, Karlyn. 2001. "This Labor Day, workers have cause to celebrate." *Wall Street Journal*, August 27, p. A14.

Bradburd, Daniel. 1982. "Volatility of animal wealth among Southwest Asian pastoralists." *Human Ecology*, 10, pp. 85–106.

Bradsher, Keith. 1995. "More on the wealth of nations." *New York Times*, August 20, p. E6.

Braithwaite, John. 1989. *Crime, Shame and Reintegration*. New York: Cambridge University Press.

Brauchli, Marcus W., and Dan Biers. 1995. "Green lanterns." *Wall Street Journal*, April 19, pp. A1, A4.

Brazelton, T. Berry. 1998. "Building a better self-image." *Newsweek* [Special Issue], pp. 76–77.

Brewer, Geoffrey. 2000. "Out to pasture, greener pasture." *New York Times*, June 21, pp. C1, C8.

Bridges, William P., and Wayne J. Villemez. 1986. "Informal hiring and income in the labor market." *American Sociological Review*, 51, pp. 574–582.

Brinson, Susan L. 1992. "The use and opposition of rape myths in prime-time television dramas." *Sex Roles*, 27, pp. 359–375.

Broh, Beckett A. 2002. "Linking extracurricular programming to academic achievement: Who benefits and why?" *Sociology of Education*, 75, pp. 69–95.

Brookhiser, Richard. 1991. *The Way of the WASP: How It Made America, and How It Can Save It, So to Speak*. New York: Free Press.

Brown, Roger. 1965. *Social Psychology*. New York: Free Press.

Bruni, Frank. 2001. "Bush pushes role of private sector in aiding the poor." *New York Times,* May 21, pp. A1, A15.

Budig, Michelle J. 2002. "Male advantage and the gender composition of jobs: Who rides the glass escalator?" *Social Problems,* 49, pp. 258–277.

Buford, Bill. 1992. *Among the Thugs.* New York: Norton.

Buller, Mary Klein, and David B. Buller. 1987. "Physicians' communication style and patient satisfaction." *Journal of Health and Social Behavior,* 28, pp. 275–388.

Burgess, Ernest W. 1967/1925. "The growth of the city: An introduction to a research project." In R. E. Park, E. W. Burgess, and R. D. McKenzie (eds.), *The City.* Chicago: University of Chicago Press.

Burkett, Elinor. 1997. "'God created me to be a slave'." *New York Times Magazine,* October 12, pp. 56–60.

Burt, Ronald S. 1983. "Corporate philanthropy as a cooptive relation." *Social Forces,* 62, pp. 419–449.

Butler, Robert. 2001. "The myth of old Age." *Newsweek,* Fall/Winter [Special Issue], p. 33.

Butler, Robert. 1984. "Interview." *U.S. News & World Report,* July 2, pp. 51–52.

Butterfield, Fox. 1996. "Gun violence may be subsiding, studies find." *New York Times,* October 14, p. A6.

Calmes, Jackie. 1997. "Fast rise in retirement age would raise money, fury." *Wall Street Journal,* February 10, p. A20.

Camarillo, Albert. 1996. *Chicanos in a Changing Society.* Cambridge, MA: Harvard University Press.

Campbell, Anne. 1993. *Men, Women, and Aggression.* New York: Basic Books.

Canary, Daniel J., and Kathryn Dindia. 1998. *Sex Differences and Similarities in Communication.* Mahwah, NJ: Erlbaum.

Cannon, Angie. 2003. "Taking liberties." *U.S. News & World Report,* May 12, pp. 44–46.

Cantril, Hadley, with Hazel Gaudet and Herta Herzog. 1982/1940. *The Invasion from Mars.* Princeton, NJ: Princeton University Press.

Carlson, Darren. 2004. "2004 campaign trail winds through cyberspace." January 20. Available online: www.gallup.com.

Carlson, Eugene. 1991. "Impact of zones for enterprise is ambiguous." *Wall Street Journal,* April 1, pp. B1, B2.

Carnoy, Martin, and Henry M. Levin. 1985. *Schooling and Work in the Democratic State.* Stanford, CA: Stanford University Press.

Carpenter, Betsy. 1990. "Living with our legacy." *U.S. News & World Report,* April 23, pp. 60–65.

Carstensen, Laura L. 2001. "On the brink of a brand-new old age." *New York Times,* January 2, p. A19.

Casper, Lynne M., Sara S. McLanahan, and Irwin Garfinkel. 1994. "The gender-gap: What we can learn from other countries." *American Sociological Review,* 59, pp. 594–605.

Cassel, Susie Lan. 2001. *The Chinese in America: A History from Gold Mountain to the New Millennium.* Walnut Creek, CA: AltaMira.

Castro, Janice. 1993. "Disposable workers." *Time,* March 29, pp. 43–47.

Chambers, Chris. 2000. "Americans largely satisfied with own health care . . ." September 20. Available online: www.gallup.com.

Chambers, Marcia. 1997. "For women, 25 years of Title IX has not leveled the playing field." *New York Times,* June 16, pp. A1, C18.

Chambliss, William J. 1969. *Crime and the Legal Process.* New York: McGraw-Hill.

Chang, Leslie. 2001. "Parental discretion." *Wall Street Journal,* February 2, pp. A1, A6.

Charon, Joel M. 1992. *Symbolic Interactionism,* 4th ed. Englewood Cliffs, NJ: Prentice-Hall.

Chaves, Mark. 2002. "Abiding faith." *Contexts,* Summer, pp. 19–26.

Cherlin, Andrew J. 1992. *Marriage, Divorce, Remarriage.* Cambridge, MA: Harvard University Press.

Cherlin, Andrew J. 1983. "Changing family and household: Contemporary lessons from historical research." *Annual Review of Sociology,* 9, pp. 51–66.

Cherlin, Andrew J., and Frank F. Furstenberg, Jr. 1994. "Stepfamilies in the United States: A reconsideration." *Annual Review of Sociology,* 20, pp. 359–381.

Cherlin, Andrew J., and Frank F. Furstenberg, Jr. 1983. "The American family in the year 2000." *Futurist,* 18, pp. 7–14.

Chilman, Catherine Street. 1993. "Hispanic families in the United States: Research perspectives." In Harriette Pipes McAdoo (ed.), *Family Ethnicity: Strength in Diversity.* Newbury Park, CA: Sage.

Chimerine, Lawrence. 1995. *Multinational Corporations and the U.S. Economy.* Washington, DC: Economic Strategy Institute.

Chirot, Daniel, and Jennifer Edwards. 2003. "Making sense of the senseless: Understanding genocide." *Contexts,* Spring, pp. 12–19.

Christensen, Andrew, and Neil S. Jacobson. 2000. *Reconcilable Differences.* New York: Guilford.

Christopher, Robert C. 1983. *The Japanese Mind: The Goliath Explained.* New York: Simon & Schuster.

Church, George J. 1993. "Gorezilla zips the system." *Time,* September 13, pp. 25–28.

Clark, Charles S. 1993. *TV Violence.* Washington, DC: Congressional Quarterly.

Clarke, B. J. 1998. *A Closer Look at Promise Keepers.* Pulaski, TN: Sain.

Clarke, Lee. 2002. "Panic: Myth or reality?" *Contexts,* Fall, pp. 21–26.

Clawson, Dan, and Naomi Gerstel. 2002. "Caring for our young: Child care in Europe and the United States." *Contexts,* Fall/Winter, pp. 28–35.

Close, Ellis. 1993. *The Rage of a Privileged Class.* New York: HarperCollins.

Cloud, John. 2003. "Guarding death's door." *Time,* July 14, pp. 46–54.

Cloud, John. 2001. "AIDS at 20." *Time,* June 11, p. 83.

Cloud, John. 2000. "A kinder, gentler death." *Time,* September 18, pp. 60–67.

Cloud, John, and Jodie Morse. 2001. "Home sweet school." *Time,* August 27, pp.47–54.

CNN. 2000. "Survey: Internet established as major news source in 2000 elections." Available online: www.CNN.com. Accessed December 4.

Cockerham, William. 2001. *Medical Sociology,* 8th ed. Englewood Cliffs, NJ: Prentice-Hall.

Cohen, Adam. 2001. "Coloring the campus." *Time,* September 17, pp. 48–49.

Cohen, James R. 2002. "Maryland's 'smart growth': Using incentives to combat sprawl." In Gregory D. Squires (ed.), *Urban Sprawl: Causes, Consequences and Policy Responses* (pp. 293–324). Washington, DC: Urban Institute Press.

Cohen, Joyce. 2001. "On the Internet, love really is blind." *New York Times,* January 18, pp. D1, D9.

Coleman, James William, and Donald R. Cressey. 1993. *Social Problems,* 5th ed. New York: HarperCollins.

Coleman, John J. 1996. *Party Decline in America: Policy, Politics, and the Fiscal State.* Princeton, NJ: Princeton University Press.

Collins, Gail. 1998. "Lust at the top: The prequel." *New York Times Magazine,* March 29, pp. 42–43.

Collins, Randall. 1975. *Conflict Sociology.* New York: Academic Press.

Commoner, Barry. 1990. *Making Peace with the Planet.* New York: Pantheon.

Conrad, Peter. 2001. *Sociology of Health and Illness: Critical Perspectives,* 6th ed. New York: Worth.

Conway, Flo, and Jim Siegelman. 1995. *Snapping: America's Epidemic of Sudden Personality Change,* 2nd ed. New York: Stillpoint Press.

Cook, Arnold. 2000. *Historical Drift: Must My Church Die?* Camp Hill, PA: Christian.

Cook, William J. 1998/1999. "American innovators." *U.S. News & World Report,* December 28/January 4, pp. 40–42.

Cooley, Charles H. 1909. *Social Organization.* New York: Scribner's.

Coontz, Stephanie. 1997. *The Way We Really Are: Coming to Terms with America's Changing Families.* New York: Basic Books.

Cooper, Kristina, et al. 1986. "Correlates of mood and marital satisfaction among dual-worker and single-worker couples." *Social Psychology Quarterly,* 49, pp. 322–329.

Cooper, Matthew. 1998. "Turning up the heat." *Newsweek,* April 13, pp. 50–51.

Corliss, Richard. 2001. "Go ahead, make her day." *Time,* March 26, pp. 64–66.

Corliss, Richard. 1993. "A few good women." *Time,* April 15, pp. 58–59.

Corsaro, William A., and Donna Eder. 1995. "Development and socialization of children and adolescents." In Karen S. Cook, Gary Alan Fine, and James S. House (eds.), *Sociological Perspectives on Social Psychology.* Boston: Allyn & Bacon.

Corsaro, William A., and Donna Eder. 1990. "Children's peer cultures." *Annual Review of Sociology,* 16, pp. 197–220.

Corsaro, William A., and Tomas A. Rizzo. 1988. "*Discussione* and friendship: Socialization processes in the peer culture of Italian nursery school children." *American Sociological Review,* 53, pp. 879–894.

Cory, Christopher T. 1979. "Women smile less for success." *Psychology Today,* March, p. 16.

Cose, Ellis. 2001. "Silver linings from a summit." *Newsweek,* September 17, p. 40.

Costello, Daniel. 2000. "Spanking makes a comeback." *Wall Street Journal,* June 9, pp. W1, W16.

Coulibaly, Modibo, Rodney Green, and David James. 1998. *Segregation in Federally Subsidized Low-Income Housing in the United States.* Westport, CT: Praeger.

Cowell, Alan. 1994. "Pope rules out debate on women as priests." *New York Times,* May 31, pp. A1, A4.

Cowgill, Donald O. 1974. "Aging and modernization: A revision of the theory." In J. F. Gubrium (ed.), *Late Life: Communities and Environmental Policy.* Springfield, IL: Thomas.

Cowley, Geoffrey, and Bill Turque. 1999. "Critical condition." *Newsweek,* November 8, pp. 59–61.

Cox, Harvey. 1966. *The Secular City.* New York: Macmillan.

Crossen, Cynthia. 1991. "Kids acting up? Don't yell, validate their tiny feelings." *Wall Street Journal,* December 10, pp. A1, A4.

Crossette, Barbara. 1998. "Most consuming more, and the rich much more." *New York Times,* September 13, p. 3.

Crosette, Barbara. 1995. "The second sex in the third world." *New York Times,* September 10, pp. 4-1, 4-3.

Cullingford, Cedric. 1993. "Children's social and moral claims." *Society,* November/December, pp. 52–54.

Currie, Elliott. 1999. "A forum—beyond legalization: New ideas for ending the war on drugs." *The Nation,* September 20, pp. 11–20.

Currie, Elliott. 1998. *Crime and Punishment in America.* New York: Metropolitan Books.

Currie, Elliott. 1993. *Reckoning: Drugs, the Cities, and the American Future.* New York: Hill and Wang.

Curry, Andrew. 2000. "Pursuing happiness by the numbers." *U.S. News & World Report,* December 18, p. 56.

Dahl, Robert A. 1981. *Democracy in the United States: Promise and Performance,* 4th ed. Boston: Houghton Mifflin.

Darnton, John. 1994. "In decolonized, destitute Africa bankers are the new overlords." *New York Times,* June 20, pp. A1, A6–A7.

Davidman, Lynn, and Arthur L. Greil. 1994. "Gender and the experience of conversion: The case of 'returnees' to modern orthodox Judaism." In William H. Swatos, Jr. (ed.), *Gender and Religion.* New Brunswick, NJ: Transaction.

Davis, James. 1991. *Who Is Black? One Nation's Definition.* University Park: Pennsylvania State University Press.

Davis, James. 1982. "Up and down opportunity's ladder." *Public Opinion,* June/July, pp. 11–15, 48–51.

Davis, Kenneth C. 1995. "Ethnic cleansing didn't start in Bosnia." *New York Times,* September 3, pp. E1, E6.

Davis, Kingsley. 1976. "The world's population crises." In Robert K. Merton and Robert Nisbet (eds.), *Contemporary Social Problems,* 4th ed. New York: Harcourt Brace Jovanovich.

Davis, Kingsley. 1955. "The origin and growth of urbanization in the world." *American Journal of Sociology,* 60, pp. 429–437.

Davis, Kingsley. 1947. "Final note on a case of extreme isolation." *American Journal of Sociology,* 52, pp. 432–437.

Davis, Kingsley, and Wilbert E. Moore. 1945. "Some principles of stratification." *American Sociological Review,* 10, pp. 242–249.

Davis, Murray S. 1993. *What's So Funny? The Comic Conception of Culture and Society.* Chicago: University of Chicago Press.

Deegan, Mary Jo. 1988. *Jane Addams and the Men of Chicago School.* New Brunswick, NJ: Transaction.

Delphy, Christine, and Diana Leonard. 1992. *Familiar Exploitation: A New Analysis of Marriage in Contemporary Western Societies.* Cambridge, England: Polity Press.

Denton, Nancy A., and Douglas S. Massey. 1989. "Racial identity among Caribbean Hispanics: The effect of double minority status on residential segregation." *American Sociological Review,* 54, pp. 790–808.

Dentzer, Susan. 1995. "Paying the price of female neglect." *U.S. News & World Report,* September 11, p. 45.

Derrida, Jacques. 1997. *Deconstruction in a Nutshell: A Conversation with Jacques Derrida.* New York: Fordham University Press.

Dershowitz, Alan. 1997. *The Vanishing American Jew.* New York: Little, Brown.

Deveny, Kathleen. 2003. "We're not in the mood." *Newsweek,* June 30, pp. 40–46.

DeWaal, Cornelis. 2001. *On Mead.* Belmont, CA: Wadsworth.

Dickerson, Debra. 1998. "An army-style prep school for minorities." *U.S. News & World Report,* December 29, pp. 76–80.

Dickey, Christopher. 2002. "Inside Suicide, Inc." *Newsweek,* April 15, pp. 26–32.

Diesenhouse, Susan. 1990. "More women are playing, but fewer call the shots." *New York Times,* December 11, pp. B11–B12.

DiIulio, John J. 1995. "Why violent crime rates have dropped." *Wall Street Journal,* September 6, p. A17.

Dobash, Russell P., et al. 1992. "The myth of sexual symmetry in marital violence." *Social Problems,* 39, pp. 71–91.

Doerr, Edd, et al. 1996. *The Case against School Vouchers.* Amherst, NY: Prometheus Books.

Domhoff, G. William. 1983. *Who Rules America Now? A View for the Eighties.* Englewood Cliffs, NJ: Prentice-Hall.

Domhoff, G. William. 1978. *The Powers That Be: Processes of Ruling-Class Domination in America.* New York: Random House.

Doskoch, Peter. 1996. "Happily ever laughter." *Psychology Today,* July/August, pp. 33–35.

Dougherty, Peter J. 2002. *Who's Afraid of Adam Smith?* New York: Wiley.

Dowd, Maureen. 1994. "Americans like G.O.P. agenda but split on how to reach goals." *New York Times,* December 15, pp. A1, A14.

Dreazen, Yochi J. 2001. "Democrats may be goring their ox as Lieberman, Hollings target Hollywood." *Wall Street Journal,* June 20, p. A20.

Dreier, Peter. 2001. "How will you spend the 21st century?" *Footnotes,* July/August, pp. 11–12.

Dresser, Norine. 1999. *Multicultural Celebrations: Today's Rules of Etiquette for Life's Special Occasions.* New York: Three Rivers Press.

Dresser, Norine. 1996. *Multicultural Manners: New Rules of Etiquette for a Changing Society.* New York: Wiley.

Dugger, Celia W. 2001. "Relying on hard and soft sells, India pushes sterilization." *New York Times,* June 22, pp. A1, A10.

Dugger, Celia W. 1996a. "Immigrant cultures raising issues of child punishment." *New York Times,* February 29, pp. A1, A12.

Dugger, Celia W. 1996b. "African ritual pain: Genital cutting." *New York Times,* October 5, pp. 1, 4–5.

Dunlap, David W. 1996. "Gay families ease into suburbia." *New York Times,* April 16, pp. B1, B6.

Durkheim, Émile. 1915/1966. *The Elementary Forms of the Religious Life.* New York: Free Press.

Durkheim, Émile. 1897/1951. *Suicide.* New York: Free Press.

Dutton, Diana B. 1978. "Explaining the low use of health services by the poor: Costs, attitudes, or delivery system?" *American Sociological Review,* 43, pp. 348–368.

Dychtwald, Ken. 1989. *Age Wave: The Challenges and Opportunities of an Aging America.* Los Angeles: Jeremy Tarcher.

Easterbrook, Gregg. 2003. *The Progress Paradox: How Life Gets Better While People Feel Worse.* New York: Random House.

Easterbrook, Gregg. 1987. "The revolution in medicine." *Newsweek,* January 26, pp. 40–74.

Edwards, Tamala M. 2000. "Flying solo." *Time,* August 28, pp. 47–53.

Egan, Timothy. 1998. "Backlash growing as Indians make a stand for sovereignty." *New York Times,* March 9, pp. A1, A16.

Ehrenreich, Barbara. 2001. *Nickel and Dimed: On (Not) Getting By in America.* New York: Henry Holt.

Ehrlich, Anne. 1984. "Critical masses: World population 1984." *Sierra,* July/August, pp. 36–40.

Eig, Jonathan. 2002. "Keeping hope." *Wall Street Journal,* December 26, pp. A1, A7.

Eisenberg, Anne. 1999. "Female M.D.'s more open with options, patients say." *New York Times,* August 17, p. D8.

Elkin, Frederick, and Gerald Handel. 1988. *The Child and Society,* 5th ed. New York: Random House.

Elkind, David. 1992. "The future of childhood." *Psychology Today,* May/June, pp. 38–81.

Elliott, Michael. 1998. "It ain't necessarily so." *Newsweek,* March 30, p. 57.

Ellis, Lee. 1985. "Religiosity and criminality." *Sociological Perspectives,* 28, pp. 501–520.

Emmons, Karen M., et al. 2004. "Predictors of smoking among college students." In Alex Thio and Thomas C. Calhoun (eds.), *Readings in Deviant Behavior,* 3rd ed. (pp. 247–250). Boston: Allyn & Bacon.

Epstein, Cynthia Fuchs. 1976. "Sex roles." In Robert K. Merton and Robert Nisbet (eds.), *Contemporary Social Problems.* New York: Harcourt Brace Jovanovich.

Epstein, Robert. 1997. "Folk wisdom: Was your grandmother right?" *Psychology Today,* November/December, pp. 46–50, 76.

Erickson, Bonnie. 2003. "Social networks: The value of variety." *Contexts,* Winter, pp. 25–31.

Erickson, Robert, and Jan O. Jonsson. 1996. *Education and Social Class.* Boulder, CO: Westview.

Espinosa, P. K. 1992. "Life in these United States." *Reader's Digest,* January, p. 68.

Estrada, Michelle, Justin Brown, and Fiona Lee. 1995. "Who gets the credit? Perceptions of idiosyncrasy credit in work groups." *Small Group Research,* 26, January, pp. 56–76.

Etzioni, Amitai. 2001. "Is bowling together sociologically lite?" *Contemporary Sociology,* 30, pp. 223–224.

Etzioni, Amitai. 1993. *The Spirit of Community: Rights, Responsibilities and the Communitarian Agenda.* New York: Crown.

Etzioni, Amitai. 1975. *A Comparative Analysis of Complex Organizations,* rev. ed. New York: Free Press.

Evans, Diana. 1996. "Before the roll call: Interest group lobbying and public policy outcomes in House committees." *Political Research Quarterly,* 49, pp. 287–304.

Faludi, Susan. 1991. *Backlash: The Undeclared War against American Women.* New York: Crown.

Farley, John E. 1995. *Majority–Minority Relations,* 3rd ed. Englewood Cliffs, NJ: Prentice-Hall.

Farley, Reynolds, and William H. Frey. 1994. "Changes in the segregation of whites from blacks during the 1980s: Small steps toward a more integrated society." *American Sociological Review,* 59, pp. 30–41.

Farran, D. C., and R. Haskins. 1980. "Reciprocal influence in the social interactions of mothers and three-year-old children from different socioeconomic backgrounds." *Child Development,* 51, pp. 780–791.

Farris, Michael P. 1997. "Solid evidence to support home schooling." *Wall Street Journal,* March 5, p. A18.

Feagin, Joe R. 1995. *White Racism: The Basics.* New York: Routledge.

Feagin, Joe R., and Clairece Booher Feagin. 1999. *Racial and Ethnic Relations,* 6th ed. Englewood Cliffs, NJ: Prentice-Hall.

Featherman, David L., and Robert M. Hauser. 1978. *Opportunity and Change.* New York: Academic Press.

Feller, Ben. 2003. "U.S. tops in school spending, not scores." September 16. Available online: www.story.news.yahoo.com.

Felson, Richard B., and Mark D. Reed. 1986. "Reference groups and self-appraisals of academic ability and performance." *Social Psychology Quarterly,* 49, pp. 103–109.

Ferguson, Niall. 2001. "2011." *New York Times Magazine,* December 2, pp. 77–79.

Ferree, Myra Marx, and Elaine J. Hall. 1996. "Rethinking stratification from a feminist perspective: Gender, race, and class in mainstream textbooks." *American Sociological Review,* 61, pp. 929–950.

Feshbach, Murray, and Alfred Friendly, Jr. 1992. *Ecocide in the U.S.S.R.* New York: Basic Books.

Fineman, Howard. 1996. "Redrawing the color lines." *Newsweek,* April 29, pp. 34–35.

Firestone, David. 2001a. "The new-look suburbs: Denser or more far-flung?" *New York Times,* April 17, pp. A1, A14.

Firestone, David. 2001b. "U.S. figures show prison population is now stabilizing." *New York Times,* June 9, pp. A2, A10.

Firor, John. 1990. *The Changing Atmosphere: A Global Challenge.* New Haven, CT: Yale University Press.

Fischer, Claude. 1984. *The Urban Experience,* 2nd ed. San Diego: Harcourt Brace Jovanovich.

Fischer, Joannie. 2001. "The first clone." *U.S. News & World Report,* December 3, pp.51–63.

Fischman, Joshua. 1986. "What are friends for?" *Psychology Today,* September, pp. 70–71.

Fish, Jefferson M. 1995. "Mixed blood." *Psychology Today,* November/December, pp. 51–61, 76, 80.

Fisher, Ian. 1999. "Sometimes a girl's best friend is not her father." *New York Times,* March 2, p. A4.

Fiske, Edward B., 1987. "Global focus on quality in education." *New York Times,* June 1, pp. 19, 23.

Flexner, Eleanor, and Ellen F. Fitzpatrick. 1996. *Century of Struggle: The Women's Rights Movement in the United States.* Cambridge, MA: Harvard University Press.

Florida, Richard, and Martin Kenney. 1991. "Transplanted organizations: The transfer of Japanese industrial organization to the U.S." *American Sociological Review,* 56, pp. 381–398.

Fogel, Robert William. 2000. *The Fourth Great Awakening and the Future of Egalitarianism.* Chicago: University of Chicago Press.

Forbes, Malcolm S., Jr. 1996. "Wrong approach," *Forbes,* March 11, pp. 25–26.

Fram, Leslie. 2003. *How to Marry a Divorced Man.* New York: Regan Books.

Francese, Peter. 2003. "Trend ticker: Investing in demographics." *American Demographics,* January, pp. 48–51.

Francese, Peter. 2002. "Continuing education." *Demographics,* April, pp. 46–47.

Frantz, Douglas. 2001. "Unofficial commission acts to ease Turkish-Armenian enmity." *New York Times,* July 10, p. A3.

Freedman, Alix M. 1990. "Deadly diet." *Wall Street Journal,* December 18, pp. A1, A4.

Freedman, Jonathan L. 1986. "Television violence and aggression: A rejoinder." *Psychological Bulletin,* 100, pp. 372–378.

French, Howard W. 2001. "Japan's refusal to revise textbooks angers its neighbors." *New York Times,* July 10, p. A3.

French, Howard W. 1996. "Africans look east for a new model." *New York Times,* February 4, pp. 4-1, 4-4.

Freudenheim, Milt. 1996. "Health care in the era of capitalism." *New York Times,* April 7, p. E6.

Fussell, Paul. 1996. "The culture of war." *Society,* 33, September/October, pp. 53–56.

Fussell, Paul. 1992. *Class: A Guide through the American Status System.* New York: Touchstone.

Gabriel, Trip. 1997. "Pack dating: For a good time, call a crowd." *New York Times: Education Life,* January 5, pp. 22–23, 38.

Gahr, Evan. 1998. "Computers are for girls." *Wall Street Journal,* October 30, p. W11.

Galanter, Marc. 1999. *Cults: Faith, Healing, and Coercion.* Oxford, England: Oxford University Press.

Gallagher, Maggie. 1996. *The Abolition of Marriage: How We Destroy Lasting Love.* New York: Regnery.

Gallagher, Winifred. 2001. "Young love: The good, the bad and the educational." *New York Times,* November 13, p. D6.

Gallagher, Winifred. 1996. *I.D.: How Heredity and Experience Make You Who You Are.* New York: Random House.

Gallup, George, Jr. 2003. "Healthcare system." June 27–29. Available online: www.gallup.com.

Gallup, George, Jr. 2001. "Poll topic and trend—religion." Available online: www.gallup.com.

Gallup, George, Jr., and Jim Castelli. 1989. *The People's Religion: American Faith in the '90s.* New York: Macmillan.

Gamson, William A. 1975. *The Strategy of Social Protest.* Homewood, IL: Dorsey.

Gans, Herbert J. 1982. *The Urban Villagers.* New York: Free Press.

Gans, Herbert J. 1971. "The uses of poverty: The poor pay all." *Social Policy,* 2, pp. 20–24.

Gans, Herbert J. 1968. *People and Plans.* New York: Basic Books.

Gardner, Howard. 1993. *Creating Minds: An Anatomy of Creativity Seen through the Lives of Freud, Einstein, Picasso, Stravinsky, Eliot, Graham, and Gandhi.* New York: Basic Books.

Gardyn, Rebecca. 2002. "The mating game." *American Demographics,* July/August, pp. 33–37.

Gardyn, Rebecca. 2001a. "Fallen faith." *American Demographics,* March, p. 25.

Gardyn, Rebecca. 2001b. "Granddaughters of feminism." *American Demographics,* April, pp. 43–47.

Gardyn, Rebecca. 2000. "Who's the boss?" *American Demographics,* September, pp. 53–58.

Garfinkel, Harold. 2002. *Ethnomethodology's Program: Working Out Durkheim's Aphorism.* Lanham, MD: Rowman & Littlefield.

Garfinkel, Harold. 1967. *Studies in Ethnomethodology.* Englewood Cliffs, NJ: Prentice-Hall.

Gelles, Richard J., and Claire Pedrick Cornell. 1990. *Intimate Violence in Families,* 2nd ed. Beverly Hills, CA: Sage.

Gelman, David. 1986. "Why we age differently." *Newsweek,* October 20, pp. 60–61.

Gerber, Gwendolyn L. 1989. "The more positive evaluation of men than women on the gender-stereotyped traits." *Psychological Reports,* 65, pp. 275–286.

Gerencher, Kristen. 2001. "Good-looks bias more potent for men." Available online: www.CBSMarketWatch.com. Accessed March 30.

Gergen, David. 1999. "A sense of belonging." *U.S. News & World Report,* December 6, p. 108.

Gerstel, Naomi, and Sally K. Gallagher. 2001. "Men's caregiving: Gender and the contigent character of care." *Gender and Society,* 15, pp. 197–217.

Gibbs, Nancy R. 1996. "Cause celeb." *Time,* June 17, pp. 28–30.

Gibbs, Nancy R. 1995. "Love and let die." In Robert Emmet Long (ed.), *Suicide.* New York: Wilson.

Gibson, Richard. 1998. "Merchants mull the long and the short of lines." *Wall Street Journal,* September 3, pp. B1, B4.

Gilbert, Dennis, and Joseph A. Kahl. 1993. *The American Class Structure,* 4th ed. Belmont, CA: Wadsworth.

Gilgoff, Dan, and Jay Tolson. 2003. "Losing friends?" *U.S. News & World Report,* March 17, p. 40.

Gilleard, Christopher John, and Ali Aslan Gurkan. 1987. "Socioeconomic development and the status of elderly men in Turkey: A test of modernization theory." *Journal of Gerontology,* 42, pp. 353–357.

Gilliard, Darrell K., and Allen J. Beck. 1996. "Prison and jail inmates, 1995." *Bureau of Justice Statistics Bulletin,* August, pp. 1–14.

Gilligan, Carol. 1989. "Mapping the moral domain: Images of self in relationship." *Cross Currents,* 39, Spring, pp. 50–63.

Gilligan, Carol. 1982. *In a Different Voice: Psychological Theory and Women's Development.* Cambridge, MA: Harvard University Press.

Gilman, Hank. 1986. "Marketers court older consumers as balance of buying power shifts." *Wall Street Journal,* April 23, p. A37.

Giordano, Joseph. 1987. "The Mafia mystique." *U.S. News & World Report,* February 16, p. 6.

Glaab, Charles N., and A. Theodore Brown. 1983. *A History of Urban America,* 3rd ed. New York: Macmillan.

Glastris, Paul. 1996. "Writing Murphy's law." *U.S. News & World Report,* October 7, pp. 30–32.

Glastris, Paul, and Bruce B. Auster. 1997. "Clinton's next trial." *U.S. News & World Report,* February 10, pp. 26–30.

Glater, Jonathan D. 2001. "Women are close to being majority of law students." *New York Times,* March 26, pp. A1, A16.

Gleick, Elizabeth. 1997. "The marker we've been . . . waiting for." *Time,* November 17, pp. 28–36.

Gleick, Elizabeth. 1995. "The costly crisis in our schools." *Time,* January 30, pp. 67–68.

Goetting, Ann. 1995. *Homicide in Families and Other Social Populations.* New York: Springer.

Goffman, Erving. 1971. *Relations in Public: Microstudies of the Public Order.* New York: Basic Books.

Goffman, Erving. 1967. *Interaction Ritual.* New York: Random House.

Goldberg, Carey. 1996. "Survey reports more drug use by teenagers." *New York Times,* August 21, p. A8.

Golden, Daniel. 2003. "What if affirmative action in education ends?" *Wall Street Journal,* March 31, pp. B1, B3.

Goldman, Ari L. 1991. "Portrait of religion in U.S. holds dozens of surprises." *New York Times,* April 10, pp. A1, A11.

Goldscheider, Calvin. 2003. "Are American Jews vanishing again?" *Contexts,* Winter, pp. 18–24.

Goldstein, Melvyn C., and Cynthia M. Beall. 1982. "Indirect modernization and the status of the elderly in a rural third-world setting." *Journal of Gerontology,* 37, pp. 743–748.

Goldstone, Jack A. 1994. *Revolutions: Theoretical, Comparative, and Historical Studies,* 2nd ed. New York: Harcourt Brace Jovanovich.

Goleman, Daniel. 1991. "Anatomy of a rumor: Fear feeds it." *New York Times,* June 4, pp. B1, B7.

Goleman, Daniel. 1990. "Stereotypes of the sexes said to persist in therapy." *New York Times,* April 10, pp. B1, B7.

Goode, William J. 1993. *World Changes in Divorce Patterns.* New Haven, CT: Yale University Press.

Goodlad, John I. 1984. *A Place Called School: Prospects for the Future.* New York: McGraw-Hill.

Goodman, Robert S. 1996. "Animal communication treasure hunt." *American Biology Teacher,* 58, pp. 224–226.

Goodstein, Laurie. 2001. "Most Americans see benefits in religion, a poll shows." *New York Times,* January 10, p. A13.

Goodstein, Laurie. 1997. "Good for the gander, but the goose isn't so sure." *New York Times,* October 5, p. 4-4.

Goodstein, Laurie, and Marjorie Connelly. 1998. "Teen-age poll finds support for tradition." *New York Times,* April 30, pp. A1, A18.

Gordon, Devin. 2001. "The dominator." *Newsweek,* June 18, pp. 42–47.

Gorman, Christine. 2003. "The no. 1 killer of women." *Time,* April 28, pp. 61–66.

Gorman, Christine. 1998. "Playing the HMO game." *Time,* July 13, pp. 22–32.

Gorman, Christine. 1992. "Sizing up the sexes." *Time,* January 20, pp. 42–51.

Gottdiener, Mark. 1994. *The New Urban Sociology.* New York: McGraw-Hill.

Gottdiener, Mark. 1985. *The Social Production of Urban Space.* Austin: University of Texas Press.

Gottdiener, Mark. 1983. "Understanding metropolitan deconcentration: A clash of paradigms." *Social Science Quarterly,* 64, pp. 227–246.

Gottfried, Paul. 1996. "Is modern democracy warlike?" *Society,* 33, September/October, pp. 64–67.

Gottlieb, Annie. 1971. "Female human beings." *New York Times Book Review,* February 21, p. 2-1.

Gottman, John. 2002. *The Mathematics of Marriage: Dynamic Nonlinear Models.* Cambridge, MA: MIT Press.

Gottman, John. 1994. *Why Marriages Succeed or Fail.* New York: Simon & Schuster.

Götz, Ignacio L. 1999. *The Culture of Sexism.* Westport, CT: Praeger.

Goy, R. W., and B. S. McEwen. 1980. *Sexual Differentiation of the Brain.* Cambridge, MA: MIT Press.

Granovetter, Mark. 1984. "Small is bountiful: Labor markets and establishment size." *American Sociological Review,* 49, pp. 323–334.

Granovetter, Mark. 1983. "The strength of weak ties: A network theory revisited." In Randall Collins (ed.), *Sociological Theory 1983.* San Francisco: Jossey-Bass.

Gray, Paul. 1995. "The Catholic paradox." *Time,* October 9, pp. 64–68.

Gray, John. 1992. *Men Are from Mars, Women Are from Venus.* New York: HarperCollins.

Greenberg, David. 1981. *Crime and Capitalism: Readings in Marxist Criminology.* Palo Alto, CA: Mayfield.

Greenberger, Ellen, and Wendy A. Goldberg. 1989. "Work, parenting, and the socialization of children." *Developmental Psychology,* 25, pp. 22–35.

Greene, Jay P. 2003. "An unfair grade for vouchers." *Wall Street Journal,* May 16, p. A8.

Greenhouse, Linda. 2002. "Ruling in Ohio case." *New York Times,* June 28, pp. A1, A17.

Greenhouse, Steven. 1994. "State Department finds widespread abuse of world's women." *New York Times,* February 3, pp. A1, A6.

Gregory, Raymond F. 2001. *Age Discrimination in the American Workplace: Old at a Young Age.* New Brunswick, NJ: Rutgers University Press.

Greider, William. 1992. *Who Will Tell the People: The Betrayal of American Democracy.* New York: Simon & Schuster.

Griffith, Jeanne E., et al. 1989. "American education: The challenge of change." *Population Bulletin,* December, pp. 2–39.

Grogan, Paul, and Tony Proscio. 2000. *Comeback Cities: A Blueprint for Urban Neighborhood Revival.* Boulder, CO: Westview.

Grossman, Divina. 1994. "Enhancing your 'cultural competence.'" *American Journal of Nursing,* July, pp. 59–62.

Grusky, David B. 2001. *Social Stratification: Class, Race, and Gender in Sociological Perspective,* 2nd ed. Boulder, CO: Westview.

Guernsey, Lisa. 2001. "Cyberspace isn't so lonely after all." *New York Times,* July 26, pp. D1, D5.

Gumbel, Nicky. 2002. *How Does the New Age Movement Relate to Christianity?* Eastbourne, England: Kingsway.

Guttman, Monika. 1994. "Separating the sisters." *U.S. News & World Report,* March 28, pp. 49–50.

Gwynne, S. C. 1998. "What a drag!" *Time,* September 14, pp. 26–35.

Hacker, Andrew. 1992. *Two Nations: Black and White, Separate, Hostile, Unequal.* New York: Scribner's.

Hadaway, C. Kirk, et al. 1993. "What the polls don't show: A closer look at U.S. church attendance." *American Sociological Review,* 58, pp. 741–752.

Hafner, Katie. 2000. "A credibility gap in the digital divide." *New York Times,* March 5, p. 4-4.

Hager, Mary. 1998. "How 'demographic fatigue' will defuse the population bomb." *Newsweek,* November 2, p. 12.

Hall, Wayne. 1986. "Social class and survival on the *S.S. Titanic.*" *Social Science and Medicine,* 22, pp. 687–690.

Hammond, Phillip E. 1985. "The curious path of conservative Protestantism." *Annals of American Academy of Political and Social Science,* 480, pp. 53–62.

Hamner, Tommie J., and Pauline H. Turner. 1996. *Parenting in Contemporary Society,* 3rd ed. Boston: Allyn & Bacon.

Hancock, LynNell. 1994. "Red, white—and blue." *Newsweek,* November 7, p. 54.

Hannon, Kerry. 1996. "The tempting life of a professional temp." *U.S. News & World Report,* October 28, pp. 80–81.

Harayda, Janice. 1986. *The Joy of Being Single.* Garden City, NY: Doubleday.

Hardin, Garrett. 1993. *Living within Limits: Ecology, Economics, and Population Taboos.* New York: Oxford University Press.

Hargrove, Barbara. 1989. *The Sociology of Religion,* 2nd ed. Arlington Heights, IL: Harlan Davidson.

Harjo, Suzan Shown. 1993. "The American Indian experience." In Harriette Pipes McAdoo (ed.), *Family Ethnicity: Strength in Diversity.* Newbury Park, CA: Sage.

Harper, Lucinda. 1993. "Good looks can mean a pretty penny on the job." *Wall Street Journal,* November 23, p. B1.

Harris, Anthony R., and Lisa R. Meidlinger. 1995. "Criminal behavior: Race and class." In Joseph F. Sheley (ed.), *Criminology: A Contemporary Handbook.* Belmont, CA: Wadsworth.

Harris, Chauncy D. 1997. "'The nature of cities' and urban geography in the last half century." *Urban Geography,* 18, pp. 15–35.

Harris, Chauncy D., and Edward L. Ullman. 1945. "The nature of cities." *Annals of the American Academy of Political and Social Science,* 242, pp. 7–17.

Harris, Judith Rich. 1999. *The Nurture Assumption: Why Children Turn Out the Way They Are.* New York: Touchstone.

Harris, Marvin. 1995. *Cultural Anthropology,* 4th ed. New York: HarperCollins.

Harris, Marvin. 1985. *Good to Eat: Riddles of Foods and Culture.* New York: Simon & Schuster.

Harris, Monica J., and Robert Rosenthal. 1985. "Mediation of interpersonal expectancy effects: 31 meta-analyses." *Psychological Bulletin,* 97, pp. 363–386.

Harrison, Lawrence E. 1999. "The cultural roots of poverty." *Wall Street Journal,* July 13, p. A22.

Harrison, Lawrence E. 1992. *Who Prospers? How Cultural Values Shape Economic and Political Success.* New York: Basic Books.

Hatch, Ruth C., et al. 1986. "Spiritual intimacy and marital satisfaction." *Family Relations,* 35, pp. 539–545.

Haub, Carl V. 1999. "Population trends." *Britannica Book of the Year,* pp. 300–301.

Hauser, Philip M. 1981. "Chicago—Urban crisis exemplar." In J. John Palen (ed.), *City Scenes,* 2nd ed. Boston: Little, Brown.

Hawkes, Kristen, and James F. O'Connell. 1981. "Affluent hunters? Some comments in light of the Alyawara case." *American Anthropologist,* 83, pp. 622–626.

Hawkins, Dana. 1996. "Homeschool battles." *U.S. News & World Report,* February 12, pp. 57–58.

Hawkins, Darnell F. 1995. "Ethnicity, race, and crime: A review of selected studies." In Darnell F. Hawkins (ed.), *Eth-*

nicity, Race, and Crime. Albany: State University of New York Press.

Headden, Susan. 1998. "The Hispanic dropout mystery." *U.S. News & Report,* October 20, pp. 64–65.

Headland, Thomas N., and Lawrence A. Reid. 1989. "Hunter-gatherers and their neighbors from prehistory to the present." *Current Anthropology,* 30, pp. 43–51.

Heath, Rebecca Piirto. 1998. "The new working class." *American Demographics,* January, pp. 51–55.

Hegedus, Rita. 1976. "Voucher plans." In Steven E. Goodman (ed.), *Handbook on Contemporary Education.* New York: Bowker.

Heilbroner, Robert L. 1980. *Marxism: For and Against.* New York: Norton.

Heilbroner, Robert L. 1972. *The Worldly Philosophers: The Lives, Times, and Ideas of the Great Economic Thinkers,* 4th ed. New York: Simon & Schuster.

Heim, Pat, and Susan Golant. 1993. *Hardball for Women.* New York: Plume.

Helitzer, Melvin. 1987. *Comedy Writing Secrets.* Cincinnati: Writer's Digest Books.

Henneberger, Melinda, and Michel Marriott. 1993. "For some, youthful courting has become a game of abuse." *New York Times,* July 11, pp. 1, 14.

Henry, William A., III. 1990. "Beyond the melting pot." *Time,* April 9, pp. 28–31.

Henslin, James M., and Mae A. Biggs. 1971. "Dramaturgical desexualization: The sociology of the vaginal examination." In James M. Henslin (ed.), *Studies in the Sociology of Sex.* New York: Appleton-Century-Crofts.

Herberg, Will. 1983. *Protestant-Catholic-Jew: An Essay in American Religions.* Chicago: University of Chicago Press.

Herbert, Bob. 1995. "Buying clothes without exploiting children." *New York Times,* August 4, p. D15.

Herbert, Wray. 1999a. "Getting close, but not too close." *U.S. News & World Report,* March 22, pp. 56–57.

Herbert, Wray. 1999b. "When strangers become family." *U.S. News & World Report,* November 29, pp. 58–67.

Herring, Cedric. 2002. "Is job discrimination dead?" *Contexts,* Summer, pp. 13–18.

Herrnstein, Richard J., and Charles Murray. 1994. *The Bell Curve: Intelligence and Class Structure in American Life.* New York: Free Press.

Heyneman, Stephen P., and William A. Loxley. 1983. "The effect of primary-school quality on academic achievement across twenty-nine high- and low-income countries." *American Journal of Sociology,* 88, pp. 1162–1194.

Hill, Michael R., and Susan Hoecker-Drysdale. 2002. *Harriet Martineau: Theoretical and Methodological Perspectives.* London, England: Routledge.

Hinds, Michael deCourcy. 2000. "Mixed signals on education." *American Demographics,* March, pp. 22–23.

Hirschi, Travis. 1969. *Causes of Delinquency.* Berkeley: University of California Press.

Hirschman, Charles, and Huu Minh Nguyen. 2002. "Tradition and change in Vietnamese family structure in the Red River Delta." *Journal of Marriage and the Family,* 64, pp. 1063–1079.

Hoare, Carol. 2001. *Erikson on Development in Adulthood: New Insights from the Unpublished Papers.* New York: Oxford University Press.

Hochschild, Arlie Russell. 1997. *The Time Bind: When Work Becomes Home and Home Becomes Work.* New York: Metropolitan Books.

Hochschild, Arlie Russell. 1989. *The Second Shift.* New York: Viking.

Hochschild, Arlie Russell. 1983. *The Managed Heart: Commercialization of Human Feeling.* Berkeley: University of California Press.

Hodge, Robert W., Paul M. Siegel, and Peter H. Rossi. 1964. "Occupational prestige in the United States: 1925–1963." *American Journal of Sociology,* 70, pp. 286–302.

Hodson, Randy. 1989. "Gender differences in job satisfaction: Why aren't women more dissatisfied?" *Sociological Quarterly,* 30, pp. 385–399.

Hoecker-Drysdale, Susan. 1992. *Harriet Martineau: First Woman Sociologist.* Oxford, England: Berg.

Hoffer, Eric. 1966. *The True Believer: Thoughts on the Nature of Mass Movements.* New York: Harper & Row.

Hofferth, Sandra. 2002. "Did welfare reform work? Implications for 2002 and beyond." *Contexts,* Spring, pp. 45–51.

Hogan, Dennis P., et al. 1990. "Race, kin networks, and assistance to mother-headed families." *Social Forces,* 68, pp. 797–812.

Hogan, Patrick Cohm. 2001. *The Culture of Conformity: Understanding Social Consent.* Durham, NC: Duke University Press.

Hollander, Edwin P. 1986. "The idiosyncrasy credit model of leadership." *Encyclopedia of Leadership.* Stuttgart, Germany: Plenum.

Holmes, Steven A. 2001. "The confusion over who we are." *New York Times,* June 3, pp. 4-1, 4-5.

Holmes, Steven A. 1998a. "1997 AIDS deaths down almost half in U.S. from 1996." *New York Times,* October 8, pp. A1, A24.

Holmes, Steven A. 1998c. "Women surpass men in educational achievement, census reports." *New York Times,* June 30, p. A18.

Holmes, Steven A. 1996. "Income disparity between poorest and richest rises." *New York Times,* June 20, pp. A1, A10.

Horn, Thelma Sternberg, and Curt Lox. 1998. "The self-fulfilling prophecy theory: When coaches' expectations become reality." In Jean M. Williams (ed.), *Applied Sport Psychology: Personal Growth to Peak Performance,* 3rd ed. Mountain View, CA: Mayfield.

Hornblower, Margot. 1998. "The boy who loved bombs." *Time,* June 1, pp. 42–44.

Hornblower, Margot. 1996. "Putting tongues in check." *Time,* October 9, pp. 41–50.

Hoult, Thomas Ford. 1979. *Sociology for a New Day,* 2nd ed. New York: Random House.

House, James S., et al. 1988. "Social relationships and health." *Science,* 241, pp. 540–545.

Hout, Michael, Andrew Greeley, and Melissa Wilde. 2001. "The demographic imperative in religious change in the United States." *American Journal of Sociology,* 107, pp. 468–500.

Howard, Michael C. 1993. *Contemporary Cultural Anthropology,* 4th ed. New York: HarperCollins.

Howard, Philip K. 2001. *The Lost Art of Drawing the Line: How Fairness Went Too Far.* New York: Random House.

Howarth, Glennys. 1996. *Last Rites: The Work of the Modern Funeral Director.* Amityville, NY: Baywood.

Hoyt, Homer. 1943. "The structure of American cities in the post-war era." *American Journal of Sociology,* 48, pp. 475–492.

Hoyt, Karen. 1987. *The New Age Rage.* Old Tappan, NJ: Fleming Revell.

Hraba, Joseph. 1979. *American Ethnicity.* Itasca, IL: Peacock.

Humphreys, Laud. 1970. *Tearoom Trade: Impersonal Sex in Public Places.* Chicago: Aldine.

Huntington, Samuel P. 1996. *The Clash of Civilizations and the Remaking of World Order.* New York: Simon & Schuster.

Hwang, Caroline. 1998. "The good daughter." *Newsweek,* September 21, p. 16.

Hymowitz, Kay S. 2001. "Parenting: The lost art." *American Educator,* Spring, pp. 4–9.

Impoco, Jim. 1996. "TV's frisky family values." *U.S. News & World Report,* April 15, pp. 58–62.

Ingrassia, Michele. 1995. "Still fumbling in the dark." *Newsweek,* March 13, pp. 60–62.

Ingrassia, Michele, and Pat Wingert. 1995. "The new providers." *Newsweek,* May 22, pp. 36–38.

Jackson, Kenneth T. 2001. "Once again, the city beckons." *New York Times,* March 30, p. A23.

Jackson, Linda A., John E. Hunter, and Carole N. Hodge. 1995. "Physical attractiveness and intellectual competence: A meta-analytic review." *Social Psychology Quarterly,* 58, pp. 108–122.

Jacobs, Charles, and Mohamed Athie. 1994. "Bought and sold." *New York Times,* July 13, p. A11.

Jacobs, Jerry A. 2003. "Detours on the road to equality: Women, work and higher education." *Contexts,* Winter, pp. 32–41.

Jacquard, Albert. 1983. "Myths under the microscope." *UNESCO Courier,* 36, pp. 25–27.

Jacobson, Mark Z. 2002. *Atmospheric Pollution: History, Science, and Regulation.* New York: Cambridge University Press.

Jacoby, Tamar. 2002. "A nation of immigrants." *Wall Street Journal,* April 29, p. A18.

Jagtenberg, Tom, and David McKie. 1997. *Eco-Impacts and the Greening of Postmodernity: New Maps for Communication Studies, Cultural Studies, and Sociology.* Thousand Oaks, CA: Sage.

Jalali, Rita, and Seymour Martin Lipset. 1993. "Racial and ethnic conflicts: A global perspective." *Political Science Quarterly,* 107, pp. 585–606.

Janis, Irving L. 1982. *Groupthink: Psychological Studies of Policy Decisions and Fiascos.* Boston: Houghton Mifflin.

Jankowski, Martin Sanchez. 1995. "The rising significance of status in U.S. race relations." In Michael Peter Smith and Joe R. Feagin (eds.), *The Bubbling Cauldron.* Minneapolis: University of Minnesota Press.

Janofsky, Michael. 2001. "Conviction of a polygamist raises fears among others." *New York Times,* May 24, p. A14.

Janus, Samuel S., and Cynthia L. Janus. 1993. *The Janus Report on Sexual Behavior.* New York: Wiley.

Jaret, Charles. 1983. "Recent neo-Marxist urban analysis." *Annual Review of Sociology,* 9, pp. 499–525.

Jason, Leila. 2001. "Are there rules of etiquette for cell phone use?" *Wall Street Journal,* September 10, p. R16.

Jauhar, Sandeep. 2001. "Hidden in the world of medicine, discrimination and stereotypes." *New York Times,* June 19, p. D6.

Jehl, Douglas. 1999. "Arab honor's price: A woman's blood." *New York Times,* June 20, pp. 1, 9.

Jencks, Christopher, et al. 1994. "Inequality: A reassessment of the effect of family and schooling in America." In David B. Grusky (ed.), *Social Stratification: Class, Race, and Gender in Sociological Perspective.* Boulder, CO: Westview.

Johnson, David W., and Frank P. Johnson. 1997. *Joining Together: Group Theory and Group Skills.* Boston: Allyn & Bacon.

Johnson, Julie, et al. 1991. "Why do blacks die young?" *Time,* September 16, pp. 50–52.

Johnson, Sally. 1995. "Continuing education: College à la carte." *New York Times: Education Life,* August 6, pp. 22–24.

Johnson, Sterling, Jr. 1987. "This is the wrong message to give." *New York Times,* December 20, p. E20.

Johnston, Ronald L. 1996. *Religion in Society,* 5th ed. Englewood Cliffs, NJ: Prentice-Hall.

Jones, Jeffrey M. 2001. "Update: Americans' views on stem cell research." August 14. Available online: www.gallup.com.

Kadlec, Daniel. 2003. "Where did my raise go?" *Time,* May 26, pp. 44–54.

Kahn, Michael. 2002. *Basic Freud: Psychoanalytic Thoughts for Twenty-First Century.* New York: Basic Books.

Kalick, S. Michael, and Thomas E. Hamilton III. 1986. "The matching hypothesis reexamined." *Journal of Personality and Social Psychology,* 51, pp. 673–682.

Kalmuss, Debra. 1984. "The intergenerational transmission of marital aggression." *Journal of Marriage and the Family,* 46, pp. 11–19.

Kammen, Michael. 1999. *American Culture, American Tastes: Social Change and the 20th Century.* New York: Knopf.

Kang, Stephanie. 2003. "Hot item or old hat?" *Wall Street Journal,* October 24, pp. B1, B4.

Kanin, Eugene J. 1983. "Rape as a function of relative sexual frustration." *Psychological Reports,* 52, pp. 133–134.

Kantrowitz, Barbara. 1996. "Gay families come out." *Newsweek,* November 4, pp. 50–57.

Kantrowitz, Barbara. 1991. "Striking a nerve." *Newsweek,* October 21, pp. 38, 40.

Kantrowitz, Barbara, and Pat Wingert, 2001. "Unmarried, with children." *Newsweek,* May 28, pp. 46–54.

Kaplan, David E. 2003. "Playing offense." *U.S. News & World Report,* June 2, pp. 18–29.

Karp, David A., Gregory P. Stone, and William C. Yoels. 1991. *Being Urban: A Sociology of City Life.* New York: Praeger.

Karp, David A., and William C. Yoels. 1998. *Sociology in Everyday Life.* Prospect Height, IL: Waveland.

Kart, Gary S. 1990. *The Realities of Aging,* 3rd ed. Boston: Allyn & Bacon.

Katz, Jack. 1988. *Seductions of Crime.* New York: Basic Books.

Katzenbach, Jon R. 2003. *Why Pride Matters More Than Money.* New York: Crown Business.

Keen, David. 1994. *The Benefits of Famine.* Princeton, NJ: Princeton University Press.

Keller, Helen. 1954. *The Story of My Life.* Garden City, NY: Doubleday.

Kelley, Tina. 1998. "Internet shopping: A mixed bag." *New York Times,* July 30, pp. D1, D5.

Kelly, Patricia Fernandez. 1994. "Broadening the scope: gender and the study of international development." In A. Douglas Kincaid and Alejandro Portes (eds.), *Comparative National Development*. Chapel Hill: University of North Carolina Press.

Kennedy, Paul M. 1991. "A declining empire goes to war." *Wall Street Journal*, January 24, p. A10.

Kennedy, Paul M. 1988. *The Rise and Fall of the Great Powers*. New York: Random House.

Kephart, William M., and Davor Jedlicka. 1991. *The Family, Society, and the Individual*, 7th ed. New York: HarperCollins.

Kerbo, Harold R. 1982. "Movements of 'crisis' and movements of 'affluence': A critique of deprivation and resource mobilization theories." *Journal of Conflict Resolution*, 26, pp. 645–663.

Kerckhoff, Alan C., Richard T. Campbell, and Idee Winfield-Laird. 1985. "Social mobility in Great Britain and the United States." *American Journal of Sociology*, 91, pp. 281–308.

Kilborn, Peter T. 2000. "Learning at home, students take the lead." *New York Times*, May 24, pp. A1, A17.

Kilborn, Peter T. 1999. "Gimme shelter: Same song, new tune." *New York Times*, December 5, p. 4-5.

Kilker, Ernest Evans. 1993. "Black and white in America: The culture and politics of racial classification." *International Journal of Politics, Culture and Society*, 7, pp. 229–258.

Kim, Henry H. 1999. *Guns and Violence*. San Diego, CA: Greenhaven.

Kimball, Meredith M. 1989. "A new perspective on women's math achievement." *Psychological Bulletin*, 105, pp. 198–214.

King, Anthony. 1985. "Transatlantic transgressions: A comparison of British and American scandals." *Public Opinion*, January, pp. 20–22, 64.

Kinzer, Stephen. 2001. "Why they don't know us." *New York Times*, November 11, p. 4-5.

Kirk, Stuart A., and Herb Kutchins. 1994. "Is bad writing a mental disorder?" *New York Times*, June 20, p. A11.

Kirk, Stuart A., and Herb Kutchins. 1992. *The Selling of DSM: The Rhetoric of Science in Psychiatry*. New York: Aldine de Gruyter.

Kisser, Cynthia. 1997. "The road to Heaven's Gate." *Wall Street Journal*, April 1, p. A18.

Kitahara, Michio. 1982. "Menstrual taboos and the importance of hunting." *American Anthropologist*, 84, pp. 901–903.

Kitano, Harry H. L. 1981. "Asian-Americans: The Chinese, Japanese, Koreans, Filipinos, and Southeast Asians." *Annals*, 454, pp. 125–149.

Kitano, Harry H. L., and Roger Daniels. 1995. *Asian Americans: Emerging Minorities*, 2nd ed. Englewood Cliffs, NJ: Prentice-Hall.

Klag, Michael J., et al. 1991. "The association of skin color with blood pressure in U.S. blacks with low socioeconomic status." *Journal of the American Medical Association*, 265, pp. 599–640.

Klaus, Patsy A., and Michael R. Rand. 1984. "Family violence." *Bureau of Justice Statistics Special Report*. Washington, DC: U.S. Department of Justice.

Kleiner, Carolyn. 2000. "A push becomes a shove." *U.S. News & World Report*, March 13, pp. 49–50.

Klinger, Scott, and Holly Sklar. 2002. "Titans of the Enron economy." *Nation*, August 5, pp. 16–17.

Kluger, Jeffrey. 2001a. "A climate of despair." *Time*, April 9, pp. 30–36.

Kluger, Jeffrey. 2001b. "How to manage teen drinking (the smart way)." *Time*, June 18, pp. 42–44.

Koenig, Fredrick. 1982. "Today's conditions make U.S. 'ripe for the rumor mill.'" *U.S. News & World Report*, December 6, p. 42.

Koerner, Brendan I. 1999. "The boys' club persists." *U.S. News & World Report*, April 5, pp. 56–57.

Kohlberg, Lawrence. 1981. *The Philosophy of Moral Development: Moral Stages and the Idea of Justice*. New York: Harper & Row.

Kohn, Alfie. 1997. "How not to teach values." *Education Digest*, 62, pp. 12–17.

Kohn, Alfie. 1988. "You know what they say." *Psychology Today*, April, pp. 36–41.

Kohn, Alfie. 1986. *No Contest: The Case against Competition*. Boston: Houghton Mifflin.

Kohn, Alfie, and Mariah Nelson. 1992. "At issue: Does athletic competition in the U.S. go too far?" *CQ Researcher*, 2, p. 209.

Kohn, Melvin L. 1983. "The benefits of bureaucracy." In Melvin L. Kohn and Carmi Schooler (eds.), *Occupational Structure and Personality*. Norwood, NJ: Ablex.

Kohn, Melvin L. 1980. "Job complexity and adult personality." In Neal Smelser and Erik Erikson (eds.), *Themes of Love and Work in Adulthood*. Cambridge, MA: Harvard University Press.

Kolbert, Elizabeth. 1994. "Television gets closer looks as a factor in real violence." *New York Times*, December 14, pp. A1, A13.

Konner, Melvin. 2001. "Have we lost the healing touch?" *Newsweek*, June 25, p. 77.

Kosters, Marvin H. 1990. "Be cool, stay in school." *American Enterprise*, March/April, pp. 60–67.

Kotkin, Joel. 2001. "Cities must change to survive." *Wall Street Journal*, October 24, p. A22.

Kramer, Peter D. 1997. "Divorce and our national values." *New York Times*, August 29, p. A15.

Krasnow, Iris. 2001. *Surrendering to Marriage*. New York: Hyperion.

Kraut, Robert, et al. 2002. "Internet paradox revisited." *Journal of Social Issues*, 58, pp. 49–75.

Krauthammer, Charles. 1990. "In praise of low voter turnout." *Time*, May 21, p. 88.

Kristof, Nicholas D. 1997. "Once prized, Japan's elderly feel dishonored and fearful." *New York Times*, August 4, pp. A1, A4.

Kristof, Nicholas D. 1996a. "Guns: One nation bars, the other requires." *New York Times*, March 10, p. E3.

Kristof, Nicholas D. 1996b. "Who needs love? In Japan, many couples don't." *New York Times*, February 11, pp. 1, 6.

Kristof, Nicholas D. 1995a. "Japan confronting gruesome war atrocity." *New York Times*, March 17, pp. A1, A4.

Kristof, Nicholas D. 1995b. "Japanese outcasts better off than in past but still outcast." *New York Times*, November 30, pp. A1, A8.

Kronholz, June. 1998. "U.S. 12th-graders rank near bottom in math, science." *Wall Street Journal*, February 25, p. B2.

Krueger, Alan, and Jitka Maleckova. 2002. "Does poverty cause terrorism?" *New Republic,* June 24, pp. 27–33.

Krugman, Paul. 2001. "Hearts and heads." *New York Times,* April 22, p. 17.

Krugman, Paul. 1996. *Pop Internationalism.* Cambridge, MA: MIT Press.

Krysan, Maria, and Reynolds Farley. 2002. "The residential preferences of blacks: Do they explain persistent segregation?" *Social Forces,* 80, pp. 937–981.

Kuchment, Anna. 2003. "Get a move on." *Newsweek,* October 20, p. E28.

Kuczynski, Alex. 1999. "Enough about feminism. Should I wear lipstick?" *New York Times,* p. 4-4.

Kübler-Ross, Elisabeth. 1969. *On Death and Dying.* New York: Macmillan.

Kulish, Nicholas. 2001. "Population of Asian-Americans surges, 1 of 4 persons is minority, census shows." *Wall Street Journal,* March 13, p. A28.

Kunen, James S. 1996. "The end of integration." *Time,* April 29, pp. 39–45.

Kurlantzick, Joshua, and Jodie T. Allen. 2002. "The trouble with globalism." *U.S. News & World Report,* February 11, pp. 38–41.

Lacayo, Richard. 2001. "Antiwar movement: Rapid response." *Time,* October 8, pp. 72–75.

Lacayo, Richard. 1987. "Whose trial is it anyway?" *Time,* May 25, p. 62.

Ladd, Everett Carll. 1983. "Politics in the 80s: An electorate at odds with itself." *Public Opinion,* December/January, pp. 2–5.

Lakoff, George. 2002. *Moral Politics: How Liberals and Conservatives Think.* Chicago: University of Chicago Press.

Landro, Laura. 2003. "Internet use for medical data shifts doctor-patient roles." *Wall Street Journal,* July 17, p. D3.

Landro, Laura. 2001. ". . . And be an educated patient." *Wall Street Journal,* November 12, p. R10.

Lane, Harlan. 1976. *The Wild Boy of Aveyron.* Cambridge, MA: Harvard University Press.

Lapham, Lewis H. 1992. "Fear of freedom." *New York Times,* June 6, p. 15.

Lareau, Annette. 2002. "Invisible inequality: Social class and childrearing in black families and white families." *American Sociological Review,* 67, pp. 747–776.

Larsen, Otto. 1981. "Need for continuing support for social sciences." *ASA Footnotes,* 9, p. 8.

Larson, Jan. 1996. "Temps are here to stay." *American Demographics,* February, pp. 26–31.

Larson, Reed. 1994. *Divergent Realities: The Emotional Lives of Mothers, Fathers, and Adolescents.* New York: Basic Books.

Lasch, Christopher. 1979. *The Culture of Narcissism: American Life in an Age of Diminishing Expectations.* New York: Norton.

Latané, Bibb, and Steve Nida. 1981. "Ten years of research on group size and helping." *Psychological Bulletin,* 89, pp. 308–324.

Lavelle, Louis, and Sheridan Prasso. 2002. "The fat wages of scandal." *Business Week,* September 9, p. 8.

Leach, Penelope. 1994. *Children First.* New York: Knopf.

Lealand, Geoff. 1994. "American popular culture and emerging nationalism in New Zealand." *National Forum,* 74, pp. 34–37.

Lee, Alfred McClung, and Elizabeth Briant Lee. 1979. *The Fine Art of Propaganda.* San Francisco: International Society for General Semantics.

Lee, Barrett A., and Avery M. Guest. 1983. "Determinants of neighborhood satisfaction: A metropolitan-level analysis." *Sociological Quarterly,* 24, pp. 287–303.

Lee, Dwight B, and Richard B. McKenzie. 1999. *Getting Rich in America.* New York: HarperBusiness.

Lee, Valerie, and Julia Smith. 2001. *Restructuring High Schools for Equity and Excellence: What Works?* New York: Teachers College Press.

Lefcourt, Herbert M. 2001a. *Humor: The Psychology of Living Buoyantly.* New York: Kluwer Academic/Plenum.

Lefcourt, Herbert M. 2001b. "The humor solution." In C. R. Snyder (ed.), *Coping with Stress: Effective People and Processes,* pp. 68–92. New York: Oxford University Press.

Lehman, Edward C., Jr. 1994. "Gender and ministry style: Things not what they seem." In William H. Swatos, Jr. (ed.), *Gender and Religion.* New Brunswick, NJ: Transaction.

Leledakis, Knakis. 2000. "Derrida, deconstruction, and social theory." *European Journal of Social Theory,* 3, pp. 175–193.

Lemarchand, René. 1994. "The apocalypse in Rwanda." *Cultural Survival Quarterly,* 18, pp. 29–33.

Lemert, Edwin M. 1951. *Social Pathology.* New York: McGraw-Hill.

Lemonick, Michael D. 2001. "Life in the greenhouse." *Time,* April 9, pp. 24–29.

Lemonick, Michael D. 1996. "Defining the right to die." *Time,* April 15, p. 82.

Lemonick, Michael D. 1995. "Heading for apocalypse?" *Time,* October 2, pp. 54–55.

Lemonick, Michael D. 1992. "The ozone vanishes." *Time,* February 17, pp. 60–63.

Lengermann, Patricia Madoo, and Jill Niebrugge-Brantley. 1992. "Contemporary feminist theory." In George Ritzer (ed.), *Sociological Theory,* 3rd ed. New York: McGraw-Hill.

Lenski, Gerhard, Jean Lenski, and Patrick Nolan. 1995. *Human Societies,* 7th ed. New York: McGraw-Hill.

Leo, John. 2001. "Learning to love terrorists." *U.S. News & World Report,* October 8, p. 48.

Leslie, Gerald R., and Sheila K. Korman. 1989. *The Family in Social Context,* 7th ed. New York: Oxford University Press.

Leslie, Leigh A. 1996. "Sexism in family therapy: Does training in gender roles make a difference?" *Journal of Marital and Family Therapy,* 22, pp. 253–269.

Levin, Jack, and Jack Alan Fox. 2001. *Dead Lines: Essays in Murder and Mayhem.* Boston: Allyn & Bacon.

Levin, Jack, and William C. Levin. 1980. *Ageism: Prejudice and Discrimination against the Elderly.* Belmont, CA: Wadsworth.

Levine, Daniel S. 1993. "Adult students, adult needs." *New York Times,* April 4, sect. 4A, pp. 32–33.

Levine, John M., and Richard L. Moreland. 1990. "Progress in small group research." *Annual Review of Psychology,* 14, pp. 585–634.

Levine, Robert, et al. September 1995. "Love and marriage in eleven cultures." *Journal of Cross-Cultural Psychology,* 26, pp. 554–571.

Levine, Saul V. 1984. *Radical Departures: Desperate Detours to Growing Up.* New York: Harcourt Brace Jovanovich.

Levinthal, Charles F. 2002. *Drugs, Behavior, and Modern Society.* Boston: Allyn & Bacon.

Levy, Becca, and Ellen Langer. 1994. "Aging free from negative stereotypes: Successful memory in China and among the American deaf." *Journal of Personality and Social Psychology,* 66, pp. 989–997.

Levy, Reynold. 1999. *Give and Take: A Candid Account of Corporate Philanthropy.* Boston: Harvard Business School Press.

Levy, S. G., and W. F. Fenley, Jr. 1979. "Audience size and likelihood and intensity of response during a humorous movie." *Bulletin of Psychonomic Society,* 13, pp. 409–412.

Lewin, Tamar. 1998. "Birth rates for teen-agers declined sharply in the 90's." *New York Times,* May 1, p. A17.

Lewinsolhn, Peter M., et al. 1993. "Adolescent psychopathology: I. Prevalence and incidence of depression and other DSM-III-R disorders in high school students." *Journal of Abnormal Psychology,* 102, pp. 133–144.

Lewis, Janet V. 2001. *Sexual Harassment: Issues and Analyses.* Huntington, NY: Nova Science.

Lewis, Michael. 1996. "God is in the packaging." *New York Times Magazine,* July 21, pp. 14, 16.

Lewis, Michael. 1995. "The rich: How they're different . . . than they used to be." *New York Times Magazine,* November 19, pp. 65–69.

Lewis, Oscar. 1961. *The Children of Sanchez.* New York: Random House.

Lieberson, Stanley. 1994. "Understanding ascriptive stratification: Some issues and principles." In David B. Grusky (ed.), *Social Stratification: Class, Race, and Gender in Sociological Perspective.* Boulder, CO: Westview.

Liebow, Elliot. 1993. *Tell Them Who I Am: The Lives of Homeless Women.* New York: Free Press.

Light, Richard J. 2001. *Making the Most of College: Students Speak Their Minds.* Cambridge, MA: Harvard University Press.

Lilleston, Randy. 2000. "Press secretaries say Internet brings change to presidential campaigns." May 9. Available online: www.CNN.com.

Lin, Chien, and William T. Liu. 1993. "Intergenerational relationships among Chinese immigrant families from Taiwan." In Harriette Pipes McAdoo (ed.), *Family Ethnicity: Strength in Diversity.* Newbury Park, CA: Sage.

Lin, Nan. 1982. "Social resources and instrumental action." In Peter V. Marsden and Nan Lin (eds.), *Social Structure and Network Analysis.* Beverly Hills, CA: Sage.

Lincoln, C. Eric. 1994. *The Black Muslims in America.* Trenton, NJ: Africa World Press.

Lincoln, C. Eric, and Lawrence H. Mamiya. 1990. *The Black Church in African American Experience.* Durham, NC: Duke University Press.

Lind, Michael. 1995. *The Next American Nation: The New Nationalism and the Fourth American Revolution.* New York: Free Press.

Linden, Eugene. 1993. "Megacities." *Time,* January 11, pp. 28–38.

Linsky, Arnold. 1995. *Stress, Culture, and Aggression.* New Haven, CT: Yale University Press.

Linzmayer, Owen W. 1999. *Apple Confidential: The Real Story of Apple Computer, Inc.* New York: No Starch Press.

Lipset, Semour Martin. 1996. *American Exceptionalism: A Double-Edged Sword.* New York: Norton.

Lipset, Seymour Martin. 1990. "The work ethic—Then and now." *Public Interest,* Winter, pp. 61–69.

Lipset, Seymour Martin. 1981. *Political Man: the Social Bases of Politics.* Baltimore: Johns Hopkins University Press.

Lipset, Seymour Martin, et al. 1994. "Social mobility in industrial society." In David B. Grusky (ed.), *Social Stratification: Class, Race, and Gender in Sociological Perspective.* Boulder, CO: Westview.

Lipset, Seymour Martin, and Earl Raab. 1995. *Jews and the New American Scene.* Cambridge, MA: Harvard University Press.

Lipset, Seymour Martin, and William Schneider. 1983. *The Confidence Gap: Business, Labor, and Government in the Public Mind.* New York: Free Press.

Livingstone, Sonia. 2003. "Children's use of the Internet: Reflections on the emerging research agenda." *New Media and Society,* 5, pp. 147–166.

Lomborg, Bjorn. 2001. *The Skeptical Environmentalist: Measuring the Real State of the World.* New York: Cambridge University Press.

Longman, Phillip J. 1999. "The world turns gray." *U.S. News & World Report,* March 1, pp. 30–39.

Lord, Mary. 2002. "A battle for children's future." *U.S. News & World Report,* February 25, pp. 35–36.

Lord, Walter. 1981. *A Night to Remember.* New York: Penguin.

Lublin, Joann S., and Timothy D. Schellhardt. 1998. "High court's harassment rulings confuse employers." *Wall Street Journal,* June 30, pp. B1, B8.

Luo, Yadong. 2000. *Multinational Corporations in China: Benefiting from Structural Transformation.* Herndon, VA: Books International.

Macdonald, Barbara, and Cynthia Rich. 2001. *Look Me in the Eye: Old Women, Aging, and Ageism.* Denver: Spinsters Ink Books.

MacFarquhar, Neil. 2001. "Bin Laden and his followers adhere to an austere, stringent form of Islam." *New York Times,* October 7, p. B7.

Mack, Raymond W., and Calvin P. Bradford. 1979. *Transforming America.* New York: Random House.

Madsen, Douglas, and Peter G. Snow. 1983. "The dispersion of charisma." *Comparative Political Studies,* 16, pp. 337–362.

Madsen, Jane M. 1982. "Racist images." *USA Today,* 111, p. 14.

Mallory, Larry. 2003. "Confidence in medical system climbs." August 19. Available online: www.gallup.com.

Malson, Lucien. 1972. *Wolf Children and the Problem of Human Nature.* New York: Monthly Review Press.

Manegold, Catherine S. 1994. "Bill seeks equality of sexes in school." *New York Times,* February 13, p. 14.

Mann, Coramae Richey. 1996. *Why Women Kill.* Albany: State University of New York Press.

Mann, Coramae Richey. 1995. "The contribution of institutionalized racism to minority crime." In Darnell F. Hawkins (ed.), *Ethnicity, Race, and Crime.* Albany: State University of New York Press.

Marano, Hara Estroff. 1997. "Another round, honey?" *Psychology Today,* September, p. 20.

Marcus, Eric. 1993. *Is It a Choice?* New York: HarperCollins.

Margulis, Stephen T. 2003. "Privacy as a social issue and behavioral concept." *Journal of Social Issues,* 59, pp. 243–261.

Mark, Noah P. 2002. "Cultural transmission, disproportionate prior exposure, and the evolution of cooperation." *American Sociological Review,* 67, pp. 323–344.

Markoff, John. 2000. "A newer, lonelier crowd emerges in Internet study." *New York Times,* February 16, pp. A1, A15.

Markides, Kyriakos S., and Charles H. Mindel. 1987. *Aging and Ethnicity.* Newbury Park, CA: Sage.

Markides, Kyriacos C., and Steven F. Cohn. 1982. "External conflict/internal cohesion: A reevaluation of an old theory." *American Sociological Review,* 47, pp. 88–98.

Markovsky, Barry, and Seymour M. Berger. 1983. "Crowd noise and mimicry." *Personality and Social Psychology Bulletin,* 9, pp. 90–96.

Marriott, Michel. 1998b. "The blossoming of Internet chat." *New York Times on the Web,* July 2, pp. 1–6.

Martin, M. Kay, and Barbara Voorhies. 1975. *Female of the Species.* New York: Columbia University Press.

Martinez, Barbara. 2003. "With medical costs climbing, workers are asked to pay more." *Wall Street Journal,* June 16, pp. A1, A6.

Marty, Martin E., and R. Scott Appleby (eds.). 1992. *Fundamentalisms Observed.* Chicago: University of Chicago Press.

Marx, Gary T. 2003. "A tack in the shoe: Neutralizing and resisting the new surveillance." *Journal of Social Issues,* 59, pp. 369–390.

Marx, Karl. 1866/1967. *Capital,* vol. 1. New York: International.

Masland, Tom. 1992. "Slavery." *Newsweek,* May 4, pp. 30–39.

Massey, Douglas S., and Nancy A. Denton. 1993. *American Apartheid.* Cambridge, MA: Harvard University Press.

Mattson, Greggor, et al. 2002. "Six degrees of horror." *Contexts,* Spring, p. 5.

Mauer, Marc. 1999. *Race to Incarcerate.* New York: New Press.

Maybury-Lewis, David. 1994. "What is the future and will it work?" *Cultural Survival Quarterly,* Summer/Fall, p. 1.

Mayer, Margit. 1995. "Social movement research in the United States: A European perspective." In Stanford M. Lyman (ed.), *Social Movements.* New York: New York University Press.

Mayo, Elton. 1933. *The Human Problems of Industrial Civilization.* New York: Macmillan.

McArdle, Thomas. 1994. "Do kids learn more at home?" *Investor's Business Daily,* March 14, pp. 1, 2.

McCormick, John. 1994. "Why parents kill." *Newsweek,* November 14, pp. 31–34.

McCormick, John, and Peter McKillop. 1989. "The other suburb." *Newsweek,* June 26, pp. 22–24.

McCoy, Ron. 1996. "Native American cultural ferment." *Britannica Book of the Year.* Chicago: Encyclopaedia Britannica, Inc.

McDonald, Marci. 1997. "My wife told me to go." *U.S. News & World Report,* October 6, pp. 28–30.

McDowell, Edwin. 1996. "Hospitality is their business." *New York Times,* March 21, pp. C1, C16.

McGlone, Matthew. 1998. "Sounds true to me." *Psychology Today,* October, pp. 12–13.

McGrath, Anne. 2003. "A better start?" *U.S. News & World Report,* March 10, p. 50.

McGuire, David. 2001. "Americans not ready for online voting—Study." *Newsbytes.* March 27. Available online: www.washingtonpost.com.

McKinlay, John B., and Sonja M. McKinlay. 1987. "Medical measures and the decline of mortality." In Howard D. Schwartz (ed.), *Dominant Issues in Medical Sociology,* 2nd ed. New York: Random House.

McMahon, Walter W. 2002. *Education and Development: Measuring the Social Benefits.* Oxford, England: Oxford University Press.

McPhail, Clark, and Ronald T. Wohlstein. 1983. "Individual and collective behaviors within gatherings, demonstrations, and riots." *Annual Review of Sociology,* 9, pp. 579–600.

McWilliams, Carey. 1948. *A Mask for Privilege.* Boston: Little, Brown.

Mead, Margaret. 1935. *Sex and Temperament in Three Primitive Societies.* Garden City, NY: Mentor.

Meer, Jeff. 1986. "The reason of age." *Psychology Today,* June, pp. 60–64.

Mensch, Barbara. 1986. "Age differences between spouses in first marriages." *Social Biology,* 33, pp. 229–240.

Merchant, Carolyn. 1995. "Ecofeminism." In Kate Mehuron and Gary Percesepe (eds.), *Free Spirits: Feminist Philosophers on Culture.* Englewood Cliffs, NJ: Prentice-Hall.

Merton, Robert K. 1976. *Sociological Ambivalence and Other Essays.* New York: Free Press.

Meyer, David S. 2003. "How social movements matter." *Contexts,* Fall, pp. 30–35.

Michael, Robert T., et al. 1994. *Sex in America: A Definitive Survey.* Boston: Little, Brown.

Michels, Robert. 1915. *Political Parties.* Glencoe, IL: Free Press.

Mifflin, Lawrie. 1999. "Many researchers say link is already clear on media and youth violence." *New York Times,* May 9, p. 23.

Mignon, Sylvia I., Calvin J. Larson, and William M. Holmes. 2002. *Family Abuse: Consequences, Theories, and Responses.* Boston: Allyn & Bacon.

Miles, Jack. 1997. "Religion makes a comeback." *New York Times Magazine,* December 7, pp. 56–59.

Milgram, Stanley. 1974. *Obedience to Authority.* New York: Harper & Row.

Miller, Jody. 2001. "Feminist theory." In Alex Thio and Thomas Calhoun (eds.), *Readings in Deviant Behavior,* 2nd ed. Boston: Allyn & Bacon.

Mills, C. Wright. 1959a. *The Power Elite.* New York: Oxford University Press.

Mills, C. Wright. 1959b. *The Sociological Imagination.* New York: Grove.

Min, Pyong Gap. 1995. *Asian Americans: Contemporary Trends and Issues.* Thousand Oaks, CA: Sage.

Mink, Gwendolyn. 1998. "Misreading sexual harassment law." *New York Times,* March 30, p. 19.

Miserandino, Marianne. 1996. "Children who do well in school: Individual differences in perceived competence and autonomy in above-average children." *Journal of Educational Psychology,* 88, pp. 203–214.

Mitchell, Alison. 1997. "Survivors of Tuskegee study get apology from Clinton." *New York Times,* May 17, p. 9.

Moberg, David O. 1984. "Review of James Hunter's *American Evangelicalism.*" *Contemporary Sociology,* 13, pp. 371–372.

Moeller, Thomas G. 1994. "What research says about self-esteem and academic performance." *Education Digest,* 59, pp. 34–37.

Molm, Linda D., Nobuyuki Takahashi, and Gretchen Peterson. 2003. "In the eye of the beholder: Procedural justice in social exchange." *American Sociological Review,* 68, pp. 128–152.

Molotsky, Irvin. 1988. "Senate votes to compensate Japanese-American internees." *New York Times,* April 21, pp. 1, 9.

Monroe, Sylvester. 2001, "Cincinnati riots: Race problems go unsolved when they go unadmitted." *San Jose Mercury News.* April 22. Available online: www.commondreams.org.

Moore, Stephen, and Julian L. Simon. 2000. *It's Getting Better All the Time: 100 Greatest Trends of the Last 100 Years.* Washington, DC: Cato Institute.

Morell, Marie A., et al. 1989. "Would a Type A date another Type A? Influence of behavior type and personal attributes in the selection of dating partners." *Journal of Applied Social Psychology,* 19, pp. 918–931.

Morelli, Gilda A., and Edward Z. Tronick. 1991. "Parenting and child development in the Efe foragers and Lese farmers of Zaire." In Marc H. Bornstein (ed.), *Cultural Approaches to Parenting.* Hillsdale, NJ: Erlbaum.

Morgan, Gareth. 1989. *Creative Organization Theory: A Resourcebook.* Newbury Park, CA: Sage.

Morgan, S. Philip. 1984. "Reply to King and Hunt." *Social Forces,* 62, pp. 1089–1090.

Morgan, S. Philip. 1983. "A research note on religion and morality: Are religious people nice people?" *Social Forces,* 61, pp. 683–692.

Morgen, Sandra. 1994. "Personalizing personnel decisions in feminist organizational theory and practice." *Human Relations,* 47, pp. 665–684.

Morris, Martina, Annette D. Bernhardt, and Mark S. Handcock. 1994. "Economic inequality: New methods for new trends." *American Sociological Review,* 59, pp. 205–219.

Morrow, Lance. 1978. "The lure of doomsday." *Time,* December 4, p. 30.

Morse, Jodie. 2001a. "Letting God back in." *Time,* October 22, p. 71.

Morse, Jodie. 2001b. "When parents drop out." *Time,* May 21, pp. 80–83.

Mortimore, Peter. 1988. *School Matters.* Berkeley: University of California Press.

Mullen, Brian, et al. 1989. "Group size, leadership behavior, and subordinate satisfaction." *Journal of General Psychology,* 116, pp. 155–169.

Mulvey, Laura. 1992. "Visual pleasure and narrative cinema." In Maggie Humm (ed.), *Modern Feminisms: Political, Literary, Cultural.* New York: Columbia University Press.

Mulvihill, Donald, and Melvin Tumin. 1969. *Crimes of Violence,* vol. 11. Washington, DC: U.S. Government Printing Office.

Murray, Matt. 2003. "Corporate goal: Ethnic variety, not quotas." *Wall Street Journal,* June 24, pp. B1, B4.

Musto, David F. 2002. *Drugs in America: A Historical Reader.* New York: New York University Press.

Myers, David G. 1993. *The Pursuit of Happiness.* New York: Avon Books.

Myers, Jerome K., et al. 1984. "Six-month prevalence of psychiatric disorders in three communities." *Archives of General Psychiatry,* 41, pp. 959–967.

Myerson, Allen R. 1998. "Energy addicted in America." *New York Times,* November 1, p. 5.

Nader, Ralph, and Robert Weissman. 2001. "Ending corporate welfare as we know it." *Wall Street Journal,* March 7, p. A22.

Naik, Gautam, et al. 2003. "Global baby bust." *Wall Street Journal,* January 24, pp. B1, B4.

Naisbitt, John, and Patricia Aburdene. 1990. *Megatrends 2000.* New York: Morrow.

Nanda, Serena. 1994. *Cultural Anthropology,* 5th ed. Belmont, CA: Wadsworth.

Nash, Susan Smith. 1996. *Dealing with Date Rape: True Stories from Survivors.* Norman, OK: Texture Press.

Nazario, Sonia L. 1992. "Medical science seeks a cure for doctors suffering from boorish bedside manner." *Wall Street Journal,* March 17, pp. B1, B8.

Nelan, Bruce W. 1998. "Sudan: Why is this happening again?" *Time,* July 27, pp. 29–32.

Nelson, Mariah Burton. 1994. *The Stronger Women Get, the More Men Love Football: Sexism and the American Culture of Sports.* New York: Harcourt Brace.

Nelson, Mark M. 1990. "Darkness at noon." *Wall Street Journal,* March 1, pp. A1, A13.

Nelson, Toben F., and Henry Wechsler. 2003. "School spirits: Alcohol and collegiate sports fans." *Addictive Behaviors,* January, pp. 1–11.

Neuman, W. Lawrence. 2000. *Social Research Methods: Qualitative and Quantitative Approaches,* 4th ed. Boston: Allyn & Bacon.

Newcomb, Theodore. 1958. "Attitude development as a function of reference group: The Bennington study." In Guy E. Swanson et al. (eds.), *Readings in Social Psychology.* New York: Holt, Rinehart and Winston.

Newman, Maria. 1996. "Course at your convenience." *New York Times,* November 3, sect. 4A, p. 13.

Newman, William M. 1973. *American Pluralism: A Study of Minority Groups and Social Theory.* New York: Harper & Row.

New York Times. 1991. "Private cures for public ills." February 28, p. A18.

Niebuhr, Gustav. 2000. "Marriage issue splits Jews, poll finds." *New York Times,* October 31, p. A18.

Niebuhr, Gustav. 1996. "Anti-Semitic acts down after climb." *New York Times,* February 17, p. 9.

Niebuhr, Gustav. 1992. "The lord's name." *Wall Street Journal,* April 27, pp. A1, A4.

Nielsen, Francois. 1994. "Income inequality and industrial development: Dualism revisited." *American Sociological Review,* 59, pp. 654–677.

Nies, Judith. 1996. *Native American History.* New York: Ballantine Books.

Nieuwenhuys, Olga. 1994. *Children's Lifeworlds: Gender, Welfare and Labour in the Developing World.* London, England: Routledge.

NIMH (National Institute of Mental Health). 2003. "Mental disorders in America." Available online: www.nimh.nih.gov/publicat/numbers.cfm.

Nisbet, Robert A. 1970. *The Social Bond.* New York: Knopf.

Nolan, Patrick, and Gerhard Lenski. 1999. *Human Societies,* 8th ed. New York: McGraw-Hill.

NORC (National Opinion Research Center). 2001. *General Social Survey, 1972–2001.* Chicago: University of Chicago Press.

NORC (National Opinion Research Center). 1994. *General Social Survey, 1972–1994.* Chicago: University of Chicago Press.

Nordheimer, Jon. 1990. "Stepfathers: The shoes rarely fit." *New York Times,* October 18, p. B6.

Nuland, Sherwin B. 1994. *How We Die: Reflections on Life's Final Chapter.* New York: Knopf.

Nussbaum, Debra. 1998. "Computer haves and have-nots in the schools." *New York Times,* October 22, pp. D1, D8.

Nye, Joseph, Jr. 1990. *Bound to Lead: The Changing Nature of American Power.* New York: Basic Books.

Oberschall, Anthony. 1992. *Social Movements: Ideologies, Interests, and Identities.* New Brunswick, NJ: Transaction.

O'Dea, Thomas F., and Janet O'Dea Aviad. 1983. *The Sociology of Religion,* 2nd ed. Englewood Cliffs, NJ: Prentice-Hall.

O'Driscoll, Gerald P., Kim R. Holmes, and Mary Anastasia O'Grady. 2002. *The 2002 Index of Economic Freedom.* Washington, DC: Heritage Foundation.

O'Grady, Mary Anastasia. 2003. "At last, a bill for treating immigrants humanely." *Wall Street Journal,* August 29, p. A9.

Omestad, Thomas. 2001. "Slipping into recession." *U.S. News & World Report,* July 23, p. 34.

O'Neill, June. 2001. "Welfare reform worked." *Wall Street Journal,* August 1, p. A14.

Orenstein, Gloria, and Doretta Zemp. 1994. "Rethinking environmental choices." *American Behavioral Scientist,* 37, pp. 1090–1103.

Orwell, George. 1949. *1984.* New York: Signet.

Osborne, Lawrence. 2001. "Regional disturbances." *New York Times Magazine,* May 6, pp. 100–102.

Ochse, Rhona, and Cornelis Plug. 1986. "Cross-cultural investigation of the validity of Erikson's theory of personality development." *Journal of Personality and Social Psychology,* 50, pp. 1240–1252.

Ostling, George. 1991. "Superchurches and how they grow." *Time,* August 5, pp. 62–63.

Page, Benjamin I. 1983. *Who Gets What from Government.* Berkeley: University of California Press.

Palen, I. John. 1995. *The Suburbs.* New York: McGraw-Hill.

Palisi, Bartolomeo J., and Claire Canning. 1983. "Urbanism and social psychological well-being: A cross-cultural test of three theories." *Sociological Quarterly,* 24, pp. 527–543.

Palmore, Erdman, and Daisaku Maeda. 1985. *The Honorable Elders Revisited: A Revised Cross-Cultural Analysis of Aging in Japan.* Durham, NC: Duke University Press.

Palser, Barb. 2003. "The scoop on kids." *American Journalism Review,* May, p. 66.

Papousek, Hanus, and Mechthild Papousek. 1991. "Innate and cultural guidance of infants' integrative competencies: China, the United States, and Germany." In Marc H. Bornstein (ed.), *Cultural Approaches to Parenting.* Hillsdale, NJ: Erlbaum.

Parker, Robert Nash. 1989. "Poverty, subculture of violence, and types of homicide." *Social Forces,* 67, pp. 983–1005.

Parkes, Peter. 1987. "Livestock symbolism and pastoral ideology among the Kafirs of the Hindu Kush." *Man,* 22, pp. 37–660.

Parsons, Talcott. 1964/1951. *The Social System.* Glencoe, IL: Free Press.

Parsons, Talcott, and Robert F. Bales. 1953. *Family, Socialization, and Interaction Process.* Glencoe, IL: Free Press.

Passell, Peter. 1995. "The wealth of nations: A 'greener' approach turns list upside down." *New York Times,* September 19, pp. B5, B12.

Patterson, Orlando. 2001. "Race by the numbers." *New York Times,* May 8, p. A31.

Patterson, Orlando. 2000. "Taking culture seriously: A framework and an Afro-American illustration." In Lawrence E. Harrison and Samuel P. Hungtington (eds.), *Culture Matters: How Values Shape Human Progress* (pp. 202–218). New York: Basic Books.

Patterson, Orlando. 1994. "Ecumenical America: Global culture and the American cosmos." *World Policy Journal,* 11, pp. 103–117.

Patterson, Orlando (quoted in Schlesinger, Arthur, Jr.) 1991. "A new era begins—but history remains." *Wall Street Journal,* December 11, p. A16.

Paul, Annie Murphy. 1998. "Kid stuff: Do parents really matter?" *Psychology Today,* January/February, pp. 46–49, 78.

Paul, Pamela. 2003. "Religious identity and mobility." *American Demographics,* March, pp. 20–21.

Pear, Robert. 2001. "Sex differences called key in medical studies." *New York Times,* April 25, p. A14.

Pear, Robert. 1997. "Academy's report says immigration benefits the U.S." *New York Times,* May 18, pp. 1, 12.

Pear, Robert. 1995. "Proposed definition of indigence could explain number of poor." *New York Times,* April 30, pp. 1, 15.

Pearce, Diana M. 1993. "The feminization of poverty: Update." In Alison M. Jaggar and Paula S. Rothenberg (eds.), *Feminist Frameworks,* 3rd ed. New York: McGraw-Hill.

Pedahzur, Ami, Arie Perliger, and Leonard Weinberg. 2003. "Altruism and fatalism: The characteristics of Palestinian suicide terrorists." *Deviant Behavior,* 24, pp. 405–423.

Pedersen, Daniel, et al. 1999. "Sprawling, sprawling . . ." *Newsweek,* July 19, pp. 22–27.

Peek, Charles W., Evans W. Curry, and H. Paul Chalfant. 1985. "Religiosity and delinquency over time: Deviance deterrence and deviance amplification." *Social Science Quarterly,* 66, pp. 120–131.

Pennebaker, J. W. 1980. "Perceptual and environmental determinants of coughing." *Basic Applied Social Psychology,* 1, pp. 83–91.

Perlo, Victor. 1996. *Economics of Racism II: The Roots of Inequality, USA.* New York: International.

Perry, Joellen. 2000. "Only the cyberlonely." *U.S. News & World Report,* February 28, p. 62.

Pescosolido, Bernice A., and Sharon Georgianna. 1989. "Durkheim, suicide, and religion: Toward a network theory of suicide." *American Sociological Review,* 54, pp. 33–48.

Peterson, Iver. 1999. "After decades of dismissal, the suburbs win converts." *New York Times,* December 5, pp. 1, 43.

Peterson, Janice. 1994. "Traditional economic theories and issues of gender: The status of women in the United States and the former Soviet Union." In Janice Peterson and Doug Brown (eds.), *The Economic Status of Women under Capitalism: Institutional Economics and Feminist Theory.* Hants, England: Edward Elgar.

Petit, Charles W. 1998. "Rediscovering America." *U.S. News & World Report,* October 12, pp. 57–64.

Pheysey, Diana C. 1993. *Organizational Cultures: Types and Transformations.* London, England: Routledge.

Pianin, Eric. 2003. "Study finds net gain from pollution rules." September 27. Available online: www.washingtonpost.com.

Pinchot, Gifford, and Elizabeth Pinchot. 1993. *The End of Bureaucracy and the Rise of the Intelligent Organization.* San Francisco: Berrett-Koehler.

Pines, Maya. 1981. "The civilizing of Genie." *Psychology Today,* September, pp. 28–34.

Pinker, Steven. 2002. *The Blank Slate: The Modern Denial of Human Nature.* New York: Viking.

Pinkney, Alphonso. 1993. *Black Americans,* 4th ed. Englewood Cliffs, NJ: Prentice-Hall.

Piven, Frances Fox, and Richard A. Cloward. 1995. "Collective protest: A critique of resource-mobilization theory." In Stanford M. Lyman (ed.), *Social Movements.* New York: New York University Press.

Pizzo, Stephen P., and Paul Muolo. 1993. "Take the money and run." *New York Times Magazine,* May 9, p. 26.

Pollak, Lauren Harte, and Peggy A. Thoits. 1989. "Processes in emotional socialization." *Social Psychology Quarterly,* 52, pp. 22–34.

Pollock, Ellen Joan. 2000. "Deportment gap." *Wall Street Journal,* February 7, pp. A1, A20.

Pope, Victoria. 1994. "To be young and pretty in Moscow." *U.S. News & World Report,* March 28, p. 56.

Porter, Bruce, and Marvin Dunn. 1984. *The Miami Riot of 1980.* Lexington, MA: Lexington Books.

Portes, Alejandro. 2002. "English-only triumphs, but the costs are high." *Contexts,* Spring, pp. 10–15.

Posner, Richard A. 1995. *Aging and Old Age.* Chicago: University of Chicago Press.

Postman, Neil. 1985. *Amusing Ourselves to Death: Public Discourse in the Age of Show Business.* New York: Viking.

Powell, Colin. 1998. "I wasn't left to myself." *Newsweek,* April 27, p. 32.

Power, Thomas G., and Josephine A. Shanks. 1989. "Parents and socializers: Maternal and paternal views." *Journal of Youth and Adolescence,* 18, pp. 203–217.

Powers, Daniel A., and Christopher G. Ellison. 1995. "Interracial contact and black racial attitudes: The contact hypothesis and selectivity bias." *Social Forces,* 74, pp. 205–226.

Provine, Robert R. 2000. *Laughter: A Scientific Investigation.* London, England: Faber.

Purdum, Todd S. 2002. "U.S. blocks money for family clinics promoted by U.S." *New York Times,* July 23, pp. A1, A6.

Purvis, Andrew. 1996. "A contagion of genocide." *Time,* July 8, pp. 38–39.

Purvis, Andrew. 1992. "A day in the death of Somalia." *Time,* September 21, pp. 32–40.

Purvis, Andrew. 1990. "A perilous gap." *Time,* Fall [Special Issue], pp. 66–67.

Putnam, Robert D. 2000. *Bowling Alone: The Collapse and Revival of American Community.* New York: Simon & Schuster.

Quinney, Richard. 1974. *Critique of Legal Order.* Boston: Little, Brown.

Race, Tim. 1998. "Building girls cyber rooms of their own." *New York Times on the Web,* March 5.

Radford, John. 1990. *Child Prodigies and Exceptional Early Achievers.* New York: Free Press.

Ramirez, Francisco O., and John W. Meyer. 1980. "Comparative education: The social construction of the modern world system." *Annual Review of Sociology,* 6, pp. 369–399.

Ramirez, O. 1997. "Mexican American children and adolescents." In Jewelle Taylor Gibbs and Larke Huang (eds.), *Children of Color.* San Francisco: Jossey-Bass.

Raney, Rebecca Fairley. 1998. "Politicians woo voters on the Web." *New York Times,* July 30, pp. D1, D10.

Rank, Mark R. 2003. "As American as apple pie: Poverty and welfare." *Contexts,* Summer, pp. 41–49.

Ranney, Austin. 1983. "Nonvoting is not a social disease." *Public Opinion,* October/November, pp. 16–19.

Raper, Arthur F. 1970. *The Tragedy of Lynching.* New York: Dover.

Ratnesar, Romesh. 1998. "A place at the table." *Time,* October 12, p. 38.

Rau, William, and Dennis W. Roncek. 1987. "Industrialization and world inequality: The transformation of the division of labor in 59 nations, 1960–1981." *American Sociological Review,* 52, pp. 359–369.

Ray, Julie. 2003. "Assisted-dying debate in U.S., Canada, Britain." September 9. Available online: www.gallup.com.

Rector, Robert. 1998. "America has the world's richest poor people." *Wall Street Journal,* September 24, p. A18.

Regier, Darrel A., et al. 1993. "The de facto U.S. mental and addictive disorders service system: Epidemiologic catchment area prospective 1-year prevalence rates of disorders and services." *Archives of General Psychiatry,* 50, pp. 85–94.

Regulus, Thomas A. 1995. "Race, class and sociobiological perspectives on crime." In Darnell F. Hawkins (ed.), *Ethnicity, Race, and Crime.* Albany: State University of New York Press.

Reibstein, Larry. 1997. "Whose right is it?" *Newsweek,* January 20, p. 36.

Reiss, David. 2000. *The Relationship Code: Deciphering Genetic and Social Influences on Adolescent Development.* Cambridge, MA: Harvard University Press.

Resnick, Michael D., et al. 1997. "Protecting adolescents from harm: Findings from the National Longitudinal Study on Adolescent Health." *Journal of the American Medical Association,* September 10, pp. 823–832.

Restak, Richard M. 1979. *The Brain: The Last Frontier.* Garden City, NY: Doubleday.

Reuters. 1998. "Getting old is getting easier—study finds." *Infoseek News,* October 1.

Rice, Mabel L., et al. 1990. "Words from 'Sesame Street': Learning vocabulary while viewing." *Developmental Psychology,* 26, pp. 421–428.

Richardson, Laurel. 1988. *The Dynamics of Sex and Gender: A Sociological Perspective.* New York: Harper & Row.

Richardson, Lynda. 1998. "Wave of laws aimed at people with H.I.V." *New York Times,* September 25, pp. A1, A25.

Ridgeway, Cecilia L., and Shelley J. Correll. 2000. "Limiting inequality through interaction: The end(s) of gender." *Contemporary Sociology,* pp. 110–120.

Ridley, Matt. 2003. "What makes you who you are." *Time,* June 2, pp. 54–63.

Riesman, David. 1950. *The Lonely Crowd.* New Haven, CT: Yale University Press.

Rimer, Sara. 2000. "A lost moment recaptured." *New York Times: Education Life,* January 9, pp. 21–24.

Ripley, Amanda. 2002. "Why suicide bombing . . . is now all the rage." *Time,* April 15, pp. 32–39.

Robbins, William. 1990. "New decade finds new hope on the farm." *New York Times,* May 18, pp. A1, A10.

Roberts, Sam. 1993. *Who We Are: A Portrait of America Based on the Latest U.S. Census*. New York: Times Books.

Roberts, Steven. 1990. "An all-American snapshot: How we count and why." *U.S. News & World Report*, April 2, p. 10.

Robins, Lee N., et al. 1984. "Lifetime prevalence of specific psychiatric disorders in three sites." *Archives of General Psychiatry*, 41, pp. 949–958.

Robinson, David. 1995. "The Hollywood conquest." *1995 Britannica Book of the Year*, p. 245. Chicago: Encyclopaedia Britannica.

Robinson, Jean C. 1992. "East Asian women and the paradoxes of development: A retrospective on the 1980s." In Marilyn Robinson Waldman et al. (eds.), *Understanding Women: The Challenge of Cross-Cultural Perspectives*. Columbus: Ohio State University Press.

Robinson, Simon, and Nancy Palus. 2001. "An awful human trade." *Time*, April 30, pp. 40–41.

Robison, Jennifer. 2003. "Homosexual parenting evenly divides Americans." July 1. Available online: www.gallup.com.

Rockwell, John. 1994. "The new colossus: American culture as power export." *New York Times*, January 30, pp. 2–1, 2–30.

Rodriguez, Gregory. 2001. "Identify yourself." *New York Times*, September 23, pp. 4-1, 4-4.

Roethlisberger, Fritz J., and William J. Dickson. 1939. *Management and the Worker*. Cambridge, MA: Harvard University Press.

Rogers, David. 2001. "Landmark campaign-reform bill nears Senate passage." *Wall Street Journal*, March 30, p. A16.

Roof, Wade Clark. 1993. *A Generation of Seekers*. New York: HarperCollins.

Roosevelt, Margot. 2001. "A setback for Medipot." *Time*, May 28, p. 50.

Rose, Arnold M. 1967. *The Power Structure*. New York: Oxford University Press.

Rosecrance, Richard. 1990. "Too many bosses, too few workers." *New York Times*, July 15, p. F11.

Rosen, Ruth. 2000. *The World Split Open*. New York: Viking.

Rosenbaum, David E. 1997b. "Corporate welfare's new enemies." *New York Times*, February 2, pp. E1, E6.

Rosenberg, Morris. 1990. "Reflexivity and emotions." *Social Psychology Quarterly*, 53, pp. 3–12.

Rosenblatt, Roger. 1994. "A killer in the eye." *New York Times Magazine*, June 5, pp. 38–47.

Rosener, Judy B. 1990. "The ways women lead." *Harvard Business Review*, 68, pp. 119–125.

Rosenfeld, Richard. 2002. "Crime decline in context." *Contexts*, Spring, pp. 25–34.

Rosenthal, A. M. 1995. "The cruelest hoax." *New York Times*, January 3, p. A11

Rosenthal, Elisabeth. 1998a. "Chinese bewildered by Lewinsky fuss." *New York Times*, August 8, p. 4-4.

Rosenthal, Elisabeth. 1998b. "For one-child policy, China rethinks iron hand." *New York Times*, November 1, pp. 1, 16.

Rosenthal, Robert. 1973. "The Pygmalion effect lives." *Psychology Today*, February, pp. 56–63.

Rosin, Hazel M. 1990. "The effects of dual career participation on men: Some determinants of variation in career and personal satisfaction." *Human Relations*, 43, pp. 169–182.

Ross, Alfred, and Lee Cokorinos. 1996. *Promise Keepers: The Third Wave of the American Religious Right*. New York: Sterling Research Associates.

Ross, Dorothy. 1991. *The Origins of American Social Science*. New York: Cambridge University Press.

Rossi, Alice S. 1984. "Gender and parenthood." *American Sociological Review*, 49, pp. 1–19.

Rossi, Peter H. 1989. *Down and Out in America: The Origins of Homelessness*. Chicago: University of Chicago Press.

Roston, Eric, et al. 2002. "How much is a living wage?" *Time*, April 8, pp. 52–54.

Rothschild, Joyce, and Celia Davies. 1994. "Organizations through the lens of gender: Introduction to the special issue." *Human Relations*, 47, pp. 583–590.

Rothschild, Joyce, and Raymond Russell. 1986. "Alternatives to bureaucracy: Democratic participation in the economy." *Annual Review of Sociology*, 12, pp. 307–328.

Rothstein, Edward. 2002. "Damning (yet desiring) Mickey and the Big Mac." *New York Times*, March 2, pp. A17, A19.

Rothstein, Richard. 2001. "Dramatic voucher findings fall short." *New York Times*, May 9, p. A26.

Rowe, David. 1995. *Popular Cultures*. Thousand Oaks, CA: Sage.

Rubenstein, Carin. 1982. "Real men don't earn less than their wives." *Psychology Today*, November, pp. 36–41.

Rubin, Beth A. 1996. *Shifts in the Social Contract: Understanding Change in American Society*. Thousand Oaks, CA: Pine Forge.

Rubin, Lillian Breslow. 1976. *Worlds of Pain: Life in the Working-Class Family*. New York: Basic Books.

Rushing, William A. 1995. *The AIDS Epidemic: Social Dimensions of an Infectious Disease*. Boulder, CO: Westview.

Russell, Diana E. H., and Rebecca M. Bolen. 2000. *The Epidemic of Rape and Child Sexual Abuse in the United States*. Thousand Oaks, CA: Sage.

Russell, George. 1984. "People, people, people." *Time*, August 6, pp. 24–25.

Russo, Francine. 2001. "Aggression loses some of its punch." *Time*, July [Bonus Section], pp. Y2–Y4.

Russo, Francine. 2000. "Bridal vows revisited." *Time*, July 24, pp. G1–G3.

Rutherford, Megan. 2000. "Catching their second wind." *Time*, January 31, pp. E5–E7.

Rutter, Michael. 1983. "School effects on pupil progress: Research findings and policy implications." *Child Development*, 54, pp. 1–29.

Rybczynski, Witold. 1995. *City Life: Urban Expectations in a New World*. New York: Scribner's.

Rymer, Russ. 1993. *Genie: An Abused Child's Flight from Silence*. New York: HarperCollins.

Sachs, Andrea. 1993. "9–Zip! I Love It!" *Time*, November 22, pp. 44–45.

Sadker, Myra, and David Sadker. 1995. *Failing at Fairness: How Our Schools Cheat Girls*. New York: Touchstone.

Sahlins, Marshall. 1972. *Stone Age Economics*. Chicago: Aldine.

SAMHSA (Substance Abuse and Mental Health Services Administration). 2002. *Annual Household Survey*. Available online: www.hhs.gov/news.

Samuelson, Robert J. 2003a. "A crackup for world trade?" *Newsweek*, August 25, p. 55.

Samuelson, Robert J. 2003b. "Globalization goes to war." *Newsweek*, February 24, p. 41.

Samuelson, Robert J. 2003c. "The spirit of America." *Newsweek*, January 13, p. 47.

Samuelson, Robert J. 1997. "Balancing act." *Newsweek*, August 11, pp. 24–27.

Sapir, Edward. 1929. "The status of linguistics as a science." *Language*, 5, pp. 207–214.

Sapolsky, Robert. 2000. "It's not 'all in the genes.'" *Newsweek*, April 10, p. 68.

Sayle, Murray. 1982. "A textbook case of aggression." *Far Eastern Economic Review*, 117, pp. 36–38.

Scarce, Rik. 1994. "(No) trial (but) tribulation: When courts and ethnography conflict." *Journal of Contemporary Ethnography*, 23, pp. 123–149.

Schaefer, Richard T. 2001. *Race and Ethnicity in the United States*. Upper Saddle River, NJ: Prentice-Hall.

Schellhardt, Timothy D. 1998. "Jury to consider if 'overqualified' signals age bias." *Wall Street Journal*, July 27, pp. B1, B8.

Schemo, Diana Jean. 2001. "In covenant marriage, forging ties that bind." *New York Times*, November 10, p. A8.

Schemo, Diana Jean. 1995. "Of modern bondage." *New York Times*, October 10, pp. A1, A5.

Schlesinger, Arthur Meier. 2002. *History of U.S. Political Parties*. Philadelphia: Chelsea House.

Schmidt, Alvin J. 1997. *The Menace of Multiculturalism: Trojan Horse in America*. New York: Praeger.

Schmitt, Eric. 2002. "The U.S. census of 2000." *Britannica Book of the Year*, pp. 514–515.

Schmitt, Eric. 2001a. "Analysis of census finds segregation along with diversity." *New York Times*, April 4, p. A15.

Schmitt, Eric. 2001b. "Census data show a sharp increase in living standard." *New York Times*, August 6, pp. A1, A10.

Schmitt, Eric. 2001c. "U.S. population has biggest 10-year rise ever." *New York Times*, April 3, p. A10.

Schmitt, Eric. 1997. "Illegal immigrants rose to 5 million in '96." *New York Times*, February 8, p. 7.

Schoemer, Karen. 1996. "Of female bondage." *Newsweek*, August 5, p. 73.

Schor, Juliet B. 1998. *The Overspent American*. New York: Basic Books.

Schor, Juliet B. 1991. *The Overworked American: The Unexpected Decline of Leisure*. New York: Basic Books.

Schrof, Joannie M. 1998a. "Married . . . with problems." *U.S. News & World Report*, January 19, pp. 56–57.

Schrof, Joannie M. 1998b. "Required course: Bedside manner 101." *U.S. News & World Report*, December 21, p. 66.

Schrof, Joannie M. 1993. "Feminism's daughters." *U.S. News & World Report*, September 27, pp. 68–71.

Schultz, Duane P. 1964. *Panic Behavior*. New York: Random House.

Schulz, David A. 1982. *The Changing Family*, 3rd ed. Englewood Cliffs, NJ: Prentice-Hall.

Schur, Edwin M. 1984. *Labeling Women Deviant: Gender, Stigma, and Social Control*. New York: Random House.

Schwab, William A. 1992. *The Sociology of Cities*. Englewood Cliffs, NJ: Prentice-Hall.

Scott, David Clark. 1986. "How 'quality circles' move from the assembly line to the office." *Christian Science Monitor*, August 4, p. 18.

Scott, John (ed.). 2002. *Social Networks: Critical Concepts in Sociology*. London, England: Routledge.

Scott, Paul. 2001. "Sacred battles." *New York Times Magazine*, September 30, p. 19.

Scully, Diana, and Joseph Marolla. 1984. "Convicted rapists' vocabulary of motive: Excuses and justifications." *Social Problems*, 31, pp. 530–544.

Seager, Joni. 2003. *The Penguin Atlas of Women in the World*. New York: Penguin.

See, Katherine O'Sullivan, and William J. Wilson. 1988. "Race and ethnicity." In Neil J. Smelser (ed.), *Handbook of Sociology*. Newbury Park, CA: Sage.

Seligmann, Jean. 1993. "Husbands no, babies yes." *Newsweek*, July 26, p. 53.

Sengupta, Subir. 1995. "The influence of culture on portrayals of women in television commercials: A comparison between the United States and Japan." *International Journal of Advertising*, 13, pp. 314–333.

Sennett, Richard. 1991. *The Conscience of the Eye: The Design and Social Life of Cities*. New York: Knopf.

Seuffert, Virginia. 1990. "Home remedy." *Policy Review*, 52, pp. 70–75.

Shapiro, Laura. 1990. "Guns and dolls." *Newsweek*, May 28, pp. 56–65.

Sheler, Jeffery L. 2001a. "Drug, scalpel . . . and faith?" *U.S. News & World Report*, July 2, pp. 46–47.

Sheler, Jeffery L. 2001b. "Muslim in America." *U.S. News & World Report*, October 29, pp. 50–52.

Sheler, Jeffery L 1994. "Spiritual America." *U.S. News & World Report*, April 4, pp. 48–59.

Sheler, Jeffery L. 1990. "Islam in America." *U.S. News & World Report*, October 8, pp. 69–71.

Shellenbarger, Sue. 1996. "Work and family." *Wall Street Journal*, February 28, p. B1.

Sherif, Muzafer. 1956. "Experiments in group conflict." *Scientific American*, 19, pp. 54–58.

Shibutani, Tamotsu. 1966. *Improvised News*. Indianapolis: Bobbs-Merrill.

Shipman, Pat. 1994. *The Evolution of Racism: Human Differences and the Use and Abuse of Science*. New York: Simon & Schuster.

Shirk, Martha, Neil G. Bennett, and J. Lawrence Aber. 1999. *Lives on the Line: American Families and the Struggle to Make Ends Meet*. Boulder, CO: Westview.

Shon, Steven P., and Davis Y. Ja. 1992. "Asian families." In Arlene S. Skolnick and Jerome H. Skolnick (eds.), *Family in Transition*, 7th ed. New York: HarperCollins.

Shorto, Russell. 1997. "Belief by the numbers." *New York Times Magazine*, December 7, pp. 60–61.

Shweder, Richard A. 1997. "It's called poor health for a reason." *New York Times*, March 9, p. E5.

Sidel, Ruth. 1990. *On Her Own: Growing Up in the Shadow of the American Dream*. New York: Viking.

Silberner, Joanne. 1990. "Health: Another gender gap." *U.S. News & World Report*, September 24, pp. 54–55.

Simenauer, Jacqueline, and David Carroll. 1982. *Singles: The New Americans*. New York: Simon & Schuster.

Simon, Julian L. 1990. *Population Matters: People, Resources, Environment, and Immigration*. New Brunswick, NJ: Transaction.

Simon, Roger. 2001. "A nation, still in pain, rallies." *U.S. News & World Report*, October 22, pp. 52–54.

Simpson, Jeffry A., et al. 1986. "The association between romantic love and marriage: Kephart (1967) twice revisited." *Personality and Social Psychology Bulletin*, 12, pp. 363–372.

Sizer, Theodore R. 1984. *Horace's Compromise: The Dilemma of the American High School*. Boston: Houghton Mifflin.

Skinner, B. F. 1983. "Creativity in old age." *Psychology Today*, September, pp. 28–29.

Skinner, Denis. 1980. "Dual-career family stress and coping: A literature review." *Family Relations,* 29, pp. 473–480.

Slonim, Maureen B. 1991. *Children, Culture, and Ethnicity.* New York: Garland.

Small, Meredith F. 2001. *Kids: How Biology and Culture Shape the Way We Raise Our Children.* New York: Doubleday.

Smelser, Neil J. 1971/1962. *Theory of Collective Behavior.* New York: Free Press.

Smith, Dinitia. 1998. "Philosopher gamely in defense of his ideas." *New York Times,* May 30, pp. A13, A15.

Smith, Garry J. 1996. "The noble sports fan." In D. Stanley Eitzen (ed.), *Sport in Contemporary Society: An Anthology,* 5th ed. New York: St. Martin's.

Smith, Merril D. 2002. *Sex without Consent: Rape and Sexual Coercion in America.* New York: New York University Press.

Smith-Lovin, Lynn. 1995. "The sociology of affect and emotion." In Karen S. Cook, Gary Alan Fine, and James S. House (eds.), *Sociological Perspectives on Social Psychology.* Boston: Allyn & Bacon.

Smock, Pamela J. 2000. "Cohabitation in the United States: An appraisal of research themes, findings, and implications." *Annual Review of Sociology,* 26, pp. 1–20.

Snow, David A., and Leon Anderson. 2003. "Street people." *Contexts,* Winter, pp. 12–17.

Snow, David A., and Leon Anderson. 1993. *Down on Their Luck: A Study of Homeless Street People.* Berkeley: University of California Press.

Sommers, Christina Hoff. 2000. *The War against Boys.* New York: Simon & Schuster.

Sowell, Thomas. 1994. *Race and Culture: A World View.* New York: Basic Books.

Spake, Amanda, and Marianne Szegedy-Maszak. 2001. "The second wave." *U.S. News & World Report,* October 8, pp. 50–52.

Spates, James L. 1983. "The sociology of values." *Annual Review of Sociology,* 9, pp. 27–49.

Spitz, René A. 1945. "Hospitalism." *Psychoanalytic Study of the Child,* 1, pp. 53–72.

Stanley, Thomas J., and William D. Danko. 1998. *The Millionaire Next Door: The Surprising Secrets of America's Wealthy.* New York: Pocket Books.

Staples, Brent. 1998. "The push to broaden God's market share." *New York Times,* October 4, p. 14.

Stavenhagen, Rodolfo. 1991. "Ethnic conflicts and their impact on international society." *International Social Science Journal,* 43, pp. 117–131.

Stearns, Marion S. 1971. *Report on Preschool Programs.* Washington, DC: U.S. Government Printing Office.

Steiss, Tara Kate. 2001. *Gender Stereotyping in Parents' Involvement in Youth Sports.* Norton, MA: Wheaton College.

Steffensmeier, Darrell, and Emilie Allan. 1995. "Criminal behavior: Gender and age." In Joseph F. Sheley (ed.), *Criminology: A Contemporary Handbook.* Belmont, CA: Wadsworth.

Steinberg, Laurence. 1994. *Crossing Paths: How Your Child's Adolescence Triggers Your Own Crisis.* New York: Simon & Schuster.

Steinberg, Laurence. 1987. "Why Japan's students outdo ours." *New York Times,* April 25, p. 15.

Steinberg, Laurence, Bradford Brown, and Sanford Dornbusch. 1996. *Beyond the Classroom: Why School Reform Has Failed and What Parents Need to Do.* New York: Simon & Schuster.

Stevens, Gillian, et al. 1990. "Education and attractiveness in marriage choices." *Social Psychology Quaterly,* 53, pp. 62–72.

Stevens, Mitchell. 2001. *Kingdom of Children: Culture and Controversy in the Homeschooling Movement.* Princeton, NJ: Princeton University Press.

Stevens, William K. 1995. "Scientists say earth's warming could set off wide disruptions." *New York Times,* September 18, pp. A1, A5

Stodghill, Ron. 1997. "God of our fathers?" *Time,* October 6, pp. 34–40.

Stodghill, Ron, and Amanda Bower. 2002. "Where everybody's a minority." *Time,* September 2, pp. 26–30.

Stokes, Myron. 1995. "The shame of the city." *Newsweek,* September 4, p. 26.

Stolberg, Sheryl Gay. 1998a. "As doctors trade shingle for marquee, cries of woe." *New York Times,* August 3, pp. A1, A14.

Stolberg, Sheryl Gay. 1998b. "Cultural issues pose obstacles in cancer fight." *New York Times,* March 14, pp. A1, A30.

Stoll, Clarice Stasz. 1978. *Female and Male.* Dubuque, IA: Brown.

Stolzenberg, Ross M. 1990. "Ethnicity, geography, and occupational achievement of Hispanic men in the United States." *American Sociological Review,* 55, pp. 143–154.

Stout, Hilary. 1996. "Gore and Kemp both focus on urban problems." *Wall Street Journal,* October 9, p. A20.

Straus, Murray A. 1995. *Physical Violence in American families: Risk Factors and Adaptations to Violence in 8,145 Families.* New Brunswick, NJ: Transaction.

Strong, Bryan. 2001. *The Marriage and Family Experience,* 8th ed. Belmont, CA: Wadsworth.

Strum, Charles. 1993. "School tracking: Efficiency or elitism?" *New York Times,* April 1, p. B5.

Sullum, Jacob. 1998. *For Your Own Good: The Anti-Smoking Crusade and the Tyranny of Public Health.* New York: Free Press.

Suro, Roberto. 1991. "Where America is growing: The suburban cities." *New York Times,* February 23, pp. 1, 10.

Sutherland, Edwin H. 1939. *Principles of Criminology.* Philadelphia: Lippincott.

Suttles, Gerald. 1970. *The Social Order of the Slum.* Chicago: University of Chicago Press.

Svestka, Sherlie S. 1996. "Head Start and early Head Start programs: What we have learned over the last 30 years about preschool, families and communities." *International Journal of Early Childhood,* 28, pp. 59–62.

Syme, S. Leonard, and Lisa F. Berkman. 1987. "Social class, susceptibility, and sickness." In Howard D. Schwartz (ed.), *Dominant Issues in Medical Sociology,* 2nd ed. New York: Random House.

Szelenyi, Szonja. 1994. "Women and the class structure." In David B. Grusky (ed.), *Social Stratification: Class, Race, and Gender in Sociological Perspective.* Boulder, CO: Westview.

Szymanski, Albert. 1978. *The Capitalist State and the Politics of Class.* Cambridge, MA: Winthrop.

Takaki, Ronald. 1993. *A Different Mirror: A History of Multicultural America.* Boston: Little, Brown.

Talbot, Margaret. 2001. "The shyness syndrome." *New York Times Magazine,* June 24, pp. 11–12.

Tannen, Deborah. 2001a. *Talking from 9 to 5: Women and Men at Work.* New York: Quill.

Tannen, Deborah. 2001b. *The Handbook of Discourse Analysis.* Malden, MA: Blackwell.

Tannen, Deborah. 2001c. *You Just Don't Understand: Women and Men in Conversation.* New York: Quill.

Tannen, Deborah. 1986. *That's Not What I Meant!* New York: Morrow.

Tannenbaum, Frank. 1938. *Crime and the Community.* New York: Columbia University Press.

Taylor, Frederick W. 1911. *Scientific Management.* New York: Harper.

Taylor, Robert Joseph, et al. 1993. "Developments in research on black families: A decade review." In Harriette Pipes McAdoo (ed.), *Family Ethnicity: Strength in Diversity.* Newbury Park, CA: Sage.

Terkel, Studs. 1992. *Race: How Blacks and Whites Think and Feel About the American Obsession.* New York: New Press.

Tharp, Mike. 1987. "Academic debate." *Wall Street Journal,* March 10, p. A1.

Thio, Alex. 2004. *Deviant Behavior,* 7th ed. Boston: Allyn & Bacon.

Thoits, Peggy A. 1989. "The sociology of emotion." *Annual Review of Sociology,* 15, pp. 317–342.

Thomas, Evan. 2002. "Descent into hell." *Newsweek,* November 4, pp. 21–38.

Thomas, Gail E. 1995. "Notes on Asian American employment." In Gail E. Thomas (ed.), *Race and Ethnicity in America: Meeting the Challenge in the 21st Century.* Washington, DC: Taylor & Francis.

Thompson, J. J. 1998. "Plugging the kegs." *U.S. News & World Report,* January 26, pp. 63–67.

Thorne, Barrie. 1993. *Gender Play: Girls and Boys in School.* New Brunswick, NJ: Rutgers University Press.

Thorne, Barrie, and Marilyn Yalom. 1992. *Rethinking the Family: Some Feminist Questions,* rev. ed. Boston: Northeastern University Press.

Thornton, Russell. 2001. "What the census doesn't count." *New York Times,* March 23, p. A21.

Thottam, Jyoti. 2003. "Where the good jobs are going." *Time,* August 4, pp. 36–39.

Thurow, Lester C. 1996. *The Future of Capitalism.* New York: Morrow.

Tiley, John J. 2000. "Cultural relativism." *Human Rights Quartertly,* 22, pp. 501–547.

Tilly, Louise A., and Joan W. Scott. 1978. *Women, Work, and the Family.* New York: Holt, Rinehart and Winston.

Time.com. 1998. "Asia business." *TIME Asia: The Cyberspace Marketplace,* 152, no. 4 (August 3).

Tobin, Jonathan N., et al. 1987. "Sex bias in considering coronary bypass surgery." *Annals of Internal Medicine,* 107, pp. 19–25.

Toch, Thomas, and Warren Cohen. 1998. "Public education: A monopoly no longer." *U.S. News & World Report,* November 23, p. 25.

Tolentino, Paz Estrella E. 2000. *Multinational Corporations: Emergence and Evolution.* London, England: Routledge.

Tolson, Jay. 2001. "Struggle for Islam." *U.S. News & World Report,* October 15, pp. 22–26.

Tolson, Jay. 2000. "No wedding? No ring? No problem." *U.S. News & World Report,* March 13, p. 48.

Tomsho, Robert. 2003. "State lawmakers give school vouchers new momentum." *Wall Street Journal,* April 7, pp. A15, A18.

Toner, Robin. 1992. "Politics of welfare: Focusing on the problem." *New York Times,* July 5, pp. 1, 13.

Toufexis, Anastasia. 1990. "A call for radical surgery." *Time,* May 7, p. 50.

Tow, James D. 2002. *Violence in Film and Television.* San Diego, CA: Greenhaven Press.

Traub, James. 1999. "The class of Prop. 209." *New York Times Magazine,* May 2, pp. 44–79.

Travers, Jeffrey, and Stanley Milgram. 1969. "An experimental study of the small world problem." *Sociometry,* 32, pp. 425–443.

Treiman, Donald J. 1977. *Occupational Prestige in Comparative Perspective.* New York: Academic Press.

Triandis, Harry C. 1989. "Cross-cultural studies of individualism and collectivism." *Nebraska Symposium on Motivation,* 37, pp. 41–133.

Trond, Petersen, Ishak Saporta, and Marc-David Seidel. 2000. "Offering a job: Meritocracy and social networks." *American Journal of Sociology,* 106, pp. 763–817.

Trotman, C. James. 2002. *Multiculturalism: Roots and Realities.* Bloomington: Indiana University Press.

Trotter, Robert J. 1987. "Mathematics: A male advantage?" *Psychology Today,* January, pp. 66–67.

Tumin, Melvin M. 1953. "Some principles of stratification: A critical analysis." *American Sociological Review,* 18, pp. 387–393.

Turco, Richard P. 2002. *Earth Under Siege: From Air Pollution to Global Change.* New York: Oxford University Press.

Turner, Barry A. 1992. "The symbolic understanding of organizations." In Michael Reed and Michael Hughes (eds.), *Rethinking Organization: New Directions in Organization Theory and Analysis.* Newbury Park, CA: Sage.

Turner, Margery Austin, Michael Fix, and Raymond J. Struyk. 1991. *Opportunities Denied: Discrimination in Hiring.* Washington, DC: Urban Institute.

Turner, Ralph H., and Lewis M. Killian. 1987. *Collective Behavior,* 4th ed. Englewood Cliffs, NJ: Prentice-Hall.

Turner, Ronny E., and Charles Edgley. 1990. "Death as theater: A dramaturgical analysis of the American funeral." In Dennis Brissett and Charles Edgley (eds.), *Life as Theater: A Dramaturgical Sourcebook.* New York: Aldine de Gruyter.

Twaddle, Andrew, and Richard Hessler. 1987. *A Sociology of Health,* 2nd ed. New York: Macmillan.

Tyrangiel, Josh. 2001. "Did you hear about . . ." *Time,* October 8, p. 77.

Uchitelle, Louis. 2001. "How to define poverty? Let us count the ways." *New York Times,* May 26, pp. A15–A17.

Uchitelle, Louis. 1999. "The American middle, just getting by." *New York Times,* August 1, pp. 3-1, 3-13.

United Nations. 2001. *Human Development Report 2001.* New York: Oxford University Press.

United Nations. 2000. *The World's Women 2000: Trends and Statistics.* New York: United Nations.

U.S. Census Bureau. 2003. *Statistical Abstract of the United States.* Washington, DC: Government Printing Office.

U.S. Census Bureau. 2002. *Statistical Abstract of the United States.* Washington, DC: Government Printing Office.

U.S. Census Bureau. 2001. *Statistical Abstract of the United States.* Washington, DC: U.S. Government Printing Office.

U.S. Census Bureau. 1998. *Statistical Abstract of the United States.* Washington, DC: U.S. Government Printing Office.

U.S. Commission on Civil Rights. 1992. *Civil Rights Issues Facing Asian Americans in the 1990s.* Washington, DC: U.S. Government Printing Office.

U.S. Department of Education. 2000. *21st Century Community Learning Centers.* Washington, DC: U.S. Government Printing Office.

U.S. General Accounting Office. 2003. "Telecommunications: Characteristics and Choices of Internet Users." Available online: www.digitaldividenetwork.org.

Usdansky, Margaret L. 1996. "Single motherhood: Stereotypes vs. statistics." *New York Times,* February 11, p. E4.

Useem, Michael. 1980. "Which business leaders help govern?" *Insurgent Sociologist,* 9, pp. 107–120.

Valian, Virginia. 1998. *Why So Slow? The Advancement of Women.* Cambridge, MA: MIT Press.

Van Biema, David. 2001. "As American as . . . " *Time,* October 1, pp. 72–74.

Van Biema, David. 1995. "Bury my heart in committee." *Time,* September 18, pp. 48–51.

Van Leeuwen, Mary Stewart. 1990. "Life after Eden." *Christianity Today,* July 16, pp. 19–21.

Varghese, Raju. 1981. "An empirical analysis of the Eriksonian bipolar theory of personality." *Psychological Reports,* 49, pp. 819–822.

Vealey, Robin S., and Susan M. Walter. 1998. "Imagery training for performance enhancement and personal development." In Jean M. Williams (ed.), *Applied Sport Psychology: Personal Growth to Peak Performance,* 3rd ed. Mountain View, CA: Mayfield.

Vega, William. 1998. "American society can cause mental illness." *Infoseek (Online News),* September 14.

Verbrugge, Lois M. 1985. "Gender and health: An update on hypotheses and evidence." *Journal of Health and Social Behavior,* 26, pp. 156–182.

Viola, Herman J. 1996. *North American Indians.* New York: Crown.

Viscusi, W. Kip. 1992. *Smoking: Making the Risky Decision.* New York: Oxford University Press.

Waite, Linda J. 1995. "Does marriage matter?" *Demography,* 32, pp. 483–507.

Waite, Linda J., and Maggie Gallagher. 2000. *The Case for Marriage: Why Married People Are Happier, Healthier, and Better Off Financially.* New York: Doubleday.

Waitzkin, Howard. 1987. "A Marxian interpretation of the growth and development of coronary care technology." In Howard D. Schwartz (ed.), *Dominant Issues in Medical Sociology,* 2nd ed. New York: Random House.

Wald, Matthew L. 1990. "Guarding environment: A world of challenges." *New York Times,* April 22, pp. 1, 16–17.

Waldie, D. J. 2001. "Catching the urban wave." *New York Times,* November 27, p. A21.

Waldman, Peter. 1996. "Pitiful fate." *Wall Street Journal,* June 20, pp. A1, A5.

Wallerstein, Judith, et al. 2000. *The Unexpected Legacy of Divorce: A 25 Year Landmark Study.* New York: Hyperion.

Walsh, Mary Williams. 2001. "Reversing decades-long trend, Americans retiring later in life." *New York Times,* February 26, pp. A1, A13.

Waltermaurer, Eve, Christina Ortega, and Louise-Anne McNutt. 2003. "Issues in estimating the prevalence of intimate partner violence." *Journal of Interpersonal Violence,* 18, pp. 959–974.

Walters, Pamela Barnhouse, and Richard Rubinson. 1983. "Educational expansion and economic output in the United States, 1890–1969: A production function analysis." *American Sociological Review,* 48, pp. 480–493.

Walters, Suzanna Danuta. 1995. *Material Girls: Making Sense of Feminist Cultural Theory.* Berkeley: University of California Press.

Walzer, Michael. 1978. "Must democracy be capitalist?" *New York Review of Books,* July 20, p. 41.

Wartzman, Rick. 1992. "Sharing gains." *Wall Street Journal,* May 4, pp. A1, A4.

Watson, Russell. 1995. "When words are the best weapon." *Newsweek,* February 27, pp. 36–40.

Wattenberg, Ben. 2001. "America by the numbers." *Wall Street Journal,* January 3, p. A14.

Waxman, Chaim I. 1990. "Is the cup half-full or half-empty?: Perspectives on the future of the American Jewish community." In Seymour Martin Lipset (ed.), *American Pluralism and the Jewish Community.* New Brunswick, NJ: Transaction.

Weart, Spencer R. 1998. *Never at War: Why Democracies Will Not Fight One Another.* New Haven, CT: Yale University Press.

Weaver, Charles N., and Michael D. Matthews. 1990. "Work satisfaction of females with full-time employment and full-time housekeeping: 15 years later." *Psychological Reports,* 66, pp. 1248–1250.

Weber, Max. 1968. *Economy and Society: An Outline of Interpretive Sociology,* vol.1, ed. Guenther Roth and Claus Wittich. New York: Bedminster Press.

Weber, Max. 1946. *From Max Weber: Essays in Sociology,* trans. and ed. H. H. Gerth and C. Wright Mills. New York: Oxford University Press.

Wechsler, Henry, 1998. "Binge drinking remains a college plague." *Infoseek (Online News),* September 10.

Wechsler, Henry, et al. 1995. "Correlates of college student binge drinking." *American Journal of Public Health,* 85, pp. 921–926.

Wehrfritz, George, and Kay Itoi. 2003. "Subterranean city." *Newsweek,* October 20, pp. E14–E16.

Weis, Lois (ed.). 1988. *Class, Race, and Gender in American Education.* Albany: State University of New York Press.

Weisheit, Ralph. 1992. "Patterns of female crime." In Robert G. Culbertson and Ralph Weisheit (eds.), *Order Under Law,* 4th ed. Prospect Heights, IL: Waveland.

Welchman, Kit. 2000. *Erik Erikson: His Life, Work and Significance.* Philadelphia: Open University Press.

Wells, Amy Stuart. 1991. "Once a desegregation tool, magnet school becoming school of choice." *New York Times,* January 9, p. B6.

Wessel, David. 2003. "Americans are buying more health care." *Wall Street Journal,* January 9, p. A2.

Westin, Alan F. 2003. "Social and political dimensions of privacy." *Journal of Social Issues,* 59, pp. 431–453.

White, Jack E. 1997. "I'm just who I am." *Time,* May 5, pp. 32–36.

White, Jack E. 1993. "Growing up in black and white." *Time,* May 17, pp. 48–49.

White, Joseph B., and Joann S. Lublin. 1996. "Some companies try to rebuild loyalty." *Wall Street Journal,* September 27, pp. B1, B7.

White, Lynn K., and John N. Edwards. 1990. "Emptying the nest and parental well-being: An analysis of national panel data." *American Sociological Review,* 55, pp. 235–242.

White, Sheldon H. 1977. "The paradox of American education." *National Elementary Principal,* 56, pp. 9, 10.

Whiteford, Michael B., and John Friedl. 1992. *The Human Portrait,* 3rd ed. Englewood Cliffs, NJ: Prentice-Hall.

Whittier, Nancy. 1995. *Feminist Generations: The Persistence of the Radical Women's Movement.* Philadelphia: Temple University Press.

Whorf, Benjamin. 1956. *Language, Thought, and Reality.* New York: Wiley.

Whyte, Martin King. 1992. "Choosing mates—the American way." *Society,* March/April, pp. 71–77.

Wildavsky, Ben. 2000. "A blow to bilingual education." *U.S. News & World Report,* September 4, p. 20.

Wiley, Norbert. 1979. "Notes on self genesis: From me to we to I." *Studies in Symbolic Interaction,* 2, pp. 87–105.

Wilkinson, Doris. 1993. "Family ethnicity in America." In Harriette Pipes McAdoo (ed.), *Family Ethnicity: Strength in Diversity.* Newbury Park, CA: Sage.

Williams, David R. 2003. "The health of men: Structured inequalities and opportunities." *American Journal of Public Health,* 93, pp. 724–732.

Williams, Robin M., Jr. 1970. *American Society: A Sociological Interpretation,* 3rd ed. New York: Knopf.

Williams, Robin M., Jr. 1994. "The sociology of ethnic conflicts: Comparative international perspectives." *Annual Review of Sociology,* 20, pp. 49–79.

Wilson, Edward O. 1980. *Sociobiology: The Abridged Edition.* Cambridge, MA: Harvard University Press.

Wilson, James Q. 2001. "Why not try vouchers?" *New York Times,* April 27, p. A27.

Wilson, Warner. 1989. "Brief resolution of the issue of similarity versus complementarity in mate selection using height preferences as a model." *Psychological Reports,* 65, pp. 387–393.

Wilson, William Julius. 1996. *When Work Disappears: The World of the New Urban Poor.* New York: Knopf.

Wilson, William Julius, and Andrew J. Cherlin. 2001. "The real test of welfare reform still lies ahead." *New York Times,* July 13, p. A19.

Wimberley, Dale W. 1984. "Socioeconomic deprivation and religious salience: A cognitive behavioral approach." *Sociological Quarterly,* 25, pp. 223–238.

Winch, Robert F. 1971. *The Modern Family.* New York: Holt, Rinehart and Winston.

Winerip, Michael. 1998. "Binge nights: The emergency on campus." *New York Times: Education Life,* January 4, pp. 29–42.

Winslow, Ron. 1989. "Sometimes, talk is the best medicine." *Wall Street Journal,* October 5, p. B1.

Witkin, Gordon, et al. 1998. "Again." *U.S. News & World Report,* June 1, pp. 16–21.

Wolf, Naomi. 1993. *Fire with Fire.* New York: Random House.

Wolfe, Alan. 2001. *Moral Freedom: The Impossible Idea That Defines the Way We Live Now.* New York: Norton.

Wood, Julia T. 1994. *Gendered Lives: Communication, Gender, and Culture.* Belmont, CA: Wadsworth.

Woodard, Michael D. 1995. "Economic rights and black entrepreneurship: A program for economic development in the post-civil-rights era." In Gail E. Thomas (ed.), *Race and Ethnicity in America: Meeting the Challenge in the 21st Century.* Washington, DC: Taylor & Francis.

Woodburn, James. 1982. "Egalitarian societies." *Man,* 17, pp. 431–451.

Woodward, Kenneth L. 2002. "Christianity's newest converts." *Britannica Book of the Year,* pp. 306–307.

Woodward, Kenneth L. 1987. "Saving souls—or a ministry?" *Newsweek,* July 13, pp. 52–53.

World Bank. 2001. *World Bank Atlas 2001.* Washington, DC: World Bank.

World Bank. 1996. *World Development Report 1996.* New York: Oxford University Press.

World Bank. 1990. *World Development Report 1990.* New York: Oxford University Press.

Wren, Christopher S. 1997. "Survey suggests leveling off in use of drugs by students." *New York Times,* December 21, p. 12.

Wright, Robert. 1995. "Who's really to blame?" *Time,* November 6, pp. 33–37.

Wright, Stuart A., and Elizabeth S. Piper. 1986. "Families and cults: Familial factors related to youth leaving or remaining in deviant religious groups." *Journal of Marriage and the Family,* 48, pp. 15–25.

Wrong, Dennis H. 1990. *Population and Society,* 4th ed. New York: Random House.

Wrong, Dennis H. 1961. "The oversocialized conception of man in modern sociology." *American Sociological Review,* 26, pp. 183–193.

Wuthnow, Robert. 1994. "Religion and economic life." In Neil J. Smelser and Richard Swedberg (eds.), *The Handbook of Economic Sociology.* Princeton, NJ: Princeton University Press.

Yoshihashi, Pauline. 1990. "Immigration law's employer sanctions prove to have little impact, study finds." *Wall Street Journal,* April 20, p. A16.

Yoshikawa, Hirokazu. 1995. "Long-term effects of early childhood programs on social outcomes and delinquency." *Future of Children,* 5, pp. 51–75.

Young, Gay, and Bette J. Dickerson (eds.). 1994. *Color, Class and Country: Experiences of Gender.* London, England: Zed Books.

Zachary, G. Pascal. 1996. "Strategic shift." *Wall Street Journal,* June 13, pp. A1, A6.

Zagorin, Adam. 1994. "The sins of a sainted bank." *Time,* August 22, pp. 54–55.

Zakaria, Fareed. 2001. "Why do they hate us?" *Newsweek,* October 15, pp. 22–40.

Zakaria, Fareed. 1998. *From Wealth to Power: The Unusual Origins of America's World Role.* Princeton, NJ: Princeton University Press.

Zangwill, Israel. 1909. *The Melting Pot.* New York: Macmillan.

Zaslow, Jeffrey. 2003a. "Staying in touch . . ." *Wall Street Journal,* June 24, p. D1.

Zaslow, Jeffrey. 2003b. "Will you still need me . . ." *Wall Street Journal,* June 17, p. D1.

Zaslow, Jeffrey. 2003c. "Divorce makes a comeback." *Wall Street Journal,* January 14, pp. D1, D10.

Zenner, Walter P. 1985. "Jewishness in America: Ascription and choice." *Ethnic and Racial Studies,* 8, pp. 117–133.

Zernike, Kate, and Melody Petersen. 2001. "School's backing of behavior drugs comes under fire." *New York Times,* August 19, pp. 1, 29.

Zigler, Edward. 2000. "The wrong read on Head Start." *New York Times,* December 23, p. A13.

Zimmerman, Carle. 1949. *The Family of Tomorrow.* New York: Harper.

Zuckerman, Mortimer. 2003. "All work and no play." *U.S. News & World Report,* September 8, p. 86.

Zwingle, Erla. 2002. "Cities: Where's everybody going?" *National Geographic,* November, pp. 70–99.

Name Index

Subject Index

PHOTO CREDITS

Chapter 1: Page xxviii, © AP/Wide World Photos; Page 4, © David Young-Wolff/Getty Images; Page 5, © Lou Dematteis/The Image Works; Pages 9 and 10, © Bettmann/CORBIS; Page 11 (top), Library of Congress; Page 11 (bottom), © Hulton Archive/Getty Images; Page 14, © Richard Carson/Reuters/CORBIS; Page 17, © Kaz Mori/Getty Images; Page 19, © Syracuse Newspapers/Li-Hua Lan/The Image Works; Page 24, © Spencer Grant/PhotoEdit.

Chapter 2: Page 32, © B.S.P.I./CORBIS; Page 35, © AFP/CORBIS; Page 38, © Myrleen Ferguson Cate/PhotoEdit; Page 39, © Anthony Bannister/Animals Animals/Earth Scenes; Page 41, © James Holland/Stock Boston; Page 42, © Lee Snider/The Image Works; Page 47, © Nicholas DeVore/Getty Images; Page 48, Digital Vision; Page 49, © Galen Rowell/CORBIS; Page 52, © Bettmann/CORBIS; Page 56 (left), © Robert Daly/Getty Images; Page 56 (right), © Sam Yeh/AFP/Getty Images; Page 58, © Carlos Alvarez/Getty Images.

Chapter 3: Page 66, Doug Menuez/Photodisc/Getty Images; Page 70, © Robert Brenner/PhotoEdit; Page 71, © Laura Dwight/CORBIS; Page 73 (far left), Kevin Peterson/Photodisc/Getty Images; Page 73 (middle left), © Photolibrary.com; Page 73 (middle right), Barbara Penoyar/Photodisc/Getty Images; Page 73 (far right), © Christopher Briscoe/Photo Researchers, Inc.; Page 78, © Brent Jones; Page 81, © Natalie Fobes/CORBIS; Page 83, © Penny Tweedie/Getty Images; Page 85, © Spencer Grant/PhotoEdit; Page 89, © George Shelley/CORBIS.

Chapter 4: Page 96, © David Young-Wolff/Getty Images; Page 99, © Jerry Irwin/Photo Researchers, Inc.; Page 100, © Duomo/CORBIS; Page 101, © Spencer Grant/PhotoEdit; Page 105, © Robert Azzi/Woodfin Camp & Associates; Page 107, © Richard Lord/The Image Works; Page 109, © Xavier Bonghi/Getty Images; Page 110, © Timothy Shonnard/Getty Images; Page 114, © Frank Micelotta/Getty Images.

Chapter 5: Page 118, © Michael Newman/PhotoEdit; Page 122, © Will & Deni McIntyre/Photo Researchers, Inc.; Page 123, © Ronald Martinez/Getty Images; Page 127, © Nancy Richmond/The Image Works; Page 130, © AP/Wide World Photos; Page 132, © Reuters NewMedia Inc./CORBIS; Page 135, Digital Vision; Page 139, © Matthew Borkoski/Stock Boston; Page 140, © AP/Wide World Photos.

Chapter 6: Page 147, © Michael Greenlar/The Image Works; Page 150, Ryan McVay/Photodisc/Getty Images; Page 153, © Joe Raedle/Getty Images; Page 154, © Spencer Platt/Getty Images; Page 159, © Fritz Hoffmann/The Image Works; Page 163, © A. Ramey/Stock Boston; Page 165, © A. Ramey/PhotoEdit.

Chapter 7: Page 178, © AP/Wide World Photos; Page 181, Lewis Hine Photo/Library of Congress; Page 182, © John Zillioux; Page 184, © SuperStock; Page 187, © Frank Siteman/Getty Images; Page 190, © Flash! Light/Stock Boston; Page 191, © Margot Granitsas/The Image Works; Page 193, © Jeff Greenberg/The Image Works; Page 198, © Elena Rooraid/PhotoEdit; Page 201, © Mark Peters/SIPA Press.

Chapter 8: Page 210, © John Eastcott & Yva Momatiuk/The Image Works; Page 213, © AP/Wide World Photos; Page 216, © Paul Conklin/PhotoEdit; Page 218, © AP/Wide World Photos; Page 219, © A. Ramey/PhotoEdit; Page 223, © Lawrence Migdale/Getty Images; Page 225, © Robert Frerck/Odyssey/Chicago; Page 226, © Robert Brenner/PhotoEdit; Page 230, © Bob Daemmrich/The Image Works.

Chapter 9: Page 240, © Yellow Dog Productions/Getty Images; Page 243, © David Frazier/Photo Researchers, Inc.; Page 245, © Joseph Nettis/Photo Researchers, Inc.; Page 247, Royalty-Free/CORBIS; Page 252, © AFP/CORBIS; Page 253, © Ira Wyman/CORBIS Sygma; Page 259, © Bob Daemmrich; Page 260, © Nancy Coplon.

Chapter 10: Page 270, © N. Frank/The Viesti Collection, Inc.; Page 273, © Lawrence Migdale/Lawrence Migdale/Pix; Page 275, © Michael Newman/PhotoEdit; Page 277, © Barbara Stitzer/PhotoEdit; Page 280, © James Kay/Index Stock Imagery, Inc.; Page 283, © Culver Pictures; Pages 286 and 289, © Bob Daemmrich/Stock Boston; Page 292, © Milt & Joan Mann/Cameramann International.

Chapter 11: Page 296, © Michael Newman/PhotoEdit; Page 300, © Bob Daemmrich/The Image Works; Page 301, © Michael Newman/PhotoEdit; Page 304, © Milt & Joan Mann/Cameramann International; Page 307, © AP/Wide World Photos; Page 309, © Bob Daemmrich/The Image Works; Page 315, © Michael Newman/PhotoEdit; Page 318, © AP/Wide World Photos; Page 323, © Mark Wilson/Getty Images; Page 327, © David R. Frazier Photolibrary.

Chapter 12: Page 332, © Lester Lefkowitz/CORBIS; Page 335, © National Museum of American History/Smithsonian Institution; Page 340, © Frederick Ayer/Photo Researchers, Inc.; Page 347, © Ginny Ganong Nichols/The Viesti Collection, Inc.; Page 351, © Brian Brake/Photo Researchers, Inc.; Page 352 (top), © Margaret Bourke-White/Time Life Pictures/Getty Images; Page 352 (bottom), © Justin Sullivan/Getty Images; Page 358, © AP/Wide World Photos; Page 361, © Reuters NewMedia Inc./CORBIS.

Chapter 13: Page 368, © Bob Daemmrich/Stock Boston; Page 372, © Greg Smith/CORBIS SABA; Page 375, © Spencer Grant/PhotoEdit; Page 378, © Jeff Greenberg/PhotoEdit; Page 379, © Robert Frerck/Odyssey/Chicago; Page 381, © AFP/CORBIS; Page 382, © Lester Lefkowitz/Getty Images; Page 385, © Bob Daemmrich/The Image Works; Page 388, © Lori Adamski Peek/Getty Images.

Chapter 14: Page 398, © Danny Lehman/CORBIS; Page 401, © Chuck Nacke/Woodfin Camp & Associates; Page 404, © AP/Wide World Photos; Page 405, © Robert Frerck/Woodfin Camp & Associates; Page 409, © Steven Hansen/Stock Boston; Page 410, © Susan Van Etten/PhotoEdit; Page 416, © Robert Brenner/PhotoEdit; Page 419, © Kevin Horan/Stock Boston.

Chapter 15: Page 426, © Monika Graf/The Image Works; Page 430, © AP/Wide World Photos; Page 433, © Jonathan Fickies/Getty Images; Page 435, © Erik Freeland/CORBIS SABA; Page 437, © Frazer Harrison/Getty Images; Page 441 (top), © AP/Wide World Photos; Page 441 (bottom), © Dilip Mehta/Contact Press Images; Page 443, © Doug Hulcher/Panos Pictures; Page 447, © AP/Wide World Photos.